ROTISSERIE® LEAGUE BASEBALL

ROTISSERIE® LEAGUE BASEBALL

1994 Edition

Edited by
Glen Waggoner

The Rotisserie League
Lee Eisenberg • Rob Fleder • Peter Gethers
Daniel Okrent • Michael Pollet • Cary Schneider
Robert Sklar • Cork Smith • Harry Stein
Glen Waggoner • Steve Wulf

Little, Brown and Company
Boston New York Toronto London

Contents

ROTISSERIE® LEAGUE BASEBALL

Introduction

Yoo-Hoo Is Sweeter Than Goodbye
by Steve Wulf

Michael Jordan is a wuss.

I was there the morning he announced his retirement at the Chicago Bulls' training site, when he said that after winning three championships "there were no more challenges left." And I snickered.

As I looked around the gymnasium in Deerfield, Illinois, I saw faces filled with anxiety, eyes moistened with tears, ears festooned with ear hairs. Hundreds of us were shoulder to shoulder, after all. Yet I felt alone, and somewhat superior, for I too had just won three championships. What's more, I was not like Mike, the weenie, because I knew that there were challenges ahead, worlds left unconquered, Kruks still undervalued.

Give up? Hah! Not as long as the mystery of Andres Galarraga remains unsolved.

And whereas it took Michael Jordan three seasons to win his three titles, it took me less than a year. The Rushin Wulf Hounds of our Rotisserie basketball league eked out a two-point victory over the Deli Llamas in the 1992–93 season, and we did it *without Michael Jordan.*

(Rotisserie basketball, by the way, is a wonderful game that deserves its own book, which it had once until some shortsighted publisher—not this one—decided to pull the plug. Here's a tip for the three of you out there who still miss the hoops book: Hakeem Olajuwon was even more valuable than Michael Jordan was last year.)

In my Rotisserie American League, Beowulf outdistanced the Bauery Bums, thanks to Tim Salmon, Pat Hentgen, Cecil Fielder, and Gabe Miller. You may not have heard of Gabe, but in September he traded us Andre Dawson and Dennis Eckersley for Manny Ramirez, who grew up in Washington Heights, and Domingo Jean, who ran through Washington Heights trying to get to Yankee Stadium, and that was enough to put us over the top, although we trust Gabe will be enjoying Manny for years to come. Sorry about Domingo going to the Astros.

But the *crème de la crème,* the *pièce de résistance, le plus grand bijou en la Triple Couronne* was the championship of the league that began some fourteen years ago in the soon-to-be-*finis* La Rotisserie Française restaurant in Manhattan. That was the league that launched the movement that will someday force a new entry in *Webster's* for *rotisserie:* 3. fantasy, as in Dan Okrent still thinks he can win in his Rotisserie league.

I had not won in the original Rotisserie League since 1981, which means I have never won that championship in a full season. Indeed, about three-fourths of the way through this past season, I fell out of first place for the first time all year, ruining my chance to become the first wire-to-wire winner in Rotissehistory. I thought that it was over, that I had quit running at the head of the stretch. Fortunately, Randy Myers started saving a game a day, Tom Glavine let me forget I traded Chipper Jones away for him, and little-used Todd Benzinger made Will Clark look like Wally Pipp. The Wulfgang reclaimed the lead after only a week and eventually pulled away to a nine-length victory at the wire.

My goodness, I'm beginning to sound like all those bore-you-to-tears Rotisserians who have infiltrated every phase of American life—doctors, lawyers, and, presumably, Indian chiefs have their own leagues—and driven even the original Rotisserians to distraction. "How's your Rotisserie League team doing?" is usually someone's entrée into how *his* Rotisserie League team is doing. Mike Lupica was always making fun of us on New York's all-sports radio station, WFAN, and it served us right. But then Lupica was taken off the air. Coincidence? We think not.

There are literally hundreds of thousands of Rotisserie Leagues all over the world, yet there is only one original Rotisserie League, and that is the league I won this year. To be a part of that league is to be a part of that famous picture of the original Hall of Famers. Indeed, when I scan the table at the draft every year, I look at Cork Smith and see Connie Mack. I look at Glen Waggoner and see the Bambino. I look at Michael Pollett and I see Eddie Collins—I think it's the large ears. To even be included in this group is an honor. To whip their sorry old butts, well, that's heaven. Let me luxuriate once again in the shower of Yoo-Hoo.

It is also a thrill to have the first-place team for the tenth anniversary of our very first Rotisserie League book. Back then, George Brett, Nolan Ryan, and Carlton Fisk, not to mention Paul Householder, were still going strong, and while it makes us sad to think we won't have them to kick around the table anymore—Waggoner is still especially upset about Householder—it does make us happy to think we have been joined in our pursuit by millions, including the likes of Mario Cuomo, Bryant Gumbel, and Wayne Gretzky.

If only Michael Jordan had played Rotisserie. He might have spent the night he went to Atlantic City studying for the draft. He might not have played so much golf with Richard Esquinas. He might have found a more benign, less expensive way to satisfy his competitive urges. Yes, if Michael Jordan had played Rotisserie, he might still be playing basketball.

And we would both be looking for four in a row.

1

Ground Rules

Rotisserie Baseball Embraces Free Market—and Thrives!

Last year in this chapter we announced revolutionary changes in the structure of Rotisserie League Baseball. Those changes were summed up in the chapter's title: "TRADE RESTRICTIONS ABOLISHED! ANTI-DUMPING RULES DUMPED! WORLD TILTS ON AXIS!"

That's right. The Founding Fathers of Rotisserie baseball woke up one morning after the 1992 season, took a long look at the pendulum on the old clubhouse wall, and decided it had swung too far in one direction. So, after a cup of coffee and five minutes of deliberation, we swept aside a decade of carefully crafted rules pertaining to trades and free agent acquisitions. We smashed the chains that bound us. We opened the floodgates. We threw out the bathwater (but hung on to the baby).

Did we also open Pandora's Box? Perhaps. But we believed that (1) extending the trade deadline to August 31, (2) abolishing the "Contiguous Trades Only" requirement, (3) eliminating the "Designated Asterisk" rule, and (4) removing restrictions on trading FAAB players would unleash a tidal wave of wheeling and dealing. And from reports we've received from Rotisserie leagues around the country, that's exactly what happened.

Risky? Sure, but Rotisserians who annually invest $35 in José Canseco and Darryl Strawberry are no strangers to risk. We figured that the potential rewards of the Free Trade Acts of 1993—more deals, more action, more volatility in the pennant race—were too great to pass up. After all, freedom is just another word for nothing left to lose. (Funny, we never did understand for sure what that meant when Janis sang it to us. Still don't.)

Every year in this space we urge Rotisserie veterans to review the **Official Constitution of Rotisserie League Baseball** for the same reason that pitchers spend so many hours in spring training working on covering first base. It's not that they forget how to do it over the winter or anything. It's that it never hurts to practice the fundamentals.

This year it's more important than ever for veteran owners to check out rules changes made since last season. So take a close look at **Article XI, Article XIV, Ultra V, Ultra VI-A,** and **Ultra VIII** before jumping ahead to the Player Ratings.

How to Play the Game

It happens every spring. Someone buys the new edition of this book. Talks to a friend. And before you can say "Eric Davis is on the DL," 10 to 12 apparently normal, reasonably intelligent, generally responsible people lock themselves in a stuffy room on a pleasant April morning—only to emerge, six hours later, groggy but eyes ablaze, cheeks flushed with passion, all babbling at once about needing more speed and being ready to trade relief for power and when do we get the first stats and how did I wind up with Mickey Morandini instead of Ryne Sandberg at second base and . . .

We know. We've been there. It comes with the (natural) turf of owning a Rotisserie League Baseball team.

Over a decade has passed since the first band of innocents went blithely into the first draft auction of the first season of what they—we—all thought would be a diverting little game. Poor babies. Little did we know that we were crossing an invisible boundary line, a one-way Checkpoint Charlie (Leibrandt? Hayes?), a point of no return into a brave new world filled with clichés that knew no end, from which no one would ever return.

Would we have done it if we had known then what we know now? That old maxims would be dashed to the ground and lifelong loyalties rent asunder? That Rotisserie League Baseball would rattle our brains, tiddle our winks? That Harry Stein would win four pennants?

No way! What do you think we are, nuts or something? We *didn't* know what we were doing, so we *did* bid $9 for Gene Richards back in 1980, even though we didn't know his first name. And we *did* embark on an uncharted journey into a peculiar world inhabited by Fenokees and Furriers, Burros and Fish, Nations and Gazers and Goners, a Wulfgang, a colony of Fleder Mice, and far, far too many Brenners.

You know what's even crazier? Upwards of a million people have followed suit. (That's what *USA Today* says, and who are we to argue with so important a scouting tool?)

If you have never played Rotisserie League Baseball before, consider this: You can stop right here, burn this book, and save yourself a lifetime of aggravation—not to mention a small fortune spent calling **900-820-1666**. Understand? This is a warning. We cannot be held responsible if you go beyond this period.

But as you have, here's what you do, rookies and second-year players afraid of the sophomore jinx: Read, then reread, "The Rules, Simplified" that follow; then jump ahead to the Scouting Report (pages 57–217) and dip into your favorite league. Now it's time to read the Constitution (pages 9–26)—slowly. After that, finish the book any damn way you please—you bought it, you can use it to line the litter box if you want—but *do* read the Constitution *one more time*. Now you're ready to join the **Rotisserie League Baseball Association** (see page 306). The rest will eventually be Rotissehistory.

PLAY BALL!

The Rules, Simplified

People are always coming up to us at the ballpark or in grocery store check-out lines and saying, "Hey, this Rotisserie League Baseball stuff is *really* complicated." "Oh, yeah?" we politely respond, "Compared to what? Getting your new VCR hooked up?"

The fact is, the *basics* of Rotisserie League Baseball are as simple as one-two-three strikes, yer OUT! And we can prove it.

1. Teams are made up of real, live major league baseball players who are selected at an auction draft that takes place at the beginning of the season (typically on the first weekend following Opening Day).

2. Each team in a Rotisserie League is composed of 23 players taken from the active rosters of National or American League teams. A Rotisserie League drawn from National League or American League players should have 12 teams. You can, however, have fewer teams.

3. A team consists of five outfielders, two catchers, one second baseman, one shortstop, one middle infielder (either 2B or SS), one first baseman, one third baseman, one corner man (1B or 3B), one utility man (NL) or designated hitter (AL), and nine pitchers.

4. Players are purchased at an open auction. Spending is limited to $260 per team. (If you don't want to use money, call them units or pocorobas or whatever. The point is resource allocation.) Teams may spend less. The first bidder opens the auction with a minimum bid of $1 for any player. The bidding then proceeds around the room (at minimum increments of $1) until only one bidder is left. The process is repeated, with successive owners introducing players to be bid on, until every team has a complement of 23 players.

5. A player is eligible to be drafted for any position at which he appeared in 20 or more games the preceding year. If he did not appear in 20 games at any one position, he is eligible for the position at which he appeared the most times. Once the season starts, a player qualifies for a position by playing it once. Multiple eligibility is okay.

6. Trading is permissible from Auction Draft Day until midnight August 31. After every trade, both teams must be whole—that is, they must have the same number of active players at each position that they had before the trade. The transaction fee for trades is $10.

7. If a major league player is put on the disabled list, sent to the minors, traded to the other league, or released, he may be replaced by a player from the free agent pool of unowned talent. The price for such a replacement is $25. Replacement must be made by position: You cannot replace a disabled catcher with an outfielder, even if the free agent pickings at catcher are slim, unless you have another player on your team who can be moved to the catcher slot. The original player may

either be released or placed on his Rotisserie team's reserve list. When he is activated by his major league team, a reserved player may be activated by his Rotisserie team, at which time the replacement player called up in his slot must either be waived or moved to another position where a natural opening exists (and for which he qualifies). A team may not release, reserve, or waive a player without replacing him with another active player.

8. Cumulative team performance is tabulated in four offensive and four pitching categories:

   - Composite batting average (BA)
   - Total home runs (HR)
   - Total runs batted in (RBI)
   - Total stolen bases (SB)
   - Composite earned run average (ERA)
   - Total wins (W)
   - Total saves (S)
   - Composite ratio: walks (BB) + hits (H) ÷ innings pitched (IP)

9. Teams are ranked from first to last in each of the eight categories. For example, in a ten-team league, the first-place team receives ten points, the second-place team nine points, on down to one point for last place. The team with the most points wins the pennant.

10. Prize money is distributed as follows: 50% for first place, 20% for second, 15% for third, 10% for fourth, and 5% for fifth. Even more important, the owner of the winning team receives a bottle of Yoo-Hoo—poured over his/her head. (See Chapter 8, Postgame Shower, pages 313–315.)

● ● ●

"Do I have to play for money?" No. We do, but unlike the big league version, Rotisserie League Baseball can be played for very little money, or none at all. Our stakes require a $350–$450 investment per team, depending on the number of trades and call-ups over the course of a season, but you can play for pennies, Cracker Jack prizes, or nothing at all and still have fun. Just be sure to keep the ratio of "acquisition units" to players at 260:23 for each team on Auction Draft Day.

"What do I do if it's May 15 and I've just gotten around to reading this book? Wait till next year?" Absolutely not! That's second-division thinking! You can start any time! Put your league together, hold your auction draft, and deduct all stats that accrue prior to that glorious day. Next year, start from scratch.

The rest of your questions are dealt with in the pages that follow. We hope. If not, write us c/o **Rotisserie League Baseball Association, 370 Seventh Avenue, Suite 312, New York, NY 10001**. Or call at **212-695-3463**. We'll do our best to get you playing what we still modestly call The Greatest Game for Baseball Fans Since Baseball.

OFFICIAL CONSTITUTION OF ROTISSERIE LEAGUE BASEBALL

PREAMBLE

We, the People of the Rotisserie League, in order to spin a more perfect Game, drive Justice home, kiss domestic Tranquility good-bye, promote the general Welfare in Tidewater—where it's been tearing up the International League—and secure the Blessings of Puberty to ourselves and those we've left on Base, do ordain and establish this Constitution for Rotisserie League Baseball, and also finish this run-on sentence.

I. OBJECT

To assemble a lineup of 23 National League or American League baseball players whose cumulative statistics during the regular season, compiled and measured by the methods described in these rules, exceed those of all other teams in the League.

II. TEAMS

There are 12 teams in a duly constituted Rotisserie League composed of either National League or American League players.

> **NOTE:** If you choose to play with fewer teams, be sure to make necessary adjustments so that you acquire approximately 80% of all available players at your auction draft. You could have a six-team league using American League players, for example, and draft only from among your seven favorite AL teams. Unless you reduce the available player pool proportionately to reflect a reduced number of teams, you'll never learn to appreciate the value of a good bench.

> **NOTE:** Do *not* mix the two leagues. It's unrealistic and silly, it's not the way the big leagues do it, it means you end up using only All-Stars and established regulars, and it's fattening. (On the other hand, if you *do* mix leagues, we're not going to call out the Rotisserie National Guard or anything.)

III. ROSTER

A team's active roster consists of the following players:

1. **NATIONAL LEAGUE PLAYERS**
   Five outfielders, two catchers, one second baseman, one shortstop, one

middle infielder (either second baseman or shortstop), one first baseman, one third baseman, one corner man (either first baseman or third baseman), one utility player (who may play any nonpitching position), and nine pitchers.

2. **AMERICAN LEAGUE PLAYERS**
The same, except that the utility player is called a designated hitter, consistent with the AL's insistence on perpetuating that perversion of the game.

IV. AUCTION DRAFT DAY

A **Major League Player Auction** is conducted on the first weekend after Opening Day of the baseball season. Each team must acquire 23 players at a total cost not to exceed $260. A team need not spend the maximum. The League by general agreement determines the order in which teams may nominate players for acquisition. The team bidding first opens with a minimum salary bid of $1 for any eligible player, and the bidding proceeds around the room at minimum increments of $1 until only one bidder is left. That team acquires the player for that amount and announces the roster position the player will fill. The process is repeated, with successive team owners introducing players to be bid on, until every team has a squad of 23 players, by requisite position.

- Don't get hung up on the bidding order; it's irrelevant. Do allow plenty of time; your first draft will take all day.
- Players eligible at more than one position may be shifted during the course of the draft.
- No team may make a bid for a player it cannot afford. For example, a team with $3 left and two openings on its roster is limited to a maximum bid of $2 for one player.
- No team may bid for a player who qualifies only at a position that the team has already filled. For example, a team that has acquired two catchers, and whose utility or DH slot is occupied, may not enter the bidding for any player who qualifies *only* at catcher.
- Players who commence the season on a major league team's disabled list *are* eligible to be drafted. If selected, they may be reserved and replaced upon completion of the auction draft. (See **Article XII**, page 17.)

NOTE: Final Opening Day rosters for all National League or American League teams will be needed on Auction Draft Day. Because some teams don't make their final roster moves until the last minute, even *USA Today*'s rosters, published on Opening Day, have holes. The best way to get the most complete, updated rosters is with membership in the **Rotisserie League Baseball Association**. (See page 306 for information on how to join.)

A **Minor League Player Draft** is conducted immediately following the major league auction, in which each Rotisserie League team may acquire players (a) who are not on any National/American League team's active roster; and (b) who still have official rookie status, as defined by major league baseball.

> **NOTE:** The major league rule reads: "A player shall be considered a rookie unless, during a previous season or seasons, he has (a) exceeded 130 at-bats or 50 innings pitched in the major leagues; or (b) accumulated more than 45 days on the active roster of a major league club or clubs during the period of a 25-player limit (excluding time in the military service)."

- Selection takes place in two rounds of a simple draft, not an auction.
- In the first season, the selection order shall be determined by drawing paired numbers from a hat (that is, positions 1 and 24, 2 and 23, and so on in a 12-team league).
- In subsequent years, the selection order in each of the two rounds is determined by the order in which the teams finished in the previous season. In leagues with 12 teams, the 6th place team selects first, proceeding in descending order to the 12th place team, which is in turn followed by the 5th, 4th, 3rd, 2nd, and 1st place teams.
- The price and subsequent salary upon activation of each farm system player drafted is $10.
- See **Article XIII**, page 19, for rules governing farm systems.

> **NOTE:** The order of selection stated above represents a change from early years of Rotisserie baseball, when teams selected in reverse order of the final standings of the preceding season's pennant race. By awarding the first selection to the highest finisher among second-division teams instead of the last-place team, we seek to offer an incentive to teams to keep plugging and a disincentive to finish last (i.e., in the past, a last place finish would be "rewarded" with the first farm system draft pick).

V. POSITION ELIGIBILITY

A player may be assigned to any position at which he appeared in 20 or more games in the preceding season. If a player did not appear in 20 games at a single position, he may be drafted only at the position at which he appeared most frequently. The 20 games/most games measure is used only to determine the position(s) at which a player may be drafted. Once the season is under way (but after Auction Draft Day), a player becomes eligible for assignment to any position at which he has appeared at least once. In American League versions, players selected as DHs may qualify at any position (i.e., they need not have appeared in 20 games as DH the preceding season). In National League versions, players selected for the utility slot may qualify at any position.

> **NOTE:** Two official major league sources for determining player eligibility are the National League's *Green Book* and the American League's

Red Book. Both list appearances by position under fielding averages. The *Red Book* lists all players who appeared as designated hitters the preceding season. Circulating an eligibility list by position before Auction Draft Day saves a lot of time. Prepare one yourself in March, when the *Green Book* and *Red Book* are published. Or obtain it with membership in the **Rotisserie League Baseball Association**—our list is available at least five months earlier, so you'll be able to spend the winter doing something worthwhile (see page 306 for details). Spend a few minutes before your auction to settle eligibility questions and assign eligibility to rookies. When in doubt, use common sense (instead of knives) to resolve disputes.

VI. FEES

The Rotisserie League has a schedule of fees covering all player personnel moves. No money passes directly from team to team. No bets are made on the outcome of any game. All fees are payable into the prize pool and are subsequently distributed to the top four teams in the final standings. (See **Articles VIII** and **IX**, page 13.)

1. **BASIC:** The cumulative total of salaries paid for acquisition of a 23-man roster on Auction Draft Day may not exceed $260.

2. **TRANSACTIONS:** $10 per trade (no matter how many players are involved) or player activation (from reserve list or farm system). In a trade, the team that pays the fee is subject to negotiation.

3. **CALL-UP FROM FREE AGENT POOL:** $25 for each player called up from the free agent pool.

4. **RESERVE:** $10 for each player placed on a team's reserve list (see **Article XII**, page 17).

5. **FARM SYSTEM:** $10 for each player in a team's farm system (see **Article XIII**, page 19).

6. **ACTIVATION:** $10 for each player activated from the reserve list or farm system.

7. **WAIVERS:** $10 for each player claimed on waivers (see **Article XV**, page 21).

8. **SEPTEMBER ROSTER EXPANSION:** $50 (see **Article XVI**, page 22).

VII. PLAYER SALARIES

The salary of a player is determined by the time and means of his acquisition and does not change unless the player becomes a free agent or is signed to a guaranteed long-term contract. (See **Article XVII**, page 23.)

- The salary of a player acquired in the major league draft is his auction price.

- The salary of a player called up from the free agent pool during the season is $10.
- The salary of a player activated from a team's farm system during the season is $10.
- The salary of a player claimed on waivers is $10.
- The salary of a player called up during September Roster Expansion to supplement the 23-man roster is $25 if he is drawn from the free agent pool. (See **Article XVI**, page 22.)

NOTE: Because you can commit only $260 for salaries on Auction Draft Day, and because you will keep some of your players from one season to the next, salaries are *extremely* important, particularly after the first season ends and winter trading begins. Would you trade Juan Gonzalez for Paul O'Neill? The Rangers wouldn't, not even if Blowhard George threw in Yankee Stadium (which he would be only too happy to do, outfield monuments and all). But a smart Rotisserie League owner just might make such a deal *in the off-season*, because the $20-plus difference between Gonzalez's and O'Neill's auction price is enough to buy a front-line starter.

Maintaining accurate, centralized player-personnel records of salary and contract status is *the most important* task of the League Secretary, who deserves hosannas from the other owners for all the work he does.

NOTE: The $260 salary limit pertains to Auction Draft Day *only*. After Auction Draft Day, free agent signings and acquisition of high-priced players in trades may well drive a team's payroll above $260.

VIII. PRIZE MONEY

All fees shall be promptly collected by the League Treasurer, who is empowered to subject owners to public humiliation and assess fines as needed to ensure that payments are made to the League in a timely fashion. The interest income from this investment can be used to defray the cost of a gala postseason awards ceremony and banquet. The principal shall be divided among the first four teams in the final standings as follows:

- 1st place—50%
- 2nd place—20%
- 3rd place—15%
- 4th place—10%
- 5th place—5%

IX. STANDINGS

The following criteria are used to determine team performance:

- Composite batting average (BA)
- Total home runs (HR)
- Total runs batted in (RBI)

- Total stolen bases (SB)
- Composite earned run average (ERA)
- Total wins (W)
- Total saves (S)
- Composite ratio: walks (BB) + hits (H) ÷ innings pitched (IP)

Teams are ranked from first to last in each of the eight categories and given points for each place. For example, in a 12-team league, the first-place team in a category receives 12 points, the second-place team 11, and so on down to 1 point for last place. The team with the most total points wins the pennant.

THE FENOKEE IP REQUIREMENT. A team must pitch a total of 900 innings to receive points in ERA and ratio. A team that does not pitch 900 innings maintains its place in ERA and ratio ranking but receives zero points in both of these categories. (Thus, a team that finished third in ERA but did not have 900 IP would receive no points in that category. The fourth-place team in ERA would still receive 9 points.) This rule was passed in 1988 in response to an "all-relief" strategy attempted by the Okrent Fenokees in the 1987 season. The strategy was not successful because Swampmaster Dan Okrent abandoned it after six weeks or so. But it might have worked, in more disciplined hands. Hence the new rule.

THE FENOKEE AB REQUIREMENT. A team must have 4250 at bats in the season. A team that does not have 4250 at bats maintains its place in the batting average ranking but receives zero points in that category. This rule was passed in 1991 in response to an "all-pitching" strategy attempted by the Okrent Fenokees in 1990. This time, the Beloved Founder and Former Commissioner-for-Life assembled an all-star pitching staff, Tony Gwynn, and 13 Ken Oberkfells (i.e., guys who didn't play enough to bring down Gwynn's "team" BA). The BFFCL hoped to amass 40 pitching points, 10 BA points, and 3 points in the other offensive categories to squeeze into the first division. The strategy was not successful because the Swampmaster abandoned it after six weeks or so. But it might have worked, in more disciplined hands. Hence the new rule.

- Pitchers' offensive stats are *not* counted, mainly because they don't appear weekly in *USA Today*. Nor are the pitching stats of the occasional position player called in to pitch when the score is 16–1 after five innings and the relief corps is hiding under the stands.
- In cases of ties in an individual category, the tied teams are assigned points by totaling points for the rankings at issue and dividing the total by the number of teams tied.
- In cases of ties in total points, final places in the standings are determined by comparing placement of teams in individual categories. Respective performances are calculated and a point given to each team

for bettering the other. Should one team total more points than the other, that team is declared the winner.

- Should the point totals still be equal, the tie is broken by adding each team's *total at-bats* at season's end, plus *triple the number of its innings pitched*. The team that scores a higher total by this measure wins the pennant.

X. STATS

The weekly player-performance summaries published in *USA Today* beginning in late April constitute the official data base for the computation of standings in Rotisserie League Baseball.

NOTE: When we first started out, we used *The Sporting News*. That was when *TSN* cared more about baseball than about all the Stanley Cup skate-offs, NBA playoffs, and NFL summer camping rolled into one (which, by the way, is what the Rotisserie League's Founding Fathers believe should be done with them). Not for nothing was the Holy Bible known to baseball people as *The Sporting News* of religion. But that was then, and this is now. *The Sporting News* has passed from the last Spink to new owners who seem intent on taking the "Sporting" part seriously—that is, covering other sports at the expense of baseball. A pity.

- The effective date of any transaction for purposes of statistical calculation is the Monday (AL) or Tuesday (NL) *before* the commencement of play on those days. This is because weekly stats appear in *USA Today* on Tuesday for AL games through the preceding Sunday and on Wednesday for NL games through the preceding Monday.
- Reporting deadlines should be established as close to these breaks as possible but not later than the start of any game at the beginning of a new reporting period. Noon on Monday (AL) or Tuesday (NL) makes sense.
- Transactions recorded *on* Auction Draft Day, including trades and call-ups to replace disabled players, are effective retroactive to Opening Day. Transactions occurring *after* Auction Draft Day but *before* the closing date of the first cumulative summaries to appear in *USA Today* in April are effective the Monday (AL) or Tuesday (NL) immediately after the first closing date.
- Performance stats of a player shall be assigned to a Rotisserie League team *only* when he is on the active 23-man roster of that team. It is common for a player to appear on the roster of more than one Rotisserie League team during the season because of trades and waiver-list moves. Even a player who is not traded may spend time on a team's reserve list, during which period any numbers he might compile for his major league team do not count for his Rotisserie League team.
- Standings shall be tabulated and issued in a regular and timely fashion, as determined by the League owners.

NOTE: Keeping score (see pages 303–304) is the only part of Rotisserie League Baseball that isn't any fun. Unless you're computerized, it's tedious and time-consuming. And even if your league does have a computer wonk on board, it still means he or she can't take a vacation between Opening Day and early October. (God forbid your league should go a week without standings!) The best solution: Let the official stat service authorized by the Founding Fathers do all the heavy lifting for you (see page 304).

XI. TRADES

From the completion of the auction draft until August 31, Rotisserie League teams are free to make trades of any kind without limit, except as stipulated below, *so long as the active rosters of both teams involved in a trade reflect the required position distribution upon completion of the transaction.* No trades are permitted from September 1 through the end of the season. Trades made from the day after the season ends until rosters are frozen on April 2 prior to Auction Draft Day are *not* bound by the position distribution requirement.

> **NOTE:** This means that if Team A wants to swap David Justice to Team B for José Rijo anytime between Auction Draft Day and the trade deadline, Team A will have to throw in a bum pitcher and Team B a duff outfielder to make the deal. During the off-season, the two could be dealt even-up.

- Trades do not affect the salaries or contract status of players.
- Each trade is subject to the $10 transaction fee. The fee is not affected by the number of players involved in the trade.
- Unless you want knife fights to break out among owners, prohibit all trades involving cash, "players to be named later," or "future considerations." Trust us.

NOTE ON DUMPING: "Dumping" is the inelegant but scientifically precise term used to describe what happens when a team out of contention gives up on the season and trades to a contending team its most expensive talent and its players who will be lost to free agency at the end of the year, typically for inexpensive players who can be kept the following season. A "dumping" trade is always unbalanced, sometimes egregiously so, with the contending team giving up far less than it gets, and the noncontending team giving up much more in order to acquire a nucleus for the following season. While this strategy makes sense for both clubs, extreme cases can potentially undermine the results of the auction draft, which should always be the primary indicator of an owner's ability to put together a successful team.

To guard against this, we have in the past employed rigid and restrictive Anti-Dumping measures to control trades between contenders and noncontenders. But in light of major shifts in international politics and economics in recent years, we decided in 1993 that these restrictive measures tended to inhibit rather than enhance the playing of the game.

Accordingly, we swept away all Anti-Dumping legislation last year. We did so with some trepidation, but we felt the benefits of a free market would outweigh the potential for abuses. We were right. Let freedom ring.

XII. THE RESERVE LIST

A team may replace any player on its 23-man roster who is:

- placed on the **disabled list,**
- **released,**
- **traded** to the other league, or
- **sent down** to the minors by his major league team.

To replace such a player, a Rotisserie League team must first release him outright or place him on its reserve list. A team reserves a player by notifying the League Secretary and paying the $10 transaction fee. A reserved player is removed from a team's active roster at the end of the stat week (on Monday or Tuesday)—when formal notification is given—and placed on the team's reserve list. There is no limit to the number of players a team may have on its reserve list. Reserving a player protects a team's rights to that player.

A team has two weeks to take action once a player is placed on the disabled list, released, traded to the other league, or sent to the minors by his major league team. If no action is taken, the position is frozen open until the original player's return, and no replacement may be made.

- *A suspended player may not be reserved, released, or replaced.*

NOTE: When we first wrote that, we were thinking about the old-fashioned things players might do to get themselves suspended—Bill Madlock hitting an umpire (1980), say, or Gaylord Perry throwing a spitter (1962 to 1983), although he was suspended for doing it only once (1982). Then came the drug suspensions of 1984 and afterward. We have decided to consider players suspended for substance abuse as if they were on the disabled list, and allow teams to replace them.

- Once a specific action has been taken to remove a player from its 23-man roster (via release or placing him on the reserve list), a team is then free to select any eligible player from the free agent pool of players not already owned by another Rotisserie League team. The salary assigned to a player so selected from the free agent pool is $10; the call-up fee is $25 (see **Article VI**, page 12).
- If the same player is claimed by more than one team in a given week, he goes to the team ranking lowest in the most recent standings.
- Every reserve move must be accompanied by a concomitant replacement move (i.e., a team may not reserve a player without replacing him).

- Placing a player *on* the reserve list and activating a player *from* the reserve list are *each* subject to a $10 transaction fee.
- The call-up takes effect as soon as it is recorded by the League Secretary, although the player's stats do not begin to accrue to his new team until Monday (AL) or Tuesday (NL) of the week the League Secretary records the call-up.
- A player on a Rotisserie League reserve list may not be traded *unless* the replacement player linked to him is also traded. Thus, a team might trade Andy Van Slyke (on reserve) and Henry Cotto (called up to replace him) for Derrick May.
- A replacement player may be traded or otherwise replaced (e.g., in case of injury, he could be reserved and a free agent called up to fill his slot). In such a case, the newly acquired player becomes linked to the original reserved player.
- When a player on a reserve list returns to active major league duty, he must be **reinstated** to the active 23-man roster of his Rotisserie League team *two weeks* after his activation or be **waived**. Failure to notify the League Secretary shall be considered a waiver of the player on the reserve list. A player may not be **reinstated** or **waived** until he has been activated by his major league team.

NOTE: Intended to prevent stockpiling of players, this rule is tricky to monitor. Daily newspaper transaction columns and telephone sports-information lines don't always catch every single major league roster move. The clock starts ticking when the League Secretary *is made aware of* a player being reactivated. By the way, "two weeks" means two full reporting periods and may actually be as much as two weeks plus six days (as in the case of a player being reactivated the day after a reporting deadline). In fairness, and because this is not full-contact karate but a game played among friends, an owner should be given warning by the League Secretary that time is up and he will lose a player if he doesn't make a move. Especially if there are extenuating circumstances (i.e., anything from retracing Livingston's steps in Africa to just plain laziness).

- When a player is reinstated to the active 23-man Rotisserie League roster from a team's reserve list, the player originally called up to replace him must be waived, unless the replacement player *or* the original player can be shifted to another natural opening on the roster for which he qualifies.
- If the replacement player is replaced (e.g., he is injured, put on reserve, and a free agent is called up), then *his* replacement becomes linked to the original player on the reserve list.
- A player reinstated from the reserve list may not displace any active player on the Rotisserie League team's 23-man roster *other than* his original replacement (or his successor).

NOTE: The intent of all this is to minimize the benefit a team might derive from an injury. Say Andres Galarraga is injured (again!) and you call up the inevitable Gerald Perry to replace him. Galarraga comes back. What you'd like to do is activate Galarraga, keep Perry, and waive your other corner man, Frank Bolick, who hasn't had a hit in six weeks. Our rules say you can't, on the premise that *a team is not ordinarily helped by an injury to a key player*. We know the big leagues don't handle it this way, but art doesn't always imitate life. Without some restriction, an owner might never have to pay the price for his bad judgment in drafting Frank Bolick in the first place.

XIII. FARM SYSTEM

If a farm system player is promoted to the active roster of a major league team at any time during the regular season *prior to* September 1 (when major league rosters may expand to 40), his Rotisserie League team has *two weeks* after his promotion to **activate** him (at any position for which he qualifies) or **waive** him.

- The fee for activating a player from a team's farm system is $10.
- If a farm system player is activated, the player displaced from the 23-man roster to make room for him must be placed on waivers, *unless* the farm system player can be activated into a natural opening, in which case no waiver is required. **Example:** One of your pitchers is placed on a major league disabled list; you reserve him and activate a pitcher from your farm system who has been called up by his major league team.
- Once brought up from its farm system by a Rotisserie League team, a player may not be returned to it, although he may be placed on a team's reserve list in the event he is returned to the minor leagues by his major league club.
- A farm system player not brought up to a team's 23-man roster during the season of his initial selection may be kept within the farm system in subsequent seasons upon payment of an additional $10 per year, so long as he retains official rookie status and the League Secretary is duly notified on April 1 each year, when rosters are frozen. (See also **Article XVIII**, page 24.)
- A team may have no more than three players in its farm system.
- A farm system player may be traded during authorized trading periods, subject to prevailing rules governing transactions, as may a team's selection rights in the minor league draft.

NOTE: This means that a team could acquire and exercise as many as three farm system draft picks, providing that it does not exceed the maximum of three players in its farm system at a given time.

XIV. SIGNING FREE AGENTS

Active major league players not on any Rotisserie League team's roster at the conclusion of the auction draft become free agents. During the course of the season the pool of free agents may also include minor league players not in any Rotisserie League's farm system (see **Article XIII**, page 19) who are promoted to an active major league roster; waived players who are not claimed; and players traded from the "other" major league. Such players may be signed in the following manner.

From Opening Day Until the All-Star Game. Free agents may be called up to replace players placed on a Rotisserie League team's reserve list as outlined in **Article XII** (see page 17). The only exception to **Article XII**'s provisions for signing free agents during this period is that players traded into the league from the "other" major league may be signed by a Rotisserie League team with its **Free Agent Acquisition Budget (FAAB)**, as described below.

After the All-Star Game. From the All-Star Game until the last weekly transaction deadline before September 1, free agents may be signed, without limit in number, but within the limitations of a Rotisserie League team's **Free Agent Acquisition Budget:**

- Each team shall have, for the purpose of acquiring free agents during the course of the season, a supplementary budget of $100.
- At the deadline established by each league for recording weekly transactions, a team may submit a *sealed* bid for one or more free agents.
- The minimum bid shall be $5; the maximum shall be the amount remaining in a team's **FAAB**.
- A free agent so selected goes to the highest bidder. If more than one team bids the same amount on a player, and if that amount is the highest bid, the player goes to the team that is lowest in the most recently compiled standings.
- The salary of a free agent signed in this manner is his acquisition price. His contract status is that of a first-year player.
- In addition to the player's acquisition price, a team signing a free agent must pay the $25 transaction fee for calling up free agents as set forth in **Article VI** (page 12).
- For each free agent that it signs, a team *must* at the same time waive or release a player at the same position from its *active* roster. (See page 9. If on a major league team's *active* roster, such a player is *waived.* If he has been placed on a major league team's disabled list, released, traded to the "other" league, or demoted to the minors, such a player is *released* and may not be acquired by a Rotisserie League team until he is once again on a major league roster.)
- A free agent signed for a salary in excess of $10 (i.e., more than the customary call-up fee for replacement players) is deemed to have a guaranteed two-year contract. If such a player is not protected the following season (i.e., if he is released into the free agent pool at the time rosters are frozen on April 1), then a contract buyout fee in the amount of twice his salary or $100, whichever is greater, shall be paid by the team owning his contract at the time.
- If a Rotisserie League team loses a player to the "other" league in an interleague trade, then the team's available **FAAB** dollars are increased by an amount equal to the lost player's salary.

NOTE: The provision regarding players acquired for a sum in excess of the customary $10 call-up fee is intended to discourage frivolous bidding for free agents. It is also intended to make teams who are most likely to benefit from signing costly free agents—that is, teams still in the race for the first division—pay for it dearly, by making such players expensive to dump the following spring.

NOTE: Set up a simple, common-sense mechanism for handling the "sealed bid" part of the **FAAB** process. Nothing elaborate is needed. Price, Waterhouse need not be called in. Don't permit bidders to make contingency bids (e.g., "If I don't get Ruth at $29, then I'll bid $25 for Gehrig, and if I don't get Gehrig . . .") unless your League Secretary doesn't have a day job

XV. WAIVERS

Under certain conditions, a Rotisserie League player may be waived.

- When a player on a Rotisserie League team's reserve list is activated by his major league team, either he or the player called up earlier to replace him *must* be placed on waivers (see **Article XII**, page 17).
- When a team activates a player from its farm system, except into a natural opening (see **Article XIII**, page 19), the player dropped from the 23-man roster to make room for him *must* be placed on waivers.
- A player no longer on the active roster of his major league team and whose Rotisserie League position is taken by a player activated from the reserve list or farm system may not be placed on waivers but *must* be released outright.

NOTE: This is to prevent a team from picking up a disabled list player on waivers merely for the purpose of releasing him and replacing him with a player of higher quality from the free agent pool.

- The waiver period begins at noon on the Monday (AL) or Tuesday (NL) after the League Secretary has been notified that a player has been waived and lasts one week, at the end of which time the player shall become the property of the lowest-ranked team to have claimed him. To make room on its roster, the team acquiring a player on waivers must assign the player to a natural opening or waive a player at the same position played by the newly acquired player.
- Waiver claims take precedence over the replacement of an injured, released, or demoted player who has been put on reserve. That is, a player on waivers may be signed by a team with a roster opening at his position only if no other team lower in the standings claims the player on waivers.
- A team may acquire on waivers *no more* than one player in a given week, but there is no limit to the number of players a team may acquire on waivers during the season.

- A player who clears waivers—that is, is not claimed by any team—returns to the free agent pool.
- The fee for acquiring a player on waivers is $10. The salary of a player acquired on waivers shall be $10 or his current salary, whichever is greater. His contract status shall remain the same.
- A player with a guaranteed long-term contract may *not* be waived during the season. He may, however, be released and replaced if he is traded to the "other" league.
- A player may be given his outright release *only* if he is
    (a) unconditionally released,
    (b) placed on the "designated for assignment" list,
    (c) sent to the minors,
    (d) placed on the "disqualified" list,
    (e) traded to the "other" major league, or
    (f) placed on the disabled list.

XVI. SEPTEMBER ROSTER EXPANSION

If it chooses, a team may expand its roster for the pennant drive by calling up additional players after September 1 from the free agent pool, its own reserve list, or its own farm system. A team may call up as many players as it wishes, subject to payment of appropriate fees as outlined below, except that at no time may the number of active players on its roster exceed 40.

- The order of selection for September Roster Expansion is determined by the most recent standings, with the last-place team having first selection, and so on. During this 24-hour period, September Roster Expansion claims take precedence over waiver claims and routine call-ups to replace players who are disabled, released, or traded to the other league by their major league teams. This selection order pertains until midnight, September 2 *only,* after which time a team forfeits its order in the selection process, though *not* its right to make a selection. Selection after midnight, September 2, is on a first-come, first-served basis. Also, after midnight, September 2, waiver claims and routine call-ups to fill natural openings take precedence over September Roster Expansion claims.
- The performance stats of players called up during September Roster Expansion start to accrue on the Monday (AL) or Tuesday (NL) after the League Secretary has been notified of the player's selection.
- The fee for expanding the roster in September is $50.
- The salary assigned to a September call-up from the free agent pool is $25. The salary of a September call-up from a team's reserve list or farm system is the salary established at the time he was previously acquired (on Auction Draft Day, or subsequently from the free agent pool, or via waivers).

NOTE: A device for heightening the excitement for contending teams and for sweetening the kitty at their expense, September Roster Expansion will generally not appeal to second-division clubs (who should, however, continue to watch the waiver wire in the hope of acquiring "keepers" for next season at a $10 salary).

XVII. THE OPTION YEAR AND
GUARANTEED LONG-TERM CONTRACTS

A player who has been under contract at the same salary during two consecutive seasons and whose service has been uninterrupted (that is, he has not been waived or released, although he may have been traded) must, prior to the freezing of rosters in his third season, be released; signed at the same salary for his option year; or signed to a guaranteed long-term contract.

If **released**, the player returns to the free agent pool and becomes available to the highest bidder at the next auction draft. If signed at the same salary for an **option year**, the player must be released back into the free agent pool at the end of that season. If signed to a **guaranteed long-term contract**, the player's salary in each year covered by the new contract (which commences with the option year) shall be the sum of his current salary plus $5 for each additional year beyond the option year. In addition, a signing bonus, equal to one half the total value of the long-term contract, but not less than $5, shall also be paid.

> **NOTE:** This rule is intended to prevent blue-chippers, low-priced rookies who blossom into superstars, and undervalued players from being tied up for the duration of their careers by the teams who originally drafted them. It guarantees periodic transfusions of top-flight talent for Auction Draft Day and provides rebuilding teams something to rebuild with. And it makes for some interesting decisions at roster-freeze time two years down the pike.
>
> Here's how it works. Let's say you drafted Neon Deion Sanders of the Atlanta Braves for $2 in 1992, a fair price then for a football player with a strikeout swing, a questionable attitude, and too much jewelry. It's now the spring of 1994 and Sanders, whose maturity has caught up with his raw talent, has become a power threat and a team player. You could let Sanders play one more season for you and get a tremendous return on your two bucks, but that would be almost as foolish as Sanders risking his knees in the NFL. Taking a longer view, you daydream about Sanders's power and speed numbers, assess your needs, project what's likely to be available in the upcoming draft, cross your fingers against football injury—and sign him to a three-year guaranteed contract. Sanders's salary zooms to $12 ($2 + $5 + $5), but he's yours through the 1996 season. His signing bonus, which does not count against your $260 Auction Draft Day limit, is $18 (one half of 3 × $12). If he continues to mature as a ballplayer, you've got a bargain.

- In determining a player's status, "season" is understood to be a full season or any fraction thereof. Thus, a player called up from the free agent pool in the middle of the 1992 season and subsequently retained at the same salary without being released in 1993 (even though he may have been traded) enters his option year in 1994 and must be released, signed at the same salary for an option year, or signed to a long-term contract.

- A team may sign a player to only one long-term contract, at the end of which he becomes a free agent.
- Option-year and long-term contracts are entirely transferable, both in rights and obligations; the trade of a player in no way affects his contract status.
- If, during the course of a long-term contract, a player is traded from the National League to the American League (or vice versa), the contract is rendered null and void. The team that loses the player's services shall be under no further financial obligations.
- In all other cases—specifically *including* sudden loss of effectiveness—a team must honor the terms of a long-term contract, as follows: A player with such a contract *may* be released back into the free agent pool (that is, not protected on a team's roster prior to Auction Draft Day), but a team that chooses to do so must pay into the prize pool, above the $260 Auction Draft Day limit, a sum equal to *twice* the remaining value of the player's contract or $100, whichever is greater.

NOTE: This is an escape hatch for the owner who buys a dog but can't stand fleas. It's costly, but it's fair.

XVIII. ROSTER PROTECTION

For the first three seasons of the League's existence, each team must retain, from one season to the next, *no fewer than* **7** but *no more than* **15** of the players on its 23-man roster. After three seasons, this minimum requirement is eliminated, the maximum retained. The minimum is removed because, after three seasons, a team might find it impossible to retain a specific minimum because too many players have played out their option.

- The names of players being retained must be recorded with the League Secretary by midnight, April 1. Specific notice must also be made at that time of any guaranteed long-term contract signings and farm system renewals.
- The cumulative salaries of players protected prior to Auction Draft Day are deducted from a team's $260 expenditure limit, and the balance is available for acquisition of the remaining players needed to complete the team's 23-man roster.
- The League Secretary should promptly notify all teams in the League of each team's protected roster, including player salaries, contract status, and amount available to spend on Auction Draft Day.
- Failure to give notice of a guaranteed long-term contract for a player in his option year will result in his being continued for one season at his prior year's salary and then released into the free agent pool. Failure to renew a farm system player's minor league contract will result in his becoming available to all other teams in the subsequent minor league draft.

- A farm system player whose minor league contract is renewed on April 1 and who subsequently makes his major league team's active roster may, at his Rotisserie League owner's option, be added to the protected list of players on Auction Draft Day (and another player dropped, if necessary, to meet the 15-player limit), or he may be dropped and made available in the auction draft. He may not be retained in his Rotisserie League team's farm system.

NOTE: The April 1 roster-protection deadline was originally set to correspond with the end of the major leagues' spring interleague trading period, a rite of spring that no longer exists. We've stuck to April 1 anyway, because it gives us a week or so to fine-tune draft strategies. Until you know who the other teams are going to keep, you won't know for sure who's going to be available. And until you know how much they will have to spend on Auction Draft Day, you won't be able to complete your own pre-draft budget. So April 1 it is; don't fool with it.

XIX. GOVERNANCE

The Rotisserie League is governed by a Committee of the Whole consisting of all team owners. The Committee of the Whole may designate as many League officials as from time to time it deems appropriate, although only two—the League Secretary and the League Treasurer—ever do any work. The Committee of the Whole also designates annually an Executive Committee composed of three team owners in good standing. The Executive Committee has the authority to interpret playing rules and to handle all necessary and routine League business. All decisions, rulings, and interpretations by the Executive Committee are subject to veto by the Committee of the Whole. Rule changes, pronouncements, and acts of whimsy are determined by majority vote of the Committee of the Whole. Member leagues of the **Rotisserie League Baseball Association** (see page 297) may appeal to the RLBA for adjudication of disputes and interpretation of rules. The Rotisserie League has three official meetings each year: Auction Draft Day (the first weekend after Opening Day), the Midsummer Trade Meeting (at the All-Star break), and the Gala Postseason Banquet and Awards Ceremony. Failure to attend at least two official meetings is punishable by trade to the Cleveland Indians.

XX. YOO-HOO

To consecrate the bond of friendship that unites all Rotisserie League owners in their pursuit of the pennant, to symbolize the eternal verities and values of the Greatest Game for Baseball Fans Since Baseball, and to soak the head of the League champion with a sticky brown substance before colleagues and friends duly assembled, the **Yoo-Hoo Ceremony** is hereby ordained as the culminating event of the baseball season. Each year, at the awards ceremony and banquet, the owner of the championship team shall have a bottle of Yoo-Hoo poured over his or her head by the preceding year's pennant winner. The Yoo-Hoo Ceremony shall be performed with the dignity and solemnity appropriate to the occasion.

NOTE: If Yoo-Hoo, the chocolate-flavored beverage once endorsed by soft-drink connoisseur Yogi Berra, is not available in your part of the country, you have two options: (a) send up an alternative beverage, one chosen in the Yoo-Hoo spirit, as a pinch-hitter, or (b) move.

STILL CONFUSED?

Call Roti·Stats, the best Rotisserie stats service in the business, for clarifications, explanations, salutations, a current weather report, and a hard sell.

800-884-7684

ROTISSERIE ULTRA
The Rules of Play

Turn Up the Volume

Rotisserie Ultra requires more scouting, more planning, more wheeling, and more dealing. You move players off and onto your active roster as often as you want to. You ride guys on hot streaks, then ditch them when they go cold. You buy free agents. You bring along youngsters all the way from the low minors. You swing complicated, multiplayer deals. You build a strong bench with waiver moves to carry you through injuries and slumps.

Does playing Rotisserie Ultra mean giving up all pretense of having a normal life? No, you should keep up that pretense as long as you can. It does mean that you're not going to have a lot of time for scuba diving the Great Barrier Reef, reading Proust, learning to play the saxophone, paneling the rec room, or having a catch with your kid this summer. You're going to be busy, Bucky—or you're going to be in the second division. (Or, if your name is Okrent and you're the BFFCL, you're going to be both.)

Remember that the Sturgeon General himself—Peter Gethers, owner of Peter's Famous Smoked Fish—has warned that playing Rotisserie Ultra *before you're ready* can lead to "sensory overload, stress-related insomnia, pattern baldness, hot flashes, and premature ejaculation."

We recommend that fledgling leagues play the regular version of the game, become acclimated to its demands and pressures, and shake out own-ers who can't stand the heat of a pennant race before moving on to Ultra. Stay within yourselves, walk before you run, take it one game at a time, and floss regularly. Only then should you consider Ultra. After all, we can't have everybody in America having too much fun all at once.

Editor's Note: *Many of the rules in the Official Constitution of Rotisserie League Baseball also apply to Rotisserie Ultra, so we decided not to repeat every line of fine print that applies to both, except as needed for clarity. That means that the "Rules of Play" that follow for Rotisserie Ultra should be read together with the original Constitution. If you can't handle that assignment, you're going to have* real *trouble with Rotisserie Ultra.*

ULTRA I. THE ROTATION DRAFT

After the conclusion of the auction draft, in which teams acquire their 23-man active rosters for a sum not to exceed $260, owners successively draft up to 17 additional players in 17 separate rounds of selection. Initially, players acquired in this fashion comprise a team's reserve roster.

- Any baseball player is eligible for this draft. *Exception:* In National League versions, no player on the roster or in the minor league organization of an American League team may be selected; and, in American League versions, the opposite is true. Eligible players include (in the NL version, by way of example) previously undrafted NL players, NL-owned minor leaguers, unsigned players, Japanese players, high-school or college players, and the kid down the block with the great arm.
- In the rotation draft, owners are not required to select players by position. They may select all pitchers, all position players, or a mix.
- The order of selection for each of the 17 rounds is determined by the order of finish in the previous season. In leagues with 12 teams, the 6th place team selects first, proceeding in descending order to the 12th place team, followed by the 5th, 4th, 3rd, 2nd, and 1st place teams.

NOTE: For leagues switching over from Rotisserie League rules to Rotisserie League Ultra rules, the first two rounds of the rotation draft follow the order of the former farm system draft. Only players who have rookie status and are not on a major league 25-man roster or disabled list may be selected in these two rounds. This protects the property rights of teams that may have acquired additional farm system draft picks or improved their draft position via trades prior to the shift to Rotisserie League Ultra.

ULTRA II. THE RESERVE ROSTER

A team's reserve roster consists of those players acquired through the rotation draft, through trades, through demotions from the active roster, or through waiver claims. Any transaction (e.g., trade, demotion, waiver claim) that increases the size of the reserve roster beyond 17 players must be accompanied by a concomitant transaction (e.g., trade, promotion, waiver) that simultaneously returns the reserve roster to its maximum 17.

ULTRA III. FEES

1. **Basic:** The cumulative total of salaries paid for acquisition of a 23-man active roster on Auction Draft Day may not exceed $260.

2. **Reserve Roster:** There are no fees payable for the acquisition of players for the 17-man reserve roster.

3. **Transactions:** $10 per trade (no matter how many players are involved), $10 per player activation or demotion.

4. **Waivers:** $10 for each player claimed on waivers.

5. **September Roster Expansion:** $50 for each player added to a team's active roster after September 1.

THE TENTH PITCHER OPTION

As everybody in the baseball world knows, a Rotisserie team is composed of 9 pitchers and 14 position players (see **Article III,** page 9). Except, of course, when it's not.

A couple of years back we experimented with a slight variation on the traditional roster configuration and permitted a team to carry 10 pitchers and 13 position players.

Most major league teams carry 10 pitchers and 15 position players. But some (e.g., the Detroit Tigers in April and May in recent years) carry only 9 pitchers, while others (e.g., the Oakland A's) carry 11. It comes down to a GM's assessment of the team's needs, its personnel, and the schedule.

If this flexibility is good for the American and National leagues, why not for the third major league—the Rotisserie League? So a couple of years back we decided to let teams fill the utility slot with a position player *or* a pitcher. The result? An unqualified success.

The Tenth Pitcher Option allows a GM to realize the full potential of Ultra. Let's say you have the usual 9 pitchers and 14 position players on your active roster, and your team starts slipping in wins. Presto! You send down the outfielder hitting .227 in your utility slot and promote a good middle innings guy from your reserve roster. In AL leagues, you must still have a DH, two catchers, and three middle infielders, so the 10th pitcher must come at the expense of a corner or an outfielder.

The Tenth Pitcher Option provides more action, sweetens the pot through additional transaction fees, and is simple to administer and monitor. You can change the mix back and forth as frequently as you wish, provided only that the total number of active players does not exceed 23, and that at no time do you have more than 14 active position players or more than 10 active pitchers.

After hearing from leagues around the country regarding their experience with the Tenth Pitcher Option, we decided to leave it as just that—an option. Some leagues, particularly those using AL players, found it awkward to implement because of the DH. Others thought it was okay for Ultra but not regular Rotisserie. Still others simply didn't like it. Many made the transition smoothly.

Hey, that's why we call it an *Option.*

ULTRA IV. PLAYER SALARIES

The salary of a player is determined by the time and means of his acquisition and does not change unless the player becomes a free agent by means of release or is signed to a guaranteed long-term contract.

- The salary of a player acquired in the auction draft is his auction price.
- The salary of a player acquired in the rotation draft is determined as

follows: If the player was selected in the first round, $15; rounds 2–6, $10; rounds 7–12, $5; rounds 13–17, $2.

- The salary of a player claimed on waivers is $10 or his previous salary, whichever is greater. His contract status remains the same.

ULTRA V. TRADES

From the completion of the rotation draft until noon on the Monday (AL) or Tuesday (NL) on or following August 31, teams are free to make trades of any kind without limit (except as indicated in **Ultra VI**, below). However, at no time can any team have on its active roster more players at a particular position than allowed under the rules of the auction draft (see **Article III**, page 9 of the Official Constitution of Rotisserie League Baseball). A team may, however, be underrepresented at a position. So long as these strictures are adhered to in the immediate wake of a trade, teams may trade any number of players, at any position, irrespective of the number or position of players being received in such trade (except, again, as indicated below in **Ultra VI**).

- At no point may a team have more than 17 players on its reserve roster or more than 40 players on its active and reserve rosters combined.
- At no point may a team have more than 23 players on its active roster, except during the September Roster Expansion period (see **Ultra X**, page 32).
- No trades of any kind may be made between September 1 and October 15, nor between April 2 (Roster Freeze Day) and the conclusion of the rotation draft on Auction Draft Day.

ULTRA VI. ANTI-DUMPING

Players in the last year of a guaranteed contract or playing out their option year and players with a salary of $25 or more are considered "asterisk" players. Such players may be traded only under the following conditions:

- One team may trade asterisk players to another team provided that for each asterisk player traded, one is received in the same deal.
- The above notwithstanding, a team may trade *one* asterisk player to another team without an asterisk player coming in return or receive *one* asterisk player without giving one up, but may only make *one* such unbalanced trade in the course of the season.
- Between October 15 and Roster Freeze Day, asterisk players on winter rosters may be traded without restrictions whatsoever.

ULTRA VI-A. ANTI-DUMPING REPEALED

Effective Opening Day, 1993, Article **Ultra VI** (above) was repealed. The text of **Ultra VI** is left in place so that newcomers to **Ultra** will know just what is being done away with.

ULTRA VII. MOVEMENT BETWEEN ACTIVE ROSTER AND RESERVE ROSTER

An owner may demote a player from the active roster to the reserve roster, or promote a player in the reverse direction, at any time and for any reason, such promotions to take effect with the subsequent stat deadline (Monday noon for AL leagues, Tuesday noon for NL leagues). However, no player may be demoted without being replaced on the active roster by an eligible player—that is, a player who fulfills position eligibility requirements (which may include shifting another active player into the demoted player's position and the promoted player into the shifted player's position) *and* who is currently on a major league roster and not on a major league disabled list.

- **Exception:** If the acquisition of an active player in a trade places the acquiring team's active roster above the positional limit (e.g., more than two catchers), a player at that position may be sent down without the need for the recall of another player.
- A player acquired by trade from another team's active roster is considered active with the acquiring team on the effective date of the trade, unless the acquiring team chooses (or is compelled by roster restrictions) to demote him. Similarly, a player acquired in a trade from another team's reserve roster is considered to be reserved with the acquiring team, unless the acquiring team promotes him.

ULTRA VIII. SIGNING FREE AGENTS

Active major league players not on any Rotisserie League team's active roster or reserve roster at the conclusion of the auction draft become free agents. During the course of the season the pool of free agents may also include minor league players not on any Rotisserie League team's reserve roster who are promoted to an active major league roster; players traded from the "other" major league; and waived players who are not claimed. Beginning one week after the first standings report, and continuing through the season until the last weekly transaction deadline before September 1, such free agents may be signed, without limit, in the following manner:

- Each team shall have, for the purpose of acquiring free agents during the course of the season, a supplementary budget of $100, known as its **Free Agent Acquisition Budget (FAAB).**
- At the deadline established by each Rotisserie League for recording weekly transactions, a Rotisserie League team may submit a *sealed* bid for one or more free agents.
- The minimum bid shall be $5; the maximum shall be the amount remaining in a team's **FAAB.**
- A free agent so selected goes to the highest bidder. If more than one team bids the same amount on a player, and if that amount is the highest bid, the player goes to the team that is lowest in the most recently compiled standings.
- The salary of a free agent signed in this manner is his acquisition price. His contract status is that of a first-year player.

- For each free agent that it signs, a team *must* at the same time waive or release a player from its *active* roster.
- If a free agent signed for a salary of $25 or more is not protected on the subsequent April 1 Roster Freeze, then the owner of his contract at the time must pay into the prize pool a buyout fee of twice his salary or $100, whichever is greater.

NOTE: The reason for the pre-September 1 deadline is to prevent a Rotisserie League team from completely restocking with $5 players when the major leagues expand their rosters to 40 in September.

NOTE: The mechanics of the "sealed bid" process will vary from league to league. Where practicable, as in leagues that have weekly meetings, the sealed bid should be just that—a bid sealed in an envelope that is opened at the meeting. In other cases, it may be more efficient to recruit a disinterested party to record all bids and report them to the League Secretary for action. Whatever mechanism you devise, keep matters in perspective. These aren't the secrets to nuclear fusion, for Einstein's sake! So try to balance the gee of security with the haw of mutual trust.

ULTRA IX. WAIVERS

Players are placed on waivers (a) when they cannot be accommodated on a team's active or reserve roster, because of space and/or positional limitations; and (b) under the rules governing the winter roster (see **Ultra XI**, page 33).

- The waiver period commences at noon on the Monday (AL) or Tuesday (NL) immediately following the team's notification of waiver to the League Secretary and extends for one full reporting period (i.e., one week). At the conclusion of that week, if the player is unclaimed, he goes into the free agent pool, and may be acquired by a team only as outlined in **Ultra VIII**, above.
- Waiver claims are honored according to the inverse order of the standings effective the week before the close of the waiver period.
- A team may reclaim a player it has waived only if all other teams in the league decline to claim him.
- The fee for acquiring a player on waivers is $10. The salary of a player acquired on waivers shall be $10 or his current salary, whichever is greater; and his contract status shall remain the same.
- Only a player currently on a 25-man major league roster (i.e., not on a disabled list) may be claimed on waivers.
- A player traded to the "other" league may not be placed on waivers.
- A player on a guaranteed long-term contract may not be placed on waivers, even in the final year of his contract.

ULTRA X. SEPTEMBER ROSTER EXPANSION

If it chooses, a team may expand its roster for the pennant drive by promoting from its reserve roster an *unlimited* number of players, as the post–September 1 active-roster size expands to a maximum of 40 players. Such players may play any position.

- September expansions can be effective no earlier than noon on the Monday (AL) or Tuesday (NL) immediately following August 31. Expansions made later in September become effective the subsequent Monday or Tuesday at noon.
- A fee of $50 must be paid for every promotion that increases the active-roster size beyond 23. Player salaries are not affected by such promotions.

ULTRA XI. WINTER ROSTER

Effective October 15, each owner is required to submit to the League Secretary a list of 23 players, irrespective of position, taken from its combined active and reserve rosters, but one not including any players who have concluded their option year or the last year of a guaranteed long-term contract. This group of players becomes the winter roster.

- Immediately after the submission of winter rosters, a waiver period concluding at noon, November 1, begins. By inverse order of the final standings in the season just ended, teams may select no more than one player from that group of players not protected on a winter roster, again with the exception of players who have concluded their option year or the final year of a guaranteed long-term contract. On claiming such a player, the claiming team must, in turn, waive a player from its own winter roster. Players thus waived become eligible for a second round of waiver claims, for a period of one week, that are conducted in the same fashion. (Unclaimed players from the first waiver period are no longer eligible.) The process continues until there is a week in which no one is claimed.
- All winter-waiver claims cost the claiming team $10, to be paid into the league treasury for the coming season.
- The salary of a player claimed on winter waivers is $10 (or his current salary, whichever is greater), and he shall be deemed to be commencing the first year of a new contract with the coming season.
- After October 23, winter rosters may exceed or fall below 23 players through trading action. Whatever size the roster, however, any successful claim of a player on waivers must be accompanied by the placing of another player from the claiming team on waivers.

ULTRA XII. ROSTER PROTECTION

Roster protection in Rotisserie League and Rotisserie League Ultra is identical (see **Article XVIII**, page 24), except as follows:

- The cumulative salaries of frozen players are deducted from a team's $260 expenditure limit in the auction draft, and the balance is available for the acquisition of the remainder of a team's active roster.

However, salaries of players frozen on April 1 who are not on 25-man major league rosters on Auction Draft Day do not count against the $260 limit.

• Frozen players not on 25-man major league rosters count against the limit of 17 players on draft day reserve rosters, and the salaries they carry must be paid into the league treasury on draft day.

• In addition to the 15 players that a team may protect from its winter roster of active and reserve roster players, a team may also protect an additional 3 players on its reserve roster, provided that such players have rookie status and have never been active on a Rotisserie League team.

• Players frozen may include players who have spent the entire previous season on a reserve roster—typically because they played only in the minor leagues. Even so, such players who are subsequently frozen are deemed to be in the *second* year of their contract with their Rotisserie League Ultra team.

• Assignment of frozen players to a reserve roster position is at the owner's discretion. That is, an owner with a $10 minor leaguer carried over from the preceding year might, for strategic reasons, assign that player to the 17th position in the rotation draft, thus forgoing a $2 pick. Or the owner might assign the player to the first round and forgo a $15 pick. The assignment of frozen players by all teams will be made before the rotation draft commences.

NOTE: Some Ultra Leagues believe that the clock on minor leaguers should not start ticking until they are promoted to the majors, as in Rotisserie Regular. We feel this would tie up too many players and eventually undermine the auction draft. Effective in 1991, we increased the number of $2 and $5 players in the rotation draft (see **Ultra IV**, page 29). That should facilitate building a farm system and encourage protection of key players without providing the blanket protection of freezing the clock. This is called a compromise.

Let There Be Lite!

Great ideas often have implausibly pedestrian beginnings.

Isaac Newton was sitting under an apple tree, thinking he would like something sweet but tart and loaded with vitamin A, when the principle of gravity fell in his lap. A man who loved martinis a bit too well, Eli Whitney got his big inspiration when his wife yelled from the kitchen, "Keep your cotton-picking hands off that gin!" And because somebody else was picking up the tab, Daniel Okrent, down from his rustic estate in western Massachusetts to join Manhattan friends for lunch, found himself eating snails and making history over a decade ago in the then-fashionable East Side bistro, La Rôtisserie Française, instead of wolfing down a grease-on-white-with-mayo at his favorite New York restaurant—and thus the world was deprived of Blimpie League Baseball.

Maybe there's something in the water up there in the Berkshire Mountains, or maybe there's just nothing else to do, but a few years back yet another bucolic Edison stumbled out of the backwoods with a new widget. Fortunately, BFFCL Okrent recognized his nearby neighbor's creation as an inspired variation on a great theme, an ingenious mechanism for filling an important sociocultural need, a cleverly constructed design with possible commercial potential.

So we stole it.

That's how we are able to bring you the newest version of The Greatest Game for Baseball Fans Since Youknowwhat, Rotisserie Lite! But before we do, common courtesy requires us to say a few words about the country bumpk . . . ah, *squire* who we city-slickered into giving away his invention for a handful of T-shirts and the promise to spell his name right.

Tony Lake (that's L-A-K-E) is a man for all seasons, though he definitely prefers summer. A hardscrabble farmer then biding his time between crops as a circuit-riding professor of international politics at several pricey New England colleges, Farmer-Professor Lake is currently President Clinton's National Security Adviser and the highest-ranking Rotisserian in the world. He is a terminal Boston Red Sox fan who started playing Rotisserie League Baseball almost a decade ago, when BFFCL Okrent sold him a copy of the rules for 40 acres and a mule. Farmer-Professor Lake says the idea for Rotisserie Lite came to him one day near the end of the 1989 season when he was sitting on his tractor thinking about the Middle East situation.

"Late that season I suddenly found myself going sane," the tiller-scholar recalls. "I caught myself reading boxscores to find out who won, not just to see how my players had done. Some days I even read the front page first. Clearly, I was in trouble."

The academic-agrarian attacked the problem by identifying what he liked best and least about Rotisserie Ultra play in the League of Nations, where his team—the Smuts Peddlers—had always been a strong contender. "I like boxscores, and I like listening to games on the radio," he says. "I don't like the lure of trading, because it appeals to extreme type-A personalities like Okrent. I was spending too much time thinking about trades instead of about foreign policy or that funny sound my tractor was making."

While unwilling to go cold turkey (he still plays in the League of Nations), Farmer-Professor Lake did go looking for a halfway house. He found it when he founded the Washington Slo-Pitch League, a six-team outfit whose owners hail mostly from the nation's capital. (The mayor of the founder's hometown was awarded a one-third ownership in a franchise as a hedge against local tax increases. So far it's worked.)

"I see the game we play in Slo-Pitch as a halfway house in either direction," Farmer-Professor Lake says. "If you've never played Rotisserie before, it's a great way to learn what it's all about. And if you've been playing it too hard or too long, it helps you recapture the whimsy, and whimsy is the whole point of Rotisserie in the first place."

Thanks, Tony. We needed that.

ROTISSERIE LITE
The Rules of Play

Same Auction Draft!
Same Stat Categories!
Same Yoo-Hoo!

No Farm System!
No Reserve List!
No Money!

Editor's Note: *The following rules were lifted from the unwritten constitution of the Washington Slo-Pitch League, with several embellishments and alterations of our own to give them a bogus air of originality. Please note that we were too lazy to repeat all the pertinent rules of Rotisserie Regular that also apply in Rotisserie Lite. That means you'll have to go back and read the **Official Constitution of Rotisserie League Baseball** (pages 9–26) to figure out what we're talking about.*

LITE I. FEWER TEAMS

A Rotisserie Lite League using National League or American League players is composed of six teams.

- With only six teams, Rotisserie Lite Leagues have shorter (and probably more orderly) auction drafts, fewer friendships to wreck, and less trouble squeezing into a telephone booth.

LITE II. ONE DIVISION ONLY

A Rotisserie Lite League uses players from only *one* NL or AL division.

- Resist the temptation to draw players from an entire league or—worse still—to mix the two leagues. "Lite" doesn't mean "soft." By restricting the talent pool to players of one division, Lite owners will need to scout as diligently as do Rotisserie Regular and Rotisserie Ultra owners. You'll have to learn which middle innings relievers can be counted on for the greatest number of quality innings, which non-regular corner men will get the most at-bats, and which fourth outfielders will deliver 40 or more RBI. In other words, you'll have to become a better, more knowledgeable fan. And isn't that the Rotisserie Way?
- Using players from only one division helps an owner new to the world of Rotisserie to draw on his or her strength. After all, we all start out as fans of a particular team, which means that we enter the Rotisserie

world knowing and liking one team—and one division—better than others. What better place to start?

LITE III. NO MONEY

Each team has 23 Lite Dollars (L$) to spend at the auction draft to acquire a full roster of 23 active major league players, with a minimum salary and minimum bidding increments of 10 cents. But real money is not used.

- "The intensity of feeling in Rotisserie is unrelated to money anyhow," sez Farmer-Professor Lake. "If you play for traditional Rotissestakes—260 real dollars for 23 real players—it's enough to be irritating if you lose, but not enough to buy a new car if you win. So what's the point?"
- Using L$ still requires an owner to manage the team budget and cope with the exigencies of free market competition for the services of Barry Bonds, Cecil Fielder, and other superstars at the auction draft. Farmer-Professor Lake promises that your throat goes dry and your heart palpitates when the bidding hits L$2.70 for Jack McDowell, the same as when it crosses $30 for baseball's number-one Rock 'n' Roller in Regular and Ultra. This means that a kid owner can have just as much Rotissefun as a parent owner without having to beg for an advance against the next six months of allowances.
- Playing for L$ also makes a team owner feel a little less hysterical when the *Baseball America* and *Baseball Weekly* subs come due.

LITE IV. MONTHLY TRANSACTIONS

Transaction Day occurs once a month, on the Monday (AL) or Tuesday (NL) before stats appear in *USA Today*. The first Transaction Day falls on the first Monday or Tuesday in May. Except for the All-Star Break Trading Period described below, all Rotisserie Lite roster moves are restricted to Transaction Day.

- On Transaction Day, a Rotisserie Lite team may release players (a) placed on a major league disabled list; (b) demoted to the minor leagues; (c) traded to the other division or to the other major league; or (d) released by their major league team, *without limit* from its current roster and replace them with players from the free agent pool who qualify at the same position. Players may not be reserved. Even players on major league disabled lists must be released if their Rotisserie Lite owner chooses to replace them. Released players go into the free agent pool and may be claimed on the *next* Transaction Day.
- Player moves on Transaction Day shall take place in reverse order of the most recent standings, with the lowest team in the standings having the right of first claim on a player from the free agent pool. While there is no limit on the number of players a team may release and replace, a team may make only one transaction at a time. That is, the last-place team in a six-team league may not make a second

transaction until all other teams in the league have had an opportunity to make a transaction.

- As there is no reserve list in Rotisserie Lite, an owner whose star player is on his major league team's disabled list and isn't scheduled to come off for another two weeks will have to make a strategic call: Ride out the injury and retain the player under contract; or release him into the free agent pool and call up a replacement immediately.
- The salary of a player claimed from the free agent pool on Transaction Day is L$1.

LITE V. TRADE RESTRICTIONS

Except for a two-week trading period ending with the last out of the All-Star Game, no trades are permitted in Rotisserie Lite.

- All trades during the trading period take effect on the first pitch of the first regular season game after the All-Star Game.
- A Rotisserie Lite team may trade only one player with a salary of L$2 or more to any one team.

LITE VI. SAME SCORING CATEGORIES

Standings shall be determined on the same basis as in Rotisserie Regular and Rotisserie Ultra—that is, according to each team's cumulative performance over the course of a full season in eight statistical categories: home runs, RBI, stolen bases, and batting average for batters; wins, saves, ERA, and ratio (hits plus walks divided by innings pitched) for pitchers.

- A team receives points in each category according to its relative position. In a six-team league, the leader in home runs would receive six points, the second-place team five points, and so on. The team with the highest point total wins the Rotisserie Lite pennant.
- Standings should be compiled and distributed weekly. As keeping score is no more fun in Lite than in Regular or Ultra, new Lite leagues should consider the special deal offered by **Roti·Stats**. As transactions only take place monthly, **Roti·Stats** is able to provide timely, accurate weekly stat reports for Rotisserie Lite Leagues at a deep discount from its regular low rates. (See pages 304–305 for details.)

LITE VII. LONG-TERM CONTRACTS

The same rules governing the option year and long-term contracts that complicate an owner's life in Rotisserie Regular and Rotisserie Ultra shall also pertain in Rotisserie Lite. (See **Article XVII** of the Official Constitution, page 23.)

- **Exception:** A player under a long-term contract in Rotisserie Lite may be released and replaced at any time without penalty, subject only to the restrictions regarding player transactions.

LITE VIII. ROSTER PROTECTION

On April 1, each team may protect a certain number of players according to the following schedule: The team that finished first the preceding year may protect a maximum of seven players; all other teams, a maximum of ten players. There is no minimum requirement.

- Yes, this makes it a lot harder to build a dynasty. But trust us: One Harry Stein loose on the land is more than enough.
- Trading is not permitted over the winter on the grounds that Rotisserie Lite owners have better things to do with their time. Particularly those who also play Rotisserie Regular or Rotisserie Ultra.

LITE IX. YOO-HOO

As there is no prize pool to divvy up in Rotisserie Lite, the Yoo-Hoo running down a Rotisserie Lite pennant-winner's face and trickling into the corners of his or her mouth will taste all the sweeter, if you can imagine such a thing.

Editor's Postscript: *As you play Rotisserie Lite, let us know what you think. It takes a long time to turn a piece of coal into a diamond, and it may take us a couple of seasons to get Lite exactly rite. We particularly want to hear from you about new wrinkles, adaptations, and changes that we might scarf up for next year's book. Just remember:* Keep it Lite!

2

The Inner Game

More New Rotisserie Voices

Two years ago we decided to turn this chapter into a soapbox for other Rotisserie owners around the country. What the heck, we figured, it'll be a lot less work for us, and our fans will get a chance to tell us how much they appreciate our noble efforts in creating the Greatest Game for Baseball Fans Since Cricket.

Ha!

We have had our judgment, our intelligence, our credentials, our looks, and our sanity challenged. We have been dissed, diced, and dumped on by Rotisserians from coast to coast. We have seen our precious Rules of the Game attacked, sneered at, and slam-dunked. "How could you possibly . . ." is the most frequent opening line of submissions received by our Literary Properties Department. "You guys are a bunch of . . ." is the way most of them sign off.

Are we upset? Are our feelings hurt? Do we sometimes cry ourselves to sleep at night? You betcha. But all in all, we figure it's worth the grief. It's *still* a lot less work for us, and we get to meet a lot of, ah, swell people.

Take **Mark Batterman.** (Somebody, please . . . !) We actually met Mark back in 1986 when he and Ken Kuta of the Farah Fawcett-Major League in sunny Southern California showed up at our First Annual Rotisserie League National Spring Training Convention and Weenie Roast in Florida. (We don't hold the spring training conventions any more for fear that Batterman and Kuta might come back.) Since then, he has pestered us regularly about everything from player prices to typos in the book to rough spots in the rules to how much nicer the weather is in Malibu. This year, however, taking his lead from other miscreants and anarchists whose words have appeared in these chapters because of misguided generosity, he has gone way over the top. He has actually suggested—nay, *demanded*—that we scrap ratio as a Rotisserie scoring category and substitute . . . well, you can find out for yourself in **The K-Factor.**

Dottie Enrico, on the other hand, is perfectly content to play Rotisserie baseball according to the rules as promulgated by Beloved Founder and Former Commisioner-for-Life Daniel Okrent. Her only gripe is that we—the Founding Fathers—are a bunch of pig-headed, male-chauvinist, misogynist, neanderthal retros. That's nonsense, of course. One of the first things Sudden

Pete Gethers, owner of Peter's Famous Smoked Fish, did when he took over the ballclub was to announce that women were welcome in all areas of the clubhouse, specifically including the trainer's room and the showers. But Dottie and a gaggle of her gal pals rudely declined that invitation and instead went out and formed their own all-girls league. Fueled by a pack of lies fed them by former token female and Founding Mother of Rotisserie League Baseball, Valerie Salembier, they have their sights set on taking over the game. Next thing you know they'll be asking for equal pay for equal work. Read all about it in **A League of Their Own.**

WHO'S ON FIRST?

**ROTI·STATS KNOWS
CALL 800-884-7684**

The K-Factor
by Mark Batterman

Rotisserie League Baseball doesn't work.

Okay, okay, okay. I know how Daniel Okrent was beaned by the muse of Abner Doubleday, and how he created the greatest game for baseball fans since, uh, baseball. That story is older than the plot of *Pride of the Yankees*. Sure, I know about the millions who play Rotisserie. Yep, I know it's not just a game, it's a lifestyle. Hey, after all, this is my tenth season at the helm of the Mark's Brothers, duking it out in the Farrah Fawcett-Major League. After a decade of ruining my eyes reading boxscores, I know shin guards from Shinola.

But the unfortunate fact remains that Rotisserie League Baseball *does not work*. To be blunt, the basic structure of the game is flawed.

Most analytical discussions—okay, overheated shouting matches—about Rotisserie rules begin with the fundamental premise that Rotisserie baseball should match the results of real baseball, if not exactly then close to it. That creates the endless, mind-numbing debates over the merits and shortcomings of the original eight scoring categories. F. X. Flinn wrote in last year's book, "The more Rotisserie League Baseball resembles major league baseball, the better." Even though I do not necessarily concur, it's fair to assume that most Rotisserians would agree with that statement with the unbridled enthusiasm of Cecil Fielder attacking a post-game meal.

If that's the case, then there is a fundamental flaw in Rotisserie baseball: disrespect for starting pitchers.

Pitching, according to the old adage, is 90% of the game. Now, the person who first articulated that old adage didn't leave any notes behind to explain how that percentage was calculated, so maybe it's exaggerated by a few points. But there is no question that in real baseball pitching—and particularly starting pitching—is much more highly valued than in Rotisserie baseball.

The fundamental flaw of Rotisserie baseball is that, even though pitching accounts for half the scoring categories, we shortchange pitching and spend most of our money on hitting.

Think about it. Pitching represents 40 of the possible 80 points in a ten-team Rotisserie league (48 of 96 if you were nuts enough to expand or misguided enough to play American League). But you never hear of a veteran Rotisserie owner doing what would seem to be mandated by logic: divide the payroll in half and spend $130 on pitching, $130 on offense. Why? Because if you did, you couldn't buy an offense, and before the end of April, the only thing you would hear would be the booming sound of the cellar door slamming down on your head.

Nor would most owners simply divide their budget by 23 and allocate $158 for the 14 offensive players and $102 for the 9 pitchers (roughly 60%

for hitting and 40% for pitching). Why? The same fate, the same booming sound, but this time . . . Memorial Day.

To verify this observation, experienced Rotisserie owners need only look at their own leagues. If you play with the original eight categories, I'll bet that at least 70% of your draft day budget goes to offense—and in most leagues, the percentage is even higher. In the Farrah Fawcett-Major League, for example, we've spent as high as 85% of our aggregate payroll on offense. One team, the Kuta Kintes, once spent $251 on their fourteen offensive players and $9 for their nine pitchers—and still finished in the money!

Right about now the Founding Fathers are probably grumbling in their beards that this No Respect Effect manifests itself, if at all, only in brand-new leagues or leagues that throw everybody back every year. Not so! It is the FF-ML experience that the opposite is true. When there are a lot of keepers, prices for offense at the auction table are even higher, and prices for pitchers are even lower. Most owners in the FF-ML—and, I suspect, most Rotisserie owners everywhere—have a tendency to keep only low-priced offensive guys and closers and throw back almost all pitchers. This has the effect of making the offense supply even smaller and the pitching pool even larger. As a result, owners spend most of their cash on hitters and peanuts on pitchers.

Consider some prices (selected not altogether randomly) from the *1991* FF-ML draft:

Hitters	Starting Pitchers
Andy Van Slyke, $40	Doug Drabek, $14
Kevin Mitchell, $47	José Rijo, $15
Von Hayes, $36 (!)	Dwight Gooden $19
Darryl Strawberry, $46	Sid Fernandez, $4
George Bell, $43	Tom Glavine, $4
Howard Johnson, $42	David Cone, $6

The message is obvious. Granted, we may love offense too well, and maybe we've had our hearts broken by fourth and fifth starters too many times. But the fact remains that, under the original scoring categories spelled out in the Official Constitution of Rotisserie League Baseball, starting pitchers do not get proper respect. Compared with their place in real baseball, *starting pitchers in Rotisserie League Baseball are unimportant.*

So where does this bingeing on batters come from? A deep-rooted cynicism created by owning Kevin Gross once too often? The fear of hearing your own voice say the words "Tim Pugh for $14?" Or perhaps a chemical flashback to the sixties ("I'd rather be a hammer than a nail . . .")? To every thing, turn, turn, turn . . .

For starters (although I'm talking about relievers, too), it's a simple matter of supply and demand: there are too many pitchers available. If your Rotisserie league has 12 teams, at the end of the draft approximately 25% of the pitching talent, and I use that word advisedly, remains unbought. If you're a 10-team league, it's over 35%. It's basic supply side economics.

(What would you expect from a game created during the Reagan era?) When the market is flooded, prices come down, and vice versa.

Second, and most important, the stat categories are unbalanced. Of the original eight, there are three offensive categories based on absolute numbers—home runs, RBI, stolen bases—and only one based on relative numbers—batting average. This means the "average" hitter contributes to three categories (the average hitter's BA being the average of all hitters), while the "great" hitter contributes in four.

Pitching, on the other hand, has just two absolute categories—wins and saves—and two relative—ERA and ratio. This means that the average pitcher contributes to just two categories; and, to make matters worse, one of the absolute stats is saves. Thus, the average *starting* pitcher contributes, at best, to only one absolute category—wins. And we all know that wins are as elusive and unpredictable as a Frank Tanana spitter.

The bottom line is that if your league uses the original eight stats, spending big money on starting pitching is stupid, and most experienced owners know it. It is smarter, cheaper, and usually much more successful to pay for a top line reliever and one ace starter, grab a pitching staff of low priced, "don't-hurt-you" middle relievers named Les, and spend most of your cash on Big Bad Barry Bonds.

The fatal flaw! Rotisserie League Baseball values hitting much more than pitching. A complex and difficult problem created by the Founding Fathers. With a simple, easy, effective solution developed by the Farrah Fawcett-Major League: **REPLACE RATIO WITH STRIKEOUTS!**

Consider these prices from the *1993* FF-ML draft:

Hitters	Starting Pitchers
Barry Bonds, $47	José Rijo, $28
Marquis Grissom, $38	Greg Maddux, $28
Gary Sheffield, $30	Tom Glavine, $23
Bobby Bonilla, $25	Doug Drabek, $26
Ron Gant, $35	John Smoltz, $26
Dave Justice, $26	Sid Fernandez, $24

In the *1991* FF-ML draft, remember, approximately 15% of our aggregate payrolls was allocated to pitching. In *1993*, we spent about 40% of our resources on pitching. The reason for the change?

We eliminated ratio and replaced it with strikeouts!

The benefits are immediate and obvious:

- Starting pitchers finally have an absolute stat they control. When Bonds blasts a dinger, it's his. When Grissom steals a base, it's his. But when a starter leaves a game with a lead . . . who knows about the win? A strikeout belongs to the pitcher that chalks it up, and only to him. He fans a guy, it's his. That is an absolute number that can't be taken away. And that creates value.
- The value of the middle reliever is instantly diminished. They don't get enough innings to mount up those K's, and with a renewed focus

on starters, the "don't-hurt-you" ERA of a middle reliever becomes inconsequential. Plus, with the middle reliever devalued and every team holding a full complement of starting pitchers, you no longer have to be concerned about amassing enough innings to meet the Fenokee IP Requirement (see **Article IX of the Official Constitution,** p. 13).

- A good starting pitcher is suddenly a three-category player: ERA, wins, and strikeouts. Would you trade Fred McGriff for Terry Mulholland? Under the original Rotisserie rules: never. Under FF-ML rules, with strikeouts as a category: maybe, because now they're *both* three-category players.
- You have to manage smarter. With the addition of strikeouts, every category is separate and discrete. The days of sliding through on two pitching categories, ERA and ratio, are over. For the first time, every player—pitcher or batter—has the opportunity to contribute in the same number of ways. The ramifications are enormous, from draft day strategies, trades, and free agent pickups to Ultra moves and beyond.
- With more of your league's budget on the pitching side, and with salaries more evenly distributed across the board, you will rediscover the $15 player. The result? Each team starts every draft day on a more level playing field.
- You will actually be able to enjoy watching a baseball game again! Without ratio, you can watch your pitcher face your hitter and enjoy it. If your hitter gets a hit, so what? Good for him, but not bad for your pitcher. Unless, of course, your hitter hits a grand slam and causes your pitcher's ERA to jump like the national debt. What can I tell you—it's not a perfect world.
- With strikeouts replacing ratio as one of the "all-new" original eight scoring categories, Rotisserie League Baseball much more closely resembles real baseball in strategy, results, and team makeup. For instance, the pitching staff of the 1993 Mark's Brothers actually had five starters, one long man, and three short relievers. Tragically, three of the starters were named Reynoso, Brummert, and Luebbers. Hey, wait until next year!

In one broad, simple, decisive stroke, replacing ratio with strikeouts rectifies a major flaw in the game, accomplishes most of the goals of the alternative scoring methods, makes Rotisserie League Baseball more competitive and more fun to play, and justifies the existence of Danny Jackson, Jack Armstrong, and José Guzman. The 1993 Farrah Fawcett-Major League race was the closest and best in our ten-year history. The lead changed hands numerous times, there were only 15 points separating nine teams, and the Fuch Ewes won the pennant with only 56 points. The Ewes' strategy? Pitching, pitching, pitching. Thirty points in wins, ERA, and strikeouts, where the three-category starter now shines in Rotisserie ball as he does in the major leagues.

Forget hits plus walks divided by innings pitched. At the old ball game, it's *one, two, three* strikes yer out. . . .

A League of Their Own
by Dottie Enrico

Half a century ago it took Hitler and a world war to jumpstart the formation of the All-American Girls Professional Baseball League. All it took in 1993 to trigger the creation of the Second Sacs League, history's first all-female Rotisserie baseball league, was a nightmare.

The nightmare began when I joined the all-male Urban League last spring and spent many sleepless nights in late March and early April cramming for my first National League draft. I was trying extra hard to keep on top of my game because I wasn't just a rookie: I was—and still am—the Urban League's first girl owner.

One afternoon I curled up on the couch with Bill James and Alex Patton (the guidebooks, not the gurus themselves) and last year's edition of this book. Within minutes I was transported to dreamland's version of My Own Private Rotisserie Idaho. It looked something like this:

[*Cue harp music. Turn on fake smoke machine.*]
Our draft is being telecast on national TV. The auctioneer is Bob Eubanks. Each owner is seated in a little booth that swirls around from backstage as Bob introduces us.

"Now let's meet this season's owners: Clarence Thomas (swirl) . . . Howard Stern (twirl) . . . Randall Terry (whirl) . . . and Dottie Enrico (kerplunk)."

Next Bob announces that extra points and a year's supply of Q-vel for Leg Cramps (promotional consideration given) are to be awarded to owners drafting players who wear camouflage-print fatigues and drive trucks with gun racks during the offseason. Halfway through the broadcast, my roster reads like a subscriber list to *Soldier of Fortune:* Randy Myers, Will the Thrill, Curt Schilling, Todd Jones. All I can think of is how relieved I am that Jack Morris isn't in the National League.

Tonight's show is full of the customary macho ballscratching. Stern, proud owner of the Tim Belch-er-Farts, tries to draft Phillies-wife-cum-Hooters-postergirl Lynn Daulton. Justice Thomas, owner of the Long Dong Dingers, threatens to pass a law requiring major league ballgirls to wear thigh-high miniskirts to each homestand.

But just as Mitch Williams, my favorite relief pitcher in the entire universe, is going-going-gone on an $80 bid by No-Choice Terry, I awake with a start.

[*Fade out harp music. Reverse zoom into reality.*]

As we girls are prone to do, I began to probe my subconscious for the deeper psychological underpinnings. I unearthed a repressed memory of

THE INNER GAME •

reading in *Ms.* (or was it *Cosmo*?) that only 1–3% of all team owners are women. I was filled with rage. Why had women been relegated to the cheap seats in Rotisserie League Baseball for so long? Is it because men think we're whiny, manipulative, mean-spirited, and argumentative? (And if we are, so what? Aren't those the qualities of a pennant-winning Rotisserie GM?)

After making several phone calls to experienced Rotisserie players, it became painfully obvious that women just weren't being asked to play. This lunacy had to end. I began calling every woman I'd ever met who knew that ERA has two meanings. Three weeks later the Second Sacs League was born.

There are nine women in our league. Six of us are journalists: Debbie Whitefield, owner of the Virginia Wolves; Dena Bunis of the Brooklyn Blues; Kathy Sizemore of the Size-o-Matics; Nancy Logan of the Alley Cats; Lois DeLong of the Lois Lanes; and me—I own the Ballbusters. In addition, there is one ad exec—Elaine Klein, who took over management of the Killer Kleins for former owner/journalist Michele Parente—and a newspaper librarian and aspiring massage therapist (easy there, guys)—Christine Baird of the Baltimore Chops.

Perhaps the most esteemed member of our league is Susan Ashmore, owner of the Barchester Trollopes. A book editor by trade, Ashmore is also a refugee from that wasteland where fantasy baseball women have traditionally toiled: Susan is a ten-year veteran in the Rotisserie *Spouse* League.

For one decade of her baseball-loving life, Susan endured midnight phone calls and messages like, "Have David call me when he gets home. It's about Howard Johnson. Not the motel, honey. He plays for the New York Mets." (Thanks, buster.)

There was plenty to gloat about in the Ashmore household last season: hubby David won the pennant in the Urban League while Susan was the proud owner of Reggie Sanders at $5 and Tommy Greene at $6. Although she would have relished the opportunity to match (or beat) David, she was philosophical about the loss: "Who needs to come in first? They don't even let you wear a shower cap during that damned Yoo-Hoo ceremony."

Next spring, Susan will establish another Rotissemilestone when she becomes the first team owner to breast-feed during a draft. Dueling team ownership, however, has created one conflict between the Ashmores: will they name the little slugger Justice or Bonds?

I suppose there are still a few knuckledragging lugs out there who have deluded themselves into believing women are bad at politicking, negotiating, and striking deals. I guess these guys must not spend much time in the office. They certainly don't spend much time in the 1990s.

Rotisserie veterans may think they've seen it all, but there are a few things they can learn from the Second Sacs League. For instance, we think women and men *do* use different criteria when evaluating players. Men are content to pore over stacks of stats. Women delve deeper. They weigh really important factors such as:

- **The player's love/family life.** Of course Mark Grace had a career year! He started dating actress Janine Turner.
- **The ratio of cellulite to muscle mass.** Look at Terry Pendleton's

1993 stats before he went on the Pennant Race Diet. And lest we forget Kevin Mitchell, Sid Fernandez, and Hector Villanueva (was he sent to the fat farm or the minor leagues?). If you lined up John Kruk, David West, and Dom DeLuise and put flags over their faces, do you really think you could tell them apart?

- **Team fashion statements.** The Marlins will never win the World Series wearing those tacky teal uniforms. As for the crappy season the Reds had—well, just chalk it up to the fact that in those goofy outfits the team was never sure if it was supposed to hit home runs or hand out Fudgesicles.

- **A rose by any other name.** Lois Delong didn't know whom to pick up for Hojo when he made his 50th trip to the DL so she settled on Phil Clark. ("Why not?" asked the owner of the Lois Lanes. "He'll fit in perfectly at the corner positions next to Jeff Kent. I like the sound of a lineup card that reads Clark Kent.")

- **Facial hair.** The Second Sacs League is convinced there is a direct correlation between the presence of facial hair and the size of a pitcher's ERA. Any sign that a player is beginning to sprout a Jack McDowell goatee or a Rod Beck/Bryan Harvey willyworm moustache transmits a subliminal message to Second Sackers: "Activate me immediately." (Attention Trevor Hoffman owners: Keep the faith. Trev's just a sideburn away from a 20-save season.)

But perhaps the most dramatic contrast that can be drawn between the sexes is that girl owners hate drafting players who are loathsome human beings. One of our Honorary Commissionerettes, Lisa Winston of *Baseball Weekly,* subjects every potential draftee to her Dinner Table Test: she only selects players she would invite into her home for dinner.

"You have to put up with these players for a whole season," she reasons. "If you couldn't stomach having a meal with them, they're really going to make you sick if they're batting .225 with 40 RBI at the end of the season."

This explains her surprising lack of Phillies. (Surprising since she won the pennant in her all-male league with a team on which every NL franchise was represented except for the NL champs.) John Kruk did Lisa a favor when he told reporters that the Phillies weren't the kind of guys you'd want to share supper with. Case closed.

We admit, however, that women don't always make ideal Rotisserie players. Our tendency to draft nice guys often leads us to become too emotionally involved with our players. Confesses Winston: "The guys in my league call me Mrs. Ron Gant because I love Ronny so much."

Sometimes these attachments defy reason. For example, I never understood why Debbie got spontaneous PMS every time I reminded her of what a great deal she made by trading me Lenny Dykstra for Gant and (a then-slumping) Pendleton. One afternoon, she closed her office door and confessed, "I don't care if Ron hits 50 homers. To me he'll always be 'Gant Can't.' He can't replace my beloved Nails."

Unlike some men we know, no Second Sacs owner would ever take unfair advantage of another owner just because she carried the torch for one

---

of her players. We learned that lesson from our other Beloved Honorary Commissionerette: Founding Mother Valerie Salembier.

As long-time camp followers of Rotisserie baseball know, Val "The Gal" Salembier was one of the founding members of the original Rotisserie League back in 1980. You will understand how proud we were on the glorious day when we called Val and told her about the formation of an all-girls league. Now a high-powered executive who could buy and sell her former Rotisserie owners in a thrice, she still bears the Dracula-like scars left by her ex-leaguemates after they sucked every ounce of talent out of her team and her farm system and left her beloved Salembier Flambés for dead.

"Those guys would've cheated their own grandmothers to get to an attractive prospect," recalls Val the Gal. "They were constantly trying to rip me off. But back in those days I was thankful for the little things. At least they never asked me to serve coffee and donuts at the draft."

We hear you, Val. We've got to accentuate the positive. The truth is, Rotisserie League Baseball is a game for everybody, and despite the gender gap, there are far more similarities between the men and women who play than there are differences. We all experience the same morning rush as we peruse the boxscores. We share a common sense of dread when we realize we've drafted two Colorado Rockies pitchers. We all closed our eyes or kicked the pooch each time John Franco, Doug Jones, or Rob Dibble took the mound last season to close a one-run game.

These are tough times in the major leagues and in Rotisserie League Baseball. The sports analysts keep saying that interest in baseball is waning, especially among young people. Others say that the wave of excitement about fantasy baseball has crested. (In other words, TV revenue isn't the only thing that could be shrinking—so could your prize pool.)

Change is unsettling, and we're in for plenty of it in this age of wild card playoffs and three regional divisions. So the next time the concepts of equality for women and social progress make you feel like you're about to upchuck, just pretend you're Tom Werner and repeat the following: women constitute 50% of the population. Their fannies can fill plenty of seats at next year's draft, and their purses are a real pretty source of future revenues.

You let us into your clubhouses, maybe we'll let you into ours.

Hunks in Spikes

Now that they know about the Second Sacs League, several macho Rotissegeeks of our acquaintance are constantly coming up to us, ostensibly to talk a little ball. But do they ask for our opinion on what was behind Will Clark's second straight off-year? Do they want to know what we think is going to happen in the Astros bullpen? Do they care about our views on Howard Johnson's mysterious decline? No. The most frequently asked question is always "So which players do you girls think have the best butts in baseball?"

(Continued)

It's demeaning. It's insulting. It's beneath us. It's also a little puzzling: why are these self-styled he-men so obessively preoccupied with that particular part of the male anatomy? But as a service to all the fellas who read this book each season, and who may share this rather narrowly focused concern, we hauled out our league Butt-o-Meter and will now answer all your questions, repressed and otherwise. What follows is a collection of all-stars that gives the "fantasy" component of Rotisserie League Baseball new meaning. At least to us.

The 1993 Second Sacs All-Hunk Team

C: **Darren Daulton.** Va-va-va-voom! Jean-Claude Van Damme merged with Troy Donahue.

C: **Todd Hundley.** The best—no, the *only*—reason to make a trip to Shea last season.

1B: **Mark Grace.** We trust implicitly in Janine Turner's good taste. Right on, Sister!

2B: **Ryno Sandberg.** The Cary Grant of the NL—a class act.

3B: **Gary Sheffield.** The only thing that turned more female heads at Joe Robbie Stadium was Wayne Huizenga doing the hokey pokey.

SS: **Barry Larkin.** Looked so sweet filling out that Good Humor–style uniform. We'll take two scoops of rocky road on a sugar cone.

COR: **Fred McGriff.** Growl.

MIF: **Mark Lemke.** Wears those funky Elvis Costello glasses.

OF: **Ron Gant.** Best bod in baseball. Period.

OF: **Jeff Conine.** Could've starred with Annette Funicello in *Beach Blanket Bingo*, one of our all-time faves. Squeaky clean, All-American good looks. Wonder if he likes dirty talk?

OF: **Len Dykstra.** First thing, we'd give him a good scrubbing.

OF: **Erik Pappas.** Eligible at C, IB, and OF, but his best position is Decorative Bench Ornament.

OF: **Ryan Thompson.** The only person outside of our league who thinks Ryan is this hot is Ryan.

UT: **Tom Foley.** Bespectacled. Civilized. Quiet. And underneath that facade, an animal.

P: **Pete Harnisch.** Because Commissionerette Winston thinks a smile and a sense of humor are worth a 1,000-point Butt-o-Meter bonus.

P: **José Rijo.** So manly, he transformed a watergun into a phallic symbol.

P: **Dennis Martinez.** El Presidente es muy delicioso.

P: **Andy Benes.** So what if the guy has only one big eyebrow? It works for Brooke Shields.

P: **Greg W. Harris.** Pitchers don't usually have good bods. He's the exception.

3

Scouting Report

1994 Player Ratings

Last year in this space we projected that in 1993 Doug Drabek, Bret Sa-berhagen, Roger Clemens, Scott Erickson, Melido Perez, John Smiley, Rob Dibble, Jeff Reardon, Mark McGwire, Howard Johnson, Felix José, Ray Lankford, Darryl Strawberry, José Canseco, and Kirby Puckett would be worth $22, $20, $28, $14, $15, $17, $28, $28, $37, $32, $27, $32, $29, $38, and $40, respectively.

Collectively, they fell a little short. About two hundred bucks short, if you want the ugly truth of it.

Part of the shortfall can be explained by injury: McGwire, HoJo, Straw-berry. Part came about because of arrogance and stupidity: Canseco. Part resulted from excessive sentiment on our part: Puckett. And part is inevitable, because this business of forecasting who's going to do what is tough.

How tough? Well, even Harry Stein and the Brenners finished out of the money last year for the third straight season. Next question?

This year we tried to do better. We taped every ESPN game and every edition of *Baseball Tonight* and spent the winter watching them frame by frame. We memorized the Final 1993 Averages (see Appendix, pages 319–341). We asked Mike Lupica. We read everything you read. We established sub-committees, had meetings, listened to expert witnesses, crunched numbers, drafted preliminary reports, and forwarded our findings to Hillary Rodham Clinton for her input. She never got back to us.

So there is an outside chance that we'll kick a few more this year. Please drop us a note after the season is over and let us know if you detected any egregious overpricing. That's the only way we can grow.

Actually, there's one more thing you can do that's even better: you can beat us at our own game. That's right, you can play in the Beat the Founding Fathers at Their Own Game League and prove that your crystal balls are bigger than ours. The details are on page 280, but essentially all you have to do is draft a Rotisserie team based on prices listed in this chapter. We put you in a league that includes one of the Founding Fathers. (If you don't want to play in Harry Stein's league, just let us know.) You get monthly standings reports. And at the All-Star break you get a chance to throw back your bums and replace them with fresh talent. Scoring is based on the traditional eight Rotisserie categories. If you win the pennant, you get a few cheap prizes and fifteen minutes of fame: your name will be listed in next year's edition of this book. Not bad for just fifty bucks, is it?

(What's that? You expected a free lunch? Sorry, champ, the kids need new shoes.)

The salary projections here are based, of course, on a zero-sum game—that is, a start-from-scratch situation. If yours is a continuing league and you carry over a certain number of players from year to year, your auction day prices will be skewed by the talent available. If all but a handful of closers are being kept, for example, the ones who are in the draft will be especially pricey. Our price projections will be less useful in such situations, and you should draw more heavily—as you undoubtedly already do—on the raw (and cooked) data we also provide.

Also note that players appear in the league in which they finished last season. Thus, look for Will Clark in the NL, Dave Magadan in the AL.

Here you get four years of major league stats (where applicable) for about 500 position players and pitchers, along with meaty (and sometimes potatoey) observations that, we hope, will be of some small benefit as you devise your draft strategy. In the next chapter we offer our new, bigger-and-better-than-ever-before Rotisserie Stat Pak, which provides lists of last season's best (and worst) performances in all the Rotisserie scoring categories.

If all that isn't enough to win you a Yoo-Hoo shower, don't call us. Call Hillary Rodham Clinton.

A NUMBERS GAME

For the fourth consecutive season, STATS, Inc. is responsible for the numbers in this chapter, the lists of best and worst 1993 performances in Chapter Four, and the final 1993 averages at the end of the book. The STATS team—headed by John Dewan and Bob Mecca—is also responsible for a lot of the fancy numerical footwork in *Sports Illustrated* and *USA Today*, and we're delighted that they're playing on our side as well. Check out page 244 for a full list of their publications and services, all of which will help you solve the mysteries of Rotisserie life.

The last line of numbers for each position player summarizes his preceding four seasons in a "Seasonal Notation." This device, invented by the great Bill James, is a way to express a player's performance over several seasons in a way that is immediately understandable—in essence, it shows what a player does every 162 games. (Not, lest there be any confusion, what he would do *if* he played all 162 games in a single season. There's a big difference. Think about it.)

For pitchers, instead of Seasonal Notation there is simply an average of his numbers in the preceding four years.

Use Seasonal Notation with caution: the veteran Rotisserian knows it to be a useful indicator, not a rock-solid guarantee of performance. It does not account for platoon differentials, injuries, getting old, change of role, change of team, or other reasons why a player's playing time and performance might fluctuate radically. Nor is it especially useful for forecasting performances of players with only a year or so in the majors.

Behind the Plate

Some Rotisserie owners budget a buck apiece for their two catchers, then take whatever backup backstops are left over at the end of the auction draft. They figure that offensive talent is so thin behind the plate that their money would be better spent where the pickings aren't so lean. Teams have won pennants with this approach.

Other Rotisserie owners spend whatever is necessary to acquire solid producers to be their two catchers. They reason that offensive talent is so thin behind the plate that getting good production from that position is an important key to Rotisserie success. Teams have won pennants with this approach.

The considered opinion of the Founding Fathers, after a decade and a half spent studying this matter, is that you never can tell.

Who could have predicted that Rick Wilkins was going to hit 30 home runs last season? Not us, by golly, or we might have projected a slightly higher salary than the $5 we put down for him in last year's book. Anybody out there figure Chad Kreuter would hit 15 dingers, bat .286, and drive in 51 runs last season? If so, you should give up Rotisserie baseball at once and head straight to the racetrack.

Or stick with Rotisserie and figure out who's going to be this year's Mike Piazza.

NATIONAL LEAGUE

BRAD AUSMUS   **Age 24/R**   **$2**

The Padres think this Dartmouth grad is their catcher of the future, which presumably began sometime last summer during the Fire Sale. The Yankees, who originally signed Ausmus and then left him exposed in the expansion draft, view him as a good defensive catcher with a marginal bat and a good college degree—sort of a Wizard of Ausmus behind the plate, a Cowardly Lion in the batter's box, a Scarecrow after he got a brain. True, the Yankees have been known to make mistakes (e.g., trading Fred McGriff for nothing). But so have the Padres (e.g., trading Fred McGriff for nothing).

Year	Team	Lg.	Pos.	G	AB	R	H	HR	RBI	SB	BA
1993	San Diego	NL	C	49	160	18	41	5	12	2	.256
Seasonal Notation					528	59	135	16	39	6	.256

BASEBALL ANAGRAM #1

Meat Loving = _____?

(Answer on page 299)

DAMON BERRYHILL   Age 30/B $5

For a second year we repeat the following advice: plan on Berryhill landing somewhere other than Atlanta, where Javy Lopez is going to take over as The Man in the Iron Mask. One of these years we'll be right. Until then, anyone looking for a backup backstop with pop will get a good return on a small investment.

Year	Team	Lg.	Pos.	G	AB	R	H	HR	RBI	SB	BA
1990	Chicago	NL	C	17	53	6	10	1	9	0	.189
1991	Chicago	NL	C	62	159	13	30	5	14	1	.189
1991	Atlanta	NL	C	1	1	0	0	0	0	0	0.000
1992	Atlanta	NL	C	101	307	21	70	10	43	0	.228
1993	Atlanta	NL	C	115	335	24	82	8	43	0	.245
Seasonal Notation					467	35	105	13	59	0	.225

DARREN DAULTON   Age 32/L $24

The best catcher in baseball the last two years. Given decent health, he should be the best catcher in baseball for the next two years as well. But good health is not exactly a given among catchers, especially 33-year-old catchers with knees like Daulton's. We're not presuming to practice medicine without a license or anything. But we are suggesting that you proceed with caution.

Year	Team	Lg.	Pos.	G	AB	R	H	HR	RBI	SB	BA
1990	Philadelphia	NL	C	143	459	62	123	12	57	7	.268
1991	Philadelphia	NL	C	89	285	36	56	12	42	5	.196
1992	Philadelphia	NL	C	145	485	80	131	27	109	11	.270
1993	Philadelphia	NL	C	147	510	90	131	24	105	5	.257
Seasonal Notation					537	82	136	23	96	8	.254

DARRIN FLETCHER   Age 27/L $6

Manager Felipe Alou and Expos pitching coach Joe Kerrigan aired Fletcher out for being lackadaisical behind the plate. Fletcher listened. Next hitting coach Tommy Harper started nagging him to move up on the plate and go for power. Fletcher listened. Then he went out and had a bang-up second half. Amazing, isn't it—a modern-day baseball player who actually listens to somebody else.

Year	Team	Lg.	Pos.	G	AB	R	H	HR	RBI	SB	BA
1990	Los Angeles	NL	C	2	1	0	0	0	0	0	0.000
1990	Philadelphia	NL	C	9	22	3	3	0	1	0	.136
1991	Philadelphia	NL	C	46	136	5	31	1	12	0	.228
1992	Montreal	NL	C	83	222	13	54	2	26	0	.243
1993	Montreal	NL	C	133	396	33	101	9	60	0	.255
Seasonal Notation					461	32	112	7	58	0	.243

JOE GIRARDI   Age 29/R $3

Poor Joe. Last season was supposed to be his big chance to prove he was a major league hitter. But then he got injured, and when he came back all he proved was that he could handle a Triple-A pitching staff.

Year	Team	Lg.	Pos.	G	AB	R	H	HR	RBI	SB	BA
1990	Chicago	NL	C	133	419	36	113	1	38	8	.270
1991	Chicago	NL	C	21	47	3	9	0	6	0	.191
1992	Chicago	NL	C	91	270	19	73	1	12	0	.270
1993	Colorado	NL	C	86	310	35	90	3	31	6	.290
Seasonal Notation					511	45	139	2	42	6	.272

CARLOS HERNANDEZ   Age 26/R $1

Anybody remember Bruce Edwards, a catcher for the Dodgers when Roy Campanella came up? He was actually Carlos Hernandez in an earlier incarnation.

Year	Team	Lg.	Pos.	G	AB	R	H	HR	RBI	SB	BA
1990	Los Angeles	NL	C	10	20	2	4	0	1	0	.200
1991	Los Angeles	NL	C	15	14	1	3	0	1	1	.214
1992	Los Angeles	NL	C	69	173	11	45	3	17	0	.260
1993	Los Angeles	NL	C	50	99	6	25	2	7	0	.253
Seasonal Notation					344	22	86	5	29	1	.252

TODD HUNDLEY   Age 24/B $4

When a guy gets benched in favor of Charlie O'Brien, it should send alarm signals. So should the presence of prospect Brooks Fordyce, whom the Mets will give every chance to win the job this spring. But Hundley showed double-digit HR power last season, and he's still only 24. We think he's worth a modest investment.

Year	Team	Lg.	Pos.	G	AB	R	H	HR	RBI	SB	BA
1990	New York	NL	C	36	67	8	14	0	2	0	.209
1991	New York	NL	C	21	60	5	8	1	7	0	.133
1992	New York	NL	C	123	358	32	75	7	32	3	.209
1993	New York	NL	C	130	417	40	95	11	53	1	.228
Seasonal Notation					471	44	100	9	49	2	.213

STEVE LAKE   Age 37/R $1

Five home runs last year? Probably a typo.

Year	Team	Lg.	Pos.	G	AB	R	H	HR	RBI	SB	BA
1990	Philadelphia	NL	C	29	80	4	20	0	6	0	.250
1991	Philadelphia	NL	C	58	158	12	36	1	11	0	.228
1992	Philadelphia	NL	C	20	53	3	13	1	2	0	.245
1993	Chicago	NL	C	44	120	11	27	5	13	0	.225
Seasonal Notation					440	32	102	7	34	0	.234

TIM LAKER   Age 24/R $1

Born in Encino, California, which makes him a Greater Los Angeles Laker.

Year	Team	Lg.	Pos.	G	AB	R	H	HR	RBI	SB	BA
1992	Montreal	NL	C	28	46	8	10	0	4	1	.217
1993	Montreal	NL	C	43	86	3	17	0	7	2	.198
Seasonal Notation					301	25	61	0	25	6	.205

KIRT MANWARING   Age 28/R $5

Okay, so we were wrong to say last year that *Fred* Waring was a better hitter. But who knows what kind of hitter Fred would have been if he'd had Bobby Bonds as his hitting coach?

Year	Team	Lg.	Pos.	G	AB	R	H	HR	RBI	SB	BA
1990	San Francisco	NL	C	8	13	0	2	0	1	0	.154
1991	San Francisco	NL	C	67	178	16	40	0	19	1	.225
1992	San Francisco	NL	C	109	349	24	85	4	26	2	.244
1993	San Francisco	NL	C	130	432	48	119	5	49	1	.275
Seasonal Notation					501	45	126	4	49	2	.253

BOB NATAL   Age 28/R $1

You've got to have a second-string catcher for a buck, right? So why not take a chance on this guy? The Marlins have fallen out of love with Benito Santiago, and Natal is a former Expos product. In an organization where virtually every top executive is a former Expos product, that's like being a Friend of Bill in Washington.

Year	Team	Lg.	Pos.	G	AB	R	H	HR	RBI	SB	BA
1992	Montreal	NL	C	5	6	0	0	0	0	0	0.000
1993	Florida	NL	C	41	117	3	25	1	6	1	.214
Seasonal Notation					433	10	88	3	21	3	.203

CHARLIE O'BRIEN   Age 32/R $1

We realize that even Dallas Green, the Foghorn Leghorn of baseball managers, must have gotten punch-drunk watching the plucky Mets reinvent the game of baseball. But what on earth was Big D thinking of when he made this guy the number two hitter?

Year	Team	Lg.	Pos.	G	AB	R	H	HR	RBI	SB	BA
1990	Milwaukee	AL	C	46	145	11	27	0	11	0	.186
1990	New York	NL	C	28	68	6	11	0	9	0	.162
1991	New York	NL	C	69	168	16	31	2	14	0	.185
1992	New York	NL	C	68	156	15	33	2	13	0	.212
1993	New York	NL	C	67	188	15	48	4	23	1	.255
Seasonal Notation					422	36	87	4	40	0	.207

JOE OLIVER   Age 28/R $9

Turned Dan Wilson into trade bait with his solid production and decent backstopping. Among NL catchers, only Daulton, Piazza, and Wilkins put up better power numbers, and each of them will cost more than twice what Oliver customarily fetches in a Rotisserie draft.

Year	Team	Lg.	Pos.	G	AB	R	H	HR	RBI	SB	BA
1990	Cincinnati	NL	C	121	364	34	84	8	52	1	.231
1991	Cincinnati	NL	C	94	269	21	58	11	41	0	.216
1992	Cincinnati	NL	C	143	485	42	131	10	57	2	.270
1993	Cincinnati	NL	C	139	482	40	115	14	75	0	.239
Seasonal Notation					521	44	126	14	73	0	.243

GREG OLSON
Age 33/R   **$1**

The Braves love Olson's attitude, but not as much as they love Javy Lopez's talent.

Year	Team	Lg.	Pos.	G	AB	R	H	HR	RBI	SB	BA
1990	Atlanta	NL	C	100	298	36	78	7	36	1	.262
1991	Atlanta	NL	C	133	411	46	99	6	44	1	.241
1992	Atlanta	NL	C	95	302	27	72	3	27	2	.238
1993	Atlanta	NL	C	83	262	23	59	4	24	1	.225
Seasonal Notation					501	52	121	7	51	1	.242

JAYHAWK OWENS
Age 25/R   **$1**

If he has the talent to match his name, we're talking first-ballot Hall of Fame.

Year	Team	Lg.	Pos.	G	AB	R	H	HR	RBI	SB	BA
1993	Colorado	NL	C	33	86	12	18	3	6	1	.209
Seasonal Notation					422	58	88	14	29	4	.209

TOM PAGNOZZI
Age 31/R   **$5**

The Cardinals flopped for a lot of reasons: bullpen injuries, a mediocre rotation, an off-year from Ray Lankford, and—most important—the tight-fisted ways of the brewery, which refuses to spend money on a franchise that has maybe the best fans and richest tradition in the game. (Put your Proud to be Your Bud right here, August Busch III.) But one of the most frequently overlooked reasons was Pags getting hurt and missing nearly half the season. His absence forced into service the immortal . . .

Year	Team	Lg.	Pos.	G	AB	R	H	HR	RBI	SB	BA
1990	St. Louis	NL	C	69	220	20	61	2	23	1	.277
1991	St. Louis	NL	C	140	459	38	121	2	57	9	.264
1992	St. Louis	NL	C	139	485	33	121	7	44	2	.249
1993	St. Louis	NL	C	92	330	31	85	7	41	1	.258
Seasonal Notation					550	44	142	6	60	4	.260

ERIK PAPPAS
Age 27/R   **$1**

. . . who played all right for a while. Looks like he's going to be a much better hitter than either Milt or Irene.

Year	Team	Lg.	Pos.	G	AB	R	H	HR	RBI	SB	BA
1991	Chicago	NL	C	7	17	1	3	0	2	0	.176
1993	St. Louis	NL	C	82	228	25	63	1	28	1	.276
Seasonal Notation					445	47	120	1	54	1	.269

MIKE PIAZZA
Age 25/R   **$27**

According to old Dodger hands such as Joey Amalfitano, Joe Ferguson, Bill Russell, and Vin Scully, Piazza is the strongest guy they've ever seen in a Dodger uniform. How strong? Well, you know those hand grippers that fitness freaks like to squeeze? The Dodgers had to order specially made ones with extra tension for Piazza because he didn't get any resistance from the conventional version. For all his muscles, Piazza is still just a baseball baby with a lot to learn. What sets him apart is a willingness—no,

Catchers
pp. 59-73

Corners
pp. 73-95

Infield
pp. 95-116

Outfield
pp. 117-150

DH
pp. 150-153

Starters
pp. 154-189

Relievers
pp. 190-217

an *obsession*—to do it, to learn about his craft. Bid the ranch on him for years to come.

Year	Team	Lg.	Pos.	G	AB	R	H	HR	RBI	SB	BA
1992	Los Angeles	NL	C	21	69	5	16	1	7	0	.232
1993	Los Angeles	NL	C	149	547	81	174	35	112	3	.318
Seasonal Notation					587	81	181	34	113	2	.308

TODD PRATT   Age 27/R $1

Two things to keep in mind: Pratt has some sock, and Darren Daulton's creaky knees are always one misstep away from six weeks on the DL.

Year	Team	Lg.	Pos.	G	AB	R	H	HR	RBI	SB	BA
1992	Philadelphia	NL	C	16	46	6	13	2	10	0	.283
1993	Philadelphia	NL	C	33	87	8	25	5	13	0	.287
Seasonal Notation					439	46	125	23	76	0	.286

TOM PRINCE   Age 29/R $1

A Frog.

Year	Team	Lg.	Pos.	G	AB	R	H	HR	RBI	SB	BA
1990	Pittsburgh	NL	C	4	10	1	1	0	0	0	.100
1991	Pittsburgh	NL	C	26	34	4	9	1	2	0	.265
1992	Pittsburgh	NL	C	27	44	1	4	0	5	1	.091
1993	Pittsburgh	NL	C	66	179	14	35	2	24	1	.196
Seasonal Notation					351	26	64	3	40	2	.184

JEFF REED   Age 31/L $2

We'd get a little excited about those six dingers if he'd had more than 13 in nine previous seasons combined.

Year	Team	Lg.	Pos.	G	AB	R	H	HR	RBI	SB	BA
1990	Cincinnati	NL	C	72	175	12	44	3	16	0	.251
1991	Cincinnati	NL	C	91	270	20	72	3	31	0	.267
1992	Cincinnati	NL	C	15	25	2	4	0	2	0	.160
1993	San Francisco	NL	C	66	119	10	31	6	12	0	.261
Seasonal Notation					391	29	100	7	40	0	.256

BENITO SANTIAGO   Age 29/R $10

Didn't take long for him to wear out his welcome, did it? The Marlins will try to trade him, but the big salary and bad attitude will be hard to move. Fortunately, bad attitude has never been a big Rotisserie concern, particularly from catchers capable of delivering double figures in HR *and* SB.

Year	Team	Lg.	Pos.	G	AB	R	H	HR	RBI	SB	BA
1990	San Diego	NL	C	100	344	42	93	11	53	5	.270
1991	San Diego	NL	C	152	580	60	155	17	87	8	.267
1992	San Diego	NL	C	106	386	37	97	10	42	2	.251
1993	Florida	NL	C	139	469	49	108	13	50	10	.230
Seasonal Notation					579	61	147	16	75	8	.255

SCOTT SERVAIS   Age 26/R $6

There is a hoary Rotisserie strategy, dating back to 1980, of drafting both your catchers from the same major league team. That was the year that the Getherswag Goners signed Ted Simmons and Terry Kennedy—the regular catcher and his backup, respectively, for the St. Louis Cardinals—and went on to win the first-ever Rotisserie pennant. Last season Servais and Eddie Taubensee combined for 20 homers and 74 RBI, and in most drafts their combined price was several bucks less than that of Benito Santiago or Joe Oliver. There's a lesson to be learned here, we think.

Year	Team	Lg.	Pos.	G	AB	R	H	HR	RBI	SB	BA
1991	Houston	NL	C	16	37	0	6	0	6	0	.162
1992	Houston	NL	C	77	205	12	49	0	15	0	.239
1993	Houston	NL	C	85	258	24	63	11	32	0	.244
Seasonal Notation					455	32	107	10	48	0	.236

DANNY SHEAFFER   Age 32/R $1

We liked what we saw last summer. So did the Rockies. Stay tuned.

Year	Team	Lg.	Pos.	G	AB	R	H	HR	RBI	SB	BA
1993	Colorado	NL	C	82	216	26	60	4	32	2	.278
Seasonal Notation					426	51	118	7	63	3	.278

DON SLAUGHT   Age 35/R $7

He can't go more than 350–400 AB a year, but Sluggo has made himself into a rock solid offensive player. Career high last year in RBI, highest HR total since 1986. A very late bloomer?

Year	Team	Lg.	Pos.	G	AB	R	H	HR	RBI	SB	BA
1990	Pittsburgh	NL	C	84	230	27	69	4	29	0	.300
1991	Pittsburgh	NL	C	77	220	19	65	1	29	1	.295
1992	Pittsburgh	NL	C	87	255	26	88	4	37	2	.345
1993	Pittsburgh	NL	C	116	377	34	113	10	55	2	.300
Seasonal Notation					481	47	149	8	66	2	.310

TIM SPEHR   Age 27/R $1

If he played opera instead of baseball, he would be a Spehr carrier.

Year	Team	Lg.	Pos.	G	AB	R	H	HR	RBI	SB	BA
1991	Kansas City	AL	C	37	74	7	14	3	14	1	.189
1993	Montreal	NL	C	53	87	14	20	2	10	2	.230
Seasonal Notation					289	37	61	9	43	5	.211

EDDIE TAUBENSEE   Age 25/L $5

There is a hoary Rotisserie strategy, dating back to 1980 ... but you know all about that, don't you? (If not, see Scott Servais.)

Year	Team	Lg.	Pos.	G	AB	R	H	HR	RBI	SB	BA
1991	Cleveland	AL	C	26	66	5	16	0	8	0	.242
1992	Houston	NL	C	104	297	23	66	5	28	2	.222
1993	Houston	NL	C	94	288	26	72	9	42	1	.250
Seasonal Notation					470	39	111	10	56	2	.237

BASEBALL ANAGRAM #2

I Slew Swat = _____?

(Answer on page 299)

Catchers
pp. 59-73

Corners
pp. 73-95

Infield
pp. 95-116

Outfield
pp. 117-150

DH
pp. 150-153

Starters
pp. 154-189

Relievers
pp. 190-217

HECTOR VILLANUEVA   Age 29/R $1

Yes, he ate himself out of the National League. But wasn't the DH rule invented for guys like Hector? And wouldn't the world be a better place if he got another chance—say, in Fenway Park?

Year	Team	Lg.	Pos.	G	AB	R	H	HR	RBI	SB	BA
1990	Chicago	NL	C	52	114	14	31	7	18	1	.272
1991	Chicago	NL	C	71	192	23	53	13	32	0	.276
1992	Chicago	NL	C	51	112	9	17	2	13	0	.152
1993	St. Louis	NL	C	17	55	7	8	3	9	0	.145
Seasonal Notation					401	44	92	21	61	0	.230

RICK WILKINS   Age 26/L $23

Can he do it again? You betcha.

Year	Team	Lg.	Pos.	G	AB	R	H	HR	RBI	SB	BA
1991	Chicago	NL	C	86	203	21	45	6	22	3	.222
1992	Chicago	NL	C	83	244	20	66	8	22	0	.270
1993	Chicago	NL	C	136	446	78	135	30	73	2	.303
Seasonal Notation					474	63	130	23	62	2	.275

DAN WILSON   Age 25/R $1

For years we've been hearing from the Reds about this guy being a big-time prospect. Then we get a look at him and he turns out to be Bob Melvin. Now he's with Seattle. Don't lose any sleep over him.

Year	Team	Lg.	Pos.	G	AB	R	H	HR	RBI	SB	BA
1992	Cincinnati	NL	C	12	25	2	9	0	3	0	.360
1993	Cincinnati	NL	C	36	76	6	17	0	8	0	.224
Seasonal Notation					340	27	87	0	37	0	.257

AMERICAN LEAGUE

SANDY ALOMAR, JR.   Age 27/R $6

Isn't it strange how these things turn out? A lot of people, most especially including the Indians front office, were ready to stick a fork in Sandy The Junior after two off years, a deteriorating work ethic, and back surgery. But then he worked his head off in post-operative rehab, returned to play his tail off in the season's final six weeks, and is now a good bet to pay off your draft day investment in him with All-Star numbers.

Year	Team	Lg.	Pos.	G	AB	R	H	HR	RBI	SB	BA
1990	Cleveland	AL	C	132	445	60	129	9	66	4	.290
1991	Cleveland	AL	C	51	184	10	40	0	7	0	.217
1992	Cleveland	AL	C	89	299	22	75	2	26	3	.251
1993	Cleveland	AL	C	64	215	24	58	6	32	3	.270
Seasonal Notation					551	55	145	8	63	4	.264

PAT BORDERS
Age 30/R   **$7**

We thought Ed Sprague would replace him, but then Sprague became a third baseman. We thought Randy Knorr would replace him, but then Knorr showed he couldn't hit. We now think Carlos Delgado will replace him as the Blue Jays catcher sometime this season. We're nothing if not consistent.

Year	Team	Lg.	Pos.	G	AB	R	H	HR	RBI	SB	BA
1990	Toronto	AL	C	125	346	36	99	15	49	0	.286
1991	Toronto	AL	C	105	291	22	71	5	36	0	.244
1992	Toronto	AL	C	138	480	47	116	13	53	1	.242
1993	Toronto	AL	C	138	488	38	124	9	55	2	.254
Seasonal Notation					513	45	131	13	61	0	.255

CARLTON FISK
Too Old/R   **$0**

Good old Pudge. We couldn't let him leave the ballpark without saying goodbye—and without lamenting how what should have been a triumphant farewell turned into a name-calling contest with White Sox owner and designated snake Jerry Reinsdorf. For some of us Fisk's departure is just one more utterly unnecessary reminder that, like old number 27/72, we're getting a little long in tooth. The problem is that, unlike him, we don't have the Hall of Fame to look forward to. There is talk that New Hampshire Republicans want Pudge to run for governor. The mind boggles. If Fisk gives speeches the way he caught games, then the good citizens of the Granite State are in for four years of Castro-like stemwinders that go on for hours.

Year	Team	Lg.	Pos.	G	AB	R	H	HR	RBI	SB	BA
1990	Chicago	AL	C	137	452	65	129	18	65	7	.285
1991	Chicago	AL	C	134	460	42	111	18	74	1	.241
1992	Chicago	AL	C	62	188	12	43	3	21	3	.229
1993	Chicago	AL	C	25	53	2	10	1	4	0	.189
Seasonal Notation					521	54	132	18	74	4	.254

BRIAN HARPER
Age 34/R   **$11**

No hitter in baseball is more frequently underrated, unnoticed, and unappreciated. Not by us, though.

Year	Team	Lg.	Pos.	G	AB	R	H	HR	RBI	SB	BA
1990	Minnesota	AL	C	134	479	61	141	6	54	3	.294
1991	Minnesota	AL	C	123	441	54	137	10	69	1	.311
1992	Minnesota	AL	C	140	502	58	154	9	73	0	.307
1993	Minnesota	AL	C	147	530	52	161	12	73	1	.304
Seasonal Notation					581	67	176	11	80	1	.304

BILL HASELMAN
Age 27/R   **$1**

If Dan Wilson can't cut the mustard, which is likely, Haselman could end up being Seattle's catcher and a nice bargain pickup. A big guy with little offensive pop.

Year	Team	Lg.	Pos.	G	AB	R	H	HR	RBI	SB	BA
1990	Texas	AL	DH	7	13	0	2	0	3	0	.154
1992	Seattle	AL	C	8	19	1	5	0	0	0	.263
1993	Seattle	AL	C	58	137	21	35	5	16	2	.255
Seasonal Notation					375	48	93	11	42	4	.249

Catchers pp. 59–73

Corners pp. 73–95

Infield pp. 95–116

Outfield pp. 117–150

DH pp. 150–153

Starters pp. 154–189

Relievers pp. 190–217

SCOTT HEMOND   Age 28/R $6

Any catcher who steals 14 bases and hits six home runs in just 215 AB causes us to sit up and take notice. So we ran a background check on Mr. Hemond—no relation, we discovered, to the Orioles' general manager—and found that back in 1989 in the Southern League he stole 45 bases. As we all know, a catcher with speed is about as rare as a lefthanded pitcher without a job. Bid accordingly.

Year	Team	Lg.	Pos.	G	AB	R	H	HR	RBI	SB	BA
1990	Oakland	AL	3B	7	13	0	2	0	1	0	.154
1991	Oakland	AL	C	23	23	4	5	0	0	1	.217
1992	Oakland	AL	C	17	27	7	6	0	1	1	.222
1992	Chicago	AL	DH	8	13	1	3	0	1	0	.231
1993	Oakland	AL	C	91	215	31	55	6	26	14	.256
Seasonal Notation					322	47	78	6	32	17	.244

CHRIS HOILES   Age 29/R $20

Notice how many home runs he's hit in the last two years combined. Then notice how few runs he's batted in those same two years. What he might well be is the latest Orioles reincarnation of Gary Roenicke, who was called "Solo" by his teammates for his uncanny knack of saving his home runs for times when the bases were empty. We're not complaining, mind you. He can be our backstop any day. We're just doing our job, pinching the numbers until the pips squeak, and making general nuisances of ourselves. Don't bother sending thank you notes.

Year	Team	Lg.	Pos.	G	AB	R	H	HR	RBI	SB	BA
1990	Baltimore	AL	C	23	63	7	12	1	6	0	.190
1991	Baltimore	AL	C	107	341	36	83	11	31	0	.243
1992	Baltimore	AL	C	96	310	49	85	20	40	0	.274
1993	Baltimore	AL	C	126	419	80	130	29	82	1	.310
Seasonal Notation					521	79	142	28	73	0	.274

RON KARKOVICE   Age 30/R $9

Karko will never be accused of being a pretty boy, and Kevin Costner won't play him in the movie. But he has made himself into a solid player with the kind of numbers that can grow on you. They certainly grew on us this year: we *never* expected to see that kind of power from him. And frankly, we doubt seriously we will see it again.

Year	Team	Lg.	Pos.	G	AB	R	H	HR	RBI	SB	BA
1990	Chicago	AL	C	68	183	30	45	6	20	2	.246
1991	Chicago	AL	C	75	167	25	41	5	22	0	.246
1992	Chicago	AL	C	123	342	39	81	13	50	10	.237
1993	Chicago	AL	C	128	403	60	92	20	54	2	.228
Seasonal Notation					450	63	106	18	60	5	.237

JOE KMAK   Age 30/R $1

Kno kway.

Year	Team	Lg.	Pos.	G	AB	R	H	HR	RBI	SB	BA
1993	Milwaukee	AL	C	51	110	9	24	0	7	6	.218
Seasonal Notation					349	28	76	0	22	19	.218

RANDY KNORR   Age 25/R $1

Shows every sign of being yet another over-ballyhooed Toronto farm prospect in the mold of Rob Ducey, Sil Campusano, and Eddie Zoskey.

Year	Team	Lg.	Pos.	G	AB	R	H	HR	RBI	SB	BA
1991	Toronto	AL	C	3	1	0	0	0	0	0	0.000
1992	Toronto	AL	C	8	19	1	5	1	2	0	.263
1993	Toronto	AL	C	39	101	11	25	4	20	0	.248
Seasonal Notation					392	38	97	16	71	0	.248

CHAD KREUTER   Age 29/R $7

For a while last spring, he led the American League in hitting. No, we didn't think it would last either. And we're not very confident that it will happen again. Still, you have to like double figures in HRs from your catcher.

Year	Team	Lg.	Pos.	G	AB	R	H	HR	RBI	SB	BA
1990	Texas	AL	C	22	22	2	1	0	2	0	.045
1991	Texas	AL	C	3	4	0	0	0	0	0	0.000
1992	Detroit	AL	C	67	190	22	48	2	16	0	.253
1993	Detroit	AL	C	119	374	59	107	15	51	2	.286
Seasonal Notation					452	63	119	13	52	1	.264

MIKE LaVALLIERE   Age 33/L $1

Spanky is with a new gang now, and he doesn't get to play much anymore. Not enough pop to be very interesting as a part-timer.

Year	Team	Lg.	Pos.	G	AB	R	H	HR	RBI	SB	BA
1990	Pittsburgh	NL	C	96	279	27	72	3	31	0	.258
1991	Pittsburgh	NL	C	108	336	25	97	3	41	2	.289
1992	Pittsburgh	NL	C	95	293	22	75	2	29	0	.256
1993	Pittsburgh	NL	C	1	5	0	1	0	0	0	.200
1993	Chicago	AL	C	37	97	6	25	0	8	0	.258
Seasonal Notation					485	38	129	3	52	0	.267

MIKE MACFARLANE   Age 29/R $12

Not the first catcher in baseball history to be a late bloomer in the power department; Carlton Fisk comes to mind. Now, we're not comparing him to Fisk. We're just trying to demonstrate through some real inside baseball knowledge that this is a guy to hang on to, while on the other hand . . .

Year	Team	Lg.	Pos.	G	AB	R	H	HR	RBI	SB	BA
1990	Kansas City	AL	C	124	400	37	102	6	58	1	.255
1991	Kansas City	AL	C	84	267	34	74	13	41	1	.277
1992	Kansas City	AL	C	129	402	51	94	17	48	1	.234
1993	Kansas City	AL	C	117	388	55	106	20	67	2	.273
Seasonal Notation					519	63	134	19	76	1	.258

BASEBALL ANAGRAM #3

Crazy Sheen = _____?

(Answer on page 299)

Catchers
pp. 59-73

Corners
pp. 73-95

Infield
pp. 95-116

Outfield
pp. 117-150

DH
pp. 150-153

Starters
pp. 154-189

Relievers
pp. 190-217

BRENT MAYNE
Age 25/L   **$1**

. . . this is a guy who won't play much because of all of the above. Of course, there's always the chance he will also turn out to be a late bloomer in the power department, in which case you can blame us for not hanging on to him. By the way, isn't Brent Mayne the name of a character in *Days of Our Lives?* Or are we thinking about one of those CNN talking heads?

Year	Team	Lg.	Pos.	G	AB	R	H	HR	RBI	SB	BA
1990	Kansas City	AL	C	5	13	2	3	0	1	0	.231
1991	Kansas City	AL	C	85	231	22	58	3	31	2	.251
1992	Kansas City	AL	C	82	213	16	48	0	18	0	.225
1993	Kansas City	AL	C	71	205	22	52	2	22	3	.254
Seasonal Notation					441	41	107	3	48	3	.243

BOB MELVIN
Age 32/R   **$1**

Who would have thunk that he would end up being the Bosox' best offensive backstop? Unfortunately, that's like being the best dresser in a nudist colony.

Year	Team	Lg.	Pos.	G	AB	R	H	HR	RBI	SB	BA
1990	Baltimore	AL	C	93	301	30	73	5	37	0	.243
1991	Baltimore	AL	C	79	228	11	57	1	23	0	.250
1992	Kansas City	AL	C	32	70	5	22	0	6	0	.314
1993	Boston	AL	C	77	176	13	39	3	23	0	.222
Seasonal Notation					446	34	110	5	51	0	.246

GREG MYERS
Age 27/L   **$3**

Change of scenery helped him creep back to so-so. Maybe he'll turn out to be a late bloomer.

Year	Team	Lg.	Pos.	G	AB	R	H	HR	RBI	SB	BA
1990	Toronto	AL	C	87	250	33	59	5	22	0	.236
1991	Toronto	AL	C	107	309	25	81	8	36	0	.262
1992	Toronto	AL	C	22	61	4	14	1	13	0	.230
1992	California	AL	C	8	17	0	4	0	0	0	.235
1993	California	AL	C	108	290	27	74	7	40	3	.255
Seasonal Notation					452	43	113	10	54	1	.250

DAVE NILSSON
Age 24/L   **$3**

Such a disappointment that Foster's Lager has been temporarily banned in Milwaukee. Too young to be a late bloomer.

Year	Team	Lg.	Pos.	G	AB	R	H	HR	RBI	SB	BA
1992	Milwaukee	AL	C	51	164	15	38	4	25	2	.232
1993	Milwaukee	AL	C	100	296	35	76	7	40	3	.257
Seasonal Notation					493	53	122	11	69	5	.248

MATT NOKES
Age 30/L   **$5**

He won't catch as much now because of Mike Stanley's many dingers. He won't DH as much because of Danny Tartabull's many boo-boos. Ergo, so long as he continues to wear pinstripes, he won't be worth as much in Rotissedollars as the thunder in his bat might otherwise dictate.

Catchers
pp. 59–73

Corners
pp. 73–95

Infield
pp. 95–116

Outfield
pp. 117–150

DH
pp. 150–153

Starters
pp. 154–189

Relievers
pp. 190–217

Year	Team	Lg.	Pos.	G	AB	R	H	HR	RBI	SB	BA
1990	Detroit	AL	DH	44	111	12	30	3	8	0	.270
1990	New York	AL	C	92	240	21	57	8	32	2	.237
1991	New York	AL	C	135	456	52	122	24	77	3	.268
1992	New York	AL	C	121	384	42	86	22	59	0	.224
1993	New York	AL	C	76	217	25	54	10	35	0	.249
Seasonal Notation					487	52	120	23	73	1	.248

JUNIOR ORTIZ　　　　　　　　　　　Age 34/R　　　$1

You might want to grab him if you need a little extra speed, but we like having him around for comic relief. In fact, should comic relief ever become a Rotisserie category, this guy is the next Johnny Bench.

Year	Team	Lg.	Pos.	G	AB	R	H	HR	RBI	SB	BA
1990	Minnesota	AL	C	71	170	18	57	0	18	0	.335
1991	Minnesota	AL	C	61	134	9	28	0	11	0	.209
1992	Cleveland	AL	C	86	244	20	61	0	24	1	.250
1993	Cleveland	AL	C	95	249	19	55	0	20	1	.221
Seasonal Notation					412	34	104	0	37	1	.252

JOHN ORTON　　　　　　　　　　　Age 28/R　　　$1

The rules say you have to have two catchers, but they don't say he has to be one of them.

Year	Team	Lg.	Pos.	G	AB	R	H	HR	RBI	SB	BA
1990	California	AL	C	31	84	8	16	1	6	0	.190
1991	California	AL	C	29	69	7	14	0	3	0	.203
1992	California	AL	C	43	114	11	25	2	12	1	.219
1993	California	AL	C	37	95	5	18	1	4	1	.189
Seasonal Notation					418	35	84	4	28	2	.202

MARK PARENT　　　　　　　　　　　Age 32/R　　　$1

We always thought of Parent as a useful guy to have around. You know, four or five homers for your buck, not enough playing time to damage your BA, good influence in your clubhouse, that sort of thing. Keep that in mind, especially since Chris Hoiles looks to be a mortal lock to get hurt every year.

Year	Team	Lg.	Pos.	G	AB	R	H	HR	RBI	SB	BA
1990	San Diego	NL	C	65	189	13	42	3	16	1	.222
1991	Texas	AL	C	3	1	0	0	0	0	0	0.000
1992	Baltimore	AL	C	17	34	4	8	2	4	0	.235
1993	Baltimore	AL	C	22	54	7	14	4	12	0	.259
Seasonal Notation					420	36	96	13	48	1	.230

TONY PENA　　　　　　　　　　　Age 36/R　　　$1

Sad but true: the famed Mendoza Line is soon going to be renamed the Peña Plateau.

Year	Team	Lg.	Pos.	G	AB	R	H	HR	RBI	SB	BA
1990	Boston	AL	C	143	491	62	129	7	56	8	.263
1991	Boston	AL	C	141	464	45	107	5	48	8	.231
1992	Boston	AL	C	133	410	39	99	1	38	3	.241
1993	Boston	AL	C	126	304	20	55	4	19	1	.181
Seasonal Notation					497	49	116	5	48	5	.234

GENO PETRALLI
Age 34/B   **$1**

Talk about specialization: he became Kenny Rogers's designated catcher. What's next, a designated third baseman for Jeff Bronkey?

Year	Team	Lg.	Pos.	G	AB	R	H	HR	RBI	SB	BA
1990	Texas	AL	C	133	325	28	83	0	21	0	.255
1991	Texas	AL	C	87	199	21	54	2	20	2	.271
1992	Texas	AL	C	94	192	11	38	1	18	0	.198
1993	Texas	AL	C	59	133	16	32	1	13	2	.241
Seasonal Notation					368	33	89	1	31	1	.244

IVAN RODRIGUEZ
Age 22/R   **$10**

There was the time when he kicked the dirt petulantly after getting the bunt sign. There was the time when the pitching coach needed to hurry to the mound because he kept calling fastballs to a pitcher who didn't want to throw one in order to protect his caught-stealing stats. There was the time he had a shoving match with teammate Gary Redus, who was rightfully upset at being forced to wait for batting practice because of Pudge's tardiness. Get the picture? What we have here is a mega-talent who sometimes behaves like a 22-year-old. We expect him to grow up.

Year	Team	Lg.	Pos.	G	AB	R	H	HR	RBI	SB	BA
1991	Texas	AL	C	88	280	24	74	3	27	0	.264
1992	Texas	AL	C	123	420	39	109	8	37	0	.260
1993	Texas	AL	C	137	473	56	129	10	66	8	.273
Seasonal Notation					546	55	145	9	60	3	.266

MIKE STANLEY
Age 30/R   **$15**

Before anyone gets snotty with us for missing the boat on the Yankees' MVP in 1993, just remember that if any of you could have predicted that Stanley would have the season he had, you would have been writing this stupid book and we could have spent more time vacationing on the Vineyard with Bill and Hillary. Also, keep in mind that before last year Stanley hit just 24 home runs in 1,160 AB in 520 games spread over seven seasons. Was last season an example of the Joe Hardy Syndrome? Or could it be that Stanley is just another late bloomer?

Year	Team	Lg.	Pos.	G	AB	R	H	HR	RBI	SB	BA
1990	Texas	AL	C	103	189	21	47	2	19	1	.249
1991	Texas	AL	C	95	181	25	45	3	25	0	.249
1992	New York	AL	C	68	173	24	43	8	27	0	.249
1993	New York	AL	C	130	423	70	129	26	84	1	.305
Seasonal Notation					395	57	108	15	63	0	.273

TERRY STEINBACH
Age 32/R   **$9**

Before we leave the subject of Mike Stanley—okay, we feel a little sheepish about dismissing him as "a solid pro" worth just $2 in last year's book—we just want to point out that in the winter of 1992 the Yankees had no plans for Stanley being their everyday catcher, otherwise they wouldn't have dangled millions of dollars around in front of then free agent Terry Steinbach, who, by the way, has never had a season like Stanley had last year, which doesn't mean Terry isn't a solid pro—and worth more than a measly two bucks.

Year	Team	Lg.	Pos.	G	AB	R	H	HR	RBI	SB	BA
1990	Oakland	AL	C	114	379	32	95	9	57	0	.251
1991	Oakland	AL	C	129	456	50	125	6	67	2	.274
1992	Oakland	AL	C	128	438	48	122	12	53	2	.279
1993	Oakland	AL	C	104	389	47	111	10	43	3	.285
Seasonal Notation					566	60	154	12	75	2	.273

MICKEY TETTLETON   Age 33/B $30

Going ... The quintessential Detroit Tiger. ... *going* ... A Rotisserian's dream come true.... *gone!* Qualifies at catcher and in the outfield as well as first base. *It's outta here! Another home run by Tettleton!* (Thanks, Ernie.)

Year	Team	Lg.	Pos.	G	AB	R	H	HR	RBI	SB	BA
1990	Baltimore	AL	C	135	444	68	99	15	51	2	.223
1991	Detroit	AL	C	154	501	85	132	31	89	3	.263
1992	Detroit	AL	C	157	525	82	125	32	83	0	.238
1993	Detroit	AL	1B	152	522	79	128	32	110	3	.245
Seasonal Notation					539	85	131	29	90	2	.243

DAVE VALLE   Age 33/R $5

The early word (i.e., before this book went to press) was that the Mariners would ditch Valle because of his big salary. And the other early word was that among the teams most interested was Boston, an outfit that everyone seems to agree could use a tad more sock behind the plate.

Year	Team	Lg.	Pos.	G	AB	R	H	HR	RBI	SB	BA
1990	Seattle	AL	C	107	308	37	66	7	33	1	.214
1991	Seattle	AL	C	132	324	38	63	8	32	0	.194
1992	Seattle	AL	C	124	367	39	88	9	30	0	.240
1993	Seattle	AL	C	135	423	48	109	13	63	1	.258
Seasonal Notation					462	52	106	12	51	0	.229

Catchers
pp. 59-73

Corners
pp. 73-95

Infield
pp. 95-116

Outfield
pp. 117-150

DH
pp. 150-153

Starters
pp. 154-189

Relievers
pp. 190-217

At the Corners

You want to hear something pathetic? Last year just three American League third basemen hit 15 or more home runs, while a like number had 75 or more RBI. Fortunately, on the other side of the diamond, 13 American League first basemen launched 15 or more downtowners and eight drove in 75 or more runs. That's more like it.

In Rotisserie as in life, the corners are traditionally a primary power source. You look to first and third for bushels of HR and pecks of RBI, the meat and potatoes of your offense. Short-circuit yourself at those two slots— come out of the auction draft with, say, Wade Boggs, Dave Segui, and Scott Cooper as your corners—and you will almost certainly suffer a power outage this summer. A Dave Magadan would need to hit about .450 in 600 plate appearances to make up for what he fails to deliver in the whomp department. Your corners are—or should be—charter members of your swat team.

Most years, there is an adequate supply of rolling thunder at first and third. For instance, in the National league last season, 15 cornermen socked

15 or more homers, while 17 drove in 75 or more runs, with the production evenly distributed between first and third.

When power is supplied at that level, the Rotisserie owner has some maneuverability. You get outbid for one big hitter, you simply buy another. But when power is in short supply at one of the corners, as with American league third basemen this year, you have to be careful not to get boxed out of the bidding for the few genuine thumpers available. Otherwise, you run the risk of leaving the table with a B. J. Surhoff and a Mike Pagliarulo. And should your third cornerstone happen to be a Wally Joyner, you are in for a summer without fireworks, not even on the Fourth of July.

NATIONAL LEAGUE

JEFF BAGWELL   Age 25/R $29

We know it's old news, but darn it, we're still perplexed. Is it really possible that a team desperately in need of a young, powerful, hard-nosed, right-handed hitter actually traded away this young, powerful, hard-nosed, right-handed hitter in order to rent Larry Andersen—*Larry Andersen!*—for six weeks? And is it really true that the dunderhead who made this decision is still gainfully employed as a general manager for the same team? There's something wrong with this story, even after three years.

Year	Team	Lg.	Pos.	G	AB	R	H	HR	RBI	SB	BA
1991	Houston	NL	1B	156	554	79	163	15	82	7	.294
1992	Houston	NL	1B	162	586	87	160	18	96	10	.273
1993	Houston	NL	1B	142	535	76	171	20	88	13	.320
Seasonal Notation					589	85	173	18	93	10	.295

KIM BATISTE   Age 26/R $2

If he accepts a utility role, which won't be all that easy to do for a player his age, he can be a valuable reserve. A good glove man, despite those errors in last year's playoffs, with a lot more stick than he showed back in 1992, his rookie season.

Year	Team	Lg.	Pos.	G	AB	R	H	HR	RBI	SB	BA
1991	Philadelphia	NL	SS	10	27	2	6	0	1	0	.222
1992	Philadelphia	NL	SS	44	136	9	28	1	10	0	.206
1993	Philadelphia	NL	3B	79	156	14	44	5	29	0	.282
Seasonal Notation					388	30	95	7	48	0	.245

TODD BENZINGER   Age 31/B $3

We were half-dozing one night around midnight, half-watching a Cubs-Giants game from the coast. (No jokes about getting a life, please. After all, Frank Castillo was pitching, and we had a personal stake in his ERA.) Out of nowhere, Thom Brenneman, the well-spoken young man who fills in for Harry Caray for three innings every night on WGN, reported that he had played basketball against Todd Benzinger in high school. It was the kind of information for which remote control was made. Click.

Year	Team	Lg.	Pos.	G	AB	R	H	HR	RBI	SB	BA
1990	Cincinnati	NL	1B	118	376	35	95	5	46	3	.253
1991	Cincinnati	NL	1B	51	123	7	23	1	11	2	.187
1991	Kansas City	AL	1B	78	293	29	86	2	40	2	.294
1992	Los Angeles	NL	OF	121	293	24	70	4	31	2	.239
1993	San Francisco	NL	1B	86	177	25	51	6	26	0	.288
Seasonal Notation					450	42	115	6	54	3	.258

Catchers
pp. 59–73

Corners
pp. 73–95

Infield
pp. 95–116

Outfield
pp. 117–150

DH
pp. 150–153

Starters
pp. 154–189

Relievers
pp. 190–217

SEAN BERRY   Age 27/R $7

He had some interesting moments, and since the Expos are very unsure about what will happen at third base he could get more chances for other such moments. Berry won't make Expos fans forget Tim Wallach, but he did make everyone forget Frank Bolick.

Year	Team	Lg.	Pos.	G	AB	R	H	HR	RBI	SB	BA
1990	Kansas City	AL	3B	8	23	2	5	0	4	0	.217
1991	Kansas City	AL	3B	31	60	5	8	0	1	0	.133
1992	Montreal	NL	3B	24	57	5	19	1	4	2	.333
1993	Montreal	NL	3B	122	299	50	78	14	49	12	.261
Seasonal Notation					384	54	96	13	50	12	.251

FRANK BOLICK   Age 28/B $1

We weren't exactly sure who he was last spring when he made the Expos roster. He didn't do anything last year to clear things up.

Year	Team	Lg.	Pos.	G	AB	R	H	HR	RBI	SB	BA
1993	Montreal	NL	1B	95	213	25	45	4	24	1	.211
Seasonal Notation					363	42	76	6	40	1	.211

SID BREAM   Age 33/L $2

Isn't it typical of baseball's infinite unpredictability that this solid player, who has two of the worst knees this side of Bobby Orr and who many scouts consider the slowest baserunner since Gus Triandos, will forever be remembered for his dash home to win the 1992 playoffs? The question now is where he winds up, because he's likely gone from Atlanta. Still capable of a clutch dinger now and then, so he'll find work somewhere.

Year	Team	Lg.	Pos.	G	AB	R	H	HR	RBI	SB	BA
1990	Pittsburgh	NL	1B	147	389	39	105	15	67	8	.270
1991	Atlanta	NL	1B	91	265	32	67	11	45	0	.253
1992	Atlanta	NL	1B	125	372	30	97	10	61	6	.261
1993	Atlanta	NL	1B	117	277	33	72	9	35	4	.260
Seasonal Notation					439	45	115	15	70	6	.262

BASEBALL ANAGRAM #4

Nasty Like Me = _____?

(Answer on page 299)

ROD BREWER
Age 28/L $1

A solid role player with enough defensive skills to get some playing time in the outfield. You could do worse for your last offensive slot.

Year	Team	Lg.	Pos.	G	AB	R	H	HR	RBI	SB	BA
1990	St. Louis	NL	1B	14	25	4	6	0	2	0	.240
1991	St. Louis	NL	1B	19	13	0	1	0	1	0	.077
1992	St. Louis	NL	1B	29	103	11	31	0	10	0	.301
1993	St. Louis	NL	OF	110	147	15	42	2	20	1	.286
Seasonal Notation					271	28	75	1	31	0	.278

STEVE BUECHELE
Age 32/R $10

If he were an ice cream flavor, he'd be plain vanilla.

Year	Team	Lg.	Pos.	G	AB	R	H	HR	RBI	SB	BA
1990	Texas	AL	3B	91	251	30	54	7	30	1	.215
1991	Texas	AL	3B	121	416	58	111	18	66	0	.267
1991	Pittsburgh	NL	3B	31	114	16	28	4	19	0	.246
1992	Pittsburgh	NL	3B	80	285	27	71	8	43	0	.249
1992	Chicago	NL	3B	65	239	25	66	1	21	1	.276
1993	Chicago	NL	3B	133	460	53	125	15	65	1	.272
Seasonal Notation					548	64	141	16	75	0	.258

FRANCISCO CABRERA
Age 27/R $1

We like Peter Gammons a lot, but when he said one night that Cabrera might be stronger than Juan Gonzalez, we decided he must have heard the "Baseball Tonight" theme song one too many times. Sayonara, Francisco.

Year	Team	Lg.	Pos.	G	AB	R	H	HR	RBI	SB	BA
1990	Atlanta	NL	1B	63	137	14	38	7	25	1	.277
1991	Atlanta	NL	C	44	95	7	23	4	23	1	.242
1992	Atlanta	NL	C	12	10	2	3	2	3	0	.300
1993	Atlanta	NL	1B	70	83	8	20	4	11	0	.241
Seasonal Notation					278	26	72	14	53	1	.258

KEN CAMINITI
Age 30/B $10

His value and his mailing address will be determined by where the Astros decide to play phenom Phil Nevin. With Luis Gonzalez's return to form and Eric Anthony's promise as a power hitter, the only place for Nevin is at third, which means this solid, hardworking player will have to pack his bags. We're just blue-skying it here, but wouldn't this native Californian look good in Oakland green and gold?

Year	Team	Lg.	Pos.	G	AB	R	H	HR	RBI	SB	BA
1990	Houston	NL	3B	153	541	52	131	4	51	9	.242
1991	Houston	NL	3B	152	574	65	145	13	80	4	.253
1992	Houston	NL	3B	135	506	68	149	13	62	10	.294
1993	Houston	NL	3B	143	543	75	142	13	75	8	.262
Seasonal Notation					601	72	157	11	74	8	.262

ARCHI CIANFROCCO
Age 27/R $6

The name sounds like an entrée in an upscale restaurant, but the guy it belongs to is something even tastier: the kind of player who wins Rotisserie pennants by delivering double-digit dingers for single-digit dollars. We'll have the Archi Cianfrocco and a tossed salad, dressing on the side, and a bottle of Yoo-Hoo.

Year	Team	Lg.	Pos.	G	AB	R	H	HR	RBI	SB	BA
1992	Montreal	NL	1B	86	232	25	56	6	30	3	.241
1993	Montreal	NL	1B	12	17	3	4	1	1	0	.235
1993	San Diego	NL	3B	84	279	27	68	11	47	2	.244
Seasonal Notation					469	48	113	16	69	4	.242

WILL CLARK   Age 30/L $24

One year older than Rafael Palmeiro. Less power. Much less speed. Coming off two straight off years. What *were* the Rangers thinking about?

Year	Team	Lg.	Pos.	G	AB	R	H	HR	RBI	SB	BA
1990	San Francisco	NL	1B	154	600	91	177	19	95	8	.295
1991	San Francisco	NL	1B	148	565	84	170	29	116	4	.301
1992	San Francisco	NL	1B	144	513	69	154	16	73	12	.300
1993	San Francisco	NL	1B	132	491	82	139	14	73	2	.283
Seasonal Notation					607	91	179	21	100	7	.295

GREG COLBRUNN   Age 24/R $5

Last year we said he was not a bad hunch bet. An injury short-circuited his season, so we don't know whether the hunch would have paid off. We're going to go out on a limb and say, once again, that Colbrunn is not a bad hunch bet.

Year	Team	Lg.	Pos.	G	AB	R	H	HR	RBI	SB	BA
1992	Montreal	NL	1B	52	168	12	45	2	18	3	.268
1993	Montreal	NL	1B	70	153	15	39	4	23	4	.255
Seasonal Notation					426	35	111	7	54	9	.262

ORESTES DESTRADE   Age 31/B $18

A solid second half convinced us that he has a future. And who knows, he might end up being better for the Marlins in the long run than . . .

Year	Team	Lg.	Pos.	G	AB	R	H	HR	RBI	SB	BA
1993	Florida	NL	1B	153	569	61	145	20	87	0	.255
Seasonal Notation					602	64	153	21	92	0	.255

ANDRES GALARRAGA   Age 32/R $26

. . . who longed for the sweltering humidity of Florida, grudgingly accepted the crisp, cool mountain air of Colorado, and coped with his disappointment by having a monster season. Veteran skeptics that we are, our knee-jerk reaction is that he won't do it a second time. On the other hand, we didn't think he'd do it a first time.

Year	Team	Lg.	Pos.	G	AB	R	H	HR	RBI	SB	BA
1990	Montreal	NL	1B	155	579	65	148	20	87	10	.256
1991	Montreal	NL	1B	107	375	34	82	9	33	5	.219
1992	St. Louis	NL	1B	95	325	38	79	10	39	5	.243
1993	Colorado	NL	1B	120	470	71	174	22	98	2	.370
Seasonal Notation					594	70	164	20	87	7	.276

Catchers
pp. 59-73

Corners
pp. 73-95

Infield
pp. 95-116

Outfield
pp. 117-150

DH
pp. 150-153

Starters
pp. 154-189

Relievers
pp. 190-217

MARK GRACE   Age 29/L $21

Never exactly one of our favorites, but last year he had a terrific season, his best ever. Still, we recall the comment made a few years ago by a veteran (and widely respected) teammate: "Gracie is one of those guys who looks great and sounds great until the team gets in the race, and it becomes a 'we' situation, not an 'I' situation." But since the Rotisserie game is all "I" and never "we," and since the Cubs aren't likely to be in the race any time in the remainder of the century, none of that should make any difference to you. Go get him. Janine Turner is a throw-in in the deal.

Year	Team	Lg.	Pos.	G	AB	R	H	HR	RBI	SB	BA
1990	Chicago	NL	1B	157	589	72	182	9	82	15	.309
1991	Chicago	NL	1B	160	619	87	169	8	58	3	.273
1992	Chicago	NL	1B	158	603	72	185	9	79	6	.307
1993	Chicago	NL	1B	155	594	86	193	14	98	8	.325
Seasonal Notation					618	81	187	10	81	8	.303

WILLIE GREENE   Age 22/L $6

The Reds originally hoped he could play shortstop. Then they hoped he could play the outfield. Next they hoped he would hit enough to be the answer at third. He's still young, and there are several other positions for which he might be considered, so get him while he's cheap. There's a big, *big* upside.

Year	Team	Lg.	Pos.	G	AB	R	H	HR	RBI	SB	BA
1992	Cincinnati	NL	3B	29	93	10	25	2	13	0	.269
1993	Cincinnati	NL	SS	15	50	7	8	2	5	0	.160
Seasonal Notation					526	62	121	14	66	0	.231

DAVE HANSEN   Age 25/L $1

He's become one of the best pinch hitters in baseball. Whoopee.

Year	Team	Lg.	Pos.	G	AB	R	H	HR	RBI	SB	BA
1990	Los Angeles	NL	3B	5	7	0	1	0	1	0	.143
1991	Los Angeles	NL	3B	53	56	3	15	1	5	1	.268
1992	Los Angeles	NL	3B	132	341	30	73	6	22	0	.214
1993	Los Angeles	NL	3B	84	105	13	38	4	30	0	.362
Seasonal Notation					300	27	75	6	34	0	.250

CHARLIE HAYES   Age 28/R $21

Do you think maybe the Yankees . . . oh, never mind. We can't think of a single reason why Hayes shouldn't continue to put up strong power numbers for the next several years.

Year	Team	Lg.	Pos.	G	AB	R	H	HR	RBI	SB	BA
1990	Philadelphia	NL	3B	152	561	56	145	10	57	4	.258
1991	Philadelphia	NL	3B	142	460	34	106	12	53	3	.230
1992	New York	AL	3B	142	509	52	131	18	66	3	.257
1993	Colorado	NL	3B	157	573	89	175	25	98	11	.305
Seasonal Notation					574	63	152	17	74	5	.265

DAVE HOLLINS   Age 27/B $23

In the Phillies' clubhouse, a cross between a local chapter of the Hell's Angels and Animal House, Hollins fits in as perfectly as he does at third base. He's not a pretty fielder, but he gets the job done, and he'd run through a brick wall to win a game. If the center fielder didn't have first dibs on it, "Nails" would be the perfect nickname for him. Keep in mind as you look at his production numbers for 1993 that he missed almost a month with injuries. His price may be a little lower this spring because of that, but this is the year he breaks out. Get him.

Year	Team	Lg.	Pos.	G	AB	R	H	HR	RBI	SB	BA
1990	Philadelphia	NL	3B	72	114	14	21	5	15	0	.184
1991	Philadelphia	NL	3B	56	151	18	45	6	21	1	.298
1992	Philadelphia	NL	3B	156	586	104	158	27	93	9	.270
1993	Philadelphia	NL	3B	143	543	104	148	18	93	2	.273
Seasonal Notation					528	91	141	21	84	4	.267

GREGG JEFFERIES   Age 26/B $35

Jealous Mets veterans dubbed him an egocentric little shit and got the club's mindless management to run him out of New York. Hal McRae didn't like his hyper approach and ran him out of Kansas City. So he ended up in St. Louis, where he had a better summer than Bud Light. Meanwhile, the same Mets have become to baseball what Chevy Chase is to late-night comedy shows, and Hal McRae is throwing telephones at sportswriters. We love human nature.

Year	Team	Lg.	Pos.	G	AB	R	H	HR	RBI	SB	BA
1990	New York	NL	2B	153	604	96	171	15	68	11	.283
1991	New York	NL	2B	136	486	59	132	9	62	26	.272
1992	Kansas City	AL	3B	152	604	66	172	10	75	19	.285
1993	St. Louis	NL	1B	142	544	89	186	16	83	46	.342
Seasonal Notation					621	86	183	13	80	28	.295

HOWARD JOHNSON   Age 33/B $8

What happened? We had him tabbed as 1993 Comeback Player of the Year, but he was heading the other direction even before the injury put an end to his summer. We're not shrinks or anything, but Hojo seems to be a very sensitive guy who internalizes a lot of stuff. There could be no coming back from the psychic damage of the past two tears. We hope we're wrong, and that he's the 1994 Comeback Player of the Year in Colorado.

Year	Team	Lg.	Pos.	G	AB	R	H	HR	RBI	SB	BA
1990	New York	NL	3B	154	590	89	144	23	90	34	.244
1991	New York	NL	3B	156	564	108	146	38	117	30	.259
1992	New York	NL	OF	100	350	48	78	7	43	22	.223
1993	New York	NL	3B	72	235	32	56	7	26	6	.238
Seasonal Notation					584	93	142	25	92	30	.244

RICKY JORDAN   Age 28/R $4

Last season he was a bit player who didn't drive in many runs. That's not exactly an enticing combination. Bad break for him that he didn't go to an expansion team. He's young enough and talented enough to be a productive

Catchers
pp. 59–73

Corners
pp. 73–95

Infield
pp. 95–116

Outfield
pp. 117–150

DH
pp. 150–153

Starters
pp. 154–189

Relievers
pp. 190–217

regular, but he'll never get the chance so long as John Kruk's knees hold up.

Year	Team	Lg.	Pos.	G	AB	R	H	HR	RBI	SB	BA
1990	Philadelphia	NL	1B	92	324	32	78	5	44	2	.241
1991	Philadelphia	NL	1B	101	301	38	82	9	49	0	.272
1992	Philadelphia	NL	1B	94	276	33	84	4	34	3	.304
1993	Philadelphia	NL	1B	90	159	21	46	5	18	0	.289
Seasonal Notation					455	53	124	9	62	2	.274

ERIC KARROS   Age 26/R $19

You couldn't call last season a sophomore slump, but you couldn't call it a giant leap toward stardom, either. Looked strangely like a leveling-off year, which shouldn't be the case for a guy so young. We're not about to do the in-depth research needed to know for sure, but doesn't it seem like the Dodgers produce a lot of rookies of the year who never get a whole lot better? That's okay if the rookie happens to be a Mike Piazza, but if Karros is going to stay at this level for the next decade or so we're going to look elsewhere for excitement. Greg Brock, where are you?

Year	Team	Lg.	Pos.	G	AB	R	H	HR	RBI	SB	BA
1991	Los Angeles	NL	1B	14	14	0	1	0	1	0	.071
1992	Los Angeles	NL	1B	149	545	63	140	20	88	2	.257
1993	Los Angeles	NL	1B	158	619	74	153	23	80	0	.247
Seasonal Notation					594	69	148	21	85	1	.250

JEFF KING   Age 29/R $13

A lot of people are perplexed that he doesn't hit more home runs. But maybe Jim Leyland is extracting the maximum from his laid-back third baseman. The RBI total last season was pretty amazing on a team as anemic offensively as the Buccos. Even more amazing was the BA, an impressive 65 points above his lifetime mark. We'll take him.

Year	Team	Lg.	Pos.	G	AB	R	H	HR	RBI	SB	BA
1990	Pittsburgh	NL	3B	127	371	46	91	14	53	3	.245
1991	Pittsburgh	NL	3B	33	109	16	26	4	18	3	.239
1992	Pittsburgh	NL	3B	130	480	56	111	14	65	4	.231
1993	Pittsburgh	NL	3B	158	611	82	180	9	98	8	.295
Seasonal Notation					568	72	147	14	84	6	.260

JOHN KRUK   Age 33/L $21

Amid a late-season slump that marred an otherwise solid season, Mr. Cholesterol was being badgered by the media. And he finally sputtered, "Hey, they're signing this peace treaty today between ... um ... you know, the POL and Egypt, so my slump ain't no big deal." If only he hailed from Arkansas instead of West Virginia, there would be a place for him in the Clinton State Department.

Year	Team	Lg.	Pos.	G	AB	R	H	HR	RBI	SB	BA
1990	Philadelphia	NL	OF	142	443	52	129	7	67	10	.291
1991	Philadelphia	NL	1B	152	538	84	158	21	92	7	.294
1992	Philadelphia	NL	1B	144	507	86	164	10	70	3	.323
1993	Philadelphia	NL	1B	150	535	100	169	14	85	6	.316
Seasonal Notation					557	88	170	14	86	7	.306

BASEBALL ANAGRAM #5

Nerdy Stalk = _____?

(Answer on page 299)

Corners
pp. 73–95

Infield
pp. 95–116

Outfield
pp. 117–150

DH
pp. 150–153

Starters
pp. 154–189

Relievers
pp. 190–217

MIKE LANSING   Age 26/R $9

If you buy him on draft day, and we recommend strongly that you do so, slot him at 2B or SS, where he also qualifies. Look for him to move to shortstop full-time this year, where his excellent range, baseball instincts, and offensive numbers will fit much better than at a power spot like third.

Year	Team	Lg.	Pos.	G	AB	R	H	HR	RBI	SB	BA
1993	Montreal	NL	3B	141	491	64	141	3	45	23	.287
Seasonal Notation					564	73	162	3	51	26	.287

FRED McGRIFF   Age 30/L $34

He's the real Chief Noc-a-homa.

Year	Team	Lg.	Pos.	G	AB	R	H	HR	RBI	SB	BA
1990	Toronto	AL	1B	153	557	91	167	35	88	5	.300
1991	San Diego	NL	1B	153	528	84	147	31	106	4	.278
1992	San Diego	NL	1B	152	531	79	152	35	104	8	.286
1993	San Diego	NL	1B	83	302	52	83	18	46	4	.275
1993	Atlanta	NL	1B	68	255	59	79	19	55	1	.310
Seasonal Notation					578	97	167	36	106	5	.289

HAL MORRIS   Age 28/L $10

Our patience is wearing thin. First he charges the mound in a spring training game—a *spring training* game!—and loses six weeks of the season to an injury. Then, when he comes back, he hits a limp, anemic, flimsy, powder-puff .317 with just seven HR and 49 RBI in 101 games. That's just one dinger more than Todd Benzinger hit in 200 *fewer* AB. This guy makes Mark Grace look like Lou Gehrig.

Year	Team	Lg.	Pos.	G	AB	R	H	HR	RBI	SB	BA
1990	Cincinnati	NL	1B	107	309	50	105	7	36	9	.340
1991	Cincinnati	NL	1B	136	478	72	152	14	59	10	.318
1992	Cincinnati	NL	1B	115	395	41	107	6	53	6	.271
1993	Cincinnati	NL	1B	101	379	48	120	7	49	2	.317
Seasonal Notation					550	74	170	12	69	9	.310

EDDIE MURRAY   Age 38/B $20

The first time Mets announcer Tim McCarver saw Eddie Murray in the clubhouse in spring training after Murray signed with the Mets, McCarver walked up to introduce himself and wish Murray well. Murray cut him dead, turned his back, refused to acknowledge McCarver's presence. Now, McCarver is both an ex-ballplayer and a genuinely nice guy. He had never said or written anything disparaging about Murray; in fact, he had praised the signing of Murray on air. Yet he got the same treatment that Murray has been giving to reporters and sportscasters for a decade. We offer this

---

anecdote as confirmation that Murray will never be a media darling. He will never turn up on the late-night talk show circuit, either as guest or host. Almost without exception, he is contemptuous, dismissive, uncooperative, rude, gratuitously and indiscriminately nasty toward the press, presumably because of wounds inflicted long ago in Baltimore. So what? Here's someone who has more career RBI than all but 16 players in baseball history. Here's someone who still drove in 100 runs on what was the worst team of the last 25 years. Here's someone who does a lot of charity work that never gets publicized. But because the pathetic Mets organization needed a scapegoat, they fingered their best player for his supposed negative influence in a clubhouse that already was poisoned long before he arrived. We only hope that he can finish out his Hall of Fame career in Cleveland.

Year	Team	Lg.	Pos.	G	AB	R	H	HR	RBI	SB	BA
1990	Los Angeles	NL	1B	155	558	96	184	26	95	8	.330
1991	Los Angeles	NL	1B	153	576	69	150	19	96	10	.260
1992	New York	NL	1B	156	551	64	144	16	93	4	.261
1993	New York	NL	1B	154	610	77	174	27	100	2	.285
Seasonal Notation					601	80	170	23	100	6	.284

TERRY PENDLETON   Age 33/B $14

In an off year, he still managed to crank it up down the stretch. But the meter is running, and word is that Chipper Jones is being groomed to play third base, if not right away then at least sometime this year. Bid cautiously.

Year	Team	Lg.	Pos.	G	AB	R	H	HR	RBI	SB	BA
1990	St. Louis	NL	3B	121	447	46	103	6	58	7	.230
1991	Atlanta	NL	3B	153	586	94	187	22	86	10	.319
1992	Atlanta	NL	3B	160	640	98	199	21	105	5	.311
1993	Atlanta	NL	3B	161	633	81	172	17	84	5	.272
Seasonal Notation					627	86	179	17	90	7	.287

CHRIS SABO   Age 32/R $22

For all his injuries and eccentricities, he is still a dangerous hitter who would look all right in a lot of lineups, including yours.

Year	Team	Lg.	Pos.	G	AB	R	H	HR	RBI	SB	BA
1990	Cincinnati	NL	3B	148	567	95	153	25	71	25	.270
1991	Cincinnati	NL	3B	153	582	91	175	26	88	19	.301
1992	Cincinnati	NL	3B	96	344	42	84	12	43	4	.244
1993	Cincinnati	NL	3B	148	552	86	143	21	82	6	.259
Seasonal Notation					607	93	164	24	84	16	.271

GARY SHEFFIELD   Age 25/R $29

Here you have a 25-year-old guy with a batting championship under his belt, a $3.1 million annual salary, maybe the best bat speed in the game, and a stateful of worshipful fans ready to elevate him to baseball sainthood. His reaction to all this? He says he might retire because he's tired of hearing too many negative comments. No wonder so many kids have pictures of basketball players hanging in their rooms.

Year	Team	Lg.	Pos.	G	AB	R	H	HR	RBI	SB	BA
1990	Milwaukee	AL	3B	125	487	67	143	10	67	25	.294
1991	Milwaukee	AL	3B	50	175	25	34	2	22	5	.194
1992	San Diego	NL	3B	146	557	87	184	33	100	5	.330
1993	San Diego	NL	3B	68	258	34	76	10	36	5	.295
1993	Florida	NL	3B	72	236	33	69	10	37	12	.292
Seasonal Notation					601	86	177	22	92	18	.295

JOHN VANDERWAL   Age 27/L $3

Just another of Montreal's seemingly endless supply of modestly talented yet quietly effective role players who toil in thankless obscurity. If he were a hockey player, they'd name an *école* after him.

Year	Team	Lg.	Pos.	G	AB	R	H	HR	RBI	SB	BA
1991	Montreal	NL	OF	21	61	4	13	1	8	0	.213
1992	Montreal	NL	OF	105	213	21	51	4	20	3	.239
1993	Montreal	NL	1B	106	215	34	50	5	30	6	.233
Seasonal Notation					341	41	79	6	40	6	.233

GUILLERMO VELASQUEZ   Age 25/L $1

Tom Werner's front office tried to sell this raw rookie as a replacement for Fred McGriff. Padres fans said they'd prefer to hear Roseanne Arnold get another shot at the "Star Spangled Banner."

Year	Team	Lg.	Pos.	G	AB	R	H	HR	RBI	SB	BA
1992	San Diego	NL	1B	15	23	1	7	1	5	0	.304
1993	San Diego	NL	1B	79	143	7	30	3	20	0	.210
Seasonal Notation					286	13	63	6	43	0	.223

TIM WALLACH   Age 36/R $6

Yet another of those shrewd Dodgers pickups. We hear that this year they have their sights set on George Bell for an outfield spot. Maybe they could also persuade Ron Cey to come back from Antarctica or wherever he's living in case Wallach gets hurt. Is anyone running this team nowadays?

Year	Team	Lg.	Pos.	G	AB	R	H	HR	RBI	SB	BA
1990	Montreal	NL	3B	161	626	69	185	21	98	6	.296
1991	Montreal	NL	3B	151	577	60	130	13	73	2	.225
1992	Montreal	NL	3B	150	537	53	120	9	59	2	.223
1993	Los Angeles	NL	3B	133	477	42	106	12	62	0	.222
Seasonal Notation					603	60	147	14	79	2	.244

MATT WILLIAMS   Age 28/R $34

He got back on track very nicely, didn't he? Think it might possibly have something to do with Barry Bonds hitting behind him in the lineup?

Year	Team	Lg.	Pos.	G	AB	R	H	HR	RBI	SB	BA
1990	San Francisco	NL	3B	159	617	87	171	33	122	7	.277
1991	San Francisco	NL	3B	157	589	72	158	34	98	5	.268
1992	San Francisco	NL	3B	146	529	58	120	20	66	7	.227
1993	San Francisco	NL	3B	145	579	105	170	38	110	1	.294
Seasonal Notation					617	85	165	33	105	5	.268

Catchers
pp. 59–73

Corners
pp. 73–95

Infield
pp. 95–116

Outfield
pp. 117–150

DH
pp. 150–153

Starters
pp. 154–189

Relievers
pp. 190–217

KEVIN YOUNG   Age 24/R $6

He was thrown to the wolves, and the wolves ate him. But a lot of baseball
people believe he will eventually become a solid player. So do we. There's
nothing in his minor league history to suggest that he will ever be a big
power guy, but we think there is a big upside this season, because after last
year he's sure to go dirt cheap.

Year	Team	Lg.	Pos.	G	AB	R	H	HR	RBI	SB	BA
1992	Pittsburgh	NL	3B	10	7	2	4	0	4	1	.571
1993	Pittsburgh	NL	1B	141	449	38	106	6	47	2	.236
Seasonal Notation					489	42	118	6	54	3	.241

TODD ZEILE   Age 28/R $24

Here's what we wrote last year: "Anyway, just a hunch, but we say Zeile
bounces back big time this year." Okay, so it was a no-brainer, but we kick
so many that we like to call attention to occasional flashes of crystal-ball
brilliance. A lot of Cardinals say that the key for Zeile was having his locker
next to the hyper Gregg Jefferies, whose go-get-'em attitude supposedly lit
a fire under Tepid Todd. Funny, the Mets had us believing that the only
thing worse than Jefferies in a clubhouse is asbestos.

Year	Team	Lg.	Pos.	G	AB	R	H	HR	RBI	SB	BA
1990	St. Louis	NL	C	144	495	62	121	15	57	2	.244
1991	St. Louis	NL	3B	155	565	76	158	11	81	17	.280
1992	St. Louis	NL	3B	126	439	51	113	7	48	7	.257
1993	St. Louis	NL	3B	157	571	82	158	17	103	5	.277
Seasonal Notation					576	75	153	13	80	8	.266

AMERICAN LEAGUE

MIKE BLOWERS   Age 28/R $6

The Mariners loved Mr. Grand Slam's season so much that they had him go
to the Instructional League to learn how to catch, hoping to add to his
versatility. Think how much money the Yankees could have saved by keeping
Blowers—or, for that matter, Charlie Hayes—instead of blowing a bundle
on . . .

Year	Team	Lg.	Pos.	G	AB	R	H	HR	RBI	SB	BA
1990	New York	AL	3B	48	144	16	27	5	21	1	.188
1991	New York	AL	3B	15	35	3	7	1	1	0	.200
1992	Seattle	AL	3B	31	73	7	14	1	2	0	.192
1993	Seattle	AL	3B	127	379	55	106	15	57	1	.280
Seasonal Notation					462	59	112	16	59	1	.244

WADE BOGGS   Age 35/L $9

. . . who, to his credit, at least seems again to be a semblance of, well, Wade
Boggs. But two home runs and 59 RBI are pretty puny for a left-handed-
hitting third baseman in Yankee Stadium, especially one who's 35 years old
and makes umpty-ump million dollars a year for another couple of seasons.
How long can the Yankees keep Russell Davis, a bona fide, power-hitting,
third-base prospect down on the farm? How can they win with so little
power from the corners?

Year	Team	Lg.	Pos.	G	AB	R	H	HR	RBI	SB	BA
1990	Boston	AL	3B	155	619	89	187	6	63	0	.302
1991	Boston	AL	3B	144	546	93	181	8	51	1	.332
1992	Boston	AL	3B	143	514	62	133	7	50	1	.259
1993	New York	AL	3B	143	560	83	169	2	59	0	.302
Seasonal Notation					620	90	185	6	61	0	.299

Catchers
pp. 59-73

Corners
pp. 73-95

Infield
pp. 95-116

Outfield
pp. 117-150

DH
pp. 150-153

Starters
pp. 154-189

Relievers
pp. 190-217

SCOTT COOPER   Age 26/L $10

Nothing sums up how faceless Lou Gorman's Red Sox have become than the gut-wrenching fact that this oh-so-average player was Boston's sole representative in the 1993 All-Star game. As we ranted last year concerning Mike Sharperson, the Dodgers' sole 1992 All Star, do the fans really need a player from every organization in the so-called midsummer classic? Would the game have really lost its luster last July if Scott Cooper hadn't been there? Weren't there about fifty guys you'd rather have seen play?

Year	Team	Lg.	Pos.	G	AB	R	H	HR	RBI	SB	BA
1990	Boston	AL	3B	2	1	0	0	0	0	0	0.000
1991	Boston	AL	3B	14	35	6	16	0	7	0	.457
1992	Boston	AL	1B	123	337	34	93	5	33	1	.276
1993	Boston	AL	3B	156	526	67	147	9	63	5	.279
Seasonal Notation					493	58	140	7	56	3	.285

GLENN DAVIS   Age 33/R $10

Gee, Glenn, you really think that was a good move, yelling at your manager when you weren't in the lineup on your first day back at work after several seasons on the DL? And with your team in a pennant race and all? We used to like this guy a lot—for all those home runs he hit in the Astrodome, for the way he overcame a lot of adversity in his personal life, and for the community things he did off the field. We stuck with him through all those injuries when he went to Baltimore, as did the Orioles front office. But now . . . who knows? Assuming he gets another chance with somebody, and assuming he stays healthy for a change, he could be worth a lot more than the stab-in-the-dark price we put on him. But those are pretty big assumptions, and he could end up being worth a whole lot less. Glad we don't have to make these kinds of calls for a living.

Year	Team	Lg.	Pos.	G	AB	R	H	HR	RBI	SB	BA
1990	Houston	NL	1B	93	327	44	82	22	64	8	.251
1991	Baltimore	AL	1B	49	176	29	40	10	28	4	.227
1992	Baltimore	AL	DH	106	398	46	110	13	48	1	.276
1993	Baltimore	AL	1B	30	113	8	20	1	9	0	.177
Seasonal Notation					590	74	146	26	86	7	.249

ALVARO ESPINOZA   Age 32/R $1

A sound utility player who will likely be around a lot of years with a lot of different teams.

Year	Team	Lg.	Pos.	G	AB	R	H	HR	RBI	SB	BA
1990	New York	AL	SS	150	438	31	98	2	20	1	.224
1991	New York	AL	SS	148	480	51	123	5	33	4	.256
1993	Cleveland	AL	3B	129	263	34	73	4	27	2	.278
Seasonal Notation					448	44	111	4	30	2	.249

CECIL FIELDER   Age 30/R $35

Not too shabby for an "off year." No, he didn't lead the league in RBI for the third straight season. And no, he can't get you that critical late-inning SB to put the tieing run in scoring position. But the big man can play in our league anytime. In a world of inconsistency, he is as dependable a Rotisserian as has ever lived.

Year	Team	Lg.	Pos.	G	AB	R	H	HR	RBI	SB	BA
1990	Detroit	AL	1B	159	573	104	159	51	132	0	.277
1991	Detroit	AL	1B	162	624	102	163	44	133	0	.261
1992	Detroit	AL	1B	155	594	80	145	35	124	0	.244
1993	Detroit	AL	1B	154	573	80	153	30	117	0	.267
Seasonal Notation					607	94	159	41	130	0	.262

TRAVIS FRYMAN   Age 25/R $25

We wish he'd strike out a little less. We wish he'd settle down defensively. We wish he'd be a tad more consistent. And we wish Sparky would put him at shortstop and leave him there, where his Rotisserie value is much greater. But so long as Alan Trammell has a pulse, Fryman will have two addresses on the left side of the Tigers infield.

Year	Team	Lg.	Pos.	G	AB	R	H	HR	RBI	SB	BA
1990	Detroit	AL	3B	66	232	32	69	9	27	3	.297
1991	Detroit	AL	3B	149	557	65	144	21	91	12	.259
1992	Detroit	AL	SS	161	659	87	175	20	96	8	.266
1993	Detroit	AL	SS	151	607	98	182	22	97	9	.300
Seasonal Notation					631	86	175	22	95	9	.277

GARY GAETTI   Age 35/R $4

He actually put up a few numbers after arriving in Kansas City. And that's how many dollars you should invest in him—a few.

Year	Team	Lg.	Pos.	G	AB	R	H	HR	RBI	SB	BA
1990	Minnesota	AL	3B	154	577	61	132	16	85	6	.229
1991	California	AL	3B	152	586	58	144	18	66	5	.246
1992	California	AL	3B	130	456	41	103	12	48	3	.226
1993	California	AL	3B	20	50	3	9	0	4	1	.180
1993	Kansas City	AL	3B	82	281	37	72	14	46	0	.256
Seasonal Notation					587	60	138	18	74	4	.236

LEO GOMEZ   Age 27/R $11

Tough year. Physical problems all season, plus some rumbling among Orioles brass about his fortitude, or shortage thereof. Big upside this season: he'll go cheap, and we *still* think he's a 30-homer hitter waiting to happen.

Year	Team	Lg.	Pos.	G	AB	R	H	HR	RBI	SB	BA
1990	Baltimore	AL	3B	12	39	3	9	0	1	0	.231
1991	Baltimore	AL	3B	118	391	40	91	16	45	1	.233
1992	Baltimore	AL	3B	137	468	62	124	17	64	2	.265
1993	Baltimore	AL	3B	71	244	30	48	10	25	0	.197
Seasonal Notation					547	64	130	20	64	1	.238

RENE GONZALES Age 32/R $3

A nice guy who wears number 99, but he shouldn't be anyone's everyday anything.

Year	Team	Lg.	Pos.	G	AB	R	H	HR	RBI	SB	BA
1990	Baltimore	AL	2B	67	103	13	22	1	12	1	.214
1991	Toronto	AL	SS	71	118	16	23	1	6	0	.195
1992	California	AL	3B	104	329	47	91	7	38	7	.277
1993	California	AL	3B	117	335	34	84	2	31	5	.251
Seasonal Notation					399	49	99	4	39	5	.249

KELLY GRUBER Age 32/R $8

Maybe the Mets will take a chance on him. Maybe he'll go to Japan. Maybe he really was hurt when Whitey Herzog somehow got duped into trading for him. Maybe he's all through. But there's no maybes about this bit of advice: don't risk big bucks on his coming back strong.

Year	Team	Lg.	Pos.	G	AB	R	H	HR	RBI	SB	BA
1990	Toronto	AL	3B	150	592	92	162	31	118	14	.274
1991	Toronto	AL	3B	113	429	58	108	20	65	12	.252
1992	Toronto	AL	3B	120	446	42	102	11	43	7	.229
1993	California	AL	3B	18	65	10	18	3	9	0	.277
Seasonal Notation					618	81	157	26	94	13	.255

CHIP HALE Age 29/L $2

Third base is a Minnesota wasteland, and this guy showed some flashes of potential. Incidentally, his given name is Walter William Hale III, which sounds like he should be a lawyer from a John Grisham novel, or at the least, an heir to some kind of fortune. For that matter, so does . . .

Year	Team	Lg.	Pos.	G	AB	R	H	HR	RBI	SB	BA
1990	Minnesota	AL	2B	1	2	0	0	0	2	0	0.000
1993	Minnesota	AL	2B	69	186	25	62	3	27	2	.333
Seasonal Notation					435	57	143	6	67	4	.330

PHIL HIATT Age 24/R $9

. . . whose name isn't spelled the write way for him to be heir to all those hotels or even to that legal services thing that advertises on Mary Tyler Moore reruns. But what else can you say about this much-praised Royals prospect who lost his job to Gary Gaetti? Plenty. Two years ago he hit 27 home runs in 487 at-bats in the Southern League. Three years ago he stole 28 bases in the Florida State League. Any 24-year-old with power and speed deserves a second look.

Year	Team	Lg.	Pos.	G	AB	R	H	HR	RBI	SB	BA
1993	Kansas City	AL	3B	81	238	30	52	7	36	6	.218
Seasonal Notation					476	60	104	14	72	12	.218

BASEBALL ANAGRAM #6

Hark! Soft Man? = _____?

(Answer on page 299)

Catchers
pp. 59–73

Corners
pp. 73–95

Infield
pp. 95–116

Outfield
pp. 117–150

DH
pp. 150–153

Starters
pp. 154–189

Relievers
pp. 190–217

KENT HRBEK

Age 33/L   **$17**

We're not ready to give up on the Herbster. He's short on vowels, but long on heart. We want him to get healthy and stay that way, because we think he still has a couple of big years left in him.

Year	Team	Lg.	Pos.	G	AB	R	H	HR	RBI	SB	BA
1990	Minnesota	AL	1B	143	492	61	141	22	79	5	.287
1991	Minnesota	AL	1B	132	462	72	131	20	89	4	.284
1992	Minnesota	AL	1B	112	394	52	96	15	58	5	.244
1993	Minnesota	AL	1B	123	392	60	95	25	83	4	.242
Seasonal Notation					552	77	147	26	98	5	.266

TIM HULETT

Age 34/R   **$2**

When Gomez staggered to the sidelines, Hulett gave the Orioles a few solid weeks. That's his job. Unfortunately, that's also his limit.

Year	Team	Lg.	Pos.	G	AB	R	H	HR	RBI	SB	BA
1990	Baltimore	AL	3B	53	153	16	39	3	16	1	.255
1991	Baltimore	AL	3B	79	206	29	42	7	18	0	.204
1992	Baltimore	AL	3B	57	142	11	41	2	21	0	.289
1993	Baltimore	AL	3B	85	260	40	78	2	23	1	.300
Seasonal Notation					449	56	118	8	46	1	.263

JOHN JAHA

Age 27/R   **$12**

For half the year, he was overmatched. But the final numbers offer hope for the gambler and dreamer in all of us.

Year	Team	Lg.	Pos.	G	AB	R	H	HR	RBI	SB	BA
1992	Milwaukee	AL	1B	47	133	17	30	2	10	10	.226
1993	Milwaukee	AL	1B	153	515	78	136	19	70	13	.264
Seasonal Notation					524	76	134	17	64	18	.256

TERRY JORGENSEN

Age 27/R   **$1**

Hits like Christine.

Year	Team	Lg.	Pos.	G	AB	R	H	HR	RBI	SB	BA
1992	Minnesota	AL	1B	22	58	5	18	0	5	1	.310
1993	Minnesota	AL	3B	59	152	15	34	1	12	1	.224
Seasonal Notation					420	40	104	2	34	4	.248

WALLY JOYNER

Age 31/L   **$13**

Last year, we rashly called him the Mark Grace of the American League. On reflection, we have decided we owe Mark Grace an apology. Joyner isn't good enough to get away with his attitude. He could have learned an awful lot about the game of baseball from a guy who used to play his position, fellow by the name of Brett. Could have, but didn't.

Year	Team	Lg.	Pos.	G	AB	R	H	HR	RBI	SB	BA
1990	California	AL	1B	83	310	35	83	8	41	2	.268
1991	California	AL	1B	143	551	79	166	21	96	2	.301
1992	Kansas City	AL	1B	149	572	66	154	9	66	11	.269
1993	Kansas City	AL	1B	141	497	83	145	15	65	5	.292
Seasonal Notation					605	82	172	16	84	6	.284

JIM LEYRITZ   Age 30/R $8

He's so cocky that one AL star from another team was heard to say, "Man, he wears wrist bands like he's a brother." Leyritz is also one of the strongest guys around and a heckuva bit player.

Year	Team	Lg.	Pos.	G	AB	R	H	HR	RBI	SB	BA
1990	New York	AL	3B	92	303	28	78	5	25	2	.257
1991	New York	AL	3B	32	77	8	14	0	4	0	.182
1992	New York	AL	DH	63	144	17	37	7	26	0	.257
1993	New York	AL	1B	95	259	43	80	14	53	0	.309
Seasonal Notation					449	55	120	14	62	1	.267

SCOTT LIVINGSTONE   Age 28/L $1

Not a major factor in your plans, we presume.

Year	Team	Lg.	Pos.	G	AB	R	H	HR	RBI	SB	BA
1991	Detroit	AL	3B	44	127	19	37	2	11	2	.291
1992	Detroit	AL	3B	117	354	43	100	4	46	1	.282
1993	Detroit	AL	3B	98	304	39	89	2	39	1	.293
Seasonal Notation					491	63	141	5	60	2	.288

DAVE MAGADAN   Age 31/L $5

The RBI are few and far between, the home runs less frequent than a new moon. But the guy must be living right: he got away from the horrible Mets, went to play in his native Florida, and, though he didn't want to be traded, landed on the club managed by his favorite uncle, Lou Piniella. Now he's back in his native Florida, where this little mini-series began.

Year	Team	Lg.	Pos.	G	AB	R	H	HR	RBI	SB	BA
1990	New York	NL	1B	144	451	74	148	6	72	2	.328
1991	New York	NL	1B	124	418	58	108	4	51	1	.258
1992	New York	NL	3B	99	321	33	91	3	28	1	.283
1993	Florida	NL	3B	66	227	22	65	4	29	0	.286
1993	Seattle	AL	1B	71	228	27	59	1	21	2	.259
Seasonal Notation					528	68	151	5	64	1	.286

CARLOS MARTINEZ   Age 28/R $1

The least valuable Martinez in the major leagues.

Year	Team	Lg.	Pos.	G	AB	R	H	HR	RBI	SB	BA
1990	Chicago	AL	1B	92	272	18	61	4	24	0	.224
1991	Cleveland	AL	DH	72	257	22	73	5	30	3	.284
1992	Cleveland	AL	1B	69	228	23	60	5	35	1	.263
1993	Cleveland	AL	3B	80	262	26	64	5	31	1	.244
Seasonal Notation					527	46	133	9	62	2	.253

EDGAR MARTINEZ   Age 31/R $22

Write off 1993 to the injuries, swallow your disappointment if you drafted him last season, and go get him again.

Year	Team	Lg.	Pos.	G	AB	R	H	HR	RBI	SB	BA
1990	Seattle	AL	3B	144	487	71	147	11	49	1	.302
1991	Seattle	AL	3B	150	544	98	167	14	52	0	.307
1992	Seattle	AL	3B	135	528	100	181	18	73	14	.343
1993	Seattle	AL	DH	42	135	20	32	4	13	0	.237
Seasonal Notation					582	99	181	16	64	5	.311

Catchers
pp. 59–73

Corners
pp. 73–95

Infield
pp. 95–116

Outfield
pp. 117–150

DH
pp. 150–153

Starters
pp. 154–189

Relievers
pp. 190–217

TINO MARTINEZ　　　　　　　　　　　　　　Age 26/L　　　$19

While you're at it, go get him, too. This guy has some serious thump, and he's just entering prime time.

Year	Team	Lg.	Pos.	G	AB	R	H	HR	RBI	SB	BA
1990	Seattle	AL	1B	24	68	4	15	0	5	0	.221
1991	Seattle	AL	1B	36	112	11	23	4	9	0	.205
1992	Seattle	AL	1B	136	460	53	118	16	66	2	.257
1993	Seattle	AL	1B	109	408	48	108	17	60	0	.265
Seasonal Notation					556	61	140	19	74	1	.252

DON MATTINGLY　　　　　　　　　　　　　Age 32/L　　　$16

For two midsummer months we watched him pick up the Yankees, put them on his aching back, and carry them into a pennant race. Alas, it couldn't last forever, not with that inside-out dink swing he has to employ against too many pitchers these days. We all just have to accept the fact that the current-year Donnie Baseball bears scant resemblance to the 1984–87 models. Eight American League first basemen hit more home runs last season; six had more RBI. That puts him in the middle of the pack at the position, even though he's at the top of the heap in class.

Year	Team	Lg.	Pos.	G	AB	R	H	HR	RBI	SB	BA
1990	New York	AL	1B	102	394	40	101	5	42	1	.256
1991	New York	AL	1B	152	587	64	169	9	68	2	.288
1992	New York	AL	1B	157	640	89	184	14	86	3	.287
1993	New York	AL	1B	134	530	78	154	17	86	0	.291
Seasonal Notation					639	80	180	13	83	1	.283

MARK McGWIRE　　　　　　　　　　　　Age 30/R　　　$34

One evening before a mid-September game last summer, McGwire sat on the Oakland bench, bored out of his gourd, his ailing foot propped up on towels. He was innocently asked about one of the season's sillier theories, that all the home runs and tape-measure monster shots were because the ball was juiced. (Who exactly decides to juice the ball in this Oliver Stone interpretation of the National Pastime—some seamstress in Costa Rica?) McGwire snarled, "You know why the ball is going so far? It's because of horseshit pitching, and it's because of this"— whereupon he flexed a forearm that was the approximate width of John Kruk's waist. The pitching didn't get any better over the winter, but Mark McGwire's foot did, so get out your wallet and pay the price.

Year	Team	Lg.	Pos.	G	AB	R	H	HR	RBI	SB	BA
1990	Oakland	AL	1B	156	523	87	123	39	108	2	.235
1991	Oakland	AL	1B	154	483	62	97	22	75	2	.201
1992	Oakland	AL	1B	139	467	87	125	42	104	0	.268
1993	Oakland	AL	1B	27	84	16	28	9	24	0	.333
Seasonal Notation					529	85	126	38	105	1	.240

KEITH MILLER　　　　　　　　　　　　　Age 30/R　　　　$5

Health care reform may have come too late to salvage much of a career for this bruised, broken, beat-up bundle of hustle. You know the line: "If he stays healthy . . ."

Year	Team	Lg.	Pos.	G	AB	R	H	HR	RBI	SB	BA
1990	New York	NL	OF	88	233	42	60	1	12	16	.258
1991	New York	NL	2B	98	275	41	77	4	23	14	.280
1992	Kansas City	AL	2B	106	416	57	118	4	38	16	.284
1993	Kansas City	AL	3B	37	108	9	18	0	3	3	.167
Seasonal Notation					508	73	134	4	37	24	.265

Catchers
pp. 59-73

Corners
pp. 73-95

Infield
pp. 95-116

Outfield
pp. 117-150

DH
pp. 150-153

Starters
pp. 154-189

Relievers
pp. 190-217

RANDY MILLIGAN   Age 32/R $7

Should be a stabilizing influence on a young Cleveland team that needs this kind of veteran role player. Solid, unspectacular performer who tends to get overlooked until the end of the draft, when he's picked up for small money by a team on its way to the pennant.

Year	Team	Lg.	Pos.	G	AB	R	H	HR	RBI	SB	BA
1990	Baltimore	AL	1B	109	362	64	96	20	60	6	.265
1991	Baltimore	AL	1B	141	483	57	127	16	70	0	.263
1992	Baltimore	AL	1B	137	462	71	111	11	53	0	.240
1993	Cincinnati	NL	1B	83	234	30	64	6	29	0	.274
1993	Cleveland	AL	1B	19	47	7	20	0	7	0	.426
Seasonal Notation					526	75	138	17	72	1	.263

JOHN OLERUD   Age 25/L $36

A unique perspective on this latter-day Roy Hobbs was offered last summer by Blue Jays coach Nick Leyva: "Now, I know I ain't Randy Johnson, but I throw BP to Olerud's group every night, and this bleeping guy is unbelievable. Every bleeping ball he hits is a line drive, every bleeping one. Un-bleeping-believable." But bleeping true.

Year	Team	Lg.	Pos.	G	AB	R	H	HR	RBI	SB	BA
1990	Toronto	AL	DH	111	358	43	95	14	48	0	.265
1991	Toronto	AL	1B	139	454	64	116	17	68	0	.256
1992	Toronto	AL	1B	138	458	68	130	16	66	1	.284
1993	Toronto	AL	1B	158	551	109	200	24	107	0	.363
Seasonal Notation					540	84	160	21	85	0	.297

MIKE PAGLIARULO   Age 34/L $4

A gamer. If you owned a real baseball team (as opposed to a hyper-real Rotisserie team), this is a guy you'd want to have in the clubhouse. Good things seem to follow him around. But big salary, shrinking revenues, and small brains among major league moguls may make it hard for him to find work.

Year	Team	Lg.	Pos.	G	AB	R	H	HR	RBI	SB	BA
1990	San Diego	NL	3B	128	398	29	101	7	38	1	.254
1991	Minnesota	AL	3B	121	365	38	102	6	36	1	.279
1992	Minnesota	AL	3B	42	105	10	21	0	9	1	.200
1993	Minnesota	AL	3B	83	253	31	74	3	23	6	.292
1993	Baltimore	AL	3B	33	117	24	38	6	21	0	.325
Seasonal Notation					492	52	133	8	50	3	.271

RAFAEL PALMEIRO   Age 29/L $40

He moved up on the plate a little, stopped worrying about hitting the ball to the opposite field, and decided to become a superstar. We think he was made for the role. We think the Rangers were nuts to let him walk.

Year	Team	Lg.	Pos.	G	AB	R	H	HR	RBI	SB	BA
1990	Texas	AL	1B	154	598	72	191	14	89	3	.319
1991	Texas	AL	1B	159	631	115	203	26	88	4	.322
1992	Texas	AL	1B	159	608	84	163	22	85	2	.268
1993	Texas	AL	1B	160	597	124	176	37	105	22	.295
Seasonal Notation					623	101	187	25	94	7	.301

DEAN PALMER   Age 25/R $30

Rangers hitting coach Willie Upshaw, one of our all-time favorite people, thinks Palmer is only scratching the surface of his talent. We advise you to listen to Mr. Upshaw and pay accordingly.

Year	Team	Lg.	Pos.	G	AB	R	H	HR	RBI	SB	BA
1991	Texas	AL	3B	81	268	38	50	15	37	0	.187
1992	Texas	AL	3B	152	541	74	124	26	72	10	.229
1993	Texas	AL	3B	148	519	88	127	33	96	11	.245
Seasonal Notation					564	85	127	31	87	8	.227

CRAIG PAQUETTE   Age 25/R $3

The A's think he has a chance to be a solid, productive player. If you avert your eyes from that batting average, you can see their point.

Year	Team	Lg.	Pos.	G	AB	R	H	HR	RBI	SB	BA
1993	Oakland	AL	3B	105	393	35	86	12	46	4	.219
Seasonal Notation					606	54	132	18	70	6	.219

EDUARDO PEREZ   Age 24/R $9

There are no better people in baseball than the Perez family. That's why it was so unfair that when Tony finally got a chance to manage, it was with a team whose owner was a cruel old bigot and whose general manager was a cover-his-butt young preppie. Then along comes Eduardo, Tony's son, who breaks in with a team owned by a senile cowboy and the cowboy's penny-pinching, shrewish wife. Maybe he'll catch a break and get traded.

Year	Team	Lg.	Pos.	G	AB	R	H	HR	RBI	SB	BA
1993	California	AL	3B	52	180	16	45	4	30	5	.250
Seasonal Notation					560	49	140	12	93	15	.250

DAVID SEGUI   Age 27/B $6

Yet another son of a former major leaguer to emerge in the past few years, Segui has a sweet stroke but not the kind of power we'd like to see in Camden Yards. We want a guy who can rain home run balls onto Boog Powell's barbecue stand and smash out windows in the Orioles' front office. So, presumably, do the Orioles. What they have instead is the American League edition of Hal Morris.

Year	Team	Lg.	Pos.	G	AB	R	H	HR	RBI	SB	BA
1990	Baltimore	AL	1B	40	123	14	30	2	15	0	.244
1991	Baltimore	AL	1B	86	212	15	59	2	22	1	.278
1992	Baltimore	AL	1B	115	189	21	44	1	17	1	.233
1993	Baltimore	AL	1B	146	450	54	123	10	60	2	.273
Seasonal Notation					407	43	107	6	47	1	.263

Catchers
pp. 59–73

Corners
pp. 73–95

Infield
pp. 95–116

Outfield
pp. 117–150

DH
pp. 150–153

Starters
pp. 154–189

Relievers
pp. 190–217

KEVIN SEITZER   Age 32/R $7

We don't include defense in the imperfect world of Rotisserie baseball, but it is illustrative that some Oakland people said upon releasing Seitzer that his defensive range was roughly equivalent to that of an ottoman. And since he isn't exactly the Platonic ideal of a DH, we wonder about his future.

Year	Team	Lg.	Pos.	G	AB	R	H	HR	RBI	SB	BA
1990	Kansas City	AL	3B	158	622	91	171	6	38	7	.275
1991	Kansas City	AL	3B	85	234	28	62	1	25	4	.265
1992	Milwaukee	AL	3B	148	540	74	146	5	71	13	.270
1993	Oakland	AL	3B	73	255	24	65	4	27	4	.255
1993	Milwaukee	AL	3B	47	162	21	47	7	30	3	.290
Seasonal Notation					574	75	155	7	60	9	.271

J. T. SNOW   Age 26/B $12

In April, he looked like Will Clark. In May, he played like Roy Clark. By June, he couldn't hit like Petula Clark. And his dad, the wide receiver, never was as good as Dwight Clark.

Year	Team	Lg.	Pos.	G	AB	R	H	HR	RBI	SB	BA
1992	New York	AL	1B	7	14	1	2	0	2	0	.143
1993	California	AL	1B	129	419	60	101	16	57	3	.241
Seasonal Notation					515	72	122	19	70	3	.238

PAUL SORRENTO   Age 28/L $16

A quiet but productive hitter in a lineup oozing with talent.

Year	Team	Lg.	Pos.	G	AB	R	H	HR	RBI	SB	BA
1990	Minnesota	AL	DH	41	121	11	25	5	13	1	.207
1991	Minnesota	AL	1B	26	47	6	12	4	13	0	.255
1992	Cleveland	AL	1B	140	458	52	123	18	60	0	.269
1993	Cleveland	AL	1B	148	463	75	119	18	65	3	.257
Seasonal Notation					496	65	127	20	68	1	.256

ED SPRAGUE   Age 26/R $14

His father was a major leaguer. His wife is an Olympian. He won a World Series game as a rookie. And in Skydome, where fans make less noise than a Bill Moyers lecture crowd, and in a lineup packed with stars, he doesn't even get noticed. Inside tip: he's going to get better.

Year	Team	Lg.	Pos.	G	AB	R	H	HR	RBI	SB	BA
1991	Toronto	AL	3B	61	160	17	44	4	20	0	.275
1992	Toronto	AL	C	22	47	6	11	1	7	0	.234
1993	Toronto	AL	3B	150	546	50	142	12	73	1	.260
Seasonal Notation					523	50	136	11	69	0	.262

B. J. SURHOFF
Age 29/L   **$9**

He rescued a season that began with him hitting .118 after the first six weeks. The pre–spring training word is that he might go back to catching. That would be a good Rotisserie move, because his numbers would look a whole lot better coming from the catcher slot.

Year	Team	Lg.	Pos.	G	AB	R	H	HR	RBI	SB	BA
1990	Milwaukee	AL	C	135	474	55	131	6	59	18	.276
1991	Milwaukee	AL	C	143	505	57	146	5	68	5	.289
1992	Milwaukee	AL	C	139	480	63	121	4	62	14	.252
1993	Milwaukee	AL	3B	148	552	66	151	7	79	12	.274
Seasonal Notation					576	69	157	6	76	14	.273

FRANK THOMAS
Age 25/R   **$42**

One scout called him "Wade Boggs with power." Another called him "a right-handed Ted Williams." A third called him "the most impossible hitter to pitch to since Jim Rice in his prime." We call him "the best hitter in baseball"—and you can quote us.

Year	Team	Lg.	Pos.	G	AB	R	H	HR	RBI	SB	BA
1990	Chicago	AL	1B	60	191	39	63	7	31	0	.330
1991	Chicago	AL	DH	158	559	104	178	32	109	1	.318
1992	Chicago	AL	1B	160	573	108	185	24	115	6	.323
1993	Chicago	AL	1B	153	549	106	174	41	128	4	.317
Seasonal Notation					571	108	183	31	116	3	.321

JEFF TREADWAY
Age 31/L   **$2**

A spare part, but a good spare part.

Year	Team	Lg.	Pos.	G	AB	R	H	HR	RBI	SB	BA
1990	Atlanta	NL	2B	128	474	56	134	11	59	3	.283
1991	Atlanta	NL	2B	106	306	41	98	3	32	2	.320
1992	Atlanta	NL	2B	61	126	5	28	0	5	1	.222
1993	Cleveland	AL	3B	97	221	25	67	2	27	1	.303
Seasonal Notation					465	52	135	6	50	2	.290

MO VAUGHN
Age 26/L   **$28**

Thanks to hitting coach Mike Easler, the Red Sox have at least one interesting player to watch. When Big Mo connects, he makes you glad you're not a baseball.

Year	Team	Lg.	Pos.	G	AB	R	H	HR	RBI	SB	BA
1991	Boston	AL	1B	74	219	21	57	4	32	2	.260
1992	Boston	AL	1B	113	355	42	83	13	57	3	.234
1993	Boston	AL	1B	152	539	86	160	29	101	4	.297
Seasonal Notation					531	71	143	21	90	4	.270

ROBIN VENTURA
Age 26/L   **$21**

Two straight years of treading water. Do you think that maybe it has something to do with Walter Hrniak, the maniacal White Sox hitting coach who teaches his hitters to swing like they're cutting wheat?

Year	Team	Lg.	Pos.	G	AB	R	H	HR	RBI	SB	BA
1990	Chicago	AL	3B	150	493	48	123	5	54	1	.249
1991	Chicago	AL	3B	157	606	92	172	23	100	2	.284
1992	Chicago	AL	3B	157	592	85	167	16	93	2	.282
1993	Chicago	AL	3B	157	554	85	145	22	94	1	.262
Seasonal Notation					585	80	158	17	88	1	.270

Up the Middle

The middle of the infield was a little rocky in the National League last season. Barry Larkin, Delino DeShields, Robby Thompson, and Ryne Sandberg missed big chunks of the season with injuries. Shawon Dunston only got back in time for a cup of coffee. The Wizard of Oz began to show his age. Tony Fernandez hit bottom.

Meanwhile, over in the American League, the middle infield must have been a lot smoother. Roberto Alomar and Carlos Baerga gave us goose bumps in their *mano a mano* to determine the best second baseman in the universe. Ozzie Guillen returned, a cause for joyous celebration. Alan Trammell and Lou Whitaker proved that the longest running act in the show still has legs. Tony Fernandez soared to the top.

In both leagues, a lot of exciting young talent emerged at second and short last season: Ándujar Cedeño, Royce Clayton, and Wil Cordero in the NL; Bret Boone, Brent Gates, and John Valentin in the AL. Also in both leagues, the trend toward more offense up the middle continued unabated: even with expansion, Steve Jeltz and Mario Mendoza were nowhere to be seen.

All in all, while there were plenty of ups and downs, 1993 was a good year for middle infielders.

Just ask Tony Fernandez.

NATIONAL LEAGUE

LUIS ALICEA
Age 28/B   **$4**

It's taken him a lot longer than the Cardinals expected, but it looks like he might have made it.

Year	Team	Lg.	Pos.	G	AB	R	H	HR	RBI	SB	BA
1991	St. Louis	NL	2B	56	68	5	13	0	0	0	.191
1992	St. Louis	NL	2B	85	265	26	65	2	32	2	.245
1993	St. Louis	NL	2B	115	362	50	101	3	46	11	.279
Seasonal Notation					439	51	113	3	49	8	.258

ALEX ARIAS   Age 26/R $2

Look at it this way: he's young, he has good defensive skills, he can handle himself at the plate, and the Marlins have no one else in the pipeline. That makes him a sound choice as your third middle infielder.

Year	Team	Lg.	Pos.	G	AB	R	H	HR	RBI	SB	BA
1992	Chicago	NL	SS	32	99	14	29	0	7	0	.293
1993	Florida	NL	2B	96	249	27	67	2	20	1	.269
Seasonal Notation					440	51	121	2	34	1	.276

KEVIN BAEZ   Age 27/R $1

Put on an old peace button, let your hair grow down to your shoulders, dig up one of your old anti–Vietnam War posters, belt out a chorus of "The Night They Drove Old Dixie Down," and wonder how on earth this no-relation-to-Joan ever got to the major leagues. (Oh. Of course. He's a Met.)

Year	Team	Lg.	Pos.	G	AB	R	H	HR	RBI	SB	BA
1990	New York	NL	SS	5	12	0	2	0	0	0	.167
1992	New York	NL	SS	6	13	0	2	0	0	0	.154
1993	New York	NL	SS	52	126	10	23	0	7	0	.183
Seasonal Notation					388	25	69	0	18	0	.179

BRET BARBERIE   Age 26/B $6

If he can stay healthy for a full season, he will flirt with .300 and drive in some runs. Came up through the Expos organization, which means he has a home forever in Florida.

Year	Team	Lg.	Pos.	G	AB	R	H	HR	RBI	SB	BA
1991	Montreal	NL	SS	57	136	16	48	2	18	0	.353
1992	Montreal	NL	3B	111	285	26	66	1	24	9	.232
1993	Florida	NL	2B	99	375	45	104	5	33	2	.277
Seasonal Notation					482	52	132	4	45	6	.274

JAY BELL   Age 28/R $10

A lot of heavy thinkers explained last year's home run binge by saying the "ball must be juiced." If so, the juice must have skipped Pittsburgh, where no one hits home runs anymore. (Back in 1991, when this consummate pro drove his Rotisserie salary into double digits by hitting home runs, well, yes, no question about it, the ball *was* juiced.)

Year	Team	Lg.	Pos.	G	AB	R	H	HR	RBI	SB	BA
1990	Pittsburgh	NL	SS	159	583	93	148	7	52	10	.254
1991	Pittsburgh	NL	SS	157	608	96	164	16	67	10	.270
1992	Pittsburgh	NL	SS	159	632	87	167	9	55	7	.264
1993	Pittsburgh	NL	SS	154	604	102	187	9	51	16	.310
Seasonal Notation					625	97	171	10	57	11	.274

FREDDIE BENAVIDES   Age 27/R $2

The Rockies grew tired of his shoddy play afield and less than diligent work habits. Take that as a warning.

Year	Team	Lg.	Pos.	G	AB	R	H	HR	RBI	SB	BA
1991	Cincinnati	NL	SS	24	63	11	18	0	3	1	.286
1992	Cincinnati	NL	2B	74	173	14	40	1	17	0	.231
1993	Colorado	NL	SS	74	213	20	61	3	26	3	.286
Seasonal Notation					422	42	112	3	43	3	.265

MIKE BENJAMIN   Age 28/R $1

Unless Robby Thompson takes a free-agent walk or suffers a major injury, Benjamin won't play enough to be a factor in your pennant plans.

Year	Team	Lg.	Pos.	G	AB	R	H	HR	RBI	SB	BA
1990	San Francisco	NL	SS	22	56	7	12	2	3	1	.214
1991	San Francisco	NL	SS	54	106	12	13	2	8	3	.123
1992	San Francisco	NL	SS	40	75	4	13	1	3	1	.173
1993	San Francisco	NL	2B	63	146	22	29	4	16	0	.199
Seasonal Notation					346	40	60	8	27	4	.175

CRAIG BIGGIO   Age 28/R $21

This guy hit 21 home runs? That's twice as many as he hit in the previous three seasons combined. Man, the ball must be juiced. (Warning note: he was caught stealing 17 times in 32 attempts, which may mean his old catcher's knees are stiffening up on him.)

Year	Team	Lg.	Pos.	G	AB	R	H	HR	RBI	SB	BA
1990	Houston	NL	C	150	555	53	153	4	42	25	.276
1991	Houston	NL	C	149	546	79	161	4	46	19	.295
1992	Houston	NL	2B	162	613	96	170	6	39	38	.277
1993	Houston	NL	2B	155	610	98	175	21	64	15	.287
Seasonal Notation					611	85	173	9	50	25	.284

JEFF BLAUSER   Age 28/R $19

It was mid-September with the Braves in the midst of their juggernaut finish. Bobby Cox and his coaches were sittin' and spittin' in the old dugout, talkin' ball and droppin' a lot of "g"s from the end of words. The chattin' got around to who was the Braves' MVP, and it sure was surprisin' when not a few started bringin' up Blauser's name. The offense was always there. The difference last year was in his defense: he went from sub-par to first-rate in the field, thereby ensurin' him enough at-bats to become an All Star—and to turn Chipper Jones into the Braves' *third baseman* of the future.

Year	Team	Lg.	Pos.	G	AB	R	H	HR	RBI	SB	BA
1990	Atlanta	NL	SS	115	386	46	104	8	39	3	.269
1991	Atlanta	NL	SS	129	352	49	91	11	54	5	.259
1992	Atlanta	NL	SS	123	343	61	90	14	46	5	.262
1993	Atlanta	NL	SS	161	597	110	182	15	73	16	.305
Seasonal Notation					514	81	143	14	65	8	.278

TIM BOGAR   Age 27/R $1

Some people around the Mets thought Bogey could be the shortstop of the future, but then he was browbeaten into a stupor by the Dallas Green Bile

Catchers
pp. 59–73

Corners
pp. 73–95

Infield
pp. 95–116

Outfield
pp. 117–150

DH
pp. 150–153

Starters
pp. 154–189

Relievers
pp. 190–217

Machine and was last seen wandering around dazed in the rubble of the Mets' season. Was 1993 the beginning of a beautiful relationship between Bogey and Mets fans? Will people shout "Here's looking at you, kid" every time he steps to the plate? Will Dallas let him "Play it again, Tim?" We'll have to wait for the sequel, coming soon to a local ballpark.

Year	Team	Lg.	Pos.	G	AB	R	H	HR	RBI	SB	BA
1993	New York	NL	SS	78	205	19	50	3	25	0	.244
Seasonal Notation					425	39	103	6	51	0	.244

JEFF BRANSON   Age 27/L $1

The Reds wanted him to take hold of the second-base job. He let it go between his legs.

Year	Team	Lg.	Pos.	G	AB	R	H	HR	RBI	SB	BA
1992	Cincinnati	NL	2B	72	115	12	34	0	15	0	.296
1993	Cincinnati	NL	SS	125	381	40	92	3	22	4	.241
Seasonal Notation					407	42	103	2	30	3	.254

CASEY CANDAELE   Age 33/B $1

Flickering out.

Year	Team	Lg.	Pos.	G	AB	R	H	HR	RBI	SB	BA
1990	Houston	NL	OF	130	262	30	75	3	22	7	.286
1991	Houston	NL	2B	151	461	44	121	4	50	9	.262
1992	Houston	NL	SS	135	320	19	68	1	18	7	.213
1993	Houston	NL	2B	75	121	18	29	1	7	2	.240
Seasonal Notation					384	36	96	2	32	8	.252

VINNY CASTILLA   Age 26/R $3

We'll pass this on for what it's worth: Braves people think this guy, who was drafted out of their organization, will someday be an everyday player with 15–home run potential. Make him one of your sleeper picks.

Year	Team	Lg.	Pos.	G	AB	R	H	HR	RBI	SB	BA
1991	Atlanta	NL	SS	12	5	1	1	0	0	0	.200
1992	Atlanta	NL	3B	9	16	1	4	0	1	0	.250
1993	Colorado	NL	SS	105	337	36	86	9	30	2	.255
Seasonal Notation					460	48	117	11	39	2	.254

ANDUJAR CEDENO   Age 24/R $13

Still one scary dude throwing the ball from shortstop, but he began to show what he can do with the bat. Last year was a big confidence builder. Our crystal ball shows a rising star.

Year	Team	Lg.	Pos.	G	AB	R	H	HR	RBI	SB	BA
1990	Houston	NL	SS	7	8	0	0	0	0	0	0.000
1991	Houston	NL	SS	67	251	27	61	9	36	4	.243
1992	Houston	NL	SS	71	220	15	38	2	13	2	.173
1993	Houston	NL	SS	149	505	69	143	11	56	9	.283
Seasonal Notation					542	61	133	12	57	8	.246

ROYCE CLAYTON
Age 24/R   **$11**

Faltered a bit down the stretch, but otherwise vindicated those of us who have predicted great things for him in the past few years. We have also predicted great things for . . .

Year	Team	Lg.	Pos.	G	AB	R	H	HR	RBI	SB	BA
1991	San Francisco	NL	SS	9	26	0	3	0	2	0	.115
1992	San Francisco	NL	SS	98	321	31	72	4	24	8	.224
1993	San Francisco	NL	SS	153	549	54	155	6	70	11	.282
Seasonal Notation					558	52	143	6	59	11	.257

WIL CORDERO
Age 22/R   **$11**

. . . who provided a few thrills last season with his bat. But his defense and the presence of Mike Lansing might eventually send Cordero to third.

Year	Team	Lg.	Pos.	G	AB	R	H	HR	RBI	SB	BA
1992	Montreal	NL	SS	45	126	17	38	2	8	0	.302
1993	Montreal	NL	SS	138	475	56	118	10	58	12	.248
Seasonal Notation					532	64	138	10	58	10	.260

DELINO DeSHIELDS
Age 25/L   **$24**

Wears his pants high to honor the stars of the old Negro League. When he was healthy, he looked and played a lot like Cool Papa Bell. Perfect tonic for the LA offense. But don't you just hate it when one of your top players gets chicken pox? Hamstring pulls and thumb injuries, they come with the game. But chicken pox? If this happens again, we're going to insist that *Baseball Register* start listing childhood diseases in its player bios.

Year	Team	Lg.	Pos.	G	AB	R	H	HR	RBI	SB	BA
1990	Montreal	NL	2B	129	499	69	144	4	45	42	.289
1991	Montreal	NL	2B	151	563	83	134	10	51	56	.238
1992	Montreal	NL	2B	135	530	82	155	7	56	46	.292
1993	Montreal	NL	2B	123	481	75	142	2	29	43	.295
Seasonal Notation					624	93	173	6	54	56	.277

MARIANO DUNCAN
Age 31/R   **$19**

The Phillies scored so many runs, he went unnoticed. But if you got him cheap, you noticed.

Year	Team	Lg.	Pos.	G	AB	R	H	HR	RBI	SB	BA
1990	Cincinnati	NL	2B	125	435	67	133	10	55	13	.306
1991	Cincinnati	NL	2B	100	333	46	86	12	40	5	.258
1992	Philadelphia	NL	OF	142	574	71	153	8	50	23	.267
1993	Philadelphia	NL	2B	124	496	68	140	11	73	6	.282
Seasonal Notation					606	83	168	13	71	15	.279

SHAWON DUNSTON
Age 31/R   **$12**

We don't have a clue. Neither do the Cubs. That's what spring training is for.

Year	Team	Lg.	Pos.	G	AB	R	H	HR	RBI	SB	BA
1990	Chicago	NL	SS	146	545	73	143	17	66	25	.262
1991	Chicago	NL	SS	142	492	59	128	12	50	21	.260
1992	Chicago	NL	SS	18	73	8	23	0	2	2	.315
1993	Chicago	NL	SS	7	10	3	4	0	2	0	.400
Seasonal Notation					579	74	154	15	62	24	.266

Catchers
pp. 59-73

Corners
pp. 73-95

Infield
pp. 95-116

Outfield
pp. 117-150

DH
pp. 150-153

Starters
pp. 154-189

Relievers
pp. 190-217

TOM FOLEY
Age 34/L　　**$1**

He'll have his hands full this spring getting the health care bill through Congress.

Year	Team	Lg.	Pos.	G	AB	R	H	HR	RBI	SB	BA
1990	Montreal	NL	SS	73	164	11	35	0	12	0	.213
1991	Montreal	NL	SS	86	168	12	35	0	15	2	.208
1992	Montreal	NL	SS	72	115	7	20	0	5	3	.174
1993	Pittsburgh	NL	2B	86	194	18	49	3	22	0	.253
Seasonal Notation					327	24	71	1	27	2	.217

CARLOS GARCIA
Age 26/R　　**$12**

Hit four more home runs last season than José Lind hit in six years with the Pirates. Stole the same number of bases that José Lind stole in the preceding three years with the Pirates. Batted 34 points higher than José Lind did his last year with the Pirates. Scored 31 more runs than José Lind averaged his last three years with the Pirates. Chico who?

Year	Team	Lg.	Pos.	G	AB	R	H	HR	RBI	SB	BA
1990	Pittsburgh	NL	SS	4	4	1	2	0	0	0	.500
1991	Pittsburgh	NL	SS	12	24	2	6	0	1	0	.250
1992	Pittsburgh	NL	2B	22	39	4	8	0	4	0	.205
1993	Pittsburgh	NL	2B	141	546	77	147	12	47	18	.269
Seasonal Notation					554	76	147	10	47	16	.266

JEFF GARDNER
Age 30/L　　**$1**

Scrappy. But there's a reason he was a 29-year-old rookie.

Year	Team	Lg.	Pos.	G	AB	R	H	HR	RBI	SB	BA
1991	New York	NL	SS	13	37	3	6	0	1	0	.162
1992	San Diego	NL	2B	15	19	0	2	0	0	0	.105
1993	San Diego	NL	2B	140	404	53	106	1	24	2	.262
Seasonal Notation					443	54	109	0	24	1	.248

RICKY GUTTIERREZ
Age 23/R　　**$2**

We think a guy who strikes out 97 times while hitting only five home runs ought to choke up a little, cut down on his swing, work with the tee, and spend some quality time in the batting cage learning to make better contact.

Year	Team	Lg.	Pos.	G	AB	R	H	HR	RBI	SB	BA
1993	San Diego	NL	SS	133	438	76	110	5	26	4	.251
Seasonal Notation					533	92	133	6	31	4	.251

LENNY HARRIS
Age 29/L　　**$1**

Has some offensive skills, but needs 350 AB to be of any Rotisserie value. Not likely unless somebody gets hurt.

Year	Team	Lg.	Pos.	G	AB	R	H	HR	RBI	SB	BA
1990	Los Angeles	NL	3B	137	431	61	131	2	29	15	.304
1991	Los Angeles	NL	3B	145	429	59	123	3	38	12	.287
1992	Los Angeles	NL	2B	135	347	28	94	0	30	19	.271
1993	Los Angeles	NL	2B	107	160	20	38	2	11	3	.237
Seasonal Notation					422	51	119	2	33	15	.282

JEFF KENT

Age 26/R   **$17**

Scorned by the media, booed by the fans, and bullied by Big Bad Dallas, the kid took a lickin' but kept on tickin'. Tied with Craig Biggio for most home runs in NL by a second baseman. Goal this year is *not* to lead the league again in errors.

Year	Team	Lg.	Pos.	G	AB	R	H	HR	RBI	SB	BA
1992	Toronto	AL	3B	65	192	36	46	8	35	2	.240
1992	New York	NL	2B	37	113	16	27	3	15	0	.239
1993	New York	NL	2B	140	496	65	134	21	80	4	.270
Seasonal Notation					536	78	138	21	87	4	.258

BARRY LARKIN

Age 29/R   **$21**

Our theory is to keep paying for his services on the assumption that one of these years he'll remain healthy, put together all those marvelous skills, and finally have the monster season we all keep expecting. But our trust in this theory is admittedly beginning to waver.

Year	Team	Lg.	Pos.	G	AB	R	H	HR	RBI	SB	BA
1990	Cincinnati	NL	SS	158	614	85	185	7	67	30	.301
1991	Cincinnati	NL	SS	123	464	88	140	20	69	24	.302
1992	Cincinnati	NL	SS	140	533	76	162	12	78	15	.304
1993	Cincinnati	NL	SS	100	384	57	121	8	51	14	.315
Seasonal Notation					620	95	189	14	82	25	.305

MARK LEMKE

Age 28/B   **$5**

A plucky player who had a career year. Now, along with all Braves infielders, he tries to hold off the challenge of the amazing Chipper Jones, not to mention the estimable Ramon Caraballo.

Year	Team	Lg.	Pos.	G	AB	R	H	HR	RBI	SB	BA
1990	Atlanta	NL	3B	102	239	22	54	0	21	0	.226
1991	Atlanta	NL	2B	136	269	36	63	2	23	1	.234
1992	Atlanta	NL	2B	155	427	38	97	6	26	0	.227
1993	Atlanta	NL	2B	151	493	52	124	7	49	1	.252
Seasonal Notation					425	44	100	4	35	0	.237

JEFF McKNIGHT

Age 31/B   **$1**

It's as if the Mets deliberately tried to be as mediocre as possible.

Year	Team	Lg.	Pos.	G	AB	R	H	HR	RBI	SB	BA
1990	Baltimore	AL	1B	29	75	11	15	1	4	0	.200
1991	Baltimore	AL	OF	16	41	2	7	0	2	1	.171
1992	New York	NL	2B	31	85	10	23	2	13	0	.271
1993	New York	NL	SS	105	164	19	42	2	13	0	.256
Seasonal Notation					326	37	77	4	28	0	.238

ROBERTO MEJIA

Age 21/R   **$4**

The Rockies think he is a real prospect. They want him to win their second-base job. They think he'll show some power. Before you take all this to the bank, remember that these are the same people who put together the Pitching Staff From Hell.

Year	Team	Lg.	Pos.	G	AB	R	H	HR	RBI	SB	BA
1993	Colorado	NL	2B	65	229	31	53	5	20	4	.231
Seasonal Notation					570	77	132	12	49	9	.231

Catchers
pp. 59-73

Corners
pp. 73-95

Infield
pp. 95-116

Outfield
pp. 117-150

DH
pp. 150-153

Starters
pp. 154-189

Relievers
pp. 190-217

MICKEY MORANDINI　　　　　　　　　Age 27/L　　　$3

If you buy him with the idea of having a solid bit player, you done good. If you pick him up with the idea of having a starting second baseman, you deserve to work for the Rockies. Note the nice little SB bonus.

Year	Team	Lg.	Pos.	G	AB	R	H	HR	RBI	SB	BA
1990	Philadelphia	NL	2B	25	79	9	19	1	3	3	.241
1991	Philadelphia	NL	2B	98	325	38	81	1	20	13	.249
1992	Philadelphia	NL	2B	127	422	47	112	3	30	8	.265
1993	Philadelphia	NL	2B	120	425	57	105	3	33	13	.247
Seasonal Notation					547	66	138	3	37	16	.253

JOSE OFFERMAN　　　　　　　　　　Age 25/B　　　$18

If you own him, look at those RBI and SB and give yourself a hug. Never mind that he led the league in errors by a wide margin for the second straight year. That doesn't matter to you any more than it does to the Dodgers, whose only other plausible shortstop alternative is Bill Russell. (The coach, not the basketball player.)

Year	Team	Lg.	Pos.	G	AB	R	H	HR	RBI	SB	BA
1990	Los Angeles	NL	SS	29	58	7	9	1	7	1	.155
1991	Los Angeles	NL	SS	52	113	10	22	0	3	3	.195
1992	Los Angeles	NL	SS	149	534	67	139	1	30	23	.260
1993	Los Angeles	NL	SS	158	590	77	159	1	62	30	.269
Seasonal Notation					540	67	137	1	42	23	.254

JOSE OQUENDO　　　　　　　　　　Age 30/B　　　$1

Stick a fork in him. And while you're at it, paint a big question mark on the forehead of . . .

Year	Team	Lg.	Pos.	G	AB	R	H	HR	RBI	SB	BA
1990	St. Louis	NL	2B	156	469	38	118	1	37	1	.252
1991	St. Louis	NL	2B	127	366	37	88	1	26	1	.240
1992	St. Louis	NL	2B	14	35	3	9	0	3	0	.257
1993	St. Louis	NL	SS	46	73	7	15	0	4	0	.205
Seasonal Notation					445	40	108	0	33	0	.244

GERONIMO PENA　　　　　　　　　Age 27/B　　　$4

. . . who has bodacious skills but no apparent inclination to use them to their fullest. Maybe he needs a change of scenery.

Year	Team	Lg.	Pos.	G	AB	R	H	HR	RBI	SB	BA
1990	St. Louis	NL	2B	18	45	5	11	0	2	1	.244
1991	St. Louis	NL	2B	104	185	38	45	5	17	15	.243
1992	St. Louis	NL	2B	62	203	31	62	7	31	13	.305
1993	St. Louis	NL	2B	74	254	34	65	5	30	13	.256
Seasonal Notation					431	67	114	10	50	26	.266

BASEBALL ANAGRAM #8

Bug Slide = _____?

(Answer on page 299)

JODY REED
Age 31/R $2

It's a sign of how the Dodgers have declined that this resoundingly average player will likely keep his job.

Year	Team	Lg.	Pos.	G	AB	R	H	HR	RBI	SB	BA
1990	Boston	AL	2B	155	598	70	173	5	51	4	.289
1991	Boston	AL	2B	153	618	87	175	5	60	6	.283
1992	Boston	AL	2B	143	550	64	136	3	40	7	.247
1993	Los Angeles	NL	2B	132	445	48	123	2	31	1	.276
Seasonal Notation					614	74	168	4	50	5	.275

RICH RENTERIA
Age 32/R $1

Expansion was invented for guys like this.

Year	Team	Lg.	Pos.	G	AB	R	H	HR	RBI	SB	BA
1993	Florida	NL	2B	103	263	27	67	2	30	0	.255
Seasonal Notation					413	42	105	3	47	0	.255

BIP ROBERTS
Age 30/B $12

A big talent going to waste. As a member of the Davey Johnson regime said one day in an assessment of the Reds, "We got the weirdest mix of players you've ever seen. And Bip? Hey, Bip is from a different planet." He'll be on a new spaceship by the time you read this. Beam him up.

Year	Team	Lg.	Pos.	G	AB	R	H	HR	RBI	SB	BA
1990	San Diego	NL	OF	149	556	104	172	9	44	46	.309
1991	San Diego	NL	2B	117	424	66	119	3	32	26	.281
1992	Cincinnati	NL	OF	147	532	92	172	4	45	44	.323
1993	Cincinnati	NL	2B	83	292	46	70	1	18	26	.240
Seasonal Notation					589	100	174	5	45	46	.295

JUAN SAMUEL
Age 33/R $3

Now just a classy shadow of his former self.

Year	Team	Lg.	Pos.	G	AB	R	H	HR	RBI	SB	BA
1990	Los Angeles	NL	2B	143	492	62	119	13	52	38	.242
1991	Los Angeles	NL	2B	153	594	74	161	12	58	23	.271
1992	Los Angeles	NL	2B	47	122	7	32	0	15	2	.262
1992	Kansas City	AL	OF	29	102	15	29	0	8	6	.284
1993	Cincinnati	NL	2B	103	261	31	60	4	26	9	.230
Seasonal Notation					535	64	136	9	54	26	.255

REY SANCHEZ
Age 26/R $2

A good third man up the middle.

Year	Team	Lg.	Pos.	G	AB	R	H	HR	RBI	SB	BA
1991	Chicago	NL	SS	13	23	1	6	0	2	0	.261
1992	Chicago	NL	SS	74	255	24	64	1	19	2	.251
1993	Chicago	NL	SS	105	344	35	97	0	28	1	.282
Seasonal Notation					524	50	140	0	41	2	.268

Catchers
pp. 59–73

Corners
pp. 73–95

Infield
pp. 95–116

Outfield
pp. 117–150

DH
pp. 150–153

Starters
pp. 154–189

Relievers
pp. 190–217

RYNE SANDBERG

Age 34/R $24

He was never himself after Mean Mike Jackson busted his hand in spring training. Look for a strong return to form. One caveat: we've all been over-paying for Ryno the last three years in hopes of seeing a repeat of 1990. Time to admit that's not in the cards.

Year	Team	Lg.	Pos.	G	AB	R	H	HR	RBI	SB	BA
1990	Chicago	NL	2B	155	615	116	188	40	100	25	.306
1991	Chicago	NL	2B	158	585	104	170	26	100	22	.291
1992	Chicago	NL	2B	158	612	100	186	26	87	17	.304
1993	Chicago	NL	2B	117	456	67	141	9	45	9	.309
Seasonal Notation					624	106	188	27	91	20	.302

DOUG SAUNDERS

Age 24/R $1

The Mets are so desperate that they're bringing in aging, brightly clad, red headed golfers with funny swings to brighten up things . . . oops, wrong spelling.

Year	Team	Lg.	Pos.	G	AB	R	H	HR	RBI	SB	BA
1993	New York	NL	2B	28	67	8	14	0	0	0	.209
Seasonal Notation					387	46	81	0	0	0	.209

STEVE SCARSONE

Age 27/R $1

Spare part.

Year	Team	Lg.	Pos.	G	AB	R	H	HR	RBI	SB	BA
1992	Philadelphia	NL	2B	7	13	1	2	0	0	0	.154
1992	Baltimore	AL	2B	11	17	2	3	0	0	0	.176
1993	San Francisco	NL	2B	44	103	16	26	2	15	0	.252
Seasonal Notation					347	49	81	5	39	0	.233

MIKE SHARPERSON

Age 32/R $1

We didn't want him two years ago when he was an All-Star by default. Why should we want him now?

Year	Team	Lg.	Pos.	G	AB	R	H	HR	RBI	SB	BA
1990	Los Angeles	NL	3B	129	357	42	106	3	36	15	.297
1991	Los Angeles	NL	3B	105	216	24	60	2	20	1	.278
1992	Los Angeles	NL	2B	128	317	48	95	3	36	2	.300
1993	Los Angeles	NL	2B	73	90	13	23	2	10	2	.256
Seasonal Notation					364	47	105	3	37	7	.290

CRAIG SHIPLEY

Age 31/R $1

Boy, those Padres are really stockpiling the talent, aren't they?

Year	Team	Lg.	Pos.	G	AB	R	H	HR	RBI	SB	BA
1991	San Diego	NL	SS	37	91	6	25	1	6	0	.275
1992	San Diego	NL	SS	52	105	7	26	0	7	1	.248
1993	San Diego	NL	SS	105	230	25	54	4	22	12	.235
Seasonal Notation					355	31	87	4	29	10	.246

OZZIE SMITH

Age 39/B $12

Less range, more errors, fewer stolen bases, but the Wiz is still a delight to watch after all these years. The Hall of Fame will just have to wait.

Year	Team	Lg.	Pos.	G	AB	R	H	HR	RBI	SB	BA
1990	St. Louis	NL	SS	143	512	61	130	1	50	32	.254
1991	St. Louis	NL	SS	150	550	96	157	3	50	35	.285
1992	St. Louis	NL	SS	132	518	73	153	0	31	43	.295
1993	St. Louis	NL	SS	141	545	75	157	1	53	21	.288
Seasonal Notation					608	87	170	1	52	37	.281

Catchers
pp. 59-73

Corners
pp. 73-95

Infield
pp. 95-116

Outfield
pp. 117-150

DH
pp. 150-153

Starters
pp. 154-189

Relievers
pp. 190-217

KEVIN STOCKER   Age 24/B $5

His biggest booster is Larry Bowa, now a Phillies coach, once a great Phillies shortstop, who was dropped from the Hall of Fame ballot by brain-dead, tunnel-visioned voters despite over 2,000 career hits and the best fielding percentage in history. Where were we? Oh, yes. Stocker. Well, Bowa fell in love with the kid in spring training a year ago. Said Bowa, "His head is always in the game. He has great instincts. He never makes the same mistake twice. He will find a way to get a runner in from third. He is one of those tough kids that reminds me of . . . well, me."

Year	Team	Lg.	Pos.	G	AB	R	H	HR	RBI	SB	BA
1993	Philadelphia	NL	SS	70	259	46	84	2	31	5	.324
Seasonal Notation					599	106	194	4	71	11	.324

TIM TEUFEL   Age 35/R $3

He can come off our bench any time.

Year	Team	Lg.	Pos.	G	AB	R	H	HR	RBI	SB	BA
1990	New York	NL	1B	80	175	28	43	10	24	0	.246
1991	New York	NL	1B	20	34	2	4	1	2	1	.118
1991	San Diego	NL	2B	97	307	39	70	11	42	8	.228
1992	San Diego	NL	2B	101	246	23	55	6	25	2	.224
1993	San Diego	NL	2B	96	200	26	50	7	31	2	.250
Seasonal Notation					395	48	91	14	50	5	.231

ROBBY THOMPSON   Age 31/R $19

Finally got some attention for being the productive player he's always been. That game-winning homer last August against Florida was one of the season's special moments. We do worry some about his durability, but not enough to keep our mouths shut when the bidding starts.

Year	Team	Lg.	Pos.	G	AB	R	H	HR	RBI	SB	BA
1990	San Francisco	NL	2B	144	498	67	122	15	56	14	.245
1991	San Francisco	NL	2B	144	492	74	129	19	48	14	.262
1992	San Francisco	NL	2B	128	443	54	115	14	49	5	.260
1993	San Francisco	NL	2B	128	494	85	154	19	65	10	.312
Seasonal Notation					573	83	154	19	64	12	.270

JOSE VIZCAINO   Age 26/B $6

The year's biggest surprise. Two things that cloud the picture: the Dunston Factor, and the weird whims of GM Larry Himes.

Year	Team	Lg.	Pos.	G	AB	R	H	HR	RBI	SB	BA
1990	Los Angeles	NL	SS	37	51	3	14	0	2	1	.275
1991	Chicago	NL	3B	93	145	7	38	0	10	2	.262
1992	Chicago	NL	SS	86	285	25	64	1	17	3	.225
1993	Chicago	NL	SS	151	551	74	158	4	54	12	.287
Seasonal Notation					455	48	120	2	36	7	.266

CHICO WALKER
Age 35/B $1

A veteran major league scout was staring bleary-eyed at the field one early afternoon. As usual, Chico was letting balls clang off his glove. Said the scout: "Give the guy credit. I've been in the game for over 40 years and this guy makes some of the worst plays I've ever seen." That's okay, though, because Chico hustles a lot and hits a little, which makes him a giant among Mets. (P.S.: His given name, in case you were wondering, is Cleotha.)

Year	Team	Lg.	Pos.	G	AB	R	H	HR	RBI	SB	BA
1991	Chicago	NL	3B	124	374	51	96	6	34	13	.257
1992	Chicago	NL	OF	19	26	2	3	0	2	1	.115
1992	New York	NL	3B	107	227	24	70	4	36	14	.308
1993	New York	NL	2B	115	213	18	48	5	19	7	.225
Seasonal Notation					372	42	96	6	40	15	.258

WALT WEISS
Age 30/B $2

Eureka! He played a full season without spending a minute on the DL! Alert the media!

Year	Team	Lg.	Pos.	G	AB	R	H	HR	RBI	SB	BA
1990	Oakland	AL	SS	138	445	50	118	2	35	9	.265
1991	Oakland	AL	SS	40	133	15	30	0	13	6	.226
1992	Oakland	AL	SS	103	316	36	67	0	21	6	.212
1993	Florida	NL	SS	158	500	50	133	1	39	7	.266
Seasonal Notation					514	55	128	1	39	10	.250

ERIC YOUNG
Age 26/R $17

A potentially explosive offensive player, but the Rockies must find him a position, ideally one not requiring him to catch or throw a baseball.

Year	Team	Lg.	Pos.	G	AB	R	H	HR	RBI	SB	BA
1992	Los Angeles	NL	2B	49	132	9	34	1	11	6	.258
1993	Colorado	NL	2B	144	490	82	132	3	42	42	.269
Seasonal Notation					522	76	139	3	44	40	.267

AMERICAN LEAGUE

ROBERTO ALOMAR
Age 26/B $38

We sent out a crack team of investigative journalists to find something he doesn't do well. After all, we don't want to come across as a bunch of slobbering, starstruck sycophants, even if we are. So far, all we have come up with is his insistence on living at the Skydome Hotel: even though it does make for a short commute, we fear it might turn him into a one-dimensional personality. Don't worry: we're still digging.

Year	Team	Lg.	Pos.	G	AB	R	H	HR	RBI	SB	BA
1990	San Diego	NL	2B	147	586	80	168	6	60	24	.287
1991	Toronto	AL	2B	161	637	88	188	9	69	53	.295
1992	Toronto	AL	2B	152	571	105	177	8	76	49	.310
1993	Toronto	AL	2B	153	589	109	192	17	93	55	.326
Seasonal Notation					629	100	191	10	78	47	.304

RICH AMARAL　　　　　　　　　　　　　Age 32/R　　　$6

The Mariners were as surprised as anybody to find out that they had a productive little second baseman in their midst. A second-round draft pick in 1983, he spent ten solid years in the minors before getting his break. And when it came, he made the most of it. We're surprised no one has made a TV movie of his life.

Year	Team	Lg.	Pos.	G	AB	R	H	HR	RBI	SB	BA
1991	Seattle	AL	2B	14	16	2	1	0	0	0	.063
1992	Seattle	AL	3B	35	100	9	24	1	7	4	.240
1993	Seattle	AL	2B	110	373	53	108	1	44	19	.290
Seasonal Notation					498	65	135	2	51	23	.272

CARLOS BAERGA　　　　　　　　　　　Age 25/B　　　$35

We sent out a second crack team of investigative journalists to find something he doesn't do well. So far, all we have come up with is his haircut, which makes him look a little like Larry of the Three Stooges.

Year	Team	Lg.	Pos.	G	AB	R	H	HR	RBI	SB	BA
1990	Cleveland	AL	3B	108	312	46	81	7	47	0	.260
1991	Cleveland	AL	3B	158	593	80	171	11	69	3	.288
1992	Cleveland	AL	2B	161	657	92	205	20	105	10	.312
1993	Cleveland	AL	2B	154	624	105	200	21	114	15	.321
Seasonal Notation					609	90	183	16	93	7	.301

JUAN BELL　　　　　　　　　　　　　　Age 26/B　　　$1

Don't get all worked up about the five homers in 286 AB. The ball was juiced. Anyway, he's in the major leagues because of his glove, not his bat.

Year	Team	Lg.	Pos.	G	AB	R	H	HR	RBI	SB	BA
1990	Baltimore	AL	SS	5	2	1	0	0	0	0	0.000
1991	Baltimore	AL	2B	100	209	26	36	1	15	0	.172
1992	Philadelphia	NL	SS	46	147	12	30	1	8	5	.204
1993	Philadelphia	NL	SS	24	65	5	13	0	7	0	.200
1993	Milwaukee	AL	2B	91	286	42	67	5	29	6	.234
Seasonal Notation					431	52	88	4	35	6	.206

BRET BOONE　　　　　　　　　　　　　Age 24/R　　　$8

His daddy—Bob Boone, the cerebral catcher—never let people around him forget how smart he was. So no one was particularly surprised when the kid proved to be stubborn and headstrong, specifically in insisting on swinging for the seats every time he walked to the plate. Lou Piniella, not exactly wishy-washy himself, banished Boone the younger to the minors to teach him a lesson. Boone returned, not noticeably chastened, and continued to swing for the fences. Only now he started clearing them with enough regularity to re-establish his credentials as a future star. The Mariners will live to regret sending him to Cincinnati, where Barry Larkin will help him grow up.

Year	Team	Lg.	Pos.	G	AB	R	H	HR	RBI	SB	BA
1992	Seattle	AL	2B	33	129	15	25	4	15	1	.194
1993	Seattle	AL	2B	76	271	31	68	12	38	2	.251
Seasonal Notation					594	68	138	23	78	4	.233

MIKE BORDICK   Age 28/R $4

Tony LaRussa's kind of guy. Ours, too. Sneaky good numbers that won't bust your budget.

Year	Team	Lg.	Pos.	G	AB	R	H	HR	RBI	SB	BA
1990	Oakland	AL	3B	25	14	0	1	0	0	0	.071
1991	Oakland	AL	SS	90	235	21	56	0	21	3	.238
1992	Oakland	AL	2B	154	504	62	151	3	48	12	.300
1993	Oakland	AL	SS	159	546	60	136	3	48	10	.249
Seasonal Notation					491	54	130	2	44	9	.265

JOEY CORA   Age 28/B $6

Here's a guy who was an everyday second baseman for a division winner last season, whereas in San Diego they thought he was no more than a fringe player. We thought it might be fun, just one more time, to throw together a team of ex–Padres farmhands, an elite group that includes John Kruk, Robbie Alomar, Carlos Baerga, Dave Hollins, Sandy Alomar, Jr., Benito Santiago, Ozzie Smith, Dave Winfield, and Shane Mack. We'd take our chances most years with that team.

Year	Team	Lg.	Pos.	G	AB	R	H	HR	RBI	SB	BA
1990	San Diego	NL	SS	51	100	12	27	0	2	8	.270
1991	Chicago	AL	2B	100	228	37	55	0	18	11	.241
1992	Chicago	AL	2B	68	122	27	30	0	9	10	.246
1993	Chicago	AL	2B	153	579	95	155	2	51	20	.268
Seasonal Notation					448	74	116	0	34	21	.259

MARIO DIAZ   Age 32/R $1

When Manuel Lee proved to be an overpaid, underachieving, hypochondriacal bust, this journeyman stepped in and played some solid shortstop. He'll probably be rewarded with a return to utility duty, so don't go hog-wild.

Year	Team	Lg.	Pos.	G	AB	R	H	HR	RBI	SB	BA
1990	New York	NL	SS	16	22	0	3	0	1	0	.136
1991	Texas	AL	SS	96	182	24	48	1	22	0	.264
1992	Texas	AL	SS	19	31	2	7	0	1	0	.226
1993	Texas	AL	SS	71	205	24	56	2	24	1	.273
Seasonal Notation					352	40	91	2	38	0	.259

GARY DiSARCINA   Age 26/R $2

His defensive problems have Whitey Herzog a little uneasy about his future. And if Whitey's uneasy, so are we. Still, 45 RBI from a middle infielder is nothing to sneeze at.

Year	Team	Lg.	Pos.	G	AB	R	H	HR	RBI	SB	BA
1990	California	AL	SS	18	57	8	8	0	0	1	.140
1991	California	AL	SS	18	57	5	12	0	3	0	.211
1992	California	AL	SS	157	518	48	128	3	42	9	.247
1993	California	AL	SS	126	416	44	99	3	45	5	.238
Seasonal Notation					532	53	125	3	45	7	.236

Catchers
pp. 59–73

Corners
pp. 73–95

Infield
pp. 95–116

Outfield
pp. 117–150

DH
pp. 150–153

Starters
pp. 154–189

Relievers
pp. 190–217

BASEBALL ANAGRAM #9

Moral? Boot Rear = _____?

(Answer on page 299)

BILLY DORAN   Age 35/B $1

Looks like the end of the line for this solid pro.

Year	Team	Lg.	Pos.	G	AB	R	H	HR	RBI	SB	BA
1990	Houston	NL	2B	109	344	49	99	6	32	18	.288
1990	Cincinnati	NL	2B	17	59	10	22	1	5	5	.373
1991	Cincinnati	NL	2B	111	361	51	101	6	35	5	.280
1992	Cincinnati	NL	2B	132	387	48	91	8	47	7	.235
1993	Milwaukee	AL	2B	28	60	7	13	0	6	1	.217
Seasonal Notation					494	67	133	8	51	14	.269

DAMION EASLEY   Age 24/R $8

If the Angels can figure out how to cure him of shin splints, they—and you, without even having to foot his medical bills—will have a dynamite offensive second baseman.

Year	Team	Lg.	Pos.	G	AB	R	H	HR	RBI	SB	BA
1992	California	AL	3B	47	151	14	39	1	12	9	.258
1993	California	AL	2B	73	230	33	72	2	22	6	.313
Seasonal Notation					514	63	149	4	45	20	.291

FELIX FERMIN   Age 30/R $2

The Indians keep hoping every spring that someone will beat El Gato out of a job. But by Memorial Day, he's usually back in there. By Labor Day, the Indians usually start looking for someone else to beat El Gato out of his job the next season. Frankly, he's not good enough for you to go through all that torture.

Year	Team	Lg.	Pos.	G	AB	R	H	HR	RBI	SB	BA
1990	Cleveland	AL	SS	148	414	47	106	1	40	3	.256
1991	Cleveland	AL	SS	129	424	30	111	0	31	5	.262
1992	Cleveland	AL	SS	79	215	27	58	0	13	0	.270
1993	Cleveland	AL	SS	140	480	48	126	2	45	4	.262
Seasonal Notation					500	49	130	0	42	3	.262

TONY FERNANDEZ   Age 31/B $12

Don't ask him to do an "I Love New York" commercial. He may not remain in Toronto, but you can bet he won't wind up in Gotham again.

Year	Team	Lg.	Pos.	G	AB	R	H	HR	RBI	SB	BA
1990	Toronto	AL	SS	161	635	84	175	4	66	26	.276
1991	San Diego	NL	SS	145	558	81	152	4	38	23	.272
1992	San Diego	NL	SS	155	622	84	171	4	37	20	.275
1993	New York	NL	SS	48	173	20	39	1	14	6	.225
1993	Toronto	AL	SS	94	353	45	108	4	50	15	.306
Seasonal Notation					628	84	173	4	55	24	.276

SCOTT FLETCHER
Age 35/R   **$5**

For much of last season, he was the Red Sox' most valuable player. That fact speaks volumes about how faceless and uninteresting the Bosox have become during the reign of Lou Gorman.

Year	Team	Lg.	Pos.	G	AB	R	H	HR	RBI	SB	BA
1990	Chicago	AL	2B	151	509	54	123	4	56	1	.242
1991	Chicago	AL	2B	90	248	14	51	1	28	0	.206
1992	Milwaukee	AL	2B	123	386	53	106	3	51	17	.275
1993	Boston	AL	2B	121	480	81	137	5	45	16	.285
Seasonal Notation					542	67	139	4	60	11	.257

GREG GAGNE
Age 32/R   **$8**

A solid player who delivers good bang for the buck, provided the buck isn't too big. One of the major reasons for the Royals' quantum improvement last year.

Year	Team	Lg.	Pos.	G	AB	R	H	HR	RBI	SB	BA
1990	Minnesota	AL	SS	138	388	38	91	7	38	8	.235
1991	Minnesota	AL	SS	139	408	52	108	8	42	11	.265
1992	Minnesota	AL	SS	146	439	53	108	7	39	6	.246
1993	Kansas City	AL	SS	159	540	66	151	10	57	10	.280
Seasonal Notation					494	58	127	8	48	9	.258

MIKE GALLEGO
Age 33/R   **$8**

The Yankees tried to dump him and his big salary all spring, but by mid-summer he had snatched the starting shortstop job away from Spike Owen and proved that he is still the tough, winning player he had been in Oakland. That same plateau could soon be scaled by . . .

Year	Team	Lg.	Pos.	G	AB	R	H	HR	RBI	SB	BA
1990	Oakland	AL	2B	140	389	36	80	3	34	5	.206
1991	Oakland	AL	2B	159	482	67	119	12	49	6	.247
1992	New York	AL	2B	53	173	24	44	3	14	0	.254
1993	New York	AL	SS	119	403	63	114	10	54	3	.283
Seasonal Notation					497	65	122	9	51	4	.247

BRENT GATES
Age 24/B   **$12**

. . . whose manager, Tony LaRussa, a skipper not given to Sparky-esque hyperbole, predicts that this good-looking kid will someday win a batting title. We assume Tony means in the American League and not in the Pacific Coast League.

Year	Team	Lg.	Pos.	G	AB	R	H	HR	RBI	SB	BA
1993	Oakland	AL	2B	139	535	64	155	7	69	7	.290
Seasonal Notation					623	74	180	8	80	8	.290

CRAIG GREBECK
Age 29/R   **$1**

Had his 15 minutes of fame in 1992. Last season it was back to his more familiar utility role.

Year	Team	Lg.	Pos.	G	AB	R	H	HR	RBI	SB	BA
1990	Chicago	AL	3B	59	119	7	20	1	9	0	.168
1991	Chicago	AL	3B	107	224	37	63	6	31	1	.281
1992	Chicago	AL	SS	88	287	24	77	3	35	0	.268
1993	Chicago	AL	SS	72	190	25	43	1	12	1	.226
Seasonal Notation					407	46	100	5	43	0	.248

Catchers
pp. 59-73

Corners
pp. 73-95

Infield
pp. 95-116

Outfield
pp. 117-150

DH
pp. 150-153

Starters
pp. 154-189

Relievers
pp. 190-217

OZZIE GUILLEN   Age 30/L $9

Not a base-stealing threat anymore after that hideous injury that ruined his 1992 season. But so long as his buoyant clubhouse spirit doesn't get worn down keeping all those massive White Sox egos from imploding, he'll be an All-Star in our book.

Year	Team	Lg.	Pos.	G	AB	R	H	HR	RBI	SB	BA
1990	Chicago	AL	SS	160	516	61	144	1	58	13	.279
1991	Chicago	AL	SS	154	524	52	143	3	49	21	.273
1992	Chicago	AL	SS	12	40	5	8	0	7	1	.200
1993	Chicago	AL	SS	134	457	44	128	4	50	5	.280
Seasonal Notation					541	57	148	2	57	14	.275

JEFF HUSON   Age 29/L $1

To give you an idea how sick things got in the days preceding the expansion draft, some of the get-a-lifers who spent months poring over scouting reports and minor league stats and reading the minds of Dave Dombrowski and Bob Gebhard (a frightening thought at best) started predicting that Colorado would make this guy their first pick in the draft. Imagine how baseball history would have altered if Gebhard had done so! Instead, he chose David Nied, who went 4–7 and spent half the season on the DL. Boy, that expansion draft was fun.

Year	Team	Lg.	Pos.	G	AB	R	H	HR	RBI	SB	BA
1990	Texas	AL	SS	145	396	57	95	0	28	12	.240
1991	Texas	AL	SS	119	268	36	57	2	26	8	.213
1992	Texas	AL	SS	123	318	49	83	4	24	18	.261
1993	Texas	AL	SS	23	45	3	6	0	2	0	.133
Seasonal Notation					405	57	95	2	31	15	.235

PAT KELLY   Age 26/R $8

Fell out of favor among some Yankees front-office folk during a generally solid first season as an everyday player, probably because he didn't quite match the hype they'd heaped on him in the last two years. Does that mean Steve Sax is going to be asked back?

Year	Team	Lg.	Pos.	G	AB	R	H	HR	RBI	SB	BA
1991	New York	AL	3B	96	298	35	72	3	23	12	.242
1992	New York	AL	2B	106	318	38	72	7	27	8	.226
1993	New York	AL	2B	127	406	49	111	7	51	14	.273
Seasonal Notation					503	60	125	8	49	16	.250

CHUCK KNOBLAUCH   Age 25/R $13

His numbers aren't worth kiting a check for, but he remains one of our favorite players. For example, there was the day last season when he approached an ESPN crew with a special request. Seems Knobbie and some of his henchmen had convinced teammate Bernardo Brito that ESPN wanted Brito to do one of those dopey "da-da-da, da-da-da" promos. Knobbie persuaded ESPN to go along with the gang, and Brito was taped doing the worst "da-da-da, da-da-da" this side of Chevy Chase. Speaking of Chevy, he didn't have any worse reviews than . . .

Year	Team	Lg.	Pos.	G	AB	R	H	HR	RBI	SB	BA
1991	Minnesota	AL	2B	151	565	78	159	1	50	25	.281
1992	Minnesota	AL	2B	155	600	104	178	2	56	34	.297
1993	Minnesota	AL	2B	153	602	82	167	2	41	29	.277
Seasonal Notation					623	93	177	1	51	31	.285

MANUEL LEE   Age 28/B $1

. . . who was, in our humble estimation, The Stiff of the Year. Odds are that Texas eats the last year of his contract and dumps him.

Year	Team	Lg.	Pos.	G	AB	R	H	HR	RBI	SB	BA
1990	Toronto	AL	2B	117	391	45	95	6	41	3	.243
1991	Toronto	AL	SS	138	445	41	104	0	29	7	.234
1992	Toronto	AL	SS	128	396	49	104	3	39	6	.263
1993	Texas	AL	SS	73	205	31	45	1	12	2	.220
Seasonal Notation					510	58	123	3	42	6	.242

SCOTT LEIUS   Age 28/R $1

If he bounces back from shoulder injury, he faces a fight for the Twins shortstop job and may well end up at third, where his lack of power makes him far less attractive.

Year	Team	Lg.	Pos.	G	AB	R	H	HR	RBI	SB	BA
1990	Minnesota	AL	SS	14	25	4	6	1	4	0	.240
1991	Minnesota	AL	3B	109	199	35	57	5	20	5	.286
1992	Minnesota	AL	3B	129	409	50	102	2	35	6	.249
1993	Minnesota	AL	SS	10	18	4	3	0	2	0	.167
Seasonal Notation					402	57	103	4	37	6	.258

JOSE LIND   Age 29/R $1

Great leather man, but Chico had the lowest on-base average of any regular second baseman in the major leagues. Offensively, a cypher.

Year	Team	Lg.	Pos.	G	AB	R	H	HR	RBI	SB	BA
1990	Pittsburgh	NL	2B	152	514	46	134	1	48	8	.261
1991	Pittsburgh	NL	2B	150	502	53	133	3	54	7	.265
1992	Pittsburgh	NL	2B	135	468	38	110	0	39	3	.235
1993	Kansas City	AL	2B	136	431	33	107	0	37	3	.248
Seasonal Notation					541	48	136	1	50	5	.253

PAT LISTACH   Age 26/B $15

The Brewers think the slide was caused by injuries, not the sophomore jinx. Indeed, it is awfully difficult to have a sophomore jinx in an expansion year, so we think it was the injuries, too. Grab him while the price is right.

Year	Team	Lg.	Pos.	G	AB	R	H	HR	RBI	SB	BA
1992	Milwaukee	AL	SS	149	579	93	168	1	47	54	.290
1993	Milwaukee	AL	SS	98	356	50	87	3	30	18	.244
Seasonal Notation					613	93	167	2	50	47	.273

TOREY LOVULLO · Age 28/B · $2

He won one April game with a home run off Roger Clemens. At the time, it seemed remarkable, but then everyone started hitting home runs off Roger Clemens. Maybe the ball was juiced.

Year	Team	Lg.	Pos.	G	AB	R	H	HR	RBI	SB	BA
1991	New York	AL	3B	22	51	0	9	0	2	0	.176
1993	California	AL	2B	116	367	42	92	6	30	7	.251
Seasonal Notation					490	49	118	7	37	8	.242

PAT MEARES · Age 25/R · $2

He was the best of a mediocre lot at shortstop for the Twins last year, but Minnesota has another young shortstop named Dennis Hocking, who should challenge for the job this spring.

Year	Team	Lg.	Pos.	G	AB	R	H	HR	RBI	SB	BA
1993	Minnesota	AL	SS	111	346	33	87	0	33	4	.251
Seasonal Notation					504	48	126	0	48	5	.251

SPIKE OWEN · Age 32/B · $1

Has the range of a park bench, swings a limp stick, and signed a huge contract that the Yankees will never be able to unload. Good thing he's such a positive influence in the clubhouse.

Year	Team	Lg.	Pos.	G	AB	R	H	HR	RBI	SB	BA
1990	Montreal	NL	SS	149	453	55	106	5	35	8	.234
1991	Montreal	NL	SS	139	424	39	108	3	26	2	.255
1992	Montreal	NL	SS	122	386	52	104	7	40	9	.269
1993	New York	AL	SS	103	334	41	78	2	20	3	.234
Seasonal Notation					504	59	125	5	38	6	.248

JEFF REBOULET · Age 29/R · $1

Might flourish if traded to Montreal—as a defenseman.

Year	Team	Lg.	Pos.	G	AB	R	H	HR	RBI	SB	BA
1992	Minnesota	AL	SS	73	137	15	26	1	16	3	.190
1993	Minnesota	AL	SS	109	240	33	62	1	15	5	.258
Seasonal Notation					335	42	78	1	27	7	.233

HAROLD REYNOLDS · Age 33/B · $5

Nice man, but the SB total is down for the fourth straight season. That doesn't leave much, Rotisserie-wise speaking.

Year	Team	Lg.	Pos.	G	AB	R	H	HR	RBI	SB	BA
1990	Seattle	AL	2B	160	642	100	162	5	55	31	.252
1991	Seattle	AL	2B	161	631	95	160	3	57	28	.254
1992	Seattle	AL	2B	140	458	55	113	3	33	15	.247
1993	Baltimore	AL	2B	145	485	64	122	4	47	12	.252
Seasonal Notation					592	83	148	4	51	22	.251

Catchers
pp. 59-73

Corners
pp. 73-95

Infield
pp. 95-116

Outfield
pp. 117-150

DH
pp. 150-153

Starters
pp. 154-189

Relievers
pp. 190-217

ERNEST RILES   Age 33/L $1

Why is he here? Oh, yes, we remember now. It's because he was Boston's best left-handed pinch-hitter.

Year	Team	Lg.	Pos.	G	AB	R	H	HR	RBI	SB	BA
1990	San Francisco	NL	SS	92	155	22	31	8	21	0	.200
1991	Oakland	AL	3B	108	281	30	60	5	32	3	.214
1992	Houston	NL	SS	39	61	5	16	1	4	1	.262
1993	Boston	AL	2B	94	143	15	27	5	20	1	.189
Seasonal Notation					311	35	65	9	37	2	.209

BILLY RIPKEN   Age 29/R $1

Injuries killed any chance of him sticking it to the Orioles for separating him from his big brother. But he did seem to fit in well with the Rangers. We happened upon the Texas clubhouse one afternoon to find Billy, wearing rubber gloves, trying to pull a bug out of teammate Geno Petralli's eye. A pretty disgusting sight to behold, if you want the truth of it.

Year	Team	Lg.	Pos.	G	AB	R	H	HR	RBI	SB	BA
1990	Baltimore	AL	2B	129	406	48	118	3	38	5	.291
1991	Baltimore	AL	2B	104	287	24	62	0	14	0	.216
1992	Baltimore	AL	2B	111	330	35	76	4	36	2	.230
1993	Texas	AL	2B	50	132	12	25	0	11	0	.189
Seasonal Notation					474	48	115	2	40	2	.243

CAL RIPKEN   Age 33/R $19

Mr. Baltimore made news last summer when it was revealed that he stayed in different hotels than the rest of his teammates and that he was met by a private limo on road stops while his teammates rode the bus. He explained that such measures were necessary because he couldn't get privacy on the road. We wonder if Orioles like Jim Palmer, Brooks Robinson, or Frank Robinson ever had the same problem—and came up with the same solution. We also wonder why he did nothing down the stretch for Baltimore the last two seasons when the Orioles desperately needed someone to carry them. And, while the power numbers are still impressive, we wonder if he hasn't become little more than just a pretty good player on the down side of his career. Finally, we wonder if he wouldn't be a lot fresher for the pennant drive if he were to sit down from time to time in day games following night games.

Year	Team	Lg.	Pos.	G	AB	R	H	HR	RBI	SB	BA
1990	Baltimore	AL	SS	161	600	78	150	21	84	3	.250
1991	Baltimore	AL	SS	162	650	99	210	34	114	6	.323
1992	Baltimore	AL	SS	162	637	73	160	14	72	4	.251
1993	Baltimore	AL	SS	162	641	87	165	24	90	1	.257
Seasonal Notation					632	84	171	23	90	3	.271

LUIS RIVERA   Age 30/R $1

We'd rather have Bombo.

Year	Team	Lg.	Pos.	G	AB	R	H	HR	RBI	SB	BA
1990	Boston	AL	SS	118	346	38	78	7	45	4	.225
1991	Boston	AL	SS	129	414	64	107	8	40	4	.258
1992	Boston	AL	SS	102	288	17	62	0	29	4	.215
1993	Boston	AL	2B	62	130	13	27	1	7	1	.208
Seasonal Notation					464	52	108	6	47	5	.233

BILL SPIERS

Age 27/L   **$2**

Yawn.

Year	Team	Lg.	Pos.	G	AB	R	H	HR	RBI	SB	BA
1990	Milwaukee	AL	SS	112	363	44	88	2	36	11	.242
1991	Milwaukee	AL	SS	133	414	71	117	8	54	14	.283
1992	Milwaukee	AL	SS	12	16	2	5	0	2	1	.313
1993	Milwaukee	AL	2B	113	340	43	81	2	36	9	.238
Seasonal Notation					496	70	127	5	56	15	.257

KURT STILLWELL

Age 28/B   **$1**

We seem to be in a rut.

Year	Team	Lg.	Pos.	G	AB	R	H	HR	RBI	SB	BA
1990	Kansas City	AL	SS	144	506	60	126	3	51	0	.249
1991	Kansas City	AL	SS	122	385	44	102	6	51	3	.265
1992	San Diego	NL	2B	114	379	35	86	2	24	4	.227
1993	San Diego	NL	SS	57	121	9	26	1	11	4	.215
1993	California	AL	2B	22	61	2	16	0	3	2	.262
Seasonal Notation					512	52	125	4	49	4	.245

DOUG STRANGE

Age 29/B   **$4**

Solid contribution in Texas last year.

Year	Team	Lg.	Pos.	G	AB	R	H	HR	RBI	SB	BA
1991	Chicago	NL	3B	3	9	0	4	0	1	1	.444
1992	Chicago	NL	3B	52	94	7	15	1	5	1	.160
1993	Texas	AL	2B	145	484	58	124	7	60	6	.256
Seasonal Notation					475	52	115	6	53	6	.244

DICKIE THON

Age 35/R   **$1**

A noble warrior, but only a bit player these days.

Year	Team	Lg.	Pos.	G	AB	R	H	HR	RBI	SB	BA
1990	Philadelphia	NL	SS	149	552	54	141	8	48	12	.255
1991	Philadelphia	NL	SS	146	539	44	136	9	44	11	.252
1992	Texas	AL	SS	95	275	30	68	4	37	12	.247
1993	Milwaukee	AL	SS	85	245	23	66	1	33	6	.269
Seasonal Notation					549	51	J40	7	55	13	.255

ALAN TRAMMELL

Age 36/R   **$12**

Started the season at third but ended up back at shortstop after another of Sparky's brainstorms. Wherever he plays, we want him on our team.

Year	Team	Lg.	Pos.	G	AB	R	H	HR	RBI	SB	BA
1990	Detroit	AL	SS	146	559	71	170	14	89	12	.304
1991	Detroit	AL	SS	101	375	57	93	9	55	11	.248
1992	Detroit	AL	SS	29	102	11	28	1	11	2	.275
1993	Detroit	AL	SS	112	401	72	132	12	60	12	.329
Seasonal Notation					599	88	176	15	89	15	.294

Catchers
pp. 59–73

Corners
pp. 73–95

Infield
pp. 95–116

Outfield
pp. 117–150

DH
pp. 150–153

Starters
pp. 154–189

Relievers
pp. 190–217

JOHN VALENTIN

Age 27/R $9

Overcame early-season jitters and his own cockiness to become one of the more productive offensive shortstops in the league. And he should get better.

Year	Team	Lg.	Pos.	G	AB	R	H	HR	RBI	SB	BA
1992	Boston	AL	SS	58	185	21	51	5	25	1	.276
1993	Boston	AL	SS	144	468	50	130	11	66	3	.278
Seasonal Notation					523	56	145	12	72	3	.277

OMAR VIZQUEL

Age 26/B $4

Got caught stealing 14 times in 26 attempts last year. Maybe he learned base-stealing from ex-teammate Harold Reynolds.

Year	Team	Lg.	Pos.	G	AB	R	H	HR	RBI	SB	BA
1990	Seattle	AL	SS	81	255	19	63	2	18	4	.247
1991	Seattle	AL	SS	142	426	42	98	1	41	7	.230
1992	Seattle	AL	SS	136	483	49	142	0	21	15	.294
1993	Seattle	AL	SS	158	560	68	143	2	31	12	.255
Seasonal Notation					540	55	139	1	34	11	.259

LOU WHITAKER

Age 36/L $12

Yes, he's slowed down, but Sweet Lou is still one of the most productive second basemen in the league. Among AL second sackers, only Roberto Alomar, Carlos Baerga, and Brent Gates had more RBI in 1993.

Year	Team	Lg.	Pos.	G	AB	R	H	HR	RBI	SB	BA
1990	Detroit	AL	2B	132	472	75	112	18	60	8	.237
1991	Detroit	AL	2B	138	470	94	131	23	78	4	.279
1992	Detroit	AL	2B	130	453	77	126	19	71	6	.278
1993	Detroit	AL	2B	119	383	72	111	9	67	3	.290
Seasonal Notation					554	99	149	21	86	6	.270

In the Outfield

Eyes glazed over after spending the winter trying to rank all the fourth and fifth starters and middle relievers in baseball? Nodding off from the exertion of figuring out which catchers are likely to hurt your batting average the least? Feeling like going for a bungee jump without a bungee after scanning the list of no-hit, no-run, no-name middle infielders from which you'll fill that all-important third up the middle slot? Thinking maybe that there's too much bleeping heavy lifting in this stupid Rotisserie League Baseball bullbleep?

Rejoice! Shout hallelujah! Lift up your eyes and gaze upon a new day! It's time to talk about outfielders.

No two ways about it: scouting outfielders is the payoff for all the drudge work that goes into building a Rotisserie juggernaut. The outfield is where you find baseball's most exciting players, the Thoroughbreds, the four-category studs, the fence-busting, base-stealing, run-producing supermen that transform boxscores into epic poetry.

Sure, there are plenty of exceptions to the rule that the best and brightest offensive talent is found in the outfield. Roberto Alomar, Carlos Baerga, Barry Larkin, and Ryne Sandberg don't exactly disgrace themselves when they take off their gloves and pick up their bats; and Frank Thomas, though not an outfielder, is a pretty good hitter.

And true, part of the appeal of outfielders, part of the reason that they get the adrenaline pumping faster at the auction draft, is that there are more of them: it takes longer to work your way down to the bottom of the barrel.

But the base reason why scouting and buying outfielders is so much fun is that outfield is a personal playground for the likes of Barry Bonds and Ken Griffey, Jr., Juan Gonzales and Ron Gant, Albert Belle and Marquis Grissom, plus an all-star supporting cast of Kenny Loftons, Dave Justices, Rickey Hendersons, and Lenny Dykstras.

Pitchers, smitchers: you can't trust 'em. No matter that my catchers and middle infielders cost five bucks, total. Who's on first? I don't know. No, he's on third.

"Okay, hold it down. Barry Bonds is on the table at $43. Do I hear $44? $44! Who'll say $45?" *You* know the answer to that last one.

HITS. RUNS. NO ERRORS.
ROTI·STATS
CALL 800-884-7684

NATIONAL LEAGUE

MOISES ALOU
Age 27/R   **$29**

Not since Lawrence Taylor snapped Joe Theismann's leg on Monday Night Football do we recall seeing a more gruesome sports injury on TV. When Alou tripped and then collapsed rounding first, the opposing team's second baseman and the second base umpire took one look at his mangled ankle and turned away in shock and horror. So did everyone who saw it replayed on *Baseball Tonight*. Can he recover fully? Let's cross our fingers, because he is a legitimate star on the rise. Price contingent on rehab.

Year	Team	Lg.	Pos.	G	AB	R	H	HR	RBI	SB	BA
1990	Pittsburgh	NL	OF	2	5	0	1	0	0	0	.200
1990	Montreal	NL	OF	14	15	4	3	0	0	0	.200
1992	Montreal	NL	OF	115	341	53	96	9	56	16	.282
1993	Montreal	NL	OF	136	482	70	138	18	85	17	.286
Seasonal Notation					511	77	144	16	85	20	.282

ERIC ANTHONY
Age 26/L   **$18**

Hovering in that zone between solidly productive regular and full-bore star. This will be the season that tells the tale.

Year	Team	Lg.	Pos.	G	AB	R	H	HR	RBI	SB	BA
1990	Houston	NL	OF	84	239	26	46	10	29	5	.192
1991	Houston	NL	OF	39	118	11	18	1	7	1	.153
1992	Houston	NL	OF	137	440	45	105	19	80	5	.239
1993	Houston	NL	OF	145	486	70	121	15	66	3	.249
Seasonal Notation					513	60	116	18	72	5	.226

KEVIN BASS
Age 34/B   **$1**

Member in good standing of the All Fish team (other teammates: Catfish Hunter, Mudcat Grant, Dizzy Trout, Sid Bream, Dickie Thon, Walleye Moon). But you'd be wise to throw him back.

Year	Team	Lg.	Pos.	G	AB	R	H	HR	RBI	SB	BA
1990	San Francisco	NL	OF	61	214	25	54	7	32	2	.252
1991	San Francisco	NL	OF	124	361	43	84	10	40	7	.233
1992	San Francisco	NL	OF	89	265	25	71	7	30	7	.268
1992	New York	NL	OF	46	137	15	37	2	9	7	.270
1993	Houston	NL	OF	111	229	31	65	3	37	7	.284
Seasonal Notation					453	52	116	10	55	11	.258

BILLY BEAN
Age 29/L   **$1**

This is not the former Mets outfielder who turned to scouting at an early age and has now become assistant general manager with Oakland, where he fits right in as an intelligent, cerebral, class guy. This is a refugee from the Tigers by way of the Dodgers by way of Japan. In his case, world traveler is just another name for journeyman.

Year	Team	Lg.	Pos.	G	AB	R	H	HR	RBI	SB	BA
1993	San Diego	NL	OF	88	177	19	46	5	32	2	.260
Seasonal Notation					325	34	84	9	58	3	.260

DEREK BELL · Age 25/R · $21

The Padres worry about his work habits. They worry about him off the field. They worry about his attitude. They worry that he makes too many mistakes in center field. They know he can't play third after a miserable late-season audition. But they also know he has the potential to be a potent offensive player. And if he cuts down on his strikeouts, grows up, and applies himself just a little more, we think he can be a four-category stud.

Year	Team	Lg.	Pos.	G	AB	R	H	HR	RBI	SB	BA
1991	Toronto	AL	OF	18	28	5	4	0	1	3	.143
1992	Toronto	AL	OF	61	161	23	39	2	15	7	.242
1993	San Diego	NL	OF	150	542	73	142	21	72	26	.262
Seasonal Notation					517	71	130	16	62	25	.253

DANTE BICHETTE · Age 30/R · $22

So what if he played in the mile-high joke of a stadium. So what if the ball was juiced. He has found a home where warning track flies sail into the stands. Go along for the fun.

Year	Team	Lg.	Pos.	G	AB	R	H	HR	RBI	SB	BA
1990	California	AL	OF	109	349	40	89	15	53	5	.255
1991	Milwaukee	AL	OF	134	445	53	106	15	59	14	.238
1992	Milwaukee	AL	OF	112	387	37	111	5	41	18	.287
1993	Colorado	NL	OF	141	538	93	167	21	89	14	.310
Seasonal Notation					561	72	154	18	79	16	.275

BARRY BONDS · Age 29/L · $44

Not a bad player.

Year	Team	Lg.	Pos.	G	AB	R	H	HR	RBI	SB	BA
1990	Pittsburgh	NL	OF	151	519	104	156	33	114	52	.301
1991	Pittsburgh	NL	OF	153	510	95	149	25	116	43	.292
1992	Pittsburgh	NL	OF	140	473	109	147	34	103	39	.311
1993	San Francisco	NL	OF	159	539	129	181	46	123	29	.336
Seasonal Notation					548	117	170	37	122	43	.310

BOBBY BONILLA · Age 31/B · $29

Big power year for Bobby Bo. Too bad he didn't enjoy it more. It might help if he would stop worrying about the New York media. No one else cares about the New York media, least of all those poor people in New York who have to put up with all those self-important blowhards every day.

Year	Team	Lg.	Pos.	G	AB	R	H	HR	RBI	SB	BA
1990	Pittsburgh	NL	OF	160	625	112	175	32	120	4	.280
1991	Pittsburgh	NL	OF	157	577	102	174	18	100	2	.302
1992	New York	NL	OF	128	438	62	109	19	70	4	.249
1993	New York	NL	OF	139	502	81	133	34	87	3	.265
Seasonal Notation					594	99	163	28	104	3	.276

Catchers pp. 59-73

Corners pp. 73-95

Infield pp. 95-116

Outfield pp. 117-150

DH pp. 150-153

Starters pp. 154-189

Relievers pp. 190-217

DARYL BOSTON   Age 31/L $8

We've always thought there was a little more here than just another spare part. In our book—and this was our book until you bought it—14 dingers in fewer than 300 at-bats ought to earn him the chance to prove it.

Year	Team	Lg.	Pos.	G	AB	R	H	HR	RBI	SB	BA
1990	Chicago	AL	DH	5	1	0	0	0	0	1	0.000
1990	New York	NL	OF	115	366	65	100	12	45	18	.273
1991	New York	NL	OF	137	255	40	70	4	21	15	.275
1992	New York	NL	OF	130	289	37	72	11	35	12	.249
1993	Colorado	NL	OF	124	291	46	76	14	40	1	.261
Seasonal Notation					381	59	100	12	44	14	.265

JACOB BRUMFIELD   Age 28/R $4

It might be easier to list all the people who *didn't* play the outfield for Cincinnati last season. We knew about the speed, but the six homers in 273 AB is as many as he hit in any full season in the minor leagues. Playing time will still be a problem.

Year	Team	Lg.	Pos.	G	AB	R	H	HR	RBI	SB	BA
1992	Cincinnati	NL	OF	24	30	6	4	0	2	6	.133
1993	Cincinnati	NL	OF	103	272	40	73	6	23	20	.268
Seasonal Notation					385	58	98	7	31	33	.255

JEROMY BURNITZ   Age 24/L $13

Talk about heavy burdens. All the Mets brass want him to do is carry the franchise for a couple of years while they frantically try to rebuild a bankrupt farm system. Oh, sure, Bobby Bonilla is the designated team star, but he was a mega-bucks free agent, not a farm product. If Burnitz makes it big, and on the strength of last year's debut he just might, then Fred Wilpon, Frank Cashen, and their partners in crime will be able to point to the lefty slugger with the misspelled first name and say, "See, we haven't been doing such a bad job after all." Hope the kid's shoulders are very strong.

Year	Team	Lg.	Pos.	G	AB	R	H	HR	RBI	SB	BA
1993	New York	NL	OF	86	263	49	64	13	38	3	.243
Seasonal Notation					495	92	120	24	71	5	.243

BRETT BUTLER   Age 36/L $17

He has one of the worst base-stealing percentages of any sack burglar base-stealer in baseball, but he keeps chopping out 180 or so hits every year, and who knows if he'll ever stop.

Year	Team	Lg.	Pos.	G	AB	R	H	HR	RBI	SB	BA
1990	San Francisco	NL	OF	160	622	108	192	3	44	51	.309
1991	Los Angeles	NL	OF	161	615	112	182	2	38	38	.296
1992	Los Angeles	NL	OF	157	553	86	171	3	39	41	.309
1993	Los Angeles	NL	OF	156	607	80	181	1	42	39	.298
Seasonal Notation					612	98	185	2	41	43	.303

CHUCK CARR   Age 25/B $24

He announced at one point last year that he might someday be in the Hall of Fame, and he wasn't talking about buying a ticket. After Carr showboated his way through an adventurous night against Philadelphia, several of the Phillies were heard to mutter, "Let's grab that little bleeper and beat the bleep out of him." Lighten up, Phils. Chuck E. reminds us a little of Willie Mays Hayes from *Major League*, the best baseball movie ever made.

Year	Team	Lg.	Pos.	G	AB	R	H	HR	RBI	SB	BA
1990	New York	NL	OF	4	2	0	0	0	0	1	0.000
1991	New York	NL	OF	12	11	1	2	0	1	1	.182
1992	St. Louis	NL	OF	22	64	8	14	0	3	10	.219
1993	Florida	NL	OF	142	551	75	147	4	41	58	.267
Seasonal Notation					565	75	146	3	40	63	.260

MARK CARREON   Age 30/R $3

Good bat. If the Giants say farewell to Willie McGee, Carreon could get a lot more playing time this year. It doesn't matter that he has the defensive range of an oak tree: Darren Lewis can just extend his coverage zone to the right field foul line.

Year	Team	Lg.	Pos.	G	AB	R	H	HR	RBI	SB	BA
1990	New York	NL	OF	82	188	30	47	10	26	1	.250
1991	New York	NL	OF	106	254	18	66	4	21	2	.260
1992	Detroit	AL	OF	101	336	34	78	10	41	3	.232
1993	San Francisco	NL	OF	78	150	22	49	7	33	1	.327
Seasonal Notation					409	45	105	13	53	3	.259

WES CHAMBERLAIN   Age 27/R $13

His season got off to a smashing start when he showed up three hours late for the Phillies' home opener. The righty half of a platoon last year, but stay tuned for bigger and better things. We didn't take a vote or anything, and we may end up eating our words, but we—some of us, at least—think this could be a breakout year for Chamberlain. He has the offensive tools; he needs to work on the attitude.

Year	Team	Lg.	Pos.	G	AB	R	H	HR	RBI	SB	BA
1990	Philadelphia	NL	OF	18	46	9	13	2	4	4	.283
1991	Philadelphia	NL	OF	101	383	51	92	13	50	9	.240
1992	Philadelphia	NL	OF	76	275	26	71	9	41	4	.258
1993	Philadelphia	NL	OF	96	284	34	80	12	45	2	.282
Seasonal Notation					550	66	142	20	77	10	.259

DAVE CLARK   Age 31/L $4

Jim Leyland has a knack for squeezing maximum performance out of marginal players. This is not meant to denigrate Clark: after all, he's in the majors and we're not. It is meant to emphasize that a smart manager knows how to pick the right situations to get the most out of his available talent. Clark is Exhibit A.

Year	Team	Lg.	Pos.	G	AB	R	H	HR	RBI	SB	BA
1990	Chicago	NL	OF	84	171	22	47	5	20	7	.275
1991	Kansas City	AL	DH	11	10	1	2	0	1	0	.200
1992	Pittsburgh	NL	OF	23	33	3	7	2	7	0	.212
1993	Pittsburgh	NL	OF	110	277	43	75	11	46	1	.271
Seasonal Notation					348	49	93	12	52	5	.267

Catchers
pp. 59-73

Corners
pp. 73-95

Infield
pp. 95-116

Outfield
pp. 117-150

DH
pp. 150-153

Starters
pp. 154-189

Relievers
pp. 190-217

JERALD CLARK   Age 30/R $9

Solid player, but last season was as good as it's likely to get.

Year	Team	Lg.	Pos.	G	AB	R	H	HR	RBI	SB	BA
1990	San Diego	NL	1B	52	101	12	27	5	11	0	.267
1991	San Diego	NL	OF	118	369	26	84	10	47	2	.228
1992	San Diego	NL	OF	146	496	45	120	12	58	3	.242
1993	Colorado	NL	OF	140	478	65	135	13	67	9	.282
Seasonal Notation					513	52	130	14	65	4	.253

PHIL CLARK   Age 25/R $5

If you make a few adjustments to equalize at-bats, it's amazing what similar years the various Clarks in the National League had in 1993. Unfortunately for the Giants and for his Rotisserie owners who paid 35 smackers for him, that includes Will. Padre Phil is no Thrill, but he put up impressive offensive numbers while playing five positions in San Diego, including catcher. Of course, the thing that they like best about him there is that he works cheap.

Year	Team	Lg.	Pos.	G	AB	R	H	HR	RBI	SB	BA
1992	Detroit	AL	OF	23	54	3	22	1	5	1	.407
1993	San Diego	NL	OF	102	240	33	75	9	33	2	.313
Seasonal Notation					381	46	125	12	49	3	.330

ALEX COLE   Age 28/L $4

Formidable Don Baylor and crusty Don Zimmer, Baylor's trusted lieutenant, watched this act for about half a season. And these two baseball men from different generations nodded their heads and agreed that they had to find other alternatives. The former Mayor-for-the-Day of Cleveland was released as soon as the season ended. Somebody else will give him a shot, and he'll play enough to steal a few bases, but don't get your hopes up.

Year	Team	Lg.	Pos.	G	AB	R	H	HR	RBI	SB	BA
1990	Cleveland	AL	OF	63	227	43	68	0	13	40	.300
1991	Cleveland	AL	OF	122	387	58	114	0	21	27	.295
1992	Cleveland	AL	OF	41	97	11	20	0	5	9	.206
1992	Pittsburgh	NL	OF	64	205	33	57	0	10	7	.278
1993	Colorado	NL	OF	126	348	50	89	0	24	30	.256
Seasonal Notation					492	75	135	0	28	44	.275

VINCE COLEMAN   Age 32/B Suspended

We don't know what—if anything—major league baseball is going to do, but we're suspending him indefinitely. That means he cannot be acquired at the 1994 auction draft or subsequently signed during the 1994 season. We'll review his case next fall.

Year	Team	Lg.	Pos.	G	AB	R	H	HR	RBI	SB	BA
1990	St. Louis	NL	OF	124	497	73	145	6	39	77	.292
1991	New York	NL	OF	72	278	45	71	1	17	37	.255
1992	New York	NL	OF	71	229	37	63	2	21	24	.275
1993	New York	NL	OF	92	373	64	104	2	25	38	.279
Seasonal Notation					621	98	172	4	46	79	.278

JEFF CONINE   Age 27/R $12

The only player in the National League to appear in all 162 games. Cal Ripken, move over.

Year	Team	Lg.	Pos.	G	AB	R	H	HR	RBI	SB	BA
1990	Kansas City	AL	1B	9	20	3	5	0	2	0	.250
1992	Kansas City	AL	OF	28	91	10	23	0	9	0	.253
1993	Florida	NL	OF	162	595	75	174	12	79	2	.292
Seasonal Notation					574	71	164	9	73	1	.286

HENRY COTTO   Age 33/R $1

A classic fringe player who will always hit for average and steal a few bases.

Year	Team	Lg.	Pos.	G	AB	R	H	HR	RBI	SB	BA
1990	Seattle	AL	OF	127	355	40	92	4	33	21	.259
1991	Seattle	AL	OF	66	177	35	54	6	23	16	.305
1992	Seattle	AL	OF	108	294	42	76	5	27	23	.259
1993	Seattle	AL	OF	54	105	10	20	2	7	5	.190
1993	Florida	NL	OF	54	135	15	40	3	14	11	.296
Seasonal Notation					422	56	111	7	41	30	.265

LENNY DYKSTRA   Age 31/L $30

His first at-bat is always the best. He doesn't have the chaw just right yet, so there he stands, spitting out little chunks of tobacco onto his chest, all the while stretching and twisting, kicking dirt, talking to himself, twitching his head back and forth, squinting out at the mound, getting ready to throw body and soul into the fray. The perfect prelude to playing the game the way it's supposed to be played.

Year	Team	Lg.	Pos.	G	AB	R	H	HR	RBI	SB	BA
1990	Philadelphia	NL	OF	149	590	106	192	9	60	33	.325
1991	Philadelphia	NL	OF	63	246	48	73	3	12	24	.297
1992	Philadelphia	NL	OF	85	345	53	104	6	39	30	.301
1993	Philadelphia	NL	OF	161	637	143	194	19	66	37	.305
Seasonal Notation					643	123	199	13	62	43	.310

JIM EISENREICH   Age 34/L $6

One of the year's great stories. A talented and brave veteran descends into the Philadelphia zoo, is quickly nicknamed "Dahmer" by his sensitive team-mates, and produces an Oscar-quality performance by a player in a supporting role.

Year	Team	Lg.	Pos.	G	AB	R	H	HR	RBI	SB	BA
1990	Kansas City	AL	OF	142	496	61	139	5	51	12	.280
1991	Kansas City	AL	OF	135	375	47	113	2	47	5	.301
1992	Kansas City	AL	OF	113	353	31	95	2	28	11	.269
1993	Philadelphia	NL	OF	153	362	51	115	7	54	5	.318
Seasonal Notation					473	56	137	4	53	9	.291

Catchers
pp. 59–73

Corners
pp. 73–95

Infield
pp. 95–116

Outfield
pp. 117–150

DH
pp. 150–153

Starters
pp. 154–189

Relievers
pp. 190–217

JUNIOR FELIX   Age 26/B $1

Didn't he used to be a big league ballplayer?

Year	Team	Lg.	Pos.	G	AB	R	H	HR	RBI	SB	BA
1990	Toronto	AL	OF	127	463	73	122	15	65	13	.263
1991	California	AL	OF	66	230	32	65	2	26	7	.283
1992	California	AL	OF	139	509	63	125	9	72	8	.246
1993	Florida	NL	OF	57	214	25	51	7	22	2	.238
Seasonal Notation					589	80	151	13	77	12	.256

STEVE FINLEY   Age 29/L $17

He got 545 at-bats, but at least 200 of them were tainted by slow recovery from
illness and injuries, and in midsummer he was still languishing in the low .230s.
To finish where he did took a strong second half, and that's what you should focus
on. Finley's price will be lower than usual this year. You take it from here.

Year	Team	Lg.	Pos.	G	AB	R	H	HR	RBI	SB	BA
1990	Baltimore	AL	OF	142	464	46	119	3	37	22	.256
1991	Houston	NL	OF	159	596	84	170	8	54	34	.285
1992	Houston	NL	OF	162	607	84	177	5	55	44	.292
1993	Houston	NL	OF	142	545	69	145	8	44	19	.266
Seasonal Notation					592	75	163	6	50	31	.276

LOU FRAZIER   Age 29/B $3

His speed is worth a few extra bucks. But an outfielder trying to get playing time
on a team with Alou, Grissom, and Walker has to worry about muscle atrophy.

Year	Team	Lg.	Pos.	G	AB	R	H	HR	RBI	SB	BA
1993	Montreal	NL	OF	112	189	27	54	1	16	17	.286
Seasonal Notation					273	39	78	1	23	24	.286

DAVE GALLAGHER   Age 33/R $2

Good baseball player. Just not a good *Rotisserie* baseball player.

Year	Team	Lg.	Pos.	G	AB	R	H	HR	RBI	SB	BA
1990	Chicago	AL	OF	45	75	5	21	0	5	0	.280
1990	Baltimore	AL	OF	23	51	7	11	0	2	1	.216
1991	California	AL	OF	90	270	32	79	1	30	2	.293
1992	New York	NL	OF	98	175	20	42	1	21	4	.240
1993	New York	NL	OF	99	201	34	55	6	28	1	.274
Seasonal Notation					352	44	94	3	39	3	.269

RON GANT   Age 29/R $34

The Crime Dog arrived to take much of the pressure off everyone around
him in the lineup. Thus liberated, Gant proceeded to be one of the four or

---

BASEBALL ANAGRAM #11

Shad Love? Nil = _____?

(Answer on page 299)

---

five best players in baseball last season. A note of caution: if he is traded, his numbers will likely dip big time.

Year	Team	Lg.	Pos.	G	AB	R	H	HR	RBI	SB	BA
1990	Atlanta	NL	OF	152	575	107	174	32	84	33	.303
1991	Atlanta	NL	OF	154	561	101	141	32	105	34	.251
1992	Atlanta	NL	OF	153	544	74	141	17	80	32	.259
1993	Atlanta	NL	OF	157	606	113	166	36	117	26	.274
Seasonal Notation					601	103	163	30	101	32	.272

BERNARD GILKEY   Age 27/R $22

For some reason, the Cardinals wanted him to be their fourth outfielder. He strangled that idea at birth by having a walloping good year. On the verge of being a big-money, four-category star, so the brewery will probably trade him for someone cheaper. A graduate of St. Louis's University High School, whose other baseball alums are Ken Holtzman, Art Shamsky, and Cory Schneider.

Year	Team	Lg.	Pos.	G	AB	R	H	HR	RBI	SB	BA
1990	St. Louis	NL	OF	18	64	11	19	1	3	6	.297
1991	St. Louis	NL	OF	81	268	28	58	5	20	14	.216
1992	St. Louis	NL	OF	131	384	56	116	7	43	18	.302
1993	St. Louis	NL	OF	137	557	99	170	16	70	15	.305
Seasonal Notation					561	85	160	12	60	23	.285

LUIS GONZALEZ   Age 26/L $19

Art Howe, a good and decent man who got shafted by the new Astros owner, was talking about his team in the season's final days. Howe could see the firing coming, but he nonetheless looked back on his season with some satisfaction. One reason was this Gonzalez. Said Howe: "You know, you work with a player for a few years, you get mad at him, you send him to the minors to shake him up, and then all of a sudden it kicks in for him. And if anything good came out of this season, it was that Luis Gonzalez turned himself into a legit major league hitter."

Year	Team	Lg.	Pos.	G	AB	R	H	HR	RBI	SB	BA
1990	Houston	NL	3B	12	21	1	4	0	0	0	.190
1991	Houston	NL	OF	137	473	51	120	13	69	10	.254
1992	Houston	NL	OF	122	387	40	94	10	55	7	.243
1993	Houston	NL	OF	154	540	82	162	15	72	20	.300
Seasonal Notation					541	66	144	14	74	14	.267

MARQUIS GRISSOM   Age 26/R $38

Years ago, when Marquis was a mere pup, some of the scouts were saying that he looked like a sawed-off version of Andre Dawson. Hoo-hah, we thought to ourselves, but it looks like they were right. The power might not yet be Hawkish, but everything else sure is.

Year	Team	Lg.	Pos.	G	AB	R	H	HR	RBI	SB	BA
1990	Montreal	NL	OF	98	288	42	74	3	29	22	.257
1991	Montreal	NL	OF	148	558	73	149	6	39	76	.267
1992	Montreal	NL	OF	159	653	99	180	14	66	78	.276
1993	Montreal	NL	OF	157	630	104	188	19	95	53	.298
Seasonal Notation					613	91	170	12	66	66	.278

Catchers
pp. 59-73

Corners
pp. 73-95

Infield
pp. 95-116

Outfield
pp. 117-150

DH
pp. 150-153

Starters
pp. 154-189

Relievers
pp. 190-217

TONY GWYNN
Age 33/L **$26**

Tony and his friend John Kruk were talking one day about the future. "They're getting rid of your whole team," Kruk said. "Why don't you come over and play with us?" "No way," Gwynn answered. "You guys are too crazy. I'm going to stay home." And so Tony stays home and keeps on hitting. But we get the feeling, even with the .358 BA, that Tony has it on cruise control.

Year	Team	Lg.	Pos.	G	AB	R	H	HR	RBI	SB	BA
1990	San Diego	NL	OF	141	573	79	177	4	72	17	.309
1991	San Diego	NL	OF	134	530	69	168	4	62	8	.317
1992	San Diego	NL	OF	128	520	77	165	6	41	3	.317
1993	San Diego	NL	OF	122	489	70	175	7	59	14	.358
Seasonal Notation					651	91	211	6	72	12	.324

GLENALLEN HILL
Age 29/R **$6**

Let's see, now—10 HR in 87 AB translates into, what, 63 homers over a full season? Talk about the Friendly Confines. . . .

Year	Team	Lg.	Pos.	G	AB	R	H	HR	RBI	SB	BA
1990	Toronto	AL	OF	84	260	47	60	12	32	8	.231
1991	Toronto	AL	DH	35	99	14	25	3	11	2	.253
1991	Cleveland	AL	OF	37	122	15	32	5	14	4	.262
1992	Cleveland	AL	OF	102	369	38	89	18	49	9	.241
1993	Cleveland	AL	OF	66	174	19	39	5	25	7	.224
1993	Chicago	NL	OF	31	87	14	30	10	22	1	.345
Seasonal Notation					506	67	125	24	69	14	.248

THOMAS HOWARD
Age 29/B **$1**

Yet another toiler in the Cincinnati fields last summer. We've always liked him as a cheap, end-of-draft buy because of his speed. But it always comes down to the same question for guys like this: playing time. If Bobby Kelly, Kevin Mitchell, and Reggie Sanders are all healthy, players like Howard end up with pine time, not prime time.

Year	Team	Lg.	Pos.	G	AB	R	H	HR	RBI	SB	BA
1990	San Diego	NL	OF	20	44	4	12	0	0	0	.273
1991	San Diego	NL	OF	106	281	30	70	4	22	10	.249
1992	San Diego	NL	OF	5	3	1	1	0	0	0	.333
1992	Cleveland	AL	OF	117	358	36	99	2	32	15	.277
1993	Cleveland	AL	OF	74	178	26	42	3	23	5	.236
1993	Cincinnati	NL	OF	38	141	22	39	4	13	5	.277
Seasonal Notation					452	53	118	5	40	15	.262

PETE INCAVIGLIA
Age 30/R **$18**

Inky is to the fine art of hitting what the Philly cheese steak is to haute cuisine. Extra onions, please.

Year	Team	Lg.	Pos.	G	AB	R	H	HR	RBI	SB	BA
1990	Texas	AL	OF	153	529	59	123	24	85	3	.233
1991	Detroit	AL	OF	97	337	38	72	11	38	1	.214
1992	Houston	NL	OF	113	349	31	93	11	44	2	.266
1993	Philadelphia	NL	OF	116	368	60	101	24	89	1	.274
Seasonal Notation					535	63	131	23	86	2	.246

DARRIN JACKSON — Age 30/R — $9

He becomes a swell defensive center fielder and bona fide power hitter in San Diego, so the Blue Jays go out and get him. Then he mysteriously loses all traces of major league skills, so the Mets go and get him. If you see a pattern there, you're not alone. Keep in mind, though, that he was ill most of the year. Don't write him off.

Year	Team	Lg.	Pos.	G	AB	R	H	HR	RBI	SB	BA
1990	San Diego	NL	OF	58	113	10	29	3	9	3	.257
1991	San Diego	NL	OF	122	359	51	94	21	49	5	.262
1992	San Diego	NL	OF	155	587	72	146	17	70	14	.249
1993	Toronto	AL	OF	46	176	15	38	5	19	0	.216
1993	New York	NL	OF	31	87	4	17	1	7	0	.195
Seasonal Notation					519	59	127	18	60	8	.245

CHRIS JONES — Age 28/R — $4

There's some offensive talent here, and Colorado is the perfect place for it to blossom.

Year	Team	Lg.	Pos.	G	AB	R	H	HR	RBI	SB	BA
1991	Cincinnati	NL	OF	52	89	14	26	2	6	2	.292
1992	Houston	NL	OF	54	63	7	12	1	4	3	.190
1993	Colorado	NL	OF	86	209	29	57	6	31	9	.273
Seasonal Notation					304	42	80	7	34	11	.263

BRIAN JORDAN — Age 27/R — $15

One of our personal highlights of the World Series occurred when a Canadian writer came up to the Phillies' *Rickey* Jordan and asked him if he "missed playing pro football." Rickey, ever a gentleman, said, "No, because I've never played pro football. You're thinking of the Jordan who plays for the Cardinals and who could be a star someday if he cuts his swing down just a little." Hey, maybe Rickey will be an advance scout after he quits playing. Meanwhile, we'd like to congratulate *Brian* Jordan on making the right choice.

Year	Team	Lg.	Pos.	G	AB	R	H	HR	RBI	SB	BA
1992	St. Louis	NL	OF	55	193	17	40	5	22	7	.207
1993	St. Louis	NL	OF	67	223	33	69	10	44	6	.309
Seasonal Notation			·		552	66	144	19	87	17	.262

DAVE JUSTICE — Age 27/L — $36

Marriage to Halle Berry agrees with him. (It's hard to imagine anyone with whom it *wouldn't* agree, but that's another matter.) Hitting behind Fred McGriff also agrees with him. So does the long-awaited maturity he demonstrated this year. He used to do a pretty fair imitation of a jerk, but he grew up in 1993. We see a lot of Hollywood parties and monster seasons in his future.

Year	Team	Lg.	Pos.	G	AB	R	H	HR	RBI	SB	BA
1990	Atlanta	NL	1B	127	439	76	124	28	78	11	.282
1991	Atlanta	NL	OF	109	396	67	109	21	87	8	.275
1992	Atlanta	NL	OF	144	484	78	124	21	72	2	.256
1993	Atlanta	NL	OF	157	585	90	158	40	120	3	.270
Seasonal Notation					574	93	155	33	107	7	.270

Catchers
pp. 59–73

Corners
pp. 73–95

Infield
pp. 95–116

Outfield
pp. 117–150

DH
pp. 150–153

Starters
pp. 154–189

Relievers
pp. 190–217

BOBBY KELLY
Age 29/R   **$29**

Until his shoulder turned into spaghetti, he was having a terrific season. This is one place where the Reds did not make a mistake.

Year	Team	Lg.	Pos.	G	AB	R	H	HR	RBI	SB	BA
1990	New York	AL	OF	162	641	85	183	15	61	42	.285
1991	New York	AL	OF	126	486	68	130	20	69	32	.267
1992	New York	AL	OF	152	580	81	158	10	66	28	.272
1993	Cincinnati	NL	OF	78	320	44	102	9	35	21	.319
Seasonal Notation					633	86	179	16	72	38	.283

RAY LANKFORD
Age 26/L   **$22**

Something happened on his way to becoming Barry Bonds. The Cardinals are worried. There was even talk about trading him last fall. We think there's too much ability here for him to flame out so soon, but as one of the St. Louis brass pointed out, "You never know about a guy like this. Baseball always came easy to him, and when he struggled, he had no idea what to do." This could be the toughest call in the auction draft. If he picks up where he left off in 1992, you're in clover at this price. If he picks up where he left off in 1993, you're in something else.

Year	Team	Lg.	Pos.	G	AB	R	H	HR	RBI	SB	BA
1990	St. Louis	NL	OF	39	126	12	36	3	12	8	.286
1991	St. Louis	NL	OF	151	566	83	142	9	69	44	.251
1992	St. Louis	NL	OF	153	598	87	175	20	86	42	.293
1993	St. Louis	NL	OF	127	407	64	97	7	45	14	.238
Seasonal Notation					584	84	155	13	73	37	.265

DARREN LEWIS
Age 26/R   **$21**

When we argue that the SB category in Rotisserie baseball is actually an acknowledgement of the importance of defense, Lewis is our star witness. Yes, he steals bases, which is the basis for his Rotisserie value. But his primary baseball value is being one of the best—if not *the* best—defensive outfielders in the game.

Year	Team	Lg.	Pos.	G	AB	R	H	HR	RBI	SB	BA
1990	Oakland	AL	OF	25	35	4	8	0	1	2	.229
1991	San Francisco	NL	OF	72	222	41	55	1	15	13	.248
1992	San Francisco	NL	OF	100	320	38	74	1	18	28	.231
1993	San Francisco	NL	OF	136	522	84	132	2	48	46	.253
Seasonal Notation					534	81	130	1	39	43	.245

AL MARTIN
Age 26/L   **$15**

The Pirates think the K's will go down and the RBI will go up. So do we.

Year	Team	Lg.	Pos.	G	AB	R	H	HR	RBI	SB	BA
1992	Pittsburgh	NL	OF	12	12	1	2	0	2	0	.167
1993	Pittsburgh	NL	OF	143	480	85	135	18	64	16	.281
Seasonal Notation					514	89	143	18	68	16	.278

DAVE MARTINEZ

Age 29/L **$2**

Solid role player, but the roles keep getting smaller and smaller.

Year	Team	Lg.	Pos.	G	AB	R	H	HR	RBI	SB	BA
1990	Montreal	NL	OF	118	391	60	109	11	39	13	.279
1991	Montreal	NL	OF	124	396	47	117	7	42	16	.295
1992	Cincinnati	NL	OF	135	393	47	100	3	31	12	.254
1993	San Francisco	NL	OF	91	241	28	58	5	27	6	.241
Seasonal Notation					491	63	132	9	48	16	.270

DERRICK MAY

Age 25/L **$14**

Not exactly a gazelle afield, a weakness shared by his mates in the Cubs outfield. Indeed, the Cubs had the worst outfield defense in baseball last summer, and the prospect is for more of the same this year. No matter. May remains the darling of the Cubs brass because of his steady development as a productive hitter. Look for even more power from him this season.

Year	Team	Lg.	Pos.	G	AB	R	H	HR	RBI	SB	BA
1990	Chicago	NL	OF	17	61	8	15	1	11	1	.246
1991	Chicago	NL	OF	15	22	4	5	1	3	0	.227
1992	Chicago	NL	OF	124	351	33	96	8	45	5	.274
1993	Chicago	NL	OF	128	465	62	137	10	77	10	.295
Seasonal Notation					512	61	144	11	77	9	.281

WILLIE McGEE

Age 35/B **$7**

He doesn't run much anymore, and when he does he gets caught half the time. He doesn't hit with power. He doesn't drive in runs the way he used to when he batted third for the Cardinals. He doesn't get many walks or score many runs. And the BA? As one Giant said last summer, echoing many others, "Willie's .300 average is the most meaningless .300 I've ever seen." All that makes him the least valuable ex-MVP this side of Dale Murphy, who's retired.

Year	Team	Lg.	Pos.	G	AB	R	H	HR	RBI	SB	BA
1990	St. Louis	NL	OF	125	501	76	168	3	62	28	.335
1990	Oakland	AL	OF	29	113	23	31	0	15	3	.274
1991	San Francisco	NL	OF	131	497	67	155	4	43	17	.312
1992	San Francisco	NL	OF	138	474	56	141	1	36	13	.297
1993	San Francisco	NL	OF	130	475	53	143	4	46	10	.301
Seasonal Notation					603	80	186	3	59	20	.310

ORLANDO MERCED

Age 27/L **$11**

The rap: not much power, lower than average defensive skills, indifferent work ethic. Not a resume that will cause anybody in Pittsburgh to forget Roberto Clemente, Dave Parker, or Bobby Bonilla.

Year	Team	Lg.	Pos.	G	AB	R	H	HR	RBI	SB	BA
1990	Pittsburgh	NL	C	25	24	3	5	0	0	0	.208
1991	Pittsburgh	NL	1B	120	411	83	113	10	50	8	.275
1992	Pittsburgh	NL	1B	134	405	50	100	6	60	5	.247
1993	Pittsburgh	NL	OF	137	447	68	140	8	70	3	.313
Seasonal Notation					501	79	139	9	70	6	.278

KEVIN MITCHELL   Age 32/R $26

And speaking of work ethic, here's a guy who, while on the DL and awaiting shoulder surgery, was spotted jet-skiing. Remember, the Mets, Padres, Giants, and Mariners traded him after arriving at the same conclusion about his attitude, albeit from radically different perspectives. What complicates the picture, of course, is that when Mitchell is reasonably healthy and reasonably motivated he is a monster hitter. Also: he can become a free agent after this season, a factor that may help in the motivation department.

Year	Team	Lg.	Pos.	G	AB	R	H	HR	RBI	SB	BA
1990	San Francisco	NL	OF	140	524	90	152	35	93	4	.290
1991	San Francisco	NL	OF	113	371	52	95	27	69	2	.256
1992	Seattle	AL	OF	99	360	48	103	9	67	0	.286
1993	Cincinnati	NL	OF	93	323	56	110	19	64	1	.341
Seasonal Notation					574	89	167	32	106	2	.292

RAUL MONDESI   Age 23/R $1

Speedy.

Year	Team	Lg.	Pos.	G	AB	R	H	HR	RBI	SB	BA
1993	Los Angeles	NL	OF	42	86	13	25	4	10	4	.291
Seasonal Notation					331	50	96	15	38	15	.291

OTIS NIXON   Age 35/B $22

Stopped whining about playing time and emerged as a major factor in the Braves' stretch run. Could steal 70 bases leading off for the Red Sox.

Year	Team	Lg.	Pos.	G	AB	R	H	HR	RBI	SB	BA
1990	Montreal	NL	OF	119	231	46	58	1	20	50	.251
1991	Atlanta	NL	OF	124	401	81	119	0	26	72	.297
1992	Atlanta	NL	OF	120	456	79	134	2	22	41	.294
1993	Atlanta	NL	OF	134	461	77	124	1	24	47	.269
Seasonal Notation					504	92	141	1	29	68	.281

JOE ORSULAK   Age 31/L $4

A pro's pro.

Year	Team	Lg.	Pos.	G	AB	R	H	HR	RBI	SB	BA
1990	Baltimore	AL	OF	124	413	49	111	11	57	6	.269
1991	Baltimore	AL	OF	143	486	57	135	5	43	6	.278
1992	Baltimore	AL	OF	117	391	45	113	4	39	5	.289
1993	New York	NL	OF	134	409	59	116	8	35	5	.284
Seasonal Notation					531	65	148	8	54	6	.280

BASEBALL ANAGRAM #12

Alamo Pear Flier = _____?

(Answer on page 299)

PHIL PLANTIER　　　　　　　　　　　　　Age 25/L　　　$29

He's for real. Halfway through last season, the Padres hitting coach was telling anybody who would listen that Plantier would someday lead the National League in home runs. Not an outrageous prediction, although San Diego will need to get a few hitters in the lineup to keep other teams from pitching around him.

Year	Team	Lg.	Pos.	G	AB	R	H	HR	RBI	SB	BA
1990	Boston	AL	DH	14	15	1	2	0	3	0	.133
1991	Boston	AL	OF	53	148	27	49	11	35	1	.331
1992	Boston	AL	OF	108	349	46	86	7	30	2	.246
1993	San Diego	NL	OF	138	462	67	111	34	100	4	.240
Seasonal Notation					504	72	128	26	86	3	.255

KEVIN ROBERSON　　　　　　　　　　　　Age 26/B　　　$3

According to one Cub official, "He has an ego way too big for someone who didn't hit his weight." Maybe, but he has the physical tools that may enable his performance to catch up with that ego. And he could get a chance to chase it in what is a very muddled Wrigley world.

Year	Team	Lg.	Pos.	G	AB	R	H	HR	RBI	SB	BA
1993	Chicago	NL	OF	62	180	23	34	9	27	0	.189
Seasonal Notation					470	60	88	23	70	0	.189

HENRY RODRIGUEZ　　　　　　　　　　　Age 26/L　　　$1

The Dodgers think he has potential as a fourth or fifth outfielder. Considering that they don't have a second or third outfielder, that's not exactly a ringing endorsement.

Year	Team	Lg.	Pos.	G	AB	R	H	HR	RBI	SB	BA
1992	Los Angeles	NL	OF	53	146	11	32	3	14	0	.219
1993	Los Angeles	NL	OF	76	176	20	39	8	23	1	.222
Seasonal Notation					404	38	89	13	46	1	.220

DEION SANDERS　　　　　　　　　　　　Age 26/L　　　$11

All of a sudden, Neon's trip to the Nike Hall of Fame took a detour toward utility duty. We don't know if his ego, not to mention his jeweler, can handle that development. Oh, well, there's always football. But with Otis Nixon gone and Dave Gallagher around to bat against tough lefties, maybe Neon will glow this year.

Year	Team	Lg.	Pos.	G	AB	R	H	HR	RBI	SB	BA
1990	New York	AL	OF	57	133	24	21	3	9	8	.158
1991	Atlanta	NL	OF	54	110	16	21	4	13	11	.191
1992	Atlanta	NL	OF	97	303	54	92	8	28	26	.304
1993	Atlanta	NL	OF	95	272	42	75	6	28	19	.276
Seasonal Notation					437	72	111	11	41	34	.256

Catchers
pp. 59–73

Corners
pp. 73–95

Infield
pp. 95–116

Outfield
pp. 117–150

DH
pp. 150–153

Starters
pp. 154–189

Relievers
pp. 190–217

REGGIE SANDERS   Age 26/R $32

A month on the shelf with an injury was all that stood between Sanders and a huge season. A superstar on the rise.

Year	Team	Lg.	Pos.	G	AB	R	H	HR	RBI	SB	BA
1991	Cincinnati	NL	OF	9	40	6	8	1	3	1	.200
1992	Cincinnati	NL	OF	116	385	62	104	12	36	16	.270
1993	Cincinnati	NL	OF	138	496	90	136	20	83	27	.274
Seasonal Notation					567	97	152	20	75	27	.269

DWIGHT SMITH   Age 30/L $6

Jim Lefebvre became Dwight's third major league manager to say the same thing: "I can't believe some of the dumb things this guy does." Now, all three of those managers got fired, so we're wondering exactly who is the dumb one here. Ideally, your fourth outfielder ought to be able to catch and throw the ball to be insured of playing time, but this is not an ideal world.

Year	Team	Lg.	Pos.	G	AB	R	H	HR	RBI	SB	BA
1990	Chicago	NL	OF	117	290	34	76	6	27	11	.262
1991	Chicago	NL	OF	90	167	16	38	3	21	2	.228
1992	Chicago	NL	OF	109	217	28	60	3	24	9	.276
1993	Chicago	NL	OF	111	310	51	93	11	35	8	.300
Seasonal Notation					373	48	101	8	40	11	.271

CORY SNYDER   Age 31/R $7

When the Straw Man's season imploded, the Dodgers had no choice but to give Snyder everyday duty. This was definitely not part of the preseason blueprint, and what happened was that they got decent part-time numbers from a full-timer. This is a recipe for disappointment, in either the NL West or your friendly local Rotisserie league.

Year	Team	Lg.	Pos.	G	AB	R	H	HR	RBI	SB	BA
1990	Cleveland	AL	OF	123	438	46	102	14	55	1	.233
1991	Chicago	AL	OF	50	117	10	22	3	11	0	.188
1991	Toronto	AL	OF	21	49	4	7	0	6	0	.143
1992	San Francisco	NL	OF	124	390	48	105	14	57	4	.269
1993	Los Angeles	NL	OF	143	516	61	137	11	56	4	.266
Seasonal Notation					530	59	131	14	65	3	.247

SAMMY SOSA   Age 25/R $30

Ninety percent of Sosa's production came in spectacular but brief bursts followed by long, yawning chasms of nothing. His outfield play can charitably be described as inconsistent. He is constitutionally incapable of hitting a cutoff man. And his teammates consider him a selfish, mindless player. Hey, nobody's perfect.

Year	Team	Lg.	Pos.	G	AB	R	H	HR	RBI	SB	BA
1990	Chicago	AL	OF	153	532	72	124	15	70	32	.233
1991	Chicago	AL	OF	116	316	39	64	10	33	13	.203
1992	Chicago	NL	OF	67	262	41	68	8	25	15	.260
1993	Chicago	NL	OF	159	598	92	156	33	93	36	.261
Seasonal Notation					558	79	134	21	72	31	.241

DARRYL STRAWBERRY

Age 32/L $20

Not exactly a banner year for the Straw Man. Depending on his back and his attitude, the salary is either $20 too low or $20 too high.

Year	Team	Lg.	Pos.	G	AB	R	H	HR	RBI	SB	BA
1990	New York	NL	OF	152	542	92	150	37	108	15	.277
1991	Los Angeles	NL	OF	139	505	86	134	28	99	10	.265
1992	Los Angeles	NL	OF	43	156	20	37	5	25	3	.237
1993	Los Angeles	NL	OF	32	100	12	14	5	12	1	.140
Seasonal Notation					576	92	148	33	108	12	.257

TONY TARASCO

Age 23/L $5

Mentioned more often in trade discussions last year than NAFTA. If Gant stays, he's an ex-Brave. If Gant goes, he's the Braves leftfielder. Keep your eye on the agate type.

Year	Team	Lg.	Pos.	G	AB	R	H	HR	RBI	SB	BA
1993	Atlanta	NL	OF	24	35	6	8	0	2	0	.229
Seasonal Notation					236	40	54	0	13	0	.229

MILT THOMPSON

Age 35/L $3

The lefty-hitting half of a platoon usually gets more at-bats than the righty, but Incaviglia's big bat kept him in the lineup more than Thompson. No matter. Thompson was the perfect role player for the role he had in Philadelphia: namely, to be a sane, level-headed, rock-solid pillar of stability in a clubhouse full of wackos.

Year	Team	Lg.	Pos.	G	AB	R	H	HR	RBI	SB	BA
1990	St. Louis	NL	OF	135	418	42	91	6	30	25	.218
1991	St. Louis	NL	OF	115	326	55	100	6	34	16	.307
1992	St. Louis	NL	OF	109	208	31	61	4	17	18	.293
1993	Philadelphia	NL	OF	129	340	42	89	4	44	9	.262
Seasonal Notation					428	56	113	6	41	22	.264

RYAN THOMPSON

Age 26/R $14

Could be a star, could be a bust. We should know a little more this time next year.

Year	Team	Lg.	Pos.	G	AB	R	H	HR	RBI	SB	BA
1992	New York	NL	OF	30	108	15	24	3	10	2	.222
1993	New York	NL	OF	80	288	34	72	11	26	2	.250
Seasonal Notation					583	72	141	20	53	5	.242

ANDY VAN SLYKE

Age 33/L $24

Slick's arm was still in the sling as he sat with us one evening. He gazed out at William Pennyfeather, who struck out three times and misplayed a fly ball, and he said, "Why don't I feel more like Wally Pipp?" All we know is that the season lost a lot when Van Slyke went down with his broken collarbone. Count on him to bounce back with great numbers and even greater one liners.

Year	Team	Lg.	Pos.	G	AB	R	H	HR	RBI	SB	BA
1990	Pittsburgh	NL	OF	136	493	67	140	17	77	14	.284
1991	Pittsburgh	NL	OF	138	491	87	130	17	83	10	.265
1992	Pittsburgh	NL	OF	154	614	103	199	14	89	12	.324
1993	Pittsburgh	NL	OF	83	323	42	100	8	50	11	.310
Seasonal Notation					609	94	180	17	94	14	.296

Catchers
pp. 59–73

Corners
pp. 73–95

Infield
pp. 95–116

Outfield
pp. 117–150

DH
pp. 150–153

Starters
pp. 154–189

Relievers
pp. 190–217

LARRY WALKER

Age 27/L **$34**

Here it comes: the big, breathtaking, breakthrough year we've all been waiting for.

Year	Team	Lg.	Pos.	G	AB	R	H	HR	RBI	SB	BA
1990	Montreal	NL	OF	133	419	59	101	19	51	21	.241
1991	Montreal	NL	OF	137	487	59	141	16	64	14	.290
1992	Montreal	NL	OF	143	528	85	159	23	93	18	.301
1993	Montreal	NL	OF	138	490	85	130	22	86	29	.265
Seasonal Notation					565	84	156	23	86	24	.276

MITCH WEBSTER

Age 34/B **$1**

Yet another example of the Dodgers' ongoing rebuilding effort.

Year	Team	Lg.	Pos.	G	AB	R	H	HR	RBI	SB	BA
1990	Cleveland	AL	OF	128	437	58	110	12	55	22	.252
1991	Cleveland	AL	OF	13	32	2	4	0	0	2	.125
1991	Pittsburgh	NL	OF	36	97	9	17	1	9	0	.175
1991	Los Angeles	NL	OF	58	74	12	21	1	10	0	.284
1992	Los Angeles	NL	OF	135	262	33	70	6	35	11	.267
1993	Los Angeles	NL	OF	88	172	26	42	2	14	4	.244
Seasonal Notation					379	49	93	7	43	13	.246

MARK WHITEN

Age 27/B **$18**

He had a big season one night last September. And that could just be the beginning.

Year	Team	Lg.	Pos.	G	AB	R	H	HR	RBI	SB	BA
1990	Toronto	AL	OF	33	88	12	24	2	7	2	.273
1991	Toronto	AL	OF	46	149	12	33	2	19	0	.221
1991	Cleveland	AL	OF	70	258	34	66	7	26	4	.256
1992	Cleveland	AL	OF	148	508	73	129	9	43	16	.254
1993	St. Louis	NL	OF	152	562	81	142	25	99	15	.253
Seasonal Notation					564	76	142	16	69	13	.252

DARRELL WHITMORE

Age 25/L **$3**

The minor league numbers aren't impressive, and he didn't blow anybody away when he came up last season. So why is everybody in the Marlins organization so excited about this guy? Expansion fever? Or do they know something we don't know? Our money is on the latter.

Year	Team	Lg.	Pos.	G	AB	R	H	HR	RBI	SB	BA
1993	Florida	NL	OF	76	250	24	51	4	19	4	.204
Seasonal Notation					532	51	108	8	40	8	.204

WILLIE WILSON

Age 38/B **$1**

Said one dazed Cubs player, "When we signed this guy, we thought we were getting a real pro. No one said anything about him being a real asshole." Guess that means he won't be elected team captain, huh? At least not by a unanimous vote.

Year	Team	Lg.	Pos.	G	AB	R	H	HR	RBI	SB	BA
1990	Kansas City	AL	OF	115	307	49	89	2	42	24	.290
1991	Oakland	AL	OF	113	294	38	70	0	28	20	.238
1992	Oakland	AL	OF	132	396	38	107	0	37	28	.270
1993	Chicago	NL	OF	105	221	29	57	1	11	7	.258
Seasonal Notation					424	53	112	1	41	27	.265

AMERICAN LEAGUE

Catchers
pp. 59–73

Corners
pp. 73–95

Infield
pp. 95–116

Outfield
pp. 117–150

DH
pp. 150–153

Starters
pp. 154–189

Relievers
pp. 190–217

BRADY ANDERSON   Age 30/L $19

So here's the way we figure it: 1992 was a career year, never to be duplicated, while 1993 was a career norm. Sound about right? Okay, we can live with that. And now we can start hounding him about the dorky sideburns.

Year	Team	Lg.	Pos.	G	AB	R	H	HR	RBI	SB	BA
1990	Baltimore	AL	OF	89	234	24	54	3	24	15	.231
1991	Baltimore	AL	OF	113	256	40	59	2	27	12	.230
1992	Baltimore	AL	OF	159	623	100	169	21	80	53	.271
1993	Baltimore	AL	OF	142	560	87	147	13	66	24	.262
Seasonal Notation					538	80	138	12	63	33	.256

ALBERT BELLE   Age 27/R $41

You know what utterly startled us about his gargantuan season last year? Those 23 stolen bases. In six previous seasons of professional baseball prior to 1993, a span that encompassed 347 major league and 298 minor league games, Belle had stolen a total of exactly 13 bases. So how do you figure 23 last year? Maybe he was trying to tell us something.

Year	Team	Lg.	Pos.	G	AB	R	H	HR	RBI	SB	BA
1990	Cleveland	AL	DH	9	23	1	4	1	3	0	.174
1991	Cleveland	AL	OF	123	461	60	130	28	95	3	.282
1992	Cleveland	AL	DH	153	585	81	152	34	112	8	.260
1993	Cleveland	AL	OF	159	594	93	172	38	129	23	.290
Seasonal Notation					606	85	167	36	123	12	.275

LANCE BLANKENSHIP   Age 30/R $2

Funny, we once thought he had a chance to become Tony Phillips.

Year	Team	Lg.	Pos.	G	AB	R	H	HR	RBI	SB	BA
1990	Oakland	AL	3B	86	136	18	26	0	10	3	.191
1991	Oakland	AL	2B	90	185	33	46	3	21	12	.249
1992	Oakland	AL	2B	123	349	59	84	3	34	21	.241
1993	Oakland	AL	OF	94	252	43	48	2	23	13	.190
Seasonal Notation					380	63	84	3	36	20	.221

HUBIE BROOKS   Age 37/R $1

If he doesn't find a job, we'll miss him. He's always played the game as if he really loved it—for the simple reason that he does.

Year	Team	Lg.	Pos.	G	AB	R	H	HR	RBI	SB	BA
1990	Los Angeles	NL	OF	153	568	74	151	20	91	2	.266
1991	New York	NL	OF	103	357	48	85	16	50	3	.238
1992	California	AL	DH	82	306	28	66	8	36	3	.216
1993	Kansas City	AL	OF	75	168	14	48	1	24	0	.286
Seasonal Notation					548	64	137	17	78	3	.250

SCOTT BROSIUS — Age 27/R — $4

The A's think he can help them off the bench at all the infield and outfield positions. If so, then it's goodbye to . . .

Year	Team	Lg.	Pos.	G	AB	R	H	HR	RBI	SB	BA
1991	Oakland	AL	2B	36	68	9	16	2	4	3	.235
1992	Oakland	AL	OF	38	87	13	19	4	13	3	.218
1993	Oakland	AL	OF	70	213	26	53	6	25	6	.249
Seasonal Notation					414	54	99	13	47	13	.239

JERRY BROWNE — Age 28/B — $1

. . . whose Tony Phillips impersonation has run out of steam.

Year	Team	Lg.	Pos.	G	AB	R	H	HR	RBI	SB	BA
1990	Cleveland	AL	2B	140	513	92	137	6	50	12	.267
1991	Cleveland	AL	2B	107	290	28	66	1	29	2	.228
1992	Oakland	AL	3B	111	324	43	93	3	40	3	.287
1993	Oakland	AL	OF	76	260	27	65	2	19	4	.250
Seasonal Notation					517	70	134	4	51	7	.260

TOM BRUNANSKY — Age 33/R — $1

Look for a mild comeback—if any team gives him a chance.

Year	Team	Lg.	Pos.	G	AB	R	H	HR	RBI	SB	BA
1990	St. Louis	NL	OF	19	57	5	9	1	2	0	.158
1990	Boston	AL	OF	129	461	61	123	15	71	5	.267
1991	Boston	AL	OF	142	459	54	105	16	70	1	.229
1992	Boston	AL	OF	138	458	47	122	15	74	2	.266
1993	Milwaukee	AL	OF	80	224	20	41	6	29	3	.183
Seasonal Notation					529	59	127	16	78	3	.241

DAMON BUFORD — Age 23/R — $1

All of a sudden baseball is being flooded with the offspring of former major leaguers, positively a plethora of progeny—from Alomar to Alou to Bonds to Boone to Griffey to Perez to McRae to May to Stottlemyre to Haney to Segui to, yes, Buford. Maybe they should form a club or something.

Year	Team	Lg.	Pos.	G	AB	R	H	HR	RBI	SB	BA
1993	Baltimore	AL	OF	53	79	18	18	2	9	2	.228
Seasonal Notation					241	55	55	6	27	6	.228

JAY BUHNER — Age 29/R — $24

Everybody has always wondered what would happen if he stayed healthy for a full year. Last season we found out. We are pleased to report that he is a down-to-earth guy who doesn't get carried away with himself. Most big league players—heck, most *people*—are able to come up with dozens of reasons—none having to do with themselves, needless to say—for failing to live up to expectations. Not Buhner: "If I don't drive in a hundred or so runs hitting around Junior in our batting order, I ought to be shot."

Year	Team	Lg.	Pos.	G	AB	R	H	HR	RBI	SB	BA
1990	Seattle	AL	OF	51	163	16	45	7	33	2	.276
1991	Seattle	AL	OF	137	406	64	99	27	77	0	.244
1992	Seattle	AL	OF	152	543	69	132	25	79	0	.243
1993	Seattle	AL	OF	158	563	91	153	27	98	2	.272
Seasonal Notation					544	78	139	27	93	1	.256

ELLIS BURKS   Age 29/R $16

Nice guy makes a big comeback. We like that.

Year	Team	Lg.	Pos.	G	AB	R	H	HR	RBI	SB	BA
1990	Boston	AL	OF	152	588	89	174	21	89	9	.296
1991	Boston	AL	OF	130	474	56	119	14	56	6	.251
1992	Boston	AL	OF	66	235	35	60	8	30	5	.255
1993	Chicago	AL	OF	146	499	75	137	17	74	6	.275
Seasonal Notation					588	83	160	19	81	8	.273

IVAN CALDERON   Age 32/R $1

What a waste.

Year	Team	Lg.	Pos.	G	AB	R	H	HR	RBI	SB	BA
1990	Chicago	AL	OF	158	607	85	166	14	74	32	.273
1991	Montreal	NL	OF	134	470	69	141	19	75	31	.300
1992	Montreal	NL	OF	48	170	19	45	3	24	1	.265
1993	Boston	AL	OF	73	213	25	47	1	19	4	.221
1993	Chicago	AL	DH	9	26	1	3	0	3	0	.115
Seasonal Notation					570	76	154	14	74	26	.271

JOSE CANSECO   Age 29/R $32

What a waste[2].

Year	Team	Lg.	Pos.	G	AB	R	H	HR	RBI	SB	BA
1990	Oakland	AL	OF	131	481	83	132	37	101	19	.274
1991	Oakland	AL	OF	154	572	115	152	44	122	26	.266
1992	Oakland	AL	OF	97	366	66	90	22	72	5	.246
1992	Texas	AL	OF	22	73	8	17	4	15	1	.233
1993	Texas	AL	OF	60	231	30	59	10	46	6	.255
Seasonal Notation					601	105	157	40	124	19	.261

JOE CARTER   Age 34/R $35

The most reliable RBI machine in the game gazed at the Blue Jays batting
order one day and sighed, "Man, I'm hitting behind two Hall of Famers and
Robbie, who's on his way there, and in front of a guy who's likely to hit .400
someday. No wonder no one knows who I am." We say it ain't so, Joe.

Year	Team	Lg.	Pos.	G	AB	R	H	HR	RBI	SB	BA
1990	San Diego	NL	OF	162	634	79	147	24	115	22	.232
1991	Toronto	AL	OF	162	638	89	174	33	108	20	.273
1992	Toronto	AL	OF	158	622	97	164	34	119	12	.264
1993	Toronto	AL	OF	155	603	92	153	33	121	8	.254
Seasonal Notation					635	90	162	31	117	15	.256

DARNELL COLES   Age 31/R $1

If he winds up on your Opening Day roster, dial 911.

Year	Team	Lg.	Pos.	G	AB	R	H	HR	RBI	SB	BA
1990	Seattle	AL	OF	37	107	9	23	2	16	0	.215
1990	Detroit	AL	DH	52	108	13	22	1	4	0	.204
1991	San Francisco	NL	OF	11	14	1	3	0	0	0	.214
1992	Cincinnati	NL	3B	55	141	16	44	3	18	1	.312
1993	Toronto	AL	OF	64	194	26	49	4	26	1	.253
Seasonal Notation					417	48	104	7	47	1	.250

Catchers
pp. 59–73

Corners
pp. 73–95

Infield
pp. 95–116

Outfield
pp. 117–150

DH
pp. 150–153

Starters
pp. 154–189

Relievers
pp. 190–217

CHAD CURTIS

Age 25/R   **$29**

A tough, hustling, base-stealing overachiever. A Whitey Herzog type of player.

Year	Team	Lg.	Pos.	G	AB	R	H	HR	RBI	SB	BA
1992	California	AL	OF	139	441	59	114	10	46	43	.259
1993	California	AL	OF	152	583	94	166	6	59	48	.285
Seasonal Notation					570	85	155	8	58	50	.273

MILT CUYLER

Age 25/B   **$3**

A soft, lazy, jaking underachiever. What's that make him, a Chris Brown type of player? There is a bright side: as a result of Cuyler's failings . . .

Year	Team	Lg.	Pos.	G	AB	R	H	HR	RBI	SB	BA
1990	Detroit	AL	OF	19	51	8	13	0	8	1	.255
1991	Detroit	AL	OF	154	475	77	122	3	33	41	.257
1992	Detroit	AL	OF	89	291	39	70	3	28	8	.241
1993	Detroit	AL	OF	82	249	46	53	0	19	13	.213
Seasonal Notation					502	80	121	2	41	29	.242

ERIC DAVIS

Age 31/R   **$23**

. . . got a chance to reveal that he is a Sparky Anderson type of player. Maybe we're suckers with long memories (1987: 37 HR, 100 RBI, 50 SB). Maybe we're just plain crazy (hey, it comes as part of the standard Rotisserie package). Whatever, we think Detroit breathed new life into Davis's career.

Year	Team	Lg.	Pos.	G	AB	R	H	HR	RBI	SB	BA
1990	Cincinnati	NL	OF	127	453	84	118	24	86	21	.260
1991	Cincinnati	NL	OF	89	285	39	67	11	33	14	.235
1992	Los Angeles	NL	OF	76	267	21	61	5	32	19	.228
1993	Los Angeles	NL	OF	108	376	57	88	14	53	33	.234
1993	Detroit	AL	OF	23	75	14	19	6	15	2	.253
Seasonal Notation					557	82	135	22	83	34	.242

ROB DEER

Age 33/R   **$13**

Last year he struck out more times (169) than he had hits and RBI combined (153). This year his goal is to strike out more times than he has at-bats. We think he can do it.

Year	Team	Lg.	Pos.	G	AB	R	H	HR	RBI	SB	BA
1990	Milwaukee	AL	OF	134	440	57	92	27	69	2	.209
1991	Detroit	AL	OF	134	448	64	80	25	64	1	.179
1992	Detroit	AL	OF	110	393	66	97	32	64	4	.247
1993	Detroit	AL	OF	90	323	48	70	14	39	3	.217
1993	Boston	AL	OF	38	143	18	28	7	16	2	.196
Seasonal Notation					559	81	117	33	80	3	.210

BASEBALL ANAGRAM #13

Eating a Bit Soon = _____?

(Answer on page 299)

MIKE DEVEREAUX   Age 30/R $17

The most shocking reversal of form by a position player in the American League. Some of it was due to injuries. But with his slide in all categories except salary, the Orioles spent the winter trying to move him. Our advice: let somebody else gamble on a big comeback.

Year	Team	Lg.	Pos.	G	AB	R	H	HR	RBI	SB	BA
1990	Baltimore	AL	OF	108	367	48	88	12	49	13	.240
1991	Baltimore	AL	OF	149	608	82	158	19	59	16	.260
1992	Baltimore	AL	OF	156	653	76	180	24	107	10	.276
1993	Baltimore	AL	OF	131	527	72	132	14	75	3	.250
Seasonal Notation					641	82	166	20	86	12	.259

DAN GLADDEN   Age 36/R $9

Career high in RBI. Valuable addition to your roster as long as he stays in Detroit.

Year	Team	Lg.	Pos.	G	AB	R	H	HR	RBI	SB	BA
1990	Minnesota	AL	OF	136	534	64	147	5	40	25	.275
1991	Minnesota	AL	OF	126	461	65	114	6	52	15	.247
1992	Detroit	AL	OF	113	417	57	106	7	42	4	.254
1993	Detroit	AL	OF	91	356	52	95	13	56	8	.267
Seasonal Notation					614	82	160	10	66	18	.261

JUAN GONZALEZ   Age 24/R $42

"We got him to start laying off those outside pitches and working deeper into a few counts, and he went out and hit .300," said Rangers hitting coach Willie Upshaw at the end of last season. "But in all honesty, what he does can't be taught. And he's just a baby." Added one awed scout: "Once he learns how to hit, he might hit 70 home runs some year."

Year	Team	Lg.	Pos.	G	AB	R	H	HR	RBI	SB	BA
1990	Texas	AL	OF	25	90	11	26	4	12	0	.289
1991	Texas	AL	OF	142	545	78	144	27	102	4	.264
1992	Texas	AL	OF	155	584	77	152	43	109	0	.260
1993	Texas	AL	OF	140	536	105	166	46	118	4	.310
Seasonal Notation					615	95	171	42	119	2	.278

MIKE GREENWELL   Age 30/L $14

Solid comeback year that proves you don't have to be Mr. Nice Guy to play this game.

Year	Team	Lg.	Pos.	G	AB	R	H	HR	RBI	SB	BA
1990	Boston	AL	OF	159	610	71	181	14	73	8	.297
1991	Boston	AL	OF	147	544	76	163	9	83	15	.300
1992	Boston	AL	OF	49	180	16	42	2	18	2	.233
1993	Boston	AL	OF	146	540	77	170	13	72	5	.315
Seasonal Notation					605	77	179	12	79	9	.297

KEN GRIFFEY, JR.   Age 24/L $43

We know enough to be a little leery about what Sparky Anderson has to say about players. Sparky's the guy, remember, who compared Mike Laga to Willie McCovey and maintained that "if you don't like David Rucker, you don't like ice cream" and gave Lou Whitaker's job to Chris Pitaro. But our

Catchers
pp. 59-73

Corners
pp. 73-95

Infield
pp. 95-116

Outfield
pp. 117-150

DH
pp. 150-153

Starters
pp. 154-189

Relievers
pp. 190-217

eyebrows didn't arch when the Sparkster started talking about Griffey: "Right now, Barry Bonds is the best player in the game. But my Lord, if Junior keeps going like he's going, when he gets to the age Bonds is now, not only will he be better than Bonds, we might have to start talking about him and that Mays guy in the same breath." When Sparky talks, we listen.

Year	Team	Lg.	Pos.	G	AB	R	H	HR	RBI	SB	BA
1990	Seattle	AL	OF	155	597	91	179	22	80	16	.300
1991	Seattle	AL	OF	154	548	76	179	22	100	18	.327
1992	Seattle	AL	OF	142	565	83	174	27	103	10	.308
1993	Seattle	AL	OF	156	582	113	180	45	109	17	.309
Seasonal Notation					611	96	190	30	104	16	.311

CHRIS GWYNN   Age 29/L $1

Career year.

Year	Team	Lg.	Pos.	G	AB	R	H	HR	RBI	SB	BA
1990	Los Angeles	NL	OF	101	141	19	40	5	22	0	.284
1991	Los Angeles	NL	OF	94	139	18	35	5	22	1	.252
1992	Kansas City	AL	OF	34	84	10	24	1	7	0	.286
1993	Kansas City	AL	OF	103	287	36	86	1	25	0	.300
Seasonal Notation					317	40	90	5	37	0	.284

DARRYL HAMILTON   Age 29/L $14

Strong season from a steadily improving player. SB were down because the Brewers were behind so often. Look for them to bounce back as soon as the Brewers do.

Year	Team	Lg.	Pos.	G	AB	R	H	HR	RBI	SB	BA
1990	Milwaukee	AL	OF	89	156	27	46	1	18	10	.295
1991	Milwaukee	AL	OF	122	405	64	126	1	57	16	.311
1992	Milwaukee	AL	OF	128	470	67	140	5	62	41	.298
1993	Milwaukee	AL	OF	135	520	74	161	9	48	21	.310
Seasonal Notation					530	79	161	5	63	30	.305

JEFFREY HAMMONDS   Age 23/R $12

Camden Yards habitués went ga-ga over his star potential. We want to see a little more before we give him the keys to the city. Injury could delay decision.

Year	Team	Lg.	Pos.	G	AB	R	H	HR	RBI	SB	BA
1993	Baltimore	AL	OF	33	105	10	32	3	19	4	.305
Seasonal Notation					515	49	157	14	93	19	.305

BILLY HATCHER   Age 33/R $7

Not the first name your eye runs to in the boxscores every morning, but a solid, unspectacular player who delivers the goods.

Year	Team	Lg.	Pos.	G	AB	R	H	HR	RBI	SB	BA
1990	Cincinnati	NL	OF	139	504	68	139	5	25	30	.276
1991	Cincinnati	NL	OF	138	442	45	116	4	41	11	.262
1992	Cincinnati	NL	OF	43	94	10	27	2	10	0	.287
1992	Boston	AL	OF	75	315	37	75	1	23	4	.238
1993	Boston	AL	OF	136	508	71	146	9	57	14	.287
Seasonal Notation					568	70	153	6	47	18	.270

DAVE HENDERSON   Age 35/R $10

The injuries may have signaled the beginning of the end. But don't weep for Hindu; he sure doesn't. "Hey, if I can't play anymore, then I'm just happy I played long enough and well enough to make some people smile." Us among them.

Year	Team	Lg.	Pos.	G	AB	R	H	HR	RBI	SB	BA
1990	Oakland	AL	OF	127	450	65	122	20	63	3	.271
1991	Oakland	AL	OF	150	572	86	158	25	85	6	.276
1992	Oakland	AL	OF	20	63	1	9	0	2	0	.143
1993	Oakland	AL	OF	107	382	37	84	20	53	0	.220
Seasonal Notation					588	75	149	26	81	3	.254

RICKEY HENDERSON   Age 35/R $35

Pat Gillick said during the World Series that if he had to do it all over again, he would not have traded for Rickey. We took that as a tipoff that Henderson wasn't coming back to Toronto. Where will he go? And how will he do? You already know the answer to the first question. The second one is a little tougher. We all have memories of Rickey at his spectacular best. We realize he played the last two months of 1993 with a bad hand. But we also remember the moods, the hamstrings, the times he tuned out. And we know that a lot of people in front offices around the league are convinced, fairly or not, that he will shift into coast before the ink on his new contract is dry.

Year	Team	Lg.	Pos.	G	AB	R	H	HR	RBI	SB	BA
1990	Oakland	AL	OF	136	489	119	159	28	61	65	.325
1991	Oakland	AL	OF	134	470	105	126	18	57	58	.268
1992	Oakland	AL	OF	117	396	77	112	15	46	48	.283
1993	Oakland	AL	OF	90	318	77	104	17	47	31	.327
1993	Toronto	AL	OF	44	163	37	35	4	12	22	.215
Seasonal Notation					570	129	166	25	69	69	.292

DAVID HULSE   Age 26/L $9

Faster than a speeding bullet. The problem, according to one of the Rangers coaches, is that "he can pull a hamstring eating breakfast."

Year	Team	Lg.	Pos.	G	AB	R	H	HR	RBI	SB	BA
1992	Texas	AL	OF	32	92	14	28	0	2	3	.304
1993	Texas	AL	OF	114	407	71	118	1	29	29	.290
Seasonal Notation					553	94	162	1	34	35	.293

BO JACKSON   Age 31/R $8

Bo's next sport might be table tennis. There's a table set up in the White Sox' clubhouse, and says Bo to all comers, "I can kick anyone's butt at this game." Thing is, he can.

Year	Team	Lg.	Pos.	G	AB	R	H	HR	RBI	SB	BA
1990	Kansas City	AL	OF	111	405	74	110	28	78	15	.272
1991	Chicago	AL	DH	23	71	8	16	3	14	0	.225
1993	Chicago	AL	OF	85	284	32	66	16	45	0	.232
Seasonal Notation					562	84	142	34	101	11	.253

Catchers
pp. 59–73

Corners
pp. 73–95

Infield
pp. 95–116

Outfield
pp. 117–150

DH
pp. 150–153

Starters
pp. 154–189

Relievers
pp. 190–217

CHRIS JAMES
Age 31/R   **$1**

Not a bad way to spend a buck at the end of the auction draft, but why not spend it instead on a younger, fresher face with a bigger upside?

Year	Team	Lg.	Pos.	G	AB	R	H	HR	RBI	SB	BA
1990	Cleveland	AL	DH	140	528	62	158	12	70	4	.299
1991	Cleveland	AL	DH	115	437	31	104	5	41	3	.238
1992	San Francisco	NL	OF	111	248	25	60	5	32	2	.242
1993	Houston	NL	OF	65	129	19	33	6	19	2	.256
1993	Texas	AL	OF	8	31	5	11	3	7	0	.355
Seasonal Notation					506	52	135	11	62	4	.267

DION JAMES
Age 31/L   **$4**

A first-round draft pick and quite a phenom a decade ago, but in his career he was traded twice for even bigger former phenoms: Brad Komminsk (1987) and Oddibe McDowell (1989). Where are *they* now?

Year	Team	Lg.	Pos.	G	AB	R	H	HR	RBI	SB	BA
1990	Cleveland	AL	1B	87	248	28	68	1	22	5	.274
1992	New York	AL	OF	67	145	24	38	3	17	1	.262
1993	New York	AL	OF	115	343	62	114	7	36	0	.332
Seasonal Notation					443	68	132	6	45	3	.299

STAN JAVIER
Age 30/B   **$2**

Born in San Francisco de Macorís, not San Pedro, which probably explains why he is not a shortstop.

Year	Team	Lg.	Pos.	G	AB	R	H	HR	RBI	SB	BA
1990	Oakland	AL	OF	19	33	4	8	0	3	0	.242
1990	Los Angeles	NL	OF	104	276	56	84	3	24	15	.304
1991	Los Angeles	NL	OF	121	176	21	36	1	11	7	.205
1992	Los Angeles	NL	OF	56	58	6	11	1	5	1	.190
1992	Philadelphia	NL	OF	74	276	36	72	0	24	17	.261
1993	California	AL	OF	92	237	33	69	3	28	12	.291
Seasonal Notation					367	54	97	2	33	18	.265

LANCE JOHNSON
Age 30/L   **$19**

The Hawkeroo and the Wimperoo in the White Sox broadcast booth call him the "One Dog." Plays a sweet center field, runs like a cheetah, and got some very big ribbies for the Chisox last season.

Year	Team	Lg.	Pos.	G	AB	R	H	HR	RBI	SB	BA
1990	Chicago	AL	OF	151	541	76	154	1	51	36	.285
1991	Chicago	AL	OF	160	588	72	161	0	49	26	.274
1992	Chicago	AL	OF	157	567	67	158	3	47	41	.279
1993	Chicago	AL	OF	147	540	75	168	0	47	35	.311
Seasonal Notation					588	76	168	1	51	36	.287

FELIX JOSE
Age 28/B   **$10**

Thud! A bad shoulder hampered him and forced him to give up switch-hitting, but we're beginning to understand why the Cardinals and Athletics were so anxious to unload him.

Year	Team	Lg.	Pos.	G	AB	R	H	HR	RBI	SB	BA
1990	Oakland	AL	OF	101	341	42	90	8	39	8	.264
1990	St. Louis	NL	OF	25	85	12	23	3	13	4	.271
1991	St. Louis	NL	OF	154	568	69	173	8	77	20	.305
1992	St. Louis	NL	OF	131	509	62	150	14	75	28	.295
1993	Kansas City	AL	OF	149	499	64	126	6	43	31	.253
Seasonal Notation					579	72	162	11	71	26	.281

Catchers
pp. 59–73

Corners
pp. 73–95

Infield
pp. 95–116

Outfield
pp. 117–150

DH
pp. 150–153

Starters
pp. 154–189

Relievers
pp. 190–217

WAYNE KIRBY   Age 30/L $9

Solid year, lots of speed, but the Indians have a stud named Manny Ramirez ready to swoop in and scarf up most of this guy's playing time.

Year	Team	Lg.	Pos.	G	AB	R	H	HR	RBI	SB	BA
1991	Cleveland	AL	OF	21	43	4	9	0	5	1	.209
1992	Cleveland	AL	DH	21	18	9	3	1	1	0	.167
1993	Cleveland	AL	OF	131	458	71	123	6	60	17	.269
Seasonal Notation					486	78	126	6	61	16	.260

GENE LARKIN   Age 31/B $1

Still the best baseball player to come out of Columbia University since Lou Gehrig.

Year	Team	Lg.	Pos.	G	AB	R	H	HR	RBI	SB	BA
1990	Minnesota	AL	OF	119	401	46	108	5	42	5	.269
1991	Minnesota	AL	OF	98	255	34	73	2	19	2	.286
1992	Minnesota	AL	1B	115	337	38	83	6	42	7	.246
1993	Minnesota	AL	OF	56	144	17	38	1	19	0	.264
Seasonal Notation					474	56	126	5	50	5	.266

KENNY LOFTON   Age 26/L $34

A scouting report from Indians base-running coach Dave Nelson: "Kenny's got a long way to go. But I saw Rickey when he was young, and while this kid might not hit the home runs, he can end up doing everything else better." The olive in the martini? There's not an obnoxious bone in his body.

Year	Team	Lg.	Pos.	G	AB	R	H	HR	RBI	SB	BA
1991	Houston	NL	OF	20	74	9	15	0	0	2	.203
1992	Cleveland	AL	OF	148	576	96	164	5	42	66	.285
1993	Cleveland	AL	OF	148	569	116	185	1	42	70	.325
Seasonal Notation					624	113	186	3	43	70	.299

SHANE MACK   Age 30/R $12

Sharp dropoff after two virtually identical seasons that seemed to have established Mack as a solid producer. Come back, Shane!

Year	Team	Lg.	Pos.	G	AB	R	H	HR	RBI	SB	BA
1990	Minnesota	AL	OF	125	313	50	102	8	44	13	.326
1991	Minnesota	AL	OF	143	442	79	137	18	74	13	.310
1992	Minnesota	AL	OF	156	600	101	189	16	75	26	.315
1993	Minnesota	AL	OF	128	503	66	139	10	61	15	.276
Seasonal Notation					545	86	166	15	74	19	.305

CANDY MALDONADO   Age 33/R $2

Don't ever talk about the Friendly Confines to Maldonado, who was practically run out of Chicago on a rail. Life was better in Municipal Stadium, but now the Indians are in a new ballpark with a lot of young talent. There may not be a place for this aging outfielder with minimal defensive skills, even though there's still some whack left in his bat.

Year	Team	Lg.	Pos.	G	AB	R	H	HR	RBI	SB	BA
1990	Cleveland	AL	OF	155	590	76	161	22	95	3	.273
1991	Milwaukee	AL	OF	34	111	11	23	5	20	1	.207
1991	Toronto	AL	OF	52	177	26	49	7	28	3	.277
1992	Toronto	AL	OF	137	489	64	133	20	66	2	.272
1993	Chicago	NL	OF	70	140	8	26	3	15	0	.186
1993	Cleveland	AL	OF	28	81	11	20	5	20	0	.247
Seasonal Notation					540	66	140	21	83	3	.259

DAVID McCARTY   Age 24/R $5

A much ballyhooed and somewhat cocky prospect out of Stanford, McCarty got into the habit of petulantly slinging his batting helmet toward the dugout after making an out. After taking one too many off the shin, Tom Kelly finally said, "Get him outta here." So he was sent down, and we'll have to wait a while to find out whether, as one scout rhapsodized, "McCarty can be a right-handed Will Clark." Minus the attitude, we hope.

Year	Team	Lg.	Pos.	G	AB	R	H	HR	RBI	SB	BA
1993	Minnesota	AL	OF	98	350	36	75	2	21	2	.214
Seasonal Notation					578	59	123	3	34	3	.214

MARK McLEMORE   Age 29/B $6

Applaud his surprising season. But keep in mind that the Orioles think they are a better club if McLemore is in a utility role. And remember also that a year ago the best he could do was share a platoon job with Billy Ripken. Those two facts suggest that a repeat performance is unlikely.

Year	Team	Lg.	Pos.	G	AB	R	H	HR	RBI	SB	BA
1990	California	AL	2B	20	48	4	7	0	2	1	.146
1990	Cleveland	AL	3B	8	12	2	2	0	0	0	.167
1991	Houston	NL	2B	21	61	6	9	0	2	0	.148
1992	Baltimore	AL	2B	101	228	40	56	0	27	11	.246
1993	Baltimore	AL	OF	148	581	81	165	4	72	21	.284
Seasonal Notation					505	72	129	2	55	17	.257

BRIAN McRAE   Age 26/B $16

Edging closer to stardom. If he cuts down on the strikeouts and stops worrying about saving his father's job, he can go the distance.

Year	Team	Lg.	Pos.	G	AB	R	H	HR	RBI	SB	BA
1990	Kansas City	AL	OF	46	168	21	48	2	23	4	.286
1991	Kansas City	AL	OF	152	629	86	164	8	64	20	.261
1992	Kansas City	AL	OF	149	533	63	119	4	52	18	.223
1993	Kansas City	AL	OF	153	627	78	177	12	69	23	.282
Seasonal Notation					634	80	164	8	67	21	.260

KEVIN McREYNOLDS

Age 34/R   **$8**

Somebody wake him up and tell him his career is over.

Year	Team	Lg.	Pos.	G	AB	R	H	HR	RBI	SB	BA
1990	New York	NL	OF	147	521	75	140	24	82	9	.269
1991	New York	NL	OF	143	522	65	135	16	74	6	.259
1992	Kansas City	AL	OF	109	373	45	92	13	49	7	.247
1993	Kansas City	AL	OF	110	351	44	86	11	42	2	.245
Seasonal Notation					562	72	144	20	78	7	.256

PEDRO MUNOZ

Age 25/R   **$10**

He had knee problems for half the season and never told the Twins, who still believe he is the real thing. Grab him now at a bargain price.

Year	Team	Lg.	Pos.	G	AB	R	H	HR	RBI	SB	BA
1990	Minnesota	AL	OF	22	85	13	23	0	5	3	.271
1991	Minnesota	AL	OF	51	138	15	39	7	26	3	.283
1992	Minnesota	AL	OF	127	418	44	113	12	71	4	.270
1993	Minnesota	AL	OF	104	326	34	76	13	38	1	.233
Seasonal Notation					515	56	133	17	74	5	.260

PAUL O'NEILL

Age 31/L   **$21**

Watch him enough and you realize that sitting him down against the tough left-handers makes sense. O'Neill gives new meaning to the word intensity. When he runs into a bad streak, the look on his face causes small children in the stands to burst into tears.

Year	Team	Lg.	Pos.	G	AB	R	H	HR	RBI	SB	BA
1990	Cincinnati	NL	OF	145	503	59	136	16	78	13	.270
1991	Cincinnati	NL	OF	152	532	71	136	28	91	12	.256
1992	Cincinnati	NL	OF	148	496	59	122	14	66	6	.246
1993	New York	AL	OF	141	498	71	155	20	75	2	.311
Seasonal Notation					560	71	151	21	85	9	.271

DAN PASQUA

Age 32/L   **$1**

Pass.

Year	Team	Lg.	Pos.	G	AB	R	H	HR	RBI	SB	BA
1990	Chicago	AL	DH	112	325	43	89	13	58	1	.274
1991	Chicago	AL	1B	134	417	71	108	18	66	0	.259
1992	Chicago	AL	OF	93	265	26	56	'6	33	0	.211
1993	Chicago	AL	OF	78	176	22	36	5	20	2	.205
Seasonal Notation					459	62	112	16	68	1	.244

BASEBALL ANAGRAM #14

Farm 'n' Varsity = _____?

(Answer on page 299)

DAN PELTIER   Age 25/L $2

The Rangers like the way he swings the bat. A name like that makes us wonder how he swings a hockey stick.

Year	Team	Lg.	Pos.	G	AB	R	H	HR	RBI	SB	BA
1992	Texas	AL	OF	12	24	1	4	0	2	0	.167
1993	Texas	AL	OF	65	160	23	43	1	17	0	.269
Seasonal Notation					387	50	98	2	39	0	.255

TONY PHILLIPS   Age 34/B $11

A marvel. Rotisserie numbers can't begin to measure his true value. Which is our subtle way of admitting our little game is not perfect.

Year	Team	Lg.	Pos.	G	AB	R	H	HR	RBI	SB	BA
1990	Detroit	AL	3B	152	573	97	144	8	55	19	.251
1991	Detroit	AL	OF	146	564	87	160	17	72	10	.284
1992	Detroit	AL	OF	159	606	114	167	10	64	12	.276
1993	Detroit	AL	OF	151	566	113	177	7	57	16	.313
Seasonal Notation					615	109	172	11	66	15	.281

LUIS POLONIA   Age 29/L $19

How can a player hit .271 and get so few RBI in so many AB? Whitey Herzog must have asked himself that when Polonia asked for a four-year, $12 million contract.

Year	Team	Lg.	Pos.	G	AB	R	H	HR	RBI	SB	BA
1990	New York	AL	DH	11	22	2	7	0	3	1	.318
1990	California	AL	OF	109	381	50	128	2	32	20	.336
1991	California	AL	OF	150	604	92	179	2	50	48	.296
1992	California	AL	OF	149	577	83	165	0	35	51	.286
1993	California	AL	OF	152	576	75	156	1	32	55	.271
Seasonal Notation					612	85	180	1	43	49	.294

KIRBY PUCKETT   Age 33/R $31

Fine year by most standards, but Kirby wasn't satisfied with his 1993 performance. Late in the season he looked back and said, "Shoot, I've been horsebleep." We'll gladly settle for a whole team of horsebleep, thank you.

Year	Team	Lg.	Pos.	G	AB	R	H	HR	RBI	SB	BA
1990	Minnesota	AL	OF	146	551	82	164	12	80	5	.298
1991	Minnesota	AL	OF	152	611	92	195	15	89	11	.319
1992	Minnesota	AL	OF	160	639	104	210	19	110	17	.329
1993	Minnesota	AL	OF	156	622	89	184	22	89	8	.296
Seasonal Notation					639	96	198	17	97	10	.311

CARLOS QUINTANA   Age 28/R $1

Too bad. He looked like he was on his way before the injury that canceled 1992. Being away for a year put him back at square one.

Year	Team	Lg.	Pos.	G	AB	R	H	HR	RBI	SB	BA
1990	Boston	AL	1B	149	512	56	147	7	67	1	.287
1991	Boston	AL	1B	149	478	69	141	11	71	1	.295
1993	Boston	AL	1B	101	303	31	74	1	19	1	.244
Seasonal Notation					524	63	146	7	63	1	.280

TIM RAINES

Age 34/B   **$22**

No one really noticed because of the eight weeks or so he missed with a broken thumb, but the Rock is back.

Year	Team	Lg.	Pos.	G	AB	R	H	HR	RBI	SB	BA
1990	Montreal	NL	OF	130	457	65	131	9	62	49	.287
1991	Chicago	AL	OF	155	609	102	163	5	50	51	.268
1992	Chicago	AL	OF	144	551	102	162	7	54	45	.294
1993	Chicago	AL	OF	115	415	75	127	16	54	21	.306
Seasonal Notation					605	102	173	11	65	49	.287

GARY REDUS

Age 37/R   **$2**

Bring him up early in the auction draft and try to slide him through for a buck.

Year	Team	Lg.	Pos.	G	AB	R	H	HR	RBI	SB	BA
1990	Pittsburgh	NL	1B	96	227	32	56	6	23	11	.247
1991	Pittsburgh	NL	1B	98	252	45	62	7	24	17	.246
1992	Pittsburgh	NL	1B	76	176	26	45	3	12	11	.256
1993	Texas	AL	OF	77	222	28	64	6	31	4	.288
Seasonal Notation					409	61	105	10	42	20	.259

TIM SALMON

Age 25/R   **$32**

Back in April, when J. T. Snow was hitting .400 and the Orange County crowd was talking about J. T. reminding them of Ted Williams, Whitey Herzog wasn't fooled. "Shoot, Snow's a fine ballplayer, but he's going to struggle. It's our right fielder who's going to be rookie of the year." We see Salmon as this generation's Dwight Evans, only with more power.

Year	Team	Lg.	Pos.	G	AB	R	H	HR	RBI	SB	BA
1992	California	AL	OF	23	79	8	14	2	6	1	.177
1993	California	AL	OF	142	515	93	146	31	95	5	.283
Seasonal Notation					583	99	157	32	99	5	.269

STEVE SAX

Age 34/R   **$1**

He's not allowed to play second base anymore. Pretty soon the ban could extend to the outfield.

Year	Team	Lg.	Pos.	G	AB	R	H	HR	RBI	SB	BA
1990	New York	AL	2B	155	615	70	160	4	42	43	.260
1991	New York	AL	2B	158	652	85	198	10	56	31	.304
1992	Chicago	AL	2B	143	567	74	134	4	47	30	.236
1993	Chicago	AL	OF	57	119	20	28	1	8	7	.235
Seasonal Notation					616	78	164	6	48	35	.266

Catchers
pp. 59-73

Corners
pp. 73-95

Infield
pp. 95-116

Outfield
pp. 117-150

DH
pp. 150-153

Starters
pp. 154-189

Relievers
pp. 190-217

RUBEN SIERRA   Age 28/B $27

Ouch. When a franchise player hits 47 points below his lifetime average, the franchise feels it. The power numbers look good on paper, but 1993 was not a good year for Sierra. Having Mark McGwire back will help a lot, as will the development of some of the A's young hitters. But Sandy Alderson was offering Sierra around over the winter, and shedding his big salary wasn't the sole reason.

Year	Team	Lg.	Pos.	G	AB	R	H	HR	RBI	SB	BA
1990	Texas	AL	OF	159	608	70	170	16	96	9	.280
1991	Texas	AL	OF	161	661	110	203	25	116	16	.307
1992	Texas	AL	OF	124	500	66	139	14	70	12	.278
1992	Oakland	AL	OF	27	101	17	28	3	17	2	.277
1993	Oakland	AL	OF	158	630	77	147	22	101	25	.233
Seasonal Notation					643	87	176	20	103	16	.275

LONNIE SMITH   Age 38/R $1

Skates is in the have-bat-will-travel phase of his career. Wherever he lands, look for him to come up with some big hits. Pennants seem to fly wherever he plays.

Year	Team	Lg.	Pos.	G	AB	R	H	HR	RBI	SB	BA
1990	Atlanta	NL	OF	135	466	72	142	9	42	10	.305
1991	Atlanta	NL	OF	122	353	58	97	7	44	9	.275
1992	Atlanta	NL	OF	84	158	23	39	6	33	4	.247
1993	Pittsburgh	NL	OF	94	199	35	57	6	24	9	.286
1993	Baltimore	AL	DH	9	24	8	5	2	3	0	.208
Seasonal Notation					437	71	124	10	53	11	.283

DANNY TARTABULL   Age 31/R $29

As with Sierra, there was less here than meets the eye. From a Rotisserie standpoint, of course, there was plenty. But we don't want you forgetting that there's more to baseball than boxscores. Isn't there?

Year	Team	Lg.	Pos.	G	AB	R	H	HR	RBI	SB	BA
1990	Kansas City	AL	OF	88	313	41	84	15	60	1	.268
1991	Kansas City	AL	OF	132	484	78	153	31	100	6	.316
1992	New York	AL	OF	123	421	72	112	25	85	2	.266
1993	New York	AL	DH	138	513	87	128	31	102	0	.250
Seasonal Notation					582	93	160	34	116	3	.276

GREG VAUGHN   Age 28/R $30

He would have fit right in with Harvey's Wallbangers. And if you think that's a cocktail, go to your room without dinner.

Year	Team	Lg.	Pos.	G	AB	R	H	HR	RBI	SB	BA
1990	Milwaukee	AL	OF	120	382	51	84	17	61	7	.220
1991	Milwaukee	AL	OF	145	542	81	132	27	98	2	.244
1992	Milwaukee	AL	OF	141	501	77	114	23	78	15	.228
1993	Milwaukee	AL	OF	154	569	97	152	30	97	10	.267
Seasonal Notation					576	88	139	28	96	9	.242

RANDY VELARDE

Age 31/R   **$5**

The Yankees missed him sorely when he was hurt. He's no Tony Phillips, but at least we're talking about him in the same breath. Give him 350 at-bats and he will bloosom.

Year	Team	Lg.	Pos.	G	AB	R	H	HR	RBI	SB	BA
1990	New York	AL	3B	95	229	21	48	5	19	0	.210
1991	New York	AL	3B	80	184	19	45	1	15	3	.245
1992	New York	AL	SS	121	412	57	112	7	46	7	.272
1993	New York	AL	OF	85	226	28	68	7	24	2	.301
Seasonal Notation					446	53	116	8	44	5	.260

JACK VOIGT

Age 27/R   **$3**

His Orioles teammates call him "The Natural" for the ease with which he mastered the art of pinch-hitting. We call that a stretch.

Year	Team	Lg.	Pos.	G	AB	R	H	HR	RBI	SB	BA
1992	Baltimore	AL	OF	1	0	0	0	0	0	0	0.000
1993	Baltimore	AL	OF	64	152	32	45	6	23	1	.296
Seasonal Notation					378	79	112	14	57	2	.296

TURNER WARD

Age 28/B   **$1**

Good fielder, should you need one.

Year	Team	Lg.	Pos.	G	AB	R	H	HR	RBI	SB	BA
1990	Cleveland	AL	OF	14	46	10	16	1	10	3	.348
1991	Cleveland	AL	OF	40	100	11	23	0	5	0	.230
1991	Toronto	AL	OF	8	13	1	4	0	2	0	.308
1992	Toronto	AL	OF	18	29	7	10	1	3	0	.345
1993	Toronto	AL	OF	72	167	20	32	4	28	3	.192
Seasonal Notation					378	52	90	6	51	6	.239

DEVON WHITE

Age 31/B   **$22**

Dynamite in postseason play, up and down and all around during the regular season. Watch him during a hot stretch and you think he's the second coming of Willie Mays. But when his game goes south, it's all the way to Tierra del Fuego.

Year	Team	Lg.	Pos.	G	AB	R	H	HR	RBI	SB	BA
1990	California	AL	OF	125	443	57	96	11	44	21	.217
1991	Toronto	AL	OF	156	642	110	181	17	60	33	.282
1992	Toronto	AL	OF	153	641	98	159	17	60	37	.248
1993	Toronto	AL	OF	146	598	116	163	15	52	34	.273
Seasonal Notation					649	106	167	16	60	34	.258

BERNIE WILLIAMS

Age 25/B   **$15**

Suffers from a touch of Devo Syndrome (see above), but looks like he's growing out of it.

Year	Team	Lg.	Pos.	G	AB	R	H	HR	RBI	SB	BA
1991	New York	AL	OF	85	320	43	76	3	34	10	.237
1992	New York	AL	OF	62	261	39	73	5	26	7	.280
1993	New York	AL	OF	139	567	67	152	12	68	9	.268
Seasonal Notation					650	84	170	11	72	14	.262

ROBIN YOUNT

Age 38/R   **$10**

Never a big charisma guy. All he's done is play hard and mind his own business and get 3,000 hits and earn a plaque in Cooperstown. This is his last year, we assume. It's been a great ride.

Year	Team	Lg.	Pos.	G	AB	R	H	HR	RBI	SB	BA
1990	Milwaukee	AL	OF	158	587	98	145	17	77	15	.247
1991	Milwaukee	AL	OF	130	503	66	131	10	77	6	.260
1992	Milwaukee	AL	OF	150	557	71	147	8	77	15	.264
1993	Milwaukee	AL	OF	127	454	62	117	8	51	9	.258
Seasonal Notation					602	85	154	12	80	12	.257

BOB ZUPCIC

Age 27/R   **$1**

Zzzzzzz. . . .

Year	Team	Lg.	Pos.	G	AB	R	H	HR	RBI	SB	BA
1991	Boston	AL	OF	18	25	3	4	1	3	0	.160
1992	Boston	AL	OF	124	392	46	108	3	43	2	.276
1993	Boston	AL	OF	141	286	40	69	2	26	5	.241
Seasonal Notation					402	50	103	3	41	4	.257

Designated Hitters

Maybe it's because we've been at this a while and some of us aren't quite as young as we once were, but we'd like to see the designated hitter rule amended so that to be a regular DH (10 games or more per season) a player would have to be at least 35 years old. Make the kids play the whole game; designate the DH for aging hitters who can still swing the bat but can't remember how to do anything else. We want Paul Molitor to go on taking his cuts until he's 50: baseball needs more class. We want Kevin Reimer to play the outfield: baseball needs more blooper highlights.

HAROLD BAINES

Age 35/L   **$21**

Your grandmother has nimbler knees, but as long as he can stand, the man will be able to hit.

Year	Team	Lg.	Pos.	G	AB	R	H	HR	RBI	SB	BA
1990	Texas	AL	DH	103	321	41	93	13	44	0	.290
1990	Oakland	AL	DH	32	94	11	25	3	21	0	.266
1991	Oakland	AL	DH	141	488	76	144	20	90	0	.295
1992	Oakland	AL	DH	140	478	58	121	16	76	1	.253
1993	Baltimore	AL	DH	118	416	64	130	20	78	0	.313
Seasonal Notation					545	75	155	21	93	0	.285

GEORGE BELL

Age 34/R   **$6**

Don't give up on him just yet. Wait at least until the All-Star break.

Year	Team	Lg.	Pos.	G	AB	R	H	HR	RBI	SB	BA
1990	Toronto	AL	OF	142	562	67	149	21	86	3	.265
1991	Chicago	NL	OF	149	558	63	159	25	86	2	.285
1992	Chicago	AL	DH	155	627	74	160	25	112	5	.255
1993	Chicago	AL	DH	102	410	36	89	13	64	1	.217
Seasonal Notation					637	70	164	24	102	3	.258

GEORGE BRETT

Age 40/L   Priceless

Late last summer, when speculation about Brett hanging up his spikes was in the air, a reporter asked how he wanted to leave the game. Like Ted Williams, with a home run in his last at-bat? Brett thought for a second, then flashed that Hall-of-Fame grin and said, "No, I want it to be a routine grounder to second base, the kind I've hit about a million times, that I run out hard. It will be my way of saying to the younger guys on the bench, 'Here, this is the way the game ought to be played.'"

Year	Team	Lg.	Pos.	G	AB	R	H	HR	RBI	SB	BA
1990	Kansas City	AL	1B	142	544	82	179	14	87	9	.329
1991	Kansas City	AL	DH	131	505	77	129	10	61	2	.255
1992	Kansas City	AL	DH	152	592	55	169	7	61	8	.285
1993	Kansas City	AL	DH	145	560	69	149	19	75	7	.266
Seasonal Notation					625	80	177	14	80	7	.284

CHILI DAVIS

Age 34/B $25

Talk about turning things around: he had one of baseball's least noticed great years. Can he do it again? We're optimists.

Year	Team	Lg.	Pos.	G	AB	R	H	HR	RBI	SB	BA
1990	California	AL	DH	113	412	58	109	12	58	1	.265
1991	Minnesota	AL	DH	153	534	84	148	29	93	5	.277
1992	Minnesota	AL	DH	138	444	63	128	12	66	4	.288
1993	California	AL	DH	152	573	74	139	27	112	4	.243
Seasonal Notation					571	81	152	23	95	4	.267

ANDRE DAWSON

Age 39/R $14

Turns 40 this summer, but his legs have been 40 a long, long time.

Year	Team	Lg.	Pos.	G	AB	R	H	HR	RBI	SB	BA
1990	Chicago	NL	OF	147	529	72	164	27	100	16	.310
1991	Chicago	NL	OF	149	563	69	153	31	104	4	.272
1992	Chicago	NL	OF	143	542	60	150	22	90	6	.277
1993	Boston	AL	DH	121	461	44	126	13	67	2	.273
Seasonal Notation					606	70	171	26	104	8	.283

JULIO FRANCO

Age 32/R $16

He needed to be chewed out for loafing. But the man can hit and he's not that old, except at the knees.

Year	Team	Lg.	Pos.	G	AB	R	H	HR	RBI	SB	BA
1990	Texas	AL	2B	157	582	96	172	11	69	31	.296
1991	Texas	AL	2B	146	589	108	201	15	78	36	.341
1992	Texas	AL	DH	35	107	19	25	2	8	1	.234
1993	Texas	AL	DH	144	532	85	154	14	84	9	.289
Seasonal Notation					608	103	185	14	80	25	.305

KIRK GIBSON
Age 36/L   **$11**

Great comeback, made possible by Sparky. Too bad the Tigers fell out of the race. We like to watch Gibson play in September when something is on the line. But we fear the tank is nearly empty.

Year	Team	Lg.	Pos.	G	AB	R	H	HR	RBI	SB	BA
1990	Los Angeles	NL	OF	89	315	59	82	8	38	26	.260
1991	Kansas City	AL	OF	132	462	81	109	16	55	18	.236
1992	Pittsburgh	NL	OF	16	56	6	11	2	5	3	.196
1993	Detroit	AL	DH	116	403	62	105	13	62	15	.261
Seasonal Notation					567	95	140	17	73	28	.248

REGGIE JEFFERSON
Age 25/B   **$3**

Getting enough at-bats to break a sweat is going to be tough, what with the influx of a whole gang of new talent.

Year	Team	Lg.	Pos.	G	AB	R	H	HR	RBI	SB	BA
1991	Cincinnati	NL	1B	5	7	1	1	1	1	0	.143
1991	Cleveland	AL	1B	26	101	10	20	2	12	0	.198
1992	Cleveland	AL	1B	24	89	8	30	1	6	0	.337
1993	Cleveland	AL	DH	113	366	35	91	10	34	1	.249
Seasonal Notation					542	52	136	13	51	0	.252

KEVIN MAAS
Age 29/L   **$1**

No Maas.

Year	Team	Lg.	Pos.	G	AB	R	H	HR	RBI	SB	BA
1990	New York	AL	1B	79	254	42	64	21	41	1	.252
1991	New York	AL	DH	148	500	69	110	23	63	5	.220
1992	New York	AL	DH	98	286	35	71	11	35	3	.248
1993	New York	AL	DH	59	151	20	31	9	25	1	.205
Seasonal Notation					502	70	116	27	69	4	.232

PAUL MOLITOR
Age 37/R   **$33**

Isn't he a tad old to be having a career year?

Year	Team	Lg.	Pos.	G	AB	R	H	HR	RBI	SB	BA
1990	Milwaukee	AL	2B	103	418	64	119	12	45	18	.285
1991	Milwaukee	AL	DH	158	665	133	216	17	75	19	.325
1992	Milwaukee	AL	DH	158	609	89	195	12	89	31	.320
1993	Toronto	AL	DH	160	636	121	211	22	111	22	.332
Seasonal Notation					651	113	207	17	89	25	.318

TROY NEEL
Age 28/L   **$15**

The A's think he's only scratched the surface of his power potential. Could have a breakout year, especially with Mark McGwire back next to him in the lineup.

Year	Team	Lg.	Pos.	G	AB	R	H	HR	RBI	SB	BA
1992	Oakland	AL	DH	24	53	8	14	3	9	0	.264
1993	Oakland	AL	DH	123	427	59	124	19	63	3	.290
Seasonal Notation					528	73	152	24	79	3	.287

MARC NEWFIELD
Age 21/R   **$2**

If you want to take a flyer on a high-risk, high-reward DH, grab this kid. The price will be low, but the Mariners' regard for him is high. If everybody is healthy in Seattle, he'll be well protected in that lineup and be given a good chance to develop.

Year	Team	Lg.	Pos.	G	AB	R	H	HR	RBI	SB	BA
1993	Seattle	AL	DH	22	66	5	15	1	7	0	.227
Seasonal Notation					486	36	110	7	51	0	.227

SHERMAN OBANDO
Age 24/R   **$1**

He's no relation to Sal Obando. He's also not worth more than an Obucko.

Year	Team	Lg.	Pos.	G	AB	R	H	HR	RBI	SB	BA
1993	Baltimore	AL	DH	31	92	8	25	3	15	0	.272
Seasonal Notation					480	41	130	15	78	0	.272

KEVIN REIMER
Age 29/L   **$14**

Last year we thought Reimer would give a major boost to the Brewers. We were wrong. Maybe we were thinking of this year.

Year	Team	Lg.	Pos.	G	AB	R	H	HR	RBI	SB	BA
1990	Texas	AL	DH	64	100	5	26	2	15	0	.260
1991	Texas	AL	OF	136	394	46	106	20	69	0	.269
1992	Texas	AL	OF	148	494	56	132	16	58	2	.267
1993	Milwaukee	AL	DH	125	437	53	109	13	60	5	.249
Seasonal Notation					488	54	127	17	69	2	.262

DAVE WINFIELD
Age 42/R   **$18**

Good numbers but not a great season for Big Dave. He was even streakier than usual. The Twins didn't play a game that meant anything after June. Even the 3,000 chase sort of drifted at the end. So this season might be our last look at a great player. If it is, we will have many fond memories and one big, unanswered question: how many more hits would he have had if he had only cut back on that big swing a smidgin?

Year	Team	Lg.	Pos.	G	AB	R	H	HR	RBI	SB	BA
1990	New York	AL	OF	20	61	7	13	2	6	0	.213
1990	California	AL	OF	112	414	63	114	19	72	0	.275
1991	California	AL	OF	150	568	75	149	28	86	7	.262
1992	Toronto	AL	DH	156	583	92	169	26	108	2	.290
1993	Minnesota	AL	DH	143	547	72	148	21	76	2	.271
Seasonal Notation					605	86	165	26	97	3	.273

BASEBALL ANAGRAM #15

Feign J.F.K. = _____?

(Answer on page 299)

Catchers
pp. 59–73

Corners
pp. 73–95

Infield
pp. 95–116

Outfield
pp. 117–150

DH
pp. 150–153

Starters
pp. 154–189

Relievers
pp. 190–217

On the Mound

Feeling a little shell-shocked after last season? Confidence in your ability to judge talent shot all to hell because the pitching staff you assembled in the spring spent the summer throwing batting practice? Outraged that the pennant-winning strategy you built around starting pitching exploded in your face because they juiced the doggone ball?

Relax. It wasn't your fault. You didn't screw up. Don't be so hard on yourself. It was expansion.

In 1992 eleven of twelve NL clubs had team ERAs of 3.74 or *lower*. Only the last-place Phillies had a higher ERA (4.13).

In 1993, eight of fourteen NL teams had ERAs of 4.05 or *higher*. The worst mark was posted, to absolutely no one's surprise, by the Colorado Rockies (5.41).

The difference? Expansion.

Over in the American League, ERAs are customarily half a run or so higher because of the detestable DH rule and more hitters' parks. But just because the AL didn't expand last year didn't mean it was immune to the effects of expansion.

In 1992 nine of fourteen AL teams had ERAs of 3.91 or *lower*. Detroit had the highest at 4.59.

In 1993 twelve of fourteen AL teams had ERAs of 4.04 or *higher*. That's right: only two AL teams had ERAs under 4.00—Boston (!) and Chicago. The Oakland A's were the worst at 4.90.

The difference? Expansion.

So you're off the hook, Bucky. Don't fire your pitching coach. Don't kick the dog. Most of all, don't blame yourself. Remember, this is America in the 1990s: you don't have to accept responsibility.

It was expansion.

NATIONAL LEAGUE

LUIS AQUINO   Age 28/R $2

A puzzle. We thought he might blossom in Miami, and he had some good outings early on. But then he got hurt, and when he returned he was used mainly in long relief. Has the stuff to be a winner, but tends to come unraveled. At times he looks like a world-beater; at other times everybody in the world beats him up. Some might say we're wishy-washy about the guy. Others would say, why the bother?

Year Team	Lg.	G	IP	H	BB	SO	W	L	ERA	SV	Ratio
1990 Kansas City	AL	20	68.1	59	27	28	4	1	3.16	0	1.259
1991 Kansas City	AL	38	157.0	152	47	80	8	4	3.44	3	1.268
1992 Kansas City	AL	15	67.2	81	20	11	3	6	4.52	0	1.493
1993 Florida	NL	38	110.2	115	40	67	6	8	3.42	0	1.401
Four-Year Average			100.0	102	34	47	5	5	3.57	1	1.340

JACK ARMSTRONG
Age 29/R   **$1**

Likely to explode the popular theory that expansion automatically extends the career of any pitcher with a heartbeat. Since that half-1990 season in Cincinnati when he was 11–3 and started the All-Star game, the All-American Boy's record is a gut-wrenching 23–51.

Year Team	Lg.	G	IP	H	BB	SO	W	L	ERA	SV	Ratio
1990 Cincinnati	NL	29	166.0	151	59	110	12	9	3.42	0	1.265
1991 Cincinnati	NL	27	139.2	158	54	93	7	13	5.48	0	1.518
1992 Cleveland	AL	35	166.2	176	67	114	6	15	4.64	0	1.458
1993 Florida	NL	36	196.1	210	78	118	9	17	4.49	0	1.467
Four-Year Average			167.0	174	65	109	9	14	4.47	0	1.425

RENE AROCHA
Age 28/R   **$7**

The Defector has more pitches than English vocabulary words. Solid performance last year prepared him for the next phase of his major league career, in which he learns words like "arbitration" and "media SOB."

Year Team	Lg.	G	IP	H	BB	SO	W	L	ERA	SV	Ratio
1993 St. Louis	NL	32	188.0	197	31	96	11	8	3.78	0	1.213
Four-Year Average			188.0	197	31	96	11	8	3.78	0	1.213

ANDY ASHBY
Age 26/R   **$1**

Quite a pickup by those shrewd Padres. Of all major league pitchers who logged over 100 innings pitched, Andy had the highest ERA *and* the highest ratio.

Year Team	Lg.	G	IP	H	BB	SO	W	L	ERA	SV	Ratio
1991 Philadelphia	NL	8	42.0	41	19	26	1	5	6.00	0	1.429
1992 Philadelphia	NL	10	37.0	42	21	24	1	3	7.54	0	1.703
1993 Colorado	NL	20	54.0	89	32	33	0	4	8.50	1	2.241
1993 San Diego	NL	12	69.0	79	24	44	3	6	5.48	0	1.493
Four-Year Average			67.0	84	32	42	2	6	6.77	0	1.718

PEDRO ASTACIO
Age 24/R   **$11**

Pedro-mania is not exactly sweeping Los Angeles, but Astacio has become a formidable pitcher who should get better. Seems to be at his best in the last third of the season, when he's good for a shutout or two.

Year Team	Lg.	G	IP	H	BB	SO	W	L	ERA	SV	Ratio
1992 Los Angeles	NL	11	82.0	80	20	43	5	5	1.98	0	1.220
1993 Los Angeles	NL	31	186.1	165	68	122	14	9	3.57	0	1.250
Four-Year Average			134.0	123	44	83	10	7	3.09	0	1.241

Catchers
pp. 59-73

Corners
pp. 73-95

Infield
pp. 95-116

Outfield
pp. 117-150

DH
pp. 150-153

Starters
pp. 154-189

Relievers
pp. 190-217

STEVE AVERY   Age 23/L $21

Want to know how competitive those Braves starters are with each other?
One afternoon last season ESPN was taping some promotional shots of Atlanta players. During the shoot John Smoltz wound up and accidentally threw
a ball through a wall. When it was Avery's turn, he asked what happened to
the wall. Told it had been drilled by Smoltz, Avery proceeded to blast an
identical hole a foot away from Smoltz's. Still too young to be The Man, but
old enough to win a Cy Young Award any day now.

Year Team	Lg.	G	IP	H	BB	SO	W	L	ERA	SV	Ratio
1990 Atlanta	NL	21	99.0	121	45	75	3	11	5.64	0	1.677
1991 Atlanta	NL	35	210.1	189	65	137	18	8	3.38	0	1.208
1992 Atlanta	NL	35	233.2	216	71	129	11	11	3.20	0	1.228
1993 Atlanta	NL	35	223.1	216	43	125	18	6	2.94	0	1.160
Four-Year Average			191.0	186	56	117	13	9	3.49	0	1.261

ANDY BENES   Age 26/R $18

Poor Andy. He went from being an emerging star on a team a couple of
players away from a pennant to the ace of a team composed of bit players,
minor leaguers, and Tony Gwynn. Worse still, it looks like he's now one of
the Padres' untouchables.

Year Team	Lg.	G	IP	H	BB	SO	W	L	ERA	SV	Ratio
1990 San Diego	NL	32	192.1	177	69	140	10	11	3.60	0	1.279
1991 San Diego	NL	33	223.0	194	59	167	15	11	3.03	0	1.135
1992 San Diego	NL	34	231.1	230	61	169	13	14	3.35	0	1.258
1993 San Diego	NL	34	230.2	200	86	179	15	15	3.78	0	1.240
Four-Year Average			219.0	200	69	164	13	13	3.44	0	1.226

BUD BLACK   Age 36/L $5

His health is iffy, but what else is new? Well, he's a year older, for one
thing. And though he got off to a good start last season, the Giants are too
gun-shy about his fragile left wing to expect much from him. So are we.

Year Team	Lg.	G	IP	H	BB	SO	W	L	ERA	SV	Ratio
1990 Cleveland	AL	29	191.0	171	58	103	11	10	3.53	0	1.199
1990 Toronto	AL	3	15.2	10	3	3	2	1	4.02	0	0.830
1991 San Francisco	NL	34	214.1	201	71	104	12	16	3.99	0	1.269
1992 San Francisco	NL	28	177.0	178	59	82	10	12	3.97	0	1.339
1993 San Francisco	NL	16	93.2	89	33	45	8	2	3.56	0	1.302
Four-Year Average			172.0	162	56	84	11	10	3.80	0	1.262

WILLIE BLAIR   Age 28/R $1

A season that pretty much sums up what expansion is all about.

Year Team	Lg.	G	IP	H	BB	SO	W	L	ERA	SV	Ratio
1990 Toronto	AL	27	68.2	66	28	43	3	5	4.06	0	1.369
1991 Cleveland	AL	11	36.0	58	10	13	2	3	6.75	0	1.889
1992 Houston	NL	29	78.2	74	25	48	5	7	4.00	0	1.258
1993 Colorado	NL	46	146.0	184	42	84	6	10	4.75	0	1.548
Four-Year Average			82.0	96	26	47	4	6	4.65	0	1.479

Catchers
pp. 59–73

Corners
pp. 73–95

Infield
pp. 95–116

Outfield
pp. 117–150

DH
pp. 150–153

Starters
pp. 154–189

Relievers
pp. 190–217

```
╔══════════════════════════════════════════════╗
║           BASEBALL ANAGRAM #16                 ║
║                                                ║
║        Oil Palm Tour = _____?         ║
║                                                ║
║            (Answer on page 299)                ║
╚══════════════════════════════════════════════╝
```

KENT BOTTENFIELD   Age 25/R $1

One of the growing number of surplus players from the fertile Expos organization to surface elsewhere. The jury's still out on whether Montreal was
smart to let him get away.

Year Team	Lg.	G	IP	H	BB	SO	W	L	ERA	SV	Ratio
1992 Montreal	NL	10	32.1	26	11	14	1	2	2.23	1	1.144
1993 Montreal	NL	23	83.0	93	33	33	2	5	4.12	0	1.518
1993 Colorado	NL	14	76.2	86	38	30	3	5	6.10	0	1.617
Four-Year Average			95.0	103	41	39	3	6	4.59	1	1.495

RYAN BOWEN   Age 26/R $3

As was the case with other Marlins starters, the lack of run support and
overall mediocrity of the team wore Bowen down after a promising start.

Year Team	Lg.	G	IP	H	BB	SO	W	L	ERA	SV	Ratio
1991 Houston	NL	14	71.2	73	36	49	6	4	5.15	0	1.521
1992 Houston	NL	11	33.2	48	30	22	0	7	10.96	0	2.317
1993 Florida	NL	27	156.2	156	87	98	8	12	4.42	0	1.551
Four-Year Average			87.0	92	51	56	5	8	5.46	0	1.641

JEFF BRANTLEY   Age 30/R $3

Pressed into a starting role when most of the rotation ended up in a hospital
ward. He'll be more valuable if he stays in that role, what with Beck sucking
up all the save opportunities.

Year Team	Lg.	G	IP	H	BB	SO	W	L	ERA	SV	Ratio
1990 San Francisco	NL	55	86.2	77	33	61	5	3	1.56	19	1.269
1991 San Francisco	NL	67	95.1	78	52	81	5	2	2.45	15	1.364
1992 San Francisco	NL	56	91.2	67	45	86	7	7	2.95	7	1.222
1993 San Francisco	NL	53	113.2	112	46	76	5	6	4.28	0	1.390
Four-Year Average			96.0	84	44	76	6	5	2.90	10	1.317

DOUG BROCAIL   Age 26/R $1

The Padres have high hopes for this guy. Considering their track record, we
don't put much stock in that opinion.

Year Team	Lg.	G	IP	H	BB	SO	W	L	ERA	SV	Ratio
1992 San Diego	NL	3	14.0	17	5	15	0	0	6.43	0	1.571
1993 San Diego	NL	24	128.1	143	42	70	4	13	4.56	0	1.442
Four-Year Average			71.0	80	24	43	2	7	4.74	0	1.454

TOM BROWNING   Age 33/L $4

Coming off knee surgery at an age when any injury becomes a major concern, he was hammered hard early in the season. Then he was arrested with some cannabis in his car—weed that he insisted belonged to someone else. So far, so bad. But then came the highlight of his season, maybe his career, when he showed up on a rooftop outside Wrigley Field—in uniform, during a game—to watch the ball game from the best seats *not* in the house. Sure, he was fined and suspended. But holy Harry Carey, what a sublime stunt! When you saw the highlight tape of him up there beyond the right-field wall, hanging out and watching the game, didn't it make your heart sing? Only in baseball. Only at Wrigley.

Year Team	Lg.	G	IP	H	BB	SO	W	L	ERA	SV	Ratio
1990 Cincinnati	NL	35	227.2	235	52	99	15	9	3.80	0	1.261
1991 Cincinnati	NL	36	230.1	241	56	115	14	14	4.18	0	1.289
1992 Cincinnati	NL	16	87.0	108	28	33	6	5	5.07	0	1.563
1993 Cincinnati	NL	21	114.0	159	20	53	7	7	4.74	0	1.570
Four-Year Average			164.0	186	39	75	11	9	4.26	0	1.364

JOHN BURKETT   Age 29/R $18

In the past we've been Burkett debunkers, routinely poo-pooing his success and insisting it couldn't last. But he's won 61 games the last four years, so maybe we've been talking through our hat. This season, after his career year to date, we're finally hopping on the Burkett bandwagon.

Year Team	Lg.	G	IP	H	BB	SO	W	L	ERA	SV	Ratio
1990 San Francisco	NL	33	204.0	201	61	118	14	7	3.79	1	1.284
1991 San Francisco	NL	36	206.2	223	60	131	12	11	4.18	0	1.369
1992 San Francisco	NL	32	189.2	194	45	107	13	9	3.84	0	1.260
1993 San Francisco	NL	34	231.2	224	40	145	22	7	3.65	0	1.140
Four-Year Average			207.0	211	52	125	15	9	3.86	0	1.260

TOM CANDIOTTI   Age 36/R $10

Only 18 decisions in 32 starts. Think about that for a minute. It's really hard to start that many games and get so few decisions. We wish we knew how he does it, and whether it matters.

Year Team	Lg.	G	IP	H	BB	SO	W	L	ERA	SV	Ratio
1990 Cleveland	AL	31	202.0	207	55	128	15	11	3.65	0	1.297
1991 Cleveland	AL	15	108.1	88	28	86	7	6	2.24	0	1.071
1991 Toronto	AL	19	129.2	114	45	81	6	7	2.98	0	1.226
1992 Los Angeles	NL	32	203.2	177	63	152	11	15	3.00	0	1.178
1993 Los Angeles	NL	33	213.2	192	71	155	8	10	3.12	0	1.231
Four-Year Average			214.0	195	66	151	12	12	3.09	0	1.213

FRANK CASTILLO   Age 25/R $1

Not exactly a popular hero among Wrigley's bleacher bums.

Year Team	Lg.	G	IP	H	BB	SO	W	L	ERA	SV	Ratio
1991 Chicago	NL	18	111.2	107	33	73	6	7	4.35	0	1.254
1992 Chicago	NL	33	205.1	179	63	135	10	11	3.46	0	1.179
1993 Chicago	NL	29	141.1	162	39	84	5	8	4.84	0	1.422
Four-Year Average			152.0	149	45	97	7	9	4.10	0	1.272

STEVE COOKE
Age 24/L   **$8**

There are certain baseball people in whom we have unbounded faith. One of them is Pirates pitching coach Ray Miller, who says that this lefthander will someday be good for at least 15 wins a year . . . that he has the tools to make this happen very soon . . . and that it might indeed be this year. That's good enough for us.

Year Team	Lg.	G	IP	H	BB	SO	W	L	ERA	SV	Ratio
1992 Pittsburgh	NL	11	23.0	22	4	10	2	0	3.52	1	1.130
1993 Pittsburgh	NL	32	210.2	207	59	132	10	10	3.89	0	1.263
Four-Year Average			116.0	115	32	71	6	5	3.85	1	1.250

RHEAL CORMIER
Age 26/L   **$4**

A control pitcher who the Cardinals think can be a solid contributor, But they're skeptical about him becoming the Rheal deal. By the way, with a moniker like that, why isn't he pitching in Montreal?

Year Team	Lg.	G	IP	H	BB	SO	W	L	ERA	SV	Ratio
1991 St. Louis	NL	11	67.2	74	8	38	4	5	4.12	0	1.212
1992 St. Louis	NL	31	186.0	194	33	117	10	10	3.68	0	1.220
1993 St. Louis	NL	38	145.1	163	27	75	7	6	4.33	0	1.307
Four-Year Average			132.0	144	23	77	7	7	3.99	0	1.251

JIM DESHAIES
Age 33/L   **$3**

Has left arm, will travel.

Year Team	Lg.	G	IP	H	BB	SO	W	L	ERA	SV	Ratio
1990 Houston	NL	34	209.1	186	84	119	7	12	3.78	0	1.290
1991 Houston	NL	28	161.0	156	72	98	5	12	4.98	0	1.416
1992 San Diego	NL	15	96.0	92	33	46	4	7	3.28	0	1.302
1993 Minnesota	AL	27	167.1	159	51	80	11	13	4.41	0	1.255
1993 San Francisco	NL	5	17.0	24	6	5	2	2	4.24	0	1.765
Four-Year Average			162.0	154	62	87	7	12	4.18	0	1.326

DOUG DRABEK
Age 31/R   **$20**

No one can figure out what happened to him last year. Maybe he was trying too hard to live up to the big contract. Maybe he was pressing in front of the hometown crowd. We prefer to dismiss it as just one of those off years every good player is entitled to once in his career. Accordingly, we're prepared to bet the farm that the real Doug Drabek will be back this year.

Year Team	Lg.	G	IP	H	BB	SO	W	L	ERA	SV	Ratio
1990 Pittsburgh	NL	33	231.1	190	56	131	22	6	2.76	0	1.063
1991 Pittsburgh	NL	35	234.2	245	62	142	15	14	3.07	0	1.308
1992 Pittsburgh	NL	34	256.2	218	54	177	15	11	2.77	0	1.060
1993 Houston	NL	34	237.2	242	60	157	9	18	3.79	0	1.271
Four-Year Average			240.0	224	58	152	15	12	3.09	0	1.174

Catchers
pp. 59-73

Corners
pp. 73-95

Infield
pp. 95-116

Outfield
pp. 117-150

DH
pp. 150-153

Starters
pp. 154-189

Relievers
pp. 190-217

JEFF FASSERO　　　　　　　　　　　　Age 31/L　　$14

Desperate for starters, the Expos wandered down into their bullpen and, *mon dieu*, look what they found! This is good news all around: Fassero is a whole lot more valuable as the number two man behind Ken Hill than as the number two man behind John Wetteland.

Year Team	Lg.	G	IP	H	BB	SO	W	L	ERA	SV	Ratio
1991 Montreal	NL	51	55.1	39	17	42	2	5	2.44	8	1.012
1992 Montreal	NL	70	85.2	81	34	63	8	7	2.84	1	1.342
1993 Montreal	NL	56	149.2	119	54	140	12	5	2.29	1	1.156
Four-Year Average			96.0	80	35	82	7	6	2.48	3	1.184

SID FERNANDEZ　　　　　　　　　　　Age 31/L　　$13

In a rare quiet moment late last summer, Dallas the Large was analyzing the Mets' future, such as it is. When he got to El Sid, the team's Designated Yeller put it in a nutshell. "Hell, everyone knows he could break down any time, but where are we going to go out and find a better arm?" Indeed. In Camden Yards, there will be the same uncertainty. Cross your fingers that he doesn't tear the bilateral cruciate pulley string in his funny bone while hefting a slab of Boog's ribs.

Year Team	Lg.	G	IP	H	BB	SO	W	L	ERA	SV	Ratio
1990 New York	NL	30	179.1	130	67	181	9	14	3.46	0	1.099
1991 New York	NL	8	44.0	36	9	31	1	3	2.86	0	1.023
1992 New York	NL	32	214.2	162	67	193	14	11	2.73	0	1.067
1993 New York	NL	18	119.2	82	36	81	5	6	2.93	0	0.986
Four-Year Average			139.0	103	45	122	7	9	3.02	0	1.056

TOM GLAVINE　　　　　　　　　　　　Age 28/L　　$24

Others throw harder, strike out more batters, allow fewer hits. But no one is a better competitor. Before Greg Maddux came along, Glavine was The Man. Now he is The Co-Man.

Year Team	Lg.	G	IP	H	BB	SO	W	L	ERA	SV	Ratio
1990 Atlanta	NL	33	214.1	232	78	129	10	12	4.28	0	1.446
1991 Atlanta	NL	34	246.2	201	69	192	20	11	2.55	0	1.095
1992 Atlanta	NL	33	225.0	197	70	129	20	8	2.76	0	1.187
1993 Atlanta	NL	36	239.1	236	90	120	22	6	3.20	0	1.362
Four-Year Average			231.0	217	77	143	18	9	3.17	0	1.268

DWIGHT GOODEN　　　　　　　　　　Age 29/R　　$13

New Yorkers have this problem: they remember Gooden when he was Doctor K. He's somebody else now. A smarter pitcher, one who uses his head as well as his arm. A grownup, no longer a wonderchild. But in the top of the ninth, when he gets two strikes on a power hitter with runners in scoring position, Mets fans get on their feet and start yelling like crazy for Doctor K to pay one more house call. And sometimes he does.

Year Team	Lg.	G	IP	H	BB	SO	W	L	ERA	SV	Ratio
1990 New York	NL	34	232.2	229	70	223	19	7	3.83	0	1.285
1991 New York	NL	27	190.0	185	56	150	13	7	3.60	0	1.268
1992 New York	NL	31	206.0	197	70	145	10	13	3.67	0	1.296
1993 New York	NL	29	208.2	188	61	149	12	15	3.45	0	1.193
Four-Year Average			209.0	200	64	167	14	11	3.64	0	1.261

Catchers
pp. 59–73

Corners
pp. 73–95

Infield
pp. 95–116

Outfield
pp. 117–150

DH
pp. 150–153

Starters
pp. 154–189

Relievers
pp. 190–217

TOMMY GREENE Age 26/R $14

In his first outing against the Braves in the playoffs last fall he looked like a deer cornered by a mountain lion. Pitched like one, too. But in his second turn in the playoffs, he was the lion. Then, in the World Series, the deer came back. That's the book on Greene: great stuff, but prone to occasional collapse. After a stretch when he seemed afraid to throw the ball over the plate, a couple of his teammates ripped him for being gutless in an effort to shake him up. Something worked. Should keep on winning now that he's proved to himself that he can.

Year	Team	Lg.	G	IP	H	BB	SO	W	L	ERA	SV	Ratio
1990	Atlanta	NL	5	12.1	14	9	4	1	0	8.03	0	1.865
1990	Philadelphia	NL	10	39.0	36	17	17	2	3	4.15	0	1.359
1991	Philadelphia	NL	36	207.2	177	66	154	13	7	3.38	0	1.170
1992	Philadelphia	NL	13	64.1	75	34	39	3	3	5.32	0	1.694
1993	Philadelphia	NL	31	200.0	175	62	167	16	4	3.42	0	1.185
Four-Year Average				130.0	119	47	95	9	4	3.80	0	1.271

KEVIN GROSS Age 32/R $7

Stood tall on the last day of the season and sent the Giants home empty-handed, but he's still your quintessential .500 pitcher who gives lousy ratio.

Year	Team	Lg.	G	IP	H	BB	SO	W	L	ERA	SV	Ratio
1990	Montreal	NL	31	163.1	171	65	111	9	12	4.57	0	1.445
1991	Los Angeles	NL	46	115.2	123	50	95	10	11	3.58	3	1.496
1992	Los Angeles	NL	34	204.2	182	77	158	8	13	3.17	0	1.265
1993	Los Angeles	NL	33	202.1	224	74	150	13	13	4.14	0	1.473
Four-Year Average				171.0	175	67	129	10	12	3.86	1	1.408

JOSE GUZMAN Age 30/R $6

Larry Himes, the arrogant scrooge who runs the Cubs, smugly predicted that signing this guy, along with a gaggle of other free-agent pitchers, would more than make up for the loss of Greg Maddux. If you believed him, then we have some nice real estate in downtown Mogadishu you might like to buy.

Year	Team	Lg.	G	IP	H	BB	SO	W	L	ERA	SV	Ratio
1991	Texas	AL	25	169.2	152	84	125	13	7	3.08	0	1.391
1992	Texas	AL	33	224.0	229	73	179	16	11	3.66	0	1.348
1993	Chicago	NL	30	191.0	188	74	163	12	10	4.34	0	1.372
Four-Year Average				194.0	190	77	156	14	9	3.71	0	1.368

CHRIS HAMMOND Age 28/L $4

If you want an utterly average lefthander who holds down a job in a major league starting rotation only because said rotation belongs to an expansion team, then here's your man.

Year	Team	Lg.	G	IP	H	BB	SO	W	L	ERA	SV	Ratio
1990	Cincinnati	NL	3	11.1	13	12	4	0	2	6.35	0	2.206
1991	Cincinnati	NL	20	99.2	92	48	50	7	7	4.06	0	1.405
1992	Cincinnati	NL	28	147.1	149	55	79	7	10	4.21	0	1.385
1993	Florida	NL	32	191.0	207	66	108	11	12	4.66	0	1.429
Four-Year Average				112.0	115	45	60	6	8	4.43	0	1.429

MIKE HARKEY   Age 27/R $5

How can a guy who looks so big and strong be so fragile?

Year Team	Lg.	G	IP	H	BB	SO	W	L	ERA	SV	Ratio
1990 Chicago	NL	27	173.2	153	59	94	12	6	3.26	0	1.221
1991 Chicago	NL	4	18.2	21	6	15	0	2	5.30	0	1.446
1992 Chicago	NL	7	38.0	34	15	21	4	0	1.89	0	1.289
1993 Chicago	NL	28	157.1	187	43	67	10	10	5.26	0	1.462
Four-Year Average			96.0	99	31	49	7	5	4.04	0	1.336

PETE HARNISCH   Age 27/R $18

Pretty good year for a guy the Astros had pegged as the number three man in their rotation. Not to appear immodest, but we told you here last year to stick with him. Did you listen?

Year Team	Lg.	G	IP	H	BB	SO	W	L	ERA	SV	Ratio
1990 Baltimore	AL	31	188.2	189	86	122	11	11	4.34	0	1.458
1991 Houston	NL	33	216.2	169	83	172	12	9	2.70	0	1.163
1992 Houston	NL	34	206.2	182	64	164	9	10	3.70	0	1.190
1993 Houston	NL	33	217.2	171	79	185	16	9	2.98	0	1.149
Four-Year Average			207.0	178	78	161	12	10	3.40	0	1.233

GREG W. HARRIS   Age 30/R $3

A logical component of a trade between the miserly Padres and the pitching-putrid Rockies.

Year Team	Lg.	G	IP	H	BB	SO	W	L	ERA	SV	Ratio
1990 San Diego	NL	73	117.1	92	49	97	8	8	2.30	9	1.202
1991 San Diego	NL	20	133.0	116	27	95	9	5	2.23	0	1.075
1992 San Diego	NL	20	118.0	113	35	66	4	8	4.12	0	1.254
1993 San Diego	NL	22	152.0	151	39	83	10	9	3.67	0	1.250
1993 Colorado	NL	13	73.1	88	30	40	1	8	6.50	0	1.609
Four-Year Average			148.0	140	45	95	8	10	3.52	2	1.247

OREL HERSHISER   Age 35/R $9

If he can resist the temptation to break off a slider on a double play ball, we say stick him at third for half a season and see what he can do. We already know that he swings the bat better than any Dodger third baseman since Ron Cey. And if he kicks a few learning the position, so what? He will blend in well with the rest of the LA infield.

Year Team	Lg.	G	IP	H	BB	SO	W	L	ERA	SV	Ratio
1990 Los Angeles	NL	4	25.1	26	4	16	1	1	4.26	0	1.184
1991 Los Angeles	NL	21	112.0	112	32	73	7	2	3.46	0	1.286
1992 Los Angeles	NL	33	210.2	209	69	130	10	15	3.67	0	1.320
1993 Los Angeles	NL	33	215.2	201	72	141	12	14	3.59	0	1.266
Four-Year Average			140.0	137	44	90	8	8	3.62	0	1.286

GREG HIBBARD   Age 29/L $9

Another one of those new Cubs pitchers last year that Larry Himes assured us would make everyone forget Greg Maddux. Well, every fourth game last season Hibbard got hammered. Really mauled. Enough to make you nauseous just looking at the box score. And that's if you *didn't* own him. But the wins were nice, so if you own him in an Ultra league, consider sitting him down for a week the first time he strings together three good outings.

Year Team	Lg.	G	IP	H	BB	SO	W	L	ERA	SV	Ratio
1990 Chicago	AL	33	211.0	202	55	92	14	9	3.16	0	1.218
1991 Chicago	AL	32	194.0	196	57	71	11	11	4.31	0	1.304
1992 Chicago	AL	31	176.0	187	57	69	10	7	4.40	1	1.386
1993 Chicago	NL	31	191.0	209	47	82	15	11	3.96	0	1.340
Four-Year Average			193.0	199	54	79	13	10	3.93	0	1.308

BRYAN HICKERSON   Age 30/L $3

When the injury bug bit the Giants, they pressed Hickerson into the rotation, and he was good enough to make Bud Black and Trevor Wilson expendable. This is not exactly the same as putting Koufax and Drysdale out of work, but beggars can't be choosers.

Year Team	Lg.	G	IP	H	BB	SO	W	L	ERA	SV	Ratio
1991 San Francisco	NL	17	50.0	53	17	43	2	2	3.60	0	1.400
1992 San Francisco	NL	61	87.1	74	21	68	5	3	3.09	0	1.088
1993 San Francisco	NL	47	120.1	137	39	69	7	5	4.26	0	1.463
Four-Year Average			85.0	88	26	60	5	3	3.74	0	1.323

KEN HILL   Age 28/R $20

Pretend last year didn't happen. He pitched for three-fourths of the season with a bad groin injury that limited his stuff to 50% efficiency. Assuming he didn't wile away the winter hours practicing his power frug, he should come back fit and ready to resume his position as king of the Hills.

Year Team	Lg.	G	IP	H	BB	SO	W	L	ERA	SV	Ratio
1990 St. Louis	NL	17	78.2	79	33	58	5	6	5.49	0	1.424
1991 St. Louis	NL	30	181.1	147	67	121	11	10	3.57	0	1.180
1992 Montreal	NL	33	218.0	187	75	150	16	9	2.68	0	1.202
1993 Montreal	NL	28	183.2	163	74	90	9	7	3.23	0	1.290
Four-Year Average			165.0	144	62	105	10	8	3.41	0	1.247

ERIC HILLMAN   Age 27/L $1

One of the few Mets taller than Dallas Green.

Year Team	Lg.	G	IP	H	BB	SO	W	L	ERA	SV	Ratio
1992 New York	NL	11	52.1	67	10	16	2	2	5.33	0	1.471
1993 New York	NL	27	145.0	173	24	60	2	9	3.97	0	1.359
Four-Year Average			98.0	120	17	38	2	6	4.33	0	1.389

CHARLIE HOUGH   Age 46/R $2

How do you tell people you're building for tomorrow and then trot out some guy from yesterday every fifth day?

Year Team	Lg.	G	IP	H	BB	SO	W	L	ERA	SV	Ratio
1990 Texas	AL	32	218.2	190	119	114	12	12	4.07	0	1.413
1991 Chicago	AL	31	199.1	167	94	107	9	10	4.02	0	1.309
1992 Chicago	AL	27	176.1	160	66	76	7	12	3.93	0	1.282
1993 Florida	NL	34	204.1	202	71	126	9	16	4.27	0	1.336
Four-Year Average			199.0	180	88	106	9	13	4.08	0	1.339

Catchers
pp. 59–73

Corners
pp. 73–95

Infield
pp. 95–116

Outfield
pp. 117–150

DH
pp. 150–153

Starters
pp. 154–189

Relievers
pp. 190–217

BRUCE HURST
Age 36/L **$5**

Many things in this complex world will always be a mystery to us, and we can accept that. But one conundrum keeping us up at night is why an expansion team would trade for a 36-year-old pitcher with a huge contract who was shelved most of the season with serious arm trouble. Maybe it has something to do with the fact that Hurst is light years better than anyone else the Rockies can send out there—when he is healthy. The salary is pegged on the likelihood that he won't be.

Year Team	Lg.	G	IP	H	BB	SO	W	L	ERA	SV	Ratio
1990 San Diego	NL	33	223.2	188	63	162	11	9	3.14	0	1.122
1991 San Diego	NL	31	221.2	201	59	141	15	8	3.29	0	1.173
1992 San Diego	NL	32	217.1	223	51	131	14	9	3.85	0	1.261
1993 San Diego	NL	2	4.1	9	3	3	0	1	12.46	0	2.769
1993 Colorado	NL	3	8.2	6	3	6	0	1	5.19	0	1.038
Four-Year Average			168.0	157	45	111	10	7	3.50	0	1.193

DANNY JACKSON
Age 32/L **$7**

Gave everyone a peek of his arrogant persona at the height of the Phillies' euphoric summer when he publicly ripped the Veterans Stadium ground crew for the condition of the pitcher's mound. Still, he stayed healthy all season, which made him a shoo-in for the Marcus Welby Award.

Year Team	Lg.	G	IP	H	BB	SO	W	L	ERA	SV	Ratio
1990 Cincinnati	NL	22	117.1	119	40	76	6	6	3.61	0	1.355
1991 Chicago	NL	17	70.2	89	48	31	1	5	6.75	0	1.939
1992 Chicago	NL	19	113.0	117	48	51	4	9	4.22	0	1.460
1992 Pittsburgh	NL	15	88.1	94	29	46	4	4	3.36	0	1.392
1993 Philadelphia	NL	32	210.1	214	80	120	12	11	3.77	0	1.398
Four-Year Average			149.0	158	61	81	7	9	4.11	0	1.464

DARRYL KILE
Age 25/R **$15**

Throw strikes and become an All-Star. Who knew it was that simple?

Year Team	Lg.	G	IP	H	BB	SO	W	L	ERA	SV	Ratio
1991 Houston	NL	37	153.2	144	84	100	7	11	3.69	0	1.484
1992 Houston	NL	22	125.1	124	63	90	5	10	3.95	0	1.492
1993 Houston	NL	32	171.2	152	69	141	15	8	3.51	0	1.287
Four-Year Average			150.0	140	72	110	9	10	3.69	0	1.411

GREG MADDUX
Age 27/R **$25**

The Man.

Year Team	Lg.	G	IP	H	BB	SO	W	L	ERA	SV	Ratio
1990 Chicago	NL	35	237.0	242	71	144	15	15	3.46	0	1.321
1991 Chicago	NL	37	263.0	232	66	198	15	11	3.35	0	1.133
1992 Chicago	NL	35	268.0	201	70	199	20	11	2.18	0	1.011
1993 Atlanta	NL	36	267.0	228	52	197	20	10	2.36	0	1.049
Four-Year Average			258.0	226	65	185	18	12	2.82	0	1.123

DENNIS MARTINEZ 　　　　　　　　　　　Age 38/R 　　　$18

Okay, El Presidente can be a little headstrong. Hey, he's earned the right.

Year Team	Lg.	G	IP	H	BB	SO	W	L	ERA	SV	Ratio
1990 Montreal	NL	32	226.0	191	49	156	10	11	2.95	0	1.062
1991 Montreal	NL	31	222.0	187	62	123	14	11	2.39	0	1.122
1992 Montreal	NL	32	226.1	172	60	147	16	11	2.47	0	1.025
1993 Montreal	NL	35	224.2	211	64	138	15	9	3.85	1	1.224
Four-Year Average			224.0	190	59	141	14	11	2.91	0	1.108

RAMON MARTINEZ 　　　　　　　　　　　Age 26/R 　　　$6

His younger brother has much better stuff. In truth, at far too early an age, Martinez the Elder has become no better than a fifth starter.

Year Team	Lg.	G	IP	H	BB	SO	W	L	ERA	SV	Ratio
1990 Los Angeles	NL	33	234.1	191	67	223	20	6	2.92	0	1.101
1991 Los Angeles	NL	33	220.1	190	69	150	17	13	3.27	0	1.175
1992 Los Angeles	NL	25	150.2	141	69	101	8	11	4.00	0	1.394
1993 Los Angeles	NL	32	211.2	202	104	127	10	12	3.44	0	1.446
Four-Year Average			204.0	181	77	150	14	11	3.35	0	1.264

MIKE MORGAN 　　　　　　　　　　　Age 34/R 　　　$8

When Larry Himes arrogantly drove Greg Maddux out of Chicago, he told all the ignorant people who questioned his baseball acumen that Morgan was fully capable of being a number one starter. Right. A guy who's a zillion games below .500 in his career being compared to the game's most consistent starting pitcher. The fact that the Tribune Company hasn't fired Himes should be reason enough to read the *Sun-Times* exclusively when you're in Chicago.

Year Team	Lg.	G	IP	H	BB	SO	W	L	ERA	SV	Ratio
1990 Los Angeles	NL	33	211.0	216	60	106	11	15	3.75	0	1.308
1991 Los Angeles	NL	34	236.1	197	61	140	14	10	2.78	1	1.092
1992 Chicago	NL	34	240.0	203	79	123	16	8	2.55	0	1.175
1993 Chicago	NL	32	207.2	206	74	111	10	15	4.03	0	1.348
Four-Year Average			223.0	206	69	120	13	12	3.24	0	1.225

TERRY MULHOLLAND 　　　　　　　　　Age 31/L 　　　$13

Maybe he should lose the facial hair. Not because we have anything against it in principle; it's just that it makes him look a little like Ming the Magnificent in the old Flash Gordon serial. On the other hand, maybe it's okay, so long as he doesn't shave his head. Among the nut cases that populated the Phillies clubhouse in their magical year, Mulholland was the stablest of citizens. Tough competitor.

Year Team	Lg.	G	IP	H	BB	SO	W	L	ERA	SV	Ratio
1990 Philadelphia	NL	33	180.2	172	42	75	9	10	3.34	0	1.185
1991 Philadelphia	NL	34	232.0	231	49	142	16	13	3.61	0	1.207
1992 Philadelphia	NL	32	229.0	227	46	125	13	11	3.81	0	1.192
1993 Philadelphia	NL	29	191.0	177	40	116	12	9	3.25	0	1.136
Four-Year Average			208.0	202	44	115	13	11	3.52	0	1.182

Catchers
pp. 59–73

Corners
pp. 73–95

Infield
pp. 95–116

Outfield
pp. 117–150

DH
pp. 150–153

Starters
pp. 154–189

Relievers
pp. 190–217

CHRIS NABHOLZ
Age 27/L $3

Had his moments.

Year Team	Lg.	G	IP	H	BB	SO	W	L	ERA	SV	Ratio
1990 Montreal	NL	11	70.0	43	32	53	6	2	2.83	0	1.071
1991 Montreal	NL	24	153.2	134	57	99	8	7	3.63	0	1.243
1992 Montreal	NL	32	195.0	176	74	130	11	12	3.32	0	1.282
1993 Montreal	NL	26	116.2	100	63	74	9	8	4.09	0	1.397
Four-Year Average			133.0	113	57	89	9	7	3.51	0	1.268

DAVID NIED
Age 25/R $5

Colorado put a load of pressure on the kid, not only by making him the expansion draft's top pick (and de facto franchise player) but also by making him their number one starting pitcher. The kid must have felt like he had the Rockies on his shoulders—the team *and* the mountains. Supposedly he tried to gut out a sore arm and pitched for a week without telling anybody about it. That led to a long stint on the DL and a washed out season. Here's hoping he recovers fully, because he has loads of ability to go with his grit. No wonder, he's a product of the Braves' system.

Year Team	Lg.	G	IP	H	BB	SO	W	L	ERA	SV	Ratio
1992 Atlanta	NL	6	23.0	10	5	19	3	0	1.17	0	0.652
1993 Colorado	NL	16	87.0	99	42	46	5	9	5.17	0	1.621
Four-Year Average			55.0	55	24	33	4	5	4.34	0	1.418

DONOVAN OSBORNE
Age 24/L $5

Two virtually identical seasons. Do we detect a pattern?

Year Team	Lg.	G	IP	H	BB	SO	W	L	ERA	SV	Ratio
1992 St. Louis	NL	34	179.0	193	38	104	11	9	3.77	0	1.291
1993 St. Louis	NL	26	155.2	153	47	83	10	7	3.76	0	1.285
Four-Year Average			167.0	173	43	94	11	8	3.77	0	1.288

MARK PORTUGAL
Age 31/R $12

We're a little skittish about lights-out numbers in free-agent years.

Year Team	Lg.	G	IP	H	BB	SO	W	L	ERA	SV	Ratio
1990 Houston	NL	32	196.2	187	67	136	11	10	3.62	0	1.292
1991 Houston	NL	32	168.1	163	59	120	10	12	4.49	1	1.319
1992 Houston	NL	18	101.1	76	41	62	6	3	2.66	0	1.155
1993 Houston	NL	33	208.0	194	77	131	18	4	2.77	0	1.303
Four-Year Average			168.0	155	61	112	11	7	3.43	0	1.281

TIM PUGH
Age 27/R $1

His favorite pitch is the circle change. The trouble is that in too many of his starts, the Reds had to circle the wagons.

Year Team	Lg.	G	IP	H	BB	SO	W	L	ERA	SV	Ratio
1992 Cincinnati	NL	7	45.1	47	13	18	4	2	2.58	0	1.324
1993 Cincinnati	NL	31	164.1	200	59	94	10	15	5.26	0	1.576
Four-Year Average			104.0	124	36	56	7	9	4.68	0	1.522

PAT RAPP
Age 26/R   **$1**

The Marlins think he is a good catch.

Year	Team	Lg.	G	IP	H	BB	SO	W	L	ERA	SV	Ratio
1992	San Francisco	NL	3	10.0	8	6	3	0	2	7.20	0	1.400
1993	Florida	NL	16	94.0	101	39	57	4	6	4.02	0	1.489
Four-Year Average				52.0	55	23	30	2	4	4.33	0	1.481

ARMANDO REYNOSO
Age 27/R   **$4**

It's not easy being a pitcher in Denver, but he did a bang-up good job. No wonder, he's a product of the Braves system.

Year	Team	Lg.	G	IP	H	BB	SO	W	L	ERA	SV	Ratio
1991	Atlanta	NL	6	23.1	26	10	10	2	1	6.17	0	1.543
1992	Atlanta	NL	3	7.2	11	2	2	1	0	4.70	1	1.696
1993	Colorado	NL	30	189.0	206	63	117	12	11	4.00	0	1.423
Four-Year Average				73.0	81	25	43	5	4	4.25	0	1.446

JOSE RIJO
Age 28/R   **$20**

Though the W-L record didn't reflect it, there wasn't a better pitcher on earth after the All-Star break.

Year	Team	Lg.	G	IP	H	BB	SO	W	L	ERA	SV	Ratio
1990	Cincinnati	NL	29	197.0	151	78	152	14	8	2.70	0	1.162
1991	Cincinnati	NL	30	204.1	165	55	172	15	6	2.51	0	1.077
1992	Cincinnati	NL	33	211.0	185	44	171	15	10	2.56	0	1.085
1993	Cincinnati	NL	36	257.1	218	62	227	14	9	2.48	0	1.088
Four-Year Average				217.0	180	60	181	15	8	2.56	0	1.102

BEN RIVERA
Age 25/R   **$4**

He drives you crazy with his bouts of wildness, but we predict that someday Big Ben will be a major force in the Phillies' rotation. No wonder, he's a product of the Braves system.

Year	Team	Lg.	G	IP	H	BB	SO	W	L	ERA	SV	Ratio
1992	Atlanta	NL	8	15.1	21	13	11	0	1	4.70	0	2.217
1992	Philadelphia	NL	20	102.0	78	32	66	7	3	2.82	0	1.078
1993	Philadelphia	NL	30	163.0	175	85	123	13	9	5.02	0	1.595
Four-Year Average				140.0	137	65	100	10	7	4.21	0	1.441

KIRK REUTER
Age 23/L   **$14**

A veteran scout, wise beyond his years and not given to hyperbole, came away after watching Reuter and exclaimed, "That kid has the best location with his fastball I've ever seen. He's gonna be the Randy Jones of the 1990s. He's a bleeping machine." Good enough for us.

Year	Team	Lg.	G	IP	H	BB	SO	W	L	ERA	SV	Ratio
1993	Montreal	NL	14	85.2	85	18	31	8	0	2.73	0	1.202
Four-Year Average				85.0	85	18	31	8	0	2.73	0	1.202

BRET SABERHAGEN
Age 29/R   **$16**

The thing with the bleach and the squirt gun was nice. So was the firecracker in the clubhouse. Ditto all the lying and covering up. What an embarrassment. What a team. And what a pitcher—when he is healthy. Thus, you

Catchers
pp. 59-73

Corners
pp. 73-95

Infield
pp. 95-116

Outfield
pp. 117-150

DH
pp. 150-153

Starters
pp. 154-189

Relievers
pp. 190-217

will be faced with the torturous dilemma of whether to grab him or take the moral high ground and pass. We say grab him.

Year Team	Lg.	G	IP	H	BB	SO	W	L	ERA	SV	Ratio
1990 Kansas City	AL	20	135.0	146	28	87	5	9	3.27	0	1.289
1991 Kansas City	AL	28	196.1	165	45	136	13	8	3.07	0	1.070
1992 New York	NL	17	97.2	84	27	81	3	5	3.50	0	1.137
1993 New York	NL	19	139.1	131	17	93	7	7	3.29	0	1.062
Four-Year Average			142.0	132	29	99	7	7	3.25	0	1.131

SCOTT SANDERSON
Age 37/R   **$3**

We know about all those home run balls, and we know that if his location isn't perfect he's going to get pounded, and we know he's getting up in years. But Sanderson won four games for the Giants down the stretch last year, and he knows how to pitch. On a team with good outfield defense and the ability to score runs, he can get you a bucket of wins for small bucks.

Year Team	Lg.	G	IP	H	BB	SO	W	L	ERA	SV	Ratio
1990 Oakland	AL	34	206.1	205	66	128	17	11	3.88	0	1.313
1991 New York	AL	34	208.0	200	29	130	16	10	3.81	0	1.101
1992 New York	AL	33	193.1	220	64	104	12	11	4.93	0	1.469
1993 California	AL	21	135.1	153	27	66	7	11	4.46	0	1.330
1993 San Francisco	NL	11	48.2	48	7	36	4	2	3.51	0	1.130
Four-Year Average			197.0	207	48	116	14	11	4.20	0	1.287

CURT SCHILLING
Age 27/R   **$16**

He seemed to be heading south last June when Darren Daulton got in his face. It worked.

Year Team	Lg.	G	IP	H	BB	SO	W	L	ERA	SV	Ratio
1990 Baltimore	AL	35	46.0	38	19	32	1	2	2.54	3	1.239
1991 Houston	NL	56	75.2	79	39	71	3	5	3.81	8	1.559
1992 Philadelphia	NL	42	226.1	165	59	147	14	11	2.35	2	0.990
1993 Philadelphia	NL	34	235.1	234	57	186	16	7	4.02	0	1.237
Four-Year Average			145.0	129	44	109	9	6	3.22	3	1.183

FRANK SEMINARA
Age 26/R   **$1**

The best Columbia University grad pitching in the majors today. Roar, Lion, roar!

Year Team	Lg.	G	IP	H	BB	SO	W	L	ERA	SV	Ratio
1992 San Diego	NL	19	100.1	98	46	61	9	4	3.68	0	1.435
1993 San Diego	NL	18	46.1	53	21	22	3	3	4.47	0	1.597
Four-Year Average			73.0	76	34	42	6	4	3.93	0	1.486

BASEBALL ANAGRAM #17

Zen Bedding Rot = _____?

(Answer on page 299)

JOHN SMILEY   Age 29/L $12

Marge Schott spent the year frowning over all the Nazi memorabilia she could have bought with the money wasted on Smiley, who spent nearly half the season on the DL. The Reds expect him to be healthy this year. If he is, there will be smiles all around.

Year Team	Lg.	G	IP	H	BB	SO	W	L	ERA	SV	Ratio
1990 Pittsburgh	NL	26	149.1	161	36	86	9	10	4.64	0	1.319
1991 Pittsburgh	NL	33	207.2	194	44	129	20	8	3.08	0	1.146
1992 Minnesota	AL	34	241.0	205	65	163	16	9	3.21	0	1.120
1993 Cincinnati	NL	18	105.2	117	31	60	3	9	5.62	0	1.401
Four-Year Average			175.0	169	44	110	12	9	3.84	0	1.212

PETE SMITH   Age 28/R $1

Everybody's candidate to be the sleeper on the Braves staff, but nobody figured he'd go comatose. Arm trouble was at the root of his problems last year. Maybe we're nuts, but we *still* believe there's a big upside. Smart move by the Mets.

Year Team	Lg.	G	IP	H	BB	SO	W	L	ERA	SV	Ratio
1990 Atlanta	NL	13	77.0	77	24	56	5	6	4.79	0	1.312
1991 Atlanta	NL	14	48.0	48	22	29	1	3	5.06	0	1.458
1992 Atlanta	NL	12	79.0	63	28	43	7	0	2.05	0	1.152
1993 Atlanta	NL	20	90.2	92	36	53	4	8	4.37	0	1.412
Four-Year Average			73.0	70	28	45	4	4	3.97	0	1.324

ZANE SMITH   Age 33/L $9

A bargain if he's healthy. That's a very big "if," by the way.

Year Team	Lg.	G	IP	H	BB	SO	W	L	ERA	SV	Ratio
1990 Montreal	NL	22	139.1	141	41	80	6	7	3.23	0	1.306
1990 Pittsburgh	NL	11	76.0	55	9	50	6	2	1.30	0	0.842
1991 Pittsburgh	NL	35	228.0	234	29	120	16	10	3.20	0	1.154
1992 Pittsburgh	NL	23	141.0	138	19	56	8	8	3.06	0	1.113
1993 Pittsburgh	NL	14	83.0	97	22	32	3	7	4.55	0	1.434
Four-Year Average			166.0	166	30	85	10	9	3.13	0	1.176

JOHN SMOLTZ   Age 26/R $20

The ace on most staffs, he can't get better than fourth billing in Atlanta. But he led the Fearsome Foursome in strikeouts and in fewest hits per nine innings (Smoltz gave up 7.68, Cy Young Maddux 7.69). Those two facts suggest that Smoltz has serious stuff. He also led the Fab Four in walks, a fact that explains why he's still fourth banana. Some day, maybe soon, if he gains better control of his tools, he could become The Man.

Year Team	Lg.	G	IP	H	BB	SO	W	L	ERA	SV	Ratio
1990 Atlanta	NL	34	231.1	206	90	170	14	11	3.85	0	1.280
1991 Atlanta	NL	36	229.2	206	77	148	14	13	3.80	0	1.232
1992 Atlanta	NL	35	246.2	206	80	215	15	12	2.85	0	1.159
1993 Atlanta	NL	35	243.2	208	100	208	15	11	3.62	0	1.264
Four-Year Average			237.0	207	87	185	15	12	3.52	0	1.233

Catchers
pp. 59-73

Corners
pp. 73-95

Infield
pp. 95-116

Outfield
pp. 117-150

DH
pp. 150-153

Starters
pp. 154-189

Relievers
pp. 190-217

BILL SWIFT Age 32/R $21

Great name. Great year. More of the same? Yes.

Year	Team	Lg.	G	IP	H	BB	SO	W	L	ERA	SV	Ratio
1990	Seattle	AL	55	128.0	135	21	42	6	4	2.39	6	1.219
1991	Seattle	AL	71	90.1	74	26	48	1	2	1.99	17	1.107
1992	San Francisco	NL	30	164.2	144	43	77	10	4	2.08	1	1.136
1993	San Francisco	NL	34	232.2	195	55	157	21	8	2.82	0	1.074
Four-Year Average				153.0	137	36	81	10	5	2.41	6	1.126

GREG SWINDELL Age 29/L $14

Astros owner Drayton McLane, Jr., is a millionaire, not an etymologist, but you could understand it if he figured that "Swindell" and "swindle" came from the same root word.

Year	Team	Lg.	G	IP	H	BB	SO	W	L	ERA	SV	Ratio
1990	Cleveland	AL	34	214.2	245	47	135	12	9	4.40	0	1.360
1991	Cleveland	AL	33	238.0	241	31	169	9	16	3.48	0	1.143
1992	Cincinnati	NL	31	213.2	210	41	138	12	8	2.70	0	1.175
1993	Houston	NL	31	190.1	215	40	124	12	13	4.16	0	1.340
Four-Year Average				214.0	228	40	142	11	12	3.67	0	1.249

BOB TEWKSBURY Age 33/R $13

The most despicable four-letter word in his vocabulary is spelled w-a-l-k.

Year	Team	Lg.	G	IP	H	BB	SO	W	L	ERA	SV	Ratio
1990	St. Louis	NL	28	145.1	151	15	50	10	9	3.47	1	1.142
1991	St. Louis	NL	30	191.0	206	38	75	11	12	3.25	0	1.277
1992	St. Louis	NL	33	233.0	217	20	91	16	5	2.16	0	1.017
1993	St. Louis	NL	32	213.2	258	20	97	17	10	3.83	0	1.301
Four-Year Average				195.0	208	23	78	14	9	3.13	0	1.181

RANDY TOMLIN Age 27/L $7

The Pirates think they can again become contenders if this bedeviling lefty with the Vulcan changeup gets healthy and stays that way. And the Pirates also think they can become contenders again if . . .

Year	Team	Lg.	G	IP	H	BB	SO	W	L	ERA	SV	Ratio
1990	Pittsburgh	NL	12	77.2	62	12	42	4	4	2.55	0	0.953
1991	Pittsburgh	NL	31	175.0	170	54	104	8	7	2.98	0	1.280
1992	Pittsburgh	NL	35	208.2	226	42	90	14	9	3.41	0	1.284
1993	Pittsburgh	NL	18	98.1	109	15	44	4	8	4.85	0	1.261
Four-Year Average				139.0	142	31	70	8	7	3.41	0	1.233

PAUL WAGNER Age 26/R $4

. . . can continue to make progress and learn how to be consistent with his excellent stuff. And the Pirates also think they can become contenders again if . . .

Year	Team	Lg.	G	IP	H	BB	SO	W	L	ERA	SV	Ratio
1992	Pittsburgh	NL	6	13.0	9	5	5	2	0	0.69	0	1.077
1993	Pittsburgh	NL	44	141.1	143	42	114	8	8	4.27	2	1.309
Four-Year Average				77.0	76	24	60	5	4	3.97	1	1.289

TIM WAKEFIELD   Age 27/R $4

... rediscovers the knuckleball that straightened out last year with such disasterous results that he was shipped down to the boondocks. And the Pirates also think they can become contenders again if ...

Year Team	Lg.	G	IP	H	BB	SO	W	L	ERA	SV	Ratio
1992 Pittsburgh	NL	13	92.0	76	35	51	8	1	2.15	0	1.207
1993 Pittsburgh	NL	24	128.1	145	75	59	6	11	5.61	0	1.714
Four-Year Average			110.0	111	55	55	7	6	4.17	0	1.502

BOB WALK   Age 37/R $5

... is no longer their most reliable starting pitcher by default, as he was at times last year. Do you get the feeling that maybe the Pirates aren't quite ready to become contenders any time soon?

Year Team	Lg.	G	IP	H	BB	SO	W	L	ERA	SV	Ratio
1990 Pittsburgh	NL	26	129.2	136	36	73	7	5	3.75	1	1.326
1991 Pittsburgh	NL	25	115.0	104	35	67	9	2	3.60	0	1.209
1992 Pittsburgh	NL	36	135.0	132	43	60	10	6	3.20	2	1.296
1993 Pittsburgh	NL	32	187.0	214	70	80	13	14	5.68	0	1.519
Four-Year Average			141.0	147	46	70	10	7	4.22	1	1.359

ALLEN WATSON   Age 23/L $4

A kid from New York who showed enough last year to make the Cardinals believe he might be a big winner someday. We have a hunch that might happen this year. But like the Cards, we are not willing to put our money where our mouth is.

Year Team	Lg.	G	IP	H	BB	SO	W	L	ERA	SV	Ratio
1993 St. Louis	NL	16	86.0	90	28	49	6	7	4.60	0	1.372
Four-Year Average			86.0	90	28	49	6	7	4.60	0	1.372

WALLY WHITEHURST   Age 29/R $1

The fifth starter in the San Diego rotation. Need we say more?

Year Team	Lg.	G	IP	H	BB	SO	W	L	ERA	SV	Ratio
1990 New York	NL	38	65.2	63	9	46	1	0	3.29	2	1.096
1991 New York	NL	36	133.1	142	25	87	7	12	4.18	1	1.253
1992 New York	NL	44	97.0	99	33	70	3	9	3.62	0	1.361
1993 San Diego	NL	21	105.2	109	30	57	4	7	3.83	0	1.315
Four-Year Average			100.0	103	24	65	4	7	3.81	1	1.270

TREVOR WILSON   Age 27/L $6

A Giants pitcher with arm trouble? What a surprise.

Year Team	Lg.	G	IP	H	BB	SO	W	L	ERA	SV	Ratio
1990 San Francisco	NL	27	110.1	87	49	66	8	7	4.00	0	1.233
1991 San Francisco	NL	44	202.0	173	77	139	13	11	3.56	0	1.238
1992 San Francisco	NL	26	154.0	152	64	88	8	14	4.21	0	1.403
1993 San Francisco	NL	22	110.0	110	40	57	7	5	3.60	0	1.364
Four-Year Average			144.0	131	58	88	9	9	3.83	0	1.305

TIM WORRELL

Age 26/R $1

The Padres think he has potential. The Padres also think they made some pretty shrewd trades.

Year Team	Lg.	G	IP	H	BB	SO	W	L	ERA	SV	Ratio
1993 San Diego	NL	21	100.2	104	43	52	2	7	4.92	0	1.460
Four-Year Average			100.0	104	43	52	2	7	4.92	0	1.460

ANTHONY YOUNG

Age 28/R $1

Look at the 3.77 ERA. Now look at the 1–16 W-L record. No, they don't compute. We're not saying he's hexed or anything, but we do advise you not to fly in the same airplane with him.

Year Team	Lg.	G	IP	H	BB	SO	W	L	ERA	SV	Ratio
1991 New York	NL	10	49.1	48	12	20	2	5	3.10	0	1.216
1992 New York	NL	52	121.0	134	31	64	2	14	4.17	15	1.364
1993 New York	NL	39	100.1	103	42	62	1	16	3.77	3	1.445
Four-Year Average			90.0	95	28	49	2	12	3.82	6	1.367

AMERICAN LEAGUE

JIM ABBOTT

Age 26/L $12

The no-hitter was great. And we all know about his courage and character. But he stunk up the joint for much of last season. His problems had their root in groceries, not grit. Pinstripes are slimming, but a lot of scouts and opposing managers think he needs to drop 15 pounds to regain his good velocity.

Year Team	Lg.	G	IP	H	BB	SO	W	L	ERA	SV	Ratio
1990 California	AL	33	211.2	246	72	105	10	14	4.51	0	1.502
1991 California	AL	34	243.0	222	73	158	18	11	2.89	0	1.214
1992 California	AL	29	211.0	208	68	130	7	15	2.77	0	1.308
1993 New York	AL	32	214.0	221	73	95	11	14	4.37	0	1.374
Four-Year Average			219.0	224	72	122	12	14	3.61	0	1.345

WILSON ALVAREZ

Age 24/L $19

The key was always getting his amazing stuff under control, and last season he made progress toward that goal. He was the South Side's best pitcher down the stretch in 1993, and we think 1994 will be a huge year for Alvarez. Ditto for the pitching-rich White Sox, who will coast through the "regular" season and into the several tiers of playoffs that will determine which teams go to the Stanley Cup Finals.

Year Team	Lg.	G	IP	H	BB	SO	W	L	ERA	SV	Ratio
1991 Chicago	AL	10	56.1	47	29	32	3	2	3.51	0	1.349
1992 Chicago	AL	34	100.1	103	65	66	5	3	5.20	1	1.674
1993 Chicago	AL	31	207.2	168	122	155	15	8	2.95	0	1.396
Four-Year Average			121.0	106	72	84	8	4	3.66	0	1.466

KEVIN APPIER Age 26/R $25

The best pitcher in the American League. Next question?

Year Team	Lg.	G	IP	H	BB	SO	W	L	ERA	SV	Ratio
1990 Kansas City	AL	32	185.2	179	54	127	12	8	2.76	0	1.255
1991 Kansas City	AL	34	207.2	205	61	158	13	10	3.42	0	1.281
1992 Kansas City	AL	30	208.1	167	68	150	15	8	2.46	0	1.128
1993 Kansas City	AL	34	238.2	183	81	186	18	8	2.56	0	1.106
Four-Year Average			210.0	184	66	155	15	9	2.80	0	1.188

WILLIE BANKS Age 25/R $8

First the Humpdome, now the Friendly Confines. If Fenway Park is his next stop, he'll have completed a pitcher's Nightmare Trifecta.

Year Team	Lg.	G	IP	H	BB	SO	W	L	ERA	SV	Ratio
1991 Minnesota	AL	5	17.1	21	12	16	1	1	5.71	0	1.904
1992 Minnesota	AL	16	71.0	80	37	37	4	4	5.70	0	1.648
1993 Minnesota	AL	31	171.1	186	78	138	11	12	4.04	0	1.541
Four-Year Average			86.0	96	42	64	5	6	4.61	0	1.594

TIM BELCHER Age 32/R $5

A bust with the White Sox after being a bust with the Reds, but some team will shell out big bucks for him anyway. Just be sure that you don't.

Year Team	Lg.	G	IP	H	BB	SO	W	L	ERA	SV	Ratio
1990 Los Angeles	NL	24	153.0	136	48	102	9	9	4.00	0	1.203
1991 Los Angeles	NL	33	209.1	189	75	156	10	9	2.62	0	1.261
1992 Cincinnati	NL	35	227.2	201	80	149	15	14	3.91	0	1.234
1993 Cincinnati	NL	22	137.0	134	47	101	9	6	4.47	0	1.321
1993 Chicago	AL	12	71.2	64	27	34	3	5	4.40	0	1.270
Four-Year Average			199.0	181	69	136	12	11	3.73	0	1.253

JASON BERE Age 22/R $17

We have a feeling that the White Sox and the Braves are going to be squaring off in every World Series through the turn of the century. The reason, of course, is pitching.

Year Team	Lg.	G	IP	H	BB	SO	W	L	ERA	SV	Ratio
1993 Chicago	AL	24	142.2	109	81	129	12	5	3.47	0	1.332
Four-Year Average			142.0	109	81	129	12	5	3.47	0	1.332

RICKY BONES Age 24/R $2

Led the major leagues in triples allowed (11). That must mean something.

Year Team	Lg.	G	IP	H	BB	SO	W	L	ERA	SV	Ratio
1991 San Diego	NL	11	54.0	57	18	31	4	6	4.83	0	1.389
1992 Milwaukee	AL	31	163.1	169	48	65	9	10	4.57	0	1.329
1993 Milwaukee	AL	32	203.2	222	63	63	11	11	4.86	0	1.399
Four-Year Average			140.0	149	43	53	8	9	4.75	0	1.371

Catchers
pp. 59–73

Corners
pp. 73–95

Infield
pp. 95–116

Outfield
pp. 117–150

DH
pp. 150–153

Starters
pp. 154–189

Relievers
pp. 190–217

CHRIS BOSIO   Age 31/R $13

Last year never happened. It was a fluke. An aberration. Forget about it.
Forget about what?

Year Team	Lg.	G	IP	H	BB	SO	W	L	ERA	SV	Ratio
1990 Milwaukee	AL	20	132.2	131	38	76	4	9	4.00	0	1.274
1991 Milwaukee	AL	32	204.2	187	58	117	14	10	3.25	0	1.197
1992 Milwaukee	AL	33	231.1	223	44	120	16	6	3.62	0	1.154
1993 Seattle	AL	29	164.1	138	59	119	9	9	3.45	1	1.199
Four-Year Average			183.0	170	50	108	11	9	3.55	0	1.198

KEVIN BROWN   Age 29/R $16

Some of his teammates think he would benefit from grit supplements. Maybe
Nolan Ryan left some in his locker.

Year Team	Lg.	G	IP	H	BB	SO	W	L	ERA	SV	Ratio
1990 Texas	AL	26	180.0	175	60	88	12	10	3.60	0	1.306
1991 Texas	AL	33	210.2	233	90	96	9	12	4.40	0	1.533
1992 Texas	AL	35	265.2	262	76	173	21	11	3.32	0	1.272
1993 Texas	AL	34	233.0	228	74	142	15	12	3.59	0	1.296
Four-Year Average			222.0	225	75	125	14	11	3.70	0	1.347

MARK CLARK   Age 25/R $2

Maybe it's not Lou Brock for Ernie Broglio, but the Indians will be reminded
of Mark Whiten for Mark Clark over the next few years. That won't be
entirely fair, since the Tribe had a lot of bats and desperately needed arms,
and Clark has a pretty good one. But since when has second-guessing in
baseball supposed to be fair?

Year Team	Lg.	G	IP	H	BB	SO	W	L	ERA	SV	Ratio
1991 St. Louis	NL	7	22.1	17	11	13	1	1	4.03	0	1.254
1992 St. Louis	NL	20	113.1	117	36	44	3	10	4.45	0	1.350
1993 Cleveland	AL	26	109.1	119	25	57	7	5	4.28	0	1.317
Four-Year Average			81.0	84	24	38	4	5	4.33	0	1.327

ROGER CLEMENS   Age 31/R $24

He finished below .500 for the first time ever. His ERA approached the
Kelly Downs Line. He blew leads. He dragged his own team out of the
pennant race. He had arm trouble. There were even rumors that he could
be made available for the right trade package. So what does all this mean?
Well, if it means his price is a little deflated, we say grab him and hold on
for dear life. We're not about to shy away from this generation's greatest
pitcher just because of one screwy season.

Year Team	Lg.	G	IP	H	BB	SO	W	L	ERA	SV	Ratio
1990 Boston	AL	31	228.1	193	54	209	21	6	1.93	0	1.082
1991 Boston	AL	35	271.1	219	65	241	18	10	2.62	0	1.047
1992 Boston	AL	32	246.2	203	62	208	18	11	2.41	0	1.074
1993 Boston	AL	29	191.2	175	67	160	11	14	4.46	0	1.263
Four-Year Average			234.0	198	62	205	17	10	2.77	0	1.107

DAVID CONE   Age 31/R $16

No, the Royals didn't score many runs for him. Yes, he had some tough
losses. But what's wrong with winning some of those 2–1 games instead of

serving up ninth-inning home runs to Reggie Jefferson? What's wrong with shutting someone out once in a while? What's wrong with winning more games than you lose with all that terrific stuff? Pitchers of his alleged caliber are supposed to transcend things like missed calls, bad luck, meager run support, defensive lapses, sunspots, holes in the ozone layer, and other cosmic disorders that affect merely good pitchers. We're not suggesting that the Royals swap Conehead for Ed Hearn or anything, but we want to go on record as being a little peeved.

Year	Team	Lg.	G	IP	H	BB	SO	W	L	ERA	SV	Ratio
1990	New York	NL	31	211.2	177	65	233	14	10	3.23	0	1.143
1991	New York	NL	34	232.2	204	73	241	14	14	3.29	0	1.191
1992	New York	NL	27	196.2	162	82	214	13	7	2.88	0	1.241
1992	Toronto	AL	8	53.0	39	29	47	4	3	2.55	0	1.283
1993	Kansas City	AL	34	254.0	205	114	191	11	14	3.33	0	1.256
Four-Year Average				236.0	197	91	232	14	12	3.16	0	1.213

DENNIS COOK
Age 31/L $1

No.

Year	Team	Lg.	G	IP	H	BB	SO	W	L	ERA	SV	Ratio
1990	Philadelphia	NL	42	141.2	132	54	58	8	3	3.56	1	1.313
1990	Los Angeles	NL	5	14.1	23	2	6	1	1	7.53	0	1.744
1991	Los Angeles	NL	20	17.2	12	7	8	1	0	0.51	0	1.075
1992	Cleveland	AL	32	158.0	156	50	96	5	7	3.82	0	1.304
1993	Cleveland	AL	25	54.0	62	16	34	5	5	5.67	0	1.444
Four-Year Average				96.0	96	32	51	5	4	3.97	0	1.333

RON DARLING
Age 33/R $1

Does anybody know whether he ever finished up those credits he needed for his Yale degree? We hope so, because it's time he started thinking about another line of work.

Year	Team	Lg.	G	IP	H	BB	SO	W	L	ERA	SV	Ratio
1990	New York	NL	33	126.0	135	44	99	7	9	4.50	0	1.421
1991	New York	NL	17	102.1	96	28	58	5	6	3.87	0	1.212
1991	Montreal	NL	3	17.0	25	5	11	0	2	7.41	0	1.765
1991	Oakland	AL	12	75.0	64	38	60	3	7	4.08	0	1.360
1992	Oakland	AL	33	206.1	198	72	99	15	10	3.66	0	1.309
1993	Oakland	AL	31	178.0	198	72	95	5	9	5.16	0	1.517
Four-Year Average				176.0	179	65	106	9	11	4.36	0	1.384

DANNY DARWIN
Age 38/R $13

Posting a 3.26 ERA while pitching half your games in Fenway Park is nothing short of phenomenal. But given his medical record and the number of innings he pitched last year, we're a little leery about making him the centerpiece of our staff.

Year	Team	Lg.	G	IP	H	BB	SO	W	L	ERA	SV	Ratio
1990	Houston	NL	48	162.2	136	31	109	11	4	2.21	2	1.027
1991	Boston	AL	12	68.0	71	15	42	3	6	5.16	0	1.265
1992	Boston	AL	51	161.1	159	53	124	9	9	3.96	3	1.314
1993	Boston	AL	34	229.1	196	49	130	15	11	3.26	0	1.068
Four-Year Average				155.0	141	37	101	10	8	3.38	1	1.143

JOHN DOHERTY

Age 26/R   **$7**

In a rotation where a 1-2-3 inning was sufficient cause for stopping the game and awarding the ball as a souvenir, this son of The Bronx, New York, deserves a big cheer.

Year Team	Lg.	G	IP	H	BB	SO	W	L	ERA	SV	Ratio
1992 Detroit	AL	47	116.0	131	25	37	7	4	3.88	3	1.345
1993 Detroit	AL	32	184.2	205	48	63	14	11	4.44	0	1.370
Four-Year Average			150.0	168	37	50	11	8	4.22	2	1.360

JOHN DOPSON

Age 30/R   **$1**

Not unless your league plays Rotisserie Contraire, in which giving up a lot of hits and earned runs is good.

Year Team	Lg.	G	IP	H	BB	SO	W	L	ERA	SV	Ratio
1990 Boston	AL	4	17.2	13	9	9	0	0	2.04	0	1.245
1991 Boston	AL	1	1.0	2	1	0	0	0	18.00	0	3.000
1992 Boston	AL	25	141.1	159	38	55	7	11	4.08	0	1.394
1993 Boston	AL	34	155.2	170	59	89	7	11	4.97	0	1.471
Four-Year Average			78.0	86	27	38	4	6	4.45	0	1.429

CAL ELDRED

Age 26/R   **$14**

Led the league in innings pitched. Kept his team in almost every game he started. On a good team he would have won about 22 games.

Year Team	Lg.	G	IP	H	BB	SO	W	L	ERA	SV	Ratio
1991 Milwaukee	AL	3	16.0	20	6	10	2	0	4.50	0	1.625
1992 Milwaukee	AL	14	100.1	76	23	62	11	2	1.79	0	0.987
1993 Milwaukee	AL	36	258.0	232	91	180	16	16	4.01	0	1.252
Four-Year Average			124.0	109	40	84	10	6	3.44	0	1.197

SCOTT ERICKSON

Age 26/R   **$3**

Led the league in defeats. Took his team out of games by giving up big innings early. On a good team he would have won around nine games.

Year Team	Lg.	G	IP	H	BB	SO	W	L	ERA	SV	Ratio
1990 Minnesota	AL	19	113.0	108	51	53	8	4	2.87	0	1.407
1991 Minnesota	AL	32	204.0	189	71	108	20	8	3.18	0	1.275
1992 Minnesota	AL	32	212.0	197	83	101	13	12	3.40	0	1.321
1993 Minnesota	AL	34	218.2	266	71	116	8	19	5.19	0	1.541
Four-Year Average			186.0	190	69	95	12	11	3.78	0	1.386

JOHN FARRELL

Age 31/R   **$1**

Ugly numbers. But the real news is that he can even comb his hair—much less pitch—after missing two seasons with major arm troubles. Don't get carried away with sentiment, but do pay close attention during spring training. This guy has guts.

Year Team	Lg.	G	IP	H	BB	SO	W	L	ERA	SV	Ratio
1990 Cleveland	AL	17	96.2	108	33	44	4	5	4.28	0	1.459
1993 California	AL	21	90.2	110	44	45	3	12	7.35	0	1.699
Four-Year Average			93.0	109	39	45	4	9	5.77	0	1.575

ALEX FERNANDEZ

Age 24/R   **$18**

The Braves didn't have the best starting rotation in baseball last year. The White Sox did.

Year Team	Lg.	G	IP	H	BB	SO	W	L	ERA	SV	Ratio
1990 Chicago	AL	13	87.2	89	34	61	5	5	3.80	0	1.403
1991 Chicago	AL	34	191.2	186	88	145	9	13	4.51	0	1.430
1992 Chicago	AL	29	187.2	199	50	95	8	11	4.27	0	1.327
1993 Chicago	AL	34	247.1	221	67	169	18	9	3.13	0	1.164
Four-Year Average			178.0	174	60	118	10	10	3.88	0	1.308

CHUCK FINLEY

Age 31/L   **$17**

You didn't have to be a rocket scientist to predict that he would come back strong. But being a terrific pitcher on a lousy team takes a toll, and we're a little jittery about assigning him a price commensurate with his talent.

Year Team	Lg.	G	IP	H	BB	SO	W	L	ERA	SV	Ratio
1990 California	AL	32	236.0	210	81	177	18	9	2.40	0	1.233
1991 California	AL	34	227.1	205	101	171	18	9	3.80	0	1.346
1992 California	AL	31	204.1	212	98	124	7	12	3.96	0	1.517
1993 California	AL	35	251.1	243	82	187	16	14	3.15	0	1.293
Four-Year Average			229.0	218	91	165	15	11	3.30	0	1.341

DAVE FLEMING

Age 24/L   **$12**

Suffered from control troubles at times last year: seven more walks in 40 fewer innings than in 1992. But he's young, so you expect him to sow a few wild oats.

Year Team	Lg.	G	IP	H	BB	SO	W	L	ERA	SV	Ratio
1991 Seattle	AL	9	17.2	19	3	11	1	0	6.62	0	1.245
1992 Seattle	AL	33	228.1	225	60	112	17	10	3.39	0	1.248
1993 Seattle	AL	26	167.1	189	67	75	12	5	4.36	0	1.530
Four-Year Average			137.0	144	43	66	10	5	3.92	0	1.362

MARK GARDNER

Age 32/R   **$1**

A former NL leader in hit batsmen (9 in 1990), he shares the major league record for most hit batsmen in one inning (3 in 1992). Our advice when his name comes up: duck.

Year Team	Lg.	G	IP	H	BB	SO	W	L	ERA	SV	Ratio
1990 Montreal	NL	27	152.2	129	61	135	7	9	3.42	0	1.245
1991 Montreal	NL	27	168.1	139	75	107	9	11	3.85	0	1.271
1992 Montreal	NL	33	179.2	179	60	132	12	10	4.36	0	1.330
1993 Kansas City	AL	17	91.2	92	36	54	4	6	6.19	0	1.396
Four-Year Average			148.0	135	58	107	8	9	4.25	0	1.302

EDDIE GUARDADO

Age 23/L   **$1**

Pass.

Year Team	Lg.	G	IP	H	BB	SO	W	L	ERA	SV	Ratio
1993 Minnesota	AL	19	94.2	123	36	46	3	8	6.18	0	1.680
Four-Year Average			94.0	123	36	46	3	8	6.18	0	1.680

Catchers
pp. 59-73

Corners
pp. 73-95

Infield
pp. 95-116

Outfield
pp. 117-150

DH
pp. 150-153

Starters
pp. 154-189

Relievers
pp. 190-217

MARK GUBICZA   Age 31/R $1

Now used primarily in middle relief as his injury-shortened career cranks down, but we prefer to think of him as one of the strong arms of those terrific Royals teams of the mid-1980s.

Year Team	Lg.	G	IP	H	BB	SO	W	L	ERA	SV	Ratio
1990 Kansas City	AL	16	94.0	101	38	71	4	7	4.50	0	1.479
1991 Kansas City	AL	26	133.0	168	42	89	9	12	5.68	0	1.579
1992 Kansas City	AL	18	111.1	110	36	81	7	6	3.72	0	1.311
1993 Kansas City	AL	49	104.1	128	43	80	5	8	4.66	2	1.639
Four-Year Average			110.0	127	40	80	6	8	4.70	1	1.505

BILL GULLICKSON   Age 35/R $3

All he does is win games. It's never pretty, and we'd be scared to death of him ending up on our team. But he does win games.

Year Team	Lg.	G	IP	H	BB	SO	W	L	ERA	SV	Ratio
1990 Houston	NL	32	193.1	221	61	73	10	14	3.82	0	1.459
1991 Detroit	AL	35	226.1	256	44	91	20	9	3.90	0	1.325
1992 Detroit	AL	34	221.2	228	50	64	14	13	4.34	0	1.254
1993 Detroit	AL	28	159.1	186	44	70	13	9	5.37	0	1.444
Four-Year Average			200.0	223	50	75	14	11	4.29	0	1.361

JUAN GUZMAN   Age 27/R $13

Just two complete games in 33 outings last season. As soon as Pat Gillick gets around to fixing the Blue Jay bullpen, Guzman will become a 20-game winner.

Year Team	Lg.	G	IP	H	BB	SO	W	L	ERA	SV	Ratio
1991 Toronto	AL	23	138.2	98	66	123	10	3	2.99	0	1.183
1992 Toronto	AL	28	180.2	135	72	165	16	5	2.64	0	1.146
1993 Toronto	AL	33	221.0	211	110	194	14	3	3.99	0	1.452
Four-Year Average			180.0	148	83	161	13	4	3.28	0	1.281

CHRIS HANEY   Age 25/L $1

He's the son of a former major leaguer. If that ERA stays up, his dad will soon be the father of a former major leaguer.

Year Team	Lg.	G	IP	H	BB	SO	W	L	ERA	SV	Ratio
1991 Montreal	NL	16	84.2	94	43	51	3	7	4.04	0	1.618
1992 Montreal	NL	9	38.0	40	10	27	2	3	5.45	0	1.316
1992 Kansas City	AL	7	42.0	35	16	27	2	3	3.86	0	1.214
1993 Kansas City	AL	23	124.0	141	53	65	9	9	6.02	0	1.565
Four-Year Average			96.0	103	41	57	5	7	5.05	0	1.497

ERIK HANSON   Age 28/R $6

Not one of Lou Piniella's favorites, so it came as no surprise when he was bundled off to Cincinnati. We're occasional believers in the Change of Scenery Effect, but we're not sure about Hanson and Riverfront.

Year Team	Lg.	G	IP	H	BB	SO	W	L	ERA	SV	Ratio
1990 Seattle	AL	33	236.0	205	68	211	18	9	3.24	0	1.157
1991 Seattle	AL	27	174.2	182	56	143	8	8	3.81	0	1.363
1992 Seattle	AL	31	186.2	209	57	112	8	17	4.82	0	1.425
1993 Seattle	AL	31	215.0	215	60	163	11	12	3.47	0	1.279
Four-Year Average			203.0	203	60	157	11	12	3.79	0	1.295

HILLY HATHAWAY   Age 24/L $2

His full name is Hillary Houston Hathaway. He comes from Florida, not Oxford, England. He throws lefthanded. He does not throw very hard. That's all we know, but we are desperately pulling for him to make it. Baseball *needs* Hilly Hathaways.

Year Team	Lg.	G	IP	H	BB	SO	W	L	ERA	SV	Ratio
1992 California	AL	2	5.2	8	3	1	0	0	7.94	0	1.941
1993 California	AL	11	57.1	71	26	11	4	3	5.02	0	1.692
Four-Year Average			31.0	40	15	6	2	2	5.29	0	1.715

PAT HENTGEN   Age 25/R $16

The ace of a shaky World Championship staff, he's also the only one in that rotation you can count on to get better.

Year Team	Lg.	G	IP	H	BB	SO	W	L	ERA	SV	Ratio
1991 Toronto	AL	3	7.1	5	3	3	0	0	2.45	0	1.091
1992 Toronto	AL	28	50.1	49	32	39	5	2	5.36	0	1.609
1993 Toronto	AL	34	216.1	215	74	122	19	9	3.87	0	1.336
Four-Year Average			91.0	90	36	55	8	4	4.11	0	1.380

JOE HESKETH   Age 35/L $1

Smeshketh.

Year Team	Lg.	G	IP	H	BB	SO	W	L	ERA	SV	Ratio
1990 Montreal	NL	2	3.0	2	2	3	1	0	0.00	0	1.333
1990 Atlanta	NL	31	31.0	30	12	21	0	2	5.81	5	1.355
1990 Boston	AL	12	25.2	37	11	26	0	4	3.51	0	1.870
1991 Boston	AL	39	153.1	142	53	104	12	4	3.29	0	1.272
1992 Boston	AL	30	148.2	162	58	104	8	9	4.36	1	1.480
1993 Boston	AL	28	53.1	62	29	34	3	4	5.06	1	1.706
Four-Year Average			103.0	109	41	73	6	6	4.08	2	1.446

SHAWN HILLEGAS   Age 29/R $1

How bad was Oakland last year? This bad.

Year Team	Lg.	G	IP	H	BB	SO	W	L	ERA	SV	Ratio
1990 Chicago	AL	7	11.1	4	5	5	0	0	0.79	0	0.794
1991 Cleveland	AL	51	83.0	67	46	66	3	4	4.34	7	1.361
1992 New York	AL	21	78.1	96	33	46	1	8	5.51	0	1.647
1992 Oakland	AL	5	7.2	8	4	3	0	0	2.35	0	1.565
1993 Oakland	AL	18	60.2	78	33	29	3	6	6.97	0	1.830
Four-Year Average			60.0	63	30	37	2	5	5.15	2	1.552

RANDY JOHNSON   Age 30/L $23

Who would have thought that just one simple suggestion from His Ryaness, something to do with the way Randy the Wild planted his foot, would transform this erratic giant into the most imposing pitcher in baseball. Just ask John Kruk.

Year Team	Lg.	G	IP	H	BB	SO	W	L	ERA	SV	Ratio
1990 Seattle	AL	33	219.2	174	120	194	14	11	3.65	0	1.338
1991 Seattle	AL	33	201.1	151	152	228	13	10	3.98	0	1.505
1992 Seattle	AL	31	210.1	154	144	241	12	14	3.77	0	1.417
1993 Seattle	AL	35	255.1	185	99	308	19	8	3.24	1	1.112
Four-Year Average			221.0	166	129	243	15	11	3.63	0	1.330

Catchers
pp. 59-73

Corners
pp. 73-95

Infield
pp. 95-116

Outfield
pp. 117-150

DH
pp. 150-153

Starters
pp. 154-189

Relievers
pp. 190-217

SCOTT KAMIENIECKI
Age 29/R $2

Solid work despite arm woes last year, but could get squeezed out of a job by free agent signees and younger Yankee prospects.

Year Team	Lg.	G	IP	H	BB	SO	W	L	ERA	SV	Ratio
1991 New York	AL	9	55.1	54	22	34	4	4	3.90	0	1.373
1992 New York	AL	28	188.0	193	74	88	6	14	4.36	0	1.420
1993 New York	AL	30	154.1	163	59	72	10	7	4.08	1	1.438
Four-Year Average			132.0	137	52	65	7	8	4.19	0	1.421

JIMMY KEY
Age 32/L $23

The Blue Jays did all right without him last year, but they're going to miss him a *lot* this season. The best free agent signing by the Yankees since Dave Winfield.

Year Team	Lg.	G	IP	H	BB	SO	W	L	ERA	SV	Ratio
1990 Toronto	AL	27	154.2	169	22	88	13	7	4.25	0	1.235
1991 Toronto	AL	33	209.1	207	44	125	16	12	3.05	0	1.199
1992 Toronto	AL	33	216.2	205	59	117	13	13	3.53	0	1.218
1993 New York	AL	34	236.2	219	43	173	18	6	3.00	0	1.107
Four-Year Average			204.0	200	42	126	15	10	3.39	0	1.184

TOM KRAMER
Age 26/R $3

Promising.

Year Team	Lg.	G	IP	H	BB	SO	W	L	ERA	SV	Ratio
1991 Cleveland	AL	4	4.2	10	6	4	0	0	17.36	0	3.429
1993 Cleveland	AL	39	121.0	126	59	71	7	3	4.02	0	1.529
Four-Year Average			62.0	68	33	38	4	2	4.51	0	1.600

MARK LANGSTON
Age 33/L $21

You always wonder how good he would be pitching for a contender. So long as he toils for the Angels, there's not much chance of your finding out. A horse—over 225 IP in nine of his ten big league seasons.

Year Team	Lg.	G	IP	H	BB	SO	W	L	ERA	SV	Ratio
1990 California	AL	33	223.0	215	104	195	10	17	4.40	0	1.430
1991 California	AL	34	246.1	190	96	183	19	8	3.00	0	1.161
1992 California	AL	32	229.0	206	74	174	13	14	3.66	0	1.223
1993 California	AL	35	256.1	220	85	196	16	11	3.20	0	1.190
Four-Year Average			238.0	208	90	187	15	13	3.54	0	1.247

TIM LEARY
Age 35/R $1

The double-figure wins notwithstanding, we're leery.

Year Team	Lg.	G	IP	H	BB	SO	W	L	ERA	SV	Ratio
1990 New York	AL	31	208.0	202	78	138	9	19	4.11	0	1.346
1991 New York	AL	28	120.2	150	57	83	4	10	6.49	0	1.715
1992 New York	AL	18	97.0	84	57	34	5	6	5.57	0	1.454
1992 Seattle	AL	8	44.0	47	30	12	3	4	4.91	0	1.750
1993 Seattle	AL	33	169.1	202	58	68	11	9	5.05	0	1.535
Four-Year Average			159.0	171	70	84	8	12	5.08	0	1.510

PHIL LEFTWICH   Age 24/R $1

Catchers
pp. 59-73

Corners
pp. 73-95

Infield
pp. 95-116

Outfield
pp. 117-150

DH
pp. 150-153

Starters
pp. 154-189

Relievers
pp. 190-217

A chance to stick, especially if the Angels deal off one of the higher-priced starters.

Year Team	Lg.	G	IP	H	BB	SO	W	L	ERA	SV	Ratio
1993 California	AL	12	80.2	81	27	31	4	6	3.79	0	1.339
Four-Year Average			80.0	81	27	31	4	6	3.79	0	1.339

CHARLIE LEIBRANDT   Age 37/L $3

The yellow flag is up—proceed with extreme caution. Ugly year ended with a shoulder injury and his outright release by the Rangers. Can he recuperate and find a new job? This is neither an HMO nor an employment agency, but we suggest you take two aspirins and look at his work history. Those three solid years with Atlanta weren't so long ago.

Year Team	Lg.	G	IP	H	BB	SO	W	L	ERA	SV	Ratio
1990 Atlanta	NL	24	162.1	164	35	76	9	11	3.16	0	1.226
1991 Atlanta	NL	36	229.2	212	56	128	15	13	3.49	0	1.167
1992 Atlanta	NL	32	193.0	191	42	104	15	7	3.36	0	1.207
1993 Texas	AL	26	150.1	169	45	89	9	10	4.55	0	1.424
Four-Year Average			183.0	184	45	99	12	10	3.60	0	1.243

AL LEITER   Age 28/L $4

A career reborn. Will get a chance to earn a spot in the Toronto rotation this spring. Keep an eye on him—he could be a Leiter bloomer.

Year Team	Lg.	G	IP	H	BB	SO	W	L	ERA	SV	Ratio
1990 Toronto	AL	4	6.1	1	2	5	0	0	0.00	0	0.474
1991 Toronto	AL	3	1.2	3	5	1	0	0	27.00	0	4.800
1992 Toronto	AL	1	1.0	1	2	0	0	0	9.00	0	3.000
1993 Toronto	AL	34	105.0	93	56	66	9	6	4.11	2	1.419
Four-Year Average			28.0	25	16	18	2	2	4.26	1	1.430

MARK LEITER   Age 30/R $1

Do not bother keeping an eye on him.

Year Team	Lg.	G	IP	H	BB	SO	W	L	ERA	SV	Ratio
1990 New York	AL	8	26.1	33	9	21	1	1	6.84	0	1.595
1991 Detroit	AL	38	134.2	125	50	103	9	7	4.21	1	1.300
1992 Detroit	AL	35	112.0	116	43	75	8	5	4.18	0	1.420
1993 Detroit	AL	27	106.2	111	44	70	6	6	4.72	0	1.453
Four-Year Average			94.0	96	37	67	6	5	4.53	0	1.399

JOE MAGRANE   Age 29/L $4

Whitey Herzog gave him a three-year contract. No, we couldn't figure it out either. But we do have a hunch that John Stuper, Mike Ramsey, George Hendrick, Dane Iorg, and Darrell Porter are feeling pretty good right about now regarding their chances of making a comeback in Anaheim.

Year Team	Lg.	G	IP	H	BB	SO	W	L	ERA	SV	Ratio
1990 St. Louis	NL	31	203.1	204	59	100	10	17	3.59	0	1.293
1992 St. Louis	NL	5	31.1	34	15	20	1	2	4.02	0	1.564
1993 St. Louis	NL	22	116.0	127	37	38	8	10	4.97	0	1.414
1993 California	AL	8	48.0	48	21	24	3	2	3.94	0	1.438
Four-Year Average			132.0	138	44	61	7	10	4.06	0	1.367

PAT MAHOMES   Age 23/R $1

The Twins say he has a lot of ability. They also say the Humpdome is a baseball park.

Year Team	Lg.	G	IP	H	BB	SO	W	L	ERA	SV	Ratio
1992 Minnesota	AL	14	69.2	73	37	44	3	4	5.04	0	1.579
1993 Minnesota	AL	12	37.1	47	16	23	1	5	7.71	0	1.688
Four-Year Average			53.0	60	27	34	2	5	5.97	0	1.617

KIRK McCASKILL   Age 32/R $2

After two years of arm problems, he began to show positive signs of recovery. By the end of last season, his velocity had come back 6 to 8 miles per hour, and his breaking stuff was much sharper. No way does this mean he's going to crack the White Sox rotation, but it may mean he could end up a valuable set-up man in the White Sox' bullpen. Whoever's in that role over the next few years is going to pick up a lot of wins.

Year Team	Lg.	G	IP	H	BB	SO	W	L	ERA	SV	Ratio
1990 California	AL	29	174.1	161	72	78	12	11	3.25	0	1.337
1991 California	AL	30	177.2	193	66	71	10	19	4.26	0	1.458
1992 Chicago	AL	34	209.0	193	95	109	12	13	4.18	0	1.378
1993 Chicago	AL	30	113.2	144	36	65	4	8	5.23	2	1.584
Four-Year Average			168.0	173	67	81	10	13	4.14	1	1.423

BEN McDONALD   Age 26/R $18

While other Orioles were spitting the bit right and left after the All-Star break last summer, Big Ben bore down and kept his team in all but a handful of starts. Opponents hit just .228 against him, which tells you he has the stuff to be a dominant pitcher. Now if he could just get his win-loss record a few games over .500, we'd really start getting excited about him.

Year Team	Lg.	G	IP	H	BB	SO	W	L	ERA	SV	Ratio
1990 Baltimore	AL	21	118.2	88	35	65	8	5	2.43	0	1.037
1991 Baltimore	AL	21	126.1	126	43	85	6	8	4.84	0	1.338
1992 Baltimore	AL	35	227.0	213	74	158	13	13	4.24	0	1.264
1993 Baltimore	AL	34	220.1	185	86	171	13	14	3.39	0	1.230
Four-Year Average			173.0	153	60	120	10	10	3.77	0	1.228

BASEBALL ANAGRAM #18

Opening Amore = _____?

(Answer on page 299)

JACK McDOWELL   Age 28/R $25

Here is what opposing AL batters hit against Chicago's Big Four last season: Jason Bere/.210; Wilson Alvarez/.230; Alex Fernandez/.240; and Jack Mc-Dowell/.266. Does this mean that Black Jack was lucky to win all those games? No, it means he was at his toughest when it counted the most. He snuffed rallies, stayed away from big innings, kept runners from getting into scoring position, and didn't hurt himself with walks. All that added up to another superb season from one of the fiercest competitors in the game. But we have one quibble: just where does this wannabe–rock star with the Stanford education and the bad goatee get off ripping Nolan Ryan?

Year Team	Lg.	G	IP	H	BB	SO	W	L	ERA	SV	Ratio
1990 Chicago	AL	33	205.0	189	77	165	14	9	3.82	0	1.298
1991 Chicago	AL	35	253.2	212	82	191	17	10	3.41	0	1.159
1992 Chicago	AL	34	260.2	247	75	178	20	10	3.18	0	1.235
1993 Chicago	AL	34	256.2	261	69	158	22	10	3.37	0	1.286
Four-Year Average			243.0	227	76	173	18	10	3.42	0	1.242

JOSE MESA   Age 27/R $3

One of the ostensible reasons Cleveland fired pitching coach Rick Adair was that Adair was unable to teach Mesa another pitch. If that sounds to you like the Indians were reaching, you're not alone. Adair isn't the first coach, and probably he won't be the last, to become frustrated trying to teach the talented Mesa how to grow into a consistent winner.

Year Team	Lg.	G	IP	H	BB	SO	W	L	ERA	SV	Ratio
1990 Baltimore	AL	7	46.2	37	27	24	3	2	3.86	0	1.371
1991 Baltimore	AL	23	123.2	151	62	64	6	11	5.97	0	1.722
1992 Baltimore	AL	13	67.2	77	27	22	3	8	5.19	0	1.537
1992 Cleveland	AL	15	93.0	92	43	40	4	4	4.16	0	1.452
1993 Cleveland	AL	34	208.2	232	62	118	10	12	4.92	0	1.409
Four-Year Average			134.0	147	55	67	7	9	4.97	0	1.501

ANGEL MIRANDA   Age 24/L $4

One day in Skydome last summer we watched as Miranda read the Blue Jays their rights with a screwball that reminded one and all of a young kid named Fernando. Give him—Angel, not Fernando—another season to mature, and we could have something very special on our hands.

Year Team	Lg.	G	IP	H	BB	SO	W	L	ERA	SV	Ratio
1993 Milwaukee	AL	22	120.0	100	52	88	4	5	3.30	0	1.267
Four-Year Average			120.0	100	52	88	4	5	3.30	0	1.267

MIKE MOORE   Age 34/R $6

Wins ugly.

Year Team	Lg.	G	IP	H	BB	SO	W	L	ERA	SV	Ratio
1990 Oakland	AL	33	199.1	204	84	73	13	15	4.65	0	1.445
1991 Oakland	AL	33	210.0	176	105	153	17	8	2.96	0	1.338
1992 Oakland	AL	36	223.0	229	103	117	17	12	4.12	0	1.489
1993 Detroit	AL	36	213.2	227	89	89	13	9	5.22	0	1.479
Four-Year Average			211.0	209	95	108	15	11	4.23	0	1.439

Catchers
pp. 59–73

Corners
pp. 73–95

Infield
pp. 95–116

Outfield
pp. 117–150

DH
pp. 150–153

Starters
pp. 154–189

Relievers
pp. 190–217

JACK MORRIS   Age 38/R $3

The elbow injury he suffered late last season probably means he won't be back. And frankly, no one around here is going to miss his arrogance, his surliness, and his frequently boorish behavior. But he's been a money pitcher for a lot of years, one of the game's best, and we salute him for that.

Year Team	Lg.	G	IP	H	BB	SO	W	L	ERA	SV	Ratio
1990 Detroit	AL	36	249.2	231	97	162	15	18	4.51	0	1.314
1991 Minnesota	AL	35	246.2	226	92	163	18	12	3.43	0	1.289
1992 Toronto	AL	34	240.2	222	80	132	21	6	4.04	0	1.255
1993 Toronto	AL	27	152.2	189	65	103	7	12	6.19	0	1.664
Four-Year Average			222.0	217	84	140	15	12	4.37	0	1.351

JAMIE MOYER   Age 31/L $3

As far as we're concerned, this was the biggest surprise of 1993, if not of the century. Come on now—*Jamie Moyer?* So who's it going to be this year? Bob McClure? Juan Agosto? We figure that this year just about anyone has a chance to step out of the lengthening shadows of a marginal career and have a season like the one Jamie Moyer had in 1993. Anyone, that is, except Jamie Moyer.

Year Team	Lg.	G	IP	H	BB	SO	W	L	ERA	SV	Ratio
1990 Texas	AL	33	102.1	115	39	58	2	6	4.66	0	1.505
1991 St. Louis	NL	8	31.1	38	16	20	0	5	5.74	0	1.723
1993 Baltimore	AL	25	152.0	154	38	90	12	9	3.43	0	1.263
Four-Year Average			95.0	102	31	56	5	7	4.13	0	1.400

MIKE MUSSINA   Age 25/R $18

He was never the same after injuring his shoulder in that vicious brawl he triggered against Seattle. Now, we all know that the owners and Players Association disagree on everything from arbitration to free agency to where the sun rises in the morning. We also know that both groups contain a bountiful supply of petty, small-minded zealots interested only in screwing the other side, National Pastime be damned. But you'd think that mutual self-interest would bring them together to find some way to discourage the proliferation of stupid bench-clearing brawls in which nothing but bad things can result. Baseball is following hockey's lead with another tier of playoffs. Why not go all the way and add a penalty box?

Year Team	Lg.	G	IP	H	BB	SO	W	L	ERA	SV	Ratio
1991 Baltimore	AL	12	87.2	77	21	52	4	5	2.87	0	1.118
1992 Baltimore	AL	32	241.0	212	48	130	18	5	2.54	0	1.079
1993 Baltimore	AL	25	167.2	163	44	117	14	6	4.46	0	1.235
Four-Year Average			165.0	151	38	100	12	5	3.25	0	1.138

JEFF MUTIS   Age 27/L $1

Only if you're playing Ultra and need a body for your 40th roster slot.

Year Team	Lg.	G	IP	H	BB	SO	W	L	ERA	SV	Ratio
1991 Cleveland	AL	3	12.1	23	7	6	0	3	11.68	0	2.432
1992 Cleveland	AL	3	11.1	24	6	8	0	2	9.53	0	2.647
1993 Cleveland	AL	17	81.0	93	33	29	3	6	5.78	0	1.556
Four-Year Average			34.0	47	15	14	1	4	6.88	0	1.777

CHARLES NAGY   Age 26/R $11

By September, the Indians were convinced he was 100% healthy. If so, then he should pick up where he left off in 1992—on the road to becoming one of the premier pitchers in the game. Gamble on a big comeback.

Year Team	Lg.	G	IP	H	BB	SO	W	L	ERA	SV	Ratio
1990 Cleveland	AL	9	45.2	58	21	26	2	4	5.91	0	1.730
1991 Cleveland	AL	33	211.1	228	66	109	10	15	4.13	0	1.391
1992 Cleveland	AL	33	252.0	245	57	169	17	10	2.96	0	1.198
1993 Cleveland	AL	9	48.2	66	13	30	2	6	6.29	0	1.623
Four-Year Average			139.0	149	39	84	8	9	3.94	0	1.352

JAIME NAVARRO   Age 26/R $7

A big step backward, but more a reflection on his team and than his ability. Any price under $10 could pay big returns.

Year Team	Lg.	G	IP	H	BB	SO	W	L	ERA	SV	Ratio
1990 Milwaukee	AL	32	149.1	176	41	75	8	7	4.46	1	1.453
1991 Milwaukee	AL	34	234.0	237	73	114	15	12	3.92	0	1.325
1992 Milwaukee	AL	34	246.0	224	64	100	17	11	3.33	0	1.171
1993 Milwaukee	AL	35	214.1	254	73	114	11	12	5.33	0	1.526
Four-Year Average			210.0	223	63	101	13	11	4.20	0	1.354

BOBBY OJEDA   Age 36/L $1

We hope he makes it back. He would be such a great guy to root for.

Year Team	Lg.	G	IP	H	BB	SO	W	L	ERA	SV	Ratio
1990 New York	NL	38	118.0	123	40	62	7	6	3.66	0	1.381
1991 Los Angeles	NL	31	189.1	181	70	120	12	9	3.18	0	1.326
1992 Los Angeles	NL	29	166.1	169	81	94	6	9	3.63	0	1.503
1993 Cleveland	AL	9	43.0	48	21	27	2	1	4.40	0	1.605
Four-Year Average			129.0	130	53	76	7	6	3.54	0	1.419

ROGER PAVLIK   Age 26/R $9

Overlooked in all the hoopla over Juan Gonzalez's hitting and José Canseco's pitching and Nolan Ryan's retirement was the development of this young righthander into a solid starter. He will get better.

Year Team	Lg.	G	IP	H	BB	SO	W	L	ERA	SV	Ratio
1992 Texas	AL	13	62.0	66	34	45	4	4	4.21	0	1.613
1993 Texas	AL	26	166.1	151	80	131	12	6	3.41	0	1.389
Four-Year Average			114.0	109	57	88	8	5	3.63	0	1.450

MELIDO PEREZ   Age 28/R $2

What happened? The Yankees wish they knew. A repeat of his 1992 season last year and the Yanks would have been Eastern Division champs. A repeat of 1993 this year and Melido will be back home in the Dominican Republic playing catch with Pascual. At this price, you could end up getting a tenfold ROI. Or you could be wasting a deuce.

Year Team	Lg.	G	IP	H	BB	SO	W	L	ERA	SV	Ratio
1990 Chicago	AL	35	197.0	177	86	161	13	14	4.61	0	1.335
1991 Chicago	AL	49	135.2	111	52	128	8	7	3.12	1	1.201
1992 New York	AL	33	247.2	212	93	218	13	16	2.87	0	1.231
1993 New York	AL	25	163.0	173	64	148	6	14	5.19	0	1.454
Four-Year Average			185.0	168	74	164	10	13	3.89	0	1.302

HIPOLITO PICHARDO   Age 24/R $3

A crossroads year for a guy with some ability but little idea how to use it consistently.

Year Team	Lg.	G	IP	H	BB	SO	W	L	ERA	SV	Ratio
1992 Kansas City	AL	31	143.2	148	49	59	9	6	3.95	0	1.371
1993 Kansas City	AL	30	165.0	183	53	70	7	8	4.04	0	1.430
Four-Year Average			154.0	166	51	65	8	7	3.99	0	1.403

ARTHUR RHODES   Age 24/L $3

No relation to the scholar, but still a legit prospect despite wildness.

Year Team	Lg.	G	IP	H	BB	SO	W	L	ERA	SV	Ratio
1991 Baltimore	AL	8	36.0	47	23	23	0	3	8.00	0	1.944
1992 Baltimore	AL	15	94.1	87	38	77	7	5	3.63	0	1.325
1993 Baltimore	AL	17	85.2	91	49	49	5	6	6.51	0	1.634
Four-Year Average			71.0	75	37	50	4	5	5.50	0	1.551

KENNY ROGERS   Age 29/L $9

Claude Osteen, the blunt-speaking and estimable pitching coach of the Rangers, said early last season, "If we can ever get Kenny Rogers to realize that he can't get people out with just one pitch, and that he has the stuff to set up hitters, he can be a heckuva starting pitcher. But that's a big if." Not anymore.

Year Team	Lg.	G	IP	H	BB	SO	W	L	ERA	SV	Ratio
1990 Texas	AL	69	97.2	93	42	74	10	6	3.13	15	1.382
1991 Texas	AL	63	109.2	121	61	73	10	10	5.42	5	1.660
1992 Texas	AL	81	78.2	80	26	70	3	6	3.09	6	1.347
1993 Texas	AL	35	208.1	210	71	140	16	10	4.10	0	1.349
Four-Year Average			123.0	126	50	89	10	8	4.04	7	1.424

NOLAN RYAN   Age 47/R   Priceless

You're the top.

Year Team	Lg.	G	IP	H	BB	SO	W	L	ERA	SV	Ratio
1990 Texas	AL	30	204.0	137	74	232	13	9	3.44	0	1.034
1991 Texas	AL	27	173.0	102	72	203	12	6	2.91	0	1.006
1992 Texas	AL	27	157.1	138	69	157	5	9	3.72	0	1.316
1993 Texas	AL	13	66.1	54	40	46	5	5	4.88	0	1.417
Four-Year Average			150.0	108	64	160	9	7	3.52	0	1.142

AARON SELE   Age 23/R $12

Don't be misled by Boston people who insist on comparing this kid to Roger Clemens. Sele, who barely hits 90 on the radar gun, is no Rocket. But he does have a great curve ball, excellent control, exceptional poise, and a glowing future. Try to be part of it.

Year Team	Lg.	G	IP	H	BB	SO	W	L	ERA	SV	Ratio
1993 Boston	AL	18	111.2	100	48	93	7	2	2.74	0	1.325
Four-Year Average			111.0	100	48	93	7	2	2.74	0	1.325

DAVE STEWART   Age 37/R $8

When the pennant was on the line and the Blue Jays pitching staff needed a lift last season, he pitched like the old Stew. At other times he just pitched old. And while still a classy guy and a great competitor, old Stew is now a year older.

Year	Team	Lg.	G	IP	H	BB	SO	W	L	ERA	SV	Ratio
1990	Oakland	AL	36	267.0	226	83	166	22	11	2.56	0	1.157
1991	Oakland	AL	35	226.0	245	105	144	11	11	5.18	0	1.549
1992	Oakland	AL	31	199.1	175	79	130	12	10	3.66	0	1.274
1993	Toronto	AL	26	162.0	146	72	96	12	8	4.44	0	1.346
Four-Year Average				213.0	198	85	134	14	10	3.87	0	1.324

TODD STOTTLEMYRE   Age 28/R $5

Had a better year than his dad, whom the Mets fired as pitching coach, presumably for not putting Sid Fernandez on a diet and making Bret Saberhagen act like a grownup. But the Blue Jays weren't satisfied, and Cito Gaston will be looking for someone to step forward during spring training to take Todd's spot in the rotation.

Year	Team	Lg.	G	IP	H	BB	SO	W	L	ERA	SV	Ratio
1990	Toronto	AL	33	203.0	214	69	115	13	17	4.34	0	1.394
1991	Toronto	AL	34	219.0	194	75	116	15	8	3.78	0	1.228
1992	Toronto	AL	28	174.0	175	63	98	12	11	4.50	0	1.368
1993	Toronto	AL	30	176.2	204	69	98	11	12	4.84	0	1.545
Four-Year Average				193.0	197	69	107	13	12	4.33	0	1.376

RICK SUTCLIFFE   Age 37/R $1

End of the line for one of our longtime favorites. If they handed out Cy Youngs for being a stand-up guy, his trophy case would be full.

Year	Team	Lg.	G	IP	H	BB	SO	W	L	ERA	SV	Ratio
1990	Chicago	NL	5	21.1	25	12	7	0	2	5.91	0	1.734
1991	Chicago	NL	19	96.2	96	45	52	6	5	4.10	0	1.459
1992	Baltimore	AL	36	237.1	251	74	109	16	15	4.47	0	1.369
1993	Baltimore	AL	29	166.0	212	74	80	10	10	5.75	0	1.723
Four-Year Average				130.0	146	51	62	8	8	4.87	0	1.513

FRANK TANANA   Age 40/L $1

About one of every four outings, this master craftsman gives a clinic on pitching. The other three, watch out.

Year	Team	Lg.	G	IP	H	BB	SO	W	L	ERA	SV	Ratio
1990	Detroit	AL	34	176.1	190	66	114	9	8	5.31	1	1.452
1991	Detroit	AL	33	217.1	217	78	107	13	12	3.69	0	1.357
1992	Detroit	AL	32	186.2	188	90	91	13	11	4.39	0	1.489
1993	New York	NL	29	183.0	198	48	104	7	15	4.48	0	1.344
1993	New York	AL	3	19.2	18	7	12	0	2	3.20	0	1.271
Four-Year Average				195.0	203	72	107	11	12	4.39	0	1.405

Catchers
pp. 59–73

Corners
pp. 73–95

Infield
pp. 95–116

Outfield
pp. 117–150

DH
pp. 150–153

Starters
pp. 154–189

Relievers
pp. 190–217

KEVIN TAPANI   Age 30/R $7

Another year of backpedaling from someone we thought was well on the road to stardom.

Year Team	Lg.	G	IP	H	BB	SO	W	L	ERA	SV	Ratio
1990 Minnesota	AL	28	159.1	164	29	101	12	8	4.07	0	1.211
1991 Minnesota	AL	34	244.0	225	40	135	16	9	2.99	0	1.086
1992 Minnesota	AL	34	220.0	226	48	138	16	11	3.97	0	1.245
1993 Minnesota	AL	36	225.2	243	57	150	12	15	4.43	0	1.329
Four-Year Average			212.0	215	44	131	14	11	3.83	0	1.216

FERNANDO VALENZUELA   Age 33/L $1

Late last September, when Fernando was removed from his final start of the season, the capacity crowd at Camden Yards shook off its trendy coolness for a moment and rose to give him a "Thanks for the Memories" ovation. Whether he can make it back again for another tour of duty is anybody's guess. But there were some magical times last summer, times when he had AL hitters off balance and tied in knots, that made you want to break into a chorus of "Take Me Out to the Ball Game."

Year Team	Lg.	G	IP	H	BB	SO	W	L	ERA	SV	Ratio
1990 Los Angeles	NL	33	204.0	223	77	115	13	13	4.59	0	1.471
1991 California	AL	2	6.2	14	3	5	0	2	12.15	0	2.550
1993 Baltimore	AL	32	178.2	179	79	78	8	10	4.94	0	1.444
Four-Year Average			129.0	139	53	66	7	8	4.88	0	1.477

TODD VAN POPPEL   Age 22/R $7

Forget last year's numbers. His future is now. This is the season the pieces fall into place. Grab him.

Year Team	Lg.	G	IP	H	BB	SO	W	L	ERA	SV	Ratio
1991 Oakland	AL	1	4.2	7	2	6	0	0	9.64	0	1.929
1993 Oakland	AL	16	84.0	76	62	47	6	6	5.04	0	1.643
Four-Year Average			44.0	42	32	27	3	3	5.28	0	1.658

FRANK VIOLA   Age 33/L $12

Always a durable sort—ten straight seasons in which he averaged 240 IP with nary a day on the DL—Sweet Music broke down last year. A portent of what's to come? The Red Sox are afraid so, but his huge contract makes him virtually untradable—except to the Blue Jays, should Pat Gillick decide next August that he needs an extra arm to win his third straight World Championship. Meanwhile, this is one lefty who can pitch well—and win—in Fenway Park.

Year Team	Lg.	G	IP	H	BB	SO	W	L	ERA	SV	Ratio
1990 New York	NL	35	249.2	227	60	182	20	12	2.67	0	1.150
1991 New York	NL	35	231.1	259	54	132	13	15	3.97	0	1.353
1992 Boston	AL	35	238.0	214	89	121	13	12	3.44	0	1.273
1993 Boston	AL	29	183.2	180	72	91	11	8	3.14	0	1.372
Four-Year Average			225.0	220	69	132	14	12	3.30	0	1.280

BILL WEGMAN

Age 31/R **$4**

Not many pitchers were paid more to produce less. Symptomatic of the across-the-board Brewer collapse. Count on at least modest comebacks from both pitcher and team.

Year Team	Lg.	G	IP	H	BB	SO	W	L	ERA	SV	Ratio
1990 Milwaukee	AL	8	29.2	37	6	20	2	2	4.85	0	1.449
1991 Milwaukee	AL	28	193.1	176	40	89	15	7	2.84	0	1.117
1992 Milwaukee	AL	35	261.2	251	55	127	13	14	3.20	0	1.169
1993 Milwaukee	AL	20	120.2	135	34	50	4	14	4.48	0	1.401
Four-Year Average			151.0	150	34	72	9	9	3.42	0	1.213

BOB WELCH

Age 37/R **$2**

Some power pitchers learn new ways to get batters out when their power fades. Others don't.

Year Team	Lg.	G	IP	H	BB	SO	W	L	ERA	SV	Ratio
1990 Oakland	AL	35	238.0	214	77	127	27	6	2.95	0	1.223
1991 Oakland	AL	35	220.0	220	91	101	12	13	4.58	0	1.414
1992 Oakland	AL	20	123.2	114	43	47	11	7	3.27	0	1.270
1993 Oakland	AL	30	166.2	208	56	63	9	11	5.29	0	1.584
Four-Year Average			187.0	189	67	85	15	9	4.00	0	1.367

DAVID WELLS

Age 30/L **$5**

Looks like a graduate of the John Kruk school of bodybuilding, but pitches tough in a hitters' park. This should not be construed as an unqualified endorsement of either his physical regimen or his mound prowess.

Year Team	Lg.	G	IP	H	BB	SO	W	L	ERA	SV	Ratio
1990 Toronto	AL	43	189.0	165	45	115	11	6	3.14	3	1.111
1991 Toronto	AL	40	198.1	188	49	106	15	10	3.72	1	1.195
1992 Toronto	AL	41	120.0	138	36	62	7	9	5.40	2	1.450
1993 Detroit	AL	32	187.0	183	42	139	11	9	4.19	0	1.203
Four-Year Average			173.0	169	43	106	11	9	3.98	2	1.218

BOB WICKMAN

Age 25/R **$5**

Will stay in the bullpen unless all the Yankee phenoms bomb. Wherever he goes, any guy who has a sawed-off finger that makes the ball sink naturally will always have a place on our staff.

Year Team	Lg.	G	IP	H	BB	SO	W	L	ERA	SV	Ratio
1992 New York	AL	8	50.1	51	20	21	6	1	4.11	0	1.411
1993 New York	AL	41	140.0	156	69	70	14	4	4.63	4	1.607
Four-Year Average			95.0	104	45	46	10	3	4.49	2	1.555

BOBBY WITT

Age 29/R **$6**

There was talk over the winter that Oakland might trade him. If that happens, deduct about five bucks from his value.

Year Team	Lg.	G	IP	H	BB	SO	W	L	ERA	SV	Ratio
1990 Texas	AL	33	222.0	197	110	221	17	10	3.36	0	1.383
1991 Texas	AL	17	88.2	84	74	82	3	7	6.09	0	1.782
1992 Texas	AL	25	161.1	152	95	100	9	13	4.46	0	1.531
1992 Oakland	AL	6	31.2	31	19	25	1	1	3.41	0	1.579
1993 Oakland	AL	35	220.0	226	91	131	14	13	4.21	0	1.441
Four-Year Average			180.0	173	97	140	11	11	4.20	0	1.491

Out of the Bullpen

It's End Game time during the auction draft. You have one open pitching slot and one buck to spend. And you hate your team.

You sit at the auction table, trying to stay awake even though there hasn't been a puff of fresh air in the room for six hours. You chew reflexively on a dry bagel, check your watch for the ninth time in the last ten minutes, and scratch names off a page-long list of pitchers that you would have been able to buy if you hadn't blown $33 on John Franco. You're waiting for everyone else to run out of money so you can pick up some stiff to fill out your roster, pack up your briefcase full of scouting notes, and go home to start planning for next year. Finally, all the other owners with a single open pitching slot are down to their last dollar. The next time it's your turn to put a guy up for auction no one will be able to outbid you: for better or worse, and it'll almost certainly be the latter, he'll be yours. So you sit up in your seat, shake your head to clear the cobwebs, and gird your loins for one last heroic effort to turn a bunch of sow's ears into silk purses. Fat chance. The only guys left are clones of Andy Ashby and Pete Schourek. Anthony Young is also available, but you've had enough bad luck for one draft, thank you. You run down the dwindling list for the gazillionth time. Better the devil you don't know than the devil you do know, you decide, grasping for straws and other clichés to live by. So you reject the Schoureks and Ashbys and Youngs on the list and look for someone new and untainted. Suddenly your eye falls on a name that you vaguely remember popping up in spring training. Surprised everybody by making the team, something like that. You had meant to find out more about him but naturally you didn't. He's a Brave—that's good. Probably won't pitch much. That's good, too—at least he won't hurt you. Plus he's got the same first name as last year's Cy Young Award winner—that could be a good sign. Why not? What have you got to lose?

"Greg McMichael, one dollar."

And thus a pennant is won.

NATIONAL LEAGUE

LARRY ANDERSEN   Age 40/R $1

"Everybody thought Atlanta would be here," Andersen said just before the 1993 NL playoffs began. "Everybody thought we'd be in prison." Ah, good old Larry. We thought for sure he was through. Thank goodness we were wrong. What would we do without a guy who worries about questions like "Why do you sing 'Take Me Out to the Ball Game' when you're already at a ball game?" And where would the Phils have been without his steadying influence on a shaky bullpen? Probably in prison.

Year Team	Lg.	G	IP	H	BB	SO	W	L	ERA	SV	Ratio
1990 Houston	NL	50	73.2	61	24	68	5	2	1.95	6	1.154
1990 Boston	AL	15	22.0	18	3	25	0	0	1.23	1	0.955
1991 San Diego	NL	38	47.0	39	13	40	3	4	2.30	13	1.106
1992 San Diego	NL	34	35.0	26	8	35	1	1	3.34	2	0.971
1993 Philadelphia	NL	64	61.2	54	21	67	3	2	2.92	0	1.216
Four-Year Average			59.0	50	17	59	3	2	2.41	6	1.116

BOBBY AYALA   Age 24/R $1

A young righthander with hellacious stuff who has little clue of where the ball is going when it leaves his hand. We thought he would get a chance to challenge the tottering Rob Dibble for the closer role in Cincinnati, but instead he's getting a chance to be The Man in Seattle.

Year Team	Lg.	G	IP	H	BB	SO	W	L	ERA	SV	Ratio
1992 Cincinnati	NL	5	29.0	33	13	23	2	1	4.34	0	1.586
1993 Cincinnati	NL	43	98.0	106	45	65	7	10	5.60	3	1.541
Four-Year Average			63.0	70	29	44	5	6	5.31	2	1.551

JOSE BAUTISTA   Age 29/R $6

Shhh! You might wake him up.

Year Team	Lg.	G	IP	H	BB	SO	W	L	ERA	SV	Ratio
1990 Baltimore	AL	22	26.2	28	7	15	1	0	4.05	0	1.313
1991 Baltimore	AL	5	5.1	13	5	3	0	1	16.88	0	3.375
1993 Chicago	NL	58	111.2	105	27	63	10	3	2.82	2	1.182
Four-Year Average			47.0	49	13	27	4	1	3.57	1	1.288

ROD BECK   Age 25/R $39

Never let it be said that all Giants pitchers are fragile. No other NL closer appeared in more games or logged more innings. Day after day, Beck guy just kept humping it up and saving games. Toward the end, we were worried that his right arm might fall off. No big deal if it had: he'd just have stomped in from the pen and grabbed the ball in his left paw. He might not have led his league in saves, but he was our Closer of the Year.

Year Team	Lg.	G	IP	H	BB	SO	W	L	ERA	SV	Ratio
1991 San Francisco	NL	31	52.1	53	13	38	1	1	3.78	1	1.261
1992 San Francisco	NL	65	92.0	62	15	87	3	3	1.76	17	0.837
1993 San Francisco	NL	76	79.1	57	13	86	3	1	2.16	48	0.882
Four-Year Average			74.0	57	14	70	2	2	2.37	22	0.952

STEVE BEDROSIAN   Age 36/R $3

One of the most pleasant developments of a great 1993 baseball season was the comeback of Bedrock, one of our all-time favorites. The way he pitched, you wonder why Bobby Cox didn't give him the ball in a single save situation the entire season.

Year Team	Lg.	G	IP	H	BB	SO	W	L	ERA	SV	Ratio
1990 San Francisco	NL	68	79.1	72	44	43	9	9	4.20	17	1.462
1991 Minnesota	AL	56	77.1	70	35	44	5	3	4.42	6	1.358
1993 Atlanta	NL	49	49.2	34	14	33	5	2	1.63	0	0.966
Four-Year Average			68.0	59	31	40	6	5	3.66	8	1.304

DAVE BURBA   Age 27/R $2

Most teams with winning records have a middle innings guy who vultures his way to double figures in wins by being in the right place at the right time. Last year Burba was one of the top vultures in the major leagues. The problem always is having such good place-time luck two years running. And one wonders if that final-day bombardment at the hands of the Dodgers will affect him down the road.

Catchers
pp. 59-73

Corners
pp. 73-95

Infield
pp. 95-116

Outfield
pp. 117-150

DH
pp. 150-153

Starters
pp. 154-189

Relievers
pp. 190-217

Year Team	Lg.	G	IP	H	BB	SO	W	L	ERA	SV	Ratio
1990 Seattle	AL	6	8.0	8	2	4	0	0	4.50	0	1.250
1991 Seattle	AL	22	36.2	34	14	16	2	2	3.68	1	1.309
1992 San Francisco	NL	23	70.2	80	31	47	2	7	4.97	0	1.571
1993 San Francisco	NL	54	95.1	95	37	88	10	3	4.25	0	1.385
Four-Year Average			52.0	54	21	39	4	3	4.40	0	1.429

JOHN CANDELARIA   Age 40/L $1

We really hate it when guys we have really liked for a really long time finally
fade away. Lest anyone forget, in 19 big league seasons this guy has a lifetime
ERA of 3.30 and a lifetime ratio of 1.161. The Candyman *could*.

Year Team	Lg.	G	IP	H	BB	SO	W	L	ERA	SV	Ratio
1990 Minnesota	AL	34	58.1	55	9	44	7	3	3.39	4	1.097
1990 Toronto	AL	13	21.1	32	11	19	0	3	5.48	1	2.016
1991 Los Angeles	NL	59	33.2	31	11	38	1	1	3.74	2	1.248
1992 Los Angeles	NL	50	25.1	20	13	23	2	5	2.84	5	1.303
1993 Pittsburgh	NL	24	19.2	25	9	17	0	3	8.24	1	1.729
Four-Year Average			39.0	41	13	35	3	4	4.26	3	1.364

OMAR DAAL   Age 22/L $1

All too often he pitched like the Dali Lama. Actually, we've never seen the
Dali Lama pitch, but we have it on good authority that he hangs a lot of
sliders to left-handed hitters.

Year Team	Lg.	G	IP	H	BB	SO	W	L	ERA	SV	Ratio
1993 Los Angeles	NL	47	35.1	36	21	19	2	3	5.09	0	1.613
Four-Year Average			35.0	36	21	19	2	3	5.09	0	1.613

MARK DAVIS   Age 33/L $1

Who says the Padres aren't going in the right direction? They picked this
guy up in hopes he could return to his Cy Young form, and doggone it if
there weren't innings here and there when it looked like he had. Next big
Padre signing is Nate Colbert.

Year Team	Lg.	G	IP	H	BB	SO	W	L	ERA	SV	Ratio
1990 Kansas City	AL	53	68.2	71	52	73	2	7	5.11	6	1.791
1991 Kansas City	AL	29	62.2	55	39	47	6	3	4.45	1	1.500
1992 Kansas City	AL	13	36.1	42	28	19	1	3	7.18	0	1.927
1992 Atlanta	NL	14	16.2	22	13	15	1	0	7.02	0	2.100
1993 Philadelphia	NL	25	31.1	35	24	28	1	2	5.17	0	1.883
1993 San Diego	NL	35	38.1	44	20	42	0	3	3.52	4	1.670
Four-Year Average			63.0	67	44	56	3	5	5.14	3	1.752

MARK DEWEY   Age 29/R $7

Unlike Tom Dewey (no relation), Mark showed he has the stuff to close the
deal. So, until further notice, he is the de facto chairperson of Pittsburgh's
bullpen by committee. Don't go hog-wild, though: Dewey had five BS to go
with his seven S.

Year Team	Lg.	G	IP	H	BB	SO	W	L	ERA	SV	Ratio
1990 San Francisco	NL	14	22.2	22	5	11	1	1	2.78	0	1.191
1992 New York	NL	20	33.1	37	10	24	1	0	4.32	0	1.410
1993 Pittsburgh	NL	21	26.2	14	10	14	1	2	2.36	7	0.900
Four-Year Average			27.0	24	8	16	1	1	3.27	2	1.186

ROB DIBBLE

Age 30/R   **$15**

A closer without confidence is like a bullfighter without a cape. Unless a closer believes in himself, he is utterly, nakedly vulnerable to the pressure that comes with stepping onto the mound *only* when the game is on the line. A starter can get knocked out in the early innings, take a quick shower, and sit around in the clubhouse with a can of beer while his teammates bat around a couple of times to take him off the hook. A closer doesn't have that luxury. He gives up an infield single, walks a guy on a bad call, has a broken-bat pop fly ball fall in for a single, and suddenly it's all over, finito, chalk up one in the L column. The only way a closer can be effective—the only way a closer can be a *closer*—is if he has the confidence to say to himself, what the hell, I'll get 'em next time. Say it and believe it. Last year Rob Dibble had arm problems for the second year in a row, but, more important, he also had confidence problems. More than once he wondered publicly why he was being used in closing situations. If the arm is healthy and the confidence comes back, he could be one of the all-time bargains in this year's auction-drafts. But if the confidence isn't there, the condition of the arm won't matter, and he'll be overpriced by at least a double sawbuck.

Year Team	Lg.	G	IP	H	BB	SO	W	L	ERA	SV	Ratio
1990 Cincinnati	NL	68	98.0	62	34	136	8	3	1.74	11	0.980
1991 Cincinnati	NL	67	82.1	67	25	124	3	5	3.17	31	1.117
1992 Cincinnati	NL	63	70.1	48	31	110	3	5	3.07	25	1.123
1993 Cincinnati	NL	45	41.2	34	42	49	1	4	6.48	19	1.824
Four-Year Average			73.0	53	33	105	4	4	3.14	22	1.173

TOM EDENS

Age 32/R   **$1**

Uneventful seasons seem to be his specialty.

Year Team	Lg.	G	IP	H	BB	SO	W	L	ERA	SV	Ratio
1990 Milwaukee	AL	35	89.0	89	33	40	4	5	4.45	2	1.371
1991 Minnesota	AL	8	33.0	34	10	19	2	2	4.09	0	1.333
1992 Minnesota	AL	52	76.1	65	36	57	6	3	2.83	3	1.323
1993 Houston	NL	38	49.0	47	19	21	1	1	3.12	0	1.347
Four-Year Average			61.0	59	25	34	3	3	3.64	1	1.346

STEVE FOSTER

Age 27/R   **$1**

No relation to the songwriter, but he may be given a chance to croon "The Party's Over" in Cincinnati.

Year Team	Lg.	G	IP	H	BB	SO	W	L	ERA	SV	Ratio
1991 Cincinnati	NL	11	14.0	7	4	11	0	0	1.93	0	0.786
1992 Cincinnati	NL	31	50.0	52	13	34	1	1	2.88	2	1.300
1993 Cincinnati	NL	17	25.2	23	5	16	2	2	1.75	0	1.091
Four-Year Average			29.0	27	7	20	1	1	2.41	1	1.160

JOHN FRANCO

Age 33/L   **$10**

It took a final-week hot streak for the Franco-led Mets bullpen to keep from compiling the first minus rating in the history of the Rolaids Reliever Rankings. It was a crusade that had us on the edge of our seats. The problem with assigning any salary to Franco, now a shadow of his former formidable self, is that the Mets are stuck with him—sore elbow, non-sinking sinker,

Catchers
pp. 59–73

Corners
pp. 73–95

Infield
pp. 95–116

Outfield
pp. 117–150

DH
pp. 150–153

Starters
pp. 154–189

Relievers
pp. 190–217

immense contract that makes him untradeable, and all. He'll get the ball a lot, at least in the first third of the season, no matter how he pitches. That could translate into a fair number of ugly saves and unwanted wins. (He practically tore the clubhouse apart last season after a couple of wins following blown saves.) And it could lead to heartache for Rotisserie owners who remember him when he was great.

Year Team	Lg.	G	IP	H	BB	SO	W	L	ERA	SV	Ratio
1990 New York	NL	55	67.2	66	21	56	5	3	2.53	33	1.286
1991 New York	NL	52	55.1	61	18	45	5	9	2.93	30	1.428
1992 New York	NL	31	33.0	24	11	20	6	2	1.64	15	1.061
1993 New York	NL	35	36.1	46	19	29	4	3	5.20	10	1.789
Four-Year Average			48.0	49	17	38	5	4	3.00	22	1.383

JIM GOTT
Age 34/R $21

A closer again, but don't let that news prompt you to rush down to your nearest ATM. Remember his history of arm trouble and Tommy Lasorda's history of preferring bullpen committees.

Year Team	Lg.	G	IP	H	BB	SO	W	L	ERA	SV	Ratio
1990 Los Angeles	NL	50	62.0	59	34	44	3	5	2.90	3	1.500
1991 Los Angeles	NL	55	76.0	63	32	73	4	3	2.96	2	1.250
1992 Los Angeles	NL	68	88.0	72	41	75	3	3	2.45	6	1.284
1993 Los Angeles	NL	62	77.2	71	17	67	4	8	2.32	25	1.133
Four-Year Average			75.0	66	31	65	4	5	2.64	9	1.281

GENE HARRIS
Age 29/R $23

As closers go, he'll come cheap. And if the Padres win any games, he's likely to save them. Sounds like a pretty good deal.

Year Team	Lg.	G	IP	H	BB	SO	W	L	ERA	SV	Ratio
1990 Seattle	AL	25	38.0	31	30	43	1	2	4.74	0	1.605
1991 Seattle	AL	8	13.1	15	10	6	0	0	4.05	1	1.875
1992 Seattle	AL	8	9.0	8	6	6	0	0	7.00	0	1.556
1992 San Diego	NL	14	21.1	15	9	19	0	2	2.95	0	1.125
1993 San Diego	NL	59	59.1	57	37	39	6	6	3.03	23	1.584
Four-Year Average			35.0	32	23	28	2	3	3.83	6	1.546

BRYAN HARVEY
Age 30/R $41

Back from arm troubles to reclaim his position as one of the game's best. He wore down a bit at the end of last season, but part of the reason was the growing infrequency of save opportunities as Florida sank below sea level. Don't be startled if the Marlins trade him for a whole school of prospects.

Year Team	Lg.	G	IP	H	BB	SO	W	L	ERA	SV	Ratio
1990 California	AL	54	64.1	45	35	82	4	4	3.22	25	1.244
1991 California	AL	67	78.2	51	17	101	2	4	1.60	46	0.864
1992 California	AL	25	28.2	22	11	34	0	4	2.83	13	1.151
1993 Florida	NL	59	69.0	45	13	73	1	5	1.70	45	0.841
Four-Year Average			60.0	41	19	73	2	4	2.21	32	0.993

XAVIER HERNANDEZ
Age 28/R   **$10**

The most underrated reliever in the league. With Doug Jones iffy and Todd Jones still a baby, the Astros might regret not giving the closer job to X-Man. But he will look swell in pinstripes.

Year Team	Lg.	G	IP	H	BB	SO	W	L	ERA	SV	Ratio
1990 Houston	NL	34	62.1	60	24	24	2	1	4.62	0	1.348
1991 Houston	NL	32	63.0	66	32	55	2	7	4.71	3	1.556
1992 Houston	NL	77	111.0	81	42	96	9	1	2.11	7	1.108
1993 Houston	NL	72	96.2	75	28	101	4	5	2.61	9	1.066
Four-Year Average			83.0	71	32	69	4	4	3.22	5	1.225

TREVOR HOFFMAN
Age 26/R   **$9**

He wears black socks to make himself look meaner. He consistently throws in the mid-90s. He's wild enough to scare the Red Man out of right-handed hitters. (Just ask Robby Thompson.) Of all the young bodies acquired in the Padres fire sale last summer, he might turn out to be the best of the bunch. Years from now, we could all be sitting around campfires telling Tales of Hoffman.

Year Team	Lg.	G	IP	H	BB	SO	W	L	ERA	SV	Ratio
1993 Florida	NL	28	35.2	24	19	26	2	2	3.28	2	1.206
1993 San Diego	NL	39	54.1	56	20	53	2	4	4.31	3	1.399
Four-Year Average			89.0	80	39	79	4	6	3.90	5	1.322

DARREN HOLMES
Age 27/R   **$28**

In the first third of last season, he was so bad that when he entered a game most of Colorado's bench players would head for the clubhouse to avoid witnessing the carnage. But then he went to the minors for a little attitude adjustment, and from midseason on he was the solid, consistent, effective closer the Rockies expected him to be all along.

Year Team	Lg.	G	IP	H	BB	SO	W	L	ERA	SV	Ratio
1990 Los Angeles	NL	14	17.1	15	11	19	0	1	5.19	0	1.500
1991 Milwaukee	AL	40	76.1	90	27	59	1	4	4.72	3	1.533
1992 Milwaukee	AL	41	42.1	35	11	31	4	4	2.55	6	1.087
1993 Colorado	NL	62	66.2	56	20	60	3	3	4.05	25	1.140
Four-Year Average			50.0	49	17	42	2	3	4.09	9	1.308

JEFF INNIS
Age 31/R   **$1**

Not your typical Met. He was just mediocre last season, not rank ugly.

Year Team	Lg.	G	IP	H	BB	SO	W	L	ERA	SV	Ratio
1990 New York	NL	18	26.1	19	10	12	1	3	2.39	1	1.101
1991 New York	NL	69	84.2	66	23	47	0	2	2.66	0	1.051
1992 New York	NL	76	88.0	85	36	39	6	9	2.86	1	1.375
1993 New York	NL	67	76.2	81	38	36	2	3	4.11	3	1.552
Four-Year Average			68.0	63	27	34	2	4	3.10	1	1.299

MIKE JACKSON
Age 29/R   **$5**

He pitched in 81 games and supposedly warmed up in over 40 others. Yikes! Our arm hurts just thinking about it. Over the years, Jackson has broken many a Rotisserie owner's heart. You look at the ERA and the ratio and the

Catchers
pp. 59–73

Corners
pp. 73–95

Infield
pp. 95–116

Outfield
pp. 117–150

DH
pp. 150–153

Starters
pp. 154–189

Relievers
pp. 190–217

strikeouts, and you think, hey, this guy has *got* to pick up a handful of saves, even if he isn't the main man out of the bullpen. Then you look a little closer and you see another number: five blown saves in six opportunities last season. That sums up Mike Jackson: always a setup man, never a closer.

Year Team	Lg.	G	IP	H	BB	SO	W	L	ERA	SV	Ratio
1990 Seattle	AL	63	77.1	64	44	69	5	7	4.54	3	1.397
1991 Seattle	AL	72	88.2	64	34	74	7	7	3.25	14	1.105
1992 San Francisco	NL	67	82.0	76	33	80	6	6	3.73	2	1.329
1993 San Francisco	NL	81	77.1	58	24	70	6	6	3.03	1	1.060
Four-Year Average			81.0	66	34	73	6	7	3.62	5	1.220

JOEL JOHNSTON   Age 27/R $2

Not always sure where the plate is, but he has a live arm. If Ray Miller can teach him to throw strikes, he could become, oh, vice-chairperson of Jim Leyland's bullpen by committee.

Year Team	Lg.	G	IP	H	BB	SO	W	L	ERA	SV	Ratio
1991 Kansas City	AL	13	22.1	9	9	21	1	0	0.40	0	0.806
1992 Kansas City	AL	5	2.2	3	2	0	0	0	13.50	0	1.875
1993 Pittsburgh	NL	33	53.1	38	19	31	2	4	3.38	2	1.069
Four-Year Average			26.0	17	10	17	1	1	2.87	1	1.021

DOUG JONES   Age 36/R $11

How does the saying go—"You can fool some of the people some of the time, but sooner or later you start hanging all those changeups?" Well, the chickens (and the changeups) came home to roost in Houston as they had done three years before in Cleveland. As a result, the Astros swapped him to Philadelphia. We think he needs a new league, not just a new town.

Year Team	Lg.	G	IP	H	BB	SO	W	L	ERA	SV	Ratio
1990 Cleveland	AL	66	84.1	66	22	55	5	5	2.56	43	1.043
1991 Cleveland	AL	36	63.1	87	17	48	4	8	5.54	7	1.642
1992 Houston	NL	80	111.2	96	17	93	11	8	1.85	36	1.012
1993 Houston	NL	71	85.1	102	21	66	4	10	4.54	26	1.441
Four-Year Average			86.0	88	19	66	6	8	3.37	28	1.242

TODD JONES   Age 25/R $5

Came up late last season and impressed Houston with his stuff. The salary is either ludicrously low or a tad high, depending on whether Mitch Williams burns up the Astrodome or flames out.

Year Team	Lg.	G	IP	H	BB	SO	W	L	ERA	SV	Ratio
1993 Houston	NL	27	37.1	28	15	25	1	2	3.13	2	1.152
Four-Year Average			37.0	28	15	25	1	2	3.13	2	1.152

LES LANCASTER   Age 31/R $1

Nice season from an archetypal journeyman.

Year Team	Lg.	G	IP	H	BB	SO	W	L	ERA	SV	Ratio
1990 Chicago	NL	55	109.0	121	40	65	9	5	4.62	6	1.477
1991 Chicago	NL	64	156.0	150	49	102	9	7	3.52	3	1.276
1992 Detroit	AL	41	86.2	101	51	35	3	4	6.33	0	1.754
1993 St. Louis	NL	50	61.1	56	21	36	4	1	2.93	0	1.255
Four-Year Average			103.0	107	40	60	6	4	4.31	2	1.426

RICHIE LEWIS
Age 28/R   **$1**

You never can tell about middle relievers. Six wins and a 3.36 ERA from a guy you buy for a buck at the end of the auction draft is pretty doggone good. But will he do it again? The same middle innings guy might pitch just as well the following year and get two wins. Or his ERA could balloon by a run as he vultures his way to ten wins. You just never can tell.

Year Team	Lg.	G	IP	H	BB	SO	W	L	ERA	SV	Ratio
1992 Baltimore	AL	2	6.2	13	7	4	1	1	10.80	0	3.000
1993 Florida	NL	57	77.1	68	43	65	6	3	3.26	0	1.435
Four-Year Average			41.0	41	25	35	4	2	3.86	0	1.560

MIKE MADDUX
Age 32/R   **$1**

Take a look at Mike Maddux's ERA for 1992 and 1991. Now look at the numbers of wins he got in those two years. As we were just saying, you never can tell about middle relievers.

Year Team	Lg.	G	IP	H	BB	SO	W	L	ERA	SV	Ratio
1990 Los Angeles	NL	11	20.2	24	4	11	0	1	6.53	0	1.355
1991 San Diego	NL	64	98.2	78	27	57	7	2	2.46	5	1.064
1992 San Diego	NL	50	79.2	71	24	60	2	2	2.37	5	1.192
1993 New York	NL	58	75.0	67	27	57	3	8	3.60	5	1.253
Four-Year Average			68.0	60	21	46	3	3	3.05	4	1.175

PEDRO MARTINEZ
Age 22/R   **$2**

Not to be confused with Pedro Martinez (see below). This Pedro Martinez—Pedro A., if you're keeping score—is a lefty Padres reliever with a live arm, whereas the other Pedro Martinez—Pedro J.—is a righty reliever (former Dodger, now an Expo) with a live arm. We don't want to say any more about Pedro A. because we think he could be somebody special and want to hold his price down. Mum's the word, okay?

Year Team	Lg.	G	IP	H	BB	SO	W	L	ERA	SV	Ratio
1992 Los Angeles	NL	2	8.0	6	1	8	0	1	2.25	0	0.875
1993 Los Angeles	NL	65	107.0	76	57	119	10	5	2.61	2	1.243
Four-Year Average			57.0	41	29	64	5	3	2.58	1	1.217

PEDRO MARTINEZ
Age 25/L   **$8**

Not to be confused with Pedro Martinez (see above). How good is Pedro J.'s stuff? Well, on the season's final weekend, Will Clark and Robby Thompson and a few of the Giants were sitting around, talking ball, and the general consensus was that the key to their chances of sweeping that final series with the Dodgers was to avoid facing this Pedro. Unfortunately, little did the Giants know that they also should have been hoping to avoid Kevin Gross as well. Could be the key to a divisional title in Montreal.

Year Team	Lg.	G	IP	H	BB	SO	W	L	ERA	SV	Ratio
1993 San Diego	NL	32	37.0	23	13	32	3	1	2.43	0	0.973
Four-Year Average			37.0	23	13	32	3	1	2.43	0	0.973

Catchers
pp. 59–73

Corners
pp. 73–95

Infield
pp. 95–116

Outfield
pp. 117–150

DH
pp. 150–153

Starters
pp. 154–189

Relievers
pp. 190–217

ROGER MASON
Age 35/R $1

He distinguished himself last season by allowing seven home runs that either tied or lost games. That has to be some kind of record for a reliever on a division champion. That also will likely make Boom-Boom an ex-reliever on a division champion.

Year Team	Lg.	G	IP	H	BB	SO	W	L	ERA	SV	Ratio
1991 Pittsburgh	NL	24	29.2	21	6	21	3	2	3.03	3	0.910
1992 Pittsburgh	NL	65	88.0	80	33	56	5	7	4.09	8	1.284
1993 San Diego	NL	34	50.0	43	18	39	0	7	3.24	0	1.220
1993 Philadelphia	NL	34	49.2	47	16	32	5	5	4.89	0	1.268
Four-Year Average			72.0	64	24	49	4	7	3.93	4	1.215

TIM MAUSER
Age 27/R $1

This is the warm body the Padres got for Mason, and we were about to make a cheap joke about Mauser rhyming with Bowser, but then we spotted those 46 K in 54 IP. We think we'll reserve judgment for a while.

Year Team	Lg.	G	IP	H	BB	SO	W	L	ERA	SV	Ratio
1991 Philadelphia	NL	3	10.2	18	3	6	0	0	7.59	0	1.969
1993 Philadelphia	NL	8	16.1	15	7	14	0	0	4.96	0	1.347
1993 San Diego	NL	28	37.2	36	17	32	0	1	3.58	0	1.407
Four-Year Average			32.0	35	14	26	0	1	4.59	0	1.485

ROGER McDOWELL
Age 33/R $2

Practical jokes and wisecracks aside, he remains a solid reliever with a winner's heart. He was also a loyal friend to Bobby Ojeda last season, maintaining close contact with his old pal all year when Bobby O was at his lowest. McDowell is prima facie evidence of how miserably wrongheaded the Mets have been as judges of character over the years.

Year Team	Lg.	G	IP	H	BB	SO	W	L	ERA	SV	Ratio
1990 Philadelphia	NL	72	86.1	92	35	39	6	8	3.86	22	1.471
1991 Philadelphia	NL	38	59.0	61	32	28	3	6	3.20	3	1.576
1991 Los Angeles	NL	33	42.1	39	16	22	6	3	2.55	7	1.299
1992 Los Angeles	NL	65	83.2	103	42	50	6	10	4.09	14	1.733
1993 Los Angeles	NL	54	68.0	76	30	27	5	3	2.25	2	1.559
Four-Year Average			84.0	93	39	42	7	8	3.32	12	1.550

CHUCK McELROY
Age 26/L $1

A once-promising career now seems headed in the wrong direction. Perhaps a new regime in Chicago can turn this hard-throwing lefty around. If so, look back to 1991 to see what you can expect.

Year Team	Lg.	G	IP	H	BB	SO	W	L	ERA	SV	Ratio
1990 Philadelphia	NL	16	14.0	24	10	16	0	1	7.71	0	2.429
1991 Chicago	NL	71	101.1	73	57	92	6	2	1.95	3	1.283
1992 Chicago	NL	72	83.2	73	51	83	4	7	3.55	6	1.482
1993 Chicago	NL	49	47.1	51	25	31	2	2	4.56	0	1.606
Four-Year Average			61.0	55	36	56	3	3	3.32	2	1.478

GREG McMICHAEL
Age 27/R $11

One of the year's great stories: a nonroster invitee to spring training pitches his way onto the big club, eventually becomes the ace closer, and helps carry his team to the division title. But a lot of people around the National League think this inspirational story will not repeat itself—that McMichael's stuff is too short for him to remain a closer, that the Braves know this, and that John Schuerholz will deal a handful of prospects for the dragon slayer who will finally bring World Championship rings to Ted and Jane.

Catchers
pp. 59–73

Corners
pp. 73–95

Infield
pp. 95–116

Outfield
pp. 117–150

DH
pp. 150–153

Starters
pp. 154–189

Relievers
pp. 190–217

Year Team	Lg.	G	IP	H	BB	SO	W	L	ERA	SV	Ratio
1993 Atlanta	NL	74	91.2	68	29	89	2	3	2.06	19	1.058
Four-Year Average			91.0	68	29	89	2	3	2.06	19	1.058

KENT MERCKER
Age 26/L $4

He's done just about every job you can do on a pitcher's mound except plant strawberries, and done each passably well. But the Braves still haven't decided what his permanent role is to be. Lefty closer? Maybe, if Mike Stanton's sorry second half is indicative of what's to come. Setup man? Maybe, but that would seem to under-utilize his talent. Fifth starter? Maybe, based on his solid performance in that capacity down the stretch. Pitching coach? Eventually, given the breadth of his experience.

Year Team	Lg.	G	IP	H	BB	SO	W	L	ERA	SV	Ratio
1990 Atlanta	NL	36	48.1	43	24	39	4	7	3.17	7	1.386
1991 Atlanta	NL	50	73.1	56	35	62	5	3	2.58	6	1.241
1992 Atlanta	NL	53	68.1	51	35	49	3	2	3.42	6	1.259
1993 Atlanta	NL	43	66.0	52	36	59	3	1	2.86	0	1.333
Four-Year Average			63.0	51	33	52	4	3	2.99	5	1.297

BLAS MINOR
Age 28/R $2

A solid first season for a bad Pittsburgh team. One Pirate had this to say: "You watch him throw and all you can think about is grabbing a bat. But he's got a lot of guts, he wants the ball, and he's a lot better than he appears at first glance." So let's all take a second look.

Year Team	Lg.	G	IP	H	BB	SO	W	L	ERA	SV	Ratio
1992 Pittsburgh	NL	1	2.0	3	0	0	0	0	4.50	0	1.500
1993 Pittsburgh	NL	65	94.1	94	26	84	8	6	4.10	2	1.272
Four-Year Average			48.0	49	13	42	4	3	4.11	1	1.277

ROB MURPHY
Age 33/L $1

Yet another example of the brewery's "Win If It Doesn't Cost Much" strategy that has made the Cardinals one of the most disappointing teams in baseball the last two years. You hate to see such great fans shortchanged by cheapskate owners.

Year Team	Lg.	G	IP	H	BB	SO	W	L	ERA	SV	Ratio
1990 Boston	AL	68	57.0	85	32	54	0	6	6.32	7	2.053
1991 Seattle	AL	57	48.0	47	19	34	0	1	3.00	4	1.375
1992 Houston	NL	59	55.2	56	21	42	3	1	4.04	0	1.383
1993 St. Louis	NL	73	64.2	73	20	41	5	7	4.87	1	1.438
Four-Year Average			56.0	65	23	43	2	4	4.63	3	1.567

RANDY MYERS
Age 31/L $40

Take out a second mortgage. Hock your grandfather's watch. Borrow against your life insurance. Knock over a convenience store. Sell your children. Do anything, even get a job. Just come up with the cash to acquire Randy Muscle-Head, the Human Save Machine.

Year Team	Lg.	G	IP	H	BB	SO	W	L	ERA	SV	Ratio
1990 Cincinnati	NL	66	86.2	59	38	98	4	6	2.08	31	1.119
1991 Cincinnati	NL	58	132.0	116	80	108	6	13	3.55	6	1.485
1992 San Diego	NL	66	79.2	84	34	66	3	6	4.29	38	1.481
1993 Chicago	NL	73	75.1	65	26	86	2	4	3.11	53	1.208
Four-Year Average			93.0	81	45	90	4	7	3.28	32	1.344

OMAR OLIVARES
Age 26/R $2

Joe Torre kicked him out of the rotation and into the bullpen, where he showed some aptitude for long relief. Candidate for Vulture of the Year?

Year Team	Lg.	G	IP	H	BB	SO	W	L	ERA	SV	Ratio
1990 St. Louis	NL	9	49.1	45	17	20	1	1	2.92	0	1.257
1991 St. Louis	NL	28	167.1	148	61	91	11	7	3.71	1	1.249
1992 St. Louis	NL	32	197.0	189	63	124	9	9	3.84	0	1.279
1993 St. Louis	NL	58	118.2	134	54	63	5	3	4.17	1	1.584
Four-Year Average			133.0	129	49	75	7	5	3.79	1	1.336

MIKE PEREZ
Age 29/R $19

The Cardinals think Perez has the stuff to replace Lee Smith. They know he'll cost less, which is the primary consideration around the brewery these days.

Year Team	Lg.	G	IP	H	BB	SO	W	L	ERA	SV	Ratio
1990 St. Louis	NL	13	13.2	12	3	5	1	0	3.95	1	1.098
1991 St. Louis	NL	14	17.0	19	7	7	0	2	5.82	0	1.529
1992 St. Louis	NL	77	93.0	70	32	46	9	3	1.84	0	1.097
1993 St. Louis	NL	65	72.2	65	20	58	7	2	2.48	7	1.170
Four-Year Average			49.0	42	16	29	4	2	2.57	2	1.161

DAN PLESAC
Age 32/L $1

By the end of last season, some Cubs people insisted that his arm was beginning to show signs of life. We don't believe that news flash should be cause for revamping your draft day strategy.

Year Team	Lg.	G	IP	H	BB	SO	W	L	ERA	SV	Ratio
1990 Milwaukee	AL	66	69.0	67	31	65	3	7	4.43	24	1.420
1991 Milwaukee	AL	45	92.1	92	39	61	2	7	4.29	8	1.419
1992 Milwaukee	AL	44	79.0	64	35	54	5	4	2.96	1	1.253
1993 Chicago	NL	57	62.2	74	21	47	2	1	4.74	0	1.516
Four-Year Average			75.0	74	32	57	3	5	4.07	8	1.396

JEFF REARDON
Age 38/R $3

Filled in admirably as the closer when Rob Dibble went south, but then became frustrated by Davey Johnson's indecisiveness about what his role should be.

Year Team	Lg.	G	IP	H	BB	SO	W	L	ERA	SV	Ratio
1990 Boston	AL	47	51.1	39	19	33	5	3	3.16	21	1.130
1991 Boston	AL	57	59.1	54	16	44	1	4	3.03	40	1.180
1992 Boston	AL	46	42.1	53	7	32	2	2	4.25	27	1.417
1992 Atlanta	NL	14	15.2	14	2	7	3	0	1.15	3	1.021
1993 Cincinnati	NL	58	61.2	66	10	35	4	6	4.09	8	1.232
Four-Year Average			57.0	57	14	38	4	4	3.44	25	1.216

STEVE REED   Age 28/R $3

Any fair-to-middling middle reliever for a team like the Rockies, *i.e.*, an outfit with lousy starting pitching and the ability to score runs, is a potentially valuable commodity. And that's the kind of middle reliever Reed was last year: fair-to-middling.

Year Team	Lg.	G	IP	H	BB	SO	W	L	ERA	SV	Ratio
1992 San Francisco	NL	18	15.2	13	3	11	1	0	2.30	0	1.021
1993 Colorado	NL	64	84.1	80	30	51	9	5	4.48	3	1.304
Four-Year Average			49.0	47	17	31	5	3	4.14	2	1.260

DAVE RIGHETTI   Age 35/L $1

Farewell, old friend. Sorry it had to end this way.

Year Team	Lg.	G	IP	H	BB	SO	W	L	ERA	SV	Ratio
1990 New York	AL	53	53.0	48	26	43	1	1	3.57	36	1.396
1991 San Francisco	NL	61	71.2	64	28	51	2	7	3.39	24	1.284
1992 San Francisco	NL	54	78.1	79	36	47	2	7	5.06	3	1.468
1993 San Francisco	NL	51	47.1	58	17	31	1	1	5.70	1	1.585
Four-Year Average			62.0	62	27	43	2	4	4.39	16	1.422

RICH RODRIGUEZ   Age 31/L $2

Another fair-to-middling middle reliever, only this one toils for a team that has lousy starting pitching but *not* the ability to score runs. Last year the Rockies scored 758 runs, the Marlins 581. That pretty much sums up why Steve Reed won nine games and Rich Rodriguez won three, even though Rodriguez's ERA was more than half a run lower. Keep that sort of thing in mind as you mull over the choices at the tail end of the auction draft.

Year Team	Lg.	G	IP	H	BB	SO	W	L	ERA	SV	Ratio
1990 San Diego	NL	32	47.2	52	16	22	1	1	2.83	1	1.427
1991 San Diego	NL	64	80.0	66	44	40	3	1	3.26	0	1.375
1992 San Diego	NL	61	91.0	77	29	64	6	3	2.37	0	1.165
1993 San Diego	NL	34	30.0	34	9	22	2	3	3.30	2	1.433
1993 Florida	NL	36	46.0	39	24	21	0	1	4.11	1	1.370
Four-Year Average			73.0	67	31	42	3	2	3.05	1	1.324

KEVIN ROGERS   Age 25/L $4

A great first full year. He could end up being a co-closer someday with Rod Beck. But be careful. At least a half-dozen scouts tell us that his delivery is tailor-made for arm problems.

Year Team	Lg.	G	IP	H	BB	SO	W	L	ERA	SV	Ratio
1992 San Francisco	NL	6	34.0	37	13	26	0	2	4.24	0	1.471
1993 San Francisco	NL	64	80.2	71	28	62	2	2	2.68	0	1.227
Four-Year Average			57.0	54	21	44	1	2	3.14	0	1.299

BASEBALL ANAGRAM #19

Lace Toy Crony = _____?

(Answer on page 299)

Catchers
pp. 59-73

Corners
pp. 73-95

Infield
pp. 95-116

Outfield
pp. 117-150

DH
pp. 150-153

Starters
pp. 154-189

Relievers
pp. 190-217

MEL ROJAS   Age 27/R $11

Nobody on the Expos throws better than this No-Relation-to-Cookie. But as one of his teammates said, "Mel could be the best reliever in the league if he weren't so goofy." Goofy or not, you'd be daffy not to want him on your club.

Year Team	Lg.	G	IP	H	BB	SO	W	L	ERA	SV	Ratio
1990 Montreal	NL	23	40.0	34	24	26	3	1	3.60	1	1.450
1991 Montreal	NL	37	48.0	42	13	37	3	3	3.75	6	1.146
1992 Montreal	NL	68	100.2	71	34	70	7	1	1.43	10	1.043
1993 Montreal	NL	66	88.1	80	30	48	5	8	2.95	10	1.245
Four-Year Average			69.0	57	25	45	5	3	2.63	7	1.184

BRUCE RUFFIN   Age 30/L $2

An alien took over his body. That's the only explanation we can think of for his solid season.

Year Team	Lg.	G	IP	H	BB	SO	W	L	ERA	SV	Ratio
1990 Philadelphia	NL	32	149.0	178	62	79	6	13	5.38	0	1.611
1991 Philadelphia	NL	31	119.0	125	38	85	4	7	3.78	0	1.370
1992 Milwaukee	AL	25	58.0	66	41	45	1	6	6.67	0	1.845
1993 Colorado	NL	59	139.2	145	69	126	6	5	3.87	2	1.532
Four-Year Average			116.0	129	53	84	4	8	4.68	1	1.555

TIM SCOTT   Age 27/R $3

As you may already have heard, you never can tell about middle relievers. (See Richie Lewis.) But we can tell you this about Scott: he's a good pitcher on a good team who will return good value on your investment.

Year Team	Lg.	G	IP	H	BB	SO	W	L	ERA	SV	Ratio
1991 San Diego	NL	2	1.0	2	0	1	0	0	9.00	0	2.000
1992 San Diego	NL	34	37.2	39	21	30	4	1	5.26	0	1.593
1993 San Diego	NL	24	37.2	38	15	30	2	0	2.39	0	1.407
1993 Montreal	NL	32	34.0	31	19	35	5	2	3.71	1	1.471
Four-Year Average			36.0	37	18	32	4	1	3.83	0	1.496

MIKE STANTON   Age 26/L $8

For half the year he threw like Sparky Lyle. For the other half he threw like Lyle Lovett, only Julia Roberts never even gave him a glance. The Braves don't know what to expect, and neither do we.

Year Team	Lg.	G	IP	H	BB	SO	W	L	ERA	SV	Ratio
1990 Atlanta	NL	7	7.0	16	4	7	0	3	18.00	2	2.857
1991 Atlanta	NL	74	78.0	62	21	54	5	5	2.88	7	1.064
1992 Atlanta	NL	65	63.2	59	20	44	5	4	4.10	8	1.241
1993 Atlanta	NL	63	52.0	51	29	43	4	6	4.67	27	1.538
Four-Year Average			50.0	47	19	37	4	5	4.26	11	1.306

DAVID WEST   Age 29/L $4

Looks like John Kruk from the double chin down. Pitches like a fair-to-middling middle reliever on a team with the ability to score a lot of runs.

Year Team	Lg.	G	IP	H	BB	SO	W	L	ERA	SV	Ratio
1990 Minnesota	AL	29	146.1	142	78	92	7	9	5.10	0	1.503
1991 Minnesota	AL	15	71.1	66	28	52	4	4	4.54	0	1.318
1992 Minnesota	AL	9	28.1	32	20	19	1	3	6.99	0	1.835
1993 Philadelphia	NL	76	86.1	60	51	87	6	4	2.92	3	1.286
Four-Year Average			83.0	75	44	63	5	5	4.58	1	1.435

JOHN WETTELAND

Age 27/R **$38**

From about July 15 on, there was no better closer on earth. If he can just avoid kicking batting screens in spring training, he will be an All-Star worth savoring for years.

Year	Team	Lg.	G	IP	H	BB	SO	W	L	ERA	SV	Ratio
1990	Los Angeles	NL	22	43.0	44	17	36	2	4	4.81	0	1.419
1991	Los Angeles	NL	6	9.0	5	3	9	1	0	0.00	0	0.889
1992	Montreal	NL	67	83.1	64	36	99	4	4	2.92	37	1.200
1993	Montreal	NL	70	85.1	58	28	113	9	3	1.37	43	1.008
Four-Year Average				55.0	43	21	64	4	3	2.57	20	1.156

MITCH WILLIAMS

Age 29/L **$37**

Star of a new soap opera entitled "As the Wild Thing Turns," the heartwarming tale of how one pitcher who has never had a good hair day causes an entire city to break out in hives while giving his own teammates bleeding ulcers. If you own him, don't watch the games; just check the boxscores the next morning. Way more often than not, you'll be pleasantly surprised. (Now, for the umpteenth and last time: Fregosi did the right thing in Game Six of the World Series. Without Williams, the Phillies would have been sucking wind in the middle of the NL East. He's the guy you bring in to close the deal. This time he didn't do it. But don't think of it as Mitch Williams failing; think of it as Joe Carter succeeding. That's what the Astros think—for now.)

Year	Team	Lg.	G	IP	H	BB	SO	W	L	ERA	SV	Ratio
1990	Chicago	NL	59	66.1	60	50	55	1	8	3.93	16	1.658
1991	Philadelphia	NL	69	88.1	56	62	84	12	5	2.34	30	1.336
1992	Philadelphia	NL	66	81.0	69	64	74	5	8	3.78	29	1.642
1993	Philadelphia	NL	65	62.0	56	44	60	3	7	3.34	43	1.613
Four-Year Average				74.0	60	55	68	5	7	3.30	30	1.549

MARK WOHLERS

Age 24/R **$3**

Okay, he hasn't panned out—yet. But isn't it worth gambling a few pocorobas on a guy who can throw 100 miles an hour?

Year	Team	Lg.	G	IP	H	BB	SO	W	L	ERA	SV	Ratio
1991	Atlanta	NL	17	19.2	17	13	13	3	1	3.20	2	1.525
1992	Atlanta	NL	32	35.1	28	14	17	1	2	2.55	4	1.189
1993	Atlanta	NL	46	48.0	37	22	45	6	2	4.50	0	1.229
Four-Year Average				34.0	27	16	25	3	2	3.58	2	1.272

TODD WORRELL

Age 34/R **$1**

If he's healthy, multiply the price by 30. If he's not, tip your hat in thanks for some great memories.

Year	Team	Lg.	G	IP	H	BB	SO	W	L	ERA	SV	Ratio
1992	St. Louis	NL	67	64.0	45	25	64	5	3	2.11	3	1.094
1993	Los Angeles	NL	35	38.2	46	11	31	1	1	6.05	5	1.474
Four-Year Average				51.0	46	18	48	3	2	3.59	4	1.237

Catchers
pp. 59-73

Corners
pp. 73-95

Infield
pp. 95-116

Outfield
pp. 117-150

DH
pp. 150-153

Starters
pp. 154-189

Relievers
pp. 190-217

RICK AGUILERA   Age 32/R $33

Good year for a guy with a bad back. Not surprising, because Aggie is one of the best. Unfortunately, his team is not. For a closer, this often means too many long intervals between gigs and a consequent loss of sharpness. It's easier to stay up psychologically on a winner than on a loser, particularly after the All-Star break. Sometimes the effect is cumulative—and the Twins don't look any better this year.

Year Team	Lg.	G	IP	H	BB	SO	W	L	ERA	SV	Ratio
1990 Minnesota	AL	56	65.1	55	19	61	5	3	2.76	32	1.133
1991 Minnesota	AL	63	69.0	44	30	61	4	5	2.35	42	1.072
1992 Minnesota	AL	64	66.2	60	17	52	2	6	2.84	41	1.155
1993 Minnesota	AL	65	72.1	60	14	59	4	3	3.11	34	1.023
Four-Year Average			68.0	55	20	58	4	4	2.77	37	1.094

PAUL ASSENMACHER   Age 33/L $5

New uniform, but he remains what he has always been: a durable lefty with a big hook who gives you quality innings, some wins, and a handful of saves.

Year Team	Lg.	G	IP	H	BB	SO	W	L	ERA	SV	Ratio
1990 Chicago	NL	74	103.0	90	36	95	7	2	2.80	10	1.223
1991 Chicago	NL	75	102.2	85	31	117	7	8	3.24	15	1.130
1992 Chicago	NL	70	68.0	72	26	67	4	4	4.10	8	1.441
1993 Chicago	NL	46	38.2	44	13	34	2	1	3.49	0	1.474
1993 New York	AL	26	17.1	10	9	11	2	2	3.12	0	1.096
Four-Year Average			82.0	75	29	81	6	4	3.30	8	1.262

STAN BELINDA   Age 27/R $3

How can you expect a guy to be a macho stud he-man ace closer if his last name is a girl's first name? We don't know whether that was a factor in the Pirates' decision, but the peremptory manner in which Pittsburgh dumped him should be a clear sign of his plummeting value. Frankly, in our estimation, his value has been nil ever since he failed to slam the door on the Braves in the seventh game of the 1992 NL playoffs. But that's ancient history, and we don't hold grudges. At least not forever.

Year Team	Lg.	G	IP	H	BB	SO	W	L	ERA	SV	Ratio
1990 Pittsburgh	NL	55	58.1	48	29	55	3	4	3.55	8	1.320
1991 Pittsburgh	NL	60	78.1	50	35	71	7	5	3.45	16	1.085
1992 Pittsburgh	NL	59	71.1	58	29	57	6	4	3.15	18	1.220
1993 Pittsburgh	NL	40	42.1	35	11	30	3	1	3.61	19	1.087
1993 Kansas City	AL	23	27.1	30	6	25	1	1	4.28	0	1.317
Four-Year Average			69.0	55	28	60	5	4	3.50	15	1.192

JOE BOEVER   Age 33/R $1

Used to rhyme with "Saver." Now it rhymes with "Journeyman." Nothing better sums up the Tigers' pitching staff than the fact that he actually made it better.

Year Team	Lg.	G	IP	H	BB	SO	W	L	ERA	SV	Ratio
1990 Atlanta	NL	33	42.1	40	35	35	1	3	4.68	8	1.772
1990 Philadelphia	NL	34	46.0	37	16	40	2	3	2.15	6	1.152
1991 Philadelphia	NL	68	98.1	90	54	89	3	5	3.84	0	1.464
1992 Houston	NL	81	111.1	103	45	67	3	6	2.51	2	1.329
1993 Oakland	AL	42	79.1	87	33	49	4	2	3.86	0	1.513
1993 Detroit	AL	19	23.0	14	11	14	2	1	2.74	3	1.087
Four-Year Average			100.0	93	49	74	4	5	3.30	5	1.411

TOM BOLTON   Age 31/L $1

He may have found his niche as a long reliever on a bad staff. Ugly things happen in that niche, so beware.

Year Team	Lg.	G	IP	H	BB	SO	W	L	ERA	SV	Ratio
1990 Boston	AL	21	119.2	111	47	65	10	5	3.38	0	1.320
1991 Boston	AL	25	110.0	136	51	64	8	9	5.24	0	1.700
1992 Boston	AL	21	29.0	34	14	23	1	2	3.41	0	1.655
1992 Cincinnati	NL	16	46.1	52	23	27	3	3	5.24	0	1.619
1993 Detroit	AL	43	102.2	113	45	66	6	6	4.47	0	1.539
Four-Year Average			101.0	112	45	61	7	6	4.37	0	1.536

CRIS CARPENTER   Age 28/R $3

The Rangers hoped he would help out more than he did. He'll get another chance. After all, just two seasons ago his ten wins in middle relief for the Cardinals earned him Vulture of the Year honors.

Year Team	Lg.	G	IP	H	BB	SO	W	L	ERA	SV	Ratio
1990 St. Louis	NL	4	8.0	5	2	6	0	0	4.50	0	0.875
1991 St. Louis	NL	59	66.0	53	20	47	10	4	4.23	0	1.106
1992 St. Louis	NL	73	88.0	69	27	46	5	4	2.97	1	1.091
1993 Florida	NL	29	37.1	29	13	26	0	1	2.89	0	1.125
1993 Texas	AL	27	32.0	35	12	27	4	1	4.22	1	1.469
Four-Year Average			57.0	48	19	38	5	3	3.54	1	1.146

LARRY CASIAN   Age 28/L $4

A rare ray of promise on a sorry Twins staff.

Year Team	Lg.	G	IP	H	BB	SO	W	L	ERA	SV	Ratio
1990 Minnesota	AL	5	22.1	26	4	11	2	1	3.22	0	1.343
1991 Minnesota	AL	15	18.1	28	7	6	0	0	7.36	0	1.909
1992 Minnesota	AL	6	6.2	7	1	2	1	0	2.70	0	1.200
1993 Minnesota	AL	54	56.2	59	14	31	5	3	3.02	1	1.288
Four-Year Average			25.0	30	7	13	2	1	3.81	0	1.404

NORM CHARLTON   Age 31/L $17

A horse when he's healthy. If he's fully recovered, double the price.

Year Team	Lg.	G	IP	H	BB	SO	W	L	ERA	SV	Ratio
1990 Cincinnati	NL	56	154.1	131	70	117	12	9	2.74	2	1.302
1991 Cincinnati	NL	39	108.1	92	34	77	3	5	2.91	1	1.163
1992 Cincinnati	NL	64	81.1	79	26	90	4	2	2.99	26	1.291
1993 Seattle	AL	34	34.2	22	17	48	1	3	2.34	18	1.125
Four-Year Average			94.0	81	37	83	5	5	2.80	12	1.244

Catchers
pp. 59–73

Corners
pp. 73–95

Infield
pp. 95–116

Outfield
pp. 117–150

DH
pp. 150–153

Starters
pp. 154–189

Relievers
pp. 190–217

DANNY COX   Age 34/R $5

A scout was in a press room watching a Blue Jays game on TV. Cox was pitching, and after one pitch the announcer proclaimed, "Our radar gun had that pitch at 94." The scout spit into a paper cup, mumbled a string of non-family-publication expletives, and snarled, "They either read that number backward or the guy who's running the gun is the same cracker policeman who got me at 68 going through Savannah, Georgia, last spring." Whether at 94 or 49, Cox has resuscitated a career once apparently ended by a devastating arm injury. He played a significant role in Toronto's second straight championship season, and that role should get bigger this year.

Year Team	Lg.	G	IP	H	BB	SO	W	L	ERA	SV	Ratio
1991 Philadelphia	NL	23	102.1	98	39	46	4	6	4.57	0	1.339
1992 Philadelphia	NL	9	38.1	46	19	30	2	2	5.40	0	1.696
1992 Pittsburgh	NL	16	24.1	20	8	18	3	1	3.33	3	1.151
1993 Toronto	AL	44	83.2	73	29	84	7	6	3.12	2	1.219
Four-Year Average			82.0	79	32	59	5	5	4.09	2	1.335

JERRY DIPOTO   Age 25/R $7

Another member in good standing of Cleveland's Bullpen Committee, he might even be chairperson some day.

Year Team	Lg.	G	IP	H	BB	SO	W	L	ERA	SV	Ratio
1993 Cleveland	AL	46	56.1	57	30	41	4	4	2.40	11	1.544
Four-Year Average			56.0	57	30	41	4	4	2.40	11	1.544

DENNIS ECKERSLEY   Age 31/R $31

Last year was tough on Eck fans. That's because he was only a darned good reliever on a pretty awful club instead of the Greatest Reliever Ever on a pretty terrific club. A guy who thrives on regular, meaningful work, Eck went long stretches last summer without a game to save, and the A's were out of the hunt by Memorial Day. With McGwire back in the lineup and the continued development of a few younger players, this season should be a lot more fun for Eck. And, consequently, for us.

Year Team	Lg.	G	IP	H	BB	SO	W	L	ERA	SV	Ratio
1990 Oakland	AL	63	73.1	41	4	73	4	2	0.61	48	0.614
1991 Oakland	AL	67	76.0	60	9	87	5	4	2.96	43	0.908
1992 Oakland	AL	69	80.0	62	11	93	7	1	1.91	51	0.913
1993 Oakland	AL	64	67.0	67	13	80	2	4	4.16	36	1.194
Four-Year Average			74.0	58	9	83	5	3	2.37	45	0.901

STEVE FARR   Age 37/R $9

It was painful to watch Buck Showalter try to convince everyone that Lee Smith's arrival was no reflection on Farr's status. It was. Farr has been a noble warrior over the years, and he had finally become top bull in the pen. But he wasn't getting the job done last season when it counted the most. Will he get another chance? That depends in the first instance on where Smith ends up casting his immense shadow. And then there is the X-factor, *i.e.*, the role Xavier Hernandez will play in Yankee Stadium. As of now, Farr's pinstripe prospects don't look promising.

Year Team	Lg.	G	IP	H	BB	SO	W	L	ERA	SV	Ratio
1990 Kansas City	AL	57	127.0	99	48	94	13	7	1.98	1	1.157
1991 New York	AL	60	70.0	57	20	60	5	5	2.19	23	1.100
1992 New York	AL	50	52.0	34	19	37	2	2	1.56	30	1.019
1993 New York	AL	49	47.0	44	28	39	2	2	4.21	25	1.532
Four-Year Average			74.0	59	29	58	6	4	2.31	20	1.179

MIKE FETTERS   Age 29/R $3

Solid year.

Year Team	Lg.	G	IP	H	BB	SO	W	L	ERA	SV	Ratio
1990 California	AL	26	67.2	77	20	35	1	1	4.12	1	1.433
1991 California	AL	19	44.2	53	28	24	2	5	4.84	0	1.813
1992 Milwaukee	AL	50	62.2	38	24	43	5	1	1.87	2	0.989
1993 Milwaukee	AL	45	59.1	59	22	23	3	3	3.34	0	1.365
Four-Year Average			58.0	57	24	31	3	3	3.46	1	1.370

STEVE FREY   Age 30/L $8

The fact that he's a lefty should guarantee him some closer work even if Joe Grahe comes all the way back from an arm injury.

Year Team	Lg.	G	IP	H	BB	SO	W	L	ERA	SV	Ratio
1990 Montreal	NL	51	55.2	44	29	29	8	2	2.10	9	1.311
1991 Montreal	NL	31	39.2	43	23	21	0	1	4.99	1	1.664
1992 California	AL	51	45.1	39	22	24	4	2	3.57	4	1.346
1993 California	AL	55	48.1	41	26	22	2	3	2.98	13	1.386
Four-Year Average			47.0	42	25	24	4	2	3.29	7	1.413

TODD FROHWIRTH   Age 31/R $3

Hammered so hard in the Orioles' late-season swoon that he said to one member of the fourth estate, "I hate seeing myself pitch right now. Imagine what everyone else must think."

Year Team	Lg.	G	IP	H	BB	SO	W	L	ERA	SV	Ratio
1990 Philadelphia	NL	5	1.0	3	6	1	0	1	18.00	0	9.000
1991 Baltimore	AL	51	96.1	64	29	77	7	3	1.87	3	0.965
1992 Baltimore	AL	65	106.0	97	41	58	4	3	2.46	4	1.302
1993 Baltimore	AL	70	96.1	91	44	50	6	7	3.83	3	1.401
Four-Year Average			74.0	64	30	47	4	4	2.76	3	1.251

TOM GORDON   Age 26/R $8

The Royals think he's a starter. No, wait, they think he's a reliever. No, wait, they think he's a starter. One thing is sure: with a bender like his, he's got to pitch *somewhere*. (We like him as a reliever.)

Year Team	Lg.	G	IP	H	BB	SO	W	L	ERA	SV	Ratio
1990 Kansas City	AL	32	195.1	192	99	175	12	11	3.73	0	1.490
1991 Kansas City	AL	45	158.0	129	87	167	9	14	3.87	1	1.367
1992 Kansas City	AL	40	117.2	116	55	98	6	10	4.59	0	1.453
1993 Kansas City	AL	48	155.2	125	77	143	12	6	3.58	1	1.298
Four-Year Average			156.0	141	80	146	10	10	3.89	1	1.404

GOOSE GOSSAGE   Age 42/R $1

It was a Sunday night in Yankee Stadium. With his entire bullpen exhausted after a string of dulling defeats, Tony LaRussa had no choice but to leave

Catchers	pp. 59–73
Corners	pp. 73–95
Infield	pp. 95–116
Outfield	pp. 117–150
DH	pp. 150–153
Starters	pp. 154–189
Relievers	pp. 190–217

Gossage in to take a horrible shellacking. It was painful to watch—the Goose as staff saver. We much prefer to remember earlier times, bigger games, heroic appearances in the ninth inning to snuff out another rally. For instance, there was another Bronx night, long ago,' in a game against Baltimore. The Goose came on to pitch the ninth, so Earl Weaver sent up John Lowenstein to hit for Gary Roenicke. Gossage was at his ferocious best that year, with a *slider* that cracked 90 when he got up a good head of steam. Lowenstein, figuring his chances of getting around on the Goose at slim to none, stepped up to the plate with a fungo bat in his hands. He swung at the first pitch, the bat disintegrated, the ball plopped into short right, Lowenstein ended up on first, the Oriole dugout collapsed with laughter, and the Goose went ballistic. One thing you did not want to do back then was get the Goose mad. Sure enough, he had the last laugh, striking out the next three batters on ten fastballs, none of which registered lower than 97 on the radar gun, and the last three of which were clocked at 100, 101, and 101. *That's* the Goose we will always remember.

Year Team	Lg.	G	IP	H	BB	SO	W	L	ERA	SV	Ratio
1991 Texas	AL	44	40.1	33	16	28	4	2	3.57	1	1.215
1992 Oakland	AL	30	38.0	32	19	26	0	2	2.84	0	1.342
1993 Oakland	AL	39	47.2	49	26	40	4	5	4.53	1	1.573
Four-Year Average			41.0	38	20	31	3	3	3.71	1	1.389

JOE GRAHE   Age 26/R $16

A solid closer, on his way to great things, and then the arm injury. If the arm's okay, he'll be a bargain at this price. Pay close attention during spring training—less to how well he pitches than to how often. If the Angels baby him, back away. If he works a couple of innings every third day or so, go for him.

Year Team	Lg.	G	IP	H	BB	SO	W	L	ERA	SV	Ratio
1990 California	AL	8	43.1	51	23	25	3	4	4.98	0	1.708
1991 California	AL	18	73.0	84	33	40	3	7	4.81	0	1.603
1992 California	AL	46	94.2	85	39	39	5	6	3.52	21	1.310
1993 California	AL	45	56.2	54	25	31	4	1	2.86	11	1.394
Four-Year Average			66.0	69	30	34	4	5	3.97	8	1.472

MARK GUTHRIE   Age 28/L $4

Last September, with the Twins' season long since down the drain, some of the Minnesota coaches were lamenting what might have been. It was amazing how they kept mentioning how much the loss of Guthrie meant to the club. Jeepers, we thought he was good, but not *that* good.

Year Team	Lg.	G	IP	H	BB	SO	W	L	ERA	SV	Ratio
1990 Minnesota	AL	24	144.2	154	39	101	7	9	3.79	0	1.334
1991 Minnesota	AL	41	98.0	116	41	72	7	5	4.32	2	1.602
1992 Minnesota	AL	54	75.0	59	23	76	2	3	2.88	5	1.093
1993 Minnesota	AL	22	21.0	20	16	15	2	1	4.71	0	1.714
Four-Year Average			84.0	87	30	66	5	5	3.80	2	1.382

JOHN HABYAN

Age 30/R $1

Just another arm.

Year	Team	Lg.	G	IP	H	BB	SO	W	L	ERA	SV	Ratio
1990	New York	AL	6	8.2	10	2	4	0	0	2.08	0	1.385
1991	New York	AL	66	90.0	73	20	70	4	2	2.30	2	1.033
1992	New York	AL	56	72.2	84	21	44	5	6	3.84	7	1.445
1993	New York	AL	36	42.1	45	16	29	2	1	4.04	1	1.441
1993	Kansas City	AL	12	14.0	14	4	10	0	0	4.50	0	1.286
Four-Year Average				56.0	57	16	39	3	2	3.24	3	1.269

GREG HARRIS

Age 38/R $4

Not bad as a spot starter and a middle reliever. Not good as a closer. His ten blown saves tied for the league lead.

Year	Team	Lg.	G	IP	H	BB	SO	W	L	ERA	SV	Ratio
1990	Boston	AL	34	184.1	186	77	117	13	9	4.00	0	1.427
1991	Boston	AL	53	173.0	157	69	127	11	12	3.85	2	1.306
1992	Boston	AL	70	107.2	82	60	73	4	9	2.51	4	1.319
1993	Boston	AL	80	112.1	95	60	103	6	7	3.77	8	1.380
Four-Year Average				144.0	130	67	105	9	9	3.63	4	1.361

NEAL HEATON

Age 34/L $1

As long as he has a left arm, he'll have a job.

Year	Team	Lg.	G	IP	H	BB	SO	W	L	ERA	SV	Ratio
1990	Pittsburgh	NL	30	146.0	143	38	68	12	9	3.45	0	1.240
1991	Pittsburgh	NL	42	68.2	72	21	34	3	3	4.33	0	1.354
1992	Kansas City	AL	31	41.0	43	22	29	3	1	4.17	0	1.585
1992	Milwaukee	AL	1	1.0	0	1	2	0	0	0.00	0	1.000
1993	New York	AL	18	27.0	34	11	15	1	0	6.00	0	1.667
Four-Year Average				70.0	73	23	37	5	3	4.00	0	1.357

TOM HENKE

Age 36/R $38

Spring training is full of idle moments, and during one of them last year in Port Charlotte, Florida, a glum Henke talked about how, months after the Blue Jays had informed him they were no longer interested in his services, he still felt disconnected and adrift. He talked about how tough it was to be with a new team, how much he missed the Blue Jays, how he would have stayed in Toronto for less money. Well, somewhere along the line, Henke got pretty doggone comfortable in his new Texas Ranger uniform. Or maybe it was that shiny badge he's earned as one of the premier aces in the game.

Year	Team	Lg.	G	IP	H	BB	SO	W	L	ERA	SV	Ratio
1990	Toronto	AL	61	74.2	58	19	75	2	4	2.17	32	1.031
1991	Toronto	AL	49	50.1	33	11	53	0	2	2.32	32	0.874
1992	Toronto	AL	57	55.2	40	22	46	3	2	2.26	34	1.114
1993	Texas	AL	66	74.1	55	27	79	5	5	2.91	40	1.103
Four-Year Average				63.0	47	20	63	3	3	2.44	35	1.039

MIKE HENNEMAN

Age 32/R $21

He's always the cheapest name-brand closer available, but he always delivers the goods. Except for 1989, when Sparky stuck him in the starting rotation for a time, Henneman has been a model of consistency. The save totals for

Catchers
pp. 59-73

Corners
pp. 73-95

Infield
pp. 95-116

Outfield
pp. 117-150

DH
pp. 150-153

Starters
pp. 154-189

Relievers
pp. 190-217

five of the last six years: 22, 22, 21, 24, 24. All you have to worry about if you own him is Sparky getting another wild hair.

Year Team	Lg.	G	IP	H	BB	SO	W	L	ERA	SV	Ratio
1990 Detroit	AL	69	94.1	90	33	50	8	6	3.05	22	1.304
1991 Detroit	AL	60	84.1	81	34	61	10	2	2.88	21	1.364
1992 Detroit	AL	60	77.1	75	20	58	2	6	3.96	24	1.228
1993 Detroit	AL	63	71.2	69	32	58	5	3	2.64	24	1.409
Four-Year Average			81.0	79	30	57	6	4	3.13	23	1.325

DOUG HENRY   Age 30/R $6

Saying that Milwaukee needs to shore up its bullpen is like saying that Kansas needs to work on its flatness problem.

Year Team	Lg.	G	IP	H	BB	SO	W	L	ERA	SV	Ratio
1991 Milwaukee	AL	32	36.0	16	14	28	2	1	1.00	15	0.833
1992 Milwaukee	AL	68	65.0	64	24	52	1	4	4.02	29	1.354
1993 Milwaukee	AL	54	55.0	67	25	38	4	4	5.56	17	1.673
Four-Year Average			51.2	49	21	39	2	3	3.87	20	1.346

JEREMY HERNANDEZ   Age 27/R $5

Here's a relief strategy for you: draft the entire Cleveland bullpen. You can probably get DiPoto, Hernandez, Derek Lilliquist, and Eric Plunk for, what, thirty bucks total? Together they saved 44 games last season. That's just one fewer than Jeff Montgomery, who will cost at least ten bucks more. All had good ERAs and ratios, and with four guys instead of one you have some insurance against injury. This doesn't work with just any team, mind you: the entire Milwaukee bullpen had only 29 saves last year. But when the bullpen committee is as good as Cleveland's, why not go for all of it?

Year Team	Lg.	G	IP	H	BB	SO	W	L	ERA	SV	Ratio
1991 San Diego	NL	9	14.1	8	5	9	0	0	0.00	2	0.907
1992 San Diego	NL	26	36.2	39	11	25	1	4	4.17	1	1.364
1993 San Diego	NL	21	34.1	41	7	26	0	2	4.72	0	1.398
1993 Cleveland	AL	49	77.1	75	27	44	6	5	3.14	8	1.319
Four-Year Average			54.0	54	17	35	2	4	3.43	4	1.310

ROBERTO HERNANDEZ   Age 29/R $37

On the other hand, owning a top bull like this Hernandez isn't such a bad strategy either, especially since the White Sox figure to be winning 90-plus games a year until Frank Thomas retires.

Year Team	Lg.	G	IP	H	BB	SO	W	L	ERA	SV	Ratio
1991 Chicago	AL	9	15.0	18	7	6	1	0	7.80	0	1.667
1992 Chicago	AL	43	71.0	45	20	68	7	3	1.65	12	0.915
1993 Chicago	AL	70	78.2	66	20	71	3	4	2.29	38	1.093
Four-Year Average			54.0	43	16	48	4	2	2.51	17	1.069

RICK HONEYCUTT   Age 39/L $1

In seventeen major league seasons he has been traded for or with the following players: Brian Allard, Rick Auerbach (an original Getherswag Goner), Tim Belcher, Ken Clay, Larry Cox, Willie Horton (the good Willie Horton), Steve Finch, Jerry Don Gleaton, Mario Mendoza (inventor of the Mendoza Line), Dave Pagan, Leon Roberts, Dave Stewart, Ricky Wright, and Richie

Zisk. Only pitches about 40 innings a year these days, almost exclusively against left-handed batters, which makes him the Bob McClure of the 1990s. That's no free ticket to Cooperstown, but it's not a bad way to spend the first third of one's adult life.

Year Team	Lg.	G	IP	H	BB	SO	W	L	ERA	SV	Ratio
1990 Oakland	AL	63	63.1	46	22	38	2	2	2.70	7	1.074
1991 Oakland	AL	43	37.2	37	20	26	2	4	3.58	0	1.513
1992 Oakland	AL	54	39.0	41	10	32	1	4	3.69	3	1.308
1993 Oakland	AL	52	41.2	30	20	21	1	4	2.81	1	1.200
Four-Year Average			45.0	39	18	29	2	4	3.12	3	1.244

STEVE HOWE   Age 36/L $1

Pass.

Year Team	Lg.	G	IP	H	BB	SO	W	L	ERA	SV	Ratio
1991 New York	AL	37	48.1	39	7	34	3	1	1.68	3	0.952
1992 New York	AL	20	22.0	9	3	12	3	0	2.45	6	0.545
1993 New York	AL	51	50.2	58	10	19	3	5	4.97	4	1.342
Four-Year Average			40.0	35	7	22	3	2	3.20	4	1.041

BILL KRUEGER   Age 35/L $1

Could he be this year's Jamie Moyer? Not likely. (But, for that matter, last year's Jamie Moyer wasn't likely either.)

Year Team	Lg.	G	IP	H	BB	SO	W	L	ERA	SV	Ratio
1990 Milwaukee	AL	30	129.0	137	54	64	6	8	3.98	0	1.481
1991 Seattle	AL	35	175.0	194	60	91	11	8	3.60	0	1.451
1992 Minnesota	AL	27	161.1	166	46	86	10	6	4.30	0	1.314
1992 Montreal	NL	9	17.1	23	7	13	0	2	6.75	0	1.731
1993 Detroit	AL	32	82.0	90	30	60	6	4	3.40	0	1.463
Four-Year Average			141.0	153	49	79	8	7	3.95	0	1.429

DEREK LILLIQUIST   Age 28/L $9

Next to Orel Hershiser, he's the best-hitting pitcher in baseball. Too bad he never gets to prove it. But he has proved to be a valuable member of Cleveland's vaunted BBC.

Year Team	Lg.	G	IP	H	BB	SO	W	L	ERA	SV	Ratio
1990 Atlanta	NL	12	61.2	75	19	34	2	8	6.28	0	1.524
1990 San Diego	NL	16	60.1	61	23	29	3	3	4.33	0	1.392
1991 San Diego	NL	6	14.1	25	4	7	0	2	8.79	0	2.023
1992 Cleveland	AL	71	61.2	39	18	47	5	3	1.75	6	0.924
1993 Cleveland	AL	56	64.0	64	19	40	4	4	2.25	10	1.297
Four-Year Average			65.0	66	21	39	4	5	3.92	4	1.325

GRAEME LLOYD   Age 26/L $5

The best left-handed Australian reliever in baseball. Closer potential.

Year Team	Lg.	G	IP	H	BB	SO	W	L	ERA	SV	Ratio
1993 Milwaukee	AL	55	63.2	64	13	31	3	4	2.83	0	1.209
Four-Year Average			63.0	64	13	31	3	4	2.83	0	1.210

Catchers
pp. 59-73

Corners
pp. 73-95

Infield
pp. 95-116

Outfield
pp. 117-150

DH
pp. 150-153

Starters
pp. 154-189

Relievers
pp. 190-217

ALAN MILLS   Age 27/R $5

Could be a steal this season. At the auction draft, he will go at a setup man's price. But *if* Gregg Olson's elbow blows out, which is always a distinct possibility, and *if* the Orioles don't go out and acquire a proven closer, which they almost certainly won't do because they need so many other things, then there is a strong likelihood that Mills will be the Baltimore closer. He has the stuff to do the job.

Year Team	Lg.	G	IP	H	BB	SO	W	L	ERA	SV	Ratio
1990 New York	AL	36	41.2	48	33	24	1	5	4.10	0	1.944
1991 New York	AL	6	16.1	16	8	11	1	1	4.41	0	1.469
1992 Baltimore	AL	35	103.1	78	54	60	10	4	2.61	2	1.277
1993 Baltimore	AL	45	100.1	80	51	68	5	4	3.23	4	1.306
Four-Year Average			65.0	56	37	41	4	4	3.20	2	1.406

JEFF MONTGOMERY   Age 32/R $40

Last year he was the best closer in the league, perhaps in all of baseball, but it will take a Kansas City pennant or two before he gets the recognition he deserves.

Year Team	Lg.	G	IP	H	BB	SO	W	L	ERA	SV	Ratio
1990 Kansas City	AL	73	94.1	81	34	94	6	5	2.39	24	1.219
1991 Kansas City	AL	67	90.0	83	28	77	4	4	2.90	33	1.233
1992 Kansas City	AL	65	82.2	61	27	69	1	6	2.18	39	1.065
1993 Kansas City	AL	69	87.1	65	23	66	7	5	2.27	45	1.008
Four-Year Average			88.0	73	28	77	5	5	2.44	35	1.135

BOBBY MUNOZ   Age 26/R $1

The Yankees harbor high hopes for this young fireballer with a 90-plus mph gun. But they weren't enamored with their first look at the big league level. At least, The Owner wasn't enamored. We heard that after one of Muñoz's futile efforts to find home plate The Owner got on the phone and started screaming at Buck Showalter not to use "that guy" ever again. Buck politely listened, thanked The Owner for his input, and silently crossed another few years off his pinstripe future.

Year Team	Lg.	G	IP	H	BB	SO	W	L	ERA	SV	Ratio
1993 New York	AL	38	45.2	48	26	33	3	3	5.32	0	1.620
Four-Year Average			45.0	48	26	33	3	3	5.32	0	1.621

GENE NELSON   Age 33/R $3

A smart veteran who's been setting up ace closers for a lot of years. Good to see him bounce back after a couple of stinko seasons.

Year Team	Lg.	G	IP	H	BB	SO	W	L	ERA	SV	Ratio
1990 Oakland	AL	51	74.2	55	17	38	3	3	1.57	5	0.964
1991 Oakland	AL	44	48.2	60	23	23	1	5	6.84	0	1.705
1992 Oakland	AL	28	51.2	68	22	23	3	1	6.45	0	1.742
1993 California	AL	46	52.2	50	23	31	0	5	3.08	4	1.386
1993 Texas	AL	6	8.0	10	1	4	0	0	3.38	1	1.375
Four-Year Average			58.0	61	22	30	2	4	4.12	3	1.396

JEFF NELSON
Age 27/R   **$1**

He throws hard, walks (and hits) a lot of batters, and strikes out about one per inning. But of eleven save opportunities last season, he blew ten. This does not look good on the resumé of an applicant for a closer's job. Still, just about anybody could end up being the Seattle closer.

Year Team	Lg.	G	IP	H	BB	SO	W	L	ERA	SV	Ratio
1992 Seattle	AL	66	81.0	71	44	46	1	7	3.44	6	1.420
1993 Seattle	AL	71	60.0	57	34	61	5	3	4.35	1	1.517
Four-Year Average			70.0	64	39	54	3	5	3.83	4	1.461

EDWIN NUNEZ
Age 30/R   **$1**

The highlight of his season was a fight on the team bus with rotund Oakland batting coach Bull Luzinski. We would have loved to have been there, as we are big fans of sumo wrestling.

Year Team	Lg.	G	IP	H	BB	SO	W	L	ERA	SV	Ratio
1990 Detroit	AL	42	80.1	65	37	66	3	1	2.24	6	1.270
1991 Milwaukee	AL	23	25.1	28	13	24	2	1	6.04	8	1.618
1992 Milwaukee	AL	10	13.2	12	6	10	1	1	2.63	0	1.317
1992 Texas	AL	39	45.2	51	16	39	0	2	5.52	3	1.467
1993 Oakland	AL	56	75.2	89	29	58	3	6	3.81	1	1.559
Four-Year Average			60.0	61	25	49	2	3	3.78	5	1.438

GREGG OLSON
Age 27/R   **$25**

The trendoids who crowd fashionable Camden Yards booed him pretty hard last year. Then he blew out his elbow and even they suddenly realized how valuable Otter is to the Orioles. The club and Olson are gambling that rest and rehab will let him avoid a Tommy John operation that would sideline him for 18 months or more. But they could always lose that gamble on his next pitch, so shop with caution. And hedge *your* bet by buying Alan Mills as well.

Year Team	Lg.	G	IP	H	BB	SO	W	L	ERA	SV	Ratio
1990 Baltimore	AL	64	74.1	57	31	74	6	5	2.42	37	1.184
1991 Baltimore	AL	72	73.2	74	29	72	4	6	3.18	31	1.398
1992 Baltimore	AL	60	61.1	46	24	58	1	5	2.05	36	1.141
1993 Baltimore	AL	50	45.0	37	18	44	0	2	1.60	29	1.222
Four-Year Average			63.0	54	26	62	3	5	2.41	33	1.243

JESSE OROSCO
Age 36/L   **$4**

A reborn reliever who could, by process of elimination, actually be the Brewers' closer. Still his best moment: throwing his glove straight up into the October sky after saving the seventh game of the 1986 World Series.

Year Team	Lg.	G	IP	H	BB	SO	W	L	ERA	SV	Ratio
1990 Cleveland	AL	55	64.2	58	38	55	5	4	3.90	2	1.485
1991 Cleveland	AL	47	45.2	52	15	36	2	0	3.74	0	1.467
1992 Milwaukee	AL	59	39.0	33	13	40	3	1	3.23	1	1.179
1993 Milwaukee	AL	57	56.2	47	17	67	3	5	3.18	8	1.129
Four-Year Average			51.0	48	21	50	3	3	3.54	3	1.325

BRAD PENNINGTON   Age 24/L $4

A big, hard-throwing lefthander with little idea where the ball is going. That's not much, but it's enough to make him another candidate for the Orioles closer position if Olson goes down.

Year Team	Lg.	G	IP	H	BB	SO	W	L	ERA	SV	Ratio
1993 Baltimore	AL	34	33.0	34	25	39	3	2	6.55	4	1.788
Four-Year Average			33.0	34	25	39	3	2	6.55	4	1.788

ERIC PLUNK   Age 30/R $9

The key to his remarkable turnaround after landing in Cleveland? Control. Coming into last year he had walked 410 batters in 654 innings over seven years for three clubs. Last season he cut that BB/IP ratio to 30 in 71. The current chairperson of Cleveland's BBC.

Year Team	Lg.	G	IP	H	BB	SO	W	L	ERA	SV	Ratio
1990 New York	AL	47	72.2	58	43	67	6	3	2.72	0	1.390
1991 New York	AL	43	111.2	128	62	103	2	5	4.76	0	1.701
1992 Cleveland	AL	58	71.2	61	38	50	9	6	3.64	4	1.381
1993 Cleveland	AL	70	71.0	61	30	77	4	5	2.79	15	1.282
Four-Year Average			81.0	77	43	74	5	5	3.63	5	1.471

JIM POOLE   Age 27/L $3

Nasty stuff: opposing batters hit just .175 against him last year. Makes you wonder why he wasn't used more.

Year Team	Lg.	G	IP	H	BB	SO	W	L	ERA	SV	Ratio
1990 Los Angeles	NL	16	10.2	7	8	6	0	0	4.22	0	1.406
1991 Texas	AL	5	6.0	10	3	4	0	0	4.50	1	2.167
1991 Baltimore	AL	24	36.0	19	9	34	3	2	2.00	0	0.778
1992 Baltimore	AL	6	3.1	3	1	3	0	0	0.00	0	1.200
1993 Baltimore	AL	55	50.1	30	21	29	2	1	2.15	2	1.013
Four-Year Average			26.0	17	11	19	1	1	2.37	1	1.044

TED POWER   Age 39/R $2

The ERA was ugly, but he did the job when Norm Charlton went down. Look for a more customary low profile year this season.

Year Team	Lg.	G	IP	H	BB	SO	W	L	ERA	SV	Ratio
1990 Pittsburgh	NL	40	51.2	50	17	42	1	3	3.66	7	1.297
1991 Cincinnati	NL	68	87.0	87	31	51	5	3	3.62	3	1.356
1992 Cleveland	AL	64	99.1	88	35	51	3	3	2.54	6	1.238
1993 Cleveland	AL	20	20.0	30	8	11	0	2	7.20	0	1.900
1993 Seattle	AL	25	25.1	27	9	16	2	2	3.91	13	1.421
Four-Year Average			70.0	71	25	43	3	3	3.53	7	1.348

PAUL QUANTRILL
Age 25/R   **$2**

He belongs in the bullpen, where his hockey-player mentality serves him much better than in the more introspective domain of a starter. But he needs to do something about those penalties for high-sticking.

Year Team	Lg.	G	IP	H	BB	SO	W	L	ERA	SV	Ratio
1992 Boston	AL	27	49.1	55	15	24	2	3	2.19	1	1.419
1993 Boston	AL	49	138.0	151	44	66	6	12	3.91	1	1.413
Four-Year Average			93.0	103	30	45	4	8	3.46	1	1.415

SCOTT RADINSKY
Age 26/L   **$3**

A so-so year for this mini–Wild Thing. Too talented and too young to be relegated to the role of designated lefty, *i.e.*, as the guy you use only against one or two left-handed hitters. But, on a staff as talented and deep as Chicago's, that's where he could end up if he doesn't bounce back sharply.

Year Team	Lg.	G	IP	H	BB	SO	W	L	ERA	SV	Ratio
1990 Chicago	AL	62	52.1	47	36	46	6	1	4.82	4	1.586
1991 Chicago	AL	67	71.1	53	23	49	5	5	2.02	8	1.065
1992 Chicago	AL	68	59.1	54	34	48	3	7	2.73	15	1.483
1993 Chicago	AL	73	54.2	61	19	44	8	2	4.28	4	1.463
Four-Year Average			59.0	54	28	47	6	4	3.33	8	1.376

JEFF RUSSELL
Age 32/R   **$28**

The best move Lou Gorman has ever made. It was a risk: a tender elbow had made Russell damaged goods in 1992. But the risk had a rich reward, in no small part because it bought more time for the development of . . .

Year Team	Lg.	G	IP	H	BB	SO	W	L	ERA	SV	Ratio
1990 Texas	AL	27	25.1	23	16	16	1	5	4.26	10	1.539
1991 Texas	AL	68	79.1	71	26	52	6	4	3.29	30	1.223
1992 Texas	AL	51	56.2	51	22	43	2	3	1.91	28	1.288
1992 Oakland	AL	8	9.2	4	3	5	2	0	0.00	2	0.724
1993 Boston	AL	51	46.2	39	14	45	1	4	2.70	33	1.136
Four-Year Average			54.0	47	20	40	3	4	2.77	26	1.236

KEN RYAN
Age 25/R   **$3**

. . . who is Boston's (or somebody's) closer of the future. Get him cheap while he's a setup man of the present.

Year Team	Lg.	G	IP	H	BB	SO	W	L	ERA	SV	Ratio
1992 Boston	AL	7	7.0	4	5	5	0	0	6.43	1	1.286
1993 Boston	AL	47	50.0	43	29	49	7	2	3.60	1	1.440
Four-Year Average			28.0	24	17	27	4	1	3.95	1	1.421

Catchers
pp. 59–73

Corners
pp. 73–95

Infield
pp. 95–116

Outfield
pp. 117–150

DH
pp. 150–153

Starters
pp. 154–189

Relievers
pp. 190–217

LEE SMITH   Age 36/R $35

He flips more breaking balls than he used to, and he gives up an occasional grand slam to the likes of Mariano Duncan. But he's still as intimidating a figure on the mound as ever toed the slab. Until he proves definitively that he's no longer a 40-save man, we're saying that he is. We'd be afraid not to.

Year Team	Lg.	G	IP	H	BB	SO	W	L	ERA	SV	Ratio
1990 Boston	AL	11	14.1	13	9	17	2	1	1.88	4	1.535
1990 St. Louis	NL	53	68.2	58	20	70	3	4	2.10	27	1.136
1991 St. Louis	NL	67	73.0	70	13	67	6	3	2.34	47	1.137
1992 St. Louis	NL	70	75.0	62	26	60	4	9	3.12	43	1.173
1993 St. Louis	NL	55	50.0	49	9	49	2	4	4.50	43	1.160
1993 New York	AL	8	8.0	4	5	11	0	0	0.00	3	1.125
Four-Year Average			72.0	64	21	69	4	5	2.77	42	1.170

MIKE TIMLIN   Age 28/R $3

The Toronto problem was not that Duane Ward had trouble replacing Tom Henke. (He didn't.) The problem was that Timlin had trouble replacing Ward. But down the stretch he got better, and most scouts still consider his stuff as good as any reliever's in the league. If he returns to the form he showed in 1991, the Blue Jays might not lose a single game this year.

Year Team	Lg.	G	IP	H	BB	SO	W	L	ERA	SV	Ratio
1991 Toronto	AL	63	108.1	94	50	85	11	6	3.16	3	1.329
1992 Toronto	AL	26	43.2	45	20	35	0	2	4.12	1	1.489
1993 Toronto	AL	54	55.2	63	27	49	4	2	4.69	1	1.617
Four-Year Average			69.0	67	32	56	5	3	3.77	2	1.440

GEORGE TSAMIS   Age 26/L $1

During the course of one of his frequent bombardments, Tsamis hit a wildness streak. Out of the dugout popped pitching coach Dick Such to tell him, "You better start getting the ball over." Tsamis responded, "No kidding. You think I'm doing this on purpose?" Refreshing attitude. But refreshing attitude by itself still leaves you about three bucks shy of a cold hot dog . . . on the fans' side of the field.

Year Team	Lg.	G	IP	H	BB	SO	W	L	ERA	SV	Ratio
1993 Minnesota	AL	41	68.1	86	27	30	1	2	6.19	1	1.654
Four-Year Average			68.0	86	27	30	1	2	6.19	1	1.654

JULIO VALERA   Age 25/R $1

Get a note from his doctor before making a move.

Year Team	Lg.	G	IP	H	BB	SO	W	L	ERA	SV	Ratio
1990 New York	NL	3	13.0	20	7	4	1	1	6.92	0	2.077
1991 New York	NL	2	2.0	1	4	3	0	0	0.00	0	2.500
1992 California	AL	30	188.0	188	64	113	8	11	3.73	0	1.340
1993 California	AL	19	53.0	77	15	28	3	6	6.62	4	1.736
Four-Year Average			64.0	72	23	37	3	5	4.46	1	1.469

DUANE WARD   Age 29/R $40

It was July 4, 1986. Ronald Reagan was in the White House trying to remember the names of his Cabinet members, and the Atlanta Braves were a game and a half out of first place in the NL West. (These two facts are not even remotely related, but we're trying to establish a little historical context here.) The Braves, aka America's Team, figured they were one starting pitcher away from the division championship. Doyle Alexander, a Toronto right-hander coming off two 17-win seasons, was available, and the Blue Jays weren't asking for much—just a green farmhand whose ERA in four minor league seasons had ranged from 4.20 to 5.32. True, the youngster had been a first-round draft pick back in 1982, but he was a long way from being ready for the big leagues, and Atlanta needed help immediately. So the deal was done on July 6. That is how Doyle Alexander, who went 6–6 the rest of the way as Atlanta faded to sixth, became a Brave. And that is how Duane Ward, who would eventually turn into exactly the sort of closer who would have given Atlanta World Championships in 1992 and 1993, became a Toronto Blue Jay.

Catchers
pp. 59-73

Corners
pp. 73-95

Infield
pp. 95-116

Outfield
pp. 117-150

DH
pp. 150-153

Starters
pp. 154-189

Relievers
pp. 190-217

Year Team	Lg.	G	IP	H	BB	SO	W	L	ERA	SV	Ratio
1990 Toronto	AL	73	127.2	101	42	112	2	8	3.45	11	1.120
1991 Toronto	AL	81	107.1	80	33	132	7	6	2.77	23	1.053
1992 Toronto	AL	79	101.1	76	39	103	7	4	1.95	12	1.135
1993 Toronto	AL	71	71.2	49	25	97	2	3	2.13	45	1.033
Four-Year Average			101.0	77	35	111	5	5	2.67	23	1.091

MATT WHITESIDE   Age 26/R $1

Piqued our interest with a promising debut in 1992, but last year was a giant step backward.

Year Team	Lg.	G	IP	H	BB	SO	W	L	ERA	SV	Ratio
1992 Texas	AL	20	28.0	26	11	13	1	1	1.93	4	1.321
1993 Texas	AL	60	73.0	78	23	39	2	1	4.32	1	1.384
Four-Year Average			50.0	52	17	26	2	1	3.65	3	1.366

CARL WILLIS   Age 33/R $4

Reliable understudy for Aguilera.

Year Team	Lg.	G	IP	H	BB	SO	W	L	ERA	SV	Ratio
1991 Minnesota	AL	40	89.0	76	19	53	8	3	2.63	2	1.067
1992 Minnesota	AL	59	79.1	73	11	45	7	3	2.72	1	1.059
1993 Minnesota	AL	53	58.0	56	17	44	3	0	3.10	5	1.259
Four-Year Average			75.0	68	16	47	6	2	2.78	3	1.113

4

By the Numbers

Rotisserie Stat-Pack:
Never Leave for the Auction
Draft Without It

Some Rotisserie owners show up at the auction draft with the *Baseball Register*, a copy of *Elias*, all the spring preview issues of *Baseball America* and *Baseball Weekly*, the National League's Green Book or the American League's Red Book, Bill James, spring training boxscores clipped from *USA Today*, a stack of computer printouts, Harry Stein's first novel, a year's worth of John Benson's newsletters along with his *Rotisserie Baseball Analyst*, an autographed Paul Householder card for good luck, an economy-size bottle of Rolaids, and a corned beef on rye with mustard.

Forget about it. You don't need all that stuff. While you're trying to look up how many SB Deion Sanders had, somebody's going to steal Reggie Sanders from right under your nose.

All you really need at the auction draft—assuming you've done a *little* homework beforehand—is this Rotisserie Stat-Pack. Introduced a couple of years ago as an addendum to the Player Ratings chapter, the Stat-Pack was an instant hit. You get the top performers in all the Rotissecategories (plus Runs Scored for batters and Strikeouts and Net Wins for pitchers). You also get the *worst* performers in ERA, Ratio, and BA so you can be reminded at a glance who might *hurt* you. And for batters, you get the top performers in each category *by position.*

Forget all that other stuff you used to carry to the auction draft table. Just tear out the following 23 pages and travel light. That way you'll have room to pack *two* sandwiches.

LEAGUE LEADERS, 1993

NATIONAL LEAGUE PITCHERS

RATIO
(Minimum 100 Innings Pitched)

1. Fernandez, S.	0.986	11. Bautista, J.	1.182	21. Cooke, S.	1.263
2. Maddux, G.	1.049	12. Greene, T.	1.185	22. Smoltz, J.	1.264
3. Saberhagen, B.	1.062	13. Gooden, D.	1.193	23. Hershiser, O.	1.266
4. Swift, B.	1.074	14. Arocha, R.	1.213	24. Drabek, D.	1.271
5. Rijo, J.	1.088	15. Martinez, D.	1.224	25. Osborne, D.	1.285
6. Mulholland, T.	1.136	16. Candiotti, T.	1.231	26. Kile, D.	1.287
7. Burkett, J.	1.140	17. Schilling, C.	1.237	27. Hill, K.	1.290
8. Harnisch, P.	1.149	18. Benes, A.	1.240	28. Tewksbury, B.	1.301
9. Fassero, J.	1.156	19. Martinez, P.	1.243	29. Portugal, M.	1.303
10. Avery, S.	1.160	20. Astacio, P.	1.250	30. Cormier, R.	1.307

WORST RATIOS
(Minimum 100 Innings Pitched)

1. Ashby, A.	1.821	11. Blair, W.	1.548	21. Young, A.	1.445
2. Wakefield, T.	1.714	12. Ruffin, B.	1.532	22. Brocail, D.	1.442
3. Schourek, P.	1.660	13. Barnes, B.	1.530	23. Hammond, C.	1.429
4. Rivera, B.	1.595	14. Walk, B.	1.519	24. Reynoso, A.	1.423
5. Olivares, O.	1.584	15. Gross, K.	1.473	25. Castillo, F.	1.422
6. Henry, B.	1.583	16. Armstrong, J.	1.467	26. Magrane, J.	1.414
7. Pugh, T.	1.576	17. Hickerson, B.	1.463	27. Smiley, J.	1.401
8. Browning, T.	1.570	18. Harkey, M.	1.462	28. Aquino, L.	1.401
9. Bottenfield, K.	1.566	19. Worrell, T.	1.460	29. Jackson, D.	1.398
10. Bowen, R.	1.551	20. Martinez, R.	1.446	30. Nabholz, C.	1.397

EARNED RUN AVERAGE
(Minimum 100 Innings Pitched)

1. Fassero, J.	2.29	11. Candiotti, T.	3.12	21. Astacio, P.	3.57
2. Maddux, G.	2.36	12. Glavine, T.	3.20	22. Hershiser, O.	3.59
3. Rijo, J.	2.48	13. Hill, K.	3.23	23. Wilson, T.	3.60
4. Martinez, P.	2.61	14. Mulholland, T.	3.25	24. Smoltz, J.	3.62
5. Portugal, M.	2.77	15. Saberhagen, B.	3.29	25. Burkett, J.	3.65
6. Bautista, J.	2.82	16. Aquino, L.	3.42	26. Osborne, D.	3.76
7. Swift, B.	2.82	17. Greene, T.	3.42	27. Jackson, D.	3.77
8. Fernandez, S.	2.93	18. Martinez, R.	3.44	28. Young, A.	3.77
9. Avery, S.	2.94	19. Gooden, D.	3.45	29. Arocha, R.	3.78
10. Harnisch, P.	2.98	20. Kile, D.	3.51	30. Benes, A.	3.78

WORST EARNED RUN AVERAGES
(Minimum 100 Innings Pitched)

1. Ashby, A.	6.80	11. Magrane, J.	4.97	21. Belcher, T.	4.47
2. Henry, B.	6.12	12. Worrell, T.	4.92	22. Bowen, R.	4.42
3. Schourek, P.	5.96	13. Castillo, F.	4.84	23. Barnes, B.	4.41
4. Walk, B.	5.68	14. Blair, W.	4.75	24. Guzman, J.	4.34
5. Smiley, J.	5.62	15. Browning, T.	4.74	25. Cormier, R.	4.33
6. Wakefield, T.	5.61	16. Hammond, C.	4.66	26. Brantley, J.	4.28
7. Harkey, M.	5.26	17. Harris, G.	4.59	27. Hough, C.	4.27
8. Pugh, T.	5.26	18. Brocail, D.	4.56	28. Wagner, P.	4.27
9. Bottenfield, K.	5.07	19. Armstrong, J.	4.49	29. Hickerson, B.	4.26
10. Rivera, B.	5.02	20. Tanana, F.	4.48	30. Olivares, O.	4.17

WINS

1. Burkett, J.	22	12. Smoltz, J.	15	22. Hershiser, O.	12
2. Glavine, T.	22	13. Hibbard, G.	15	23. Guzman, J.	12
3. Swift, B.	21	14. Benes, A.	15	24. Jackson, D.	12
4. Maddux, G.	20	15. Kile, D.	15	25. Swindell, G.	12
5. Portugal, M.	18	16. Rijo, J.	14	26. Mulholland, T.	12
6. Avery, S.	18	17. Astacio, P.	14	27. Fassero, J.	12
7. Tewksbury, B.	17	18. Walk, B.	13	28. Reynoso, A.	12
8. Schilling, C.	16	19. Gross, K.	13	29. Harris, G.	11
9. Harnisch, P.	16	20. Rivera, B.	13	30. Hammond, C.	11
10. Greene, T.	16	21. Gooden, D.	12	31. Arocha, R.	11
11. Martinez, D.	15				

SAVES

1. Myers, R.	53	12. Dibble, R.	19	23. Hoffman, T.	5
2. Beck, R.	48	13. Belinda, S.	19	24. Davis, M.	4
3. Harvey, B.	45	14. McMichael, G	19	25. Innis, J.	3
4. Smith, L.	43	15. Franco, J.	10	26. West, D.	3
5. Williams, M.	43	16. Rojas, M.	10	27. Rodriguez, R.	3
6. Wetteland, J.	43	17. Hernandez, X.	9	28. Barnes, B.	3
7. Stanton, M.	27	18. Reardon, J.	8	29. Young, A.	3
8. Jones, D.	26	19. Dewey, M.	7	30. Williams, B.	3
9. Gott, J.	25	20. Perez, M.	7	31. Reed, S.	3
10. Holmes, D.	25	21. Worrell, T.	5	32. Ayala, B.	3
11. Harris, G.	23	22. Maddux, M.	5		

STRIKEOUTS

1. Rijo, J.	227	11. Candiotti, T.	155	21. Martinez, R.	127
2. Smoltz, J.	208	12. Gross, K.	150	22. Hough, C.	126
3. Maddux, G.	197	13. Gooden, D.	149	23. Ruffin, B.	126
4. Schilling, C.	186	14. Burkett, J.	145	24. Avery, S.	125
5. Harnisch, P.	185	15. Hershiser, O.	141	25. Swindell, G.	124
6. Benes, A.	179	16. Kile, D.	141	26. Harris, G.	123
7. Greene, T.	167	17. Fassero, J.	140	27. Rivera, B.	123
8. Guzman, J.	163	18. Martinez, D.	138	28. Astacio, P.	122
9. Swift, B.	157	19. Cooke, S.	132	29. Jackson, D.	120
10. Drabek, D.	157	20. Portugal, M.	131	30. Glavine, T.	120

Catchers
pp. 59–73

Corners
pp. 73–95

Infield
pp. 95–116

Outfield
pp. 117–150

DH
pp. 150–153

Starters
pp. 154–189

Relievers
pp. 190–217

1. Glavine, T.	16	13. Burba, D.	7	25. Hibbard, G.	4
2. Burkett, J.	15	14. Kile, D.	7	26. Wohlers, M.	4
3. Portugal, M.	14	15. Fassero, J.	7	27. Rivera, B.	4
4. Swift, B.	13	16. Black, B.	6	28. Reed, S.	4
5. Greene, T.	12	17. Martinez, D.	6	29. Telgheder, D.	4
6. Avery, S.	12	18. Wetteland, J.	6	30. Bedrosian, S.	3
7. Maddux, G.	10	19. Rijo, J.	5	31. DeLeon, J	3
8. Schilling, C.	9	20. Perez, M.	5	32. Mulholland, T.	3
9. Rueter, K.	8	21. Scott, T.	5	33. Jones, J.	3
10. Tewksbury, B.	7	22. Astacio, P.	5	34. Belcher, T.	3
11. Bautista, J.	7	23. Martinez, P.	5	35. Lancaster, L.	3
12. Harnisch, P.	7	24. Smoltz, J.	4		

NATIONAL LEAGUE POSITION PLAYERS

HOME RUNS

1. Bonds, B.	46	12. Hayes, C.	25	22. Bell, D.	21
2. Justice, D.	40	13. Whiten, M.	25	23. Kent, J.	21
3. Williams, M.	38	14. Daulton, D.	24	24. Destrade, O.	20
4. McGriff, F.	37	15. Incaviglia, P.	24	25. Sheffield, G.	20
5. Gant, R.	36	16. Karros, E.	23	26. Bagwell, J.	20
6. Piazza, M.	35	17. Galarraga, A.	22	27. Sanders, R.	20
7. Bonilla, B.	34	18. Walker, L.	22	28. Mitchell, K.	19
8. Plantier, P.	34	19. Bichette, D.	21	29. Dykstra, L.	19
9. Sosa, S.	33	20. Sabo, C.	21	30. Thompson, R.	19
10. Wilkins, R.	30	21. Biggio, C.	21	31. Grissom, M.	19
11. Murray, E.	27				

RUNS BATTED IN

1. Bonds, B.	123	11. Whiten, M.	99	21. Bagwell, J.	88
2. Justice, D.	120	12. Galarraga, A.	98	22. Bonilla, B.	87
3. Gant, R.	117	13. Grace, M.	98	23. Destrade, O.	87
4. Piazza, M.	112	14. Hayes, C.	98	24. Walker, L.	86
5. Williams, M.	110	15. King, J.	98	25. Kruk, J.	85
6. Daulton, D.	105	16. Grissom, M.	95	26. Alou, M.	85
7. Zeile, T.	103	17. Sosa, S.	93	27. Pendleton, T.	84
8. McGriff, F.	101	18. Hollins, D.	93	28. Jefferies, G.	83
9. Murray, E.	100	19. Incaviglia, P.	89	29. Sanders, R.	83
10. Plantier, P.	100	20. Bichette, D.	89	30. Sabo, C.	82

STOLEN BASES

1. Carr, C.	58	12. Davis, E.	33	22. Smith, O.	21
2. Grissom, M.	53	13. Cole, A.	30	23. Kelly, R.	21
3. Nixon, O.	47	14. Offerman, J.	30	24. Gonzalez, L.	20
4. Jefferies, G.	46	15. Bonds, B.	29	25. Brumfield, J.	20
5. Lewis, D.	46	16. Walker, L.	29	26. Finley, S.	19
6. DeShields, D.	43	17. Sanders, R.	27	27. Sanders, D.	19
7. Young, E.	42	18. Roberts, B.	26	28. Garcia, C.	18
8. Butler, B.	39	19. Gant, R.	26	29. Sheffield, G.	17
9. Coleman, V.	38	20. Bell, D.	26	30. Alou, M.	17
10. Dykstra, L.	37	21. Lansing, M.	23	31. Frazier, L.	17
11. Sosa, S.	36				

RUNS SCORED

1. Dykstra, L.	143	11. Gilkey, B.	99	21. Grace, M.	86
2. Bonds, B.	129	12. Biggio, C.	98	22. Thompson, R.	85
3. Gant, R.	113	13. Bichette, D.	93	23. Walker, L.	85
4. McGriff, F.	111	14. Sosa, S.	92	24. Martin, A.	85
5. Blauser, J.	110	15. Daulton, D.	90	25. Lewis, D.	84
6. Williams, M.	105	16. Justice, D.	90	26. Clark, W.	82
7. Grissom, M.	104	17. Sanders, R.	90	27. King, J.	82
8. Hollins, D.	104	18. Jefferies, G.	89	28. Zeile, T.	82
9. Bell, J.	102	19. Hayes, C.	89	29. Gonzalez, L.	82
10. Kruk, J.	100	20. Sabo, C.	86	30. Young, E.	82

BATTING AVERAGE
(Minimum 300 At Bats)

1. Galarraga, A.	.370	11. Morris, H.	.317	21. Gilkey, B.	.305
2. Gwynn, T.	.358	12. Kruk, J.	.316	22. Blauser, J.	.305
3. Jefferies, G.	.342	13. Larkin, B.	.315	23. Dykstra, L.	.305
4. Mitchell, K.	.341	14. Merced, O.	.313	24. Wilkins, R.	.303
5. Bonds, B.	.336	15. Thompson, R.	.312	25. McGee, W.	.301
6. Grace, M.	.325	16. Bichette, D.	.310	26. Smith, D.	.300
7. Bagwell, J.	.320	17. Bell, J.	.310	27. Gonzalez, L.	.300
8. Kelly, R.	.319	18. Van Slyke, A.	.310	28. Slaught, D.	.300
9. Piazza, M.	.318	19. Sandberg, R.	.309	29. Grissom, M.	.298
10. Eisenreich, J.	.318	20. Hayes, C.	.305	30. Butler, B.	.298

WORST BATTING AVERAGES
(Minimum 300 At Bats)

1. Wallach, T.	.222	11. Morandini, M.	.247	21. Castilla, V.	.255
2. Hundley, T.	.228	12. Karros, E.	.247	22. Cole, A.	.256
3. Santiago, B.	.230	13. Cordero, W.	.248	23. Daulton, D.	.257
4. Davis, E.	.234	14. Anthony, E.	.249	24. Pagnozzi, T.	.258
5. Young, K.	.236	15. Gutierrez, R.	.251	25. Sabo, C.	.259
6. Lankford, R.	.238	16. Lemke, M.	.252	26. Sosa, S.	.261
7. Oliver, J.	.239	17. Whiten, M.	.253	27. Caminiti, K.	.262
8. Plantier, P.	.240	18. Lewis, D.	.253	28. Thompson, M.	.262
9. Branson, J.	.241	19. Destrade, O.	.255	29. Bell, D.	.262
10. Berryhill, D.	.245	20. Fletcher, D.	.255	30. Gardner, J.	.262

AMERICAN LEAGUE PITCHERS

RATIO
(Minimum 100 Innings Pitched)

1. Darwin, D.	1.068	11. Eldred, C.	1.252	21. Gordon, T.	1.298
2. Appier, K.	1.106	12. Deshaies, J.	1.255	22. Mills, A.	1.306
3. Key, J.	1.107	13. Cone, D.	1.256	23. Clark, M.	1.317
4. Johnson, R.	1.112	14. Clemens, R.	1.263	24. Sele, A.	1.325
5. Fernandez, A.	1.164	15. Moyer, J.	1.263	25. Tapani, K.	1.329
6. Langston, M.	1.190	16. Miranda, A.	1.267	26. Sanderson, S.	1.330
7. Bosio, C.	1.199	17. Hanson, E.	1.279	27. Bere, J.	1.332
8. Wells, D.	1.203	18. McDowell, J.	1.286	28. Hentgen, P.	1.336
9. McDonald, B.	1.230	19. Finley, C.	1.293	29. Stewart, D.	1.346
10. Mussina, M.	1.235	20. Brown, K.	1.296	30. Rogers, K.	1.349

WORST RATIOS
(Minimum 100 Innings Pitched)

1. Sutcliffe, R.	1.723	11. Banks, W.	1.541	21. Perez, M.	1.454
2. Morris, J.	1.664	12. Bolton, T.	1.539	22. Leiter, M.	1.453
3. Gubicza, M.	1.639	13. Leary, T.	1.535	23. Guzman, J.	1.452
4. Downs, K.	1.630	14. Fleming, D.	1.530	24. Valenzuela, F.	1.444
5. Wickman, B.	1.607	15. Kramer, T.	1.529	25. Gullickson, B.	1.444
6. Welch, B.	1.584	16. Navarro, J.	1.526	26. Witt, B.	1.441
7. McCaskill, K.	1.584	17. Darling, R.	1.517	27. Kamieniecki, S.	1.438
8. Haney, C.	1.565	18. Trombley, M.	1.504	28. Pichardo, H.	1.430
9. Stottlemyre, T.	1.545	19. Moore, M.	1.479	29. Leibrandt, C.	1.424
10. Erickson, S.	1.541	20. Dopson, J.	1.471	30. Leiter, A.	1.419

EARNED RUN AVERAGE
(Minimum 100 Innings Pitched)

1. Appier, K.	2.56	12. Miranda, A.	3.30	22. Brown, K.	3.59
2. Sele, A.	2.74	13. Cone, D.	3.33	23. Boever, J.	3.61
3. Alvarez, W.	2.95	14. McDowell, J.	3.37	24. Harris, G.	3.77
4. Key, J.	3.00	15. McDonald, B.	3.39	25. Hentgen, P.	3.87
5. Fernandez, A.	3.13	16. Pavlik, R.	3.41	26. Quantrill, P.	3.91
6. Viola, F.	3.14	17. Moyer, J.	3.43	27. Guzman, J.	3.99
7. Finley, C.	3.15	18. Bosio, C.	3.45	28. Eldred, C.	4.01
8. Langston, M.	3.20	19. Bere, J.	3.47	29. Kramer, T.	4.02
9. Mills, A.	3.23	20. Hanson, E.	3.47	30. Pichardo, H.	4.04
10. Johnson, R.	3.24	21. Gordon, T.	3.58	31. Banks, W.	4.04
11. Darwin, D.	3.26				

WORST EARNED RUN AVERAGES
(Minimum 100 Innings Pitched)

1. Morris, J.	6.19	11. Erickson, S.	5.19	21. Gubicza, M.	4.66
2. Haney, C.	6.02	12. Darling, R.	5.16	22. Wickman, B.	4.63
3. Sutcliffe, R.	5.75	13. Leary, T.	5.05	23. Leibrandt, C.	4.55
4. Downs, K.	5.64	14. Dopson, J.	4.97	24. Wegman, B.	4.48
5. Gullickson, B.	5.37	15. Valenzuela, F.	4.94	25. Bolton, T.	4.47
6. Navarro, J.	5.33	16. Mesa, J.	4.92	26. Clemens, R.	4.46
7. Welch, B.	5.29	17. Trombley, M.	4.88	27. Sanderson, S.	4.46
8. McCaskill, K.	5.23	18. Bones, R.	4.86	28. Mussina, M.	4.46
9. Moore, M.	5.22	19. Stottlemyre, T.	4.84	29. Stewart, D.	4.44
10. Perez, M.	5.19	20. Leiter, M.	4.72	30. Doherty, J.	4.44

WINS

1. McDowell, J.	22	13. Alvarez, W.	15	25. Tapani, K.	12
2. Johnson, R.	19	14. Witt, B.	14	26. Fleming, D.	12
3. Hentgen, P.	19	15. Guzman, J.	14	27. Pavlik, R.	12
4. Key, J.	18	16. Mussina, M.	14	28. Bere, J.	12
5. Appier, K.	18	17. Doherty, J.	14	29. Leary, T.	11
6. Fernandez, A.	18	18. Wickman, B.	14	30. Viola, F.	11
7. Langston, M.	16	19. Gullickson, B.	13	31. Clemens, R.	11
8. Finley, C.	16	20. Moore, M.	13	32. Deshaies, J.	11
9. Rogers, K.	16	21. McDonald, B.	13	33. Cone, D.	11
10. Eldred, C.	16	22. Stewart, D.	12	34. Wells, D.	11
11. Darwin, D.	15	23. Moyer, J.	12	35. Stottlemyre, T.	11
12. Brown, K.	15	24. Gordon, T.	12		

SAVES

1. Ward, D.	45	12. Henry, D.	17	22. Butcher, M.	8
2. Montgomery, J.	45	13. Plunk, E.	15	23. Nelson, G.	5
3. Henke, T.	40	14. Power, T.	13	24. Willis, C.	5
4. Hernandez, R.	38	15. Frey, S.	13	25. Howe, S.	4
5. Eckersley, D.	36	16. Grahe, J.	11	26. Davis, S.	4
6. Aguilera, R.	34	17. Dipoto, J.	11	27. Radinsky, S.	4
7. Russell, J.	33	18. Lilliquist, D.	10	28. Mills, A.	4
8. Olson, G.	29	19. Orosco, J.	8	29. Valera, J.	4
9. Farr, S.	25	20. Harris, G.	8	30. Wickman, B.	4
10. Henneman, M.	24	21. Hernandez, J.	8	31. Pennington, B.	4
11. Charlton, N.	18				

STRIKEOUTS

1. Johnson, R.	308	11. Hanson, E.	163	21. Banks, W.	138
2. Langston, M.	196	12. Clemens, R.	160	22. Witt, B.	131
3. Guzman, J.	194	13. McDowell, J.	158	23. Pavlik, R.	131
4. Cone, D.	191	14. Alvarez, W.	155	24. Darwin, D.	130
5. Finley, C.	187	15. Tapani, K.	150	25. Bere, J.	129
6. Appier, K.	186	16. Perez, M.	148	26. Hentgen, P.	122
7. Eldred, C.	180	17. Gordon, T.	143	27. Bosio, C.	119
8. Key, J.	173	18. Brown, K.	142	28. Mesa, J.	118
9. McDonald, B.	171	19. Rogers, K.	140	29. Mussina, M.	117
10. Fernandez, A.	169	20. Wells, D.	139	30. Erickson, S.	116

NET WINS

1. Key, J.	12	13. Rogers, K.	6	25. Viola, F.	3
2. McDowell, J.	12	14. Gordon, T.	6	26. Willis, C.	3
3. Johnson, R.	11	15. Radinsky, S.	6	27. Monteleone, R.	3
4. Guzman, J.	11	16. Pavlik, R.	6	28. Boever, J.	3
5. Appier, K.	10	17. Langston, M.	5	29. Moyer, J.	3
6. Hentgen, P.	10	18. Ryan, K.	5	30. Brown, K.	3
7. Wickman, B.	10	19. Sele, A.	5	31. Leiter, A.	3
8. Fernandez, A.	9	20. Gullickson, B.	4	32. Carpenter, C.	3
9. Mussina, M.	8	21. Stewart, D.	4	33. Schooler, M.	3
10. Alvarez, W.	7	22. Darwin, D.	4	34. Grahe, J.	3
11. Fleming, D.	7	23. Moore, M.	4	35. Kamieniecki, S.	3
12. Bere, J.	7	24. Kramer, T.	4		

Sidebar

Catchers
pp. 59-73

Corners
pp. 73-95

Infield
pp. 95-116

Outfield
pp. 117-150

DH
pp. 150-153

Starters
pp. 154-189

Relievers
pp. 190-217

AMERICAN LEAGUE POSITION PLAYERS

HOME RUNS

1. Gonzalez, J.	46	13. Hoiles, C.	29	24. Ventura, R.	22
2. Griffey Jr., K.	45	14. Vaughn, M.	29	25. Fryman, T.	22
3. Thomas, F.	41	15. Davis, C.	27	26. Winfield, D.	21
4. Belle, A.	38	16. Buhner, J.	27	27. Henderson, R.	21
5. Palmeiro, R.	37	17. Stanley, M.	26	28. Deer, R.	21
6. Carter, J.	33	18. Hrbek, K.	25	29. Baerga, C.	21
7. Palmer, D.	33	19. Ripken, C.	24	30. Baines, H.	20
8. Tettleton, M.	32	20. Olerud, J.	24	31. Henderson, D.	20
9. Tartabull, D.	31	21. Molitor, P.	22	32. Karkovice, R.	20
10. Salmon, T.	31	22. Puckett, K.	22	33. O'Neill, P.	20
11. Fielder, C.	30	23. Sierra, R.	22	34. Macfarlane, M.	20
12. Vaughn, G.	30				

RUNS BATTED IN

1. Belle, A.	129	11. Olerud, J.	107	21. Ventura, R.	94
2. Thomas, F.	128	12. Palmeiro, R.	105	22. Alomar, R.	93
3. Carter, J.	121	13. Tartabull, D.	102	23. Ripken, C.	90
4. Gonzalez, J.	118	14. Sierra, R.	101	24. Puckett, K.	89
5. Fielder, C.	117	15. Vaughn, M.	101	25. Mattingly, D.	86
6. Baerga, C.	114	16. Buhner, J.	98	26. Franco, J.	84
7. Davis, C.	112	17. Vaughn, G.	97	27. Stanley, M.	84
8. Molitor, P.	111	18. Fryman, T.	97	28. Hrbek, K.	83
9. Tettleton, M.	110	19. Palmer, D.	96	29. Hoiles, C.	82
10. Griffey Jr., K.	109	20. Salmon, T.	95	30. Surhoff, B.	79

STOLEN BASES

1. Lofton, K.	70	12. Anderson, B.	24	22. Listach, P.	18
2. Polonia, L.	55	13. Belle, A.	23	23. Griffey Jr., K.	17
3. Alomar, R.	55	14. McRae, B.	23	24. Kirby, W.	17
4. Henderson, R.	53	15. Molitor, P.	22	25. Fletcher, S.	16
5. Curtis, C.	48	16. Palmeiro, R.	22	26. Phillips, T.	16
6. Johnson, L.	35	17. Raines, T.	21	27. Gibson, K.	15
7. White, D.	34	18. McLemore, M.	21	28. Fernandez, T.	15
8. Jose, F.	31	19. Hamilton, D.	21	29. Felder, M.	15
9. Knoblauch, C.	29	20. Cora, J.	20	30. Mack, S.	15
10. Hulse, D.	29	21. Amaral, R.	19	31. Baerga, C.	15
11. Sierra, R.	25				

RUNS SCORED

1. Palmeiro, R.	124	11. Gonzalez, J.	105	21. Puckett, K.	89
2. Molitor, P.	121	12. Baerga, C.	105	22. Palmer, D.	88
3. White, D.	116	13. Fryman, T.	98	23. Ripken, C.	87
4. Lofton, K.	116	14. Vaughn, G.	97	24. Tartabull, D.	87
5. Henderson, R.	114	15. Cora, J.	95	25. Anderson, B.	87
6. Phillips, T.	113	16. Curtis, C.	94	26. Vaughn, M.	86
7. Griffey Jr., K.	113	17. Belle, A.	93	27. Franco, J.	85
8. Alomar, R.	109	18. Salmon, T.	93	28. Ventura, R.	85
9. Olerud, J.	109	19. Carter, J.	92	29. Boggs, W.	83
10. Thomas, F.	106	20. Buhner, J.	91	30. Joyner, W.	83

BATTING AVERAGE
(Minimum 300 At Bats)

1. Olerud, J.	.363	11. Baines, H.	.313	21. Harper, B.	.304
2. James, D.	.332	12. O'Neill, P.	.311	22. Pagliarulo, M.	.303
3. Molitor, P.	.332	13. Johnson, L.	.311	23. Boggs, W.	.302
4. Trammell, A.	.329	14. Hoiles, C.	.310	24. Fryman, T.	.300
5. Alomar, R.	.326	15. Gonzalez, J.	.310	25. Vaughn, M.	.297
6. Lofton, K.	.325	16. Hamilton, D.	.310	26. Puckett, K.	.296
7. Baerga, C.	.321	17. Griffey Jr., K.	.309	27. Palmeiro, R.	.295
8. Thomas, F.	.317	18. Raines, T.	.306	28. Livingstone, S.	.293
9. Greenwell, M.	.315	19. Fernandez, T.	.306	29. Joyner, W.	.292
10. Phillips, T.	.313	20. Stanley, M.	.305	30. Mattingly, D.	.291

WORST BATTING AVERAGES
(Minimum 300 At Bats)

1. Pena, T.	.181	12. DiSarcina, G.	.238	22. Tettleton, M.	.245
2. Deer, R.	.210	13. Spiers, B.	.238	23. Lind, J.	.248
3. Felder, M.	.211	14. Snow, J.	.241	24. Jefferson, R.	.249
4. McCarty, D.	.214	15. Hrbek, K.	.242	25. Bordick, M.	.249
5. Bell, G.	.217	16. Davis, C.	.243	26. Reimer, K.	.249
6. Paquette, C.	.219	17. Quintana, C.	.244	27. Tartabull, D.	.250
7. Henderson, D.	.220	18. Listach, P.	.244	28. Devereaux, M.	.250
8. Karkovice, R.	.228	19. Palmer, D.	.245	29. Lovullo, T.	.251
9. Munoz, P.	.233	20. Gaetti, G.	.245	30. Gonzales, R.	.251
10. Sierra, R.	.233	21. McReynolds, K.	.245	31. Meares, P.	.251
11. Owen, S.	.234				

BEAT THE FOUNDING FATHERS
AT THEIR OWN GAME!
(See page 280)

TOP POSITION PLAYERS, 1993

NL CATCHERS
(20 Games or More)

HOME RUNS

1. Piazza, M.	35	8. Slaught, D.	10	15. Manwaring, K.	5
2. Wilkins, R.	30	9. Fletcher, D.	9	16. Pratt, T.	5
3. Daulton, D.	24	10. Taubensee, E.	9	17. Ausmus, B.	5
4. Oliver, J.	14	11. Berryhill, D.	8	18. O'Brien, C.	4
5. Santiago, B.	13	12. Pagnozzi, T.	7	19. Sheaffer, D.	4
6. Hundley, T.	11	13. Reed, J.	6	20. Olson, G.	4
7. Servais, S.	11	14. Lake, S.	5		

BATTING AVERAGE

1. Piazza, M.	.318	8. Manwaring, K.	.275	15. Hernandez, C.	.252
2. Wilkins, R.	.303	9. Reed, J.	.261	16. Taubensee, E.	.250
3. Slaught, D.	.300	10. Pagnozzi, T.	.258	17. Berryhill, D.	.245
4. Girardi, J.	.291	11. Daulton, D.	.257	18. Servais, S.	.244
5. Pratt, T.	.288	12. Ausmus, B.	.256	19. Oliver, J.	.239
6. Sheaffer, D.	.278	13. O'Brien, C.	.255	20. Santiago, B.	.230
7. Pappas, E.	.276	14. Fletcher, D.	.255	21. Spehr, T.	.230

RUNS BATTED IN

1. Piazza, M.	112	9. Manwaring, K.	49	16. Pappas, E.	28
2. Daulton, D.	105	10. Berryhill, D.	43	17. Prince, T.	24
3. Oliver, J.	75	11. Taubensee, E.	42	18. Olson, G.	24
4. Wilkins, R.	73	12. Pagnozzi, T.	41	19. O'Brien, C.	23
5. Fletcher, D.	60	13. Sheaffer, D.	32	20. Lake, S.	13
6. Slaught, D.	55	14. Servais, S.	32	21. Pratt, T.	13
7. Hundley, T.	53	15. Girardi, J.	31	22. Higgins, K.	13
8. Santiago, B.	50				

STOLEN BASES

1. Santiago, B.	10	8. Spehr, T.	2	15. Olson, G.	1
2. Girardi, J.	6	9. Laker, T.	2	16. Hundley, T.	1
3. Daulton, D.	5	10. Ausmus, B.	2	17. Taubensee, E.	1
4. Piazza, M.	3	11. O'Brien, C.	1	18. Pappas, E.	1
5. Slaught, D.	2	12. Manwaring, K.	1	19. Natal, B.	1
6. Sheaffer, D.	2	13. Pagnozzi, T.	1	20. Owens, J.	1
7. Wilkins, R.	2	14. Prince, T.	1		

RUNS SCORED

1. Daulton, D.	90	8. Girardi, J.	35	15. Berryhill, D.	24
2. Piazza, M.	81	9. Slaught, D.	34	16. Servais, S.	24
3. Wilkins, R.	78	10. Fletcher, D.	33	17. Olson, G.	23
4. Santiago, B.	49	11. Pagnozzi, T.	31	18. Ausmus, B.	18
5. Manwaring, K.	48	12. Sheaffer, D.	26	19. Higgins, K.	17
6. Oliver, J.	40	13. Taubensee, E.	26	20. O'Brien, C.	15
7. Hundley, T.	40	14. Pappas, E.	25		

HOME RUNS

1. Tettleton, M.	32	8. Harper, B.	12	15. Alomar Jr, S.	6		
2. Hoiles, C.	29	9. Nokes, M.	10	16. Hemond, S.	6		
3. Stanley, M.	26	10. Steinbach, T.	10	17. Haselman, B.	5		
4. Karkovice, R.	20	11. Rodriguez, I.	10	18. Pena, T.	4		
5. Macfarlane, M.	20	12. Borders, P.	9	19. Parent, M.	4		
6. Kreuter, C.	15	13. Myers, G.	7	20. Lampkin, T.	4		
7. Valle, D.	13	14. Nilsson, D.	7	21. Knorr, R.	4		

BATTING AVERAGE

1. Hoiles, C.	.310	8. Rodriguez, I.	.273	15. Haselman, B.	.255
2. Stanley, M.	.305	9. Alomar Jr, S.	.270	16. LaValliere, M.	.255
3. Harper, B.	.304	10. Parent, M.	.259	17. Borders, P.	.254
4. Kreuter, C.	.286	11. Valle, D.	.258	18. Mayne, B.	.253
5. Steinbach, T.	.285	12. Nilsson, D.	.257	19. Nokes, M.	.249
6. Turner, C.	.280	13. Hemond, S.	.256	20. Knorr, R.	.248
7. Macfarlane, M.	.273	14. Myers, G.	.255		

RUNS BATTED IN

1. Tettleton, M.	110	8. Borders, P.	55	15. Alomar Jr, S.	32
2. Stanley, M.	84	9. Karkovice, R.	54	16. Hemond, S.	26
3. Hoiles, C.	82	10. Kreuter, C.	51	17. Lampkin, T.	25
4. Harper, B.	73	11. Steinbach, T.	43	18. Melvin, B.	23
5. Macfarlane, M.	67	12. Myers, G.	40	19. Mayne, B.	22
6. Rodriguez, I.	66	13. Nilsson, D.	40	20. Ortiz, J.	20
7. Valle, D.	63	14. Nokes, M.	35	21. Knorr, R.	20

STOLEN BASES

1. Hemond, S.	14	10. Nilsson, D.	3	19. Ortiz, J.	1
2. Rodriguez, I.	8	11. Petralli, G.	2	20. Tingley, R.	1
3. Lampkin, T.	7	12. Karkovice, R.	2	21. Valle, D.	1
4. Kmak, J.	6	13. Macfarlane, M.	2	22. Stanley, M.	1
5. Tettleton, M.	3	14. Borders, P.	2	23. Hoiles, C.	1
6. Steinbach, T.	3	15. Kreuter, C.	2	24. Orton, J.	1
7. Myers, G.	3	16. Haselman, B.	2	25. Webster, L.	1
8. Alomar Jr, S.	3	17. Harper, B.	1	26. Turner, C.	1
9. Mayne, B.	3	18. Pena, T.	1		

RUNS SCORED

1. Hoiles, C.	80	8. Harper, B.	52	15. Nokes, M.	25
2. Tettleton, M.	79	9. Valle, D.	48	16. Alomar Jr, S.	24
3. Stanley, M.	70	10. Steinbach, T.	47	17. Lampkin, T.	22
4. Karkovice, R.	60	11. Borders, P.	38	18. Mayne, B.	22
5. Kreuter, C.	59	12. Nilsson, D.	35	19. Haselman, B.	21
6. Rodriguez, I.	56	13. Hemond, S.	31	20. Pena, T.	20
7. Macfarlane, M.	55	14. Myers, G.	27		

Catchers
pp. 59–73

Corners
pp. 73–95

Infield
pp. 95–116

Outfield
pp. 117–150

DH
pp. 150–153

Starters
pp. 154–189

Relievers
pp. 190–217

NL CORNERS
(20 Games or More)

HOME RUNS

1. Williams, M.	38	15. Jefferies, G.	16	29. Clark, P.	9
2. McGriff, F.	37	16. Buechele, S.	15	30. Merced, O.	8
3. Bonilla, B.	34	17. Clark, W.	14	31. Johnson, H.	7
4. Murray, E.	27	18. Kruk, J.	14	32. Morris, H.	7
5. Hayes, C.	25	19. Grace, M.	14	33. Benzinger, T.	6
6. Karros, E.	23	20. Berry, S.	14	34. Young, K.	6
7. Galarraga, A.	22	21. Caminiti, K.	13	35. Walker, C.	5
8. Sabo, C.	21	22. Clark, J.	13	36. Jordan, R.	5
9. Destrade, O.	20	23. Wallach, T.	12	37. Batiste, K.	5
10. Sheffield, G.	20	24. Conine, J.	12	38. VanderWal, J.	5
11. Bagwell, J.	20	25. Cianfrocco, A.	12	39. Shipley, C.	4
12. Hollins, D.	18	26. Snyder, C.	11	40. Vizcaino, J.	4
13. Pendleton, T.	17	27. Bream, S.	9	41. Colbrunn, G.	4
14. Zeile, T.	17	28. King, J.	9	42. Bolick, F.	4

BATTING AVERAGE

1. Galarraga, A.	.370	15. McGriff, F.	.291	28. Pendleton, T.	.271
2. Jefferies, G.	.342	16. Jordan, R.	.290	29. Arias, A.	.269
3. Grace, M.	.325	17. Benzinger, T.	.288	30. Snyder, C.	.266
4. Pecota, B.	.323	18. Lansing, M.	.287	31. Bonilla, B.	.265
5. Bagwell, J.	.320	19. Vizcaino, J.	.287	32. Caminiti, K.	.262
6. Morris, H.	.316	20. Brewer, R.	.286	33. Berry, S.	.261
7. Kruk, J.	.316	21. Murray, E.	.285	34. Bream, S.	.260
8. Merced, O.	.313	22. Clark, W.	.283	35. Sabo, C.	.259
9. Clark, P.	.313	23. Clark, J.	.282	36. Donnels, C.	.257
10. Hayes, C.	.305	24. Batiste, K.	.282	37. Renteria, R.	.255
11. King, J.	.294	25. Zeile, T.	.277	38. Destrade, O.	.255
12. Williams, M.	.293	26. Hollins, D.	.272	39. Colbrunn, G.	.255
13. Sheffield, G.	.293	27. Buechele, S.	.272	40. Karros, E.	.247
14. Conine, J.	.292				

RUNS BATTED IN

1. Williams, M.	110	15. Jefferies, G.	83	29. Berry, S.	49
2. Zeile, T.	103	16. Sabo, C.	82	30. Cianfrocco, A.	48
3. McGriff, F.	101	17. Karros, E.	80	31. Young, K.	47
4. Murray, E.	100	18. Conine, J.	79	32. Lansing, M.	45
5. Galarraga, A.	98	19. Caminiti, K.	75	33. Bream, S.	35
6. Grace, M.	98	20. Clark, W.	73	34. Clark, P.	33
7. Hayes, C.	98	21. Sheffield, G.	73	35. Renteria, R.	30
8. King, J.	98	22. Merced, O.	70	36. VanderWal, J.	30
9. Hollins, D.	93	23. Clark, J.	67	37. Batiste, K.	29
10. Bagwell, J.	88	24. Buechele, S.	65	38. Johnson, H.	26
11. Bonilla, B.	87	25. Wallach, T.	62	39. Benzinger, T.	26
12. Destrade, O.	87	26. Snyder, C.	56	40. Donnels, C.	24
13. Kruk, J.	85	27. Vizcaino, J.	54	41. Bolick, F.	24
14. Pendleton, T.	84	28. Morris, H.	49		

STOLEN BASES

1. Jefferies, G.	46	16. Sabo, C.	6	30. Hollins, D.	2		
2. Lansing, M.	23	17. VanderWal, J.	6	31. Conine, J.	2		
3. Sheffield, G.	17	18. Pendleton, T.	5	32. Donnels, C.	2		
4. Bagwell, J.	13	19. McGriff, F.	5	33. Cianfrocco, A.	2		
5. Shipley, C.	12	20. Zeile, T.	5	34. Clark, P.	2		
6. Vizcaino, J.	12	21. Bream, S.	4	35. Young, K.	2		
7. Berry, S.	12	22. Snyder, C.	4	36. Buechele, S.	1		
8. Hayes, C.	11	23. Colbrunn, G.	4	37. Pecota, B.	1		
9. Clark, J.	9	24. Bonilla, B.	3	38. Williams, M.	1		
10. Caminiti, K.	8	25. Merced, O.	3	39. Brewer, R.	1		
11. Grace, M.	8	26. Murray, E.	2	40. Arias, A.	1		
12. King, J.	8	27. Galarraga, A.	2	41. Bolick, F.	1		
13. Walker, C.	7	28. Clark, W.	2	42. Castellano, P.	1		
14. Johnson, H.	6	29. Morris, H.	2	43. Marrero, O.	1		
15. Kruk, J.	6						

RUNS SCORED

1. McGriff, F.	111	15. Bagwell, J.	76	29. Morris, H.	48
2. Williams, M.	105	16. Caminiti, K.	75	30. Wallach, T.	42
3. Hollins, D.	104	17. Conine, J.	75	31. Young, K.	38
4. Kruk, J.	100	18. Vizcaino, J.	74	32. VanderWal, J.	34
5. Jefferies, G.	89	19. Karros, E.	74	33. Bream, S.	33
6. Hayes, C.	89	20. Galarraga, A.	71	34. Clark, P.	33
7. Grace, M.	86	21. Merced, O.	68	35. Johnson, H.	32
8. Sabo, C.	86	22. Sheffield, G.	67	36. Cianfrocco, A.	30
9. Clark, W.	82	23. Clark, J.	65	37. Renteria, R.	27
10. King, J.	82	24. Lansing, M.	64	38. Arias, A.	27
11. Zeile, T.	82	25. Snyder, C.	61	39. Shipley, C.	25
12. Pendleton, T.	81	26. Destrade, O.	61	40. Benzinger, T.	25
13. Bonilla, B.	81	27. Buechele, S.	53	41. Bolick, F.	25
14. Murray, E.	77	28. Berry, S.	50		

AL CORNERS
(20 Games or More)
HOME RUNS

1. Thomas, F.	41	15. Mattingly, D.	17	29. Gomez, L.	10
2. Palmeiro, R.	37	16. Martinez, T.	17	30. Pagliarulo, M.	9
3. Palmer, D.	33	17. Snow, J.	16	31. McGwire, M.	9
4. Tettleton, M.	32	18. Joyner, W.	15	32. Cooper, S.	9
5. Fielder, C.	30	19. Blowers, M.	15	33. Surhoff, B.	7
6. Vaughn, M.	29	20. Gaetti, G.	14	34. Thome, J.	7
7. Hrbek, K.	25	21. Leyritz, J.	14	35. Hiatt, P.	7
8. Olerud, J.	24	22. Trammell, A.	12	36. Milligan, R.	6
9. Molitor, P.	22	23. Sprague, E.	12	37. Brosius, S.	6
10. Ventura, R.	22	24. Paquette, C.	12	38. Pasqua, D.	5
11. Fryman, T.	22	25. Seitzer, K.	11	39. Magadan, D.	5
12. Neel, T.	19	26. Gallego, M.	10	40. Martinez, C.	5
13. Jaha, J.	19	27. Aldrete, M.	10	41. Espinoza, A.	4
14. Sorrento, P.	18	28. Segui, D.	10	42. Perez, E.	4

BATTING AVERAGE

1. Olerud, J.	.363	15. Vaughn, M.	.297	28. Segui, D.	.273
2. McGwire, M.	.333	16. Palmeiro, R.	.295	29. Magadan, D.	.272
3. Hale, C.	.333	17. Livingstone, S.	.293	30. Thon, D.	.270
4. Molitor, P.	.332	18. Joyner, W.	.292	31. Seitzer, K.	.269
5. Trammell, A.	.329	19. Mattingly, D.	.291	32. Fielder, C.	.267
6. Thomas, F.	.317	20. Neel, T.	.291	33. Aldrete, M.	.267
7. Leyritz, J.	.309	21. Amaral, R.	.290	34. Thome, J.	.266
8. Treadway, J.	.303	22. Gallego, M.	.283	35. Martinez, T.	.265
9. Pagliarulo, M.	.303	23. Barnes, S.	.281	36. Jaha, J.	.264
10. Boggs, W.	.302	24. Blowers, M.	.280	37. Larkin, G.	.264
11. Hulett, T.	.300	25. Cooper, S.	.279	38. Ventura, R.	.262
12. Fryman, T.	.300	26. Espinoza, A.	.277	39. Sprague, E.	.260
13. Milligan, R.	.299	27. Surhoff, B.	.273	40. Reboulet, J.	.258
14. Litton, G.	.299				

RUNS BATTED IN

1. Thomas, F.	128	15. Jaha, J.	70	28. Leyritz, J.	53
2. Fielder, C.	117	16. Joyner, W.	65	29. Gaetti, G.	50
3. Molitor, P.	111	17. Sorrento, P.	65	30. Magadan, D.	50
4. Tettleton, M.	110	18. Cooper, S.	63	31. Paquette, C.	46
5. Olerud, J.	107	19. Neel, T.	63	32. Pagliarulo, M.	44
6. Palmeiro, R.	105	20. Trammell, A.	60	33. Amaral, R.	44
7. Vaughn, M.	101	21. Segui, D.	60	34. Livingstone, S.	39
8. Fryman, T.	97	22. Martinez, T.	60	35. Milligan, R.	36
9. Palmer, D.	96	23. Boggs, W.	59	36. Hiatt, P.	36
10. Ventura, R.	94	24. Seitzer, K.	57	37. Thon, D.	33
11. Mattingly, D.	86	25. Blowers, M.	57	38. Aldrete, M.	33
12. Hrbek, K.	83	26. Snow, J.	57	39. Gonzales, R.	31
13. Surhoff, B.	79	27. Gallego, M.	54	40. Martinez, C.	31
14. Sprague, E.	73				

STOLEN BASES

1. Molitor, P.	22	17. Cooper, S.	5	33. Hale, C.	2
2. Palmeiro, R.	22	18. Reboulet, J.	5	34. Segui, D.	2
3. Amaral, R.	19	19. Perez, E.	5	35. Thome, J.	2
4. Jaha, J.	13	20. Hrbek, K.	4	36. McCarty, D.	2
5. Trammell, A.	12	21. Thomas, F.	4	37. Gaetti, G.	1
6. Surhoff, B.	12	22. Vaughn, M.	4	38. Hulett, T.	1
7. Palmer, D.	11	23. Paquette, C.	4	39. Aldrete, M.	1
8. Fryman, T.	9	24. Tettleton, M.	3	40. Treadway, J.	1
9. Seitzer, K.	7	25. Gallego, M.	3	41. Martinez, C.	1
10. Thon, D.	6	26. Miller, K.	3	42. Quintana, C.	1
11. Pagliarulo, M.	6	27. Sorrento, P.	3	43. Blowers, M.	1
12. Brosius, S.	6	28. Neel, T.	3	44. Jorgensen, T.	1
13. Hiatt, P.	6	29. Snow, J.	3	45. Ventura, R.	1
14. Barnes, S.	5	30. Espinoza, A.	2	46. Sprague, E.	1
15. Gonzales, R.	5	31. Pasqua, D.	2	47. Livingstone, S.	1
16. Joyner, W.	5	32. Magadan, D.	2		

RUNS SCORED

1. Palmeiro, R.	124	15. Sorrento, P.	75	28. Magadan, D.	49
2. Molitor, P.	121	16. Trammell, A.	72	29. Martinez, T.	48
3. Olerud, J.	109	17. Cooper, S.	67	30. Seitzer, K.	45
4. Thomas, F.	106	18. Surhoff, B.	66	31. Leyritz, J.	43
5. Fryman, T.	98	19. Gallego, M.	63	32. Gaetti, G.	40
6. Palmer, D.	88	20. Hrbek, K.	60	33. Hulett, T.	40
7. Vaughn, M.	86	21. Snow, J.	60	34. Aldrete, M.	40
8. Ventura, R.	85	22. Neel, T.	59	35. Livingstone, S.	39
9. Boggs, W.	83	23. Pagliarulo, M.	55	36. Milligan, R.	37
10. Joyner, W.	83	24. Blowers, M.	55	37. McCarty, D.	36
11. Fielder, C.	80	25. Segui, D.	54	38. Paquette, C.	35
12. Tettleton, M.	79	26. Amaral, R.	53	39. Espinoza, A.	34
13. Mattingly, D.	78	27. Sprague, E.	50	40. Gonzales, R.	34
14. Jaha, J.	78				

NL MIDDLE INFIELDERS
(20 Games or More)

HOME RUNS

1. Biggio, C.	21	16. Walker, C.	5	30. Branson, J.	3
2. Kent, J.	21	17. Pena, G.	5	31. Young, E.	3
3. Thompson, R.	19	18. Barberie, B.	5	32. Bogar, T.	3
4. Blauser, J.	15	19. Batiste, K.	5	33. Lansing, M.	3
5. Garcia, C.	12	20. Gutierrez, R.	5	34. Renteria, R.	2
6. Duncan, M.	11	21. Mejia, R.	5	35. Liriano, N.	2
7. Cedeno, A.	11	22. Samuel, J.	4	36. Reed, J.	2
8. Cordero, W.	10	23. Shipley, C.	4	37. Sharperson, M.	2
9. Sandberg, R.	9	24. Benjamin, M.	4	38. Harris, L.	2
10. Bell, J.	9	25. Vizcaino, J.	4	39. McKnight, J.	2
11. Castilla, V.	9	26. Foley, T.	3	40. DeShields, D.	2
12. Larkin, B.	8	27. Alicea, L.	3	41. Arias, A.	2
13. Teufel, T.	7	28. Morandini, M.	3	42. Scarsone, S.	2
14. Lemke, M.	7	29. Benavides, F.	3	43. Stocker, K.	2
15. Clayton, R.	6				

BATTING AVERAGE

1. Stocker, K.	.324	15. Duncan, M.	.282	28. Jones, T.	.262
2. Larkin, B.	.315	16. Batiste, K.	.282	29. Gardner, J.	.262
3. Thompson, R.	.312	17. Clayton, R.	.282	30. McKnight, J.	.256
4. Bell, J.	.310	18. Sanchez, R.	.282	31. Pena, G.	.256
5. Sandberg, R.	.309	19. Alicea, L.	.279	32. Sharperson, M.	.255
6. Blauser, J.	.305	20. Barberie, B.	.277	33. Castilla, V.	.255
7. Liriano, N.	.305	21. Reed, J.	.276	34. Renteria, R.	.255
8. DeShields, D.	.295	22. Kent, J.	.270	35. Ready, R.	.254
9. Smith, O.	.288	23. Offerman, J.	.270	36. Foley, T.	.252
10. Biggio, C.	.287	24. Young, E.	.270	37. Scarsone, S.	.252
11. Lansing, M.	.287	25. Garcia, C.	.269	38. Lemke, M.	.251
12. Vizcaino, J.	.287	26. Arias, A.	.269	39. Gutierrez, R.	.251
13. Benavides, F.	.287	27. Weiss, W.	.266	40. Teufel, T.	.250
14. Cedeno, A.	.283				

RUNS BATTED IN

#	Player	RBI	#	Player	RBI	#	Player	RBI
1.	Kent, J.	80	15.	Garcia, C.	47	29.	DeShields, D.	29
2.	Duncan, M.	73	16.	Alicea, L.	46	30.	Batiste, K.	29
3.	Blauser, J.	73	17.	Sandberg, R.	45	31.	Sanchez, R.	28
4.	Clayton, R.	70	18.	Lansing, M.	45	32.	Samuel, J.	26
5.	Thompson, R.	65	19.	Young, E.	42	33.	Benavides, F.	26
6.	Biggio, C.	64	20.	Weiss, W.	39	34.	Gutierrez, R.	26
7.	Offerman, J.	62	21.	Morandini, M.	33	35.	Bogar, T.	25
8.	Cordero, W.	58	22.	Barberie, B.	33	36.	Gardner, J.	24
9.	Cedeno, A.	56	23.	Teufel, T.	31	37.	Foley, T.	22
10.	Vizcaino, J.	54	24.	Reed, J.	31	38.	Shipley, C.	22
11.	Smith, O.	53	25.	Stocker, K.	31	39.	Branson, J.	22
12.	Bell, J.	51	26.	Renteria, R.	30	40.	Arias, A.	20
13.	Larkin, B.	51	27.	Pena, G.	30	41.	Mejia, R.	20
14.	Lemke, M.	49	28.	Castilla, V.	30			

STOLEN BASES

#	Player	SB	#	Player	SB	#	Player	SB
1.	DeShields, D.	43	16.	Cordero, W.	12	30.	Kent, J.	4
2.	Young, E.	42	17.	Alicea, L.	11	31.	Gutierrez, R.	4
3.	Offerman, J.	30	18.	Clayton, R.	11	32.	Mejia, R.	4
4.	Roberts, B.	26	19.	Thompson, R.	10	33.	Harris, L.	3
5.	Lansing, M.	23	20.	Sandberg, R.	9	34.	Yelding, E.	3
6.	Smith, O.	21	21.	Samuel, J.	9	35.	Benavides, F.	3
7.	Garcia, C.	18	22.	Cedeno, A.	9	36.	Ready, R.	2
8.	Bell, J.	16	23.	Walker, C.	7	37.	Teufel, T.	2
9.	Blauser, J.	16	24.	Weiss, W.	7	38.	Candaele, C.	2
10.	Biggio, C.	15	25.	Duncan, M.	6	39.	Sharperson, M.	2
11.	Larkin, B.	14	26.	Liriano, N.	6	40.	Jones, T.	2
12.	Morandini, M.	13	27.	Vina, F.	6	41.	Barberie, B.	2
13.	Pena, G.	13	28.	Stocker, K.	5	42.	Castilla, V.	2
14.	Shipley, C.	12	29.	Branson, J.	4	43.	Gardner, J.	2
15.	Vizcaino, J.	12						

RUNS SCORED

#	Player	R	#	Player	R	#	Player	R
1.	Blauser, J.	110	15.	Kent, J.	65	29.	Branson, J.	40
2.	Bell, J.	102	16.	Lansing, M.	64	30.	Castilla, V.	36
3.	Biggio, C.	98	17.	Larkin, B.	57	31.	Sanchez, R.	35
4.	Thompson, R.	85	18.	Morandini, M.	57	32.	Pena, G.	34
5.	Young, E.	82	19.	Cordero, W.	56	33.	Samuel, J.	31
6.	Offerman, J.	77	20.	Clayton, R.	54	34.	Mejia, R.	31
7.	Garcia, C.	77	21.	Gardner, J.	53	35.	Liriano, N.	28
8.	Gutierrez, R.	76	22.	Lemke, M.	52	36.	Renteria, R.	27
9.	Smith, O.	75	23.	Weiss, W.	50	37.	Arias, A.	27
10.	DeShields, D.	75	24.	Alicea, L.	50	38.	Teufel, T.	26
11.	Vizcaino, J.	74	25.	Reed, J.	48	39.	Shipley, C.	25
12.	Cedeno, A.	69	26.	Roberts, B.	46	40.	Ready, R.	22
13.	Duncan, M.	68	27.	Stocker, K.	46	41.	Benjamin, M.	22
14.	Sandberg, R.	67	28.	Barberie, B.	45			

QUESTIONS? CALL
800-884-7684 FOR ANSWERS

HOME RUNS

1. Ripken, C.	24	17. Fletcher, S.	5	32. Diaz, M.	2	**Catchers** pp. 59-73	
2. Fryman, T.	22	18. Fernandez, T.	5	33. Fermin, F.	2	**Corners** pp. 73-95	
3. Baerga, C.	21	19. Riles, E.	5	34. Blankenship, L.	2		
4. Alomar, R.	17	20. Bell, J.	5	35. Spiers, B.	2	**Infield** pp. 95-116	
5. Trammell, A.	12	21. Reynolds, H.	4	36. Vizquel, O.	2		
6. Boone, B.	12	22. Espinoza, A.	4	37. Knoblauch, C.	2		
7. Valentin, J.	11	23. Guillen, O.	4	38. Rossy, R.	2	**Outfield** pp. 117-150	
8. Gagne, G.	10	24. McLemore, M.	4	39. Easley, D.	2		
9. Gallego, M.	10	25. DiSarcina, G.	3	40. Thon, D.	1	**DH** pp. 150-153	
10. Whitaker, L.	9	26. Hale, C.	3	41. Lee, M.	1		
11. Phillips, T.	7	27. Litton, G.	3	42. Rivera, L.	1		
12. Velarde, R.	7	28. Bordick, M.	3	43. Stillwell, K.	1	**Starters** pp. 154-189	
13. Strange, D.	7	29. Listach, P.	3	44. Grebeck, C.	1		
14. Kelly, P.	7	30. Owen, S.	2	45. Amaral, R.	1	**Relievers** pp. 190-217	
15. Gates, B.	7	31. Cora, J.	2	46. Reboulet, J.	1		
16. Lovullo, T.	6						

BATTING AVERAGE

1. Hale, C.	.333	15. Gallego, M.	.283	29. Ripken, C.	.257
2. Trammell, A.	.329	16. Guillen, O.	.280	30. Strange, D.	.256
3. Alomar, R.	.326	17. Gagne, G.	.280	31. Vizquel, O.	.255
4. Baerga, C.	.320	18. Fernandez, T.	.279	32. Reynolds, H.	.251
5. Easley, D.	.313	19. Valentin, J.	.278	33. Meares, P.	.251
6. Phillips, T.	.313	20. Espinoza, A.	.277	34. Boone, B.	.251
7. Velarde, R.	.301	21. Knoblauch, C.	.277	35. Lovullo, T.	.250
8. Fryman, T.	.300	22. Kelly, P.	.273	36. Gomez, C.	.250
9. Litton, G.	.299	23. Diaz, M.	.273	37. Bordick, M.	.249
10. Whitaker, L.	.290	24. Thon, D.	.270	38. Lind, J.	.248
11. Amaral, R.	.290	25. Cora, J.	.268	39. Listach, P.	.244
12. Gates, B.	.290	26. Correia, R.	.266	40. Spiers, B.	.238
13. Fletcher, S.	.286	27. Fermin, F.	.263	41. DiSarcina, G.	.238
14. McLemore, M.	.284	28. Reboulet, J.	.258		

RUNS BATTED IN

1. Baerga, C.	114	15. Cora, J.	51	28. Spiers, B.	36
2. Fryman, T.	97	16. Kelly, P.	51	29. Thon, D.	33
3. Alomar, R.	93	17. Guillen, O.	50	30. Meares, P.	33
4. Ripken, C.	90	18. Bordick, M.	48	31. Vizquel, O.	31
5. McLemore, M.	72	19. Reynolds, H.	47	32. Lovullo, T.	30
6. Gates, B.	69	20. Fletcher, S.	45	33. Listach, P.	30
7. Whitaker, L.	67	21. Fermin, F.	45	34. Espinoza, A.	27
8. Valentin, J.	66	22. DiSarcina, G.	45	35. Hale, C.	27
9. Fernandez, T.	64	23. Amaral, R.	44	36. Litton, G.	25
10. Trammell, A.	60	24. Knoblauch, C.	41	37. Diaz, M.	24
11. Strange, D.	60	25. Boone, B.	38	38. Velarde, R.	24
12. Phillips, T.	57	26. Lind, J.	37	39. Blankenship, L.	23
13. Gagne, G.	57	27. Bell, J.	36	40. Easley, D.	22
14. Gallego, M.	54				

STOLEN BASES

1. Alomar, R.	55	16. Gagne, G.	10	31. Meares, P.	4
2. Knoblauch, C.	29	17. Bordick, M.	10	32. Whitaker, L.	3
3. Fernandez, T.	21	18. Spiers, B.	9	33. Owen, S.	3
4. McLemore, M.	21	19. Fryman, T.	9	34. Schofield, D.	3
5. Cora, J.	20	20. Lovullo, T.	7	35. Gallego, M.	3
6. Amaral, R.	19	21. Gates, B.	7	36. Lind, J.	3
7. Listach, P.	18	22. Thon, D.	6	37. Valentin, J.	3
8. Fletcher, S.	16	23. Stillwell, K.	6	38. Espinoza, A.	2
9. Phillips, T.	16	24. Bell, J.	6	39. Lee, M.	2
10. Baerga, C.	15	25. Strange, D.	6	40. Velarde, R.	2
11. Kelly, P.	14	26. Easley, D.	6	41. Hale, C.	2
12. Blankenship, L.	13	27. Guillen, O.	5	42. Boone, B.	2
13. Trammell, A.	12	28. DiSarcina, G.	5	43. Correia, R.	2
14. Reynolds, H.	12	29. Reboulet, J.	5	44. Gomez, C.	2
15. Vizquel, O.	12	30. Fermin, F.	4		

RUNS SCORED

1. Phillips, T.	113	16. Gates, B.	64	30. Lovullo, T.	42
2. Alomar, R.	109	17. Gallego, M.	63	31. Owen, S.	41
3. Baerga, C.	105	18. Bordick, M.	60	32. Espinoza, A.	34
4. Fryman, T.	98	19. Strange, D.	58	33. Lind, J.	33
5. Cora, J.	95	20. Amaral, R.	53	34. Reboulet, J.	33
6. Ripken, C.	87	21. Listach, P.	50	35. Easley, D.	33
7. Knoblauch, C.	82	22. Valentin, J.	50	36. Meares, P.	33
8. Fletcher, S.	81	23. Kelly, P.	49	37. Lee, M.	31
9. McLemore, M.	81	24. Fermin, F.	48	38. Boone, B.	31
10. Trammell, A.	72	25. Bell, J.	47	39. Velarde, R.	28
11. Whitaker, L.	72	26. Guillen, O.	44	40. Hale, C.	25
12. Vizquel, O.	68	27. DiSarcina, G.	44	41. Litton, G.	25
13. Gagne, G.	66	28. Blankenship, L.	43	42. Grebeck, C.	25
14. Fernandez, T.	65	29. Spiers, B.	43	43. Diaz, M.	24
15. Reynolds, H.	64				

NL OUTFIELDERS
(20 Games or More)

HOME RUNS

1. Bonds, B.	46	22. Boston, D.	14	42. Gwynn, T.	7
2. Justice, D.	40	23. Clark, J.	13	43. Carreon, M.	7
3. Gant, R.	36	24. Burnitz, J.	13	44. Felix, J.	7
4. Bonilla, B.	34	25. Chamberlain, W.	12	45. Howard, T.	7
5. Plantier, P.	34	26. Conine, J.	12	46. Lankford, R.	7
6. Sosa, S.	33	27. Clark, D.	11	47. Jackson, D.	6
7. Whiten, M.	25	28. Snyder, C.	11	48. Gallagher, D.	6
8. Incaviglia, P.	24	29. Smith, D.	11	49. Sanders, D.	6
9. Walker, L.	22	30. Thompson, R.	11	50. Jones, C.	6
10. Bichette, D.	21	31. May, D.	10	51. Brumfield, J.	6
11. Bell, D.	21	32. Jordan, B.	10	52. Strawberry, D.	5
12. Sanders, R.	20	33. Kelly, R.	9	53. Cotto, H.	5
13. Mitchell, K.	19	34. Clark, P.	9	54. Martinez, D.	5
14. Dykstra, L.	19	35. Roberson, K.	9	55. Bean, B.	5
15. Grissom, M.	19	36. Orsulak, J.	8	56. VanderWal, J.	5
16. Alou, M.	18	37. Van Slyke, A.	8	57. McGee, W.	4
17. Martin, A.	18	38. Finley, S.	8	58. Thompson, M.	4
18. Gilkey, B.	16	39. Merced, O.	8	59. Carr, C.	4
19. Anthony, E.	15	40. Rodriguez, H.	8	60. Whitmore, D.	4
20. Hill, G.	15	41. Eisenreich, J.	7	61. Mondesi, R.	4
21. Gonzalez, L.	15				

BATTING AVERAGE

1. Gwynn, T.	.358	21. Mondesi, R.	.291	41. Brumfield, J.	.269		
2. Mitchell, K.	.340	22. Alou, M.	.286	42. Carr, C.	.267		
3. Bonds, B.	.336	23. Brewer, R.	.286	43. Finley, S.	.266		
4. Carreon, M.	.327	24. Frazier, L.	.286	44. Snyder, C.	.266		
5. Kelly, R.	.319	25. Bass, K.	.284	45. Bonilla, B.	.265		
6. Eisenreich, J.	.318	26. Orsulak, J.	.284	46. Walker, L.	.265		
7. Merced, O.	.313	27. Clark, J.	.282	47. Hill, G.	.264		
8. Clark, P.	.313	28. Chamberlain, W.	.282	48. Bell, D.	.262		
9. Bichette, D.	.311	29. Martin, A.	.281	49. Thompson, M.	.262		
10. Van Slyke, A.	.310	30. Coleman, V.	.279	50. Boston, D.	.261		
11. Jordan, B.	.310	31. Sanders, D.	.276	51. Sosa, S.	.261		
12. Gilkey, B.	.305	32. Incaviglia, P.	.274	52. White, R.	.260		
13. Dykstra, L.	.305	33. Sanders, R.	.274	53. Bean, B.	.260		
14. McGee, W.	.301	34. Gant, R.	.274	54. Wilson, W.	.258		
15. Smith, D.	.300	35. Gallagher, D.	.273	55. Cole, A.	.256		
16. Gonzalez, L.	.300	36. Jones, C.	.273	56. Howard, T.	.254		
17. Butler, B.	.298	37. Clark, D.	.271	57. Lewis, D.	.253		
18. Grissom, M.	.298	38. Justice, D.	.270	58. Whiten, M.	.252		
19. May, D.	.294	39. Young, E.	.270	59. Cotto, H.	.250		
20. Conine, J.	.292	40. Nixon, O.	.269	60. Thompson, R.	.250		

Catchers
pp. 59–73

Corners
pp. 73–95

Infield
pp. 95–116

Outfield
pp. 117–150

DH
pp. 150–153

Starters
pp. 154–189

Relievers
pp. 190–217

RUNS BATTED IN

1. Bonds, B.	123	22. Anthony, E.	66	42. Burnitz, J.	38
2. Justice, D.	120	23. Mitchell, K.	64	43. Bass, K.	37
3. Gant, R.	117	24. Martin, A.	64	44. Howard, T.	36
4. Plantier, P.	100	25. Gwynn, T.	59	45. Orsulak, J.	35
5. Whiten, M.	99	26. Snyder, C.	56	46. Kelly, R.	35
6. Grissom, M.	95	27. Eisenreich, J.	54	47. Smith, D.	35
7. Sosa, S.	93	28. Van Slyke, A.	50	48. Carreon, M.	33
8. Incaviglia, P.	89	29. Lewis, D.	48	49. Clark, P.	33
9. Bichette, D.	89	30. Hill, G.	47	50. Bean, B.	32
10. Bonilla, B.	87	31. McGee, W.	46	51. Jones, C.	31
11. Walker, L.	86	32. Clark, D.	46	52. VanderWal, J.	30
12. Alou, M.	85	33. Lankford, R.	45	53. Gallagher, D.	28
13. Sanders, R.	83	34. Chamberlain, W.	45	54. Sanders, D.	28
14. Conine, J.	79	35. Thompson, M.	44	55. Martinez, D.	27
15. May, D.	77	36. Finley, S.	44	56. Roberson, K.	27
16. Gonzalez, L.	72	37. Jordan, B.	44	57. Jackson, D.	26
17. Bell, D.	72	38. Butler, B.	42	58. Thompson, R.	26
18. Merced, O.	70	39. Young, E.	42	59. Coleman, V.	25
19. Gilkey, B.	70	40. Carr, C.	41	60. Nixon, O.	24
20. Clark, J.	67	41. Boston, D.	40	61. Cole, A.	24
21. Dykstra, L.	66				

STOLEN BASES

1. Carr, C.	58	23. Cotto, H.	16	45. Eisenreich, J.	5
2. Grissom, M.	53	24. Martin, A.	16	46. Orsulak, J.	5
3. Nixon, O.	47	25. Whiten, M.	15	47. Webster, M.	4
4. Lewis, D.	46	26. Gilkey, B.	15	48. Snyder, C.	4
5. Young, E.	42	27. Gwynn, T.	14	49. Plantier, P.	4
6. Butler, B.	39	28. Bichette, D.	14	50. Whitmore, D.	4
7. Coleman, V.	38	29. Lankford, R.	14	51. Mondesi, R.	4
8. Dykstra, L.	37	30. Van Slyke, A.	11	52. Bonilla, B.	3
9. Sosa, S.	36	31. McGee, W.	10	53. Anthony, E.	3
10. Cole, A.	30	32. Howard, T.	10	54. Justice, D.	3
11. Bonds, B.	29	33. May, D.	10	55. Merced, O.	3
12. Walker, L.	29	34. Thompson, M.	9	56. Brown, J.	3
13. Sanders, R.	27	35. Clark, J.	9	57. Burnitz, J.	3
14. Gant, R.	26	36. Jones, C.	9	58. Tubbs, G.	3
15. Bell, D.	26	37. Hill, G.	8	59. Bean, B.	2
16. Kelly, R.	21	38. Smith, D.	8	60. Felix, J.	2
17. Gonzalez, L.	20	39. Wilson, W.	7	61. Chamberlain, W.	2
18. Brumfield, J.	20	40. Bass, K.	7	62. Conine, J.	2
19. Finley, S.	19	41. Martinez, D.	6	63. Clark, P.	2
20. Sanders, D.	19	42. Briley, G.	6	64. Thompson, R.	2
21. Alou, M.	17	43. VanderWal, J.	6	65. Sherman, D.	2
22. Frazier, L.	17	44. Jordan, B.	6		

RUNS SCORED

1. Dykstra, L.	143	21. Bell, D.	73	41. Howard, T.	48
2. Bonds, B.	129	22. Gwynn, T.	70	42. Boston, D.	46
3. Gant, R.	113	23. Anthony, E.	70	43. Kelly, R.	44
4. Grissom, M.	104	24. Alou, M.	70	44. Clark, D.	43
5. Gilkey, B.	99	25. Finley, S.	69	45. Van Slyke, A.	42
6. Bichette, D.	93	26. Merced, O.	68	46. Thompson, M.	42
7. Sosa, S.	92	27. Plantier, P.	67	47. Sanders, D.	42
8. Justice, D.	90	28. Clark, J.	65	48. Brumfield, J.	40
9. Sanders, R.	90	29. Coleman, V.	64	49. Gallagher, D.	34
10. Walker, L.	85	30. Lankford, R.	64	50. Chamberlain, W.	34
11. Martin, A.	85	31. May, D.	62	51. VanderWal, J.	34
12. Lewis, D.	84	32. Snyder, C.	61	52. Thompson, R.	34
13. Gonzalez, L.	82	33. Incaviglia, P.	60	53. Hill, G.	33
14. Young, E.	82	34. Orsulak, J.	59	54. Jordan, B.	33
15. Bonilla, B.	81	35. Mitchell, K.	56	55. Clark, P.	33
16. Whiten, M.	81	36. McGee, W.	53	56. Bass, K.	31
17. Butler, B.	80	37. Eisenreich, J.	51	57. Wilson, W.	29
18. Nixon, O.	77	38. Smith, D.	51	58. Jones, C.	29
19. Carr, C.	75	39. Cole, A.	50	59. Martinez, D.	28
20. Conine, J.	75	40. Burnitz, J.	49	60. Frazier, L.	27

PLAY BALL—AGAINST THE FOUNDING FATHERS
(See page 280)

AL OUTFIELDERS
(20 Games or More)
HOME RUNS

Catchers
pp. 59–73

Corners
pp. 73–95

Infield
pp. 95–116

Outfield
pp. 117–150

DH
pp. 150–153

Starters
pp. 154–189

Relievers
pp. 190–217

1. Gonzalez, J.	46	22. Devereaux, M.	14	43. Phillips, T.	7
2. Griffey Jr, K.	45	23. Leyritz, J.	14	44. James, D.	7
3. Belle, A.	38	24. Dawson, A.	13	45. Surhoff, B.	7
4. Carter, J.	33	25. Gibson, K.	13	46. Velarde, R.	7
5. Tettleton, M.	32	26. Gladden, D.	13	47. Brunansky, T.	6
6. Tartabull, D.	31	27. Greenwell, M.	13	48. Redus, G.	6
7. Salmon, T.	31	28. Anderson, B.	13	49. Jose, F.	6
8. Vaughn, G.	30	29. Reimer, K.	13	50. Brosius, S.	6
9. Buhner, J.	27	30. Munoz, P.	13	51. Kirby, W.	6
10. Puckett, K.	22	31. McRae, B.	12	52. Curtis, C.	6
11. Sierra, R.	22	32. Williams, B.	12	53. Voigt, J.	6
12. Winfield, D.	21	33. McReynolds, K.	11	54. Pasqua, D.	5
13. Henderson, R.	21	34. Canseco, J.	10	55. Coles, D.	4
14. Deer, R.	21	35. Aldrete, M.	10	56. McLemore, M.	4
15. Henderson, D.	20	36. Mack, S.	10	57. Ward, T.	4
16. Davis, E.	20	37. Hatcher, B.	9	58. Davis, B.	3
17. O'Neill, P.	20	38. James, C.	9	59. Javier, S.	3
18. Burks, E.	17	39. Hamilton, D.	9	60. Litton, G.	3
19. Raines, T.	16	40. Yount, R.	8	61. Mieske, M.	3
20. Jackson, B.	16	41. Smith, L.	8	62. Hammonds, J.	3
21. White, D.	15	42. Maldonado, C.	8		

BATTING AVERAGE

1. James, D.	.333	21. Belle, A.	.290	41. Kirby, W.	.269
2. Lofton, K.	.325	22. Henderson, R.	.289	42. Peltier, D.	.269
3. Diaz, A.	.319	23. Redus, G.	.288	43. Williams, B.	.268
4. Greenwell, M.	.315	24. Hatcher, B.	.288	44. Gladden, D.	.267
5. Phillips, T.	.313	25. Brooks, H.	.286	45. Vaughn, G.	.267
6. O'Neill, P.	.311	26. Curtis, C.	.285	46. Aldrete, M.	.267
7. Johnson, L.	.311	27. McLemore, M.	.284	47. Larkin, G.	.264
8. Hamilton, D.	.310	28. Salmon, T.	.284	48. Anderson,B.	.263
9. Gonzalez, J.	.310	29. Ducey, R.	.282	49. Gibson, K.	.261
10. Griffey Jr, K.	.309	30. McRae, B.	.282	50. Pulliam, H.	.258
11. Leyritz, J.	.309	31. Smith, L.	.278	51. Yount, R.	.258
12. Raines, T.	.306	32. Mack, S.	.276	52. Canseco, J.	.255
13. Hammonds, J.	.305	33. James, C.	.275	53. Carter, J.	.254
14. Velarde, R.	.301	34. Burks, E.	.274	54. Coles, D.	.252
15. Gwynn, C.	.300	35. Dawson, A.	.273	55. Jose, F.	.252
16. Litton, G.	.299	36. Surhoff, B.	.273	56. Devereaux, M.	.250
17. Puckett, K.	.296	37. White, D.	.272	57. Browne, J.	.250
18. Voigt, J.	.296	38. Buhner, J.	.272	58. Turang, B.	.250
19. Javier, S.	.291	39. Polonia, L.	.271	59. Tartabull, D.	.250
20. Hulse, D.	.290	40. Winfield, D.	.271	60. Reimer, K.	.250

SEE APPENDIX, PAGES 319–341,
FOR FINAL 1993 AVERAGES

RUNS BATTED IN

1. Belle, A.	129	22. Dawson, A.	67	43. Jose, F.	43
2. Carter, J.	121	23. Anderson, B.	66	44. McReynolds, K.	42
3. Gonzalez, J.	118	24. Gibson, K.	62	45. Lofton, K.	42
4. Tettleton, M.	110	25. Mack, S.	61	46. Munoz, P.	38
5. Griffey Jr, K.	109	26. Reimer, K.	60	47. James, D.	36
6. Tartabull, D.	102	27. Kirby, W.	60	48. Maldonado, C.	35
7. Sierra, R.	101	28. Henderson, R.	59	49. Aldrete, M.	33
8. Buhner, J.	98	29. Curtis, C.	59	50. Polonia, L.	32
9. Vaughn, G.	97	30. Phillips, T.	57	51. Redus, G.	31
10. Salmon, T.	95	31. Hatcher, B.	57	52. Brunansky, T.	29
11. Puckett, K.	89	32. Gladden, D.	56	53. Hulse, D.	29
12. Surhoff, B.	79	33. Deer, R.	55	54. Javier, S.	28
13. Winfield, D.	76	34. Raines, T.	54	55. Ward, T.	28
14. O'Neill, P.	75	35. Henderson, D.	53	56. Smith, L.	27
15. Devereaux, M.	75	36. Leyritz, J.	53	57. Coles, D.	26
16. Burks, E.	74	37. White, D.	52	58. James, C.	26
17. Greenwell, M.	72	38. Yount, R.	51	59. Zupcic, B.	26
18. McLemore, M.	72	39. Hamilton, D.	48	60. Gwynn, C.	25
19. McRae, B.	69	40. Johnson, L.	47	61. Litton, G.	25
20. Davis, E.	68	41. Canseco, J.	46	62. Brosius, S.	25
21. Williams, B.	68	42. Jackson, B.	45		

STOLEN BASES

1. Lofton, K.	70	25. Cuyler, M.	13	49. Browne, J.	4
2. Polonia, L.	55	26. Javier, S.	12	50. Gonzalez, J.	4
3. Henderson, R.	53	27. Surhoff, B.	12	51. Hammonds, J.	4
4. Curtis, C.	48	28. Vaughn, G.	10	52. Brunansky, T.	3
5. Davis, E.	35	29. Yount, R.	9	53. Davis, B.	3
6. Johnson, L.	35	30. Smith, L.	9	54. Tettleton, M.	3
7. White, D.	34	31. Williams, B.	9	55. Devereaux, M.	3
8. Jose, F.	31	32. Carter, J.	8	56. Ward, T.	3
9. Hulse, D.	29	33. Gladden, D.	8	57. Winfield, D.	2
10. Sierra, R.	25	34. Puckett, K.	8	58. Dawson, A.	2
11. Anderson, B.	24	35. Sax, S.	7	59. McReynolds, K.	2
12. Belle, A.	23	36. Thurman, G.	7	60. O'Neill, P.	2
13. McRae, B.	23	37. Canseco, J.	6	61. Pasqua, D.	2
14. Raines, T.	21	38. Burks, E.	6	62. James, C.	2
15. McLemore, M.	21	39. Brosius, S.	6	63. Buhner, J.	2
16. Hamilton, D.	21	40. Turang, B.	6	64. Ducey, R.	2
17. Griffey Jr, K.	17	41. Deer, R.	5	65. Velarde, R.	2
18. Kirby, W.	17	42. Greenwell, M.	5	66. Dascenzo, D.	2
19. Phillips, T.	16	43. Reimer, K.	5	67. Humphreys, M.	2
20. Gibson, K.	15	44. Zupcic, B.	5	68. Williams, G.	2
21. Felder, M.	15	45. Diaz, A.	5	69. Buford, D.	2
22. Mack, S.	15	46. Salmon, T.	5	70. McCarty, D.	2
23. Hatcher, B.	14	47. Redus, G.	4	71. Lydy, S.	2
24. Blankenship, L.	13	48. Calderon, I.	4		

RUNS SCORED

1. White, D.	116	21. Raines, T.	75	41. Reimer, K.	53	**Catchers** pp. 59–73
2. Lofton, K.	116	22. Burks, E.	75	42. Gladden, D.	52	
3. Henderson, R.	114	23. Johnson, L.	75	43. Cuyler, M.	46	**Corners** pp. 73–95
4. Phillips, T.	113	24. Polonia, L.	75	44. Dawson, A.	44	
5. Griffey Jr, K.	113	25. Hamilton, D.	74	45. McReynolds, K.	44	**Infield** pp. 95–116
6. Gonzalez, J.	105	26. Winfield, D.	72	46. Smith, L.	43	
7. Vaughn, G.	97	27. Devereaux, M.	72	47. Blankenship, L.	43	
8. Curtis, C.	94	28. Davis, E.	71	48. Leyritz, J.	43	**Outfield** pp. 117–150
9. Belle, A.	93	29. Hatcher, B.	71	49. Aldrete, M.	40	
10. Salmon, T.	93	30. O'Neill, P.	71	50. Zupcic, B.	40	**DH** pp. 150–153
11. Carter, J.	92	31. Kirby, W.	71	51. Henderson, D.	37	
12. Buhner, J.	91	32. Hulse, D.	71	52. Gwynn, C.	36	**Starters** pp. 154–189
13. Puckett, K.	89	33. Williams, B.	67	53. McCarty, D.	36	
14. Tartabull, D.	87	34. Deer, R.	66	54. Munoz, P.	34	
15. Anderson, B.	87	35. Mack, S.	66	55. Javier, S.	33	**Relievers** pp. 190–217
16. McLemore, M.	81	36. Surhoff, B.	66	56. Jackson, B.	32	
17. Tettleton, M.	79	37. Jose, F.	64	57. Voigt, J.	32	
18. McRae, B.	78	38. Yount, R.	62	58. Felder, M.	31	
19. Greenwell, M.	77	39. Gibson, K.	62	59. Quintana, C.	31	
20. Sierra, R.	77	40. James, D.	62	60. Canseco, J.	30	

AL DESIGNATED HITTERS
(20 Games or More)

HOME RUNS

1. Tartabull, D.	31	8. Winfield, D.	21	15. Leyritz, J.	14
2. Fielder, C.	30	9. Baines, H.	20	16. Dawson, A.	13
3. Vaughn, G.	30	10. Henderson, D.	20	17. Gibson, K.	13
4. Davis, C.	27	11. Brett, G.	19	18. Bell, G.	13
5. Olerud, J.	24	12. Neel, T.	19	19. Reimer, K.	13
6. Molitor, P.	22	13. Jackson, B.	16	20. Jefferson, R.	10
7. Sierra, R.	22	14. Franco, J.	14		

BATTING AVERAGE

1. Olerud, J.	.363	8. Dawson, A.	.273	15. O'Brien, P.	.257
2. Molitor, P.	.332	9. Obando, S.	.272	16. Tartabull, D.	.250
3. Baines, H.	.313	10. Winfield, D.	.271	17. Reimer, K.	.250
4. Leyritz, J.	.309	11. Fielder, C.	.267	18. Jefferson, R.	.249
5. Livingstone, S.	.293	12. Vaughn, G.	.267	19. Martinez, C.	.244
6. Neel, T.	.291	13. Brett, G.	.266	20. Davis, C.	.243
7. Franco, J.	.290	14. Gibson, K.	.261		

RUNS BATTED IN

1. Fielder, C.	117	8. Franco, J.	84	15. Gibson, K.	62
2. Davis, C.	112	9. Baines, H.	78	16. Reimer, K.	60
3. Molitor, P.	111	10. Winfield, D.	76	17. Henderson, D.	53
4. Olerud, J.	107	11. Brett, G.	75	18. Leyritz, J.	53
5. Tartabull, D.	102	12. Dawson, A.	67	19. Jackson, B.	45
6. Sierra, R.	101	13. Bell, G.	64	20. Livingstone, S.	39
7. Vaughn, G.	97	14. Neel, T.	63		

STOLEN BASES

1. Sierra, R.	25	8. Reimer, K.	5	14. Bell, G.	1
2. Molitor, P.	22	9. Davis, C.	4	15. Sasser, M.	1
3. Gibson, K.	15	10. Calderon, I.	4	16. Martinez, C.	1
4. Vaughn, G.	10	11. Neel, T.	3	17. Maas, K.	1
5. Franco, J.	9	12. Winfield, D.	2	18. Jefferson, R.	1
6. Brett, G.	7	13. Dawson, A.	2	19. Livingstone, S.	1
7. Sax, S.	7				

RUNS SCORED

1. Molitor, P.	121	8. Davis, C.	74	15. Dawson, A.	44
2. Olerud, J.	109	9. Winfield, D.	72	16. Leyritz, J.	43
3. Vaughn, G.	97	10. Brett, G.	69	17. Livingstone, S.	39
4. Tartabull, D.	87	11. Baines, H.	64	18. Henderson, D.	37
5. Franco, J.	85	12. Gibson, K.	62	19. Bell, G.	36
6. Fielder, C.	80	13. Neel, T.	59	20. Jefferson, R.	35
7. Sierra, R.	77	14. Reimer, K.	53		

STATS INK

All the stats in the Scouting Report (Chapter 3) plus all the stats in the Rotisserie Stat-Pak (Chapter 4) that you've just finished memorizing come from STATS, Inc., a band of merry number noodlers whose client list reads like a Who's Who of baseball publications: *Sports Illustrated, The Sporting News,* ESPN, *USA Today,* and, yours truly, *Rotisserie League Baseball.*

STATS, Inc. also publishes several books that belong in every Rotisserie owner's library. Among them:

- *Major League Handbook.* The first baseball annual to hit the bookstores every year (November 1), with player stats for the year just ended plus projections by Bill James for the year coming up.
- *Minor League Handbook.* An essential tool for building your farm system. Year-by-year data for AAA and AA players, plus Bill James's "Major League Equivalencies."
- *Player Profiles.* Detailed situational analyses, including month-by-month performance breakdowns.
- *Matchups!* A compendium of batter vs. pitcher matchups that gives you the lowdown on the game within the game.
- *The Scouting Report.* A mix of stats and analysis, this hardy annual includes "Stars, Bums, and Sleepers," a look at who's on the way up and who's on the way down.

And that's only for starters! For a complete catalog of STATS, Inc. publications and fantasy games (including something called "football"), call the STATS inksters at 800-63-STATS.

5

Down on the Farm

How Ya Gonna Keep 'Em
Down on the Farm?

The 1994 Minor League Report
by John Benson

Editor's Note: *John Benson needs no introduction to veteran players of Rotisserie baseball, but he insisted we give him one anyhow. For the last three years John has appeared in this spot in the batting order with a report on the current crop of farm system prospects, suspects, phenoms, and sleepers. But that's only the beginning. He is the founder, general manager, and clubhouse attendant of Diamond Library, a Rotisserie think-tank that must never be allowed to fall into enemy hands. Among Diamond Library's list of publications are* Rotisserie Baseball Annual *($22.95),* The Benson A to Z Baseball Player Guide *($15.95), and* Benson Baseball Monthly *($59/year), a monthly newsletter worth its weight in Red Man. For information on how to order and a ferociously hard sell, call John at 800-707-9090.*

Time for a little self-evaluation, the Founding Fathers said. You've been plowing this field for three years now. Time to take a long, hard look at the crops you've brought in during your stint as Secretary of (Rotisserie) Agriculture. Let's have a gander at your P/L sheet. Our readers need to know how good the farm-to-market predictions in this space have been.

Okay. No sweat. It's the nineties: reflection and introspection are good. I can deal with it, I tell myself. So why am I suddenly recalling John Dean's assignment to write a report telling what a good job the White House was doing with their internal investigation? Funny how things pop into your mind for no apparent reason. Anyway, let's proceed.

Every good forecaster looks at the future through the prism of the past. You have to know what succeeded (and failed) in the past to have a clue about what might work in the future. At the end of the day, you're evaluated not by how artfully you weave a fantasy but by how many of your dreams come true. Fortunately, we now have enough of a track record in Rotisserie husbandry to draw some instructive conclusions, the first of which is that we are doing a pretty doggone good job. No kidding.

(The "we" here comes not from any royal pretentions but from the fact that I confer with a lot of people—scouts, general managers, minor league managers, even the Founding Fathers sometimes—before reaching my conclusions. Also, if you think there is a whole gang of us to blame when a can't-miss rookie rave turns sour, maybe you won't come looking for me.)

Two questions measure performance in this farm-crop estimating business . . .

Of the good young players who reach the major leagues, how many of them are previously identified here? Answer: virtually all. The one or two exceptions are noted below, with appropriate explanations, excuses, and assignments of blame elsewhere.

How many of the players described in this report actually go on to become real major league players? Answer: the vast majority. Better than 80% of the players we've highlighted in these pages the past three years went on to play in the majors the same season they appeared here—and we haven't given up on the rest. Even among those identified as longshots or down-the-road candidates, fully two-thirds made it to the bigs the same year we recommended them.

Figuring out which minor leaguers are going to come up is only half the battle, of course. With hindsight, and viewing the Farm Report within the larger context of what happened in the major leagues and in Rotisserie baseball each year, there are some fundamental lessons to be learned about selecting freshly harvested farm products for one's Rotisserie franchise:

1. *As a general rule, do not pursue rookies.* The best ones will always be overpriced. *Always.* How much would Clint Hartung have gone for if Rotisserie baseball had been around in 1947? Does anyone know what David Green is doing these days? Is Paul Householder in the Hall of Fame yet? (The Getherswag Goners must have thought he was on his way there when they paid $33 for him way back in the profligate eighties.) Sooner or later, and usually sooner, most rookies will rip your heart out and stomp on it.

   That happens over and over again for the simple reason that draft day prices for rookies are driven by potential, not proven performance. We all know this truism to be true—in our heads, if rarely in our hearts. Every rookie who looks like he might be worth $15 will sell for $15, sometimes for $20. (Remember J. T. Snow and Kevin Young?) Rookie mania during the auction often makes it look like the object of the game is to buy all the best rookies, not to build the best team. Don't forget your real objective.

2. *In particular, avoid Dodger rookies.* Every year it seems we—I—get sucked in by the L.A. publicity blitz for the likes of Dave Hansen, Henry Rodriguez, Tom Goodwin, Carlos Hernandez, and José Muñoz. Sure, we've been right occasionally—Eric Karros and Mike Piazza have done great, José Offerman and Eric Young have done okay, and Raul

Mondesi and Billy Ashley have done nothing to diminish our hopes—but overall, we've ballyhooed far too many Dodger farmhands in these pages. Part of the problem is that Los Angeles has such a strong organization: the Dodgers grow more talent than they can fit into a major league lineup studded with overpriced veterans. Another factor is that the Dodgers have such a fine minor league newsletter for us writers: obviously, I am far too aware of their players.

3. **Only pursue rookies after they're no longer rookies.** Just as hype inflates prices when a player first comes up, disappointment depresses the market when a player fails to live up to unrealistic expectations. When that $15 talent produces only $8 of value as a rookie, he may sell for only $9 in his second year . . . and then proceed to put up $15 worth of stats. How much will Kevin Young cost in your draft this year? He'll probably be a bargain.

Our Farm Report has been especially accurate when looking two to three years into the future. While many of our three-star (* * *) players were unsurprising or overpriced the year we recommended them, there has been a quiet but highly favorable trend for most of our one-star (*) players to develop into good major leaguers—not the year we identified them, but a year or two later.

For example, the one-star specials in 1991 included Rick Wilkins, Jeff Conine, Luís Gonzalez, Eric Karros, Orlando Merced, Pat Kelly, Chuck Knoblauch, Scott Cooper, Ed Sprague, Ándujar Cedeño, Moises Alou, Derek Bell, Derrick May, Bernie Williams, Pat Hentgen, and Charles Nagy. You would have the nucleus of a pretty good ball club with that crew.

In 1992 we gave one star to Dave Nilsson, John Jaha, Bret Boone, Eric Young, Gary DiSarcina, Royce Clayton, Carlos García, Rey Sanchez, Jeromy Burnitz, Tim Salmon, Pedro Martinez, Donovan Osborne, and Armando Reynoso. Not quite as deep, but not shabby.

Consequently, instead of using these pages to fire up your backyard grill after auction draft day this year, perhaps you should hang on to this book and consult the 1994 Farm Report again in 1995 or 1996. If you were thinking about pulling out your 1993 edition to look again now, don't bother: we already did it in preparing this year's report.

One of the one-star players from last year (Brent Gates) has already made it to the majors and appears headed for a fine career. Another (Gerald Williams) looks to be permanently cast as a marginal utility player. All of the others worth knowing are listed again below, in this year's report—most of them, of course, having moved up to * * or * * * levels.

Aside from the general lessons we have learned, there are some specific players deserving mention in these chronicles of the Farm Bureau:

Told You So . . .

Juan Gonzalez and Ray Lankford got our highest (* * *) rating in 1992 and proceeded to have huge seasons. Last year we singled out Mike Piazza and Tim Salmon for stardom. Other top touts: Kenny Lofton, Derek Bell, Tino Martinez, and Reggie Sanders. Big deal, right? Everybody does a good job of tabbing the easy ones. But go back to any rookie preview from last year, and see if you can find Brent Gates, Ricky Gutierrez, Mike Lansing, and Derrick White. They were all here.

Did We Really Say That? . . .

But there were others here as well, and truth-in-advertising statutes require us to come clean about some of them.

Nominations for our all-time-worst recommendation would certainly include Mike Miller, a Mets farmhand who was on our 1991 list of best prospects for 1993. Well, 1993 has come and gone, and we're trying to forget him; organized baseball already has. Of course, we have an excuse for that pick: he is (or was?) a member of that most unpredictable species, *Homo pitcheralius*.

Other candidates for worst-ever: In 1992, we gave three stars—count 'em, * * *—to Lee Stevens, who was last seen fighting off the mosquitoes in left field at MacArthur Stadium in Syracuse. And we wish we could eat the words we used praising Johnny Guzman, Steve Adkins, and Chris George. The George case in particular taught us that getting invited to the major leagues' annual orientation seminar (only two players per team earn this privilege) doesn't matter half as much as getting command of your breaking pitches.

(By the way, don't feel bad if you haven't heard of all—or any—of the names cited above. They haven't exactly become household names, not even in their own households.)

Finally, we guessed wrong about the impact of expansion on younger players in 1993. We had far too many rookies projected to be regular players last year. This was not a result of foolish guesswork, but of overthinking. We had scrutinized the player population before and after the last major league expansion, back in 1977, and found that most of the beneficiaries in that era were rising stars, age 22–24, who got promoted a year or two early. Examples: Ruppert Jones, Jim Clancy, Steve Kemp. While there were a few such cases in 1993, the category of players who benefited most from the latest expansion included Mike Aldrete, Darnell Coles, Kirk Gibson, and Fernando Valenzuela.

In 16 years, America has learned how to recycle.

Not to Mention . . .

For some reason, Jeff Bagwell did not appear in our 1991 report. We knew about Bagwell, liked him a lot, and didn't deliberately exclude him. Could it have been a typesetting glitch? Sunspots affecting the old computer modem, maybe? Lou Gorman trying to blot out any record of what he had done?

One 1992 omission, for which your chastened farm reporter accepts full responsibility, was Pat Listach. We had a lengthy *mea culpa* on that one last year, so I'll just repeat the basic lesson learned: when a hitter has a low batting average and no power, check further to see if he has stolen 152 bases in three years. If he has, include him anyway.

Speaking of lessons learned, here are some topics we have emphasized for 1994 in our effort to make this year's picks the best ever:

1. **Speed Thrills.** Call it the Listach Response, but rest assured that the running game has been given utmost attention in the selection of this year's recommendations.

---

2. **Pitchers Can Be Hazardous to Your Health.** Even though we remain convinced that the best way to torpedo your team is by drafting rookie pitchers, we have devoted more time, energy, and space than ever to the black art. Try as we might to isolate the most important indicators of pitching promise (and we do have a few new tricks), we always find that pitchers tend to come up with sore arms at the most inopportune times. You may recognize the names Alan Embree, David Nied, and Roger Salkeld, who made our list of hot 1993 prospects but figured even more prominently last year on the disabled list. Even so, we're still in there pitching.

3. **Not So Great Expectations.** Countering last year's burst of enthusiasm about the number of rookies likely to make instant splashes, we have cut back on the number of three-star recommendations this year. The impact of expansion has dissipated—and wasn't what we expected it to be in the first place.

4. **Seeing Is Believing.** Everyone reads about minor league phenoms. We like to watch them, clock them, talk to them, and ask their opponents and coaches what they think about them. The growing resources of the Diamond Analytics scouting department, including especially Larry Bump and Bill Gray, are behind this report. There is no substitute for actually seeing players perform, and we've done that—from coast to coast, from A-ball to AAA, and from spring training to the September callups.

1994 Farm System Prospects

Here they are, the Class of 1994. Some will make it to the majors this year. Some will be pushed up before they're ready and have to be sent back down. Others won't hit the bigs for a couple of seasons. And a few won't ever make it at all. Your job now is to decide Who's on First—and I Don't Know is not a good enough answer. Each player's age is as of Opening Day, 1994. Profiles do not include 1993 major league stats (if any), which appear on pages 319–341.

RATING GUIDE

* * * Ready to be a productive regular now.
* * Fine talent, should make it to the majors in 1994.
* Good idea for 1995–1996.

CATCHERS

CARLOS DELGADO   BLUE JAYS   Age 21/L   * *

Not just a powerful bat, but a powerful *left-handed* bat. The only thing holding him back is defense, and he's learning.

Team	Level		AB	HR	RBI	SB	BA
Knoxville	AA		468	25	102	10	.303

BROOK FORDYCE   METS   Age 23/R   *

Has already pushed aside former number one draft pick Alan Zinter. Will he pass number two pick Todd Hundley too? We like his chances.

Team	Level		AB	HR	RBI	SB	BA
Norfolk	AAA		409	2	40	2	.259

TYLER HOUSTON   BRAVES   Age 23/L   *

Drafted before Frank Thomas is 1989, Houston has taken longer to mature, but he came a long way in 1993. Unfortunately, Javy Lopez is just two months older than Houston.

Team	Level		AB	HR	RBI	SB	BA
Greenville	AA		262	5	33	5	.279
Richmond	AAA		13	1	3	0	.139

MIKE LIEBERTHAL   PHILLIES   Age 22/R   *

Another first-round draft pick (1990). Didn't hit nearly as well in AAA as he did in AA the year before, but he's still young. Darren Daulton is only 32 and shows no signs of slowing down, but the guy has had *seven* knee operations, so Lieberthal's chance could come sooner than expected.

Team	Level		AB	HR	RBI	SB	BA
Scranton	AAA		382	7	40	2	.262

JAVIER LOPEZ   BRAVES   Age 23/R   * * *

For two years, Atlanta management has been content to let Lopez develop at a measured pace and build his reputation as the best minor league catching prospect since protective cups were invented. Except, that is, when Greg Olson has temporarily lost the use of an arm or leg. In 1994 and for years to come, people will be asking: "What took them so long?"

Team	Level		AB	HR	RBI	SB	BA
Richmond	AAA		380	17	74	1	.305

FIRST BASEMEN

MARCOS ARMAS   ATHLETICS   Age 24/R   * *

Did almost exactly the same at AAA as he had at AA the year before. Actually, he did somewhat better, cutting down his strikeouts. (Yes, this is Tony Armas's kid brother.)

Team	Level		AB	HR	RBI	SB	BA
Tacoma	AAA		434	15	89	4	.290

RICH AUDE   PIRATES   Age 22/R   * *

Was having a monster season in AA when he moved up to fill a vacancy at AAA Buffalo. But then Russ Morman, who was making a run at the American Association batting title, returned and pushed Aude back down to Carolina. If Kevin Young picks up where he left off last year, Aude could get the call.

Team	Level	AB	HR	RBI	SB	BA
Carolina	AA	422	18	73	8	.289
Buffalo	AAA	64	4	16	0	.375

D. J. BOSTON   BLUE JAYS   Age 22/L   *

Daryl's younger and taller (6'7" vs. 6'3") brother. The stolen base totals will drop at the major league level, but the power should develop further with maturity. Needs some work on defense. A good long-range investment.

Team	Level	AB	HR	RBI	SB	BA
Hagerstown	A	464	13	92	31	.315

TIM COSTO   REDS   Age 25/R   * *

Not getting any younger, and still looking for a position. Cincinnati had him in its makeshift outfield late in 1993 just long enough to prove that outfield is not the right position for him. Hits enough to hang on somewhere, likely as a cheaper replacement for a veteran utility player whose salary has made him expendable. Don't get your hopes up, though.

Team	Level	AB	HR	RBI	SB	BA
Indianapolis	AAA	362	11	57	3	.326

STEVE DUNN   TWINS   Age 23/L   *

Kent Hrbek and David McCarty are in the way now, but in another year or two, the Twins will have an interesting decision to make. If you play Ultra, take him in a late round at $2 and check back in a year.

Team	Level	AB	HR	RBI	SB	BA
Nashville	AA	366	14	60	1	.262

TROY FRYMAN   WHITE SOX   Age 22/L   *

Travis's younger and taller (6'3" vs. 6'1") brother. The second time around in Fighting Irish country (he batted .174 at South Bend in 1992) turned out a little better. Good bloodlines.

Team	Level	AB	HR	RBI	SB	BA
South Bend	A	173	7	41	2	.318
Sarasota	A	285	5	46	0	.239

RYAN KLESKO   BRAVES   Age 22/L   * *

No sooner had the Braves acquired Fred McGriff than there was talk about trading Crime Dog to make room for Klesko. Uh-uh. Then there was talk about moving Klesko to left field if Ron Gant walked away. Uh-uh. (Picture Kent Hrbek in left field, if you want an idea of what Klesko looked like out there.) Then there was talk about trading him to an American League team where he could DH and play a little first base. Hmm. . . .

Team	Level	AB	HR	RBI	SB	BA
Richmond	AAA	343	22	74	4	.274

MARC NEWFIELD **MARINERS** Age 21/R ★ ★

Another first baseman for whom outfielding has been an adventure. The key number here is the age. Dave Winfield and Eddie Murray didn't start in the majors until they were 21. Newfield made it at 20. They'll find a place for him somewhere.

Team	Level	AB	HR	RBI	SB	BA
Jacksonville	AA	336	19	51	1	.307

ROBERTO PETAGINE **ASTROS** Age 22/L ★ ★

Excellent patience at the plate belies that "can't-walk-off-the-island" stereotype of Latin players. Besides, Venezuela isn't an island. Just starting to develop as a power hitter. One problem: so is Jeff Bagwell.

Team	Level	AB	HR	RBI	SB	BA
Jackson	AA	437	15	90	6	.334

GREG PIRKL **MARINERS** Age 23/R ★

Got a brief trial when Tino Martinez hurt his knee last summer, but got sent back down again following an 0 for 11 minislump. Will get a longer look in 1994. By the way, do you think maybe Seattle is developing a little bit of a logjam at first?

Team	Level	AB	HR	RBI	SB	BA
Calgary	AAA	445	21	94	3	.308

GENE SCHALL **PHILLIES** Age 23/R ★

If his career continues to progress as it did in 1993, it won't be long before he'll be signing autographs at one of those big card shows in his hometown of Willow Grove, Pennsylvania.

Team	Level	AB	HR	RBI	SB	BA
Reading	AA	285	15	60	2	.326
Scranton	AAA	139	4	16	4	.237

JOE VITIELLO **ROYALS** Age 23/R ★

A number one pick in 1991, the Royals started him immediately (and somewhat prematurely) at AA Memphis. He needed a year in A-ball to get on track. Did much better in his second try at Memphis.

Team	Level	AB	HR	RBI	SB	BA
Memphis	AA	413	15	66	2	.288

DERRICK WHITE **EXPOS** Age 24/R ★ ★

Took less than two years to go from short-season Jamestown all the way to Montreal. The Expos didn't keep him long, mumbling something about the need to play defense, but he will be back.

Team	Level	AB	HR	RBI	SB	BA
Harrisburg	AA	79	2	12	2	.228
Ottawa	AAA	249	4	29	10	.281

SECOND BASEMEN

RAMON CARABALLO **BRAVES** Age 24/B * *

Classic example of steady progress up the minor league ladder, and he's doing it on the best ladder in baseball. Mark Lemke is a local hero in Atlanta, but Caraballo can flat out play.

Team	Level	AB	HR	RBI	SB	BA
Richmond	AAA	470	3	41	20	.272

DARREL DEAK **CARDINALS** Age 24/B * *

What are the Cardinals doing with a power-hitting middle infielder? He strikes out too much to fit into the St. Louis lineup. Maybe they'll trade him.

Team	Level	AB	HR	RBI	SB	BA
Arkansas	AA	414	19	73	4	.242

TONY GRAFFAGNINO **BRAVES** Age 21/R *

Don't worry about how to pronounce it, not just yet. He will have to pass another Braves 2B prospect, Ramon Caraballo, on the way up.

Team	Level	AB	HR	RBI	SB	BA
Durham	A	459	15	69	24	.275

JIM MOUTON **ASTROS** Age 25/R * *

Jumped cross-country from the Florida State League (A) to the Pacific Coast League (AAA) with improvement in all hitting categories. Ballpark effect had something to do with that, but good speed and good batting eye had more. Shaky glovework could hold him back.

Team	Level	AB	HR	RBI	SB	BA
Tucson	AAA	546	16	92	40	.315

RUBEN SANTANA **MARINERS** Age 24/R * *

From out of nowhere—or from out of Peninsula—this guy became a horse. For now he's stuck behind Bret Boone, so look for his name to pop up in trade talks.

Team	Level	AB	HR	RBI	SB	BA
Jacksonville	AA	499	21	84	13	.301

QUILVIO VERAS **METS** Age 22/B * *

We can take last year's comment and bring it up to date: In four seasons as a pro, Veras has batted over .300 four times and has stolen 183 bases. And you know how we love speed. He has fielding range reminiscent of José Lind.

Team	Level	AB	HR	RBI	SB	BA
Binghamton	AA	444	2	51	52	.306

THIRD BASEMEN

MIKE BUSCH   **DODGERS**   Age 25/R   * *

What? A Dodgers farmhand? Hey, we didn't say we were going to eliminate them completely. This one has three things going for him: large size (6'5", 243 lbs.), greatly improved strike-zone judgment, and the big hole around third base in Dodger Stadium. Is that directly over the San Andreas Fault? Has anybody checked lately?

Team	Level		AB	HR	RBI	SB	BA
Albuquerque	AAA		431	22	70	1	.283

RUSSELL DAVIS   **YANKEES**   Age 24/R   * *

For several years, the Yankees have been reciting this litany: "We won't trade Russell Davis. Russell Davis is our third baseman of the future." Sort of makes you wonder why the Yanks gave Wade Boggs that multiyear contract, doesn't it?

Team	Level		AB	HR	RBI	SB	BA
Columbus	AAA		424	26	83	1	.255

WILLIE GREENE   **REDS**   Age 22/L   * * *

After a slow start, Greene became one of the hottest hitters in the American Association last summer. His six-week tear ended when the Reds called him in August, and his season ended when he promptly dislocated his left thumb. Greene played shortstop in place of the injured Barry Larkin, but his future lies in left field in place of the injured Kevin Mitchell. You say Mitchell isn't injured? We say: just wait. If Mitchell isn't hurt, he'll be traded anyway.

Team	Level		AB	HR	RBI	SB	BA
Indianapolis	AAA		341	22	58	2	.267

BUTCH HUSKEY   **METS**   Age 22/R   * *

Didn't show much when he came up for a cup of coffee at the end of last season, but that shouldn't deter you. If he can improve his glovework just a little, the Mets will have the big-impact third baseman they want to replace the late, lamented Howard Johnson. Great power hitter, good speed, and early signs of the sort of leadership qualities so sorely missing in Shea Stadium these past several years.

Team	Level		AB	HR	RBI	SB	BA
Binghamton	AA		526	25	98	11	.251

1994 ROOKIE ALL-STAR TEAM—AMERICAN LEAGUE

C Carlos Delgado (Blue Jays)
1B Marc Newfield (Mariners)
2B Ruben Santana (Mariners)
3B Jim Thome (Indians)
SS Denny Hocking (Twins)

OF Rich Becker (Twins)
OF Jeffrey Hammonds (Orioles)
OF Manny Ramirez (Indians)
P Roger Salkeld (Mariners)
P Chad Ogea (Indians)

PHIL NEVIN   **ASTROS**   **Age 23/R**   ∗ ∗ ∗

The number one pick in the 1992 draft, he sat out until the spring of 1993. His first pro season had some rough spots, but very few players have gone from college to AAA and done as well as Nevin did. The real goods.

Team	Level	AB	HR	RBI	SB	BA
Tucson	AAA	448	10	93	8	.286

JOSE OLIVA   **BRAVES**   **Age 23/R**   ∗ ∗

The Braves like to have a credible major league backup for every position in their farm system at all times. Missing a prospect at third before last season, they stole this guy from the Rangers for Pat Gomez. Befitting a player from San Pedro de Macorís, Oliva can pick it. His quick hands also proved useful on offense last season. But where will he play?

Team	Level	AB	HR	RBI	SB	BA
Richmond	AAA	412	21	65	1	.235

LUIS ORTIZ   **RED SOX**   **Age 23/R**   ∗ ∗ ∗

Made the jump from A to AAA last year look about as tough as stepping over a crack in the sidewalk. He didn't break his mother's back, but broke the backs of some aspiring pitchers' careers. Scott Cooper is much better with the glove, so Ortíz may have to find a new position. No problem: Boston always has room for another DH.

Team	Level	AB	HR	RBI	SB	BA
Pawtucket	AAA	402	18	81	1	.294

JIM THOME   **INDIANS**   **Age 23/L**   ∗ ∗ ∗

The old Indians never would have let this guy languish long enough to lead the International League in batting average and RBI. Come to think of it, the Indians didn't leave him down in 1992. Now AL pitchers will be suffering from (dare we say it?) Thomaine.

Team	Level	AB	HR	RBI	SB	BA
Charlotte	AAA	410	25	102	1	.332

SHORTSTOPS

MANNY ALEXANDER   **ORIOLES**   **Age 23/R**   ∗ ∗

Even among the population of infielders from San Pedro de Macorís, Alexander has exceptional range. But there's this holdover named Ripken who prevents this guy from getting our three-star rating.

Team	Level	AB	HR	RBI	SB	BA
Rochester	AAA	471	6	51	19	.244

DOMINGO CEDENO BLUE JAYS Age 25/B ★ ★

May be just a caretaker until Alex Gonzalez arrives, but Cedeño is about as good as a caretaker can be. Rifle arm. Some patience at the plate and a shorter swing would help his offense a lot.

Team	Level	AB	HR	RBI	SB	BA
Syracuse	AAA	382	2	28	15	.272

BENJI GIL RANGERS Age 21/R ★ ★

Struggled when rushed into the Rangers' lineup to help an infield decimated by injuries early last year. Gil could have beaten out Larry Hanlon for the Triple-A starting job, but Oklahoma City's team was so bad the Rangers didn't want to subject a real prospect to playing there.

Team	Level	AB	HR	RBI	SB	BA
Tulsa	AA	342	17	59	20	.275

ALEX GONZALEZ BLUE JAYS Age 20/R ★ ★

The shortstop of the future north of the border. Tony Fernandez has the job for one more year, tops. With Gonzalez's power output came more than 100 strikeouts, but he could grow out of that—or hit enough homers that no one will care.

Team	Level	AB	HR	RBI	SB	BA
Knoxville	AA	561	16	69	38	.289

DENNY HOCKING TWINS Age 23/B ★ ★

Slipped a bit from his .331 season in the California League in 1992, but he still was plenty good enough to lead Nashville into the Southern League playoffs. If there is an opening at shortstop in Minnesota this year, this guy can fill it.

Team	Level	AB	HR	RBI	SB	BA
Nashville	AA	409	8	50	15	.267

CHIPPER JONES BRAVES Age 21/B ★ ★ ★

Long regarded as the best minor league prospect in baseball. If Jeff Blauser hadn't produced such a big 1993 season, you would now be reading about Jones up front in the major league profiles, not here in the Farm Report. The early line has him sticking with the big team this spring, playing a little backup infield, then moving over to third if Pendleton continues to show signs of slowing down. Another scenario has Jones pushing Blauser over to second. Still another has the Chipster going straight to Cooperstown without bothering to play major league ball.

Team	Level	AB	HR	RBI	SB	BA
Richmond	AAA	536	13	89	23	.325

MARK LEWIS INDIANS Age 24/R ★ ★ ★

A number one draft pick whose time has come. Not so much pressure on him this time, what with the emergence of so many good young Indians players.

Team	Level	AB	HR	RBI	SB	BA
Charlotte	AAA	507	17	67	9	.284

TITO NAVARRO   METS   Age 23/R

Fair defense, good speed. Only with a team that needs so much so fast would he be getting so much attention.

Team	Level	AB	HR	RBI	SB	BA
Norfolk	AAA	273	0	16	19	.282

BRANDON WILSON   WHITE SOX   Age 25/R   * *

A shortstop who can field, hit, and run, he has also received high marks as a team leader. Unfortunately for Wilson, Ozzie Guillen's resumé reads just like that, only more so.

Team	Level	AB	HR	RBI	SB	BA
Birmingham	AA	500	2	48	43	.270

OUTFIELDERS

BILLY ASHLEY   DODGERS   Age 23/R   * *

What? Another Dodger? Sure. This one belongs. Ashley is a top hitter, and last year he reduced his K/W ratio from about 7:1 down to 4:1. The defense is still a problem, but the Dodgers never seem to care about that sort of thing.

Team	Level	AB	HR	RBI	SB	BA
Albuquerque	AAA	482	26	100	6	.297

RICH BECKER   TWINS   Age 22/B   * *

The Twins' top OF prospects (Becker, Marty Cordova, Rex Delanuez), all of whom had such great years at Visalia in 1992, cooled off considerably last season. Becker had the best year of the bunch, and is the best bet for the future. Reminds some scouts of Len Dykstra because of his stocky build and all-out playing style.

Team	Level	AB	HR	RBI	SB	BA
Nashville	AA	516	15	66	29	.287

1994 ROOKIE ALL-STAR TEAM—NATIONAL LEAGUE

C	Javier Lopez (Braves)	OF	Melvin Nieves (Padres)
1B	Tim Costo (Reds)	OF	Cliff Floyd (Expos)
2B	Ramon Caraballo (Braves)	OF	Raul Mondesi (Dodgers)
3B	Willie Greene (Reds)	P	Bobby Jones (Mets)
SS	Chipper Jones (Braves)	P	Salomon Torres (Giants)

MIDRE CUMMINGS PIRATES Age 22/B ★ ★

The prospect traded by the Twins for John Smiley. Cummings doesn't have exceptional power or speed, but he's a line-drive hitter who plays the game hard. Jim Leyland will love him.

Team	Level	AB	HR	RBI	SB	BA
Carolina	AA	237	6	26	5	.295
Buffalo	AAA	232	9	21	5	.276

CARL EVERETT MARLINS Age 23/B ★

A former Yankees number one draft pick taken in the expansion draft. He was playing outstanding defense in the California League when Florida called him up last year to fill in briefly for the injured Chuck Carr. Surprised everyone with his bat work in AAA.

Team	Level	AB	HR	RBI	SB	BA
High Desert	A	253	10	52	24	.289
Edmonton	AAA	136	6	16	12	.309

RIKKERT FANEYTE GIANTS Age 24/R ★ ★

If we were in the nickname business, we'd call him Typo. The Giants promoted this Dutchman late last year to plug the hole in their outfield dike created by the injury to Darren Lewis. Just a year removed from A-ball, Faneyte has good strike-zone judgment to go along with his power and speed. Could be the Giants' rightfielder this year.

Team	Level	AB	HR	RBI	SB	BA
Phoenix	AAA	426	11	71	15	.312

CLIFF FLOYD EXPOS Age 22/L ★ ★ ★

Although he looked like he belonged when called up last last year, the Expos felt that Floyd needs more work on his defense and may have trouble at first hitting against some lefty pitchers. When these minor kinks get worked out, start thinking Hall of Fame.

Team	Level	AB	HR	RBI	SB	BA
Harrisburg	AA	380	26	101	31	.329
Ottawa	AAA	125	2	18	2	.240

JEFFREY HAMMONDS ORIOLES Age 23/R ★ ★ ★

Made the jump from amateur to major leaguer faster than anyone since John Olerud.

Team	Level	AB	HR	RBI	SB	BA
Rochester	AAA	151	5	23	6	.311
Bowie	AA	92	3	10	4	.283

JOSE HERRERA ATHLETICS Age 21/L ★

The other prospect who came with Steve Karsay in the Rickey Henderson trade. At Hagerstown, Herrera formed a devastating 1-2 punch with D. J. Boston. Only a baby, but growing fast.

Team	Level	AB	HR	RBI	SB	BA
Hagerstown	A	388	5	42	36	.317
Madison	A	14	0	0	1	.214

STEVE HOSEY　　　　　　　　GIANTS　　　Age 24/R　　　* * *

How many years does a prospect have to pound the ball in the PCL to get a chance in the majors? We'll just keep putting him here until he gets that chance or begins receiving Social Security, whichever comes first.

Team	Level	AB	HR	RBI	SB	BA
Phoenix	AAA	455	16	85	16	.292

MIKE KELLY　　　　　　　　BRAVES　　　Age 23/R　　　* *

The top hitter drafted in 1991, Kelly was one of the untouchable prospects the Braves wouldn't trade to get Fred McGriff. When he begins making contact more consistently, Kelly will be a great power hitter.

Team	Level	AB	HR	RBI	SB	BA
Richmond	AAA	424	19	58	11	.243

JOSE MALAVE　　　　　　　RED SOX　　　Age 22/R　　　*

In 1992, his third year as a pro, Malave was struggling along in the short-season New York–Penn League when suddenly everything clicked. A broken hand cut short his 1993 season, but Malave is the best hitting prospect in the Boston organization after Luís Ortíz.

Team	Level	AB	HR	RBI	SB	BA
Lynchburg	A	312	8	54	2	.301

RAY McDAVID　　　　　　　PADRES　　　Age 22/L　　　* *

With his good strike-zone judgment and superior speed, this San Diego native will soon be playing in his hometown. Assuming, of course, that his hometown still has a major league team.

Team	Level	AB	HR	RBI	SB	BA
Wichita	AA	441	11	55	33	.270

RAUL MONDESI　　　　　　DODGERS　　　Age 23/R　　　* * *

How long has it been since the Dodgers had a homegrown player as an outfield regular? Sorry, none of us goes back that far. Mondesi will end that long drought.

Team	Level	AB	HR	RBI	SB	BA
Albuquerque	AAA	425	12	65	12	.280

VINCE MOORE　　　　　　　PADRES　　　Age 22/B　　　*

Give credit to *Baseball America* for recognizing talent. They ranked Moore the Braves' 10th-best prospect after he batted only .227 and struck out 118 times in the Sally League in 1992, and he made them look good in 1993. Moore was part of the payment for Fred McGriff. As everyone knows, the situation is sort of, ah, fluid in San Diego, so he'll get his chance there, probably next year.

Team	Level	AB	HR	RBI	SB	BA
Durham	A	319	14	64	21	.292
Rancho Cucamonga	A	128	4	19	8	.266

CHAD MOTTOLA   REDS   Age 22/R   *

The fifth player taken in the 1992 draft, but only two of the top 15 got smaller bonuses. Could it be this guy just wants to play? The folks around Winston-Salem's Ernie Shore Stadium think so.

Team	Level	AB	HR	RBI	SB	BA
Winston-Salem	A	493	21	91	13	.280

MELVIN NIEVES   PADRES   Age 22/B   * *

The senior member of the trio traded for Fred McGriff. Before that deal, the Richmond lineup was known as The Great Eight, every one of them a legitimate major league prospect. Some scouts say Nieves reminds them of Ruben Sierra. You hear stuff like that, and you think, wow! You know it's crazy, you know those scouts are just filling empty air on a lazy spring afternoon, but you can't help thinking, what if they're right? Wow!

Team	Level	AB	HR	RBI	SB	BA
Richmond	AAA	273	10	36	4	.278
Las Vegas	AAA	159	7	24	2	.308

ROBERT PEREZ   BLUE JAYS   Age 24/R   * *

While the more highly regarded Juan De la Rosa bombed at Syracuse last year, Perez bloomed.

Team	Level	AB	HR	RBI	SB	BA
Syracuse	AAA	524	12	64	13	.294

MANNY RAMIREZ   INDIANS   Age 21/R   * * *

Not a bad major league debut in his hometown, was it? Kid from New York shows up in a Cleveland uniform to play in Yankee Stadium for the first time, packs the stands with friends from the old neighborhood, and proceeds to hit two home runs and a double and drive in five runs. That's the way *we* want to break in. At the plate, he resembles Juan Gonzalez, with his front-leg kick and solid 190-pound frame. His numbers also remind us of Gonzalez. We're pretty excited.

Team	Level	AB	HR	RBI	SB	BA
Canton	AA	344	17	79	2	.340
Charlotte	AAA	145	14	36	1	.317

OMAR RAMIREZ   INDIANS   Age 23/R   * *

This "other" Ramirez is no slouch, either. As the center fielder and leadoff hitter he keyed the offense for the Tribe's solid Double-A entry.

Team	Level	AB	HR	RBI	SB	BA
Canton	AA	516	7	53	24	.314

TODD STEVERSON   BLUE JAYS   Age 22/R   *

Toronto's number one draft pick in 1992 hasn't yet put up glowing numbers, but he more than held his own in the tough Florida State League.

Team	Level	AB	HR	RBI	SB	BA
Dunedin	A	413	11	54	15	.271

OZZIE TIMMONS CUBS Age 23/R *

Pure power, but with good strike-zone judgment and enough speed and athletic ability to play center field. Could help Wrigley's bleacher bums get the bad taste of Jerome Walton out of their mouths.

Team	Level	AB	HR	RBI	SB	BA
Orlando	AA	359	18	58	5	.284

RONDELL WHITE EXPOS Age 22/R * * *

Floyd may have grabbed all the headlines in the Eastern League, but after the two moved up to AAA, White had the better numbers.

Team	Level	AB	HR	RBI	SB	BA
Harrisburg	AA	372	12	52	21	.328
Ottawa	AAA	150	7	32	10	.380

NIGEL WILSON MARLINS Age 24/L * * *

Any wonder why he was Florida's first pick in the expansion draft? When he comes down to sea level in Miami, his numbers won't be as impressive as they were at Edmonton, but the Marlins would settle for even 80% of what he did in his AAA debut.

Team	Level	AB	HR	RBI	SB	BA
Edmonton	AAA	370	17	68	8	.292

JOEL WOLFE ATHLETICS Age 23/R * *

An oddity: Wolfe was promoted within the same league. In 1992, he played at Reno, Oakland's poorer entry in the California League. Last year, he moved up to Modesto, the better of the two Athletics franchises in the league, and then finished the 1993 season in Double-A. This is the kind of factoid you can dazzle people with in years to come if Wolfe becomes a leader of the pack.

Team	Level	AB	HR	RBI	SB	BA
Modesto	A	300	6	56	18	.350
Huntsville	AA	134	3	18	6	.299

PITCHERS

CORY BAILEY RED SOX Age 23/R * *

The absence of Jeff Russell last September focused attention on Bailey, who had 59 saves in three years on the Boston farm. While it's rare for a minor league closer to move directly to the top of a major league bullpen, Bailey has an outside chance to do just that.

Team	Level	W	L	ERA	IP	H	BB	K
Pawtucket	AAA	4	5	2.88	65.2	48	31	59

JAMES BALDWIN   WHITE SOX   Age 22/R   * *

Baldwin will be mentioned in the next update of the essay "The Best Trades Are the Ones You Don't Make." He was penciled in to go to the Mets for Sid Fernandez, before the Sox traded another top pitching prospect, Johnny Ruffin, for Tim Belcher.

Team	Level	W	L	ERA	IP	H	BB	K
Birmingham	AA	8	5	2.25	120.0	94	43	107
Nashville	AAA	5	4	2.61	69.0	43	36	61

ANDRES BERUMEN   PADRES   Age 22/R   * *

For a guy nobody had heard of before he was taken in the expansion draft, Berumen has made a lot of news. He even made the rare transition from effective closer to effective starter.

Team	Level	W	L	ERA	IP	H	BB	K
High Desert	A	9	2	3.62	92.0	85	36	74
Wichita	AA	3	1	5.74	26.2	35	11	17

JOHN BURKE   ROCKIES   Age 24/R   * *

Colorado's first draft pick, the year before expansion. However, no Rockies pitcher can get three stars. How can anybody be ready to pitch in that place?

Team	Level	W	L	ERA	IP	H	BB	K
Central Valley	A	7	8	3.18	119.0	104	64	114
Colorado Springs	AAA	3	2	3.14	48.2	44	23	38

JOEY EISCHEN   EXPOS   Age 23/L   * *

The Expos used the same prospects to thrash the competition in two leagues last year. First they built up an insurmountable lead at AA Harrisburg. Then they sent the prospects up to take over the International League, where Ottawa had spotted the other teams a head start. Eischen was one of those prospects.

Team	Level	W	L	ERA	IP	H	BB	K
Harrisburg	AA	14	4	3.62	119.1	122	60	110
Ottawa	AAA	2	2	3.54	40.2	34	15	29

BEST LONG-TERM PROSPECTS

C	Tyler Houston (Braves)	OF	Rondell White (Expos)
C	Brook Fordyce (Mets)	OF	Mike Kelly (Braves)
1B	Ryan Klesko (Braves)	OF	José Malave (Red Sox)
1B	Derrick White (Expos)	OF	Chad Mottola (Reds)
2B	Tony Graffagnino (Braves)	P	Steve Karsay (Athletics)
3B	Butch Huskey (Mets)	P	Scott Ruffcorn (White Sox)
3B	Phil Nevin (Astros)	P	Cory Bailey (Red Sox)
SS	Manny Alexander (Orioles)	P	Gabe White (Expos)
OF	Nigel Wilson (Marlins)		

DOMINGO JEAN   ASTROS   Age 25/R   * *

The final installment in the Steve Sax trade. How many throw-ins come with a 94 MPH fastball? Could be great in the Astrodome.

Team	Level	W	L	ERA	IP	H	BB	K
Prince William	A	0	0	0.00	1.2	1	0	1
Albany	AA	5	3	2.51	61.0	42	33	41
Columbus	AAA	2	2	2.82	44.2	40	13	39

BOBBY JONES   METS   Age 24/R   * * *

The Mets made him their number one draft choice in 1991, even though he didn't impress the scouts, who rely extensively on radar guns. In his case, the Mets may actually have done something right.

Team	Level	W	L	ERA	IP	H	BB	K
Norfolk	AAA	12	10	3.63	166.0	149	32	126

STEVE KARSAY   ATHLETICS   Age 22/R   * * *

After the Jays traded away Karsay to get Rickey Henderson, there were comments coming out of Toronto saying Karsay wasn't such a hot prospect. The Athletics, however, had been listening to the earlier reports that had made Karsay a number one pick. Our money's on Sandy Alderson and the A's.

Team	Level	W	L	ERA	IP	H	BB	K
Knoxville	AA	8	4	3.38	104.0	98	32	100
Huntsville	AA	0	0	5.14	14.0	13	3	22

JOSE MARTINEZ   PADRES   Age 23/R   *

1993 was a lost year, in which Martinez was shuttled from the Mets to the Marlins to the Padres (for Gary Sheffield). In 1992, he pitched a lot like his Binghamton teammate, Bobby Jones.

Team	Level	W	L	ERA	IP	H	BB	K
Edmonton	AAA	6	4	4.28	80.0	92	24	29
Las Vegas	AAA	2	3	9.93	35.1	56	15	16

KURT MILLER   MARLINS   Age 21/R   * *

Another well-traveled young pitcher. Former Pittsburgh number one draft pick, acquired by Florida from Texas, for Cris Carpenter. We think the Marlins are a smart organization, so we're going to keep an eye on Miller.

Team	Level	W	L	ERA	IP	H	BB	K
Tulsa	AA	6	8	5.06	96.0	102	45	68
Edmonton	AAA	3	3	4.50	48.0	42	34	19

OSCAR MUNOZ   TWINS   Age 24/R   * *

Doesn't any team hold on to its pitching prospects anymore? This one started in the Indians organization, and was traded for Paul Sorrento. Twins need arms, so stay tuned.

Team	Level	W	L	ERA	IP	H	BB	K
Nashville	AA	11	4	3.08	131.2	123	51	139
Portland	AAA	2	2	4.31	31.1	29	17	29

CHAD OGEA   INDIANS   Age 23/R   * * *

Because he signed late after being drafted out of LSU in 1991, the Indians sat Ogea out that season. That meant they could keep him away from arbitration for another year if they didn't bring him up in 1993. Now they have no such reason not to install the curveballer in their 1994 rotation.

Team	Level	W	L	ERA	IP	H	BB	K
Charlotte	AAA	13	8	3.81	181.2	169	54	135

BILL PULSIPHER   METS   Age 20/L   *

In his two pro seasons, he made steady progress from short-season A to low A, to high A, seeming to get stronger as he moved up. And in case you haven't been paying attention, the Mets could use a little help on the mound.

Team	Level	W	L	ERA	IP	H	BB	K
Capital City	A	2	3	2.08	43.1	34	12	29
St. Lucie	A	7	3	2.24	96.1	63	39	102

JOE ROSSELLI   GIANTS   Age 21/L   *

Great talent with a warning label: he underwent shoulder surgery last year and was sidelined longer than expected.

Team	Level	W	L	ERA	IP	H	BB	K
Shreveport	AA	0	1	3.13	23.0	22	7	19

SCOTT RUFFCORN   WHITE SOX   Age 24/R   * *

Even when the Sox were willing to trade pitching prospects for established players, they still thought this former Baylor Bear was a keeper.

Team	Level	W	L	ERA	IP	H	BB	K
Birmingham	AA	9	4	2.73	135.0	108	52	141
Nashville	AAA	2	2	2.80	45.0	30	8	44

ROGER SALKELD   MARINERS   Age 23/R   * * *

Missed all of 1992 with arm miseries. Before that, he was often compared to Roger Clemens. Promising comeback in 1993. Keep a close eye on developments in spring training.

Team	Level	W	L	ERA	IP	H	BB	K
Jackson	AA	4	3	3.27	77.0	71	29	56

DARRYL SCOTT   ANGELS   Age 25/R   * *

Negative: a minor league closer rarely becomes a major league closer without working his way up as a middle reliever and setup man. Positive: the Angels really need a closer, and most of their middle relievers had problems in 1993.

Team	Level	W	L	ERA	IP	H	BB	K
Vancouver	AAA	7	1	2.09	51.2	35	19	57

PAUL SPOLJARIC BLUE JAYS Age 23/L ★ ★ ★

Advanced from A to AA to AAA, and Toronto considered calling him up after just two AAA starts. (His Syracuse numbers partly reflect his pitching for a bad team.) Plus he's Canadian, eh?

Team	Level	W	L	ERA	IP	H	BB	K
Dunedin	A	3	0	1.38	26.0	16	12	29
Knoxville	AA	4	1	2.28	43.1	30	22	51
Syracuse	AAA	8	7	5.29	95.1	97	52	88

BRIEN TAYLOR YANKEES Age 22/L ★ ★

His heater and off-speed breaking ball are good enough to get out any batter in baseball right now—as long as there's no one on base.

Team	Level	W	L	ERA	IP	H	BB	K
Albany	AA	13	7	3.48	163.0	127	102	150

MARK THOMPSON ROCKIES Age 22/R ★ ★

Moved up fast in the fledgling farm system as the Rockies' second-ever draft pick, after John Burke. Maybe too fast. Thompson underwent arthroscopic surgery on his right shoulder after reaching AAA.

Team	Level	W	L	ERA	IP	H	BB	K
Central Valley	A	3	2	2.20	69.2	46	18	72
Colorado Springs	AAA	3	0	2.70	33.1	31	11	22

SALOMON TORRES GIANTS Age 22/R ★ ★ ★

This curveballer straightened himself out after a nightmarish second half in 1992. A good fielder, too, probably because he's from San Pedro de Macorís. No shortage of courage: he took the ball in the Giants' single most important game of the year last season. He'll get it plenty more times in the future.

Team	Level	W	L	ERA	IP	H	BB	K
Shreveport	AA	7	4	2.70	83.1	67	12	67
Phoenix	AAA	7	4	3.50	105.1	105	27	99

BEN VANRYN DODGERS Age 22/L ★ ★

After four seasons in the minors, he's still only 22. First made famous as a high school prospect in Mark Winegardner's "Prophet of the Sandlots." Then the Expos drafted him with a supplemental first-round pick for losing free agent Pascual Perez. Vanryn came into his own last season.

Team	Level	W	L	ERA	IP	H	BB	K
San Antonio	AA	14	4	2.21	134.1	118	38	144
Albuquerque	AAA	1	4	10.73	24.1	35	17	9

GABE WHITE EXPOS Age 22/L ★ ★

The third top prospect named White in the Montreal system. Sneaky fast, rather than overpowering.

Team	Level	W	L	ERA	IP	H	BB	K
Harrisburg	AA	7	2	2.16	100.0	80	28	80
Ottawa	AAA	2	1	3.12	40.1	38	6	28

6

Around the Horn

You're the Top
by Daniel Okrent
(With an Assist from Rotisserie Hall of Famer Cole Porter)

You're the top, you're a flag repeater
You're the top, Randy Johnson's heater
You're Charlie Hough, John Smoltz's stuff, Rod Beck
You're an O named Rip, Bo Jackson's hip
You're Dennis Eck!

You're the top, like Mrs. Walker's Larry
You're the top, Mrs. Bonds's Barry
You hit it higher than McGwire, Mark
Why—Mazel Tov! You're Ozzie's glove!
You're Fenway Park!

You're the top, you're Roberto Kelly
You're just huge, you're Cece Fielder's belly
You're Rickey's speed, or Reinsdorf's greed, the knack . . .
. . . For pitching tight with curves that bite
You're on the black!

You're the ear where Rog Clemens stuck it
You're the rear of ol' Kirby Puckett
You're Nolan's Ks, Toronto's Jays: no flop!
And if baby I'm the Marlins
You're the top!

Anyone interested in becoming a Broadway sugar daddy? Beloved Founder and Former Commissioner for Life Dan Okrent is looking for backers for two original musical comedies for the Broadway stage, *Okrenthoma!* and *Guys and Fenokees*. His a capella version of "You're the Top" is available on eight-track tape and monaural record at selected convenience stores and bait shops.

Ten Years After

Remember that group? Made a big splash at Woodstock. Wonder what they're doing now? Probably playing Rotisserie and talking about their prostates.

Rotisserie League Baseball, on the other hand, is thriving ten years after. That's right, it was ten years ago this spring that the first edition of *Rotisserie League Baseball* was published. While the National Book Awards and Pulitzer people inexplicably passed us over, several dozen of you bought that first book, and the rest—as we are wont to say at the drop of a cliché—is Rotissehistory. As that first book is now unavailable except in occult bookshops, we thought you might like to take a trip down memory lane with a few highlights from the original, 1984 edition. Do you remember where *you* were when it hit the bookstores?

• • •

The following essay by BFFCL Okrent appeared in the magazine Inside Sports *in 1981 and introduced the world to Rotisserie League Baseball. The world yawned. We reprinted it as the introduction to the 1984 book. We reprinted it again—annotated this time, in the manner of the* Oxford Guide to Shakespeare *in the 1990 book. Here it is again—and you know the best part? Okrent only got paid for it once!*

The Year George Foster Wasn't Worth $36

An Introduction to Rotisserie League Baseball
by Daniel Okrent

Was George Foster worth bags of money? He'd bashed the horsehide so hard for so long that you knew he wasn't coming cheap. He'd been an MVP, he'd nabbed homer and ribby crowns, he'd won pennants for the Reds. And it was 1980. He hadn't yet become a Met.

But, I asked myself, sitting alone in the dark night of the soul that only my fellow general managers could recognize, could Foster do it for the Okrent Fenokees? Could George's hefty Louisville Slugger carry our team— we already had Gary Templeton shining bright at short (he hadn't yet become a .250 hitter), Burt Hooton on the mound, Bruce Sutter on call in the Fenokee pen—over the top? Pennants are not won by the faint of heart or the tight of pocket, so I opened the vault and bought George. A championship was in reach.

If only, that is. Looking back on that dismaying 1980 season, I remember most vividly the June evening when George's thigh gave way and how he limped through the long summer. Who could have known this would happen? Or that Dennis Bleeping Lamp would throw more gopher balls than strikes? Or that no amount of relief pitching could help my club, bereft of power, leaden on the bases, suspect in the rotation?

Yeah, I know a GM can't be held responsible for injuries, or sudden reversals of form, or the unpredictable flowering of the other guy's rookies. But when I finally admitted no flag would flutter over Fenokee Park in October, my excuses were like rain checks in my mouth. Worse, we finished behind the sorry Fleder Mice, the woeful Pollet Burros, even the ragtag Smith Coronas, who passed us in August, smirking with glee. It was a dreadful season, eighth in the ten-team Rotisserie League.

The origins of the Rotisserie League, chronicled in the official league archives in my desk drawer, were inauspicious enough: Six of us gathered on a dreary January day at La Rotisserie Française, a restaurant on Manhattan's East Side, now defunct. Later there would be eleven—a few editors, a few writers, a lawyer, a college professor, a university administrator, and a couple of people out of the advertising business. All of us had a firm belief that we could do what Al Campanis could do—or John McHale, or Paul Owens. Hadn't we been appraising talent all our lives? I mean, being a GM was *easy*.

One could say we merely wanted to raise the ineluctable movements of generations enthralled by baseball to another, higher plateau. Assembling a collection of baseball cards, playing two-man stoopball while doing an eight-year-old's version of a play-by-play, proposing trades to hypercritical radio talk-show hosts—what were all of these preadolescent endeavors but preparation for the Rotisserie League? It wasn't enough to watch baseball, or to study it in the box scores and leaders lists: we all wished, in some way, to possess it, to control it. Lacking twenty million bucks, membership in the right country clubs, and a pair of plaid pants, I was clearly never going to own a major league club—unless I invented my own major league.

It was film historian and critic Bob Sklar, now a tenured professor at a bona fide institution of higher learning, who, with a couple of other eggheads, had laid the groundwork for the Rotisserie League years before, in Ann Arbor, Michigan. Using "imaginary money" (whatever the hell *that* is), Sklar and a few sociologists and historians selected various major league players at the beginning of each season, and their performance—batting average for hitters, ERA for pitchers—determined the winner, who got a blue ribbon, or something.

With tedious stories of these wonderful times repeated to me over the years (Sklar had been a teacher of mine at the University of Michigan, my parents actually paying hard-earned tuition dollars so that I could receive Official Wisdom from some nut who picked players for a nonbetting contest), I had long sought a way to improve on the Assistant Professors League, or whatever it was called. In 1980, I found the answer. True, Sklar laid the seed, but his game was to the Rotisserie League as rounders is to the 1927 Yankees.

Our idea was that each of us would assemble a team of 23 National League players—nine pitchers, five outfielders, two catchers, seven infielders. By trading, waiving, and even creatively juggling players on the disabled list, we'd all try for a championship. The pennant would go to the team whose players collected—in real-life baseball—the most home runs, stolen bases, wins, saves, and the like, all solid indices of baseball performance. The prize turned out to be a seedy trophy and a check for $1,662.

The auction was held in April, on a pleasant Sunday morning. And afternoon. And evening. There being no Marvin Miller to look over our shoulders, we had agreed to a form of price-fixing, prohibiting any one GM/owner from spending more than $260 to assemble a team. That was, we thought, very ownerlike. Bowie would have been proud. But then the Rennie Stennett phenomenon set in. We each had slightly more than $11 to spend, on the average, per player, but the sound of chops being licked filled the room at every drop of a ho-hum name. Would $38 buy enough Gravy Train for Dave Kingman? How about $33 for Bobby Bonds? The wiser among us waited for the fever to subside, and the Sklar Gazers picked up Mike Schmidt for $26. In the waning moments, Bob Welch was acquired for $3. The Getherswag Goners, owned by editor and novelist Peter Gethers and university administrator Glen Waggoner, got Neil Allen, whose 22 saves would win them the pennant, for a lousy two bucks. And to think I spent $36 for George Foster.

Trades? The talk never stopped. The Eisenberg Furriers swapped like rug merchants, dealing a sorry collection of nobodies into a team that led for four months. The conservative Salembier Flambés—owned by our only woman exec, Valerie Salembier, the Lorinda de Roulet of the juvenile circuit—made not a single deal and nabbed fourth-place money. I took the middle path, nudging my beloved Fenokees this way and that, trading delicately, moderately—and abysmally. On the way to my dismal finish, I contemplated firing myself. Bruce McCall, of the Collects, did even worse, dealing Omar Moreno to the Goners for Dave Goltz and Elliott Maddox. (You wonder how Goltz got his zillions from the Dodgers? Ask my friend Bruce.) When McCall asked to be suspended from making further trades, I, as commissioner, obliged, announcing the proscription by citing the best interests of baseball and the integrity of the game.

The game—The Rotisserie League—occupied the lives of all of us that first summer as no mere job or family ever could. "I am possessed by Mike Ivie," said one original Rotissarian, who called the San Francisco Giants' publicity office daily to get the latest on the reluctant slugger's physical and mental health. When Bill Madlock was suspended for duking an umpire, Lee Eisenberg of the Furriers contemplated filing a friend-of-the-court brief with the National League. McCall issued a weekly newspaper about his warriors, spicing it with a Rotisserie gossip column by "C. Nile Hack III" and dotting it with pictures cribbed from sports pages, each airbrushed so Steve Garvey, Johnny Bench, and their teammates appeared to be wearing Collects uniforms.

Each morning, all of us ran to the box scores, manically searching the agate type for news, say, of a three-for-four day from Mike Ramsey. And, on a league outing to Shea Stadium, there, for one, was Michael Pollet, attorney, father, civic activist, yelling wildly for Steve Henderson; a minute later cheering even more vociferously as the Dodgers brought in Rick Sutcliffe to pitch (hoo-ha! Fifteen bucks he'd paid for Sutcliffe and his 5.56 ERA that year!). When Henderson stepped in against Sutcliffe, Burro against Burro, Michael nearly wept in perplexity.

As commissioner and owner, I probably put more energy into this glorious nonsense than any other Rotissarian, although Glen Waggoner repeatedly said, "This is the best thing that ever happened to me," and spent the summer sending away for glossies from big league teams, memorizing Rick Auerbach's birthdate, Johnnie LeMaster's hat size. It was not hard to make rulings on various disputes, even though my interests as owner and commissioner were in conflict. Invariably, I ruled in my favor. Did Walter O'Malley abstain when the National League voted to transfer the Dodgers westward? And, after all, I was the one who had to put in endless hours each week, compiling and computing our stats from the pages of *The Sporting News*. Of course, until I dropped out of the race and into the Three-Eye League, this was a task of such compelling interest that I didn't wait for the regular Friday mail delivery of the good ol' Bible. Instead, I'd drive twenty miles each way to a newsstand that got the paper on Thursday.

We had a good pennant race in 1980. When Ellis Valentine's jaw was shattered by a rising fastball, so were the Furriers' hopes for a championship. The Gazers never quite recovered from Ivie's walkabout, the Flambés from J. R. Richard's tragedy. The Goners, who played the waiver wire like a harp, who assembled a Tekulve-Allen-Sambito bullpen, who purloined Moreno from the Collects, grabbed the flag, the trophy, and fifty percent of the kitty.

It was not until after the World Series in "other" baseball—we stopped calling it "real" baseball about an hour and a half into the total absorption of Rotisserie life—that we gathered to pour the ceremonial bottle of Yoo-Hoo over the heads of the victorious Waggoner and Gethers. It was a solemn moment, a consecration of our summer of fellowship. Then we started to argue over rules changes, to propose obscene trades to our competitors, and, finally, to divide up the prize money—owners to the core.

So it has been for three summers since. We have sharpened our baseball wits, expanded rosters, developed farm systems, welcomed new leagues to Rotisserie baseball, fine-tuned our rules, and seen new management come to two franchises. The charm of baseball, though, is its slowness to change. Before last season I signed George Foster to another contract, this one just shy of the maximum twenty percent cut allowed under major league rules. Perhaps if he's hungry, I reasoned, he'll respond to the challenge. He didn't, but his teammates did. The Fenokees finished third.

George may not be back with the Swampmen this year, but I will—this time, armed with a pennant-winning strategy, named Darryl Strawberry. The way I read the scouting reports, there'll be plenty of power in the draft, and

I can trade for speed. The bullpen's okay, but I'm going to need three starters. The Brenners are loaded again, and the Goners and Furriers are always tough. But maybe, just maybe . . .

Play ball!

● ● ●

Before Chris Berhman, there was the Rotisserie League . . .

ROTISSERIE LEAGUE ALL-TIME, ALL-DODGER NICKNAME TEAM

Dusty "Josephine" Baker
Jack "Goose" Fimple
Alejandro "Hal O'" Pena
Steve "Tenor" Sax
Manny "General" Mota
Roy "Sunrise" Campanella
Wes "Valet" Parker
Larry "Cooking" Sherry
Preacher "Shad" Roe
Jackie "Mrs." Robinson
Sal "Gift of the" Maglie

Pedro "C'est la" Guerrero
Fernando "Oil Rich" Valenzuela
Greg "Lou" Brock
Joe "Lebaseball" Lefebvre
Maury "Last" Wills
Ernie "Guy" Lombardi
Norm "Spanish" Sherry
Pee Wee "Jacob" Reese
Joe "Justice" Black
Ed "Sears" Roebuck
Bill "Bill" Russell

Charlie "Salad" Dressen (Mgr.)

● ● ●

From the outset, we thought of ourselves as educators . . .

Did You Know

. . . that *The Bible* is *The Sporting News* of religion?

. . . that Steve Nicosia is the only major leaguer whose last name is the same as the capital of a Mediterranean island republic?

. . . that Aurelio Lopez is the only pitcher in major league history with all five vowels in his first name?

. . . that Ed Figueroa was the only pitcher in major league history with all five vowels in his last name?

. . . that "Lefty" is the most common nickname in baseball history, but there's never been a player called "Righty"?

. . . that there is no nonpitcher in the Hall of Fame named "Bob"?

. . . that "Toby Harrah" spelled backward is "Harrah Ybot"?

• • •

During rain delays we made lists . . .

ROTISSERIE LEAGUE ALL-SEXUAL DIVERSITY TEAM

Coco Laboy • Jim Fairey • Mel Queen
Pete LaCock • Rollie Fingers • Pinky May
Jim O'Toole • Ewell (The Whip) Blackwell • Jim French
Boots Poffenberger • Tommy John • Ed Head
Urban Shocker • Wally Moon • Heinie Manush
Greg Gross
Mordecai (Three Finger) Brown
Gene Brabender • Steve Swisher • Jimmy Dykes
Bill Hands • Rusty Kuntz
and, collectively, the Montreal Expos

• • •

*Bruce McCall, legendary owner of the hapless McCall Collects (1980) and
the even more hapless McCall De Sax (1993), recorded for posterity the
following conversation between two former presidents of the National and
American leagues. You may need to haul out your* Encyclopedia of Baseball
*to refresh your memory (Shooty Babbit?), but we think you'll agree that this
goes a long way toward settling once and for all an age-old debate.*

The Great Rotisserie Debate:
NL vs. AL

Is the Rotisserie League founded on a myth? Is the Senior Circuit *really*
superior to the American League, as Rotisserians allege, or is their sense of
superiority nothing more than prejudice and snobbery? Last fall we invited
then AL Prexy Lee MacPhail and his NL opposite number, Chub Feeney,
to state the case for their respective leagues with cold, clear facts—and
without the childish name-calling and cliché-mongering that has so often
traded insult for insight in discussions of the two loops' relative merits and
styles. Having won the toss of the coin, Chub earned the privilege of kicking
off the chinwag. Chub?

FEENEY: Well let me just say, on behalf of the National League, what
a pleasure it is to be here among what I feel are friends, and
to help enlighten all the fine fans who are home right now,
reading this book.

MacPHAIL: I'll second that, Fats.

FEENEY: It's Chub, and what else is new? Of course you'll second that. The ALs made a career out of coming in second. Especially on a certain night in July . . .

MacPHAIL: I gather by that exquisitely subtle reference that you mean the All-Freak . . . er, All-Star Game?

FEENEY: Takes a freak to know a freak, and anybody from the league that gave us a one-armed outfielder *and* a midget *and* at least two tin-legged pitchers, well, I rest my case.

MacPHAIL: But not your yap.

FEENEY: Wasn't *our* league that threw a World Series and discriminated against black players . . . hey, the Red Sox sign any yet?

MacPHAIL: You wake up a National Leaguer in the middle of the night, first thing out of his mouth—after the chaw, I mean—is gonna be "All-Star Game."

FEENEY: I love that name, "MacPhail." Goes so good with the American League and the All-Star Game, as in "another MacPhailure."

MacPHAIL: And what kind of a bozo name is "Chub," anyways?

FEENEY: Listen, pal, when it comes to chubs, any league that's got Luzinski and Hoyt on the same team is in Fat City, literally. The Chicago Lard Sox. I hear the reason Luzinski went to the AL was that he finally got too fat to fit through the clubhouse door in Philly. They had to send him air freight on trips to the Coast, too. When he played first base last September, all the seats along the line had to be sold as "obstructed view."

MacPHAIL: The Senile Circuit babbling again.

FEENEY: They had to waive Rick Reuschel out of our league because he was making the mound at Wrigley Field concave.

MacPHAIL: Yeah, and we sent him back when he lost ten pounds off his fastball. But let's talk homers.

FEENEY: As in "AL umps are all homers," you mean? But actually, Lee, I take it back. The American isn't really the Fat League.

MacPHAIL: Mighty big of you, Blimp.

FEENEY: It's the Little League. Eddie Gaedel, Albie Pearson, Freddie Patek . . . how come your farm system's not in Taiwan?

MacPHAIL: For your information, Eddie Gaedel is dead.

FEENEY: Another mark of a true American Leaguer. Sure explains the AL's running game. "Dead men don't steal second," we say in the National. Surprised you guys haven't instituted a Designated Puller to haul your base runners around in a coaster wagon or something.

MacPHAIL: Way I understand it, most of your speed comes in little green capsules.

FEENEY: Oh, go reinterpret the pine-tar ruling again. Some league, when the biggest news of the season is a squabble about some goo on a bat and the President double-crosses his own umpires.

MacPHAIL: Dead men don't steal bases, huh? Well, real men don't need Astroturf.

FEENEY:	You guys really oughta wise up. Get the rugs off Autry's and Steinbrenner's heads and put 'em on your playing fields ... your ballparks are *so* small it won't cost any more than carpeting the locker rooms.
MacPHAIL:	Mister Steinbrenner does not wear a rug.
FEENEY:	Ah, that explains everything! The hole in his head is left open to the sky. Birdshit, rain, all sorts of stuff gets in there and that's what gums up the works!
MacPHAIL:	That is beneath even you, Feeney.
FEENEY:	Well, like I said, looking at the AL I find *everything's* beneath me. Pint-sizers wall-to-wall.
MacPHAIL:	Better than artificial turf carpeting wall-to-wall.
FEENEY:	You know what really separates the NL from the AL? We get San Francisco and you guys get ... Oakland. That says it all.
MacPHAIL:	Yeah, and Brooklyn and New York get the shaft back in Fifty-eight. Wall-to-wall carpeting *and* wall-to-wall carpetbagging, that's the National.
FEENEY:	If *we* had to spend *our* summers traipsing from places like Cleveland to Detroit to Baltimore to Arlington, Texas, we'd probably play boring baseball, too.
MacPHAIL:	You forget Seattle, one of the most ...
FEENEY:	You got a franchise in Seattle? Oh, sure, you got twenty-five guys and a Steinbrenner clone running them, but you haven't got a major league team as we in the National League define a major league team.
MacPHAIL:	At least we hide it in Seattle, while you guys stink up New York with the Mets.
FEENEY:	Your players ought to strike for boredom pay. Toronto in April. Minneapolis–St. Paul in May. Oakland, anytime. Brrrrr.
MacPHAIL:	Chief Noc-a-Homa, the San Diego Chicken. Real good taste, that's the NL all over.
FEENEY:	George and Billy and Reggie—the kind of folks you'd like to have to dinner.
MacPHAIL:	At least *they* wouldn't steal the silverware like some NL'ers we could mention.
FEENEY:	Gaylord Perry, Don Sutton ... they'd just get spit all over everything. No dinner invites for them.
MacPHAIL:	How come a different National League team every year wins the championship?
FEENEY:	Balance! We ...
MacPHAIL:	*Choke,* I call it. Four teams in four years, championship winners. That means to me that three out of four teams choked. Couldn't stand prosperity.
FEENEY:	And your teams can't even *find* prosperity.
MacPHAIL:	For your information, Toronto reported ...
FEENEY:	... its first signs of life in six years. Meanwhile Buddy LeRoux does for Boston what Attila the Hun did for Rome. I give you Calvin Griffith, Eddie Chiles.
MacPHAIL:	And if Ted Turner and Ray Kroc are the alternatives, I'll take 'em.

FEENEY:	Let's see, the AL has fourteen teams. I understand you're going to offer franchises with every box of Wheaties in your next expansion. Every time the AL expands, the quality contracts.
MacPHAIL:	Boston, Milwaukee, Brooklyn ... every time the NL shifts town, somebody sues.
FEENEY:	It isn't as simple as that.
MacPHAIL:	In fact it's Fimple. What a ...
FEENEY:	Shooty Babbit, I suppose that's a household name?
MacPHAIL:	He isn't in the majors anymore.
FEENEY:	Neither is the American League.
MacPHAIL:	How do you know? You never see AL teams in action.
FEENEY:	*Nobody* sees AL teams in action. You guys invented the DH, which created the sore-armed pitcher, which produces lots of home runs in your bandbox parks, which encourages more DHs, so most of the action in the AL comes from the third-base coach scratching his jock.
MacPHAIL:	I don't follow.
FEENEY:	That's a first!

Beat the Founding Fathers
at Their Own Game!

That's right—play head-to-head against one of the Founding Fathers of Rotisserie League Baseball. Believe you can snap the Wulfgang's baton? Want a chance at draining the Okrent Fenokees' swamp? Think you're just the cat to catch the Fleder Mice? Here's your chance.

1. Pick a 23-man Rotisserie roster based on player salaries in Chapter 3, and submit it on an official Founding Fathers League registration form along with your entry fee of $50 by May 1.

2. Play National League, American League, or Mixed League—your call. Your club will be placed in a 12-team league that includes a team owned by one of the Founding Fathers (*e.g.*, the Pollet Burro League, the Stein Brenner League, *etc.*).

3. You may spend a maximum total of 260 Rotissedollars (*i.e.*, NOT real dollars) to assemble your team, using the salaries indicated in the Scouting Report, Chapter 3. You must have the customary Rotisserie alignment: 2 catchers, 3 corners, 3 middle infielders, 5 outfielders, and 1 utility/DH; and 9 pitchers.

4. Scoring will be according to the standard Rotisserie categories: Home Runs, Runs Batted In, Stolen Bases, and Batting Average for batters; Wins, Saves, Earned Run Average, and Ratio for pitchers.

5. You will receive a complete standings report every month so that you can track your team's progress in the Founding Fathers pennant race. Each report will contain a complete performance report on every player on every team in your league, as well as standings in each of the eight statistical categories.

6. At the All-Star Break, you get a chance to ditch any bums who have been dragging your team down. Each owner will be sent an updated salary list for all the eligible players in both leagues. You can release up to seven players that you currently own and use their salaries (based on their original book prices) to acquire seven new players (based on the updated salary list). After this All-Star Break transaction period, your team must still have a full 23-man Rotisserie team and your payroll may not exceed 260 Rotissedollars.

7. Pennant-winners receive a free pass to play in the Founding Fathers League in 1995, a free copy of the next edition of this book, an official Rotisserie League T-shirt, and a wall plaque testifying to your victory. Plus you will be listed right here in next year's book as a Rotisserie owner who beat the Founding Fathers at their own game!

For your official entry registration form for the Founding Fathers League, contact the **Rotisserie League Baseball Association.** The address is **370 Seventh Avenue, Suite 312, New York, NY 10001.** The telephone number is **212–695-3463.** The fax number is **212-643-8083.** Write, call, or fax—NOW!

1993 Rotisserie League Media Guide

The Wulfgang led the pack from Opening Day and won going away, but the 1993 race for the other first-division slots was the closest in Rotisserie League history. Just four points separated second through fifth—and if the season had lasted another two weeks, the Stein Brenners might have leaped all the way from sixth to second. The explanation? Except for the Wulfgang, *nobody had a very good team.* After last year's auction draft we all agreed we'd been to happier funerals: the prices were sky high, the pickings were slim, and the consensus was that nobody had a chance to win. Know what? The consensus was almost right.

ROTISSERIE LEAGUE, 1993

FINAL STANDINGS

1. WULFGANG	73.5		7. POLLET BURROS	53.0
2. ABEL BAKERS	64.5		8. SKLAR GAZERS*	50.0
3. GLENWAG GONERS	61.5		9. FLEDER MICE*	50.0
4. SMOKED FISH	61.0		10. OKRENT FENOKEES	43.0
5. EISENBERG FURRIERS	60.5		11. CARY NATIONS	39.0
6. STEIN BRENNERS	55.5		12. MCCALL DE SAX	12.0

*Order of finish determined by tie-breaker: Gazers beat Mice in five of eight scoring categories.

PITCHING RECORDS

EARNED RUN AVERAGE			RATIO		
EISENBERG FURRIERS	3.55	12.0	EISENBERG FURRIERS	1.282	12.0
WULFGANG	3.73	11.0	SKLAR GAZERS	1.300	11.0
OKRENT FENOKEES	3.74	10.0	ABEL BAKERS	1.301	10.0
SKLAR GAZERS	3.78	9.0	POLLET BURROS	1.307	9.0
GLENWAG GONERS	3.91	8.0	SMOKED FISH	1.317	8.0
FLEDER MICE	3.92	7.0	GLENWAG GONERS	1.332	7.0
STEIN BRENNERS	3.94	6.0	CARY NATIONS	1.337	6.0
CARY NATIONS	3.96	5.0	FLEDER MICE	1.338	5.0
ABEL BAKERS	4.02	4.0	OKRENT FENOKEES	1.341	4.0
SMOKED FISH	4.03	3.0	STEIN BRENNERS	1.358	3.0
POLLET BURROS	4.11	2.0	WULFGANG	1.397	2.0
MCCALL DE SAX	4.26	1.0	MCCALL DE SAX	1.407	1.0

SAVES			WINS		
CARY NATIONS	83	12.0	POLLET BURROS	99	12.0
WULFGANG	80	11.0	ABEL BAKERS	86	10.5
STEIN BRENNERS	75	10.0	GLENWAG GONERS	86	10.5
FLEDER MICE	74	9.0	EISENBERG FURRIERS	84	9.0
EISENBERG FURRIERS	60	8.0	SKLAR GAZERS	83	8.0
SKLAR GAZERS	49	7.0	FLEDER MICE	76	7.0
SMOKED FISH	46	6.0	SMOKED FISH	75	6.0
OKRENT FENOKEES	38	5.0	OKRENT FENOKEES	69	5.0
ABEL BAKERS	33	4.0	CARY NATIONS	67	3.5
GLENWAG GONERS	10	3.0	WULFGANG	67	3.5
MCCALL DE SAX	3	2.0	MCCALL DE SAX	63	2.0
POLLET BURROS	0	1.0	STEIN BRENNERS	60	1.0

(Continued)

BATTING RECORDS

RUNS BATTED IN			STOLEN BASES		
WULFGANG	920	12.0	SMOKED FISH	210	12.0
STEIN BRENNERS	810	11.0	WULFGANG	180	11.0
SMOKED FISH	771	10.0	FLEDER MICE	167	10.0
GLENWAG GONERS	760	9.0	ABEL BAKERS	164	9.0
POLLET BURROS	756	8.0	EISENBERG FURRIERS	135	7.5
ABEL BAKERS	739	7.0	STEIN BRENNERS	135	7.5
FLEDER MICE	709	6.0	GLENWAG GONERS	134	6.0
EISENBERG FURRIERS	705	5.0	CARY NATIONS	108	5.0
CARY NATIONS	592	4.0	POLLET BURROS	107	4.0
OKRENT FENOKEES	547	3.0	OKRENT FENOKEES	99	3.0
SKLAR GAZERS	530	2.0	MCCALL DE SAX	83	2.0
MCCALL DE SAX	495	1.0	SKLAR GAZERS	65	1.0

HOME RUNS			BATTING AVERAGE		
STEIN BRENNERS	207	12.0	WULFGANG	.284	12.0
WULFGANG	193	11.0	GLENWAG GONERS	.281	11.0
ABEL BAKERS	176	10.0	ABEL BAKERS	.280	10.0
SMOKED FISH	171	9.0	POLLET BURROS	.275	9.0
POLLET BURROS	158	8.0	OKRENT FENOKEES	.274	8.0
GLENWAG GONERS	157	7.0	SMOKED FISH	.274	7.0
SKLAR GAZERS	130	6.0	SKLAR GAZERS	.272	6.0
OKRENT FENOKEES	129	5.0	STEIN BRENNERS	.271	5.0
EISENBERG FURRIERS	128	4.0	FLEDER MICE	.270	4.0
CARY NATIONS	124	3.0	EISENBERG FURRIERS	.269	3.0
FLEDER MICE	119	2.0	MCCALL DE SAX	.268	2.0
MCCALL DE SAX	80	1.0	CARY NATIONS	.261	1.0

1993 Rotisserie League Rosters

In the team rosters that follow, an asterisk (°) by a player's name indicates that he finished the season on the reserve list, while a number sign (#) signifies that the player was traded, waived, or released earlier in the season. Two asterisks (°°) identify a group of players whose 1993 contributions to their Rotisserie team were lumped together to keep this chapter shorter than the collected works of Charles Dickens.

You will note several additional stats beyond the "Original Eight" Rotisserie categories that we employ in keeping score. We put them there to suggest the range of **Roti·Stats,** which this year becomes the officially authorized stat service of the Rotisserie League Baseball Association. **Roti·Stats (800-884-7684)** can add these and other extra categories for leagues that want them.

Fine-tooth combers will note that some teams finished last season with more than 23 active players: that's because of September Expansion. Other teams finished with fewer than 23 active players: that is perfectly legal and relatively commonplace in leagues playing Rotisserie Ultra.

Wulfgang
Owner: Steve Wulf

1993 Highlights: If you lead wall-to-wall (save for one week in August), *everything* is a highlight ... Solid seasons from unexpected sources: Carlos Garcia, Todd Benzinger, Kurt Manwaring ... Big comeback from Matt Williams ... Smart trades for Tom Glavine and Terry Pendleton (Gang got the good third of Pendleton's season). **1994 Outlook:** Randy Myers ($32), Gene Harris ($6), Reggie Sanders ($10), Brian Jordan ($5), Darren Lewis ($8), and Eric Anthony ($2) form core of Gang's back-to-back pennant hopes.

FINAL ROSTER

BATTERS	AB	H	BB	HR	RBI	SB	R	OBA	BA
ANTHONY, ERIC	486	121	49	15	66	3	70	.317	.248
BAGWELL, JEFF	535	171	62	20	88	13	76	.390	.319
BENZINGER, TODD	91	28	8	5	18	0	16	.363	.307
CEDENO, ANDUJAR	505	143	48	11	56	9	69	.345	.283
FOLEY, TOM	75	18	4	1	4	0	7	.278	.240
GARCIA, CARLOS	546	147	31	12	47	18	77	.308	.269
GWYNN, TONY	489	175	36	7	59	14	70	.401	.357
JORDAN, BRIAN	210	65	10	10	43	5	28	.340	.309
KRUK, JOHN	535	169	111	14	85	6	100	.433	.315
LEWIS, DARREN	522	132	30	2	48	46	84	.293	.252
MANWARING, KIRT	432	119	41	5	49	1	48	.338	.275
PENA, GERONIMO	254	65	25	5	30	13	34	.322	.255
PENDLETON, TERRY	212	62	15	9	37	4	30	.339	.292
SANDERS, REGGIE	496	136	51	20	83	27	90	.341	.274
SANTIAGO, BENITO	469	108	37	13	50	10	49	.286	.230
WILLIAMS, MATT	579	170	27	38	110	1	105	.325	.293
#SNYDER, CORY	309	82	24	6	38	4	34	.318	.265
#VIZCAINO, JOSE	156	54	10	0	9	6	20	.385	.346
TOTALS	**6901**	**1965**	**619**	**193**	**920**	**180**	**1007**	**.343**	**.284**

PITCHERS	W	L	S	IP	H	ER	BB	K	ERA	RATIO
GLAVINE, TOM	10	2	0	90.66	100	37	29	59	3.67	1.423
HARRIS, GENE	6	6	23	59.33	57	20	37	39	3.03	1.584
HILLMAN, ERIC	2	7	0	115.67	134	47	17	47	3.66	1.305
HOFFMAN, TREVOR	2	3	2	46.00	47	24	19	44	4.70	1.435
MARTINEZ, RAMON	10	12	0	211.67	202	81	104	127	3.44	1.446
MCDOWELL, ROGER	5	3	1	63.67	74	17	30	26	2.40	1.633
MYERS, RANDY	2	4	53	75.33	65	26	26	86	3.11	1.208
OLIVERAS, OMAR	3	3	1	74.67	77	30	38	46	3.62	1.540
RAPP, PAT	4	5	0	88.33	96	39	38	53	3.97	1.517
RUETER, KIRK	7	0	0	77.33	83	26	15	26	3.03	1.267
STANTON, MIKE	0	3	0	14.33	17	11	11	14	6.91	1.954
*ASHBY, ANDY	0	2	0	34.00	44	17	16	20	4.50	1.765
#SABERHAGEN, BRET	7	7	0	139.33	131	51	17	93	3.29	1.062
#SCHILLING, CURT	9	6	0	150.33	147	70	37	104	4.19	1.224
#SMILEY, JOHN	0	2	0	25.33	44	23	9	10	8.17	2.092
#YOUNG, ANTHONY	0	12	0	73.00	79	37	31	45	4.56	1.507
TOTALS	**67**	**77**	**80**	**1339.00**	**1397**	**556**	**474**	**839**	**3.74**	**1.397**

#2

Abel Bakers
Owner: Dominick Abel

1993 Highlights: Shrewd late-season pickups of Glenallen Hill and Dave Clark ... Emergence of Jeff Kent ... Return to form of Luis Gonzales ... With stronger bullpen and less generous starters (9th in Saves and ERA), Bakery would be afloat in Yoo-Hoo. **1994 Outlook:** Gary Sheffield ($12), Kent ($14), and Al Martin ($14) provide nucleus of offense, but Pete Harnisch ($21) and Rene Arocha ($2) are only two returning Baker starters worth a donut hole. Biggest question—can Doug Jones be reborn a third time in Philadelphia?

FINAL ROSTER

BATTERS	AB	H	BB	HR	RBI	SB	R	OBA	BA
ARIAS, ALEX	249	67	27	2	20	1	27	.340	.269
BELL, JAY	604	187	77	9	51	16	102	.387	.309
BRANSON, JEFF	297	65	15	2	16	3	33	.256	.218
BREAM, SID	262	65	29	8	30	4	30	.323	.248
CHAMBERLAIN, WES	275	76	17	12	42	2	33	.318	.276
CLARK, DAVE	131	38	14	8	23	1	24	.358	.290
GIRARDI, JOE	300	87	23	3	30	5	35	.340	.290
GONZALEZ, LUIS	540	162	47	15	72	20	82	.356	.300
HILL, GLENALLEN	82	29	6	10	22	1	14	.397	.353
KELLY, ROBERTO	320	102	17	9	35	21	44	.353	.318
KENT, JEFF	496	134	30	21	80	4	65	.311	.270
MARTIN, AL	480	135	42	18	64	16	85	.339	.281
SERVAIS, SCOTT	243	56	21	10	28	0	21	.291	.230
SHEFFIELD, GARY	494	145	47	20	73	17	67	.354	.293
WHITE, RONDELL	73	19	7	2	15	1	9	.325	.260
#COLBRUNN, GREG	109	29	4	3	17	2	11	.292	.266
#COLEMAN, VINCE	373	104	21	2	25	38	64	.317	.278
#MAY, DERRICK	353	109	25	9	62	7	48	.354	.308
#VELASQUEZ, GUILLERMO	87	19	9	2	12	0	5	.291	.218
**OTHERS (4)	197	47	16	11	22	5	29	.320	.239
TOTALS	**5965**	**1675**	**494**	**176**	**739**	**164**	**828**	**.335**	**.280**

PITCHERS	W	L	S	IP	H	ER	BB	K	ERA	RATIO
AROCHA, RENE	11	8	0	188.00	197	79	31	96	3.78	1.213
FRANCO, JOHN	1	3	2	10.33	18	12	5	13	10.45	2.226
HARNISCH, PETE	10	5	0	122.33	89	34	44	100	2.50	1.087
HICKERSON, BRYAN	2	3	0	48.00	57	17	14	36	3.19	1.479
JACKSON, MIKE	5	5	1	69.66	53	24	22	64	3.10	1.077
JONES, DOUG	4	8	24	74.00	89	37	16	57	4.50	1.419
MAGRANE, JOE	8	10	0	116.00	127	64	37	38	4.97	1.414
NIED, DAVID	5	9	0	87.00	99	50	42	46	5.17	1.621
REED, STEVE	6	3	3	66.00	59	27	23	43	3.68	1.242
SWINDELL, GREG	12	13	0	187.33	213	88	40	121	4.23	1.351
*PLESAC, DAN	0	0	0	2.33	5	2	1	1	7.72	2.572
*TOMLIN, RANDY	4	8	0	96.33	101	49	15	43	4.58	1.204
#BELCHER, TIM	9	6	0	137.00	134	68	47	96	4.47	1.321
#PEREZ, MIKE	4	2	3	47.33	42	12	16	41	2.28	1.225
#WOHLERS, MARK	5	0	0	17.66	9	4	7	15	2.04	0.906
TOTALS	**86**	**83**	**33**	**1269.33**	**1292**	**567**	**360**	**810**	**4.02**	**1.301**

Glenwag Goners
Owner: Glen Waggoner

1993 Highlights: Definitely not Howard Johnson ($34), John Franco ($34), or Eric Davis ($32), the first three players selected in auction draft by defending champions . . . Nor did late-season trades for Barry Larkin and Ryne Sandberg help in quest for three-peat . . . Bullpen a fiasco, starting pitching shaky . . . How come third place? Tradition. Goners have finished in first division 12 of 14 Rotisserie League seasons. **1994 Outlook:** Bleak, even if Todd Jones ($1) bumps Mitch Williams as Astros closer . . . Goners to begin rebuilding plan as soon as auction draft is over.

FINAL ROSTER

BATTERS	AB	H	BB	HR	RBI	SB	R	OBA	BA
BIGGIO, CRAIG	610	175	77	21	64	15	98	.366	.286
BLAUSER, JEFF	597	182	85	15	73	16	110	.391	.304
CABRERA, FRANCISCO	83	20	8	4	11	0	8	.307	.240
CLARK, JERALD	478	135	20	13	67	9	65	.311	.282
CLAYTON, ROYCE	522	149	37	6	68	11	51	.332	.285
COTTO, HENRY	81	24	2	2	7	5	10	.313	.296
DUNCAN, MARIANO	213	64	4	4	33	1	28	.313	.300
FINLEY, STEVE	530	143	27	8	43	18	67	.305	.269
OLIVER, JOE	482	115	27	14	75	0	40	.278	.238
ORSULAK, JOE	409	116	28	8	35	5	59	.329	.283
SANDBERG, RYNE	176	57	14	2	10	1	29	.373	.323
TEUFEL, TIM	200	50	27	7	31	2	26	.339	.250
THOMPSON, MILT	340	89	40	4	44	9	42	.339	.261
THOMPSON, ROB	177	54	21	10	24	0	32	.378	.305
#DAVIS, ERIC	376	88	41	14	53	33	57	.309	.234
#GALARRAGA, ANDRES	293	115	18	14	65	2	46	.427	.392
#JOHNSON, HOWARD	235	56	43	7	26	6	32	.356	.238
#MAGADAN, DAVE	227	65	44	4	29	0	22	.402	.286
**OTHERS (3)	37	11	6	0	2	1	7	.459	.297
TOTALS	**6066**	**1708**	**569**	**157**	**760**	**134**	**829**	**.343**	**.281**

PITCHERS	W	L	S	IP	H	ER	BB	K	ERA	RATIO
AQUINO, LUIS	3	6	0	78.00	83	31	25	45	3.58	1.385
ASTACIO, PEDRO	14	7	0	168.33	150	66	59	109	3.53	1.242
GREENE, TOMMY	16	4	0	196.00	170	72	59	163	3.31	1.168
HEREDIA, GIL	2	0	1	26.66	28	9	7	22	3.04	1.313
HIBBARD, GREG	15	11	0	191.00	209	84	47	82	3.96	1.340
JONES, TODD	1	2	2	22.66	19	11	10	13	4.37	1.280
MASON, ROGER	4	5	0	34.67	28	18	13	27	4.67	1.183
OSBORNE, DONOVAN	10	7	0	155.67	153	65	47	83	3.76	1.285
RIVERA, BEN	2	2	0	37.67	30	16	22	35	3.82	1.380
SANDERSON, SCOTT	2	2	0	34.67	35	16	7	29	4.15	1.211
*BALLARD, JEFF	1	0	0	24.00	31	11	5	6	4.13	1.500
*BLACK, BUD	8	2	0	93.67	89	37	33	45	3.56	1.302
*HERNANDEZ, JEREMY	0	2	0	25.00	34	14	3	20	5.04	1.480
*RIGHETTI, DAVE	1	1	0	32.33	44	21	11	21	5.85	1.701
#FRANCO, JOHN	3	0	6	23.67	23	8	12	14	3.04	1.479
#PARRETT, JEFF	3	3	1	73.33	78	44	44	65	5.40	1.664
**OTHERS (3)	1	4	0	26	39	19	14	6	6.58	2.038
TOTALS	**86**	**58**	**10**	**1246.33**	**1243**	**542**	**418**	**785**	**3.91**	**1.333**

Peter's Famous Smoked Fish

Owner: Peter Gethers

1993 Highlights: "I think we have a chance to win," said Sturgeon General Peter Gethers in mid-August when Fish swam into first place for a week . . . "Blub, blub" was all he could manage six weeks later as team sank like rock . . . Deep-sixed by starters Mike Harkey, Frank Tanana, and Allen Watson.

1994 Outlook: Big Fish include Fred McGriff ($34), Lenny Dykstra ($32), Sammy Sosa ($32), Jose Offerman ($10), and Chuck Carr ($10) . . . Harkey, Tanana, and Watson *won't* be back . . . Neither will Rich Wilkins ($3), dealt away in Fish pennant push.

FINAL ROSTER

BATTERS	AB	H	BB	HR	RBI	SB	R	OBA	BA
BELL, DEREK	190	55	7	7	26	11	27	.314	.289
CARR, CHUCK	551	147	49	4	41	58	75	.326	.266
DYKSTRA, LEN	637	194	129	19	66	37	143	.421	.304
GARDNER, JEFF	404	106	45	1	24	2	53	.336	.262
KING, JEFF	611	180	59	9	98	8	82	.356	.294
LAKE, STEVE	61	12	1	2	6	0	4	.209	.196
LAKER, TIM	84	17	2	0	7	2	3	.220	.202
MCGRIFF, FRED	557	162	76	37	101	5	111	.375	.290
OFFERMAN, JOSE	590	159	71	1	62	30	77	.347	.269
SOSA, SAMMY	598	156	38	33	93	36	92	.305	.260
STOCKER, KEVIN	235	75	28	1	29	5	41	.391	.319
THOMPSON, RYAN	287	72	19	11	26	2	34	.297	.250
VANDERWAL, JOHN	173	39	18	5	26	4	25	.298	.225
WHITMORE, DARRELL	238	49	10	4	18	4	22	.237	.205
ZEILE, TODD	571	158	70	17	103	5	82	.355	.276
*OQUENDO, JOSE	53	13	10	0	2	0	6	.365	.245
#WILKINS, RICH	281	86	31	20	43	1	46	.375	.290
**OTHERS (2)	14	3	3	0	0	0	2	.429	.224
TOTALS	**6135**	**1683**	**666**	**171**	**771**	**210**	**925**	**.345**	**.274**

PITCHERS	W	L	S	IP	H	ER	BB	K	ERA	RATIO
AVERY, STEVE	18	6	0	223.33	216	73	43	125	2.94	1.160
CORMIER, RHEAL	7	6	0	123.66	137	56	23	69	4.08	1.294
GOODEN, DWIGHT	12	15	0	208.67	188	80	61	149	3.45	1.193
HARKEY, MIKE	10	10	0	157.33	187	92	43	67	5.26	1.462
HOWELL, JAY	2	3	0	54.66	47	15	15	37	2.47	1.134
MULHOLLAND, TERRY	3	1	0	55.00	54	27	12	34	4.42	1.200
ROJAS, MEL	5	8	10	88.33	80	29	30	48	2.95	1.245
TANANA, FRANK	6	12	0	146.00	167	78	43	86	4.81	1.438
WATSON, ALLEN	6	7	0	86.00	90	44	28	49	4.60	1.372
WILLIAMS, MITCH	1	4	17	25.00	24	10	27	28	3.60	2.040
WORRELL, TIM	2	7	0	91.33	98	52	40	47	5.12	1.511
*BELINDA, STAN	3	1	19	42.33	35	17	11	30	3.61	1.087
*GARDINER, MIKE	0	1	0	11.67	14	8	7	7	6.17	1.799
#MASON, ROGER	0	7	0	18.00	25	12	7	12	6.00	1.778
**OTHERS (2)	0	0	0	8.67	12	7	2	5	7.27	1.614
TOTALS	**75**	**88**	**46**	**1339.99**	**1374**	**600**	**392**	**793**	**4.03**	**1.318**

Eisenberg Furriers
Owner: Lee Eisenberg

1993 Highlights: Filled six open offensive slots at draft with Dan Walters, Mike Scioscia, Tim Wallach, Kevin Bass, Tom Goodwin, and Greg Briley . . . With that Murderers' Row, what's surprising is that Furriers finished at all, much less in first division . . . Led league for 14th consecutive season in roster moves. That's *no* surprise. **1994 Outlook:** Any Furrier team with speed (Delino DeShields, $31) and a closer (John Wetteland, $15) figures to be in contention . . . Phil Plantier ($21), Dave Hollins ($15), and Dante Bichette ($17) guarantee it.

FINAL ROSTER

BATTERS	AB	H	BB	HR	RBI	SB	R	OBA	BA
AUSMUS, BRAD	89	26	3	3	9	0	13	.315	.292
BARBERIE, BRET	370	104	33	5	33	2	44	.339	.281
DESHIELDS, DELINO	481	142	72	2	29	43	75	.386	.295
DORSETT, BRIAN	58	15	3	2	10	0	6	.295	.258
HOLLINS, DAVE	539	148	85	18	93	2	104	.373	.274
HOWARD, THOMAS	129	35	10	3	12	4	20	.323	.271
LANSING, MIKE	491	141	46	3	45	23	64	.348	.287
MCGEE, WILLIE	462	139	38	4	43	10	51	.354	.300
MORRIS, HAL	373	118	34	7	49	2	47	.373	.316
PLANTIER, PHIL	448	111	58	34	100	4	67	.333	.247
ROBERSON, KEVIN	162	31	11	7	24	0	18	.242	.191
SMITH, OZZIE	545	157	43	1	53	21	75	.340	.288
WALLACH, TIM	454	98	30	11	61	0	41	.264	.215
*BICHETTE, DANTE	538	167	28	21	89	14	92	.344	.310
#BASS, KEVIN	103	24	5	1	15	1	11	.268	.233
#BRILEY, GREG	143	31	8	3	11	6	14	.258	.216
#GEREN, BOB	89	18	9	0	1	0	5	.275	.202
#HIGGINS, KEVIN	131	30	13	0	6	0	12	.298	.229
#WALTERS, DAN	94	19	7	1	10	0	6	.257	.202
**OTHERS (9)	148	16	10	1	12	3	11	.176	.108
TOTALS	**5847**	**1575**	**546**	**128**	**705**	**135**	**776**	**.331**	**.269**

PITCHERS	W	L	S	IP	H	ER	BB	K	ERA	RATIO
ANDERSEN, LARRY	3	0	0	44.67	36	7	12	46	1.41	1.075
DAVIS, MARK	0	3	2	26.00	32	14	15	29	4.85	1.808
DEWEY, MARK	1	2	5	21.67	13	7	10	14	2.91	1.061
HERNANDEZ, XAVIER	3	5	7	79.67	67	24	27	84	2.71	1.180
JOHNSTON, JOEL	1	3	2	33.00	21	12	14	13	3.27	1.061
MADDUX, GREG	20	10	0	267.00	228	70	52	197	2.36	1.049
REYNOSO, ARMANDO	9	8	0	125.67	137	58	42	77	4.15	1.424
ROGERS, KEVIN	0	2	0	58.67	51	18	23	45	2.76	1.261
ROPER, JOHN	0	2	0	34.00	41	21	15	24	5.56	1.647
SCANLAN, BOB	2	3	0	32.66	24	13	9	22	3.58	1.010
SMOLTZ, JOHN	15	11	0	243.67	208	98	100	208	3.62	1.264
WETTELAND, JOHN	9	3	43	85.33	58	13	28	113	1.37	1.008
WILLIAMS, BRIAN	2	2	1	50.33	53	31	29	37	5.54	1.629
*CASTILLO, FRANK	5	8	0	133.33	152	69	36	79	4.66	1.410
#RIVERA, BEN	10	7	0	116.66	137	71	57	86	5.48	1.663
**OTHERS (6)	4	7	0	76.00	77	38	28	51	4.50	1.382
TOTALS	**84**	**76**	**60**	**1428.33**	**1335**	**564**	**497**	**1125**	**3.55**	**1.283**

#6

Stein Brenners
Owner: Harry Stein

1993 Highlights: Coming off ninth-place finish in 1992, once-mighty Brenners invested $11 in Jack Clark. Yes, *Jack* Clark ... Front office reasoning went something like this: Montreal had signed Clark to minor league contract at end of spring training and didn't have anybody to play first base, so Clark would be called up in May, hit 30–35 home runs, and spearhead Brenners' climb back to top of Rotisserie heap. **1994 Outlook:** Counting on Willie McCovey to come back and fill hole left by *Will* Clark in San Francisco.

FINAL ROSTER

BATTERS	AB	H	BB	HR	RBI	SB	R	OBA	BA
ALOU, MOISES	482	138	38	18	85	17	70	.338	.286
BASS, KEVIN	63	21	12	0	8	2	11	.440	.333
BERRY, SEAN	137	36	19	8	24	7	29	.352	.262
BRUMFIELD, JACOB	148	37	7	3	15	12	17	.283	.250
BUTLER, BRETT	607	181	86	1	42	39	80	.385	.298
CASTILLA, VINNY	337	86	13	9	30	2	36	.282	.255
GANT, RON	606	166	67	36	117	26	113	.346	.273
JUSTICE, DAVE	585	158	78	40	120	3	90	.355	.270
MCKNIGHT, JEFF	133	38	9	1	9	0	16	.330	.285
MURRAY, EDDIE	610	174	40	27	100	2	77	.329	.285
PIAZZA, MIKE	547	174	46	35	112	3	81	.370	.318
SCARSONE, STEVE	68	13	1	1	8	0	7	.202	.191
SMITH, LONNIE	199	57	43	6	24	9	35	.413	.286
TAUBENSEE, EDDIE	288	72	21	9	42	1	26	.300	.250
YOUNG, KEVIN	449	106	36	6	47	2	38	.292	.236
*SAUNDERS, DOUG	38	7	2	0	0	0	3	.225	.184
*TUBBS, GERRY	38	7	8	1	2	2	7	.326	.184
#FERNANDEZ, TONY	173	39	25	1	14	6	20	.323	.225
#STRAWBERRY, DARRYL	93	14	16	5	11	1	12	.275	.150
**OTHERS (2)	24	2	1	0	0	1	1	.125	.083
TOTALS	**5625**	**1526**	**568**	**207**	**810**	**135**	**769**	**.338**	**.271**

PITCHERS	W	L	S	IP	H	ER	BB	K	ERA	RATIO
BROCAIL, DOUG	2	8	0	81.66	94	42	25	48	4.63	1.457
CANDIOTTI, TOM	8	10	0	213.67	192	74	71	155	3.12	1.231
DRABEK, DOUG	2	6	0	71.33	85	36	21	53	4.54	1.486
HARRIS, GREG	11	17	0	225.33	239	115	69	123	4.59	1.367
HARVEY, BRYAN	0	2	14	23.00	11	3	5	20	1.17	0.696
HILL, KEN	2	4	0	60.00	63	28	25	30	4.20	1.467
HOLMES, DARREN	3	3	25	66.67	56	30	20	60	4.05	1.140
MERCKER, KENT	2	0	0	26.00	23	8	18	27	2.77	1.577
PORTUGAL, MARK	18	4	0	208.00	194	64	77	131	2.77	1.303
*AYALA, BOBBY	4	4	3	53.33	50	33	25	40	5.57	1.406
*LUEBBERS, LARRY	0	3	0	37.00	40	21	19	16	5.11	1.595
#BECK, ROB	2	1	31	50.33	34	8	6	61	1.43	0.795
#RODRIGUEZ, RICH	2	3	2	24.00	28	11	9	18	4.13	1.542
#WAKEFIELD, TIM	4	8	0	95.00	112	67	61	43	6.35	1.821
**OTHERS (2)	0	0	0	3.33	4	3	7	4	8.10	3.303
TOTALS	**60**	**73**	**75**	**1238.67**	**1225**	**543**	**458**	**829**	**3.95**	**1.359**

Pollet Burros
Owner: Michael Pollet

1993 Highlights: Holy Kool-Aid! Left draft table with nine starters and Jimmy Jones . . . Burros made exactly one roster move during entire season—and it wasn't to replace Scott Pose, who remained a Burro all season despite being sent to minors in April. In June, they sat down Frank Seminara and brought up Dave Otto. Rotisserie fans the world over asked one question: Why? **1994 Outlook:** John Burkett ($10) and Billy Swift ($11) make great one-two punch, but after that the Burro staff is nothing but Frank Seminaras and Dave Ottos . . . Offense? Two stallions, Orestes Destrade ($22) and Mark Grace ($18), and a bunch of donkeys.

FINAL ROSTER

BATTERS	AB	H	BB	HR	RBI	SB	R	OBA	BA
BONILLA, BOBBY	502	133	72	34	87	3	81	.357	.264
CAMINITI, KEN	543	142	49	13	75	8	75	.322	.261
CONINE, JEFF	595	174	52	12	79	2	75	.349	.292
CORDERO, WIL	475	118	34	10	58	12	56	.298	.248
DESTRADE, ORESTES	569	145	58	20	87	0	61	.323	.254
GRACE, MARK	594	193	71	14	98	8	86	.396	.324
GRISSOM, MARQUIS	630	188	52	19	95	53	104	.351	.298
HUNDLEY, TODD	417	95	23	11	53	1	40	.268	.227
PECOTA, BILL	62	20	2	0	5	1	17	.343	.322
POSE, SCOTT	41	8	2	0	3	0	0	.232	.195
SAMUEL, JUAN	261	60	23	4	26	9	31	.292	.229
SLAUGHT, DON	377	113	29	10	55	2	34	.349	.299
SMITH, DWIGHT	310	93	25	11	35	8	51	.352	.300
TOTALS	**5376**	**1482**	**492**	**158**	**756**	**107**	**711**	**.336**	**.275**

PITCHERS	W	L	S	IP	H	ER	BB	K	ERA	RATIO
BURKETT, JOHN	22	7	0	231.67	224	94	40	145	3.65	1.140
FERNANDEZ, SID	5	6	0	119.67	82	39	36	81	2.93	0.986
HAMMOND, CHRIS	11	12	0	191.00	207	99	66	108	4.66	1.429
JONES, JIMMY	4	1	0	39.67	47	28	9	21	6.35	1.412
MORGAN, MIKE	10	15	0	207.67	206	93	74	111	4.03	1.348
OTTO, DAVE	2	2	0	47.00	65	28	21	20	5.36	1.830
SMITH, ZANE	3	7	0	83.00	97	42	22	32	4.55	1.434
SWIFT, BILL	21	8	0	232.67	195	73	55	157	2.82	1.074
WALK, BOB	13	14	0	187.00	214	118	70	80	5.68	1.519
WILSON, TREVOR	7	5	0	110.00	110	44	40	57	3.60	1.364
*SEMINARA, FRANK	1	2	0	32.67	43	20	14	13	5.51	1.745
TOTALS	**99**	**79**	**0**	**1482.00**	**1490**	**678**	**447**	**825**	**4.12**	**1.307**

Sklar Gazers
Owner: Robert Sklar

1993 Highlights: Back in big leagues after year-long sabbatical spent in Soho observatory watching old movies ... Barry Bonds won Oscar for actually being worth the 47 bucks Gazers shelled out to get him ... New book by chief astronomer, *Film: An International History of the Medium,* earned rave reviews. **1994 Outlook:** Once again free to concentrate on baseball, Gazers front office hopes to build smash hit around Jeff Fassero ($5), Greg McMichael ($7), Pedro Martinez ($5), and Charlie Hayes ($17) ... Should Gazers hold on to Bonds in hope of even better sequel?

FINAL ROSTER

BATTERS	AB	H	BB	HR	RBI	SB	R	OBA	BA
BENAVIDES, FREDDIE	102	30	1	2	14	1	7	.300	.294
BENJAMIN, MIKE	138	27	8	3	14	0	19	.239	.195
BONDS, BARRY	539	181	126	46	123	29	129	.461	.335
CARREON, MARK	150	49	13	7	33	1	22	.380	.326
CIANFROCCO, ARCI	282	71	17	12	48	2	30	.294	.251
COSTO, TIM	81	19	4	3	9	0	12	.270	.234
HARRIS, LENNY	160	38	15	2	11	3	20	.302	.237
HAYES, CHARLIE	573	175	43	25	98	11	89	.353	.305
LEMKE, MARK	493	124	65	7	49	1	52	.338	.251
LOPEZ, JAVIER	9	3	0	0	0	0	0	.333	.333
MARTINEZ, DAVE	241	58	27	5	27	6	28	.317	.240
RODRIGUEZ, HENRY	169	39	10	8	23	1	20	.273	.230
WILSON, DAN	76	17	9	0	8	0	6	.305	.223
*BELL, JUAN	65	13	5	0	7	0	5	.257	.200
*TATUM, JIM	78	18	4	1	11	0	5	.268	.230
*VILLANUEVA, HECTOR	55	8	4	3	9	0	7	.203	.145
#MURPHY, DALE	42	6	5	0	7	0	1	.234	.142
#VAN SLYKE, ANDY	242	78	20	6	39	10	32	.374	.322
TOTALS	**3495**	**954**	**376**	**130**	**530**	**65**	**484**	**.343**	**.272**

PITCHERS	W	L	S	IP	H	ER	BB	K	ERA	RATIO
BENES, ANDY	15	15	0	230.67	200	97	86	179	3.78	1.240
BOTTENFIELD, KENT	4	9	0	131.00	147	82	64	48	5.63	1.611
BURBA, DAVE	5	1	0	62.33	61	29	28	63	4.19	1.428
DIBBLE, ROB	1	4	18	39.67	34	30	38	48	6.81	1.815
FASSERO, JEFF	12	5	1	149.67	119	38	54	140	2.29	1.156
HERSHISER, OREL	12	14	0	215.67	201	86	72	141	3.59	1.266
MARTINEZ, DENNIS	15	9	1	224.67	211	96	64	138	3.85	1.224
MARTINEZ, PEDRO	10	5	2	107.00	76	31	57	119	2.61	1.243
MCMICHAEL, GREG	2	3	19	91.67	68	21	29	89	2.06	1.058
REARDON, JEFF	4	6	8	61.67	66	28	10	35	4.09	1.232
#PUGH, TIM	3	9	0	78.33	101	47	25	39	5.40	1.609
TOTALS	**83**	**80**	**49**	**1392.33**	**1284**	**585**	**527**	**1039**	**3.78**	**1.301**

Fleder Mice
Owner: Rob Fleder

1993 Highlights: Cheese whiz! The Mice genuinely believed that Darrell Sherman would prove to be steal of 1993 draft ... They also believed Ray Lankford and Will Clark would have normal seasons (i.e., with numbers befitting their salaries) ... Gregg Jefferies unanimous choice as Most Valuable Mouse. **1994 Outlook:** Count on 30 wins for two bucks from Curt Schilling ($1) and Kevin Gross ($1) ... Count on Mark Whiten ($1) to leap tall buildings in a single bound ... And count on Mice to bounce back to traditional and appropriate finish: fourth place.

FINAL ROSTER

BATTERS	AB	H	BB	HR	RBI	SB	R	OBA	BA
ALICEA, LUIS	362	101	47	3	46	11	50	.361	.279
BERRYHILL, DAMON	335	82	21	8	43	0	24	.289	.244
CLARK, WILL	491	139	63	14	73	2	82	.364	.283
DAULTON, DARREN	179	47	36	6	27	2	28	.386	.262
EISENREICH, JIM	362	115	26	7	54	5	51	.363	.317
FRAZIER, LOU	167	48	12	1	14	14	20	.335	.287
JEFFERIES, GREGG	544	186	62	16	83	46	89	.409	.341
JONES, CHRIS	172	43	9	2	22	8	19	.287	.250
LANKFORD, RAY	401	96	81	7	45	14	63	.367	.239
MORANDINI, MICKEY	425	105	34	3	33	13	57	.302	.247
SABO, CHRIS	552	143	43	21	82	6	86	.312	.259
SANCHEZ, REY	344	97	15	0	28	1	35	.311	.281
WHITEN, MARK	562	142	58	25	99	15	81	.322	.252
#OLSON, GREG	237	52	24	4	23	1	19	.291	.219
#YOUNG, ERIC	357	92	38	1	28	27	58	.329	.257
**OTHERS (3)	92	24	11	1	9	2	11	.380	.261
TOTALS	**5582**	**1512**	**580**	**119**	**709**	**167**	**773**	**.339**	**.270**

PITCHERS	W	L	S	IP	H	ER	BB	K	ERA	RATIO
BAUTISTA, JOSE	5	1	2	35.00	37	15	10	19	3.86	1.343
BOSKIE, SHAWN	3	2	0	38.00	39	13	12	23	3.08	1.342
COOKE, STEVE	10	10	0	210.67	207	91	59	132	3.89	1.263
GROSS, KEVIN	13	13	0	202.33	224	93	74	150	4.14	1.473
NABHOLZ, CHRIS	7	7	0	84.67	80	40	47	54	4.25	1.500
RIJO, JOSE	14	9	0	257.33	218	71	62	227	2.48	1.088
SANFORD, MO	0	2	0	23.33	27	18	17	25	6.94	1.886
SCHILLING, CURT	7	1	0	85.00	87	35	20	82	3.71	1.259
SMITH, LEE	2	4	43	50.00	49	25	9	49	4.50	1.160
*CADARET, GREG	2	1	1	25.00	33	16	18	15	5.76	2.040
*MCELROY, CHUCK	2	1	0	22.67	18	12	12	18	4.76	1.323
*NEAGLE, DENNY	1	4	0	37.33	48	31	21	31	7.47	1.848
*TURNER, MATT	0	0	0	2.67	0	0	1	4	0.00	0.375
#BEDROSIAN, STEVE	1	0	0	18.33	12	2	6	12	0.98	0.982
#HEREDIA, GIL	1	2	0	18.33	28	14	3	11	6.87	1.691
#STANTON, MIKE	4	3	27	37.67	34	16	18	29	3.82	1.380
#WHITEHURST, WALLY	3	4	0	74.00	73	32	25	35	3.89	1.324
**OTHERS (4)	1	0	1	21.00	28	17	7	11	7.29	1.667
TOTALS	**76**	**65**	**74**	**1243.33**	**1242**	**541**	**421**	**927**	**3.92**	**1.338**

#10

Okrent Fenokees
Owner: Daniel Okrent

1993 Highlights: Injuries to Kevin Mitchell, Ryne Sandberg, and Barry Larkin knocked Fenokees out of pennant race while the dew was still on the roses ... Brightest spots of season were All-Star play of Little League second-sacker John Okrent and bravura debut of dazzling Flamenco dancer Lydia Okrent. **1994 Outlook:** Rich Wilkins ($3) and Darryl Kile ($2) form great battery, but after that come 21 question marks ... For instance: Cliff Floyd ($10), Chipper Jones ($10), and Shawon Dunston ($4) ... Big years from all three and Fenokees are in hunt.

FINAL ROSTER

BATTERS	AB	H	BB	HR	RBI	SB	R	OBA	BA
BOLICK, FRANK	213	45	23	4	24	1	25	.288	.211
BOSTON, DARYL	291	76	26	14	40	1	46	.321	.261
CLARK, PHIL	198	58	29	9	32	1	29	.383	.292
GALARRAGA, ANDRES	161	53	6	7	28	0	23	.353	.329
INCAVIGLIA, PETE	368	101	21	24	89	1	60	.313	.274
MAY, DERRICK	112	28	6	1	15	3	14	.288	.250
NIXON, OTIS	461	124	61	1	24	47	77	.354	.268
PRATT, TODD	82	24	5	4	12	0	7	.333	.292
SHARPERSON, MIKE	90	23	5	2	10	2	13	.294	.255
WILKINS, RICH	165	49	19	10	30	1	32	.369	.296
*HUNTER, BRIAN	79	11	2	0	8	0	4	.160	.139
#BELL, DEREK	352	87	16	14	46	15	46	.279	.247
#DUNCAN, MARIANO	283	76	8	7	40	5	40	.288	.268
#HERNANDEZ, CARLOS	53	12	2	2	3	0	4	.254	.226
#LARKIN, BARRY	354	112	45	8	49	13	52	.393	.316
#MITCHELL, KEVIN	262	93	19	15	58	1	47	.398	.354
#SANDBERG, RYNE	269	80	21	7	34	8	37	.348	.297
**OTHERS (3)	60	9	2	0	5	0	11	.183	.150
TOTALS	**3860**	**1061**	**316**	**129**	**547**	**99**	**567**	**.329**	**.274**

PITCHERS	W	L	S	IP	H	ER	BB	K	ERA	RATIO
BARNES, BRIAN	2	6	3	100.00	105	49	48	60	4.41	1.530
BRANTLEY, JEFF	5	6	0	113.67	112	54	46	76	4.28	1.390
KILE, DARRYL	15	8	0	171.67	152	67	69	141	3.51	1.287
OSUNA, AL	0	1	0	15.00	10	4	8	12	2.40	1.200
RUFFIN, JOHNNY	1	0	2	35.00	30	11	11	24	2.83	1.171
SCOTT, TIM	7	2	1	71.67	69	24	34	65	3.01	1.437
THIGPEN, BOBBY	2	1	0	17.33	22	12	9	9	6.23	1.788
WAGNER, PAUL	8	8	2	141.33	143	67	42	114	4.27	1.309
WAYNE, GARY	3	0	0	25.00	24	13	9	21	4.68	1.320
WOHLERS, MARK	1	2	0	24.67	23	18	15	22	6.57	1.540
*MADDUX, MIKE	0	5	2	31.67	30	19	15	25	5.40	1.421
#GLAVINE, TOM	12	4	0	148.67	136	48	61	61	2.91	1.325
#MULHOLLAND, TERRY	9	8	0	136.00	123	42	28	82	2.78	1.110
#WILLIAMS, MITCH	2	3	26	37.00	32	13	17	32	3.16	1.324
**OTHERS (3)	2	0	2	12.00	16	8	11	8	6.00	2.250
TOTALS	**69**	**54**	**38**	**1080.67**	**1027**	**449**	**423**	**752**	**3.74**	**1.342**

#11

Cary Nations
Owner: Cary Schneider

NATIONS

1993 Highlights: When handwriting appeared on clubhouse wall, Nations front office got on phone. Nobody rebuilds faster and better with late-season deals; last season was no exception, as Nations wheeled and dealed like latter-day Frank Lane (the GM, not the singer). When dust settled, Nations had nucleus of 1994 pennant winner. **1994 Outlook:** Evidence? Try Bernard Gilkey ($7), Deion Sanders ($3), Eric Karros ($7), Bob Tewksbury ($9), Salomon Torres ($5), and *three* cheap closers—Rod Beck ($5), Jim Gott ($1), and Mike Perez ($5).

FINAL ROSTER

BATTERS	AB	H	BB	HR	RBI	SB	R	OBA	BA
BATISTE, KIM	156	44	3	5	29	0	14	.295	.282
GILKEY, BERNARD	557	170	56	16	70	15	99	.368	.305
JACKSON, DARRIN	79	17	2	1	7	0	4	.234	.215
KARROS, ERIC	619	153	34	23	80	0	74	.286	.247
MCCLENDON, LLOYD	75	18	8	0	9	0	7	.313	.240
PAGNOZZI, TOM	313	77	19	6	37	1	27	.289	.246
PAPPAS, ERIK	158	38	25	1	17	0	20	.344	.240
PRINCE, TOM	94	18	8	2	15	1	11	.254	.191
SANDERS, DEION	272	75	16	6	28	19	42	.315	.275
SNYDER, CORY	202	54	20	5	18	0	26	.333	.267
VAN SLYKE, ANDY	81	22	4	2	11	1	10	.305	.271
WALKER, CHICO	79	18	4	2	7	4	7	.265	.227
YOUNG, ERIC	133	40	25	2	14	15	24	.411	.300
*WILSON, WILLIE	193	46	10	0	6	7	24	.275	.238
#BERRY, SEAN	162	42	22	6	25	5	21	.347	.259
#DAULTON, DARREN	331	84	81	18	78	3	62	.400	.253
#MALDONADO, CANDY	118	22	13	3	13	0	8	.267	.186
#PENDLETON, TERRY	421	110	21	8	47	1	51	.296	.261
#ROBERTS, BIP	292	70	38	1	18	26	45	.327	.239
#THOMPSON, ROB	317	100	24	9	41	10	53	.363	.315
**OTHERS (4)	137	36	17	8	22	0	19	.387	.263
TOTALS	**4789**	**1254**	**450**	**124**	**592**	**108**	**648**	**.325**	**.261**

PITCHERS	W	L	S	IP	H	ER	BB	K	ERA	RATIO
BECK, ROB	1	0	17	29.00	23	11	7	25	3.41	1.034
BEDROSIAN, STEVE	4	2	0	28.33	21	7	6	19	2.22	0.953
GOTT, JIM	4	8	25	77.67	71	20	17	67	2.32	1.133
PEREZ, MIKE	3	0	4	25.33	23	8	4	17	2.84	1.066
SMITH, PETE	3	8	0	89.67	92	44	36	53	4.42	1.427
TEWKSBURY, BOB	17	10	0	213.67	258	91	20	97	3.83	1.301
TORRES, SALOMON	2	5	0	37.67	32	17	25	17	4.06	1.513
*BOWEN, RYAN	7	12	0	143.67	147	76	81	91	4.76	1.587
*EILAND, DAVE	0	2	0	41.33	54	28	14	11	6.10	1.645
#DRABEK, DOUG	7	12	0	166.33	157	64	39	104	3.46	1.178
#GIBSON, PAUL	0	1	0	4.00	9	5	1	4	11.25	2.500
#HARVEY, BRYAN	1	3	31	46.00	34	10	8	53	1.96	0.913
#HICKERSON, BRYAN	5	1	0	49.33	57	31	15	23	5.66	1.459
#JACKSON, DANNY	7	6	0	122.33	125	55	42	66	4.05	1.365
**OTHERS (10)	6	9	6	100.00	117	52	35	68	4.68	1.520
TOTALS	**67**	**77**	**83**	**1166.33**	**1211**	**514**	**349**	**711**	**3.97**	**1.338**

McCall De Sax
Owner: Bruce McCall

1993 Highlights: Predictably enough, De Sax GM shelled out $41 for fellow Canadian Larry Walker. From that point, it was all downhill ... Bullpen led by Jeff Innis ... Outfield patrolled by Ozzie Canseco, Alex Cole, Junior Felix, and Mitch Webster (along with Orlando Merced and Walker) ... Rotation headed by Ken Hill and John Smiley ... Middle anchored by Walt Weiss and Jody Reed ... Thud! **1994 Outlook:** New owner (Jay Lovinger), new name (Lovinger Spoonfuls), new hopes (world peace, end to poverty, shorter movie lines, *etc.*) ... Can Jeromy Burnitz ($2) shoulder load?

FINAL ROSTER

BATTERS	AB	H	BB	HR	RBI	SB	R	OBA	BA
BUECHELE, STEVE	460	125	48	15	65	1	53	.340	.271
CANSECO, OZZIE	17	3	1	0	0	0	0	.222	.176
COLE, ALEX	348	89	43	0	24	30	50	.337	.255
FELIX, JUNIOR	214	51	10	7	22	2	25	.272	.238
FLETCHER, DARREN	396	101	34	9	60	0	33	.313	.255
JORDAN, RICKY	159	46	8	5	18	0	21	.323	.289
LAVALLIERE, MIKE	5	1	0	0	0	0	0	.200	.200
MERCED, ORLANDO	447	140	77	8	70	3	68	.414	.313
MILLIGAN, RANDY	234	64	46	6	29	0	30	.392	.273
REED, JODY	445	123	38	2	31	1	48	.333	.276
VIZCAINO, JOSE	356	93	33	3	36	6	52	.323	.261
WALKER, LARRY	490	130	80	22	86	29	85	.368	.265
WEBSTER, MITCH	172	42	11	2	14	4	26	.289	.244
WEISS, WALT	500	133	79	1	39	7	50	.366	.266
*CANDAELE, CASEY	37	7	2	0	1	0	4	.230	.189
TOTALS	**4280**	**1148**	**510**	**80**	**495**	**83**	**545**	**.346**	**.268**

PITCHERS	W	L	S	IP	H	ER	BB	K	ERA	RATIO
ARMSTRONG, JACK	5	12	0	118.33	134	64	55	59	4.87	1.597
ASSENMACHER, PAUL	2	1	0	38.67	44	15	13	34	3.49	1.474
BROWNING, TOM	7	7	0	114.00	159	60	20	53	4.74	1.570
GUZMAN, JOSE	12	10	0	191.00	188	92	74	163	4.34	1.372
HOUGH, CHARLIE	9	16	0	204.33	202	97	71	126	4.27	1.336
INNIS, JEFF	2	3	3	76.67	81	35	38	36	4.11	1.552
JACKSON, DANNY	5	5	0	88.00	89	33	38	54	3.38	1.443
LANCASTER, LES	1	1	0	22.33	16	5	7	14	2.01	1.030
SCHOUREK, PETE	5	12	0	128.33	168	85	45	72	5.96	1.660
#HARNISCH, PETE	6	4	0	95.33	82	38	35	85	3.59	1.227
#HILL, KEN	6	2	0	99.67	75	29	40	45	2.62	1.154
#SMILEY, JOHN	3	7	0	80.33	73	43	22	50	4.82	1.183
TOTALS	**63**	**80**	**3**	**1257.00**	**1311**	**596**	**458**	**791**	**4.27**	**1.407**

NOW YOU SEE HIM, NOW YOU DON'T

October 12, 1993

The Hon. Cary Schneider
President
The Rotisserie League

Dear Cary,

Enclosed is the McCall De Sax Base Ball Club's entry and exit fee into and out of the Original Rotisserie Base Ball League Inc., minus transaction fees, of which we have no record, having fired our general manager in April as part of the rebuilding program announced on Opening Day.

Perhaps the club should have heeded critics and nicknamed itself the McCall De Bacles. Perhaps Marge Schott's dog should have been in charge of day-to-day operations, as also suggested. Attendance was virtually nonexistent, and merchandise sales tended to reflect the failure of the "de Sax" moniker to not only catch on but to be, as one observer noted, comprehensible.

And yet, as if fulfilling a prophecy, the De Sax did quickly move into and never left the dead-end street that was their namesake. Not since the Seattle Pilots piloted themselves into a craggy reef has a club nickname been so aptly, chillingly accurate. Of this at least, we can be proud, or at least conscious.

Thanking you for your patience and forbearance during this period of grief and agony that some called the 1993 season, we remain,

The McCall De Sax

Editor's Note: *The president of the former McCall De Sacks was a founding member of The Rotisserie League. He went out for a cigar after the 1980 season and did not return until last year. We expect to hear from him again in, oh, 2006 or so.*

ROTI·STATS TOP TEAMS OF 1993

Here are some of the top 1993 Rotisserie teams around the country as tracked by Roti·Stats and the RLBA's former stats service. These teams managed to capture the highest percentage of their leagues' possible points. A standard league is one with twelve teams that use the original eight Rotisserie scoring categories.

STANDARD NATIONAL LEAGUES

#	% Pts.	TEAM	LEAGUE	ST	HR	RBI	SB	AVG	W	SV	ERA	RTO
1.	97.4	Mississippi Mud	Great Desert Rotisserie	CA	232	913	179	.288	93	64	3.29	1.21
2.	89.6	Rumson Jeremys	Catch 22 League	VA	180	810	170	.283	72	104	3.39	1.22
3.	88.0	LA Fog	249 Rotisserie League	MA	196	823	186	.282	68	51	3.64	1.24
4.	86.5	Mudhens	Memorial Hospital Docs	NJ	178	787	157	.276	83	63	3.57	1.27
5.	86.5	Rebels	Golden Hind Baseball Assoc.	CA	161	737	181	.281	80	79	3.14	1.17
6.	86.5	Delta Force	13th Street League	NY	175	809	165	.279	78	60	3.27	1.21
7.	85.4	Spectacles	Golden Hind Baseball Assoc.	CA	210	943	167	.287	89	48	3.69	1.25
8.	85.4	Shiite Muslims	Atlanta Rot-Ball League	GA	209	854	126	.275	96	86	3.73	1.28
9.	85.4	Donald's Ducks	Bowling League	CA	192	953	156	.278	81	69	3.78	1.28
10.	85.4	Saperstone Agers	Knickerbocker Pioneer	NY	182	835	147	.269	103	89	3.47	1.27

STANDARD AMERICAN LEAGUES

#	% Pts.	TEAM	LEAGUE	ST	HR	RBI	SB	AVG	W	SV	ERA	RTO
1.	94.3	Martin Eeks	Mesquite League	CT	174	851	198	.283	92	73	3.71	1.28
2.	91.7	Battle's Bombers	Bramble Bush League	FL	178	854	213	.270	85	79	3.50	1.29
3.	90.1	Senators	Junior League	NY	200	951	214	.274	81	67	3.96	1.29
4.	90.1	Knuckleheads	Armchair League	CA	232	914	177	.275	85	61	3.99	1.33
5.	88.0	Wagner Trains	Dublin League	NJ	222	964	195	.287	89	61	4.18	1.37
6.	86.9	Minneapolis	Branch Rickey League	MA	181	920	177	.270	84	73	4.03	1.36
7.	86.9	Bandwagon	Say Know To Drugs	NY	196	866	177	.268	93	59	3.76	1.32
8.	86.5	T-Balls	Steals & Deals League	CA	201	868	135	.270	71	71	4.05	1.32
9.	85.9	Beast From The East	Big AL From So Cal	CA	203	905	164	.279	86	51	3.87	1.34
10.	85.4	Solly Manders	Tony's Italian Kitchen	NY	204	861	147	.281	76	58	4.12	1.35

NOTABLE NON-STANDARD LEAGUES

#	% Pts.	TEAM	LEAGUE	ST	HR	RBI	SB	AVG	W	SV	ERA	RTO
1.	97.7	Sharks	Coast To Coast	TX	298	1213	261	.288	113	98	3.39	1.23
2.	94.8	Bombay Sapphires	Virgin Americans	VI	287	1126	244	.305	90	120	3.27	1.19
3.	93.8	Delta Cardinals LTD	Mudder of All Rotisserie	MD	210	920	165	.271	97	77	3.74	1.30
4.	93.8	Heavy Wangs	Mudder of All Rotisserie	MD	179	920	180	.281	84	68	3.70	1.28
5.	93.1	Dem Bums	No Turf, Domes or DH's	CA	241	994	207	.287	93	96	3.36	1.20
6.	93.1	Merhorn Rats	The Showbiz League	CA	227	1025	211	.281	79	81	3.16	1.17
7.	93.1	LAPD Sultans of SWAT	Creeping Alzheimer's	CA	218	961	213	.279	107	77	3.38	1.23
8.	93.1	Grunts	Bay Area Rotisserie Fiends	CA	210	999	230	.281	85	74	3.32	1.22
9.	93.0	Bradford Bradicals	Trans-America Roti All-Stars	CA	192	956	208	.283	101	96	3.24	1.22
10.	92.5	Pete's Putrocities	TBC Rotisserie League	MA	229	972	167	.277	79	45	3.71	1.27

ROTI·STATS MOST COMPETITIVE LEAGUES 1993

Talk about close pennant races! Here are some of the most competitive leagues around the country as tracked by Roti·Stats and the RLBA's former stats service. The "DIF" figure is the average point difference between the top five teams in a league. A standard league is one with twelve teams that uses the original eight Rotisserie scoring categories.

STANDARD NATIONAL LEAGUES

#	DIF	LEAGUE	ST	WINNER	1st	2nd	3rd	4th	5th
1.	2.25	First Church of the Holy Game	OR	ABC Bush Bombers	72.0	68.5	65.0	64.0	63.0
2.	2.25	MidLife Crisis League	IL	Big Stixx	67.0	66.5	64.5	59.0	58.0
3.	2.88	Johannsen Rotisserie League	CA	Great Danes	72.0	67.0	63.0	60.5	60.5
4.	3.25	Rotisserie League	NY	Wulfgang	73.5	64.5	61.5	61.0	60.5
5.	3.50	Greater Shreveport Rotisserie	LA	N.C. Hammers	70.0	70.0	61.0	57.0	56.0
6.	3.50	Cabarrus County League	NC	Steve's G-Men	72.0	62.0	61.5	59.5	58.0
7.	3.50	Legislative League	NY	Magic Moments	70.0	63.0	61.5	57.5	55.5
8.	3.63	Laguna National League	CA	Good Old Boys	78.0	76.0	72.0	63.5	63.5
9.	3.75	Blood & Guts League	CA	Hunt 4 Green October	73.5	69.5	68.0	61.5	58.5
10.	3.88	The Engel League	TN	Pierce Arrows	76.5	67.5	66.0	62.0	61.0

STANDARD AMERICAN LEAGUES

#	DIF	LEAGUE	ST	WINNER	1st	2nd	3rd	4th	5th
1.	2.13	Laguna American League	CA	Quick Turtles	71.5	71.0	70.5	68.5	63.0
2.	2.75	Bush League	MD	Caz Traders	77.0	75.5	75.0	67.0	66.0
3.	2.88	Found A Good Stat Service	ME	Budmen Brewers	72.0	69.0	66.5	62.5	60.5
4.	3.00	Greater Shreveport Rotisserie	LA	Thunder Lizards	77.0	74.0	70.0	69.0	65.0
5.	3.25	The Super Freak RBL	CA	Dan's Clan	76.0	74.0	69.0	68.5	63.0
6.	3.50	Beltway Bush League	VA	PH Balkers	76.0	70.0	68.5	64.0	62.0
7.	3.63	Athletes Relying on TV	CA	Whangkers	73.5	66.0	65.0	60.0	59.0
8.	3.63	Pro Bowlers AL Rotball League	IN	BeLoMe	73.5	68.5	67.0	60.5	59.0
9.	4.00	Bethesda League	MD	Marquette Yankees	73.0	70.0	69.5	58.0	57.0
10.	4.13	Say Know To Drugs	NY	Bandwagon	83.5	80.0	70.0	67.0	67.0

NOTABLE NON-STANDARD LEAGUES

#	DIF	LEAGUES	ST	WINNER	1st	2nd	3rd	4th	5th
1.	1.25	Mike & Ed's League	CA	Shotzies	53.0	52.0	50.5	50.5	48.0
2.	1.50	Beach Bum League	CA	Yogi Bears	62.0	60.0	57.5	57.0	56.0
3.	1.63	Notimer's League	CA	Brendan's Ball Bashers	49.5	48.0	45.5	43.5	43.0
4.	1.63	McKinsey & Company	NY	Outlanders	39.5	37.0	36.5	34.0	33.0
5.	1.75	Universal Baseball	CA	Diamond House Camerons	92.0	92.0	88.0	87.0	85.0
6.	1.75	Anal Retent Gents	CA	Bruins	56.5	56.0	55.0	53.0	49.5
7.	1.75	Platte River League	MO	Wheaton Hams	53.0	51.0	50.0	47.5	46.0
8.	1.75	Tenenballs	KS	Troy & Kirk	44.0	42.0	40.5	39.0	37.0
9.	1.88	Son Of Lamppost	CA	Toast III	67.5	66.0	61.5	60.5	60.0
10.	1.88	Miami Heat	FL	Mayce's Maulers	65.0	64.0	60.0	59.0	57.5

SMARGANA 1994

Stumped? Like to punch out official Rotisserie anagramist Leon di Trinka's lights? Well, get in line . . . and while you're waiting, here are the solutions to SMARGANA 1994:

BASEBALL ANAGRAM #1: Meat Loving = Tom Glavine

BASEBALL ANAGRAM #2: I Slew Swat = Walt Weiss

BASEBALL ANAGRAM #3: Crazy Sheen = Rey Sanchez

BASEBALL ANAGRAM #4: Nasty Like Me = Mike Stanley

BASEBALL ANAGRAM #5: Nerdy Stalk = Len Dykstra

BASEBALL ANAGRAM #6: Hark! Soft Man? = Frank Thomas

BASEBALL ANAGRAM #7: Should Gnat? = Don Slaught

BASEBALL ANAGRAM #8: Bug Slide = Bud Selig

BASEBALL ANAGRAM #9: Moral? Boot Rear = Roberto Alomar

BASEBALL ANAGRAM #10: Round and Later = Darren Daulton

BASEBALL ANAGRAM #11: Shad Love? Nil = Dave Hollins

BASEBALL ANAGRAM #12: Alamo Pear Flier = Rafael Palmeiro

BASEBALL ANAGRAM #13: Eating a Bit Soon = Benito Santiago

BASEBALL ANAGRAM #14: Farm 'n' Varsity = Travis Fryman

BASEBALL ANAGRAM #15: Feign J.F.K. = Jeff King

BASEBALL ANAGRAM #16: Oil Palm Tour = Paul Molitor

BASEBALL ANAGRAM #17: Zen Bedding Rot = Todd Benzinger

BASEBALL ANAGRAM #18: Opening Amore = Geronimo Peña

BASEBALL ANAGRAM #19: Lace Toy Crony = Royce Clayton

BASEBALL ANAGRAM #20: S.O.B. Chairs = Chris Sabo

7

Front Office

How to Keep Score

Once upon a time, the entire front office complex of Rotisserie League
Baseball consisted of Beloved Founder and Former Commissioner-for-Life
Daniel Okrent. There is a fading daguerreotype of Marse Dan, one hand
clinching an unfiltered Camel, the other slowly stroking his abacus, sitting
alone in his Berkshire woodshed, from which post he spewed out—we use
the word advisedly—our fledgling league's biweekly standings every third
fortnight or so. We were having too much fun to know any better that first
season, but eventually we got smart and figured that the BFFCL would
never compile and distribute the standings in a timely fashion until his team,
the hapless Fenokees, got themselves in a pennant race and gave him something to crow about. Not willing to wait 'til the end of time or hell froze
over, whichever came first, we fired him.

That single, surgical act marked the yawning of a new Rotisserie Era.

You can still do your league's stats by hand, of course—if the task
required a mathematical genius, we'd still be waiting for our first standings
report for the 1980 season. All you need is a calculator and about four hours
of free time a week, every week of the season. (You're going to want weekly
standings, whether you know it now or not.) But it's tiresome, tedious work,
the only thing about Rotisserie League Baseball that isn't a whole gang of
fun. We don't recommend keeping score by hand, but if you want to give
it a shot, we'll be happy to send you a simple "Keeping Score" pamphlet
for free; just write **Rotisserie League Baseball Association, 370 Seventh
Avenue, Suite 312, New York, NY 10001.**

You can hire someone to do the stats by hand for you. We did that
from 1981 through 1983, and our first (and only) Director of Statistical
Services, Sandra Krempasky, was immortalized by election to the Rotisserie
Hall of Fame on the first ballot in recognition of her yeowoman effort.
Problem is, Sandra retired (actually, she was phased out by a computer), and
you're never going to find anyone as good as she was.

You can develop your own computer program for crunching Rotisserie
stats and put the family computer to better use than prepping for the SATs,
keeping track of the family fortune, or playing "Jeopardy." At least we think
you can. When it comes to computers, the Founding Fathers are still trying
to figure out why the light in the refrigerator comes on when you open the

---

door. Other people say it can be done, though—something to do with spreading sheets, we think.

The *best* thing you can do, of course, is to have **Roti•Stats** compile and compute your league's stats. **Roti•Stats** is now the exclusive, officially authorized stats service for Rotisserie League Baseball—the *only* stats service sanctioned by the Founding Fathers of the game. Most important, it's the *best* stats service in the business.

We know. Last year, after a decade of running our own stats service, we decided to hang up our spikes. We went looking for a new stats service. We examined them all, and we liked what we saw in **Roti•Stats**. They've been in business just about as long as Rotisserie League Baseball, and they have an unparalleled record for accuracy and timeliness. This year, in honor of Rotisserie League Baseball's anniversary, **Roti•Stats** designed a new report format, added new features, and even lowered some of their prices. Find out for yourself what they can do for your league. Call **Roti•Stats** toll-free at **800-884-7684**.

Roti•Stats!
(You Play. Let Roti•Stats Do the Hard Stuff.)

Each week **Roti•Stats** records your transactions, computes your standings, and rushes a report via first-class mail to your league secretary. (Fax, overnight express, and modem service available for the terminally anxious.) Each weekly report contains the standings, up-to-the-minute rosters for all teams, and a transactions update. American League and Mixed League reports go out Mondays (stats through Sunday's games). National League stats go out Tuesdays (stats through Monday's games). Your league can make free, unlimited transactions that may be made retroactively at any time. Player salaries, contract status, and positions are tracked at no additional cost. No hidden charges. Just one flat fee at the beginning of the season.

- *Guaranteed 24-Hour Turnaround of Opening Day Rosters!* Call **Roti•Stats**' 800 number within 24 hours of submitting your rosters and get your standings right over the phone. Most services make you wait two to three weeks for your first standings report. **Roti•Stats** knows how anxious your owners are to find out where they stand from the first crack of the bat.
- *Free Agent List!* Each weekly report includes a list of unowned players in your league, complete with weekly and year-to-date stats for *every* player in the league.
- *Free Custom Comment Page!* You may add an extra page to your weekly report containing important information for your league mem-

bers. Many leagues use this page to reflect up-to-the-minute waiver information or to conduct general business among league members.

- **How Your Team Stacks Up Nationwide!** Periodically you'll receive special reports such as "Top Teams" in the country, "Tightest Pennant Races," and much more (see pages 297–298). You'll see how well your team and league stack up against other **Roti•Stats** leagues nationwide.

- **Additional Stat Categories!** Want more than the original eight scoring categories? No problem. Their state-of-the art software lets you include any alternate scoring categories you want—at no extra charge.

- **Same Day & Overnight Fax Service!** Reduced fax charges permit your owners to receive their standings report the fastest and most efficient way possible—the same day they are generated. (Monday for AL and Mixed; Tuesday for NL).

- **Player Value and Position Eligibility Reports!** Player values are generated by **Roti•Stats'** own proven formulas based on stats for the last two years for each player (by position). An invaluable tool on auction-draft day. Also free: a Position Eligibility Report that shows all positions for which each player is eligible to be drafted.

- **Farm System Update!** Every month, an up-to-date stats review of 50 top minor leaguers. You'll know who's been doing what down on the farm when midsummer callups hit the free agent pool.

- **Free League Administration Software!** You can use this program to submit moves to **Roti•Stats** each week or just use it to track your league fees. The fee reports alone make this a tremendous aid for your secretary.

- **The Roti•Tiller Newsletter!** Dig the latest dirt in Rotisserie baseball with **Roti•Stats'** highly unofficial, semi-irregular, not-always-polite newsletter called **The Roti•Tiller.** Designed to keep the Rotissespirit alive in your league, **The Roti•Tiller** spreads gossip, stirs up rumors, and occasionally even dispenses nuggets of useful information. Don't be surprised to see your name in headlines!

- **Multiple League Discounts!** Play in more than one league? The RLBA will discreetly provide you with a list of counselors in your region who might be able to help. Better still, **Roti•Stats** will provide significant discounts when all your leagues sign up for the best service in the game.

For complete information about **Roti•Stats**, the only stats service officialy authorized by the Founding Fathers of Rotisserie League Baseball, call toll free: **800-884-7684.** You'll get a sign-up kit, sample standings and special reports, and a lot more reasons why **Roti•Stats** should be *your* stats service. Did you get that number? It's still **800-884-7684**.

The RLBA Wants You!

You've collared a roomful of other baseball fanatics, memorized this book, subscribed to *Baseball America,* made *USA Today* a daily habit, found a newsstand that carries *USA Today Baseball Weekly,* bought every baseball mag on the racks, sent off for *Big Lew's Farm Report* (see page 307), and appointed someone else to bring chow for your first Auction Draft Day. What's next? Membership in the **Rotisserie League Baseball Association**. Join now and beat the Christmas rush. Here's what your league gets with membership in the **RLBA**:

1. ***Commissioner's Services.*** No need for your league to be rent asunder by rules disputes and internecine fighting: one Civil War was quite enough, thank you. For member leagues of the **RLBA,** we adjudicate disputes, interpret rules, issue Solomonic judgments, and otherwise maintain law and order so you can concentrate on playing the game.

2. ***Position Eligibility List.*** Complete and up-to-date. Updated every month during the season.

3. ***Quarterly Updates.*** Information on rules changes, news from other leagues, baseball gossip, and happenings around the Rotisseworld.

4. ***Opening Day Rosters.*** Official 25-man rosters, complete with last-minute disabled list moves and minor league promotions and demotions. Mailed to you Opening Day.

5. ***Monthly Farm System Updates.*** Progress reports and stat updates on the top 50 minor leaguers so you'll always know who's hot and who's not.

6. ***Championship Certificate.*** Signed by Beloved Founder and Former Commissioner-for-Life Daniel Okrent, this suitable-for-framing certificate is the perfect grace note for your pennant winner's rec room wall.

7. ***Company Store.*** The right to purchase an astonishing range of Rotisserie products at full retail price. (See the following pages.)

8. ***Yoo-Hoo.*** If you live outside the Yoo-Hoo belt, we'll send you a bottle of the precious nectar to pour over your pennant winner's head, in solemn observance of that most sacred of Rotisserituals.

How does your league join? Easy. Just fill out the form on page 309 and send it with your league's check or money order for $50 (only $25 for renewals) to the **Rotisserie League Baseball Association, 370 Seventh Avenue, Suite 312, New York, NY 10001.**

Rotisserie Baseball—The Video!
"Great!"—Siskel "Terrible!"—Ebert

That's right. We made a video. Go ahead and laugh. But hey—it works for Madonna, why not us?

Hosted by Reggie Jackson (yeah, *that* Reggie Jackson), **Rotisserie Baseball—The Video** is 30 minutes of rollicking, swashbuckling, gut-wrenching excitement, with enough car chases, frontal nudity, and violence to satisfy even Peter "Sudden Pete" Gethers ("Two thumbs!"). It features Glen "Iron Horse" Waggoner ("Two cheeseburgers!"), Harry Stein ("Not since *Gone with the Wind* . . ."), BFFCL Daniel Okrent ("Not since *Deep Throat* . . ."), and all the fun-loving Rotissegang, talking about the game they love so well.

For people new to The Greatest Game etc., **Rotisserie Baseball—The Video** is an informative, vaguely useful overview of the obsession that will soon take over their lives. For veteran Rotisserie players, it's a handy way to explain what the game is all about to people who don't know a baseball from a bass fiddle. (Just invite them over, cook up a tubful of popcorn, and pop The Video into the old VCR. They'll never be able to thank you enough, so they probably won't even try.) It's also a perfect gift idea for weddings, anniversaries, divorces, bar mitzvahs, and M-O-T-H-E-R on *Her* Day!

Just $15 plus postage and handling. See order form on page 309.

Rotisserie Ready-to-Wear!

Even if you draft like a Pollet Burro, there's no reason you can't dress like a pennant winner. Just order a few dozen official **Rotisserie T-shirts**. Available in a variety of designer colors, all of them white, this top-quality 100% cotton shirt has the famous Rotisserie coat-of-arms emblazoned across the chest in four dazzling colors. Perfect for any social occasion, but especially suitable for Auction Draft Day. A trifling $15 (plus postage and handling). Get a couple in case you slop mustard on yourself at the ball park.

And what's an official Rotisserie T-shirt without an official **Rotisserie Cap**? Only half a uniform, that's what. The Rotisserie Cap is a top-quality number in breathtaking white with the famous four-color Rotisserie logo. Only $18 (plus postage and handling)—and get this: One size fits all! See page 309 for information on how to order.

Rotisserie Farm Report

Farming is hard work, so why not let Lew Fidler, general manager of the **Baseball Association** of **Rotisserie League Stats,** help you with the sowing and reaping?

Every spring Big Lew takes a last-minute look at hundreds of minor league prospects (and suspects!). He consults his ouija board, throws the tai chi, reads his tarot cards, and pores over scouting reports. He sifts rumors, examines tea leaves, sacrifices a chicken in Central Park, and speaks to Nancy Reagan's personal astrologer (via a medium). Then, just in time for Auction Draft Day, Big Lew separates the wheat from the chaff.

The result: **Lew Fidler's Rotisserie Farm Report,** the most up-to-the-minute farm system scouting tool in Rotisserie baseball. The **Report** ranks the top 100 prospects in each league, making it an invaluable crutch for Rotisserie GMs, particularly those who play Ultra.

To order, send check or money order for $7.50 to **Rotisserie League Baseball Association, 370 Seventh Avenue, Suite 312, New York, NY 10001.**

TEAR OUT THIS PAGE!

YES! Enroll our league immediately in the **Rotisserie League Baseball Association** and send us the official **1994 Position Eligibility List** by return mail! Enclosed is our check or money order for $50 payable to **RLBA.** (Renewal leagues, send $25.)

HOLD ON! We're not sure yet, we haven't had our organizational meeting, and all we want right now is information about **Roti•Stats,** the **RLBA's** officially authorized stats service.

(Please Print)

Name of League _____

c/o Commissioner _____

Address _____

City _____ State _____ Zip _____

Telephone _____ AL/NL _____

ROTISSERIE T-SHIRTS

Size	Quantity	Price
Small	_____	$15 each
Medium	_____	2 for $28
Large	_____	3 for $39
X-Large	_____	4 for $48
XX-Large	_____	5+ $10 each

ROTISSERIE CAPS

Size	Quantity	Price
One size fits all	_____	$18 each

ROTISSERIE VIDEOS

	Quantity	Price
	_____	$15 each

Guarantee
If not completely satisfied with any Official Rotisserie product, send it back. We'll replace it or refund your money.

Shirts	$_____
Caps	$_____
Videos	$_____
Postage/Hdlg.	$ 3.50
Total	$_____ *

($US only; Check or M/O)
*NY residents add sales tax.

Name _____

Address _____

City _____ State _____ Zip _____

Mail to:
Rotisserie League Baseball Association
370 Seventh Avenue, Suite 312
New York, NY 10001

DON'T FORGET THE WINTER GAMES!

ROTISSERIE LEAGUE

BASKETBALL

- Compete in eight offensive and defensive categories based on the Official Rule Book.

- Categories include Total Points, Field Goal Percentage, 3-pointers, Free Throws Made, Assists, Rebounds, Steals, and Blocked Shots.

- Designate weekly lineups.

- Make trades. The Mailman for the Glide, anyone?

- Form your own league or let us form one for you.

- Weekly standings reports and transactions.

- Form leagues from four teams on up.

ROTISSERIE LEAGUE

HOCKEY

- Compete in six categories for skaters and two categories for goaltenders based on the Official Rotisserie League Rule Book.

- Categories include Goals, Assists, +/−, Shots on Goal, Shot Percentage, Specialty Team Play (power play and shorthanded goals), Save Percentage, and Goalie Points.

- Make trades. What about Lemieux for Lindross?

- Form your own league or let us form one for you.

- Weekly reports and transactions.

- Form leagues from four teams on up.

Yes, save me from long, cold, lonely winter nights!
Send information about:

☐ **Rotisserie League Basketball**   ☐ **Rotisserie League Hockey**

Name _____

Address _____

City _____ State _____ Zip _____

Telephone _____

Mail to:
Rotisserie League Baseball Association
370 Seventh Avenue, Suite 312
New York, NY 10001

8

Postgame Shower

A Yoo-Hoo to Arms

Editor's Note: *We ended our first book ten years ago with the following dispatch from Maestro Steve Wulf of the Wulfgang. We ended all our other books the same way. It's how we're ending this book. And it's the way we'll end our next book. That's because tradition is everything in Rotisserie League Baseball . . . unless you have to throw it into a deal for a stud power hitter.*

Unseen hands hold you, force your head down and pour water, dairy whey, corn sweetener, nonfat milk, sugar, coconut oil, cocoa, sodium caseinate, salt, sodium bicarbonate, dipotassium phosphates, calcium phosphates, guar gum, natural flavors, xanthan gum, vanillin (an artificial flavor), sodium ascorbate, ferric orthophosphate, palmitate, niacinamide, vitamin D, and, yes, *riboflavin* all over your hair. The bizarre ritual is a Yoo-Hoo shampoo, and it is what you get for winning the Rotisserie League pennant.

The chocolate-flavored rinse will not leave your locks radiant and soft to the touch, and squirrels will probably follow you around for a day or two. All in all, the ritual is pretty distasteful. But there's not a member of the Rotisserie League who wouldn't gladly suffer the rite so long as it came at the end of a championship season.

Since we traditionally end each Rotisseseason with an outpouring of the chocolate drink of our youth, we figured we may as well end the book the same way. Besides, as the beverage company's former executive vice president for promotions, Lawrence Peter Berra, once noted, or at least we think he noted, "Yoo-Hoo tastes good. And it's good for you, too."

Yoo-Hoo does taste good if your taste buds also happen to be impressed with the nose on strawberry fizzies. To sophisticated palates, Yoo-Hoo tastes a little like the runoff in the gutter outside a Carvel store.

As for Yoo-Hoo being good for you, well, Yogi says he let his kids drink it, and one of them grew up to be the .255-hitting shortstop for the Pittsburgh Pirates. But then, maybe if Dale *hadn't* touched the stuff, he might actually be worth more than the $7 the Fleder Mice paid for him in 1983.

Yoo-Hoo is not unlike the Rotisserie League. Both of them taste good, and both of them are good for you. Just don't tell anybody that. Whenever one of us tries to explain just what the Rotisserie League is, we all get the same kind of look. It's the look one might get from a bartender if one ordered, say, a Kahlua and Yoo-Hoo. The look says, "Aren't you a little too old to be partaking of that stuff?" Our look invariably replies, "But it tastes good, and it's good for you."

Yoo-Hoo's current slogan is "Yoo-Hoo's Got Life." Catchy, isn't it? But then, Yogi Berra used to be a catchy. The Rotisserie League's got life, too. It enlivens not only boxscores, but "Kiner's Korner," as well. Why, the game adds color to every fiber of your being, it gives you a sense of purpose in this crazy, cockeyed world, it puts a spring in your step and a song in your heart, and it makes you care, deeply care, for your fellow man, especially if your fellow man's name is Biff Pocoroba. So the Rotisserie League is childish, is it? Yoo-Hoo and a bottle of rum, barkeep.

In case you're wondering where Yoo-Hoo comes from, we thought we'd tell you. It comes from Carlstadt, N.J. Yoo-Hoo also goes back to the days of Ruth and Gehrig. It first arrived on the American scene as a fruit drink named after a popular greeting of that day. Founder Natale Olivieri was obsessed with making a stable chocolate drink, and after years of experimentation, he hit upon the idea of heating the chocolate. The rest is soft-drink history.

In the '50s, Yoo-Hoo's Golden Age, the product came to be associated with Yogi. A billboard of Yogi and a bottle of Yoo-Hoo greeted fans in Yankee Stadium. And Yogi wasn't the only Yankee who endorsed Yoo-Hoo—Whitey, Mickey, and the Moose could all be seen on the insides of Yoo-Hoo bottle caps. Nowadays, nobody inhabits the inside of the bottle cap. However, if you turn the cap upside down, it reads, "ooh-ooy," which is Yiddish for Rod Scurry's ERA.

Yoo-Hoo is also like baseball: You don't want to know too much about it. In the interests of this chapter, we sent an envoy out to Yankee Stadium to talk to Yogi. Yes, you've read all those funny Berra quotes over the years, about how it's not over until it's over, and about how nobody goes to that restaurant any more because it's too crowded. To tell you the truth, Yogi is not the man that people suppose him to be. He is actually two different people, depending on his mood. When he is on guard, he is full of monosyllables, and when he is relaxed, he can be genuinely engaging. But the star of "The Hathaways"° he is not.

We—actually, it was only one of us, who shall remain nameless, and if the *New Yorker* can do it, why can't we—asked Yogi if he would mind talking about Yoo-Hoo. He said, "Sorry, I can't." This caught us by surprise, but being quick on our tongue, we asked, "You can't?" Yogi said, "Nope. Ask Cerone."

At which point, we approached Rick Cerone, the catcher who took Yogi's place as executive vice president for promotions. For all their sterling qualities, Berra and Cerone do not strike us as being pillars of the corporate structure, but Yoo-Hoo obviously saw through to their executive talents. We asked Cerone if he would mind talking about Yoo-Hoo. He said, "I can't." This time, we asked, "Why?" and Cerone said, "Because I'm suing them, that's why."

°Does anybody remember who "The Hathaways" were? We've forgotten.

As it turns out, the company has changed hands, and Cerone claims that Yoo-Hoo never paid him for certain appearances. Yogi ran into similar problems, but he settled out of court. So that's why Yoo-Hoo is just like baseball: if you look too closely, it can get ugly on you.

We went back to Yogi and pleaded with him. All we cared about, we said, were the old days of Yoo-Hoo. He warmed to the subject in much the same way Natale Olivieri warmed Yoo-Hoo—slowly. Through his grunts and moans, we determined that Yogi thought Yoo-Hoo tasted good, that his kids drank it, that he wishes he had some money invested in it, and that people still link him with Yoo-Hoo, and vice versa. Then he said, "What's this for, anyway?"

We explained to him about the Rotisserie League and the book. When we said, "Then, at the end of the year, we pour Yoo-Hoo over the head of the winner," Yogi—dripping tobacco juice out of the left side of his mouth—gave us a look of partial disgust and said something like "ooh-ooy."

So, if you decide to take up baseball as played by the Rotisserie League, be warned. People will look at you funny. Pay them no mind. Just pay the Treasurer.

We hate long good-byes. When we meet again, perhaps at a theater near you showing *The Rotisserie League Goes to Japan,* let's just say, "Yoo-Hoo."

Postscript: *Now Batting for Yoo-Hoo . . .*

The payoff for outsmarting and outlucking your fellow GMs in the Greatest Game for Baseball Fans Since Baseball is a Yoo-Hoo shower, duly administered by the preceding year's champion. Without it, the winner's check is not negotiable, the victory not official, the season not over.

But what if you live outside the Yoo-Hoo Belt? What are you supposed to do? Rip the kiddos out of school and move to the East Coast?

Don't despair. The game's Founding Fathers, got together a few years ago on Mount Olympus for their annual winter meetings and ruled that substitutions are permissible, "so long as they are chosen in the spirit of Yoo-Hoo."

To untangle the legal mumbo jumbo, this means "a regionally indigenous potable—that is, a local brew." Examples: in Detroit and its environs, a bottle of Vernor's . . . in Texas, a cold Lone Star beer . . . in Maine, a filthy-tasting soft drink called Moxie . . . in northern California, a perky little Chardonnay . . . in Pittsburgh, a flagon of Rolling Rock. Get the pitcher? Sure you do, although a six-ounce bottle will suffice.

Whatever you pour, think of it as Yoo-Hoo—and do your doggone best to be under it!

APPENDIX

Final 1993 Averages

NATIONAL LEAGUE: BATTERS

NL Batter	Team	BA	HR	RBI	SB	CS	G	AB	R	BB	OBP
Alicea, L.	StL	.279	3	46	11	1	115	362	50	47	.362
Allanson, A.	SF	.167	0	2	0	0	13	24	3	1	.200
Alou, M.	Mon	.286	18	85	17	6	136	482	70	38	.340
Amaro, R.	Phi	.333	1	6	0	0	25	48	7	6	.400
Anthony, E.	Hou	.249	15	66	3	5	145	486	70	49	.319
Arias, A.	Fla	.269	2	20	1	1	96	249	27	27	.344
Ashley, B.	LA	.243	0	0	0	0	14	37	0	2	.282
Aude, R.	Pit	.115	0	4	0	0	13	26	1	1	.148
Ausmus, B.	SD	.256	5	12	2	0	49	160	18	6	.283
Baez, K.	NYN	.183	0	7	0	0	52	126	10	13	.259
Bagwell, J.	Hou	.320	20	88	13	4	142	535	76	62	.388
Barberie, B.	Fla	.277	5	33	2	4	99	375	45	33	.344
Bass, K.	Hou	.284	3	37	7	1	111	229	31	26	.359
Batiste, K.	Phi	.282	5	29	0	1	79	156	14	3	.298
Bean, B.	SD	.260	5	32	2	4	88	177	19	6	.284
Bell, D.	SD	.262	21	72	26	5	150	542	73	23	.303
Bell, J.	Pit	.310	9	51	16	10	154	604	102	77	.392
Bell, J.	Phi	.200	0	7	0	1	24	65	5	5	.268
Belliard, R.	Atl	.228	0	6	0	0	91	79	6	4	.291
Benavides, F.	Col	.286	3	26	3	2	74	213	20	6	.305
Benjamin, M.	SF	.199	4	16	0	0	63	146	22	9	.264
Benzinger, T.	SF	.288	6	26	0	0	86	177	25	13	.332
Berroa, G.	Fla	.118	0	0	0	0	14	34	3	2	.167
Berry, S.	Mon	.261	14	49	12	2	122	299	50	41	.348
Berryhill, D.	Atl	.245	8	43	0	0	115	335	24	21	.291
Bichette, D.	Col	.310	21	89	14	8	141	538	93	28	.348
Biggio, C.	Hou	.287	21	64	15	17	155	610	98	77	.373
Blauser, J.	Atl	.305	15	73	16	6	161	597	110	85	.401
Bogar, T.	NYN	.244	3	25	0	1	78	205	19	14	.300
Bolick, F.	Mon	.211	4	24	1	0	95	213	25	23	.298
Bonds, B.	SF	.336	46	123	29	12	159	539	129	126	.458
Bonilla, B.	NYN	.265	34	87	3	3	139	502	81	72	.352
Boston, D.	Col	.261	14	40	1	6	124	291	46	26	.325
Bournigal, R.	LA	.500	0	3	0	0	8	18	0	0	.500
Branson, J.	Cin	.241	3	22	4	1	125	381	40	19	.275
Bream, S.	Atl	.260	9	35	4	2	117	277	33	31	.332
Brewer, R.	StL	.286	2	20	1	0	110	147	15	17	.359
Briley, G.	Fla	.194	3	12	6	2	120	170	17	12	.250
Brooks, J.	LA	.222	1	1	0	0	9	9	2	0	.222
Brown, J.	SD	.233	0	8	3	3	47	133	21	15	.335
Brumfield, J.	Cin	.268	6	23	20	8	103	272	40	21	.321
Brumley, M.	Hou	.300	0	2	0	1	8	10	1	1	.364
Buechele, S.	ChN	.272	15	65	1	1	133	460	53	48	.345
Bullett, S.	Pit	.200	0	4	3	2	23	55	2	3	.237
Burnitz, J.	NYN	.243	13	38	3	6	86	263	49	38	.339
Butler, B.	LA	.298	1	42	39	19	156	607	80	86	.387
Cabrera, F.	Atl	.241	4	11	0	0	70	83	8	8	.308
Caminiti, K.	Hou	.262	13	75	8	5	143	543	75	49	.321

NL Batter	Team	BA	HR	RBI	SB	CS	G	AB	R	BB	OBP
Candaele, C.	Hou	.240	1	7	2	3	75	121	18	10	.298
Canseco, O.	StL	.176	0	0	0	0	6	17	0	1	.222
Caraballo, R.	Atl	.000	0	0	0	0	6	0	0	0	.000
Carr, C.	Fla	.267	4	41	58	22	142	551	75	49	.327
Carreon, M.	SF	.327	7	33	1	0	78	150	22	13	.373
Carrillo, M.	Fla	.255	0	3	0	0	24	55	4	1	.281
Castellano, P.	Col	.183	3	7	1	1	34	71	12	8	.266
Castilla, V.	Col	.255	9	30	2	5	105	337	36	13	.283
Cedeno, A.	Hou	.283	11	56	9	7	149	505	69	48	.346
Chamberlain, W.	Phi	.282	12	45	2	1	96	284	34	17	.320
Cianfrocco, A.	Mon	.235	1	1	0	0	12	17	3	0	.235
Cianfrocco, A.	SD	.244	11	47	2	0	84	279	27	17	.289
Clark, D.	Pit	.271	11	46	1	0	110	277	43	38	.358
Clark, J.	Col	.282	13	67	9	6	140	478	65	20	.324
Clark, P.	SD	.313	9	33	2	0	102	240	33	8	.345
Clark, W.	SF	.283	14	73	2	2	132	491	82	63	.367
Clayton, R.	SF	.282	6	70	11	10	153	549	54	38	.331
Colbert, C.	SF	.162	1	5	0	0	23	37	2	3	.225
Colbrunn, G.	Mon	.255	4	23	4	2	70	153	15	6	.282
Cole, A.	Col	.256	0	24	30	13	126	348	50	43	.339
Coleman, V.	NYN	.279	2	25	38	13	92	373	64	21	.316
Conine, J.	Fla	.292	12	79	2	2	162	595	75	52	.351
Cordero, W.	Mon	.248	10	58	12	3	138	475	56	34	.308
Costo, T.	Cin	.224	3	12	0	0	31	98	13	4	.250
Cotto, H.	Fla	.296	3	14	11	1	54	135	15	3	.312
Cromer, T.	StL	.087	0	0	0	0	10	23	1	1	.125
Cummings, M.	Pit	.111	0	3	0	0	13	36	5	4	.195
Daugherty, J.	Hou	.333	0	0	0	0	4	3	0	0	.333
Daugherty, J.	Cin	.220	2	9	0	0	46	59	7	11	.338
Daulton, D.	Phi	.257	24	105	5	0	147	510	90	117	.392
Davis, E.	LA	.234	14	53	33	5	108	376	57	41	.308
Decker, S.	Fla	.000	0	1	0	0	8	15	0	3	.000
DeShields, D.	Mon	.295	2	29	43	10	123	481	75	72	.389
Destrade, O.	Fla	.255	20	87	0	2	153	569	61	58	.324
Donnels, C.	Hou	.257	2	24	2	0	88	179	18	19	.327
Dorsett, B.	Cin	.254	2	12	0	0	25	63	7	3	.288
Duncan, M.	Phi	.282	11	73	6	5	124	496	68	12	.304
Dunston, S.	ChN	.400	0	2	0	0	7	10	3	0	.400
Dykstra, L.	Phi	.305	19	66	37	12	161	637	143	129	.420
Eisenreich, J.	Phi	.318	7	54	5	0	153	362	51	26	.363
Espy, C.	Cin	.233	0	5	2	2	40	60	6	14	.368
Everett, C.	Fla	.105	0	0	1	0	11	19	0	1	.150
Faneyte, R.	SF	.133	0	0	0	0	7	15	2	2	.235
Faries, P.	SF	.222	0	4	2	0	15	36	6	1	.237
Fariss, M.	Fla	.172	0	2	0	0	18	29	3	5	.294
Felix, J.	Fla	.238	7	22	2	1	57	214	25	10	.276
Fernandez, T.	NYN	.225	1	14	6	2	48	173	20	25	.323
Finley, S.	Hou	.266	8	44	19	6	142	545	69	28	.304
Fletcher, D.	Mon	.255	9	60	0	0	133	396	33	34	.320
Floyd, C.	Mon	.226	1	2	0	0	10	31	3	0	.226
Foley, T.	Pit	.253	3	22	0	0	86	194	18	11	.287
Frazier, L.	Mon	.286	1	16	17	2	112	189	27	16	.340
Gainer, J.	Col	.171	3	6	1	1	23	41	4	4	.244
Galarraga, A.	Col	.370	22	98	2	4	120	470	71	24	.403

NL Batter	Team	BA	HR	RBI	SB	CS	G	AB	R	BB	OBP
Gallagher, D.	NYN	.274	6	28	1	1	99	201	34	20	.338
Gant, R.	Atl	.274	36	117	26	9	157	606	113	67	.345
Garcia, C.	Pit	.269	12	47	18	11	141	546	77	31	.316
Gardner, J.	SD	.262	1	24	2	6	140	404	53	45	.337
Geren, B.	SD	.214	3	6	0	0	58	145	8	13	.278
Gilkey, B.	StL	.305	16	70	15	10	137	557	99	56	.370
Girardi, J.	Col	.290	3	31	6	6	86	310	35	24	.346
Goff, J.	Pit	.297	2	6	0	0	14	37	5	8	.422
Gonzalez, L.	Hou	.300	15	72	20	9	154	540	82	47	.361
Goodwin, T.	LA	.294	0	1	1	2	30	17	6	1	.333
Gordon, K.	Cin	.167	0	0	0	0	3	6	0	0	.167
Grace, M.	ChN	.325	14	98	8	4	155	594	86	71	.393
Greene, W.	Cin	.160	2	5	0	0	15	50	7	2	.189
Gregg, T.	Cin	.167	0	1	0	0	10	12	1	0	.154
Grissom, M.	Mon	.298	19	95	53	10	157	630	104	52	.351
Gutierrez, R.	SD	.251	5	26	4	3	133	438	76	50	.334
Gwynn, T.	SD	.358	7	59	14	1	122	489	70	36	.398
Hansen, D.	LA	.362	4	30	0	1	84	105	13	21	.465
Harris, L.	LA	.237	2	11	3	1	107	160	20	15	.303
Hayes, C.	Col	.305	25	98	11	6	157	573	89	43	.355
Hernandez, C.	LA	.253	2	7	0	0	50	99	6	2	.267
Hernandez, C.	Cin	.083	0	1	1	2	27	24	3	1	.120
Higgins, K.	SD	.221	0	13	0	1	71	181	17	16	.294
Hill, G.	ChN	.345	10	22	1	0	31	87	14	6	.387
Hollins, D.	Phi	.273	18	93	2	3	143	543	104	85	.372
Hosey, S.	SF	.500	0	1	0	0	3	2	0	1	.667
Housie, W.	NYN	.188	0	1	0	0	18	16	2	1	.235
Howard, T.	Cin	.277	4	13	5	6	38	141	22	12	.331
Hughes, K.	Cin	.000	0	0	0	0	3	4	0	0	.000
Hundley, T.	NYN	.228	11	53	1	1	130	417	40	23	.269
Hunter, B.	Atl	.138	0	8	0	0	37	80	4	2	.153
Huskey, B.	NYN	.146	0	3	0	0	13	41	2	1	.159
Incaviglia, P.	Phi	.274	24	89	1	1	116	368	60	21	.318
Jackson, D.	NYN	.195	1	7	0	0	31	87	4	2	.211
James, C.	Hou	.256	6	19	2	0	65	129	19	15	.333
Jefferies, G.	StL	.342	16	83	46	9	142	544	89	62	.408
Jennings, D.	ChN	.250	2	8	0	0	42	52	8	3	.316
Johnson, E.	SF	.400	0	0	0	0	4	5	1	0	.400
Johnson, H.	NYN	.238	7	26	6	4	72	235	32	43	.354
Jones, C.	Atl	.667	0	0	0	0	8	3	2	1	.750
Jones, C.	Col	.273	6	31	9	4	86	209	29	10	.305
Jones, T.	StL	.262	0	1	2	2	29	61	13	9	.366
Jordan, B.	StL	.309	10	44	6	6	67	223	33	12	.351
Jordan, R.	Phi	.289	5	18	0	0	90	159	21	8	.324
Justice, D.	Atl	.270	40	120	3	5	157	585	90	78	.357
Karros, E.	LA	.247	23	80	0	1	158	619	74	34	.287
Kelly, R.	Cin	.319	9	35	21	5	78	320	44	17	.354
Kent, J.	NYN	.270	21	80	4	4	140	496	65	30	.320
Kessinger, K.	Cin	.259	1	3	0	0	11	27	4	4	.344
King, J.	Pit	.295	9	98	8	6	158	611	82	59	.356
Klesko, R.	Atl	.353	2	5	0	0	22	17	3	3	.450
Koelling, B.	Cin	.067	0	0	0	0	7	15	2	0	.125
Kruk, J.	Phi	.316	14	85	6	2	150	535	100	111	.430

NL Batter	Team	BA	HR	RBI	SB	CS	G	AB	R	BB	OBP
Lake, S.	ChN	.225	5	13	0	0	44	120	11	4	.250
Laker, T.	Mon	.198	0	7	2	0	43	86	3	2	.222
Landrum, C.	NYN	.263	0	1	0	0	22	19	2	0	.263
Lankford, R.	StL	.238	7	45	14	14	127	407	64	81	.366
Lansing, M.	Mon	.287	3	45	23	5	141	491	64	46	.352
Larkin, B.	Cin	.315	8	51	14	1	100	384	57	51	.394
LaValliere, M.	Pit	.200	0	0	0	0	1	5	0	0	.200
Lemke, M.	Atl	.252	7	49	1	2	151	493	52	65	.335
Lewis, D.	SF	.253	2	48	46	15	136	522	84	30	.302
Lindeman, J.	Hou	.348	0	0	0	0	9	23	2	0	.348
Lindsey, D.	Phi	.500	0	0	0	0	2	2	0	0	.500
Liriano, N.	Col	.305	2	15	6	4	48	151	28	18	.376
Longmire, T.	Phi	.231	0	1	0	0	11	13	1	0	.231
Lopez, J.	Atl	.375	1	2	0	0	8	16	1	0	.412
Lopez, L.	SD	.116	0	1	0	0	17	43	1	0	.114
Lyden, M.	Fla	.300	1	1	0	0	6	10	2	0	.300
Maclin, L.	StL	.077	0	1	1	0	12	13	2	0	.071
Magadan, D.	Fla	.286	4	29	0	1	66	227	22	44	.400
Maldonado, C.	ChN	.186	3	15	0	0	70	140	8	13	.260
Manto, J.	Phi	.056	0	0	0	0	8	18	0	0	.105
Manwaring, K.	SF	.275	5	49	1	3	130	432	48	41	.345
Marrero, O.	Mon	.210	1	4	1	3	32	81	10	14	.326
Martin, A.	Pit	.281	18	64	16	9	143	480	85	42	.338
Martinez, D.	SF	.241	5	27	6	3	91	241	28	27	.317
May, D.	ChN	.295	10	77	10	3	128	465	62	31	.336
McClendon, L.	Pit	.221	2	19	0	3	88	181	21	23	.306
McGee, W.	SF	.301	4	46	10	9	130	475	53	38	.353
McGriff, F.	SD	.275	18	46	4	3	83	302	52	42	.361
McGriff, F.	Atl	.310	19	55	1	0	68	255	59	34	.392
McGriff, T.	Fla	.000	0	0	0	0	3	7	0	1	.000
McIntosh, T.	Mon	.095	0	2	0	0	20	21	2	0	.095
McKnight, J.	NYN	.256	2	13	0	0	105	164	19	13	.311
McNamara, J.	SF	.143	0	1	0	0	4	7	0	0	.143
Mejia, R.	Col	.231	5	20	4	1	65	229	31	13	.275
Merced, O.	Pit	.313	8	70	3	3	137	447	68	77	.414
Mercedes, L.	SF	.160	0	3	0	1	18	25	1	1	.250
Millette, J.	Phi	.200	0	2	0	0	10	10	3	1	.273
Milligan, R.	Cin	.274	6	29	0	2	83	234	30	46	.394
Mitchell, K.	Cin	.341	19	64	1	0	93	323	56	25	.385
Mondesi, R.	LA	.291	4	10	4	1	42	86	13	4	.322
Montoyo, C.	Mon	.400	0	3	0	0	4	5	1	0	.400
Morandini, M.	Phi	.247	3	33	13	2	120	425	57	34	.309
Morris, H.	Cin	.317	7	49	2	2	101	379	48	34	.371
Murphy, D.	Col	.143	0	7	0	0	26	42	1	5	.224
Murray, E.	NYN	.285	27	100	2	2	154	610	77	40	.325
Natal, B.	Fla	.214	1	6	1	0	41	117	3	6	.273
Navarro, T.	NYN	.059	0	1	0	0	12	17	1	0	.059
Nieves, M.	SD	.191	2	3	0	0	19	47	4	3	.255
Nixon, O.	Atl	.269	1	24	47	13	134	461	77	61	.351
O'Brien, C.	NYN	.255	4	23	1	1	67	188	15	14	.312
Offerman, J.	LA	.269	1	62	30	13	158	590	77	71	.346
Oliver, J.	Cin	.239	14	75	0	0	139	482	40	27	.276
Olson, G.	Atl	.225	4	24	1	0	83	262	23	29	.304
Oquendo, J.	StL	.205	0	4	0	0	46	73	7	12	.314
Orsulak, J.	NYN	.284	8	35	5	4	134	409	59	28	.331
Owens, J.	Col	.209	3	6	1	0	33	86	12	6	.277

NL Batter	Team	BA	HR	RBI	SB	CS	G	AB	R	BB	OBP
Pagnozzi, T.	StL	.258	7	41	1	0	92	330	31	19	.296
Pappas, E.	StL	.276	1	28	1	3	82	228	25	35	.368
Parker, R.	Hou	.333	0	4	1	2	45	45	11	3	.375
Patterson, J.	SF	.188	1	2	0	1	16	16	1	0	.188
Pecota, B.	Atl	.323	0	5	1	1	72	62	17	2	.344
Pena, G.	StL	.256	5	30	13	5	74	254	34	25	.330
Pendleton, T.	Atl	.272	17	84	5	1	161	633	81	36	.311
Pennyfeather, W.	Pit	.206	0	2	0	1	21	34	4	0	.206
Perry, G.	StL	.337	4	16	1	1	96	98	21	18	.440
Phillips, J.	SF	.313	1	4	0	0	11	16	1	0	.313
Piazza, M.	LA	.318	35	112	3	4	149	547	81	46	.370
Plantier, P.	SD	.240	34	100	4	5	138	462	67	61	.335
Polidor, G.	Fla	.167	0	0	0	0	7	6	0	0	.167
Pose, S.	Fla	.195	0	3	0	2	15	41	0	2	.233
Pratt, T.	Phi	.287	5	13	0	0	33	87	8	5	.330
Pride, C.	Mon	.444	1	5	1	0	10	9	3	0	.444
Prince, T.	Pit	.196	2	24	1	1	66	179	14	13	.272
Ready, R.	Mon	.254	1	10	2	1	40	134	22	23	.367
Reed, J.	SF	.261	6	12	0	1	66	119	10	16	.346
Reed, J.	LA	.276	2	31	1	3	132	445	48	38	.333
Renteria, R.	Fla	.255	2	30	0	2	103	263	27	21	.314
Rhodes, K.	Hou	.000	0	0	0	0	5	2	0	0	.000
Rhodes, K.	ChN	.288	3	7	2	0	15	52	12	11	.413
Roberson, K.	ChN	.189	9	27	0	1	62	180	23	12	.251
Roberts, B.	Cin	.240	1	18	26	6	83	292	46	38	.330
Rodriguez, H.	LA	.222	8	23	1	0	76	176	20	11	.266
Ronan, M.	StL	.083	0	0	0	0	6	12	0	0	.083
Royer, S.	StL	.304	1	8	0	1	24	46	4	2	.333
Sabo, C.	Cin	.259	21	82	6	4	148	552	86	43	.315
Samuel, J.	Cin	.230	4	26	9	7	103	261	31	23	.298
Sanchez, R.	ChN	.282	0	28	1	1	105	344	35	15	.316
Sandberg, R.	ChN	.309	9	45	9	2	117	456	67	37	.359
Sanders, D.	Atl	.276	6	28	19	7	95	272	42	16	.321
Sanders, R.	Cin	.274	20	83	27	10	138	496	90	51	.343
Santiago, B.	Fla	.230	13	50	10	7	139	469	49	37	.291
Saunders, D.	NYN	.209	0	0	0	0	28	67	8	3	.243
Scarsone, S.	SF	.252	2	15	0	1	44	103	16	4	.278
Servais, S.	Hou	.244	11	32	0	0	85	258	24	22	.313
Sharperson, M.	LA	.256	2	10	2	0	73	90	13	5	.299
Sheaffer, D.	Col	.278	4	32	2	3	82	216	26	8	.299
Sheffield, G.	SD	.295	10	36	5	1	68	258	34	18	.344
Sheffield, G.	Fla	.292	10	37	12	4	72	236	33	29	.378
Shelton, B.	Pit	.250	2	7	0	0	15	24	3	3	.333
Sherman, D.	SD	.222	0	2	2	1	37	63	8	6	.315
Shields, T.	ChN	.176	0	1	0	0	20	34	4	2	.222
Shipley, C.	SD	.235	4	22	12	3	105	230	25	10	.275
Siddall, J.	Mon	.100	0	1	0	0	19	20	0	1	.143
Slaught, D.	Pit	.300	10	55	2	1	116	377	34	29	.356
Smith, D.	ChN	.300	11	35	8	6	111	310	51	25	.355
Smith, L.	Pit	.286	6	24	9	4	94	199	35	43	.422
Smith, O.	StL	.288	1	53	21	8	141	545	75	43	.337
Snyder, C.	LA	.266	11	56	4	1	143	516	61	47	.331
Sosa, S.	ChN	.261	33	93	36	11	159	598	92	38	.309
Spehr, T.	Mon	.230	2	10	2	0	53	87	14	6	.281
Stairs, M.	Mon	.375	0	2	0	0	6	8	1	0	.375
Staton, D.	SD	.262	5	9	0	0	17	42	7	3	.326

NL Batter	Team	BA	HR	RBI	SB	CS	G	AB	R	BB	OBP
Stillwell, K.	SD	.215	1	11	4	3	57	121	9	11	.286
Stocker, K.	Phi	.324	2	31	5	0	70	259	46	30	.409
Strawberry, D.	LA	.140	5	12	1	0	32	100	12	16	.267
Tarasco, T.	Atl	.229	0	2	0	1	24	35	6	0	.243
Tatum, J.	Col	.204	1	12	0	0	92	98	7	5	.245
Taubensee, E.	Hou	.250	9	42	1	0	94	288	26	21	.299
Teufel, T.	SD	.250	7	31	2	2	96	200	26	27	.338
Thompson, M.	Phi	.262	4	44	9	4	129	340	42	40	.341
Thompson, R.	SF	.312	19	65	10	4	128	494	85	45	.375
Thompson, R.	NYN	.250	11	26	2	7	80	288	34	19	.302
Tomberlin, A.	Pit	.286	1	5	0	0	27	42	4	2	.333
Tubbs, G.	Cin	.186	1	2	3	1	35	59	10	14	.351
Tucker, S.	Hou	.192	0	3	0	0	9	26	1	2	.250
Uribe, J.	Hou	.245	0	3	1	0	45	53	4	8	.355
Van Slyke, A.	Pit	.310	8	50	11	2	83	323	42	24	.357
VanderWal, J.	Mon	.233	5	30	6	3	106	215	34	27	.320
Varsho, G.	Cin	.232	2	11	1	0	77	95	8	9	.302
Velasquez, G.	SD	.210	3	20	0	0	79	143	7	13	.274
Villanueva, H.	StL	.145	3	9	0	0	17	55	7	4	.203
Vizcaino, J.	ChN	.287	4	54	12	9	151	551	74	46	.340
Walbeck, M.	ChN	.200	1	6	0	0	11	30	2	1	.226
Walker, C.	NYN	.225	5	19	7	0	115	213	18	14	.271
Walker, L.	Mon	.265	22	86	29	7	138	490	85	80	.371
Wallach, T.	LA	.222	12	62	0	2	133	477	42	32	.271
Walters, D.	SD	.202	1	10	0	0	27	94	6	7	.255
Webster, M.	LA	.244	2	14	4	6	88	172	26	11	.293
Wedge, E.	Col	.182	0	1	0	0	9	11	2	0	.182
Wehner, J.	Pit	.143	0	0	0	0	29	35	3	6	.268
Weiss, W.	Fla	.266	1	39	7	3	158	500	50	79	.367
White, D.	Mon	.224	2	4	2	0	17	49	6	2	.269
White, R.	Mon	.260	2	15	1	2	23	73	9	7	.321
Whiten, M.	StL	.253	25	99	15	8	152	562	81	58	.323
Whitmore, D.	Fla	.204	4	19	4	2	76	250	24	10	.249
Wilkins, R.	ChN	.303	30	73	2	1	136	446	78	50	.376
Williams, M.	SF	.294	38	110	1	3	145	579	105	27	.325
Wilson, D.	Cin	.224	0	8	0	0	36	76	6	9	.302
Wilson, G.	Pit	.143	0	0	0	0	10	14	0	1	.143
Wilson, N.	Fla	.000	0	0	0	0	7	16	0	0	.000
Wilson, W.	ChN	.258	1	11	7	2	105	221	29	11	.301
Womack, T.	Pit	.083	0	0	2	0	15	24	5	3	.185
Wood, T.	Mon	.192	0	3	0	0	13	26	4	3	.276
Woodson, T.	StL	.208	0	2	0	0	62	77	4	1	.215
Yelding, E.	ChN	.204	1	10	3	2	69	108	14	11	.277
Young, E.	Col	.269	3	42	42	19	144	490	82	63	.355
Young, G.	Col	.053	0	1	0	1	19	19	5	4	.217
Young, K.	Pit	.236	6	47	2	2	141	449	38	36	.300
Zambrano, E.	ChN	.294	0	2	0	0	8	17	1	1	.333
Zeile, T.	StL	.277	17	103	5	4	157	571	82	70	.352

NATIONAL LEAGUE: PITCHERS

NL Pitcher	Team	W	L	SV	ERA	Ratio	GS	IP	H	BB	K
Agosto, J.	Hou	0	0	0	6.00	1.333	0	6.0	8	0	3
Aldred, S.	Col	0	0	0	10.80	3.000	0	6.2	10	9	5
Aldred, S.	Mon	1	0	0	6.75	1.875	0	5.1	9	1	4
Andersen, L.	Phi	3	2	0	2.92	1.232	0	61.2	54	21	67
Anderson, M.	Cin	0	0	0	18.56	2.813	0	5.1	12	3	4
Aquino, L.	Fla	6	8	0	3.42	1.446	13	110.2	115	40	67
Armstrong, J.	Fla	9	17	0	4.49	1.503	33	196.1	210	78	118
Arocha, R.	StL	11	8	0	3.78	1.229	29	188.0	197	31	96
Ashby, A.	Col	0	4	1	8.50	2.296	9	54.0	89	32	33
Ashby, A.	SD	3	6	0	5.48	1.507	12	69.0	79	24	44
Assenmacher, P.	ChN	2	1	0	3.49	1.474	0	38.2	44	13	34
Astacio, P.	LA	14	9	0	3.57	1.277	31	186.1	165	68	122
Avery, S.	Atl	18	6	0	2.94	1.160	35	223.1	216	43	125
Ayala, B.	Cin	7	10	3	5.60	1.612	9	98.0	106	45	65
Ayrault, B.	Phi	2	0	0	9.58	2.806	0	10.1	18	10	8
Ballard, J.	Pit	4	1	0	4.86	1.621	5	53.2	70	15	16
Barnes, B.	Mon	2	6	3	4.41	1.530	8	100.0	105	48	60
Batchelor, R.	StL	0	0	0	8.10	1.700	0	10.0	14	3	4
Bautista, J.	ChN	10	3	2	2.82	1.227	7	111.2	105	27	63
Beck, R.	SF	3	1	48	2.16	0.920	0	79.1	57	13	86
Bedrosian, S.	Atl	5	2	0	1.63	1.007	0	49.2	34	14	33
Belcher, T.	Cin	9	6	0	4.47	1.372	22	137.0	134	47	101
Belinda, S.	Pit	3	1	19	3.61	1.110	0	42.1	35	11	30
Bell, E.	Hou	0	1	0	6.14	1.636	0	7.1	10	2	2
Benes, A.	SD	15	15	0	3.78	1.257	34	230.2	200	86	179
Black, B.	SF	8	2	0	3.56	1.324	16	93.2	89	33	45
Blair, W.	Col	6	10	0	4.75	1.568	18	146.0	184	42	84
Borbon, P.	Atl	0	0	0	21.60	3.600	0	1.2	3	3	2
Boskie, S.	ChN	5	3	0	3.43	1.386	2	65.2	63	21	39
Bottenfield, K.	Mon	2	5	0	4.12	1.578	11	83.0	93	33	33
Bottenfield, K.	Col	3	5	0	6.10	1.630	14	76.2	86	38	30
Boucher, D.	Mon	3	1	0	1.91	0.953	5	28.1	24	3	14
Bowen, R.	Fla	8	12	0	4.42	1.570	27	156.2	156	87	98
Brantley, J.	SF	5	6	0	4.28	1.452	12	113.2	112	46	76
Brennan, B.	ChN	2	1	0	4.20	1.667	1	15.0	16	8	11
Brink, B.	Phi	0	0	0	3.00	1.000	0	6.0	3	3	8
Brocail, D.	SD	4	13	0	4.56	1.473	24	128.1	143	42	70
Bross, T.	SF	0	0	0	9.00	2.000	0	2.0	3	1	1
Browning, T.	Cin	7	7	0	4.74	1.579	20	114.0	159	20	53
Brummett, G.	SF	2	3	0	4.70	1.435	8	46.0	53	13	20
Bullinger, J.	ChN	1	0	1	4.32	1.620	0	16.2	18	9	10
Burba, D.	SF	10	3	0	4.25	1.416	5	95.1	95	37	88
Burkett, J.	SF	22	7	0	3.65	1.187	34	231.2	224	40	145
Burns, T.	StL	0	4	0	6.16	1.337	0	30.2	32	9	10
Bushing, C.	Cin	0	0	0	12.46	3.000	0	4.1	9	4	3
Cadaret, G.	Cin	2	1	1	4.96	1.959	0	32.2	40	23	23
Candelaria, J.	Pit	0	3	1	8.24	1.780	0	19.2	25	9	17
Candiotti, T.	LA	8	10	0	3.12	1.259	32	213.2	192	71	155
Carpenter, C.	Fla	0	1	0	2.89	1.179	0	37.1	29	13	26
Castillo, F.	ChN	5	8	0	4.84	1.486	25	141.1	162	39	84
Cooke, S.	Pit	10	10	0	3.89	1.277	32	210.2	207	59	132
Cormier, R.	StL	7	6	0	4.33	1.335	21	145.1	163	27	75
Corsi, J.	Fla	0	2	0	6.64	1.869	0	20.1	28	10	7

NL Pitcher	Team	W	L	SV	ERA	Ratio	GS	IP	H	BB	K
Daal, O.	LA	2	3	0	5.09	1.613	0	35.1	36	21	19
Davis, M.	Phi	1	2	0	5.17	1.915	0	31.1	35	24	28
Davis, M.	SD	0	3	4	3.52	1.670	0	38.1	44	20	42
DeLeon, J.	Phi	3	0	0	3.26	1.511	3	47.0	39	27	34
Deshaies, J.	SF	2	2	0	4.24	1.824	4	17.0	24	6	5
DeSilva, J.	LA	0	0	0	6.75	1.313	0	5.1	6	1	6
Dewey, M.	Pit	1	2	7	2.36	1.013	0	26.2	14	10	14
Dibble, R.	Cin	1	4	19	6.48	1.872	0	41.2	34	42	49
Dixon, S.	StL	0	0	0	33.75	4.500	0	2.2	7	5	2
Drabek, D.	Hou	9	18	0	3.79	1.283	34	237.2	242	60	157
Draper, M.	NYN	1	1	0	4.25	1.583	1	42.1	53	14	16
Edens, T.	Hou	1	1	0	3.12	1.347	0	49.0	47	19	21
Eiland, D.	SD	0	3	0	5.21	1.572	9	48.1	58	17	14
Ettles, M.	SD	1	0	0	6.50	1.500	0	18.0	23	4	9
Fassero, J.	Mon	12	5	1	2.29	1.156	15	149.2	119	54	140
Fernandez, S.	NYN	5	6	0	2.93	1.011	18	119.2	82	36	81
Fletcher, P.	Phi	0	0	0	0.00	0.000	0	0.1	0	0	0
Foster, K.	Phi	0	1	0	14.85	3.000	1	6.2	13	7	6
Foster, S.	Cin	2	2	0	1.75	1.130	0	25.2	23	5	16
Franco, J.	NYN	4	3	10	5.20	1.817	0	36.1	46	19	29
Fredrickson, S.	Col	0	1	0	6.21	1.759	0	29.0	33	17	20
Freeman, M.	Atl	2	0	0	6.08	1.479	0	23.2	24	10	25
Gardiner, M.	Mon	2	3	0	5.21	1.579	2	38.0	40	19	21
Gibson, P.	NYN	1	1	0	5.19	1.846	0	8.2	14	2	12
Glavine, T.	Atl	22	6	0	3.20	1.370	36	239.1	236	90	120
Gomez, P.	SD	1	2	0	5.12	1.705	1	31.2	35	19	26
Gooden, D.	NYN	12	15	0	3.45	1.236	29	208.2	188	61	149
Gott, J.	LA	4	8	25	2.32	1.146	0	77.2	71	17	67
Gozzo, M.	NYN	0	1	1	2.57	1.143	0	14.0	11	5	6
Grant, M.	Hou	0	0	0	0.82	1.455	0	11.0	11	5	6
Grant, M.	Col	0	1	1	12.56	2.023	0	14.1	23	6	8
Green, T.	Phi	0	0	0	7.36	2.864	2	7.1	16	5	7
Greene, T.	Phi	16	4	0	3.42	1.200	30	200.0	175	62	167
Greer, K.	NYN	1	0	0	0.00	0.000	0	1.0	0	0	2
Gross, K.	LA	13	13	0	4.14	1.498	32	202.1	224	74	150
Gross, K.	LA	0	0	0	0.60	1.133	0	15.0	13	4	12
Guetterman, L.	StL	3	3	1	2.93	1.283	0	46.0	41	16	19
Guzman, J.	ChN	12	10	0	4.34	1.387	30	191.0	188	74	163
Hammond, C.	Fla	11	12	0	4.66	1.435	32	191.0	207	66	108
Harkey, M.	ChN	10	10	0	5.26	1.481	28	157.1	187	43	67
Harnisch, P.	Hou	16	9	0	2.98	1.176	33	217.2	171	79	185
Harris, G.	SD	6	6	23	3.03	1.601	0	59.1	57	37	39
Harris, G.	SD	10	9	0	3.67	1.270	22	152.0	151	39	83
Harris, G.	Col	1	8	0	6.50	1.664	13	73.1	88	30	40
Harvey, B.	Fla	1	5	45	1.70	0.841	0	69.0	45	13	73
Henry, B.	Col	2	8	0	6.59	1.677	15	84.2	117	24	39
Henry, B.	Mon	1	1	0	3.93	1.200	1	18.1	18	4	8
Henry, D.	Cin	0	1	0	3.86	2.143	0	4.2	6	4	2
Heredia, G.	Mon	4	2	2	3.92	1.430	9	57.1	66	14	40
Hernandez, J.	SD	0	2	0	4.72	1.398	0	34.1	41	7	26
Hernandez, X.	Hou	4	5	9	2.61	1.076	0	96.2	75	28	101
Hershiser, O.	LA	12	14	0	3.59	1.298	33	215.2	201	72	141
Hibbard, G.	ChN	15	11	0	3.96	1.356	31	191.0	209	47	82
Hickerson, B.	SF	7	5	0	4.26	1.471	15	120.1	137	39	69

NL Pitcher	Team	W	L	SV	ERA	Ratio	GS	IP	H	BB	K
Hill, K.	Mon	9	7	0	3.23	1.323	28	183.2	163	74	90
Hill, M.	Cin	3	0	0	5.65	1.500	0	28.2	34	9	23
Hillman, E.	NYN	2	9	0	3.97	1.386	22	145.0	173	24	60
Hoffman, T.	Fla	2	2	2	3.28	1.206	0	35.2	24	19	26
Hoffman, T.	SD	2	4	3	4.31	1.417	0	54.1	56	20	53
Holmes, D.	Col	3	3	25	4.05	1.170	0	66.2	56	20	60
Hope, J.	Pit	0	2	0	4.03	1.500	7	38.0	47	8	8
Hough, C.	Fla	9	16	0	4.27	1.375	34	204.1	202	71	126
Howell, J.	Atl	3	3	0	2.31	1.097	0	58.1	48	16	37
Hurst, B.	SD	0	1	0	12.46	2.769	2	4.1	9	3	3
Hurst, B.	Col	0	1	0	5.19	1.038	3	8.2	6	3	6
Innis, J.	NYN	2	3	3	4.11	1.630	0	76.2	81	38	36
Jackson, D.	Phi	12	11	0	3.77	1.417	32	210.1	214	80	120
Jackson, M.	SF	6	6	1	3.03	1.099	0	77.1	58	24	70
Johnston, J.	Pit	2	4	2	3.38	1.069	0	53.1	38	19	31
Johnstone, J.	Fla	0	2	0	5.91	2.156	0	10.2	16	7	5
Jones, B.	NYN	2	4	0	3.65	1.378	9	61.2	61	22	35
Jones, D.	Hou	4	10	26	4.54	1.500	0	85.1	102	21	66
Jones, J.	Mon	4	1	0	6.35	1.412	6	39.2	47	9	21
Jones, T.	Hou	1	2	2	3.13	1.179	0	37.1	28	15	25
Juden, J.	Hou	0	1	0	5.40	1.600	0	5.0	4	4	7
Kaiser, J.	Cin	0	0	0	2.70	1.800	0	3.1	4	2	4
Kaiser, J.	NYN	0	0	0	11.57	1.929	0	4.2	6	3	5
Kile, D.	Hou	15	8	0	3.51	1.375	26	171.2	152	69	141
Kilgus, P.	StL	1	0	1	0.63	0.942	1	28.2	18	8	21
Klink, J.	Fla	0	2	0	5.02	1.619	0	37.2	37	24	22
Knudson, M.	Col	0	0	0	22.24	3.706	0	5.2	16	5	3
Lancaster, L.	StL	4	1	0	2.93	1.272	0	61.1	56	21	36
Landrum, B.	Cin	0	2	0	3.74	1.108	0	21.2	18	6	14
Layana, T.	SF	0	0	0	22.50	4.000	0	2.0	7	1	1
Leskanic, C.	Col	1	5	0	5.37	1.544	8	57.0	59	27	30
Lewis, R.	Fla	6	3	0	3.26	1.448	0	77.1	68	43	65
Looney, B.	Mon	0	0	0	3.00	1.667	1	6.0	8	2	7
Luebbers, L.	Cin	2	5	0	4.54	1.461	14	77.1	74	38	38
Maddux, G.	Atl	20	10	0	2.36	1.071	36	267.0	228	52	197
Maddux, M.	NYN	3	8	5	3.60	1.307	0	75.0	67	27	57
Magrane, J.	StL	8	10	0	4.97	1.457	20	116.0	127	37	38
Manzanillo, J.	NYN	0	0	0	3.00	1.417	0	12.0	8	9	11
Martinez, D.	Mon	15	9	1	3.85	1.273	34	224.2	211	64	138
Martinez, P.	LA	10	5	2	2.61	1.280	2	107.0	76	57	119
Martinez, P.	SD	3	1	0	2.43	1.000	0	37.0	23	13	32
Martinez, R.	LA	10	12	0	3.44	1.465	32	211.2	202	104	127
Mason, R.	SD	0	7	0	3.24	1.260	0	50.0	43	18	39
Mason, R.	Phi	5	5	0	4.89	1.268	0	49.2	47	16	32
Mauser, T.	Phi	0	0	0	4.96	1.408	0	16.1	15	7	14
Mauser, T.	SD	0	1	0	3.58	1.407	0	37.2	36	17	32
McClure, B.	Fla	1	1	0	7.11	2.842	0	6.1	13	5	6
McDowell, R.	LA	5	3	2	2.25	1.588	0	68.0	76	30	27
McElroy, C.	ChN	2	2	0	4.56	1.627	0	47.1	51	25	31
McMichael, G.	Atl	2	3	19	2.06	1.058	0	91.2	68	29	89
Menendez, T.	Pit	2	0	0	3.00	1.190	0	21.0	20	4	13
Mercker, K.	Atl	3	1	0	2.86	1.364	6	66.0	52	36	59
Miceli, D.	Pit	0	0	0	5.06	1.688	0	5.1	6	3	4

NL Pitcher	Team	W	L	SV	ERA	Ratio	GS	IP	H	BB	K
Miller, P.	Pit	0	0	0	5.40	1.700	2	10.0	15	2	2
Minor, B.	Pit	8	6	2	4.10	1.314	0	94.1	94	26	84
Minutelli, G.	SF	0	1	0	3.77	1.535	0	14.1	7	15	10
Moeller, D.	Pit	1	0	0	9.92	2.082	0	16.1	26	7	13
Moore, M.	Col	3	1	0	6.84	1.937	0	26.1	30	20	13
Morgan, M.	ChN	10	15	0	4.03	1.382	32	207.2	206	74	111
Mulholland, T.	Phi	12	9	0	3.25	1.152	28	191.0	177	40	116
Munoz, M.	Col	2	1	0	4.50	1.667	0	18.0	21	9	16
Murphy, R.	StL	5	7	1	4.87	1.454	0	64.2	73	20	41
Myers, R.	ChN	2	4	53	3.11	1.221	0	75.1	65	26	86
Nabholz, C.	Mon	9	8	0	4.09	1.466	21	116.2	100	63	74
Neagle, D.	Pit	3	5	1	5.31	1.500	7	81.1	82	37	73
Nen, R.	Fla	1	0	0	7.02	1.650	1	33.1	35	20	27
Nichols, R.	LA	0	1	0	5.68	1.737	0	6.1	9	2	3
Nied, D.	Col	5	9	0	5.17	1.632	16	87.0	99	42	46
Olivares, O.	StL	5	3	1	4.17	1.660	9	118.2	134	54	63
Osborne, D.	StL	10	7	0	3.76	1.330	26	155.2	153	47	83
Osuna, A.	Hou	1	1	2	3.20	1.224	0	25.1	17	13	21
Otto, D.	Pit	3	4	0	5.03	1.706	8	68.0	85	28	30
Painter, L.	Col	2	2	0	6.00	1.564	6	39.0	52	9	16
Pall, D.	Phi	1	0	0	2.55	1.019	0	17.2	15	3	11
Parrett, J.	Col	3	3	1	5.38	1.697	6	73.2	78	45	66
Perez, M.	StL	7	2	7	2.48	1.183	0	72.2	65	20	58
Petkovsek, M.	Pit	3	0	0	6.96	1.608	0	32.1	43	9	14
Plesac, D.	ChN	2	1	0	4.74	1.516	0	62.2	74	21	47
Portugal, M.	Hou	18	4	0	2.77	1.322	33	208.0	194	77	131
Powell, R.	Cin	0	3	0	4.41	1.163	1	16.1	13	6	17
Pugh, T.	Cin	10	15	0	5.26	1.619	27	164.1	200	59	94
Rapp, P.	Fla	4	6	0	4.02	1.511	16	94.0	101	39	57
Reardon, J.	Cin	4	6	8	4.09	1.314	0	61.2	66	10	35
Reed, S.	Col	9	5	3	4.48	1.340	0	84.1	80	30	51
Reynolds, S.	Hou	0	0	0	0.82	1.545	1	11.0	11	6	10
Reynoso, A.	Col	12	11	0	4.00	1.471	30	189.0	206	63	117
Righetti, D.	SF	1	1	1	5.70	1.606	0	47.1	58	17	31
Rijo, J.	Cin	14	9	0	2.48	1.096	36	257.1	218	62	227
Risley, B.	Mon	0	0	0	6.00	1.667	0	3.0	2	2	2
Rivera, B.	Phi	13	9	0	5.02	1.632	28	163.0	175	85	123
Robertson, R.	Pit	0	1	0	6.00	2.111	0	9.0	15	4	5
Rodriguez, R.	SD	2	3	2	3.30	1.467	0	30.0	34	9	22
Rodriguez, R.	Fla	0	1	1	4.11	1.391	0	46.0	39	24	21
Rogers, K.	SF	2	2	0	2.68	1.277	0	80.2	71	28	62
Rojas, M.	Mon	5	8	10	2.95	1.291	0	88.1	80	30	48
Roper, J.	Cin	2	5	0	5.63	1.650	15	80.0	92	36	54
Rueter, K.	Mon	8	0	0	2.73	1.202	14	85.2	85	18	31
Ruffin, B.	Col	6	5	2	3.87	1.539	12	139.2	145	69	126
Ruffin, J.	Cin	2	1	2	3.58	1.274	0	37.2	36	11	30
Ruskin, S.	Cin	0	0	0	18.00	5.000	0	1.0	3	2	0
Saberhagen, B.	NYN	7	7	0	3.29	1.084	19	139.1	131	17	93
Sanders, S.	SD	3	3	0	4.13	1.490	9	52.1	54	23	37
Sanderson, S.	SF	4	2	0	3.51	1.151	8	48.2	48	7	36
Sanford, M.	Col	1	2	0	5.30	1.794	6	35.2	37	27	36
Scanlan, B.	ChN	4	5	0	4.54	1.460	0	75.1	79	28	44
Schilling, C.	Phi	16	7	0	4.02	1.254	34	235.1	234	57	186

NL Pitcher	Team	W	L	SV	ERA	Ratio	GS	IP	H	BB	K
Schourek, P.	NYN	5	12	0	5.96	1.683	18	128.1	168	45	72
Scott, T.	SD	2	0	0	2.39	1.513	0	37.2	38	15	30
Scott, T.	Mon	5	2	1	3.71	1.471	0	34.0	31	19	35
Seanez, R.	SD	0	0	0	13.50	3.000	0	3.1	8	2	1
Seminara, F.	SD	3	3	0	4.47	1.662	7	46.1	53	21	22
Service, S.	Col	0	0	0	9.64	2.143	0	4.2	8	1	3
Service, S.	Cin	2	2	2	3.70	1.258	0	41.1	36	15	40
Shaw, J.	Mon	2	7	0	4.14	1.359	8	95.2	91	32	50
Shepherd, K.	Col	1	3	1	6.98	1.603	1	19.1	26	4	7
Shouse, B.	Pit	0	0	0	9.00	2.250	0	4.0	7	2	3
Slocumb, H.	ChN	1	0	0	3.38	1.031	0	10.2	7	4	4
Smiley, J.	Cin	3	9	0	5.62	1.420	18	105.2	117	31	60
Smith, B.	Col	2	4	0	8.49	2.056	5	29.2	47	11	9
Smith, L.	StL	2	4	43	4.50	1.160	0	50.0	49	9	49
Smith, P.	Atl	4	8	0	4.37	1.434	14	90.2	92	36	53
Smith, Z.	Pit	3	7	0	4.55	1.434	14	83.0	97	22	32
Smoltz, J.	Atl	15	11	0	3.62	1.289	35	243.2	208	100	208
Spradlin, J.	Cin	2	1	2	3.49	1.082	0	49.0	44	9	24
Stanton, M.	Atl	4	6	27	4.67	1.538	0	52.0	51	29	43
Swift, B.	SF	21	8	0	2.82	1.100	34	232.2	195	55	157
Swindell, G.	Hou	12	13	0	4.16	1.345	30	190.1	215	40	124
Tanana, F.	NYN	7	15	0	4.48	1.393	29	183.0	198	48	104
Taylor, K.	SD	0	5	0	6.45	1.829	7	68.1	72	49	45
Telgheder, D.	NYN	6	2	0	4.76	1.414	7	75.2	82	21	35
Tewksbury, B.	StL	17	10	0	3.83	1.329	32	213.2	258	20	97
Thigpen, B.	Phi	3	1	0	6.05	1.707	0	19.1	23	9	10
Toliver, F.	Pit	1	0	0	3.74	1.385	0	21.2	20	8	14
Tomlin, R.	Pit	4	8	0	4.85	1.312	18	98.1	109	15	44
Torres, S.	SF	3	5	0	4.03	1.455	8	44.2	37	27	23
Trachsel, S.	ChN	0	2	0	4.58	0.966	3	19.2	16	3	14
Trlicek, R.	LA	1	2	1	4.08	1.281	0	64.0	59	21	41
Turner, M.	Fla	4	5	0	2.91	1.206	0	68.0	55	26	59
Urbani, T.	StL	1	3	0	4.65	1.597	9	62.0	73	26	33
Valdez, S.	Mon	0	0	0	9.00	1.667	0	3.0	4	1	2
Wagner, P.	Pit	8	8	2	4.27	1.316	17	141.1	143	42	114
Wakefield, T.	Pit	6	11	0	5.61	1.784	20	128.1	145	75	59
Walk, B.	Pit	13	14	0	5.68	1.545	32	187.0	214	70	80
Walton, B.	Mon	0	0	0	9.53	2.471	0	5.2	11	3	0
Watson, A.	StL	6	7	0	4.60	1.407	15	86.0	90	28	49
Wayne, G.	Col	5	3	1	5.05	1.524	0	62.1	68	26	49
Weathers, D.	Fla	2	3	0	5.12	1.555	6	45.2	57	13	34
Wendell, T.	ChN	1	2	0	4.37	1.412	4	22.2	24	8	15
West, D.	Phi	6	4	3	2.92	1.344	0	86.1	60	51	87
Weston, M.	NYN	0	0	0	7.94	2.294	0	5.2	11	1	2
Wetteland, J.	Mon	9	3	43	1.37	1.031	0	85.1	58	28	113
Whitehurst, W.	SD	4	7	0	3.83	1.344	19	105.2	109	30	57
Wickander, K.	Cin	1	0	0	6.75	2.092	0	25.1	32	19	20
Williams, B.	Hou	4	4	3	4.83	1.439	5	82.0	76	38	56
Williams, M.	Phi	1	3	0	5.29	1.412	4	51.0	50	22	33
Williams, M.	Phi	3	7	43	3.34	1.645	0	62.0	56	44	60
Wilson, S.	LA	1	0	1	4.56	1.753	0	25.2	30	14	23
Wilson, T.	SF	7	5	0	3.60	1.418	18	110.0	110	40	57
Wohlers, M.	Atl	6	2	0	4.50	1.250	0	48.0	37	22	45

NL Pitcher	Team	W	L	SV	ERA	Ratio	GS	IP	H	BB	K
Worrell, T.	SD	2	7	0	4.92	1.460	16	100.2	104	43	52
Worrell, T.	LA	1	1	5	6.05	1.474	0	38.2	46	11	31
Young, A.	NYN	1	16	3	3.77	1.455	10	100.1	103	42	62
Young, P.	Mon	1	0	0	3.38	0.750	0	5.1	4	0	3

AMERICAN LEAGUE: BATTERS

AL Batter	Team	BA	HR	RBI	SB	CS	G	AB	R	BB	OBP
Abbott, K.	Oak	.246	3	9	2	0	20	61	11	3	.281
Aldrete, M.	Oak	.267	10	33	1	1	95	255	40	34	.353
Alexander, M.	Bal	.000	0	0	0	0	3	0	1	0	.000
Alomar, R.	Tor	.326	17	93	55	15	153	589	109	80	.408
Alomar Jr, S.	Cle	.270	6	32	3	1	64	215	24	11	.318
Amaral, R.	Sea	.290	1	44	19	11	110	373	53	33	.348
Anderson, B.	Bal	.262	13	66	24	12	142	560	87	82	.363
Armas, M.	Oak	.194	1	1	1	0	15	31	7	1	.242
Backman, W.	Sea	.138	0	0	0	0	10	29	2	1	.167
Baerga, C.	Cle	.321	21	114	15	4	154	624	105	34	.355
Baines, H.	Bal	.313	20	78	0	0	118	416	64	57	.390
Balboni, S.	Tex	.600	0	0	0	0	2	5	0	0	.600
Barnes, S.	Det	.281	2	27	5	5	84	160	24	11	.318
Bautista, D.	Det	.311	1	9	3	1	17	61	6	1	.317
Becker, R.	Min	.286	0	0	1	1	3	7	3	5	.583
Bell, G.	ChA	.217	13	64	1	1	102	410	36	13	.243
Bell, J.	Mil	.234	5	29	6	6	91	286	42	36	.321
Belle, A.	Cle	.290	38	129	23	12	159	594	93	76	.370
Blankenship, L.	Oak	.190	2	23	13	5	94	252	43	67	.363
Blosser, G.	Bos	.071	0	1	1	0	17	28	1	2	.133
Blowers, M.	Sea	.280	15	57	1	5	127	379	55	44	.357
Boggs, W.	NYA	.302	2	59	0	1	143	560	83	74	.378
Boone, B.	Sea	.251	12	38	2	3	76	271	31	17	.301
Borders, P.	Tor	.254	9	55	2	2	138	488	38	20	.285
Bordick, M.	Oak	.249	3	48	10	10	159	546	60	60	.332
Brett, G.	KC	.266	19	75	7	5	145	560	69	39	.312
Brito, B.	Min	.241	4	9	0	0	27	54	8	1	.255
Brooks, H.	KC	.286	1	24	0	1	75	168	14	11	.331
Brosius, S.	Oak	.249	6	25	6	0	70	213	26	14	.296
Browne, J.	Oak	.250	2	19	4	0	76	260	27	22	.306
Bruett, J.	Min	.250	0	1	0	0	17	20	2	1	.318
Brunansky, T.	Mil	.183	6	29	3	4	80	224	20	25	.265
Buford, D.	Bal	.228	2	9	2	2	53	79	18	9	.315
Buhner, J.	Sea	.272	27	98	2	5	158	563	91	100	.379
Burks, E.	ChA	.275	17	74	6	9	146	499	75	60	.352
Bush, R.	Min	.156	0	3	0	0	35	45	1	7	.269
Butler, R.	Tor	.271	0	2	2	2	17	48	8	7	.375
Byrd, J.	Bos	.000	0	0	0	0	2	0	0	0	.000
Calderon, I.	Bos	.221	1	19	4	2	73	213	25	21	.291
Calderon, I.	ChA	.115	0	3	0	0	9	26	1	0	.115
Canate, W.	Tor	.213	1	3	1	1	38	47	12	6	.309
Canseco, J.	Tex	.255	10	46	6	6	60	231	30	16	.308
Carey, P.	Bal	.213	0	3	0	0	18	47	1	5	.288
Carter, J.	Tor	.254	33	121	8	3	155	603	92	47	.312
Cedeno, D.	Tor	.174	0	7	1	0	15	46	5	1	.188
Coles, D.	Tor	.253	4	26	1	1	64	194	26	16	.319

AL Batter	Team	BA	HR	RBI	SB	CS	G	AB	R	BB	OBP
Cooper, S.	Bos	.279	9	63	5	2	156	526	67	58	.355
Cora, J.	ChA	.268	2	51	20	8	153	579	95	67	.351
Correia, R.	Cal	.266	0	9	2	4	64	128	12	6	.319
Cotto, H.	Sea	.190	2	7	5	4	54	105	10	2	.213
Curtis, C.	Cal	.285	6	59	48	24	152	583	94	70	.361
Cuyler, M.	Det	.213	0	19	13	2	82	249	46	19	.276
Dascenzo, D.	Tex	.199	2	10	2	0	76	146	20	8	.239
Davis, B.	Tex	.245	3	20	3	1	62	159	24	5	.273
Davis, C.	Cal	.243	27	112	4	1	152	573	74	71	.327
Davis, E.	Det	.253	6	15	2	2	23	75	14	14	.371
Davis, G.	Bal	.177	1	9	0	1	30	113	8	7	.230
Dawson, A.	Bos	.273	13	67	2	1	121	461	44	17	.313
Deer, R.	Det	.217	14	39	3	2	90	323	48	38	.302
Deer, R.	Bos	.196	7	16	2	0	38	143	18	20	.303
Delgado, C.	Tor	.000	0	0	0	0	2	1	0	1	.000
Denson, D.	ChA	.200	0	0	0	0	4	5	0	0	.200
Devereaux, M.	Bal	.250	14	75	3	3	131	527	72	43	.306
Diaz, A.	Mil	.319	0	1	5	3	32	69	9	0	.319
Diaz, M.	Tex	.273	2	24	1	0	71	205	24	8	.297
DiSarcina, G.	Cal	.238	3	45	5	7	126	416	44	15	.273
Doran, B.	Mil	.217	0	6	1	0	28	60	7	6	.284
Ducey, R.	Tex	.282	2	9	2	3	27	85	15	10	.351
Easley, D.	Cal	.313	2	22	6	6	73	230	33	28	.392
Edmonds, J.	Cal	.246	0	4	0	2	18	61	5	2	.270
Espinoza, A.	Cle	.278	4	27	2	2	129	263	34	8	.298
Felder, M.	Sea	.211	1	20	15	9	109	342	31	22	.262
Fermin, F.	Cle	.262	2	45	4	5	140	480	48	24	.303
Fernandez, T.	Tor	.306	4	50	15	8	94	353	45	31	.361
Fielder, C.	Det	.267	30	117	0	1	154	573	80	90	.368
Fisk, C.	ChA	.189	1	4	0	1	25	53	2	2	.228
Flaherty, J.	Bos	.120	0	2	0	0	13	25	3	2	.214
Fletcher, S.	Bos	.285	5	45	16	3	121	480	81	37	.341
Fox, E.	Oak	.143	1	5	0	2	29	56	5	2	.172
Franco, J.	Tex	.289	14	84	9	3	144	532	85	62	.360
Fryman, T.	Det	.300	22	97	9	4	151	607	98	77	.379
Gaetti, G.	Cal	.180	0	4	1	0	20	50	3	5	.250
Gaetti, G.	KC	.256	14	46	0	3	82	281	37	16	.309
Gagne, G.	KC	.280	10	57	10	12	159	540	66	33	.319
Gallego, M.	NYA	.283	10	54	3	2	119	403	63	50	.364
Gates, B.	Oak	.290	7	69	7	3	139	535	64	56	.357
Gibson, K.	Det	.261	13	62	15	6	116	403	62	44	.337
Gil, B.	Tex	.123	0	2	1	2	22	57	3	5	.194
Gladden, D.	Det	.267	13	56	8	5	91	356	52	21	.312
Gomez, C.	Det	.250	0	11	2	2	46	128	11	9	.304
Gomez, L.	Bal	.197	10	25	0	1	71	244	30	32	.295
Gonzales, L.	Cal	.500	0	1	0	0	2	2	0	1	.667
Gonzales, R.	Cal	.251	2	31	5	5	117	335	34	49	.346
Gonzalez, J.	Tex	.310	46	118	4	1	140	536	105	37	.368
Grebeck, C.	ChA	.226	1	12	1	2	72	190	25	26	.319
Green, S.	Tor	.000	0	0	0	0	3	6	0	0	.000
Greenwell, M.	Bos	.315	13	72	5	4	146	540	77	54	.379
Griffey Jr, K.	Sea	.309	45	109	17	9	156	582	113	96	.408
Griffin, A.	Tor	.211	0	3	0	0	46	95	15	3	.235
Gruber, K.	Cal	.277	3	9	0	0	18	65	10	2	.309

FINAL 1993 AVERAGES •

AL Batter	Team	BA	HR	RBI	SB	CS	G	AB	R	BB	OBP
Guillen, O.	ChA	.280	4	50	5	4	134	457	44	10	.292
Gwynn, C.	KC	.300	1	25	0	1	103	287	36	24	.354
Hale, C.	Min	.333	3	27	2	1	69	186	25	18	.408
Hamelin, B.	KC	.224	2	5	0	0	16	49	2	6	.309
Hamilton, D.	Mil	.310	9	48	21	13	135	520	74	45	.367
Hammonds, J.	Bal	.305	3	19	4	0	33	105	10	2	.312
Harper, B.	Min	.304	12	73	1	3	147	530	52	29	.347
Harris, D.	Tex	.197	1	8	0	1	40	76	10	5	.253
Haselman, B.	Sea	.255	5	16	2	1	58	137	21	12	.316
Hatcher, B.	Bos	.287	9	57	14	7	136	508	71	28	.336
Helfand, E.	Oak	.231	0	1	0	0	8	13	1	0	.231
Hemond, S.	Oak	.256	6	26	14	5	91	215	31	32	.353
Henderson, D.	Oak	.220	20	53	0	3	107	382	37	32	.275
Henderson, R.	Oak	.327	17	47	31	6	90	318	77	85	.469
Henderson, R.	Tor	.215	4	12	22	2	44	163	37	35	.356
Hiatt, P.	KC	.218	7	36	6	3	81	238	30	16	.285
Hill, G.	Cle	.224	5	25	7	3	66	174	19	11	.268
Hocking, D.	Min	.139	0	0	1	0	15	36	7	6	.262
Hoiles, C.	Bal	.310	29	82	1	1	126	419	80	69	.416
Horn, S.	Cle	.455	4	8	0	0	12	33	8	1	.472
Howard, C.	Sea	.000	0	0	0	0	4	1	0	0	.000
Howard, D.	KC	.333	0	2	1	0	15	24	5	2	.370
Howard, T.	Cle	.236	3	23	5	1	74	178	26	12	.278
Howitt, D.	Sea	.211	2	8	0	0	32	76	6	4	.250
Hrbek, K.	Min	.242	25	83	4	2	123	392	60	71	.357
Huff, M.	ChA	.182	1	6	1	0	43	44	4	9	.321
Hulett, T.	Bal	.300	2	23	1	2	85	260	40	23	.361
Hulse, D.	Tex	.290	1	29	29	9	114	407	71	26	.333
Humphreys, M.	NYA	.171	1	6	2	1	25	35	6	4	.250
Huson, J.	Tex	.133	0	2	0	0	23	45	3	0	.133
Jackson, B.	ChA	.232	16	45	0	2	85	284	32	23	.289
Jackson, D.	Tor	.216	5	19	0	2	46	176	15	8	.250
Jaha, J.	Mil	.264	19	70	13	9	153	515	78	51	.337
James, C.	Tex	.355	3	7	0	0	8	31	5	3	.412
James, D.	NYA	.332	7	36	0	0	115	343	62	31	.390
Javier, S.	Cal	.291	3	28	12	2	92	237	33	27	.362
Jefferson, R.	Cle	.249	10	34	1	3	113	366	35	28	.310
Johnson, L.	ChA	.311	0	47	35	7	147	540	75	36	.354
Jorgensen, T.	Min	.224	1	12	1	0	59	152	15	10	.270
Jose, F.	KC	.253	6	43	31	13	149	499	64	36	.303
Joyner, W.	KC	.292	15	65	5	9	141	497	83	66	.375
Karkovice, R.	ChA	.228	20	54	2	2	128	403	60	29	.287
Kelly, P.	NYA	.273	7	51	14	11	127	406	49	24	.317
Kirby, W.	Cle	.269	6	60	17	5	131	458	71	37	.323
Kmak, J.	Mil	.218	0	7	6	2	51	110	9	14	.317
Knoblauch, C.	Min	.277	2	41	29	11	153	602	82	65	.354
Knorr, R.	Tor	.248	4	20	0	0	39	101	11	9	.309
Koslofski, K.	KC	.269	1	2	0	1	15	26	4	4	.387
Kreuter, C.	Det	.286	15	51	2	1	119	374	59	49	.371
Lampkin, T.	Mil	.198	4	25	7	3	73	162	22	20	.280
Larkin, G.	Min	.264	1	19	0	1	56	144	17	21	.357
LaValliere, M.	ChA	.258	0	8	0	1	37	97	6	4	.282
Lee, D.	Min	.152	0	4	0	0	15	33	3	1	.176
Lee, M.	Tex	.220	1	12	2	4	73	205	31	22	.300

AL Batter	Team	BA	HR	RBI	SB	CS	G	AB	R	BB	OBP
Leius, S.	Min	.167	0	2	0	0	10	18	4	2	.227
Leonard, M.	Bal	.067	0	3	0	0	10	15	1	3	.190
Levis, J.	Cle	.175	0	4	0	0	31	63	7	2	.197
Lewis, M.	Cle	.250	1	5	3	0	14	52	6	0	.250
Leyritz, J.	NYA	.309	14	53	0	0	95	259	43	37	.410
Lind, J.	KC	.248	0	37	3	2	136	431	33	13	.271
Lindsey, D.	ChA	.000	0	0	0	0	2	1	0	0	.000
Listach, P.	Mil	.244	3	30	18	9	98	356	50	37	.319
Litton, G.	Sea	.299	3	25	0	1	72	174	25	18	.366
Livingstone, S.	Det	.293	2	39	1	3	98	304	39	19	.328
Lofton, K.	Cle	.325	1	42	70	14	148	569	116	81	.408
Lovullo, T.	Cal	.251	6	30	7	6	116	367	42	36	.318
Lydy, S.	Oak	.225	2	7	2	0	41	102	11	8	.288
Lyons, S.	Bos	.130	0	0	1	2	28	23	4	2	.200
Maas, K.	NYA	.205	9	25	1	1	59	151	20	24	.316
Macfarlane, M.	KC	.273	20	67	2	5	117	388	55	40	.360
Mack, S.	Min	.276	10	61	15	5	128	503	66	41	.335
Magadan, D.	Sea	.259	1	21	2	0	71	228	27	36	.356
Maksudian, M.	Min	.167	0	2	0	0	5	12	2	4	.353
Maldonado, C.	Cle	.247	5	20	0	1	28	81	11	11	.333
Martin, N.	ChA	.357	0	2	0	0	8	14	3	1	.400
Martinez, C.	Cle	.244	5	31	1	1	80	262	26	20	.295
Martinez, C.	Bal	.000	0	0	0	0	8	15	0	4	.000
Martinez, D.	Tor	.286	1	3	0	0	8	14	2	1	.333
Martinez, E.	Sea	.237	4	13	0	0	42	135	20	28	.366
Martinez, T.	Sea	.265	17	60	0	3	109	408	48	45	.343
Mattingly, D.	NYA	.291	17	86	0	0	134	530	78	61	.364
Mayne, B.	KC	.254	2	22	3	2	71	205	22	18	.317
McCarty, D.	Min	.214	2	21	2	6	98	350	36	19	.257
McGwire, M.	Oak	.333	9	24	0	1	27	84	16	21	.467
McIntosh, T.	Mil	.000	0	0	0	0	1	0	0	0	.000
McLemore, M.	Bal	.284	4	72	21	15	148	581	81	64	.353
McNeely, J.	Bos	.297	0	1	6	0	21	37	10	7	.409
McRae, B.	KC	.282	12	69	23	14	153	627	78	37	.325
McReynolds, K.	KC	.245	11	42	2	2	110	351	44	37	.316
Meares, P.	Min	.251	0	33	4	5	111	346	33	7	.266
Melvin, B.	Bos	.222	3	23	0	0	77	176	13	7	.251
Mercedes, H.	Oak	.213	0	3	1	1	20	47	5	2	.260
Mercedes, L.	Bal	.292	0	0	1	1	10	24	1	5	.414
Merullo, M.	ChA	.050	0	0	0	0	8	20	1	0	.050
Meulens, H.	NYA	.170	2	5	0	1	30	53	8	8	.279
Mieske, M.	Mil	.241	3	7	0	2	23	58	9	4	.290
Miller, K.	KC	.167	0	3	3	1	37	108	9	8	.229
Milligan, R.	Cle	.426	0	7	0	0	19	47	7	14	.557
Molitor, P.	Tor	.332	22	111	22	4	160	636	121	77	.402
Munoz, P.	Min	.233	13	38	1	2	104	326	34	25	.294
Myers, G.	Cal	.255	7	40	3	3	108	290	27	17	.298
Naehring, T.	Bos	.331	1	17	1	0	39	127	14	10	.377
Neel, T.	Oak	.290	19	63	3	5	123	427	59	49	.367
Newfield, M.	Sea	.227	1	7	0	1	22	66	5	2	.257
Newson, W.	ChA	.300	2	6	0	0	26	40	9	9	.429
Nilsson, D.	Mil	.257	7	40	3	6	100	296	35	37	.336
Nokes, M.	NYA	.249	10	35	0	0	76	217	25	16	.303
O'Brien, P.	Sea	.257	7	27	0	0	72	210	30	26	.335
O'Leary, T.	Mil	.293	0	3	0	0	19	41	3	5	.370

AL Batter	Team	BA	HR	RBI	SB	CS	G	AB	R	BB	OBP
O'Neill, P.	NYA	.311	20	75	2	4	141	498	71	44	.367
Obando, S.	Bal	.272	3	15	0	0	31	92	8	4	.309
Olerud, J.	Tor	.363	24	107	0	2	158	551	109	114	.473
Ortiz, J.	Cle	.221	0	20	1	0	95	249	19	11	.267
Ortiz, L.	Bos	.250	0	1	0	0	9	12	0	0	.250
Orton, J.	Cal	.189	1	4	1	2	37	95	5	7	.252
Owen, S.	NYA	.234	2	20	3	2	103	334	41	29	.294
Pagliarulo, M.	Min	.292	3	23	6	6	83	253	31	18	.350
Pagliarulo, M.	Bal	.325	6	21	0	0	33	117	24	8	.373
Palmeiro, R.	Tex	.295	37	105	22	3	160	597	124	73	.371
Palmer, D.	Tex	.245	33	96	11	10	148	519	88	53	.321
Paquette, C.	Oak	.219	12	46	4	2	105	393	35	14	.245
Parent, M.	Bal	.259	4	12	0	0	22	54	7	3	.293
Parks, D.	Min	.200	0	1	0	0	7	20	3	1	.238
Parrish, L.	Cle	.200	1	2	1	0	10	20	2	4	.333
Pasqua, D.	ChA	.205	5	20	2	2	78	176	22	26	.302
Peltier, D.	Tex	.269	1	17	0	4	65	160	23	20	.352
Pena, T.	Bos	.181	4	19	1	3	126	304	20	25	.246
Perez, E.	Cal	.250	4	30	5	4	52	180	16	9	.292
Petralli, G.	Tex	.241	1	13	2	0	59	133	16	22	.348
Phillips, T.	Det	.313	7	57	16	11	151	566	113	132	.443
Pirkl, G.	Sea	.174	1	4	0	0	7	23	1	0	.174
Polonia, L.	Cal	.271	1	32	55	24	152	576	75	48	.328
Puckett, K.	Min	.296	22	89	8	6	156	622	89	47	.349
Pulliam, H.	KC	.258	1	6	0	0	27	62	7	2	.292
Quintana, C.	Bos	.244	1	19	1	0	101	303	31	31	.317
Raines, T.	ChA	.306	16	54	21	7	115	415	75	64	.401
Ramirez, M.	Cle	.170	2	5	0	0	22	53	5	2	.200
Reboulet, J.	Min	.258	1	15	5	5	109	240	33	35	.356
Redus, G.	Tex	.288	6	31	4	4	77	222	28	23	.351
Reimer, K.	Mil	.249	13	60	5	4	125	437	53	30	.303
Reynolds, H.	Bal	.252	4	47	12	11	145	485	64	66	.343
Richardson, J.	Bos	.208	0	2	0	0	15	24	3	1	.240
Riles, E.	Bos	.189	5	20	1	3	94	143	15	20	.292
Ripken, B.	Tex	.189	0	11	0	2	50	132	12	11	.270
Ripken, C.	Bal	.257	24	90	1	4	162	641	87	65	.329
Rivera, L.	Bos	.208	1	7	1	2	62	130	13	11	.273
Rodriguez, I.	Tex	.273	10	66	8	7	137	473	56	29	.315
Rossy, R.	KC	.221	2	12	0	0	46	86	10	9	.302
Rowland, R.	Det	.217	0	4	0	0	21	46	2	5	.294
Russell, J.	Tex	.227	1	3	0	0	18	22	1	2	.292
Salmon, T.	Cal	.283	31	95	5	6	142	515	93	82	.382
Santovenia, N.	KC	.125	0	0	0	0	4	8	0	1	.222
Sasser, M.	Sea	.218	1	21	1	0	83	188	18	15	.274
Sax, S.	ChA	.235	1	8	7	3	57	119	20	8	.283
Schofield, D.	Tor	.191	0	5	3	0	36	110	11	16	.294
Segui, D.	Bal	.273	10	60	2	1	146	450	54	58	.351
Seitzer, K.	Oak	.255	4	27	4	7	73	255	24	27	.324
Seitzer, K.	Mil	.290	7	30	3	0	47	162	21	17	.359
Shave, J.	Tex	.319	0	7	1	3	17	47	3	0	.306
Sheets, L.	Sea	.118	0	1	0	0	11	17	0	2	.250
Shumpert, T.	KC	.100	0	0	1	0	8	10	0	2	.250
Sierra, R.	Oak	.233	22	101	25	5	158	630	77	52	.288
Silvestri, D.	NYA	.286	1	4	0	0	7	21	4	5	.423

AL Batter	Team	BA	HR	RBI	SB	CS	G	AB	R	BB	OBP
Smith, L.	Bal	.208	2	3	0	0	9	24	8	8	.406
Snow, J.	Cal	.241	16	57	3	0	129	419	60	55	.328
Sojo, L.	Tor	.170	0	6	0	0	19	47	5	4	.231
Sorrento, P.	Cle	.257	18	65	3	1	148	463	75	58	.340
Spiers, B.	Mil	.238	2	36	9	8	113	340	43	29	.302
Sprague, E.	Tor	.260	12	73	1	0	150	546	50	32	.310
Stahoviak, S.	Min	.193	0	1	0	2	20	57	1	3	.233
Stankiewicz, A.	NYA	.000	0	0	0	0	16	9	5	1	.000
Stanley, M.	NYA	.305	26	84	1	1	130	423	70	57	.389
Steinbach, T.	Oak	.285	10	43	3	3	104	389	47	25	.333
Stillwell, K.	Cal	.262	0	3	2	0	22	61	2	4	.299
Strange, D.	Tex	.256	7	60	6	4	145	484	58	43	.318
Suero, W.	Mil	.286	0	0	0	1	15	14	0	1	.333
Surhoff, B.	Mil	.274	7	79	12	9	148	552	66	36	.318
Sveum, D.	Oak	.177	2	6	0	0	30	79	12	16	.316
Tackett, J.	Bal	.172	0	9	0	0	38	87	8	13	.277
Tartabull, D.	NYA	.250	31	102	0	0	138	513	87	92	.363
Tettleton, M.	Det	.245	32	110	3	7	152	522	79	109	.372
Thomas, F.	ChA	.317	41	128	4	2	153	549	106	112	.426
Thome, J.	Cle	.266	7	22	2	1	47	154	28	29	.385
Thon, D.	Mil	.269	1	33	6	5	85	245	23	22	.324
Thurman, G.	Det	.213	0	13	7	0	75	89	22	11	.297
Tingley, R.	Cal	.200	0	12	1	2	58	90	7	9	.277
Tinsley, L.	Sea	.158	1	2	0	0	11	19	2	2	.238
Trammell, A.	Det	.329	12	60	12	8	112	401	72	38	.388
Treadway, J.	Cle	.303	2	27	1	1	97	221	25	14	.347
Turang, B.	Sea	.250	0	7	6	2	40	140	22	17	.340
Turner, C.	Cal	.280	1	13	1	1	25	75	9	9	.360
Valentin, J.	Bos	.278	11	66	3	4	144	468	50	49	.346
Valentin, J.	Mil	.245	1	7	1	0	19	53	10	7	.344
Valle, D.	Sea	.258	13	63	1	0	135	423	48	48	.354
Van Burkleo, T.	Cal	.152	1	1	1	0	12	33	2	6	.282
Vaughn, G.	Mil	.267	30	97	10	7	154	569	97	89	.369
Vaughn, M.	Bos	.297	29	101	4	3	152	539	86	79	.390
Velarde, R.	NYA	.301	7	24	2	2	85	226	28	18	.360
Ventura, R.	ChA	.262	22	94	1	6	157	554	85	105	.379
Vina, F.	Sea	.222	0	2	6	0	24	45	5	4	.327
Vizquel, O.	Sea	.255	2	31	12	14	158	560	68	50	.319
Voigt, J.	Bal	.296	6	23	1	0	64	152	32	25	.395
Walewander, J.	Cal	.125	0	3	1	1	12	8	2	5	.429
Walton, J.	Cal	.000	0	0	1	0	5	2	2	1	.000
Ward, T.	Tor	.192	4	28	3	3	72	167	20	23	.287
Webster, L.	Min	.198	1	8	1	0	49	106	14	11	.274
Whitaker, L.	Det	.290	9	67	3	3	119	383	72	78	.412
White, D.	Tor	.273	15	52	34	4	146	598	116	57	.341
Wilkerson, C.	KC	.143	0	0	2	0	12	28	1	1	.172
Williams, B.	NYA	.268	12	68	9	9	139	567	67	53	.333
Williams, G.	NYA	.149	0	6	2	0	42	67	11	1	.183
Wilson, C.	KC	.265	1	3	1	1	21	49	6	7	.357
Winfield, D.	Min	.271	21	76	2	3	143	547	72	45	.325
Wrona, R.	ChA	.125	0	1	0	0	4	8	0	0	.125
Yount, R.	Mil	.258	8	51	9	2	127	454	62	44	.326
Zupcic, B.	Bos	.241	2	26	5	2	141	286	40	27	.308

AMERICAN LEAGUE: PITCHERS

AL Pitcher	Team	W	L	SV	ERA	Ratio	GS	IP	H	BB	K
Abbott, J.	NYA	11	14	0	4.37	1.388	32	214.0	221	73	95
Abbott, P.	Cle	0	1	0	6.38	1.636	5	18.1	19	11	7
Aguilera, R.	Min	4	3	34	3.11	1.037	0	72.1	60	14	59
Alvarez, W.	ChA	15	8	0	2.95	1.430	31	207.2	168	122	155
Anderson, B.	Cal	0	0	0	3.97	1.147	1	11.1	11	2	4
Appier, K.	KC	18	8	0	2.56	1.110	34	238.2	183	81	186
Assenmacher, P.	NYA	2	2	0	3.12	1.154	0	17.1	10	9	11
Austin, J.	Mil	1	2	0	3.82	1.273	0	33.0	28	13	15
Ayrault, B.	Sea	1	1	0	3.20	1.220	0	19.2	18	6	7
Bailey, C.	Bos	0	1	0	3.45	1.532	0	15.2	12	12	11
Bankhead, S.	Bos	2	1	0	3.50	1.368	0	64.1	59	29	47
Banks, W.	Min	11	12	0	4.04	1.558	30	171.1	186	78	138
Belcher, T.	ChA	3	5	0	4.40	1.284	11	71.2	64	27	34
Belinda, S.	KC	1	1	0	4.28	1.354	0	27.1	30	6	25
Bere, J.	ChA	12	5	0	3.47	1.367	24	142.2	109	81	129
Bergman, S.	Det	1	4	0	5.67	1.790	6	39.2	47	23	19
Bielecki, M.	Cle	4	5	0	5.90	1.675	13	68.2	90	23	38
Boddicker, M.	Mil	3	5	0	5.67	1.778	10	54.0	77	15	24
Boever, J.	Oak	4	2	0	3.86	1.563	0	79.1	87	33	49
Boever, J.	Det	2	1	3	2.74	1.087	0	23.0	14	11	14
Bohanon, B.	Tex	4	4	0	4.76	1.694	8	92.2	107	46	45
Bolton, R.	ChA	2	6	0	7.44	1.701	8	42.1	55	16	17
Bolton, T.	Det	6	6	0	4.47	1.607	8	102.2	113	45	66
Bones, R.	Mil	11	11	0	4.86	1.439	31	203.2	222	63	63
Bosio, C.	Sea	9	9	1	3.45	1.235	24	164.1	138	59	119
Brewer, B.	KC	2	2	0	3.46	1.308	0	39.0	31	20	28
Briscoe, J.	Oak	1	0	0	8.03	2.108	0	24.2	26	26	24
Bronkey, J.	Tex	1	1	1	4.00	1.417	0	36.0	39	11	18
Brow, S.	Tor	1	1	0	6.00	1.667	3	18.0	19	10	7
Brown, K.	Tex	15	12	0	3.59	1.361	34	233.0	228	74	142
Brummett, G.	Min	2	1	0	5.74	1.650	5	26.2	29	15	10
Burgos, E.	KC	0	1	0	9.00	2.400	0	5.0	5	6	6
Burns, T.	Tex	0	4	0	4.57	1.492	5	65.0	63	32	35
Butcher, M.	Cal	1	0	8	2.86	1.341	0	28.1	21	15	24
Cadaret, G.	KC	1	1	0	2.93	1.435	0	15.1	14	7	2
Campbell, K.	Oak	0	0	0	7.31	2.000	0	16.0	20	11	9
Carpenter, C.	Tex	4	1	1	4.22	1.531	0	32.0	35	12	27
Cary, C.	ChA	1	0	0	5.23	1.742	0	20.2	22	11	10
Casian, L.	Min	5	3	1	3.02	1.306	0	56.2	59	14	31
Castillo, T.	Tor	3	2	0	3.38	1.303	0	50.2	44	22	28
Charlton, N.	Sea	1	3	18	2.34	1.125	0	34.2	22	17	48
Christopher, M.	Cle	0	0	0	3.86	1.371	0	11.2	14	2	8
Clark, M.	Cle	7	5	0	4.28	1.326	15	109.1	119	25	57
Clemens, R.	Bos	11	14	0	4.46	1.320	29	191.2	175	67	160
Cone, D.	KC	11	14	0	3.33	1.295	34	254.0	205	114	191
Converse, J.	Sea	1	3	0	5.31	1.820	4	20.1	23	14	10
Cook, A.	NYA	0	1	0	5.06	2.063	0	5.1	4	7	4
Cook, D.	Cle	5	5	0	5.67	1.481	6	54.0	62	16	34
Cook, M.	Bal	0	0	0	0.00	1.000	0	3.0	1	2	3
Cox, D.	Tor	7	6	2	3.12	1.219	0	83.2	73	29	84
Crim, C.	Cal	2	2	0	5.87	1.565	0	15.1	17	5	10
Cummings, J.	Sea	0	6	0	6.02	1.662	8	46.1	59	16	19
Darling, R.	Oak	5	9	0	5.16	1.545	29	178.0	198	72	95
Darwin, D.	Bos	15	11	0	3.26	1.081	34	229.1	196	49	130

AL Pitcher	Team	W	L	SV	ERA	Ratio	GS	IP	H	BB	K
Davis, S.	Oak	2	6	0	6.18	1.644	8	62.2	68	33	37
Davis, S.	Det	0	2	4	3.06	1.160	0	35.1	25	15	36
Dayley, K.	Tor	0	0	0	0.00	7.500	0	0.2	1	4	2
DeLeon, J.	ChA	0	0	0	1.74	0.871	0	10.1	5	3	6
DeLucia, R.	Sea	3	6	0	4.64	1.641	1	42.2	46	23	48
Deshaies, J.	Min	11	13	0	4.41	1.291	27	167.1	159	51	80
DeSilva, J.	Det	0	0	0	9.00	2.000	0	1.0	2	0	0
DiPino, F.	KC	1	1	0	6.89	1.851	0	15.2	21	6	5
Dipoto, J.	Cle	4	4	11	2.40	1.562	0	56.1	57	30	41
Doherty, J.	Det	14	11	0	4.44	1.397	31	184.2	205	48	63
Dopson, J.	Bos	7	11	0	4.97	1.484	28	155.2	170	59	89
Downs, K.	Oak	5	10	0	5.64	1.646	12	119.2	135	60	66
Drahman, B.	ChA	0	0	1	0.00	1.688	0	5.1	7	2	3
Dreyer, S.	Tex	3	3	0	5.71	1.683	6	41.0	48	20	23
Eckersley, D.	Oak	2	4	36	4.16	1.224	0	67.0	67	13	80
Eichhorn, M.	Tor	3	1	0	2.72	1.390	0	72.2	76	22	47
Eldred, C.	Mil	16	16	0	4.01	1.291	36	258.0	232	91	180
Erickson, S.	Min	8	19	0	5.19	1.587	34	218.2	266	71	116
Fajardo, H.	Tex	0	0	0	0.00	0.000	0	0.2	0	0	1
Farr, S.	NYA	2	2	25	4.21	1.574	0	47.0	44	28	39
Farrell, J.	Cal	3	12	0	7.35	1.776	17	90.2	110	44	45
Fernandez, A.	ChA	18	9	0	3.13	1.189	34	247.1	221	67	169
Fetters, M.	Mil	3	3	0	3.34	1.399	0	59.1	59	22	23
Finley, C.	Cal	16	14	0	3.15	1.317	35	251.1	243	82	187
Fleming, D.	Sea	12	5	0	4.36	1.566	26	167.1	189	67	75
Flener, H.	Tor	0	0	0	4.05	1.650	0	6.2	7	4	2
Fossas, T.	Bos	1	1	0	5.18	1.375	0	40.0	38	15	39
Frey, S.	Cal	2	3	13	2.98	1.448	0	48.1	41	26	22
Frohwirth, T.	Bal	6	7	3	3.83	1.433	0	96.1	91	44	50
Garces, R.	Min	0	0	0	0.00	1.500	0	4.0	4	2	3
Gardiner, M.	Det	0	0	0	3.97	1.676	0	11.1	12	7	4
Gardner, M.	KC	4	6	0	6.19	1.440	16	91.2	92	36	54
Gibson, P.	NYA	2	0	0	3.06	1.132	0	35.1	31	9	25
Gohr, G.	Det	0	0	0	5.96	1.853	0	22.2	26	14	23
Gordon, T.	KC	12	6	1	3.58	1.304	14	155.2	125	77	143
Gossage, G.	Oak	4	5	1	4.53	1.594	0	47.2	49	26	40
Grahe, J.	Cal	4	1	11	2.86	1.429	0	56.2	54	25	31
Granger, J.	KC	0	0	0	27.00	5.000	0	1.0	3	2	1
Grater, M.	Det	0	0	0	5.40	2.000	0	5.0	6	4	4
Grimsley, J.	Cle	3	4	0	5.31	1.724	6	42.1	52	20	27
Groom, B.	Det	0	2	0	6.14	1.718	3	36.2	48	13	15
Guardado, E.	Min	3	8	0	6.18	1.690	16	94.2	123	36	46
Gubicza, M.	KC	5	8	2	4.66	1.658	6	104.1	128	43	80
Gullickson, B.	Det	13	9	0	5.37	1.462	28	159.1	186	44	70
Guthrie, M.	Min	2	1	0	4.71	1.714	0	21.0	20	16	15
Guzman, J.	Tor	14	3	0	3.99	1.466	33	221.0	211	110	194
Haas, D.	Det	1	2	0	6.11	1.893	0	28.0	45	8	17
Habyan, J.	NYA	2	1	1	4.04	1.441	0	42.1	45	16	29
Habyan, J.	KC	0	0	0	4.50	1.286	0	14.0	14	4	10
Hampton, M.	Sea	1	3	1	9.53	2.647	3	17.0	28	17	8
Haney, C.	KC	9	9	0	6.02	1.589	23	124.0	141	53	65
Hanson, E.	Sea	11	12	0	3.47	1.302	30	215.0	215	60	163
Harris, G.	Bos	6	7	8	3.77	1.469	0	112.1	95	60	103
Hartley, M.	Min	1	2	1	4.00	1.593	0	81.0	86	36	57

AL Pitcher	Team	W	L	SV	ERA	Ratio	GS	IP	H	BB	K
Hathaway, H.	Cal	4	3	0	5.02	1.779	11	57.1	71	26	11
Heaton, N.	NYA	1	0	0	6.00	1.778	0	27.0	34	11	15
Henke, T.	Tex	5	5	40	2.91	1.117	0	74.1	55	27	79
Henneman, M.	Det	5	3	24	2.64	1.437	0	71.2	69	32	58
Henry, D.	Mil	4	4	17	5.56	1.727	0	55.0	67	25	38
Henry, D.	Sea	2	1	2	6.67	1.722	1	54.0	56	35	35
Hentgen, P.	Tor	19	9	0	3.87	1.368	32	216.1	215	74	122
Hernandez, J.	Cle	6	5	8	3.14	1.319	0	77.1	75	27	44
Hernandez, R.	ChA	3	4	38	2.29	1.093	0	78.2	66	20	71
Hesketh, J.	Bos	3	4	1	5.06	1.706	5	53.1	62	29	34
Higuera, T.	Mil	1	3	0	7.20	2.000	8	30.0	43	16	27
Hillegas, S.	Oak	3	6	0	6.97	1.896	11	60.2	78	33	29
Hitchcock, S.	NYA	1	2	0	4.65	1.516	6	31.0	32	14	26
Holman, B.	Sea	1	3	3	3.72	1.321	0	36.1	27	16	17
Holzemer, M.	Cal	0	3	0	8.87	2.143	4	23.1	34	13	10
Honeycutt, R.	Oak	1	4	1	2.81	1.224	0	41.2	30	20	21
Horsman, V.	Oak	2	0	0	5.40	1.720	0	25.0	25	15	17
Howard, C.	ChA	1	0	0	0.00	2.143	0	2.1	2	3	1
Howe, S.	NYA	3	5	4	4.97	1.401	0	50.2	58	10	19
Hutton, M.	NYA	1	1	0	5.73	1.909	4	22.0	24	17	12
Ignasiak, M.	Mil	1	1	0	3.65	1.486	0	37.0	32	21	28
Jean, D.	NYA	1	1	0	4.46	1.388	6	40.1	37	19	20
Jimenez, M.	Oak	1	0	0	4.00	1.630	4	27.0	27	16	13
Johnson, D.	Det	1	1	0	12.96	2.400	0	8.1	13	5	7
Johnson, J.	NYA	0	2	0	30.38	5.250	2	2.2	12	2	0
Johnson, R.	Sea	19	8	1	3.24	1.175	34	255.1	185	99	308
Jones, B.	ChA	0	1	0	8.59	2.318	0	7.1	14	3	7
Kamieniecki, S.	NYA	10	7	1	4.08	1.458	20	154.1	163	59	72
Karsay, S.	Oak	3	3	0	4.04	1.367	8	49.0	49	16	33
Key, J.	NYA	18	6	0	3.00	1.111	34	236.2	219	43	173
Kiefer, M.	Mil	0	0	1	0.00	0.964	0	9.1	3	5	7
Kiely, J.	Det	0	2	0	7.71	2.314	0	11.2	13	13	5
King, K.	Sea	0	1	0	6.17	1.200	0	11.2	9	4	8
Knudsen, K.	Det	3	2	2	4.78	1.619	0	37.2	41	16	29
Kramer, T.	Cle	7	3	0	4.02	1.545	16	121.0	126	59	71
Krueger, B.	Det	6	4	0	3.40	1.512	7	82.0	90	30	60
Langston, M.	Cal	16	11	0	3.20	1.194	35	256.1	220	85	196
Leach, T.	ChA	0	0	1	2.81	1.125	0	16.0	15	2	3
Leary, T.	Sea	11	9	0	5.05	1.583	27	169.1	202	58	68
Lefferts, C.	Tex	3	9	0	6.05	1.572	8	83.1	102	28	58
Leftwich, P.	Cal	4	6	0	3.79	1.376	12	80.2	81	27	31
Leibrandt, C.	Tex	9	10	0	4.55	1.450	26	150.1	169	45	89
Leiter, A.	Tor	9	6	2	4.11	1.457	12	105.0	93	56	66
Leiter, M.	Det	6	6	0	4.72	1.481	13	106.2	111	44	70
Lewis, S.	Cal	1	2	0	4.22	1.594	4	32.0	37	12	10
Lilliquist, D.	Cle	4	4	10	2.25	1.313	2	64.0	64	19	40
Linton, D.	Tor	0	1	0	6.55	1.909	1	11.0	11	9	4
Linton, D.	Cal	2	0	0	7.71	1.909	0	25.2	35	14	19
Lloyd, G.	Mil	3	4	0	2.83	1.257	0	63.2	64	13	31
Lopez, A.	Cle	3	1	0	5.98	1.651	9	49.2	49	32	25
MacDonald, B.	Det	3	3	3	5.35	1.538	0	65.2	67	33	39
Magnante, M.	KC	1	2	0	4.08	1.387	6	35.1	37	11	16
Magrane, J.	Cal	3	2	0	3.94	1.438	8	48.0	48	21	24

AL Pitcher	Team	W	L	SV	ERA	Ratio	GS	IP	H	BB	K
Mahomes, P.	Min	1	5	0	7.71	1.714	5	37.1	47	16	23
Maldonado, C.	Mil	2	2	1	4.58	1.527	0	37.1	40	17	18
Manzanillo, J.	Mil	1	1	1	9.53	2.000	1	17.0	22	10	10
Maysey, M.	Mil	1	2	1	5.73	1.909	0	22.0	28	13	10
McCaskill, K.	ChA	4	8	2	5.23	1.592	14	113.2	144	36	65
McDonald, B.	Bal	13	14	0	3.39	1.253	34	220.1	185	86	171
McDowell, J.	ChA	22	10	0	3.37	1.297	34	256.2	261	69	158
McGehee, K.	Bal	0	0	0	5.94	1.620	0	16.2	18	7	7
Meacham, R.	KC	2	2	0	5.57	1.857	0	21.0	31	5	13
Melendez, J.	Bos	2	1	0	2.25	0.938	0	16.0	10	5	14
Merriman, B.	Min	1	1	0	9.67	2.296	0	27.0	36	23	14
Mesa, J.	Cle	10	12	0	4.92	1.442	33	208.2	232	62	118
Milacki, B.	Cle	1	1	0	3.38	1.875	2	16.0	19	11	7
Militello, S.	NYA	1	1	0	6.75	2.036	2	9.1	10	7	5
Mills, A.	Bal	5	4	4	3.23	1.346	0	100.1	80	51	68
Minchey, N.	Bos	1	2	0	3.55	1.303	5	33.0	35	8	18
Miranda, A.	Mil	4	5	0	3.30	1.283	17	120.0	100	52	88
Mlicki, D.	Cle	0	0	0	3.38	1.425	3	13.1	11	6	7
Mohler, M.	Oak	1	6	0	5.60	1.601	9	64.1	57	44	42
Monteleone, R.	NYA	7	4	0	4.94	1.401	0	85.2	85	35	50
Montgomery, J.	KC	7	5	45	2.27	1.031	0	87.1	65	23	66
Moore, M.	Det	13	9	0	5.22	1.493	36	213.2	227	89	89
Morris, J.	Tor	7	12	0	6.19	1.683	27	152.2	189	65	103
Moyer, J.	Bal	12	9	0	3.43	1.303	25	152.0	154	38	90
Munoz, B.	NYA	3	3	0	5.32	1.620	0	45.2	48	26	33
Munoz, M.	Det	0	1	0	6.00	3.333	0	3.0	4	6	1
Mussina, M.	Bal	14	6	0	4.46	1.252	25	167.2	163	44	117
Mutis, J.	Cle	3	6	0	5.78	1.642	13	81.0	93	33	29
Nagy, C.	Cle	2	6	0	6.29	1.664	9	48.2	66	13	30
Navarro, J.	Mil	11	12	0	5.33	1.577	34	214.1	254	73	114
Nelson, G.	Cal	0	5	4	3.08	1.424	0	52.2	50	23	31
Nelson, G.	Tex	0	0	1	3.38	1.375	0	8.0	10	1	4
Nelson, J.	Sea	5	3	1	4.35	1.650	0	60.0	57	34	61
Nen, R.	Tex	1	1	0	6.35	2.382	3	22.2	28	26	12
Nielsen, J.	Cal	0	0	0	8.03	1.865	0	12.1	18	4	8
Novoa, R.	Mil	0	3	0	4.50	1.500	7	56.0	58	22	17
Nunez, E.	Oak	3	6	1	3.81	1.639	0	75.2	89	29	58
O'Donoghue, J.	Bal	0	1	0	4.58	1.678	1	19.2	22	10	16
Ojeda, B.	Cle	2	1	0	4.40	1.605	7	43.0	48	21	27
Oliver, D.	Tex	0	0	0	2.70	0.900	0	3.1	2	1	4
Olson, G.	Bal	0	2	29	1.60	1.222	0	45.0	37	18	44
Ontiveros, S.	Sea	0	2	0	1.00	1.333	0	18.0	18	6	13
Oquist, M.	Bal	0	0	0	3.86	1.371	0	11.2	12	4	8
Orosco, J.	Mil	3	5	8	3.18	1.182	0	56.2	47	17	67
Pall, D.	ChA	2	3	1	3.22	1.278	0	58.2	62	11	29
Patterson, B.	Tex	2	4	1	4.78	1.348	0	52.2	59	11	46
Patterson, K.	Cal	1	1	1	4.58	1.508	0	59.0	54	35	36
Pavlik, R.	Tex	12	6	0	3.41	1.419	26	166.1	151	80	131
Pennington, B.	Bal	3	2	4	6.55	1.848	0	33.0	34	25	39
Perez, M.	NYA	6	14	0	5.19	1.460	25	163.0	173	64	148
Pichardo, H.	KC	7	8	0	4.04	1.467	25	165.0	183	53	70
Plantenberg, E.	Sea	0	0	1	6.52	2.483	0	9.2	11	12	3
Plunk, E.	Cle	4	5	15	2.79	1.282	0	71.0	61	30	77
Poole, J.	Bal	2	1	2	2.15	1.013	0	50.1	30	21	29
Powell, D.	Sea	0	0	0	4.15	1.406	2	47.2	42	24	32

AL Pitcher	Team	W	L	SV	ERA	Ratio	GS	IP	H	BB	K
Power, T.	Cle	0	2	0	7.20	1.900	0	20.0	30	8	11
Power, T.	Sea	2	2	13	3.91	1.421	0	25.1	27	9	16
Quantrill, P.	Bos	6	12	1	3.91	1.428	14	138.0	151	44	66
Radinsky, S.	ChA	8	2	4	4.28	1.482	0	54.2	61	19	44
Rasmussen, D.	KC	1	2	0	7.45	1.897	4	29.0	40	14	12
Reed, R.	KC	0	0	0	9.82	2.182	0	3.2	6	1	3
Reed, R.	Tex	1	0	0	2.25	2.000	0	4.0	6	1	2
Rhodes, A.	Bal	5	6	0	6.51	1.646	17	85.2	91	49	49
Rogers, K.	Tex	16	10	0	4.10	1.368	33	208.1	210	71	140
Ruffcorn, S.	ChA	0	2	0	8.10	1.900	2	10.0	9	10	2
Russell, J.	Bos	1	4	33	2.70	1.157	0	46.2	39	14	45
Ryan, K.	Bos	7	2	1	3.60	1.500	0	50.0	43	29	49
Ryan, N.	Tex	5	5	0	4.88	1.432	13	66.1	54	40	46
Salkeld, R.	Sea	0	0	0	2.51	1.256	2	14.1	13	4	13
Sampen, B.	KC	2	2	0	5.89	2.073	0	18.1	25	9	9
Sanderson, S.	Cal	7	11	0	4.46	1.367	21	135.1	153	27	66
Schooler, M.	Tex	3	0	0	5.55	1.644	0	24.1	30	10	16
Schwarz, J.	ChA	2	2	0	3.71	1.490	0	51.0	35	38	41
Scott, D.	Cal	1	2	0	5.85	1.550	0	20.0	19	11	13
Scudder, S.	Cle	0	1	0	9.00	2.500	1	4.0	5	4	1
Sele, A.	Bos	7	2	0	2.74	1.388	18	111.2	100	48	93
Shinall, Z.	Sea	0	0	0	3.38	2.250	0	2.2	4	2	0
Slocumb, H.	Cle	3	1	0	4.28	1.610	0	27.1	28	16	18
Slusarski, J.	Oak	0	0	0	5.19	2.308	1	8.2	9	11	1
Smith, L.	NYA	0	0	3	0.00	1.125	0	8.0	4	5	11
Smithberg, R.	Oak	1	2	3	2.75	1.068	0	19.2	13	7	4
Springer, R.	Cal	1	6	0	7.20	1.800	9	60.0	73	32	31
Stewart, D.	Tor	12	8	0	4.44	1.370	26	162.0	146	72	96
Stieb, D.	ChA	1	3	0	6.04	1.836	4	22.1	27	14	11
Stottlemyre, T.	Tor	11	12	0	4.84	1.562	28	176.2	204	69	98
Sutcliffe, R.	Bal	10	10	0	5.75	1.759	28	166.0	212	74	80
Swan, R.	Sea	3	3	0	9.15	2.288	0	19.2	25	18	10
Swingle, P.	Cal	0	1	0	8.38	2.172	0	9.2	15	6	6
Tanana, F.	NYA	0	2	0	3.20	1.271	3	19.2	18	7	12
Tapani, K.	Min	12	15	0	4.43	1.356	35	225.2	243	57	150
Tavarez, J.	Cle	2	2	0	6.57	1.838	7	37.0	53	13	19
Taylor, S.	Bos	0	1	0	8.18	2.455	0	11.0	14	12	8
Telford, A.	Bal	0	0	0	9.82	1.773	0	7.1	11	1	6
Thigpen, B.	ChA	0	0	1	5.71	1.962	0	34.2	51	12	19
Timlin, M.	Tor	4	2	1	4.69	1.635	0	55.2	63	27	49
Trombley, M.	Min	6	6	2	4.88	1.531	10	114.1	131	41	85
Tsamis, G.	Min	1	2	1	6.19	1.698	0	68.1	86	27	30
Valenzuela, F.	Bal	8	10	0	4.94	1.466	31	178.2	179	79	78
Valera, J.	Cal	3	6	4	6.62	1.774	5	53.0	77	15	28
Van poppel, T.	Oak	6	6	0	5.04	1.667	16	84.0	76	62	47
Viola, F.	Bos	11	8	0	3.14	1.405	29	183.2	180	72	91
Wainhouse, D.	Sea	0	0	0	27.00	5.571	0	2.1	7	5	2
Ward, D.	Tor	2	3	45	2.13	1.047	0	71.2	49	25	97
Wegman, B.	Mil	4	14	0	4.48	1.417	18	120.2	135	34	50
Welch, B.	Oak	9	11	0	5.29	1.626	28	166.2	208	56	63
Wells, D.	Det	11	9	0	4.19	1.241	30	187.0	183	42	139
Wertz, B.	Cle	2	3	0	3.62	1.458	0	59.2	54	32	53

AL Pitcher	Team	W	L	SV	ERA	Ratio	GS	IP	H	BB	K
Whiteside, M.	Tex	2	1	1	4.32	1.397	0	73.0	78	23	39
Wickander, K.	Cle	0	0	0	4.15	2.077	0	8.2	15	3	3
Wickman, B.	NYA	14	4	4	4.63	1.643	19	140.0	156	69	70
Williams, W.	Tor	3	1	0	4.38	1.703	0	37.0	40	22	24
Williamson, M.	Bal	7	5	0	4.91	1.489	1	88.0	106	25	45
Willis, C.	Min	3	0	5	3.10	1.259	0	58.0	56	17	44
Witt, B.	Oak	14	13	0	4.21	1.455	33	220.0	226	91	131
Witt, M.	NYA	3	2	0	5.27	1.561	9	41.0	39	22	30
Young, C.	Cle	3	3	1	4.62	1.575	7	60.1	74	18	31
Young, C.	Oak	1	1	0	4.30	1.364	3	14.2	14	6	4
Young, M.	Cle	1	6	0	5.21	1.816	8	74.1	75	57	65